THE PESTS AND BLIGHTS OF THE TEA PLANT

THE PESTS AND BLIGHTS OF THE TEA PLANT

SIR GEORGE WATT
&
HAROLD H. MANN

GYAN

Published by

GYAN

Gyan Publishing House
5, Ansari Road
Daryaganj, New Delhi-110002
Phone: 011-47034999, 9811692060
E-mail: books@gyanbooks.com

Distribution Network
gyanbooks.com
India, USA, Canada, UK, Australia

ISBN: 978-93-7447-924-7 (PB)

First Published, 1903

2nd Impression 2026

Printed at: Gyan Press, Delhi.

THE PESTS AND BLIGHTS OF THE TEA PLANT
Author: SIR GEORGE WATT AND HAROLD H. MANN

THE
PESTS AND BLIGHTS
OF THE
TEA PLANT

(SECOND EDITION)

AGENTS.

In Britain.

Messrs.

E. A. Arnold, 37, Bedford Street, Strand, London, W.C.

Constable & Co., 2, Whitehall Gardens, London, S.W.

Sampson Low, Marston & Co., St. Dunstan's House, Fetter Lane, London, E.C.

P. S. King & Son, 2 & 4, Great Smith Street, London, Westminster, S.W.

Luzac & Co., 46, Great Russell Street, London, W.C.

Kegan Paul, Trench, Trübner & Co., Charing Cross Road, London, W.C.

B. Alfred Quaritch, 15, Piccadilly, London, E.

Williams and Norgate, Oxford.

Deighton Bell & Co., Cambridge.

On the Continent.

Messrs.

R. Friedländer & Sohn, Carlstrasse, 11, Berlin, N.W.

Otto Harrassowitz, Leipzig.

Karl W. Hiersemann, Leipzig.

Ernest Leroux, 28, Rue Bonaparte, Paris.

Martinus Nijhoff, The Hague.

In India.

Messrs.

Thacker, Spink & Co., Calcutta and Simla.

Newman & Co., Calcutta.

V. Kalyanarama Aiyar & Co., Madras.

R. Cambray & Co., Calcutta.

S. K. Lahiri & Co., Calcutta.

Thacker & Co., Ld., Bombay.

Higginbotham & Co., Madras.

Superintendent, American Baptist Mission Press, Rangoon.

Rai Sahib M. Gulab Singh & Sons, Mufid-i-Am Press, Lahore.

A. J. Combridge & Co., Bombay.

Mrs. Radhabai Atmaram Sagoon, Bombay.

D. B. Taraporevala, Sons & Co., Bombay.

THE PESTS AND BLIGHTS

OF THE

TEA PLANT

(SECOND EDITION)

BY

SIR GEORGE WATT, M.B., C.M., F.L.S., C.I.E.,

OFFICIER D'ACADEMIE; CORRESPONDING MEMBER, ROYAL HORTICULTURAL SOCIETY OF ENGLAND;
REPORTER ON ECONOMIC PRODUCTS TO THE GOVERNMENT OF INDIA;

AND

HAROLD H. MANN, M.Sc., F.I.C., F.L.S.,

SCIENTIFIC OFFICER TO THE INDIAN TEA ASSOCIATION.

CALCUTTA:
OFFICE OF THE SUPERINTENDENT, GOVERNMENT PRINTING, INDIA.
1903.

PREFACE TO THE SECOND EDITION.

"The Pests and Blights of the Tea Plant" was first issued in 1898, and the edition then published became exhausted in less than two years. Numerous demands from planters in all parts of the tea districts showed that another was called for, and it was finally decided to accede to these various requests.

In deciding to do so, advantage was taken of the appointment of a Scientific Officer by the Indian Tea Association in 1900, whose investigations, since that date, have carried him over all the more important tea districts of North India, and he was associated with the senior author in the work.

The book takes therefore a much wider view of the questions discussed than the former edition, which only professed to be a report of particular investigations conducted on special tours under orders of the Government of India in the Kangra Valley and Assam. In the present, on the other hand, not only has a considerable amount of information obtained since 1898 been utilised, but the book has been almost entirely re-written, and is no longer a report on certain specific journeys, but a general account of the pests and blights affecting the tea plant in India, and to a certain extent in Ceylon. We hope it may be found of service both in making the culture of tea more scientific than heretofore, and in placing in the hands of planters the best means of dealing with enemies and diseases of the plant, which seem to be growing in number and in virulence every season.

GEORGE WATT.

HAROLD H. MANN.

CALCUTTA, *March 1903.*

CONTENTS.

LIST OF PLATES.

LIST OF ILLUSTRATIONS IN TEXT.

THE

PESTS AND BLIGHTS

OF THE

TEA PLANT.

CHAPTER I.

INTRODUCTION.

INTRODUCTION. Peculiar character of industry.

1. The culture of the tea plant is of such a special character—perhaps not reproduced in any other agricultural industry in the world—that it is surrounded by difficulties the meaning and force of which can hardly be judged by the standards of ordinary agriculture either in India or elsewhere. First, the tea plant itself is a perennial tree brought by cultivation to a shrub form, and then grown for leaf, while nearly all cultures of similar plants are made for the production of fruit or seed. Again, while this bush will *grow* on the greatest variety of soil, and with considerable variation of climate, yet such growth can only *profitably* take place under very strictly defined conditions, and variations which would often be ignored in ordinary agriculture would be fatal to the commercial production of tea in any district or country. If we add to these considerations the fact that the pests and blights which prey on the leaf and which hence can often be partially, at any rate, ignored in the usual crops, are here of vital importance as removing that for which the crop is primarily grown, an idea can be formed of the very special character of the industry, as agriculture, from whatever point of view it may be surveyed.

Introduction.

INTRODUCTION.

Isolation of industry.

2. These facts have led, with others, to the commercial growth of the plant in very narrow and well-defined areas, and partly as a result of this isolation, comparatively little is known of the real principles which underlie the success or failure of the industry in a particular place, and less of the methods of preventing or dealing with these enemies of the tea plant which have arisen as an inevitable consequence of the devotion of a large area in one district to the crop.

Scientific investigations needed.

3. In the succeeding chapters we have endeavoured to represent certain aspects of the cultivation of the plant so far as they are known, but which, all of them, call for more careful investigation with a view to reforms. There exists sufficient presumptive evidence to justify the opinion that certain misapprehensions and defective methods of procedure have originated constitutional weaknesses that may be said to constantly predispose the plant to actual disease, or, in other words, to render the depredations of its enemies and parasites more alarming than they might be otherwise. We have, therefore, in discussing the subject of the tea plant, its enemies and its diseases, advocated some such reforms in the treatment of the plant that may be found desirable and practicable and should necessarily accompany more specific efforts to battle with the pests and blights.

SOURCES of INFORMATION.

II.—Sources of Information and Assistance.

Tours in Tea Districts by Authors.

4. In presenting the observations which we now propose to offer, it should be explained that those which are new are primarily based on the notes made during the journeys of the authors in the Indian Tea Districts from the year 1894 to 1902. These journeys were conducted by Dr. Watt, on behalf of the Indian Government, in the Kangra Valley (October and November 1894), in Assam (March to July 1895 and again in 1897), and in Darjeeling and the Dooars (October and November 1900), and by Mr. Mann, travelling for the Indian Tea Association, in Assam, Cachar, Sylhet and Chittagong (in 1900), in Assam and Darjeeling (in 1901), and in the Surma Valley and the Darjeeling Terai (in 1902). The present work is, however, intended purely and simply as a *popular statement*, since it would take many years to do justice to the subject or even to fully work up the mass of material that has been collected during the few months we have had in the districts. It is issued, as was the first edition, in the hope that it may prove of some slight

practical value, and also that it may awaken interest in subjects of enquiry that need to be very considerably extended before definite results in many directions can be obtained.

SOURCES of INFORMATION.

5. But while the primary responsibility for any novel statements made is our own, we have freely used the sources of information on the subject accessible to us. The following are the chief of these:—

General.

1st.—The Journals and Proceedings of the Agri-Horticultural Society of India, more specially from 1865-1885,—the period of greatest interest by the Society in the subject of tea.

2nd.—Special publications of the Indian Tea Industry, including the annual reports of the Indian Tea Association from 1882 to 1901.

3rd.—Newspaper correspondence from 1873 to the present date, more especially the letters which originally appeared in the "*Tea Gazette,*" but which may now be conveniently consulted in the "*Tea Cyclopedia*" and the "*Tea Planter's Vade Mecum.*" The "*Tropical Agriculturist*" of Colombo has been found a mine of information for confirming or correcting observations made in India.

4th.—The planting papers of Calcutta—*The Indian Planter's Gazette,*" "*The Planter,*" and "*Indian Gardening and Planting*" and of South India—"*Planting Opinion.*"

5th.—The *Indian Museum Notes*, more especially **Mr. E. C. Cotes's** account of the *Insects and Mites which attack the Tea Plant in India.*

Botany.

6th.—The invaluable aid of **Sir W. T. Thiselton Dyer**, the Director of, and of **Mr. G. Massee**, Cryptogamic Botanist in, the Kew Gardens, London, for several reports on Tea Blights. Among the most valuable papers on the Fungal Diseases of Tea are those written by **Dr. D. D. Cunningham** some years ago, and of these we have made the fullest use. In recent years **Dr. Butler**, the Cryptogamic Botanist to the Government of India, has given extremely valuable aid in the working out of several previously obscure diseases.

Entomology.

7th.—The very great assistance, most generously afforded by **Mr. E. E. Green**, the Government Entomologist of Ceylon, who has for many years identified himself with the study of tea pests, and has, in consequence, discovered and investigated the life histories of a large number of obscure species. **Mr. Green** has not only examined practically all our pests, but has in return presented a most valuable set of the pests collected by him in Ceylon. Similarly, **Dr. A. S. R. Anderson** and **Mr. E. Barlow**, formerly of the Indian Museum,

Introduction.

SOURCES of INFORMATION.

Co-operation of Planters.

have helped a good deal in the identification of species. To the late Mr. L. de Nicéville, of the Indian Museum, we owe a special debt of gratitude, as it was on a journey suggested by one of the authors, that he contracted the disease which carried him off in a few days.

8th.—The greatest debt is, however, owing to the large circle of planters whom it has been our good fortune to meet during our tours, and from whom the most valuable assistance has been obtained. Where so much valuable aid has been afforded one can hardly mention particular cases, but to Mr. James Buckingham, C.I.E., of Amgoorie, for general help, to Mr. T. H. Hall, now of Borsillah, for a good many photographs reproduced in these pages, and to Mr. Lindsay Alexander, now in England, but formerly at Pathalipam, Assam, for similar help, we are, among others, very specially indebted.

9th.—Finally, the files of correspondence in the office of the Reporter on Economic Products to the Government of India have been freely drawn upon and have been of great assistance.

III.—Need for further Investigation and Experiment.

RESULTS not final.

6. In this work we however make no pretence of finality in any way. The methods of cultivation described, or recommended where they differ from those usually in vogue, require the most thorough and critical examination in the field before use on a large scale. We perfectly recognise that it is impossible to know whether a method eminently successful under one set of conditions will be equally successful, or successful at all, in another district or under another set of conditions. This being the case, we should be the first to deprecate radical departures on a large scale from regular practices until on a small area in the same district such departures have proved to be a success. But, on the other hand, there seems little doubt that deterioration of the tea in existence on most, though not on all, gardens, to whatever cause it may be due, has been, and is, taking place, and this deterioration indicates that some part of the usual procedure of planting is defective. It may be laid down as a universal rule in agriculture that where, owing to the utilisation of land for some years, that land becomes agriculturally less valuable, something is wrong either in the method of treating the soil or the plant,—or else a change is occurring in the climate.

Introduction.

7. That any change of moment is occurring in the climate of the Indian Tea Districts is, as yet, not proved. The deterioration which is undoubtedly occurring in most old gardens is probably, therefore, due to one or the other of the remaining two causes named, or to both, and the remedy seems to be to examine the soil which has long grown tea and ascertain the nature of the exhaustion which has taken place; and furthermore to examine the bushes and obtain information as to the effect, which the usual methods of planting—cultivation, pruning and plucking—have had on the wood, the leaf, and the general character of the plant. So far perhaps work has been carried, but it needs very careful experimental as well as observational work on land and on bushes under actual tea garden conditions before it can be said that the results are always really and absolutely applicable. It has not been possible to carry out such experimental work as yet, though there seems a distinct probability that this may be feasible in the near future. In the meantime the results obtained by careful observation in the field, by laboratory analyses and experiments, and by a certain number of field experiments are here placed on record in a succession of chapters on—

RESULTS not final.

Possible climatic changes.

Need for examination of soil and bush.

Conf. with paras, 171, 183, 211, 213.

(*a*) Plant Life in general, with special reference to the growth of a plant for leaf production.

(*b*) Seeds and Seed Gardens.

(*c*) Hoeing and Weeding.

(*d*) Drainage.

(*e*) Principles of Pruning.

(*f*) Plucking.

(*g*) Manuring.

Summary of chapters.

After this follows a more detailed description of the various insect pests and fungal blights which attack the bush, and the methods which have been or may be found useful in dealing with them, distinction being made between those of primary and of secondary importance at present.

PLANT LIFE.

CHAPTER II.

PLANT LIFE.

Conf. with para. 98.

8. While fully conscious that it would be both undesirable and unsatisfactory to attempt in a few pages a scientific account of even the leading features of Plant Life, it may serve a useful purpose, nevertheless, if we endeavour to bring to mind some of the leading facts that should guide the tea-planter in his out-door operations. We shall, therefore, only touch on those aspects of this very instructive study that have a direct bearing on Hoeing and Weeding, Draining, Pruning, Plucking and Manuring. It should accordingly be understood that the few brief paragraphs that comprise this chapter have been offered with one object, namely, to heip to elucidate certain practical recommendations which we feel called upon to lay before those interested in tea-planting. Our remarks must not, therefore, be judged according to the standard of advanced research into the physiology of plants.

IV.—Nutritive and Reproductive Systems.

Nutritive and reproductive functions.

9. ***Parts of the plant.***—It is customary to speak of the parts of a plant as consisting of two sets, Nutritive and Reproductive. The former are concerned with the life of the individual, the latter with perpetuation of the species. The nutritive organs may be said to be the Roots, Stem, Branches and Leaves; the reproductive, the Flowers and Fruits with their ultimate offspring—the Seed.

Mouths of the plant.

Food of plant.

Although not absolutely correct, it may be said that the roots are the mouths of the plant, and that the leaves are both the lungs and the stomach. The food of plants may be expressed briefly as Air, Water and Mineral Substances. The atmosphere being but indirectly under the control of the agriculturist, his attention is mainly directed to the soil. Under the chapters on Hoeing and Draining, an effort will be made to indicate the manner in which the cultivator may take full advantage of the valuable properties of air. By drainage, moreover, not only can the soil temperature be raised, but even climatic conditions beneficially influenced.

Value of air.

Composition of air.

Air may be regarded as consisting of oxygen and nitrogen, two gases that are intimately mixed up, but which remain chemically

Plant Life.

free from each other—a wonderful fact and one of the greatest importance. During thunderstorms, however, actual union takes place between a certain amount of these two gases, and a compound results which by a further union with the elements of water becomes Nitric Acid. That acid is of the greatest value to the plants since it contributes toward the decompositions of the soil by which insoluble substances are rendered soluble. But the air also contains a very considerable amount of Carbonic Acid gas, and a lesser amount of an equally valuable compound, Ammonia.

NUTRITIVE and REPRODUCTIVE.

Nitric acid. *Conf. with para. 15.*

10. ***Respiration.***—Animals inhale the air in order that its free oxygen may be combined with the waste carbon of their bodies forming carbonic acid, and this is exhaled. Plants breathe by precisely the same principle, but added to their respiration they have a process of digestion. Under the influence of the light rays of the sun, acting on the green colouring matter of the leaves, the carbonic acid of their exhalation, as also the carbonic acid of the atmosphere, is decomposed, the carbon retained as a food material, and pure oxygen exhaled. During night, however, this absorption of carbon does not take place, so that the respiration of plants is then demonstrable as identical with that of animals.

Respiration. *Conf. with para. 13.*

Chlorophyll. *Conf. with para. 13.*

11. ***Food Materials.***—The food of animals has to undergo a regular series of chemical changes collectively designated *Digestion*, before it can be absorbed or utilized. Moreover, the food materials of animals are very different from those of plants, since animals are unable to live upon earthy or inorganic substances. The animal is in fact entirely dependent on the plant for the preparation of its food. Plant food may be said to be oxygen, hydrogen, nitrogen and carbon, (all derived from air and water) also certain earthy materials obtained from the soil. The plant possesses no stomach, strictly so speaking, but nevertheless its food materials have to undergo chemical changes, by a process designated *Assimilation*, which closely corresponds to digestion, before they can be built up in the tissues of the plant. Although the proportion of mineral matter eaten by plants is comparatively small, the higher plants at least cannot live without certain mineral substances. Each plant may be said to demand certain inorganic substances, otherwise it will not grow. The agriculturist, in his efforts to improve the soil, has, therefore, to direct attention chiefly to these indispensable inorganic

Food materials.

Assimilation. *Conf. with para. 98.*

NUTRITIVE and REPRODUCTIVE.

food substances. During the process of assimilation the food materials are built up into various organic compounds, and these again are utilized in the formation of plant tissues. Briefly, the organic compounds of plants may be said to be:—

Chemical compounds of plant tissue.

1st.—***Starches*** and compounds of a similar type, built up of oxygen, hydrogen and carbon, in varying proportions. Of this nature may be mentioned starch proper; cellulose or the constituent of wood and fibre; gum; and lastly, sugar.

2nd.—***Protein*** compounds. These contain nitrogen in addition to the oxygen, hydrogen and carbon of the starches, as also smaller proportions of sulphur, phosphorus, etc. Of this nature may be mentioned gluten; albumen; casein, etc., etc. All living and growing vegetable tissues contain a certain proportion of protein matter and a liberal supply of nitrogen is, therefore, indispensable to the life of plants. Let it be added in passing that nitrogen may be regarded as derived mainly, if not entirely, by the roots.

3rd.—***Oils or Fats.***—These all agree in containing less oxygen than would be necessary to convert their hydrogen into water.

4th.—***Water,*** an article of food the elements of which are occasionally separated and utilized in the formation of certain compounds.

CIRCULATION. *Conf. with para. 99.*

V.—Circulation of sap.

12. ***Growth.***—On placing a seed under the conditions of germination, the first change that takes place may be said to be that a portion of its protein undergoes a sort of fermentation by which a part of it is converted into a substance very generally designated *Diastase.* That substance is no sooner produced than it acts upon the store of starch (also contained within the seed) and converts it into a form of sugar, which being soluble thus increases the specific gravity of the cell-contents. *Osmose* is in this way brought into action, that is to say, water is absorbed. It passes through the component cell-walls of the seed, obedient to a law of nature that a balance must be at once struck, should the specific gravities of two adjacent fluids be disturbed.

Growth. *Conf. with para. 21.*

13. The latent embryo being thus supplied with soluble food materials commences to grow. No sooner has its young stem and

leaves ascended above ground than their cells become charged with a green colouring matter (*Chlorophyll*) the services of which are now eminently required. With the exception of the moisture and the small amount of soluble substances absorbed, growth hitherto must be viewed as simply the result of the embryo having been able to use the materials which had been stored up for it within the seed. It may in fact be defined as growth, as the result of re-arrangement. But no sooner have the roots penetrated the soil and the leaves unfolded in the atmosphere than three distinct phenomena make their appearance:— **CIRCULATION of SAP.** **Action of chlorophyll.** *Conf. with para. 10.*

1st.—The sun by evaporation withdraws moisture from the leaves and thus the specific gravity of their cell-contents becomes increased owing to concentration.

2nd.—The leaves commence to breathe and purify thereby what may even already be impure.

3rd.—The leaves decompose the carbonic acid of the atmosphere inhaled by them, retain the carbon and set free the oxygen.

14. ***Ascent of Sap.***—For convenience we may view these conditions as originating the circulation of the sap and commencing the process of assimilation. It has been stated that by osmose the specific gravity of the cell-contents of the delicate roots that had emerged from the seed, was lowered. But by transpiration from the cells of the leaves, the specific gravity of *their* cell-contents is now raised. In consequence the cells above draw on the cells below for an extra supply of moisture. This suction from above and osmotic pressure from below may thus be viewed as sufficient to originate a circulation of fluid through the plant tissue. The ascending current is called the *Crude Sap*, because, while it contains many of the necessary food materials, they exist in a condition that cannot be utilized. The crude sap has to undergo a series of changes which, as already stated, are collectively designated the assimilation or digestion of plants. **Ascending or crude sap.** *Conf. with paras. 98, 100.*

15. But let us see what the crude sap contains, before we proceed to discuss the changes of assimilation. Water of course constitutes by far its largest proportion and is in addition the medium, through which other substances have been absorbed—for the food materials of plants must be soluble. Held in solution, then, the **Water.**

CIRCULATION of SAP.

Origin of Nitrates.

Conf. with para. 9.

crude sap contains compounds of nitrogen and nitrates. These nitrates have been derived from various sources, such as the ammonia of decomposing organic matter and of the air, nitrates formed by the nitric acid of the air, and last but perhaps the most important of all from the nitrogen fixing organisms of the soil which originate in part, at any rate, from the roots of leguminous plants. Lastly, the crude sap contains the mineral substances derived from the soil.

Position of current.

16. Avoiding all controversial points, it may not incorrectly then be regarded that the current of water, laden with these food materials, ascends through the young layer of wood, immediately underneath the bark, being propelled by the following amongst other forces :— osmotic pressure below, suction due to transpiration above, the chemical affinity that the cell-walls possess for water, capillary attraction between layers of cells and tissues, and, lastly, the decomposition of water and the utilization of its component elements during assimilation.

Causes of circulation.

Assimilation.

17. ***Assimilation and Descent of Sap.***—By whatever means it *may be*, this is certain, that a steady current of sap ascends amongst the young wood cells and, on reaching the leaves, is acted on in the three ways already mentioned. It is concentrated by perspiration, it is purified by respiration, and it is carbonised by decomposition of the carbonic acid gas of the atmosphere. This carbon entering into combination directly with the elements of water, forms one or other of the starches. By union with water, with carbon and with the nitrogen from a nitrate, protein matter is produced. In this way, then, many nutritious food-stuffs are formed. The sap is now digested or as it is called assimilated, and it slowly makes its way downwards by diffusing itself through the entire substance of the plant. From the elaborated *Descending Sap* the various tissues and structures are able to pick out the compounds which they require and these built up within the cells, cause them to grow, and finally, when mature to multiply, so that with vigorous circulation of sap rapid growth takes place.

Descending sap.

VI.—Conditions of Maturity.

Plant structures.

18. ***Plant Tissue.***—The cell may be said to be the ultimate structure. It is a small sac, the containing wall of which is composed of cellulose. One of the most striking peculiarities of the cell-wall has already been mentioned, but may be here more pointedly recapitulated. Although devoid of pores of any kind, fluids pass

Plant Life.

freely through in obedience to the law of osmose. The cell-contents are of a liquid nature with sometimes solid materials formed within. CONDITIONS of MATURITY.

Many microscopic plants consist simply of one cell. Others are built up of cells all of one shape and size, like the bricks of a wall, only that they are living bricks that increase in number by cell division. In still a third class of plants the cells are of different shapes, many compacted together and even fused, end on end, into tubes that ultimately form fibrous tissue and wood. These changes in the shape and also in the special adaptations of the cell, are brought into existence in obedience to the demand for the accomplishment of fixed and definite functions, attributed to the various organs of plant structure. The walls of the cells are thickened when the object is to form wood; the cell-walls in that case gradually become impervious to fluids and thus cease to participate in the circulation of sap. Wood is, therefore, developed to give strength and support to the young growing shoots and to bear the flowers and fruits. Formation of wood.

19. ***Reproduction.***—But the formation of wood, *beyond certain limits*, when the object aimed at by the cultivator is a free circulation of sap and rapid production of shoots, may be regarded as an unfavourable and undesirable symptom. It is an unmistakeable sign of the advance of age and will assuredly be followed by the production of flowers and fruits. When, therefore, a plant has attained maturity, reproduction becomes the governing principle of its future life. Should it be prematurely aged, by adverse circumstances, it may similarly be seen to put forth an effort to make up for the fast approach of its own death by the production of the germs for a new generation. Production of flowers

VII.—Practical Lessons to be Learned.

20. ***Continuous Growth—Flushing.***—To the tea-planter, therefore, the production of unnecessary wood or of flowers should be looked upon as untoward circumstances. In both cases pruning becomes a necessity. But pruning must go hand and glove with soil improvement, for if a check be given to the natural desires of the plant *viz.*, to provide for a new generation, without supplying it with the materials necessary for continued growth, the shock may prove fatal. But it should never be forgotten that the cultivation of the tea plant, figuratively speaking, might be characterised as a forced procrastination in the fulfilment of a universal law of nature. And the simile which Continuous growth—flushing. Improvement of soil. *Conf. with para. 95.*

PRACTICAL LESSONS.

it is here desired to draw is but partially true. The lower portion of the stem may represent a seared old age, forced through pruning and cultivation, to continually renew its youth. But the presence of old wood in the stem, by retarding circulation and constantly forcing on the younger upper shoots the necessity to flower and fruit, must be injurious to the planter's aims and objects.

Old Wood.

Roots.

21. Under the Chapters on Pruning and Drainage, an effort will be made to exemplify the chief peculiarities of the roots. It may here, however, be explained that absorption takes place chiefly in the minute hairs that surround the ultimate fibrils. Hairs are in many cases greatly elongated simple cells. They suck in the moisture of the soil charged with food materials. This is transmitted from the young roots along the older roots to the stem and onward to the leaves. The activity of absorption depends, however, almost entirely on the demands of growth and is regulated by the leaves. Transpiration and assimilation are not physical phenomena. The mouths of the leaf are minute openings in the epidermis (stomata), mostly situate on the under-surface. These open, to allow of free transpiration, or close when a rest is desired, and thus directly control the roots. The strength of the ascending current of sap is accordingly dependent on the extent and activity of the young growing shoots and the number of fresh hungry leaves.

Demands of growth. *Conf. with paras. 12–13.*

Flushing.

22. In the Chapter devoted to Plucking, an explanation will be offered as to the meaning of flushing. But in passing it may be said that the knife having secured for the planter the effort, on the part of the plant, to produce new shoots (instead of maturing those already in existence, with the view to the production of seed), a vigour has been given to the roots which must either result in "bleeding" from the cut surfaces or in the production of more and still more shoots to take the place of those plucked off.

Bleeding.

23. From what has been said it, therefore, may now be fully understood that pruning for the production of leaf is, and must be, a very hurtful and exhausting proceeding. It should, accordingly, be pursued with either of two objects in view:—

Uprooting and replanting. *Conf. with para. 248.*

(*a*) The death of the plant being accepted as a necessity, after a fixed number of years, the system of pruning should be that best calculated to secure the utmost return during the life of the plant.

Plant Life.

PRACTICAL LESSONS.

Preservation of Health.

(*b*) The object being to preserve the plant indefinitely, the system of pruning pursued should be that calculated to give the highest annual return, commensurate with the health of the plant.

Deterioration.

The method pursued in the past has to a very great extent been an attempt to obtain the benefit of both systems. Hence, as might have been expected, deterioration has set in, and, in a large measure, the unsatisfactory condition of many old tea properties is due to the non-recognition of the fundamental botanical principles which we have just set out.

CHAPTER III.

RACES OF THE TEA PLANT.

Seed Gardens, and Improvement of Seed.

VIII.—Varieties of seed.

VARIETIES of SEED.

24. The relative merits of the indigenous to the hybrid, and the China varieties as plants in tea gardens have been discussed *ad nauseam* almost from the first commencement of the tea planting industry. And yet at this late date there is little agreement as to the meaning attached to the words used. For instance, a type of plant dignified with the title "indigenous" in the Darjeeling District, might be considered but a medium hybrid in the Upper Assam Valley, and what was reckoned high class indigenous seed twenty years ago, when planted, is now looked upon again as very medium hybrid after growing for a number of years.

Indigenous Tea in Assam. *Conf. with para. 56.*

25. The so-called original indigenous tea of Assam was found on raised banks of light soil in most cases skirting the base of the Naga Hills, or in the basin of the Dehing River. In 1839 Mr. C. A. Bruce, who was then acting as Superintendent of the Government Tea plantations in Assam, described how he had found it at a large number of what are still the centres of so-called pure Assam indigenous seed. He notes particularly, for instance, Namsang, Tingri, Keyhung, Jaipur, Noholia, Muttuck in the Dehing Valley, and Cherideo and Gabro Purbut among others at the base of the hills.

Isolated Patches.

Even before this however the commissioners appointed by Government to enquire into the existence of tea in Assam in 1835 (Drs. Wallich, Griffiths, and McClelland) had found tea on the same or similar spots. In none of these particular places do the conditions exist which would satisfy a botanist that the plants are strictly speaking indigenous. There is very little in fact to remove the suspicion that they might originally have been planted. One naturally has to face the very pertinent question—How comes it that in the places of Assam, the so-called indigenous tea covers only small isolated patches of 5, 20, or at most 100 acres, while many miles of precisely similar jungle and forest extend around? It is necessary, in fact, to leave the valley and to penetrate into the Naga Hills and

Naga Hills and Manipur Teas.

Manipur before the tea plant can be said to form a feature of the prevailing vegetation over fairly extensive tracts of country.

VARIETIES of SEED

26. Then again the swampy jungles or damp forest tracts, in which most of these isolated plots of seed tea occur, are about as dissimilar as it is possible to imagine from the conditions that prevail in what may be viewed as the forests of truly wild tea in the Naga Hills and Manipur. We do not think that it has been satisfactorily made out that there never was, on the fringe of high land that skirts the mountainous walls of Assam, a condition of native tea cultivation, such as exists at present in the Shan States, long anterior to the existence of the European industry. If this idea be allowed to gain credence, the observation repeatedly recorded by one of us (G. W.) while examining seed gardens, that in few indeed of these gardens could the *jat* of tea be pronounced uniform, would at once be accounted for. It does not by any means follow that the first China tea plant that reached the valley of Assam came to it, as the result of the enlightened action of Lord William Bentinck in his efforts to organize the modern tea industry. Unmistakeable hybrid teas can, not unfrequently, be seen in some of these so-called indigenous seed-gardens, but even were these removed it could hardly be said that the remainder manifested throughout a constant type. "Assam indigenous" even, or "indigenous" is, in our opinion, a very comprehensive term indeed, so that we should speak of bad "Assam indigenous" just as we freely admit the term bad hybrid.

Possible early cultivation.

Assam indigenous is variable term.

27. The same argument applies in a modified way to the Cachar and Sylhet plant, but here its hybrid nature, as found wild in jungles, is less likely in most cases, and these plants represent, more probably than those in the Brahmaputra Valley, the natural spread of the vegetation in the Lushai hills towards their foot; and this is confirmed by the fact that it has not been able to cross to the north of the river Barak, where indeed wild tea has never been found in Cachar.

IX.—Deterioration of Jat.

Deterioration of Jat.

28. But though the so-called stocks of Assam Indigenous Tea may not be indigenous in the strict sense of the terms they represent what one may call one of the cultural races of the plant. Among all agricultural plants such races exist of very different cultural

CHANGE of JAT.

Potatoes.

value, though this cultural value is not always of a very permanent character. Thus, for instance, it is well known that a potato which, when first grown from seed and introduced into the market, may give an excellent yield of large flavoury produce, will after repeated culture from the tubers "degrade" to an altogether inferior position. The same is probably the case with tea. We have often been told by planters that what appeared to be very second-rate type of plant was put out with high class Assam indigenous seed. The reason of the inferior appearance was probably that the plant had, by constant cultivation under unfavourable conditions, gone down the scale of *jat*.

Example in Tea.

An excellent example of this was noticed in the Jorhat District. A block of tea was put out some twenty years ago from precisely the same stock of seed so far as records show. It is noticed now that whenever there has been a good deal of wash, and hence the soil has become poorer, the *jat* of tea, judged by the size of the leaves, has also become lower than that on the more favourably situated portions of the plot.

X.—Recognition of Different Forms.

Recognition. of forms.

29. Size of leaf is not, however, the only means, nor is it the best means, of distinguishing differences of type of plant. The study of the number of veins on the leaf forms a much more satisfactory, though by no means an absolute test. Whether, judged by this standard, the jat of a plant deteriorates on growth under unfavourable conditions, would require a good deal of careful observation to say, but there is strong reason for supposing that it does do so.

The wild plant.

30. In the wild state the so-called Assam indigenous tea plant may be described as a somewhat remarkable large bush; in exceptional cases it might even be called a small tree. It rarely forms a pronounced stem, but gives off near the ground, say, from 2 feet upwards, three, five, or as many as ten branches which ascend and are sparsely, though similarly, branched, so that the tall narrow bush of 20 to 50 feet in height becomes not unlike a miniature poplar tree. It fruits freely on last year's wood (or near the extremities of the twigs) and the fruits are 1, 2, 3, or 4 seeded with occasionally two seeds within each section of the fruit. The leaves are for the most part not more than 3 to 4 inches long and 1½ to 2 broad. They are of a dark green colour, concave on the upper

Races of the Tea Plant.

surface, that is to say, the sides of the leaf ascend slightly so as to form a depression towards the mid-rib. The margins are sharply serrate and the apex considerably elongated. The veins of the leaf when examined by transmitted light show eight primary branches (on either side of the mid-rib) and eight subordinate veins. The veins of one side very nearly alternate with those of the other. The first pair and the last pair are very minute. These sixteen veins arch upwards in loops that unite together a little within the margin. There are often still more subordinate ramifications seen in some forms of the plant, but only the veins that form the loops here mentioned should be counted.

RACES of TEA PLANT.

The wild plant.

Veins of leaf.

Conf. with para. 48.

31. ***Races (Jats) of the Tea Plant.***—The number of the veins is a *fairly* constant and an interesting feature of the various forms of the tea plant. Thus, for example, it will be found that in the so-called China tea plant, only eight veins loop round in the way mentioned and in hybrid teas there may be 9, 10, 11, 12, 13, or 14 pairs. We do not advance these statements as applicable to every leaf that may be plucked off a tea bush, but we do affirm that the vast majority of the leaves of the "pure Assam indigenous plant" will be seen to have 16 pairs of veins, "good hybrids" will have from 12 to 14, and all "bad hybrids" less than that, while the majority of the leaves of "pure China" will have only eight veins or sometimes even fewer. The "Manipur" or "Burma" plant (and the "Cachar" or "Lushai" stock which *may* originally have been derived from the Manipur) has more than sixteen pairs of veins. In some cases twenty-two veins may be counted. But the Manipur plant has altogether a larger habit than the Assam. It may be said that judged by this standard there are, now recognisable, about five distinct races of wild tea apparently independent of hybridisation, if indeed "China" may count as one. These, with their characteristics, may be described as follows :—

China Hybrid.

Assam indigenous.

Manipur.

Lushai.

(*a*) "*China.*"—The mature leaf is $1\frac{1}{16}$ to $2\frac{1}{2}$ inches long, and varies in width from $\frac{3}{4}$ to $\frac{7}{16}$ inches. As stated above, it rarely counts more than eight veins on either side of the mid-rib of the leaf, four principal and four subordinate ones. As a whole, the plant is essentially a bush, and even if given the opportunity, rarely, if ever, takes the "poplar" tree form of the other races.

China plant.

Races of the Tea Plant.

RACES of TEA PLANT.

Assam indigenous.

(*b*) "*Assam Indigenous.*"—The mature leaf is much larger than the above, ranging from 6 to 7¾ in length, and from 2⅜ to 2⅞ inches in width. It contains about 16 veins on each side of the mid-rib.

Manipur.

(*c*) "*Manipur*" or "*Burma.*"—Here we get what is altogether a larger leafed plant even than the Assam indigenous. The leaves vary a good deal in shape, but are broader in proportion to their length than the last-mentioned kind, as well as being much darker in colour, and probably more coarse in texture. The average leaf will probably be from 6 to 8 inches in length, and 2½ to 3¼ in width, and it may contain up to 22 veins on either side.

Naga.

(*d*) "*Naga.*"—This type possesses a long, narrow leaf, say, from 6 to 9 inches in length, and 2 to 3½ inches in width. Its veins number from 20 to 24 on each side. Very little of the pure jat has come into cultivation, but a large amount of "hybridised Naga" may be seen on Mr. Buckingham's garden at Amgoorie.

Lushai.

(*e*) "*Lushai*" or "*Cachar Indigenous.*"—The leaf of this type is the largest of all, growing often to a length of 12 to 14 inches and a breadth of 6 to 7½ inches. It is not found wild, so far as we know, out of the Lushai Hills and South Cachar, and possibly in Burma, and has not as yet come into cultivation to a very great extent, though a great many indigenous bushes of this variety remain in cultivation in Cachar. Its venation gives 20 to 24 on each side of the leaf. It is a rather delicate type and will not safely bear the hard cutting to which most of the other varieties easily submit.

XI.—Peculiarities produced in the Garden.

The Garden Plant

32. According to botanists all these forms of the tea plant belong to one species. Whether we are to regard them as natural races or not, cultivation can be seen to have produced almost as great departures as exist between the very small thick-leaved China stock and the large, soft, leathery-leaved Manipur plant Setting on one side the botanical problem here indicated, attention may be directed to the subject of the changes in the character of the tea plant, under the

RACES of TEA PLANT.

The Garden plant.

hands of the planter. When grown for its leaf-flushing power it is a bush not more than 4 to 5 feet in height. In some cases a short thick stem, from 4 to 9 inches in diameter and 2 feet in height, has been produced; in others it has been made to branch very early into a skeleton of five or six main branches, each perhaps 2 inches in diameter; and in still another condition a broom of perhaps 50 to 100 shoots not thicker than the thumb have been made to ascend from the ground parallel to each other to a height of 3 or 4 feet. In all these cases the plant has lost its natural habit of a sparsely branched tall bush. The China plant of the Assam and Darjeeling gardens is for the most part a low, much-branched bush which only very occasionally is seen to have a distinct stem. In Kangra, however, it is often tall, erect, and very much more like the hybrid than the China plant met with in Assam.

China plant in Kangra.

33. But in addition to a complete change in primary structure or form, it has become densely covered with a multitude of minute branchlets that bear leaves nearly twice the size of the average leaves of the wild plant, and in the better jats of "Assam indigenous" these are pale coloured, soft, less distinctly serrated and concave below. It has to a large extent been deprived of the power of flowering and fruiting, its whole energies have been concentrated in the flushing or production, during part of the season at least, of complete new sets of shoots, which each bear a terminal bud and three to seven leaves according to the system of plucking that may be pursued. Not only have the leaves become soft and pale green, but, together with the whole of the young shoots, they are very succulent and only slightly lignified.

Flushing.

XII.—Origin of Disease.

Origin of disease.

34. The entire nature of the plant has been changed. It is of course grown for its young leafy shoots, and success depends on their quantity and the rapidity with which these are formed. There is reason to believe that in the early years of tea planting, the Assam indigenous afforded only some four or five pluckings* during the season. It now yields on an average from 20 to 30. And if this fact alone does not appeal to most planters as denoting a radical change in the plant, the well-known further fact may be added that for some years

* See Bruce's Reports.

Races of the Tea Plant.

ORIGIN OF of DISEASE.

Mid-season.

past it has been observed that mid-season in all good jat gardens at least appears to be gradually becoming later. We are aware that some planters think this is due to the plants not being so severely plucked in the early months of the season, a change of practice on that point having taken place owing to the more extended cultivation of Assam indigenous. There may be some truth in that, but still there would appear no doubt the period of the plant's activity is being altered, perhaps in adaptation to climatic changes (consequent on the opening out of large tracts). It may seem paradoxical, however, to say that success consists in the production and development of a diseased state, but such is the case. The fattened ox is in reality an animal in a condition of disease, quite as much so as blanched celery is a diseased vegetable product. In both cases they could not exist but for the protecting care that is bestowed on them. In other words, animals and plants are, strictly speaking, diseased whenever their natural functions are disarranged. In such a condition they can exist when carefully tended only. It might, however, more correctly express this view of the case to say they are in an unhealthy condition and to thus reserve the term "disease" to the specific ailments that supervene. They are, in other words, living in a state of predisposition to the organic diseases that may ultimately effect their destruction.

Diseased state.

Predisposition to disease.

Conf. with paras. 100, 189, 298.

Domestication.

35. This is true, of course, of nearly all cultivation, and is in other words an expression of the effects of domestication. But it is doubly true in this case. The tea is forced to produce an abnormal or disproportionate amount of leaf; and it has been removed from the shade of the forest and from association with other plants. Indeed it seems very likely that the so-called rest that the plants get in winter is more than obliterated by the annually recurring effort that is required shortly thereafter to recover the severe shock of the pruning (and probably also the deep hoeing) to which it has been subjected.

Winter rest.

36. The fact of this change of habit in the plant under cultivation would be sufficient to condemn the system, which perhaps hardly now exists any longer, but which has been very common in the past, of taking seed for planting from the leaf bushes of the garden. In doing so, apart from the danger of hybridizing with some wretched low jat bush alongside, one takes seed from what may be called a tainted source. In a similar manner the leaving,

Seed from leaf bushes.

over certain portions of a tea garden, a selected number of bushes to grow up for seed production is, in our opinion, distinctly reprehensible, as a rule, as compared with the opening out of the special seed-gardens. Even were all plants in the garden of one uniform jat, so that, in this case also, the risk of crossing might be regarded as entirely removed, the seed-bearing plants, under these conditions, cannot obtain, without injury to the leaf-bearing stock, the necessary treatment. **ORIGIN of DISEASE.**

XIII.—Improvement of Stock.

IMPROVEMENT of STOCK.

37. We have thus already pointed out the wild races of tea that exist, and shown how these are modified under cultivation. There seems, however, no reason why the whole of these should not be improved upon by a process of selection of those stocks in the garden which produce the most leaf and are the most free from disease. It is needless to attempt to give here an essay on the principles usually followed in selecting and perfecting cultivated races of plants. Suffice it to say that it seems a much more rational and satisfactory way to work back from the tea garden itself instead of forward from the so-called jungle seed-garden. The tall unpruned plants in the seed-garden (or in fact all tea bushes left to grow at will) have lost most of the external peculiarities of form and colour of leaf, and habit of branching, by which they are recognizable, the one from the other. It is accordingly a matter of considerable difficulty to identify the prized forms of the tea garden in the seed-producing state, since all become in the seed-garden very much alike. It follows that the various jats of tea found in the leaf-garden should be carefully studied and their various merits ascertained by comparative tests before any start is made with the seed-garden.

Selection. *Conf. with paras. 52, 53.*

Work back from leaf-garden.

38. If by these means it were observed that one bush possessed certain properties of merit, such as, that it flushed exceptionally freely or early; that it enjoyed immunity or perhaps only suffered less severely from particular blights; or that it succeeded better on a peculiar soil (for which it was desired to have a special stock), than any of the other forms in the garden, we should single out that individual plant for experiment. So again if we found a bush that flowered and fruited freely in the stunted form of the tea garden, we should look upon that as a possible advantageous property that

Methods of selection.

Races of the Tea Plant.

IMPROVEMENT of STOCK.

Methods of selection.

might be perpetuated with the view of producing from the Assam indigenous a plant that would in some respect resemble the China stock. We should have each bush that manifested special properties deemed worthy of investigation isolated, by an enclosure, so that it should not be plucked or otherwise interfered with. It could then be studied carefully with the view to ascertain whether the peculiarity it possessed was more or less fixed. It might then become necessary to cover it completely with a fine wire gauze frame so as to prevent cross fertilization on its reaching the stage. After a sufficient supply of well-formed seed had been obtained from it, we should remove the enclosure and treat it like the other bushes, but have that individual plant numbered and recorded as the standard upon which improvement was to be effected and with which comparisons were in the future to be made of the results obtained.

Propagation by cuttings.

39. Another method would be to produce by cuttings if possible a large number of plants from some particular bush in order to see if its special property was preserved. Having previously selected and prepared a bit of good tea land in the jungles, say, a mile away from the garden, we should now sow the seed there or plant out the rooted cuttings.

40. Doubtless many of the seedlings, after a year or two, would give indications that the seed had been hybridized in spite of every precaution. Every seedling or cutting that manifested the slightest departure from the arbitrarily selected standard I should have instantly removed, and after a time only some half a dozen of the best and purest retained. These we should allow to run to seed, but when the flowers began to form would pluck off a large number, and in order to secure fertilization within the specially selected individuals and to obviate the risk of external influence, would mechanically fertilize the flowers from which this second stage of seed was desired. After obtaining the required quantity we very possibly might next exterminate the plants in the seed-garden and trust to the new and less hybridized supply. Repeating the process of sowing we should again eliminate all the seedlings, say, when they were two or three years old, that manifested the slightest tendency to depart from the structural peculiarities that it was desired to develop. This would take many years no doubt; but, by a process of careful selection, a definite type of plant could easily be developed

and fixed. A supply of seed might then be obtained to plant out a fairly large seed-garden.

UNIFORMITY of STOCK.

XIV.—Advantages of Uniformity of Stock.

Advantages of uniformity.

Conf. with paras. 46, 52.

41. It is perhaps hardly necessary to reiterate the fact that gardens of mixed jats are far less productive than those in which greater care has been manifested in the selection of seed. It is also well known that gardens of fairly uniform and good jat are usually very nearly exempt from the ravages of mosquito, red-spider, etc. We have been taken over many such gardens and had convincing proof in others that it is in the inferior portions, with poor jat teas, where these and other pests first make their appearance, and from whence they spread to the better parts of the garden. To plant out a garden with some half a dozen jats of tea, one bush China, another Assam, and a third an inferior hybrid, or shall we put it two-thirds Assam and one-third inferior jats (dispersed through the better jats), is to provide the conditions necessary for blights to attack the entire garden simultaneously. It was a mistaken notion that to plant Assam and China bushes together secured a good blend of the properties of the two stocks. It has long since been proved to satisfaction that there are mechanical difficulties in collecting and manufacturing leaves of mixed size, age and thickness. Moreover, differences of jat involve a further difficulty in the season of flushing and time necessary to mature each successive flush. If plucked when the one jat is ready, the others may be too old or too young and a loss that may be appalling is thereby sustained. If it be thought desirable to have early flushing as well as late flushing plant, let these be in separate plots where they can be plucked at their respective seasons. Blending cannot be successfully accomplished at the garden and should never be attempted since under the climatic conditions that prevail during the manufacturing season, the sooner each day's produce is packed the better.

Evils of mixed Jats.

Flushing season.

Blending.

Recognisable forms.

42. ***Certain Forms of Tea found in most Gardens.***—Any person who may be disposed to doubt our statements, regarding the wide diversity of quality and yield of the different bushes that compose the vast majority of the gardens in Assam, need only walk into the nearest plot of tea and compare bush by bush. He will find the greatest possible differences in the shape, colour, texture,

UNIFORMITY of STOCK. degree of prominence of the veins and of the marginal serration of the leaves. If next he turns attention to the flushing power of two bushes of different jats, but of as near as possible equal size, he will find that one has only, say, 20 flushing shoots, while the other may have 100. Here, for example, is a bush with fine large, broad, thick and shining dark-coloured leaves, with coarse serration and with deep depressions between the widely arching veins. At a distance it looks not unlike a Cachar jat bush, but is larger and coarser built and spreads into stouter lateral branches than is customary with the Cachar. It was obtained, however, from the same seed-garden as the others and treated absolutely in the same manner as this other plant with smaller paler leaves and minute serration. The former may be seen to be liable to a peculiar blight. This may be described. A constriction occurs at the base of the leaf, the sides are compressed upwards, the leaf turns over to one side under the wind, the now upturned under-surface becomes at first purple, then brown and dies; it is then attacked by a fungus. We have never seen that peculiar disease except on the Assam indigenous plant which we trust our description may bring to the mind's eye of the practical man. It may be asked—Is that large clumsy plant anything like as productive as the smaller leaved, more erect bush growing alongside of it? The two forms of tea here indicated are to be found in nearly every garden in Assam.

Laurel-leaved Tea.

Peculiar disease.

Holly-leaved Tea. 43. The planter will now please turn round and look at this other bush, for behind him is a third form, a stunted plant with broad leaves that are deeply cut on the margin, until they almost look like those of the holly. These holly-like leaves will be seen to be abruptly terminated, instead of being gradually tapered. The newly formed wood has become prematurely brown and the plant is copiously branched and densely covered with ever-green leaves, but it flushes very indifferently. That is to say, the buds do not elongate quickly, the leaves rapidly become too thick and hard to be used as tea; the buds in fact sometimes look like small green roses, and the plant for all the good that it does might just as well be dug up.

Varying quality. 44. Neither the laurel-leaved large bush nor the holly-leaved plant here indicated are profitable, compared with many other forms that might easily enough be substituted. Their dense dark green foliage gives a vigorous look to the garden, however, and thereby they escape the condemnation that they richly deserve. No treatment will ever succeed in bringing bushes that are by nature non-productive into a state of efficiency. But one is told it will never pay to uproot even useless plants. That may be so (though it is very much to be doubted), but why plant useless bushes? A very short inspection of any tea garden will suffice to show most persons that there are different qualities of tea bushes both as to flavour of tea afforded and yield of leaf. If that be so, why should advantage not be taken of so ordinary an observation by developing the seed supply from selected stock?

UNIFORMITY of STOCK.

Uprooting bushes.

XV.—Hybrids.

HYBRIDS.

45. The usual expression "hybrid" has been employed in some of the remarks above, though of course the tea "crosses" are not, botanically speaking, "hybrids" unless the China plant be regarded as a distinct species from the Assam, which it certainly is not. The term is, however, convenient and need not be objected to. While the popular cry of the present day, in the plains at any rate, is to exterminate all China tea and all hybrids and to substitute indigenous jats, we venture to think there may be a danger in carrying this ideal too far. There are, undoubtedly, good as well as bad hybrids, and for some soils and certain climatic conditions a good hybrid may be better than the purest and best Assam indigenous. The very worst argument against the hybrid teas is their greater liability to mosquito; their advantages are that they flush earlier and are less affected by deficient rainfall than the poorer jats. As already pointed out, they are dangerous when intermixed with Assam indigenous, but under proper control might, in our opinion, be grown on special plots of land for which they have undoubted advantages.

Extermination of China Jats

Peculiarities of Hybrids.

46. The object at present in view, however, is to indicate the mixed character of the plants to be found in most gardens, in the hope of being able to convey the idea that a vast improvement in yield would result, were the gardens of the future planted with one form of tea only, and that, the one that had been ascertained of most value. With old gardens where uprooting and replanting are considered financially impossible, every vacancy should be filled up

Uniformity vastly improves outturn.

Conf. with paras. 41–44, 52, 55.

Races of the Tea Plant.

HYBRIDS.

by the right jat, and it is possible much sooner than might be supposed at first sight a complete renovation may be effected.

47. But to return to the subject of the races of the plant, it may be said there is an infinitely more extensive series of hybrid than of pure forms. Here, for example, is a thick-leaved hybrid, with prominent veins, with the leaves exceptionally narrow for their length, pointed at both extremities, and with the sides of the leaf closed upwards so as to show the lighter under-surfaces. The whole attitude of the plant conveys the idea of being parched or of suffering from heat and want of rain. Many planters point to these peculiarities as indicative of the approach of green-fly. The conditions here mentioned may be seen scores of times without a trace of green-fly and that too from March to July. But we have never seen the peculiarities mentioned occur in any form of plant except the narrow, pointed, dark-green-leaved hybrid here described. Like many other forms of the tea plant, this has very frequently a disease of its own which may indeed be the cause of the convolute closing up of the leaves. Over the surfaces of the upturned portions will frequently be seen a multitude of brown or black spots that give the plant a very unsightly appearance. These spots are due to the growth of pustules imbedded within the tissue that contain a wart-forming mite which may possibly be peculiar to this form of plant.

(Margin: Inferior Hybrids. — Coarse Parched plant. — Green-fly. — Wart-forming mite.)

Are hybrids of that character profitable? Count the number of flushing buds and you will see that whatever be the cause of the parched condition, the plant is "*banjhi*" (barren), that is, its buds have been arrested in their growth and are unproductive. The particular form of plant here described is in fact infinitely more liable to become banjhi than is any other jat in the garden.

(Margin: Banjhi bushes.)

48. But there are other hybrids which in point of shape and size of leaf can only be definitely classified by counting the veins. They are sometimes called good hybrids, at other times bad jats of Assam. From the indigenous teas they may be recognized at a distance by their thicker texture, more parallel venation and darker colour of foliage, and also by the important fact that they come into bearing at a much earlier date.

(Margin: Veins of the Leaf. *Conf. with para. 30.*)

49. But we forbear to mention further the long list of hybrids that might be described in this place—hybrids that differ from each other in shape of bush and size and texture of leaf until they

gradually merge from the pure Assam into the pure China. An infinite series might be picked out in any one garden, many of the forms of which, if carefully studied, would each be found to have properties of its own. **HYBRIDS.**

50. ***Process of Hybridization.***—Before leaving the subject of these hybrids it may be as well to say that there is probably no planter who has actually mechanically hybridized different forms and ascertained for himself the advantages or disadvantages of this method of dealing with the jats of tea. What is more surprising, some planters deny that the forms commonly called hybrid have been produced by crossing the Assam indigenous and the China. There can, in our opinion, be no room for doubt that they usually are crosses between the various races mentioned, but it is surprising that the production of these crosses should so completely have been left to accident. **Hybridism.** **Crosses not Hybrids.**

51. It seems possible that the female element in the inferior hybrids may have been the China stock. But this could only be determined by actual experiment. We desire pointedly to draw attention to the uncertainty that exists regarding the origin of the hybrids, in order to convey the idea that in crossing one Assam jat with another, Assam with Cachar, Assam with Manipur, Assam with Naga, Assam with Lushai, or Assam with China, etc., etc., very different results may be obtained in each of these cases from the two stock plants, according as seed is gathered, say in the case of Assam and China, from (*a*) Assam or from (*b*) China. So again the strengthening effects of crossing the resultant with (*a*) or with (*b*) has not apparently been systematically tested. A very extensive series of such experiments might be tried, and who can say that he who follows these up may not produce a jat of tea infinitely superior to any stock at present in existence? Hybridization has hitherto been left to nature; it has in fact been regarded as an unavoidable evil instead of being recognized as one of the possible means of solving the question of blights or of effecting improvements in the yield and quality of tea. **Experiment necessary.**

52. The above remarks on the mixed nature of the stock in most gardens must be held as sufficient for the present purpose. Since it can be demonstrated that one plant is less productive than another, an importance is at once given to a more careful selection of seed, **Mixed stock.** *Conf. with paras. 41–44, 46.*

HYBRIDS.

that should commend itself to all persons interested in tea cultivation. How the many difficulties that beset the adoption of measures of reform are to be overcome must be left for practical men to determine. It seems likely, however, that were a stipulation made, in seed transactions *as to percentage of quality as well as of germination*, the companies who do a business in supplying seed would soon find it to their interest to free their seed-gardens of all doubtful plants. So far as we understand, the contracts simply stipulate for seed of a particular seed-garden (such as Bazaloni, Tingri, Namsang, Kalline, Singlo, etc.), but make no provision for uniformity of jat. It is apparently accepted that seed from a certain seed-garden is of uniform quality.

Percentage of quality in Seed.

Conf. with paras. 37–44, 55.

XVI.–Different districts require different Jats.

Different districts require different Jats.

53. One more point in this connection. It is well to insist on the fact that the plant, whether it be hybrid or a wild race, which may be the best in one district will very likely be totally out of place in another. The delicate jats of Upper Assam are eminently suitable for the climate of that district, but in hotter districts with less rainfall, especially where long six months' droughts are matters of course, they are totally out of place. In the Brahmaputra Valley for instance, in any part below Golaghat on the one bank and Bishnath on the other, it seems probable that they should be replaced by the hardier Manipur types or by some new stock evolved on the principles above laid down. Bazaloni plant, splendid jat as it is, has several times absolutely died out when an attempt was made to plant it in Chittagong. Quite recently a very fine jat was sent to the Terai for planting, but even in the nursery showed its susceptibility to mosquito blight, and hence unsuitability, for in a place like this where mosquito is almost the ruin of the district, the susceptibility or not to this blight should have formed the most essential element in the choice of seed. Instances might be multiplied with regard to almost any district, and it is therefore evident that it is most unwise to buy seed on the reputation it enjoys elsewhere without ascertaining its special applicability to the climate and soil conditions in which it is to be planted.

Chittagong Terai.

XVII.–Seed-Gardens.

Seed-Gardens.

54. ***Seed-Gardens.***– From what has been said therefore it would appear that seed-gardens lying in the jungle, unapproachable

during a large part of the year, and incapable of coming under careful supervision are not to be recommended or encouraged. The idea that seed should come direct from the jungle is one which is now giving way, and rightly so, to that of requiring its production under known conditions. The reason for this is at least twofold - in the first place diseases could be eradicated which might pass from the seed to a new garden, as seems to be quite possible at least in the case of one fungus disease (Brown Blight), for here the fungus was distinctly seen by one of us (G. W.) on the ripe seed itself; in the second, the production of the best seed demands careful cultivation and pruning—the latter of course being conducted on entirely different principles from those in vogue in the leaf-garden, and in a similar manner to that used in a fruit orchard.

SEED-GARDENS.

Too isolated Seed-Gardens.

Brown blight.

55. It would undoubtedly, therefore, be preferable to the present system for every large company to open out a seed-garden of its own, in some suitable situation and within manageable distance of head-quarters. The first step in that direction should be the selection of the stock, and in this the very greatest care should be manifested. Advantage in every direction might be expected to follow an almost hypercritical study of the seedlings intended for the future seed-garden.

Selection of stock. *Conf. with paras. 37–44, 52.*

56. ***Selection of Site for a Seed-Garden.***—In its truly wild state tea occurs on a rich red rather heavy loam or even a clay, red in colour, and perhaps approaching the Tezpur bank soil in type. The soil selected should approximate as near as possible to this kind of land. Lowlying, swampy, black, heavy soils with much decomposing matter are to be avoided. It is evident that seed tea does not appreciate the presence of heavy jungle. It occurs in the wild state in association with open mixed scrubby vegetation, and hence the seed-garden might with advantage be interplanted with "*Sau*," "*Kala siris*," or similar trees.

Site of Seed-Garden.

Habitat of wild Tea. *Conf. with paras. 25–27.*

57. The pruning that should be annually given to the bushes should be the removal periodically of all branches that had already borne a sufficient amount of fruit or that were giving indications of becoming exhausted. The primary aim should be to produce a healthy well-formed bush, with as little superfluous wood as possible. It is a matter of some practical importance to prevent the bushes from running into unmanageable large sizes, since in that state they

Pruning for Seed. *Conf. with para. 134.*

Size of bushes.

SEED-GARDENS.

incur the risk of being broken during the rough handling they are often subjected to, in the collection of seed. That object would very possibly be attained by the systematic removal of one or more branches every three or four years.

Collection of Seed.

58. In fact the lopping off or thinning out of a certain percentage of overgrown boughs would do less harm to seed-production, where quality of seed was aimed at, than a more extensive system of light pruning. The pruning that should be pursued may briefly be said to be similar to orchard cultivation generally. Deep cultivation is also essential, and the opportunity should then be taken to cut a certain percentage of the roots. The deep hoeing and root-pruning, if the latter is done, should, as a rule, be accomplished not later than January and should only be undertaken when the soil is comparatively speaking dry. Deep hoeing in damp clay soils is distinctly injurious though sub-soil drainage with or without pipes placed at a distance from the roots would vastly improve the majority of seed-gardens.

Exchange of Seed.

59. ***Exchanges.***—But there is one point that must still be mentioned in connection with the subject of seed-production. It is the all but universal experience in agriculture that seed had better not be raised in the locality where it is to be sown. An advantage is universally admitted as secured by an exchange of seed. But were all the larger companies to accept, as an obligation laid on them, the duty of opening out seed-gardens and scientifically studying the best methods of producing the most approved jats of tea, exchanges might easily and profitably be effected. Indeed, the extent of property held by many of the larger companies is such that with two or three small seed-gardens in different corners of their estate they need have no fear in using their own seed.

Improvement in yield.

Conf. with para. 46.

60. ***Conclusion.***—It is known that certain blights show a decided preference for certain races of the tea plant. Where such blights prevail to a ruinous extent selection of stock might amount to a successful remedial measure. The subject of seed-production should therefore not only commend itself to every one interested in tea, because of the high prices demanded for good seed, but because of the radical reforms and economies that would soon be effected were all future gardens, extensions, and replantations, made with carefully selected and approved stock. An undoubted increase of yield, with a

corresponding reduced cost would take place and blights become of very much lessened consequence. SURPLUS TEA SEED.

XVIII.-Utilisation of surplus Tea Seed.

61. During the past two or three years (1899-1901) a very large amount of seed has been produced which is not needed for planting, and must be utilised, if utilised at all, in some other way than for sowing. The value of seed of this character almost entirely depends on the usefulness of the oil and on the possibility of getting good feeding or manurial material from the residual cake. It was attempted in 1885 to put tea seed, as such, on the London market under the name "*tanne.*" Great interest, we understand, was manifested, but the seed found no buyer, and the price asked sank quickly to a level far below the cost of importation. At the present day the seed does not come into commerce at all, except for the production of new bushes.

Excess of seed produced.

'Tanne.'

62. The following analysis by Mr. D. Hooper ("*South of India Observer,*" 1894) of Tea seed from the Nilgiris, previously dried, shows the composition of the material :—

Analysis of seed.

Fixed Oil	22·9
Albuminoids	8·5
Saponin	9·1
Carbohydrates	19·9
Starch	32·5
Fibre	3·8
Mineral matter	3·3
	100·0

Of these constituents, those of interest for our purpose are the fixed oil, the saponin, the albuminoids (*i.e.,* the nitrogen) and the mineral matter. Let us take these seriatim.

63. ***The Fixed Oil***—Is present in small amount compared with that in most other oil seeds, such as linseed, cotton or castor. It is necessary to say, however, that many samples appear to contain much more oil than the seeds quoted above, but an estimated yield of 25 per cent. obtainable by hot pressure is probably an extreme one for practical working. If high quality oil is wished, the seed will

Tea seed oil.

Quantity.

SURPLUS TEA SEED.

have to be pressed cold, and not more than 20 per cent. may be anticipated. Even this may be taken as higher than would, on the average, be obtained under commercial conditions.

Properties of oil.

64. The oil itself is a clear, light yellow, liquid, non-drying oil, approaching olive oil in character, but which always has a more or less acrid taste. A sample recently examined appears to be free from saponin—a poisonous substance (see below) which nearly always occurs in it, but in order to get this freedom great care has to be taken in pressing. Though when heated the poisonous properties of the saponin are destroyed, yet the small quantity which may be present would condemn it as an edible oil for use in western countries. The Chinese, it appears, have long used it for cooking purpose, and it might possibly be employed by the people in the tea districts in a similar manner if it were easily obtainable.

Uses of oil.

65. As a lamp oil it answers very well, and would seem to be quite capable of local introduction for this purpose. We say "local introduction" because burning oils are at present rather at a discount in the markets of the world compared with their former position,—kerosene and petroleum products having largely taken the market in the great centres which was formerly theirs. At the same time the fact that it is satisfactory for this purpose should not be forgotten. The oil produces an excellent soap, hard and white. For this purpose the presence of saponin would be no disadvantage, but would rather add to the lathering power of the soap. If the oil could be produced in quantity, and a supply guaranteed at a rate which would compete with the other vegetable oils, there is no doubt an opening for it in this direction.

Saponin

66. ***The Saponin.***—This poisonous constituent of the tea seed is all but entirely contained in the cake, after expression of the oil. It is white, solid, sweetish to the taste at first, but rapidly becoming bitter and acrid in the mouth, and it leaves a biting sensation in the throat for some time. It is exceedingly poisonous, and its presence at once destroys any chance of using the cake or the seed as a feeding stuff for animals.

lbuminoids and Nitrogen.

67. ***The Albuminoids and Nitrogen.***—To the nitrogen contained in the albuminoids the cake would owe the greatest part of its manurial value. In this respect, however, it does not for one moment compare with most other oil cakes. Compare for instance

SURPLUS TEA SEED.

the following figures representing the average amount of nitrogen in other manure cakes with that given by Tea Seed Oil Cake :—

Manurial value. Nitrogen. *Conf. with paras. 265—271.*

	Nitrogen per cent.
Mustard Cake	4 to 5
Linseed Cake	4 to 5·5
Castor Cake	5·5 to 6·5
Decorticated Cotton Cake . . .	6·5 to 8
Undecorticated Cotton Cake . . .	3·5 to 4·5
Tea Seed Cake	1·92

Thus, if castor cake were worth 2 rupees per maund in Calcutta, calculating on the basis of the nitrogen alone, the Tea Seed Cake would probably not be worth, at the most, ten to twelve annas for the same quantity.

68. Tea Seed Cake is likewise inferior in other manurial constituents. Comparing again the following figures for mineral matter and phosphoric acid in several manure cakes, this will be clearly seen :—

Mineral matter and Phosphoric Acid.

	Mineral Matter per cent.	Phosphoric Acid per cent.
Mustard Cake	8 to 10	2 to 3
Linseed Cake . . .	4 to 6	1·5 to 3
Castor Cake	9 to 10	2 to 3
Cotton Cake . . .	7 to 8	3 to 4
Tea Seed Cake	3·3 to 4·07	0·58

Summary.

69. Taking these various points into consideration, it will at once be seen that as a manure the cake produced by pressing tea seed is of very inferior character, and would hardly pay for carriage over very long distances for this purpose,—nor can it compete in any market with cakes produced from other oil seeds. On the other hand it is quite good enough to use locally, provided the net cost does not exceed 8 to 12 annas per maund on the garden. It (the cake) is however supposed to have insecticidal properties, and might be useful for this purpose. In the paper above quoted, Mr. Hooper suggests spraying the bushes with a decoction of the seed, or dusting the plants with a powder made by grinding them up. Such a decoction is likely to be serviceable against red spider, but exactly of what value it is can only be determined by trial. Spread on the ground round the bushes the cake would be likely to keep away some types of

SURPLUS TEA SEED.

caterpillar, and other pests which spread by creeping from bush to bush, or which make their home in the ground during the day. A strip covered with this cake between the tea and the jungle would probably keep out many of the pests which creep from the surrounding land into the tea. The utility of the cake itself as an efficient substitute for soap is very doubtful. Though it lathers well, on account of its saponin content, yet this does not necessarily mean that it has great cleansing properties. Nevertheless it has been used for many years in China instead of soap, and it would probably be of some value for this purpose. One more use is made of the cake in China. It is there stated to be very effective as a poison for fish.

Summary.

70. On the whole, therefore, while it appears that there would be a market for the oil if it could be obtained in quantity and fairly cheaply, it must, for the present, be a local one, and the material could hardly compete with oils already in general commerce, unless it be for the production of superior soaps. As a lamp oil it has distinct advantages which should recommend it for local consumption. The press cake is useless for feeding, and forms an inferior manure, though one quite good enough to apply to the land and also to cart for some distance, provided the cost on the garden does not exceed 8 to 12 annas per maund. It would probably be useful as an insecticide—both as cake against certain caterpillars, and as a decoction which might replace that of a wild fern now used in Dibrugarh against Red Spider.

Analysis of tea seed cake.

71. The analysis of a sample of tea seed cake recently obtained was as follows:—

Moisture	11·99
Oil	10·48
* Albuminoids	12·00
Carbohydrates, etc.	58·80
Woody Fibre	2·66
† Phosphoric Acid	·58
Lime	·11
Alkaline Salts, etc.	2·78
Sand	·60
	100·00

* Containing Nitrogen . . . . 1·92
† Phosphate of Lime . . . . 1·26

NECESSITY of TILLAGE.

CHAPTER IV.

HOEING, WEEDING AND TILLAGE GENERALLY.

(In the chapters which follow it does not seem necessary to repeat the reference given in the last edition of this work to the earlier authors on hoeing, draining, and other agricultural operations carried on the tea garden, unless they have some special bearing on the argument here set out. Those interested in these matters of purely historical importance are referred to the former edition.)

XIX.—Necessity of a friable soil and of tillage.

Conf. with para. 271.

Soil required for tea.

72. A point in the history of the tea cultivation has now been reached at which it is possible to lay down with some approach to confidence the soil conditions which are necessary for the production of the most vigorous tea bushes and the maximum production of leaf. The first of these is undoubtedly the friability, or at any rate the easy penetrability of the land to a considerable depth to the plant roots and also to water. Tillage becomes therefore necessary under Indian conditions, and though the amount, the methods, and the character of the tillage vary from district to district and also with the character of the land in one district, yet in some measure, it seems essential almost everywhere. Tillage of the soil may be said to be undertaken with the two-fold object of opening it up in order that water may penetrate freely, and of turning up and exposing again and again fresh portions of it to the direct action of heat, sunlight and air, in order that disintegration may take place. By these means the soil is mechanically pulverised, and at the same time undergoes certain very necessary chemical and physical changes that are essential before it can become available as plant food. Rain-water may be said to be nature's chief manurial agent. It holds in solution a large quantity of air which, as we know, contains oxygen, nitrogen, carbonic acid, nitric acid and ammonia. Rain-water, moreover, has been warmed both in passing through the air and by its contact with the warm surface soil. Heat and oxygen bring about important decomposition in the organic ingredients of the soil, the acids enter into union with its insoluble matter and

Objects of Tillage. *Conf. with para. 75.*

Chemical and Physical changes.

Rain-water.

OBJECTS of TILLAGE.

render much of it soluble, while the nitrogen of the air feeds the organisms of the soil that are indispensable to the life of the higher plants. It is thus self-evident that if the soil be not fully and freely permeated by the rain-water, it cannot be in a full measure productive, though, of course, some plants demand much more thorough permeation than others. Further, the more frequently and completely that the surface soil is broken up and exposed to the sun, air and water, the greater will be the disintegration of its insoluble mineral ingredients and the higher its immediate fertility.

Fertility.

Retention of Friability of Soil.

73. But tillage alone will not produce, in by any means all soils, the desirable results here set out. There exist soils now under tea in India which, when hoed, only remain friable until the next shower of rain, and then run down again into an absolute puddle. It is therefore necessary not only to consider the necessity of cultivation, which no one in India would now deny, but also the amount and kind necessary under different conditions, the treatment supplementary to hoeing in certain cases in order to *retain* the friability and permeability of the soil, and the final effect on the soil itself of long continued and constantly recurring cultivation.

XX.—Annual Deep Hoeing.

Deep Hoe necessary.

74. In the first place, it may be stated as an absolutely general rule throughout the Indian Tea Districts, with the exception of the case of tea planted in peat bheels, and in lands of allied character, that deep cultivation to at least a depth of eight or nine inches should be given after the end of the rains in each autumn or early cold weather.

Objects of Deep Hoe.

Prevents Evaporation. *Conf. with paras. 99, 101.*

Increases Fertility. *Conf. with para. 72.*

75. The object primarily to be attained by this cultivation is the protection of the land and hence of the bushes against the long drought which follows in most districts, for the soil turned up by this hoeing, especially if it is immediately pulverised, forms a sort of blanket preventing the evaporation of the water in the lower strata of the soil during the ensuing months. But this is not the only object in view. The cultivation of tea makes very large demands on the available fertility of the land, and, if outside measures are not added, the only way in which the soil can recoup itself from the loss caused by the tea crop is by rendering a further portion of its reserve stock of plant-food ready for use. This conversion of non-available into available food can only be accomplished by

PLATE I. (*To face Page 37.*)

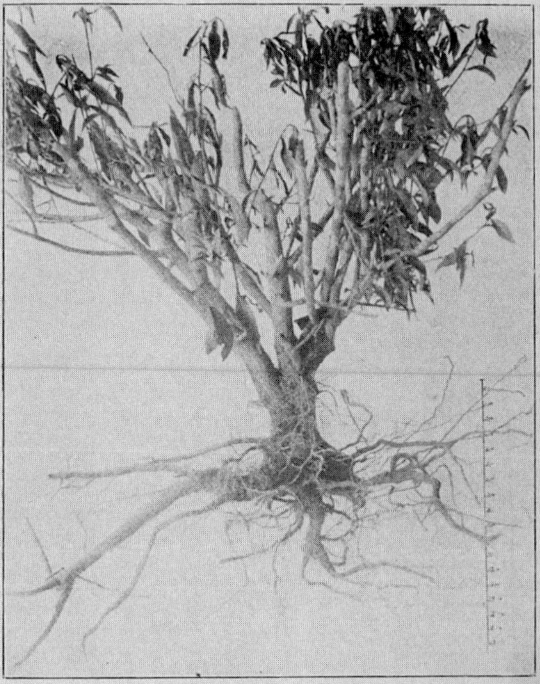

No. 1.—Bush shewing formation of roots on hard pan subsoil.
(From Photograph by H. H. Mann.)

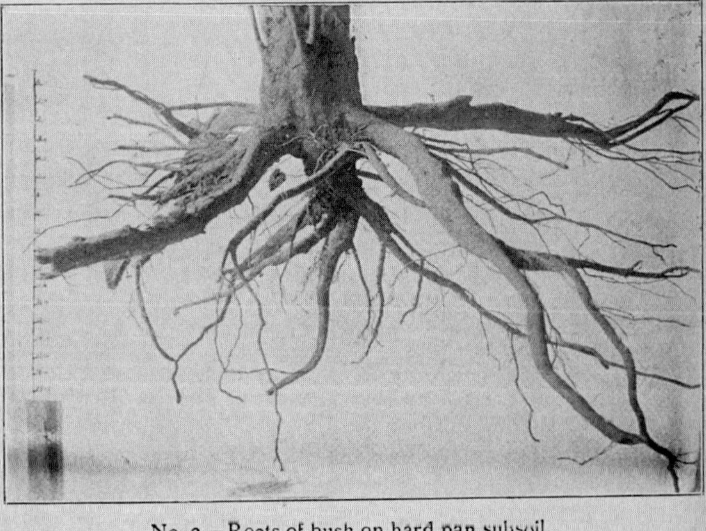

No. 2.—Roots of bush on hard pan subsoil.
(From Photograph by H. H. Mann.)

Hoeing, Weeding and Tillage generally.

exposure of the lower strata of the soil to air, to light, and to the changes in temperature necessarily connected with such exposure. To what extent this rendering available of reserve materials takes place under Indian conditions has never been the subject of investigations, but judging from analyses made by one of the authors (H. H. M.) on the Oxford clay subsoils of England, the *available* amount of Potash and Phosphoric Acid will probably often double itself by three months' exposure even without any rain. **OBJECTS of TILLAGE.**

76. A third object is served however by this autumn cultivation in many of the lands now under tea which show a strong tendency to the formation of a hard subsoil "pan." The presence of this leads to unhealthiness and hence to various diseases such as Red Rust, and causes rapid deterioration of the plant. Such a tendency can be controlled only by cultivation to a different depth in different seasons. For instance, if the normal cold weather hoe is nine inches, the "pan" will form at this depth, and it will need deeper cultivation, say, once in three years, to properly prevent its formation. This is partly the reason, for instance, why it has become customary on the Tezpur bank to put in a hoe of 14 to 15 inches once, say, in three years, a depth of cultivation which would be totally unnecessary on a garden where the soil was naturally more friable, and hence showed no tendency to the formation of a "pan" layer. **Prevention of 'Hard pan.'** **'Tezpur Deep Hoe.'**

77. This excessively deep hoe, however suitable for gardens which have been commenced and treated in frank acknowledgment of its need, is too dangerous a method of dealing with old existing gardens for it to be universally recommended in such cases. The necessary cutting of roots, and large roots too, which is often required to carry it out, involves such a shock to the bushes that in some cases it is many years before they recover their tone,—if indeed they ever do. The other alternative of deep trench hoeing down alternate rows of tea each year, and so of allowing the descent of the roots, is here much more to be recommended, and, if experiments now in progress turn out the success which seems probable, will afford a most valuable means of dealing with cases which have been almost beyond recovery by any other means. **Hoeing in Old Gardens.** **Trench Hoeing.**

78. In summary, therefore, deep tillage once a year is not only advisable but practically necessary in almost every type of land, except that classified as "peat." Its usual depth should be at least **Summary.**

TILLAGE. 8 to 10 inches, but in the case of lands with a tendency to form hard pan its depth should be varied from year to year. In cases where excessively deep hoeing is not advisable the same effect will probably be produced by cutting deep trenches between the rows.

Objects. The objects of this annual deep cultivation are these :—

(*a*) it is a protection from drought;
(*b*) it renders the fertility of the soil more available for the plant;
(*c*) it is a means of preventing the formation of hard pan.

XXI.—Light Hoeing.

Light Hoeing. 79. If a good yield of tea is to be obtained, not only is a winter deep hoe necessary, but it is equally essential to cultivate regularly during the time when the leaf is growing. The object of such cultivation is, of course, primarily to keep down rank weed and jungle growth among the tea, but it has another function equally if not more important. The fact is often brought to notice that a new garden needs little hoeing to make it yield, but that after a number of years in order to keep up the usual rate of yield of tea per acre, more and more cultivation becomes necessary. The reason for this, is simply that the roots have sufficient food in their vicinity when the soil is virgin and rich, but that in after years, when exhaustion has begun to be felt, they cannot get it nearly so easily unless, by hoeing, a fresh supply is constantly brought into contact with them. Hence the function of the hoe as a means of putting plant food into the most favourable position for absorption, is at least equally important with its use as a means of keeping down weed growth.

New Garden needs little Hoeing.

Cultivation on Peat. 80. This function is well illustrated by the known fact that on exceedingly rank land such as the peat flats of Cachar and Sylhet little or no cultivation is either needed or given. Here the roots are surrounded by what is a mass of little else than plant food, and so long as the peat is present there will always be amply sufficient for the bush, and that in an easily available form. When one considers further that the extreme rankness of the growth causes the soil to be quickly shaded so that little weed herbage can grow under the bushes, the use of the hoe is found to be needed very little during the growing season for either of the above-mentioned purposes.

No Weeds on Peat.

81. But apart from the exceptional circumstances which these

Hoeing, Weeding and Tillage generally.

present, there is no more discussed question among planters as to the amount of cultivation necessary on a garden. Some hold, and in many cases we suspect rightly, that in the majority of gardens the error tends to lie on the side of over, rather than under, hoeing. Indeed, it seems an unfortunate circumstance that tea-cultivation has come to mean surface hoeing. But still the moot points remain. How many hoeings form the best allowance on light, medium, and heavy land? Is it better to hoe three times to 6 inches deep than six times to 4 inches deep? Is it wise to hoe during the whole growing season at the same rate or go ahead with the work vigorously in spring and allow jungle to grow in the autumn?

TILLAGE. Over-Cultivation.

82. ***Experiment to prove extent of hoeing and weeding desirable.***—We should like to see the experiment tried for, say, eight or ten years, of a plot of land 30 acres in extent, consisting of a fairly uniform soil throughout, similar drainage all over, and with exactly the same age and jat of bushes being divided into two equal sections and experimentally tested as follows:—

Experiment necessary.

One half to be deep hoed three times a year, and light hoed once every month and carefully weeded so that not a trace of weed could be seen anywhere throughout the entire experimental term. The other, once deep hoed and light hoed not more than four times a year, weeds being kept down during July, August and September when thought excessive, and at each hoeing carefully buried in the soil. The returns preserved should show:—

Nature of Returns.

(*a*) the total expense of cultivation of each plot separately;
(*b*) the average price obtained for the tea of each plot separately;
(*c*) the total yield per acre of tea of each plot separately.

Of course such a plot would have previously to be freed from all deep-rooted injurious weeds, such as "*ulu*" grass, and the systems of plucking and pruning would have to be precisely similar. At first the return from the highly cultivated and absolutely clean plot would very possibly be higher than from the other, but it is very probable that a decidedly greater exhaustion of soil would be demonstrated even in ten years, by the decline both in the price and in the weight of the tea, while the extra cost of production would be found to bear heavily against the financial results of the so-called high cultivation.

83. The introduction of green manuring crops into the system of growing tea in recent years forms a departure from what has been

Green Manuring.

TILLAGE.

hitherto reckoned as good planting practice. For the use of these crops as aids to tea cultivation involves the land being under a crop of "green manure" in May and June when otherwise it would have been as clean as at any time in the year. We believe, however, that this is a step in the right direction and that the avoidance of what often was a totally unnecessary "round of the hoe," except to get rid of a small amount of jungle growth, will, entirely apart even from the manurial value of the green crop itself, be of benefit both from a planting and financial point of view. While we do not approve of the growth of a mixed weed herbage in a garden, the presence of a known selected type of plant for growing among tea as a green manure will decidedly be of the highest benefit to the tea bushes.

Green Manuring. *Conf. with paras. 89, 124, 126, 238–252, 282.*

Effects of Over-Hoeing.

84. It will therefore be seen that we are strongly of opinion that there is a limit to the extent that hoeing is beneficial. Every time the soil is turned up and pulverised it is exposed to the action of the atmosphere. It is dried, made porous, and oxidised. If the soil be already too porous, hoeing beyond a certain limit may become positively hurtful. Porous soils have usually a very low percentage of organic matter, and as being porous, their organic materials are always rapidly oxidised and used up.

Amount of Hoeing needed.

85. For these reasons rules for the hoeing of all gardens cannot be laid down either as to the depth of hoeing, or as to the number of hoes. Generally speaking the stiffer a soil the more cultivation it will require, *provided it be not carried out when the soil is wet,* which is worse than useless. Thus while four light hoeings in the season will be ample on some sandy lands, double this amount will be by no means excessive on stiff plateau or flat. It is usually useless to turn over land in the spring when it is already perfectly loose and dry simply because the time has come for the hoeing. We have heard planters boast that their "second round of hoeing was almost finished" when owing to lack of rain the said hoeing could do little or no good. It is only possible to carry out agricultural operations of this sort by the exercise of a considerable amount of discretion, which can only be exercised by the man on the spot, for hoeing in almost all soils will be found most useful when the soil hoed is, in the case of stiff land, about half dry, or in the case of sandy light land, is from half to three-quarters saturated with moisture.

Kodalli *versus* Fork.

86. Into the vexed question of the "*kodalli*" *versus* the "fork"

hoe—a theme hotly contested by men of long experience, it is hardly our function to enter. The one simulates the European plough, the other the cultivator; with the one the soil is turned over, with the other it is merely loosened (though it may, in stiff soils, be equally turned over); the one means the cutting of nearly all lateral roots, in the other case a great many are not injured. Both systems have their value and in general one may say that whatever has been the system it will be wise to continue it. On slopes the question takes another aspect, and this will be mentioned a little later.

CULTIVATION of SLOPES.

XXII.—Cultivation of slopes.

Wash of Soil. *Conf. with paras. 127–129, 271.*

87. The principles thus laid down may be applicable to flat land; on slopes they are complicated by a problem which is a vital one in a hilly region,—how to prevent wash of soil down the slopes. The question of how to combine the greatest amount of cultivation with the minimum of wash is the most important problem in the culture of tea in the Darjeeling and similarly situated districts, where an excess of hoeing means gradual destruction of the garden, while too great a limitation of cultivation means low yield, poor bushes, and general lack of vigour in the garden. Without daring to lay down any system in detail, which is indeed beyond the scope of this chapter, the following system suggested by a well-known Darjeeling planter might perhaps be indicated as representing a good plan for that district. He says. "It seems, therefore, that the proper way to tackle cultivation on these slopes, not terraced, where terracing now would be almost prohibitive in cost on account of loss of soil, would be to hoe as soon after the rains as possible, try and get a light hoe in immediately after the pruning, and then not touch the slopes again to ensure a sward covering the surface before the first sharp showers of spring occur. In July and August a regular turf will have formed after a sickling or two, and then all slopes not too steep might have the soil turned over almost with immunity from wash, as the surface soil is then a mass of green jungle and roots."

Method suggested.

88. The same system would apply to slopes of the same kind in other districts which have not been terraced. But a slope not terraced should be an anomaly instead of being the rule, and when one sees a garden ruined owing to surface wash, owing to no attempt having been made to terrace the land, one is inclined to consider it as

Terracing. *Conf. with para. 129.*

SUPPLEMENTARY TREATMENT.

the just reward of neglect in the garden's early days before it was too late. Terracing will however be dealt with in the next chapter.

XXIII.—Treatment supplementary to hoeing.

Loss of Organic Matter.

89. Hoeing will not keep some tea soils friable if applied alone. Owing to their originally finely divided condition they tend, as they lose organic matter owing to exposure, plant growth, and leakages of many kinds, to become more and more consolidated and hence more and more unsuitable for the growth of tea. Under these circumstances the plan of growing a crop of some green plant, preferably one of the leguminous or pea tribe, can be most strongly recommended as returning or giving to the soil the organic matter which will render it again friable and suitable for tea. The best crop for this purpose hitherto tried in the plains is "*Kalai*" or "*Mati kalai*" (**Phaseolus mungo** or **Phaseolus aconitifolius**) of which more will be said under manuring, but the function of such crops in retaining the open texture of land is exceedingly important.

Use of Green Crops. *Conf. with paras. 83, 124, 126, 238-252, 282.*

Weeds as Green Crops. *Conf. with paras. 90-92, 240-241.*

It might at once be asked,—Will not the same purpose be served by allowing the natural weeds of the land to grow, and hoeing them in the same way as the *kalai* is hoed in?—To this it may be answered that in a certain measure the same purpose will be served but not altogether, and for two reasons. Of these the first is that the root development of the ordinary tea garden weeds is excessively small (*see Plate II*) when compared with the *Kalais*, and secondly, that the organic matter when hoed in is very poor in manurial value compared with the leguminous plants, as these latter have the power of fixing valuable matters from the air. The burial of organic matter, of any sort, however, tends to increase the friability of the soil and hence on stiff land is very valuable.

Burial of Organic Matter.

XXIV.—Weeds.

Weeds. *Conf. with paras. 80, 89, 240-241.*

90. ***Advantages and Disadvantages of Weeds.***—Though it is advisable to have a crop, as suggested above, on the land between the tea during part of the season, it by no means follows that a crop of weeds is desirable, and the greater and greater avoidance of such a crop of weeds seems to be one of the great points of development in the tea industry of the past few years. The general

PLATE II. (*To face Page 43.*)

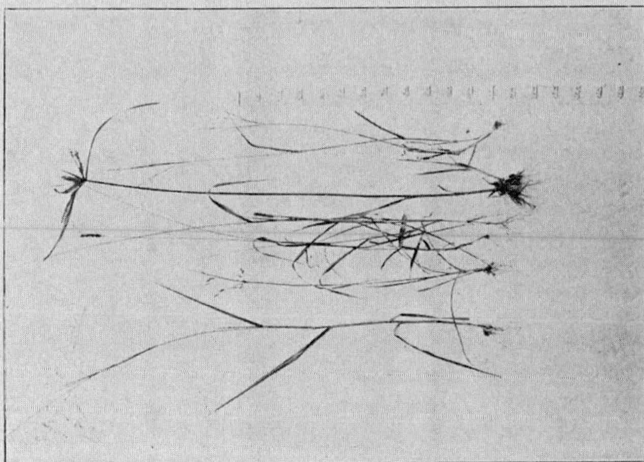

No. 2.—Various Grasses of Tea Gardens.
(From Photograph by H. H. Mann.)

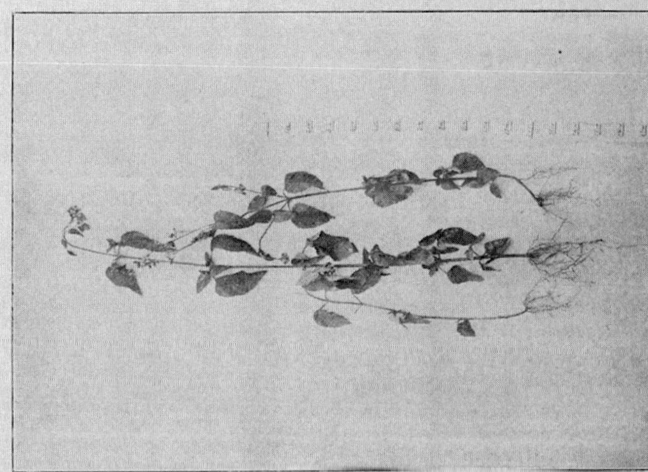

No. 1.—Ageratum ('cold-weather weed,' '*ilami*') of Tea Gardens.
(From Photograph by H. H. Mann.)

Hoeing, Weeding and Tillage generally.

view throughout the tea growing districts at present is that weeds are undesirable in any quantity, and as applied to the mixture of more or less useless (even when not harmful) vegetation usually found, we are quite in agreement with this view, though we think that the presence of a definite selected crop between the bushes for part, even, of every season to be eminently desirable. The weeds naturally growing up may and do harbour many of the pests (such as the Orange Beetle) of the tea, and this in itself would condemn their growth. One may say in general that their disadvantages are their choking effect on the tea, and their harbouring of pests and blight, and their sole advantage—the return of organic matter to the soil—can be better accomplished by a crop specially grown for the purpose. WEEDS. Encourage Pests.

91. ***Weeds of Tea Gardens.***—It may be of advantage here to give an enumeration of the more common weeds of tea gardens in India. The list has no pretension to be complete, but gives, we fancy, the most important of those found.

(*i*) Undoubtedly the most common weed is the **Ageratum** known as "cold weather weed" in Assam, and as "*Ilami*" in the Dooars and Darjeeling (see Plate II). It seems universal where tea is grown, is a sign of cultivated land, and flourishes where tea flourishes. As its root development is shallow, it is of little value as a green manure. Ageratum. *Conf. with para. 240.*

(*ii*) **Imperata arundinacea.**—*Ulu* grass (Assam), *Sunn* grass (Assam), "*Kur*" (Darjeeling), "*Ciru*" (Dooars and Terai) is the worst weed of tea culture. It occurs practically everywhere, but yields to constant hoeing. It occupies the place in tea culture that "couch" grass or "twitch" does in English agriculture. 'Ulu' Grass.

(*iii*) Other grasses of various kinds are also found (see Plate II). "*Doob*" grass (**Cynodon dactylon**) is often noticed, but does not seem important. Among annual grasses **Paspalum sanguinale** is much the most common and is known as "*bunsu*" among the Nepalese and also in the plains. It is the first weed growth in a garden after hoeing in the rains very often, and occurs from Sylhet to an elevation of 5,000 feet in Darjeeling. Another most common grass is **Setaria Glauca,**—and together these form the most frequently found grasses of tea gardens. Other Grasses.

Hoeing, Weeding and Tillage generally.

WEEDS.

Polygonum spp.

(*iv*) Polygonaceous plants often form a large part of the annual weed herbage. **Polygonum runcinatum** and **Polygonum alatum** (known as "*Kuru*" in Nepalese) are especially common on the lower Himalaya.

Bidens pilosa.

(*v*) **Bidens pilosa,** the seeds of which are exceedingly irritating to coolies and all others, is one of the most objectionable weeds, and occurs everywhere.

Sensitive Plant. *Conf. with para. 249.*

(*vi*) **Mimosa pudica** or "Sensitive Plant" is not often found among the tea, but by the side of tea garden roads is very common. To its thorns are attributed a large amount of the ulcers on the feet among the coolies in the late rains. Among other leguminous plants the *Sida* (**Sida rhombifolia**) was prominent in all districts from Dibrugarh to the Terai.

Ferns.

(*vii*) Ferns are very common in all sections of the tea area, and are much objected to. They get into the inside of the bushes and are very difficult to eradicate.

Colocasia antiquorum.

(*viii*) **Colocasia antiquorum** is common everywhere. It, with ferns, forms the principal undergrowth on the Sylhet bheels, and it seems specially fond of damp places, but flourishes everywhere. Owing to its bulbous root, it only yields to hand pulling, and should be thrown out on to the roads.

Titiapat.

(*ix*) The Worm wood (**Artemisia**) or "*Titiapat*" is also excessively common and very luxuriant.

Abijal.

(*x*) A very objectionable caryophyllaceous weed is **Drymaria sp.** or "*Abijal*" which climbs inside the bushes, more especially in the hilly districts, and in one case on record the seeds and small pieces of the weed got into the tea, were manufactured with it, and were concentrated in sorting into the finer grades, and ruined them. It is only bad in the second half of the season.

Artificial Nature of Weeds on Tea Estates.

92. For some reason or other therefore tea garden weeds are of a very artificial and uniform character, and are, as a whole, of a very useless type. A consideration of the usual weed herbage confirms most strongly the view that it is not wise to allow weeds to grow, and that if it be desired to have green plants on the soil at any time of the year they should be specially planted ones such as those recommended previously, and not the weed herbage of the garden.

DRAINAGE.

CHAPTER V.

DRAINAGE OF TEA GARDENS.

Objects of Drainage. *Conf. with para. 101.*

93. It has been said that "to drain land is to rid it of its superfluous moisture." That is the most generally accepted idea, but the objects aimed at in addition are to increase the depth and improve the condition of the arable soil. The drainage of agricultural land thus differs essentially from that of the streets of a town. The removal of surplus water is undertaken with a definite object in view, the fulfilment of which determines the position and number of the drains that may be necessary. To understand, therefore, the principle involved by the conception of superfluous moisture in agriculture, it becomes necessary to devote, first, some attention to the study of water and its influences on the soil, and, second, to consider the functions it performs in the economy of plant life.

XXV.—Water and its Relation to the soil.

Conf. with paras. 95, 107, 108. **Solvent of Food Materials.**

94. In the first place, then, water may be said to be the solvent by means of which the food materials of the soil are taken up by the roots. But in addition to water passing into and being diffused through the soil, by virtue of this dissolving power, it is very much more largely drawn down by another physical law, namely, the affinity for water which the various ingredients of the soil possess. All soils, it may be said, have the power to absorb and retain water apart from the temporary disappearance of certain of their ingredients in the state of solution. Soils may be regarded as built up of mineral particles of varying sizes and properties with interspaces occupied by water and air. No soil, however dry it may appear, is totally devoid of water and air. A soil is saturated when it contains the maximum quantity of water that its interspaces are capable of holding naturally. And this again is regulated by the chemical and mechanical conditions of its mineral particles. Water is diffused through the soil by what is called "capillary attraction," the interspaces act like tubes within which the water is rapidly distributed. The shape and size of these interspaces is entirely dependent on the mechanical condition of the mineral particles. But the chemical and physical properties of soil ingredients

Movement of Water in Soil. **Soils.** **Saturated Soils.** **Soil Moisture.** **Capillary Attraction.**

WATER in RELATION to SOIL. Soil Affinity for Water.

aid materially in this absorption of moisture. Sugar will be dissolved if placed in contact with water, but castor oil is neither dissolved nor will it mechanically mix with water—it has no affinity for it. Clayey soils manifest a strong affinity and sandy or gritty soils a very weak affinity for water. Dry clay will absorb from the atmosphere as much as 5 per cent. of moisture in 24 hours, while sand, unless in a very fine state of division, will hardly absorb any. Water is thus attracted to, retained by, and distributed within the soil, until the maximum absorbing point has been attained. With clayey soils this is much higher and therefore reached considerably later than with sandy soils. Soils that soon become saturated are those that are soonest parched. In soils with a due portion of clay the moisture rises up gradually from below to replace surface evaporation, and such soils, therefore, dry slowly, because of the strong affinity for water possessed by clay. So again clayey soils absorb the night dews, and thus to a certain extent compensate for the daily surface evaporation by night absorption. During heavy rains an excess over saturation still passes through the soil to the underground channels of transmission by simple gravitation, but even still very largely in consequence of the peculiar affinity of clay for water. The excess does not at all events tend so readily to flow on the surface of clayey loams as is the case with saturated sandy soils, the ingredients of which possess little or no affinity for water. From these considerations, therefore, it may be said that a soil is water-logged when it retains a surplus proportion of moisture over saturation, the surplus existing not as moisture but as actual water.

Sandy Soil. Parching of Soils. Evaporation and Absorption. Water-logged Soils.

Improvement of Soil Conditions. *Conf. with para. 20.*

95. ***Improvement of the Soil.***—Having thus briefly indicated what is meant by superfluous water, it may be as well similarly to exemplify the principles involved in the improvement of the physical and chemical condition of the soil through drainage. When superfluous water exists in a soil for any length of time, terrestrial plants are drowned. The effect on the tea plant of water-logged soil will be at once apparent when it is recollected that, in its wild habitat, it is a native of slopes. By way of illustration, therefore, if water accumulated in a tea garden, at a certain depth below the surface, its presence must restrict the extent of culturable soil, for the roots of the tea plant will certainly not live in water. It follows that an agency that will carry the water to the lower depth than it might

Culturable Depth and Water. *Conf. with paras. 94, 107, 108, 254.*

flow naturally, will increase by that extent the culturable depth of the soil. So again should the removal of surplus water from the soil be left to evaporation, many very injurious influences are brought to bear on the crop and on the soil. It is a well known fact that evaporation lowers the temperature. Water, before it can be expanded into the condition of vapour, must obtain a large amount of heat. A badly drained soil that contains an excess of water has its temperature lowered through the utilization of the earth's heat and the absorption of the sun's rays in the accomplishment of evaporation. As the spring advances and the sun's rays become hotter and hotter, evaporation increases and the soil becomes colder and colder. A fall in soil temperature makes the crops late, and hence badly drained soils are cold and late; perfectly drained soils warm and early. But there is another circumstance that had better be here mentioned. Just as rain carries the soluble materials into the soil, evaporation during the dry season tends to bring these again to the surface, sometimes in the form of saline efflorescence. Should the soil not be porous and readily absorbent, owing to defective drainage, the first heavy showers, with the burst of the monsoons, will carry away these accumulations of soluble matter and thus gradually impoverish the soil.

WATER in RELATION to SOIL.

Fall in Temperature.

Cold Soils—Late Crops.

Surface Soluble Matter.

96. These are surely considerations of the first importance to the tea planter that scarcely require to be further exemplified. It will at once be admitted, however, that the contrast between neighbouring gardens as to the commencement of the flushing season is often very striking. In many instances that difference may be accepted as a prognostication of defective drainage in the one as compared with the other. The complaint is often heard that one garden gives a poor return as compared with another, owing to its having a shallow soil. Drainage, while removing the surplus water and lessening the evils of evaporation, extends the arable depth to a far greater extent than could be accomplished by the expenditure of the same amount of capital in deep hoeing.

Indications of Defective Drainage.

Saving in Hoeing.

97. The descent of the water to the drains opens up the soil, carries air and heat down to the level of the drains, and distributes the soluble materials of the surface throughout the entire stratum permeated. This is accomplished through the all important circumstance that the ingredients of the soil (more especially the

WATER in RELATION to SOIL.

clay) act as a chemical filter. The warm water, charged with the products of the surface soil disintegration and with air (that is, Oxygen, Nitrogen, Carbonic Acid, Nitric Acid and Ammonia) is immediately seized upon and deprived of its food materials. Physical and chemical changes of the soil also at once ensue. Poisonous decomposing organic matter is oxidised; the insoluble iron salts are converted into soluble food substances; and the nitrogen of the air is brought down to nourish and develop the indispensably necessary nitrogen-fixing organisms of the soil. Physical modifications of the soil of a no less valuable character also take place. The continuous passage of water through the soil opens it up, and its capillarity is thus vastly improved. By drawing the rain down surface wash is prevented. The arable depth of the soil being increased, the roots are able to penetrate to a greater extent and are thus protected by the additional layer of soil from the evil consequence of excessive surface evaporation, and they have the further advantage that, occupying a larger extent of the soil, they have increased facilities of obtaining food. Plants growing, therefore, on a well drained soil, are better able to withstand the effect of drought than those on a water-logged soil. A continuous supply of moisture is brought up to meet the necessities of the plant, the surface soil does not become caked, and in consequence rain, when it does fall, is at once absorbed, instead of being carried away as surface wash.

Chemical Actions of Rain-water. — *Nitrogen-fixing Organisms.* — *Effect on Roots.* — *Surface Caking Prevented.*

XXVI.—Water and its Relation to the Plant.

Conveys Food.

98. Turning now to the *second* consideration, namely, the functions water performs in the economy of plant life, it need hardly be repeated that it is the solvent chiefly utilised to facilitate the nutritious solid materials of the soil being absorbed by the roots. As already remarked, when rain falls on a properly drained soil, it carries down to the roots not only the mineral ingredients of the surface (rendered soluble through the action of the sun and air), but also oxygen in the form of air dissolved in the water, and, an equally important necessity to the life of the plant, heat, absorbed from the atmosphere and from the warm surface soil. In its descent through the soil, the water distributes these food materials of the plant and thus carries fresh supplies to every little fibril. It

would be beyond the scope of the present chapter to trace out in detail the further functions of water, as it next ascends through the tissues of the plant, participates in the phenomena of digestion (or as it is called assimilation) and of transpiration (that is, perspiration and respiration), and finally once more descends to be built up in the growing tissues. But it may be said a free circulation of water in and through the soil is an essential condition of successful cultivation. The minute hairs on the rootlets suck up the moisture charged with nutritive materials. By exuding an acid principle they at the same time decompose and render soluble some of the ingredients of the soil that are necessary for the plant and which otherwise might not be rendered available. But in their search for moisture and food the roots are not passive agents obedient to mechanical or accidental environment. They are directly controlled by the leaves above ground.

WATER in RELATION to PLANT. *Conf. with para. 14.*

Control by Leaves.

99. Transpiration (or as it might popularly be described perspiration) takes place literally within the tissue of the leaf and is thus a widely different phenomenon from the drying by evaporation of a piece of damp wood. It is a vital, not a physical, phenomenon. Small mouths called stomata are distributed over the epidermis of the leaves (of land plants), more especially on the under surfaces, and these open into passages that radiate through the cellular structure of the leaf. Water in the form of vapour is given off into these passages and makes its escape through the stomata so long as they remain open. But under certain circumstances they can be closed and transpiration thereby checked. The moment this takes place the demand for fresh supplies of moisture ceases and the rootlets with their absorbent hairs remain inactive or nearly so. Transpiration is necessarily very largely influenced by the conditions of the atmosphere in relation to the degree of humidity in the soil. But these are purely accidental phenomena controlled by physical attributes. A dry atmosphere brought to bear on the leaves of a plant whose roots are in a damp soil should cause rapid transpiration, conversely a damp atmosphere with the roots in a dry soil should retard transpiration. But it must not be forgotten that the circulation of water through the tissue of the plant is primarily in consequence of *its being the medium of conveyance of food.* If, therefore, its circulation was governed exclusively by such physical conditions as

Evaporation and Transpiration. *Conf. with paras. 75, 101.*

Circulation varies with Demand for Food. *Conf. with paras. 12–17.*

WATER in RELATION to PLANT.

have been mentioned, the plant would be surcharged with food materials to an injurious extent and might be even forced to continue the function of assimilation during its periods of repose. It will thus be seen that vitality is and must be the power that utilizes and controls the physical laws that are brought to bear on the plant.

Excessive Supplies.

100. When transpiration is not desired the stomata are closed and the suction within the roots discontinued. But while that is so there can be no doubt that with plants as with animals circumstances often arise that induce excessive absorption of both food and liquid. When that takes place disease must of necessity supervene sooner or later, and when once the plant loses its activity, physical and not vital influences predominate until death occurs. It cannot, therefore, be doubted but that an abnormally damp soil is a condition to be carefully guarded against since it must of necessity expose the plant to an injurious resistance to the operation of natural laws. That the leaves may in consequence become charged with an excess of moisture (a sort of dropsical condition) seems highly probable. It might even be supposed that a too rapid evaporation (transpiration) would injuriously lower the plant temperature. Every one who has given the subject any degree of study is familiar with the sticky appearance of land plants growing on an over damp soil, and it is possible the sun blistering of the leaves to which tea planters often allude is due to this circumstance.

Resistance to Natural Laws.

Disease. *Conf. with paras. 34, 189, 198.*

Sun Blistering.

Objects of Drainage. *Conf. with para. 93.*

101. It will thus be seen that there are good reasons for the affirmation that drainage is undertaken with a two-fold purpose, *viz.*,—to remove excessive moisture and to increase the culturable depth as well as to improve the physical and chemical conditions of the soil. It is a mistake, therefore, to suppose that under any circumstances a perfect system of drainage is calculated to dry the soil abnormally and thus to expose the crop to the evil consequence of drought. Actual water only is carried away by drains, and before the excess can reach the channels of exit a far greater depth of soil than would have been the case otherwise has been raised to the point of saturation. The capillarity of the soil is vastly improved by drainage no doubt, but the affinity for water (possessed more especially by its component proportion of clay) is so strong that the presence of an elaborate system of underground drains will not deprive it of its moisture. The deeper portions of the soil part

Actual Water Removed.

Capillarity.

reluctantly in fact with their moisture, and do so only at the demands of surface evaporation, not underground drainage. Evaporation is a direct disturbance in the equilibrium of soil humidity that must be adjusted. The ascending return current of moisture through the soil (caused by surface evaporation) thus brings to the roots the soluble food materials, also the water, air, and heat, which had been carried down and imprisoned within the lower depth of soil through the action of the drain.

INDIAN AUTHORS.

Soil Moisture Removed by Evaporation. *Conf. with paras. 75, 99.*

XXVII.—Indian Authors on Tea Drainage.

102\. Having thus indicated very briefly the scientific principle involved by drainage, we might now turn attention to review the attitude assumed by Indian writers on tea planting regarding this very important subject. It seems, however, useless to again reprint the substance of what are in many cases radically incorrect opinions, and we would refer those who wish for such a summary to the first edition of this work. Among views constantly expressed which have led to enormous loss to the tea industry are two which it is especially desirable to finally mark out as radically wrong. These are the opinion that there is not any need for dealing with slopes; the other that districts with only medium rainfall require no drainage. The acceptance of the first of these positions has meant the ruin of numbers of gardens both in Cachar, Assam, and Darjeeling; the second position has led to the omission of drainage in districts, such as Nowgong, where, if anywhere, a thorough system is emphatically needed.

Incorrect Opinions. *Conf. with para. 106.*

103\. The most valuable of the literature on the subject of drainage of tea gardens is a series of articles published in 1878 by Mr. E. C. Schrottky on "*Agriculture with especial reference to tea planting.*" It is needless to attempt to give passages from Mr. Schrottky's paper to show how completely he understood the true value of drainage, but, as an instance, in one passage he refutes the idea that drains dry the soil injuriously in the words, "the drainer's object is to remove stagnant water from the soil only in order to give access to more water." Most soils are drained, *not so much to get water out of the land as to get it into the land.* More water will pass through a drained than through an undrained soil, drainage opening thoroughly even the most tenacious soil, giving a free passage to water through it and thus securing to it the entire rainfall, part of which before, on

Schrottky. *Conf. with para. 117.*

Drains do not injuriously dry the Soil.

Drains carry Water to the Soil.

Drainage of Tea Gardens.

INDIAN AUTHORS.

Manurial Value of Rain-water.

all but sandy soils, found its way over the surface of the land into ditches and *nullahs* carrying away with it some of the most fertilising elements of the soil." "It is a very common notion, especially among tea-planters, that rain when it comes down in heavy showers is injurious and should be carried off the land as soon as possible. They do not consider that rain-water contains most valuable elements, and that the luxuriant vegetation of the tropics is due, to a certain extent, to the presence of these in every shower that falls."

Rows of Bushes.

104. Had the early writers on the subject of tea planting, and drainage in connection with it, ever urged that in the laying out of an estate and in the direction given to the rows of bushes, a direct and fixed relationship should be established to the natural drainage of the soil, much good would have resulted. We should have heard nothing of the controversy as to whether the rows should run east and west, north and south, or diagonally to the sun's path. They would have been so arranged that drains, should they have subsequently become imperatively necessary, could have been run between the rows as their natural and proper positions. It was really of primary importance from the earliest undertakings, as it is to the present day, that in laying out an estate spaces should be reserved for drains quite as much as for roads. If found unnecessary these reserve spaces could subsequently have been planted or, if necessary, furnished with drains connecting on to and completing a preconceived system. In surveying the land for a new extension, the survey officer should be directed to take the water levels with the greatest care and to indicate on his plan the trunk and mains with their chief tributary feeder or connecting drains, required to secure a perfect drainage. The planter with such a plan before him could then easily decide the direction of the rows of bushes and the spaces to be reserved for possible future lateral drains to carry surplus water from the various undulations of the soil to the connecting drains. But it is very likely that the total absence, in the past, of any preconceived plan of drainage may be employed as an argument against a complete reformation of the older gardens, in this aspect of tea cultivation.

Spacing for Drains.

Objections likely to be raised.

XXVIII.—Conditions of Successful Drainage.

105. These considerations and recommendations lead naturally therefore to the study of the means by which so very great advan-

tages may be attained, namely, the methods by which water may be most freely distributed and the excess most conveniently removed. Rivers and streams are the great arteries and veins in the circulation of water. Rain-water will percolate through most soils and appear again on the surface in the form of springs. SUCCESSFUL DRAINAGE. Springs.

106. Artificial drainage may be said to consist in giving improved facilities in the conveyance of surplus water to the rivers and the substitution of a better sub-soil drainage than may happen to exist in the plot of land under consideration. In other words, it means the construction of improvements in the outflow and in the underground currents. Let it, however, be added these must be developed essentially on the lines of existing natural conditions. A successful system of artificial drainage therefore consists of :— *Conf. with para. 116.* Artificial Drainage. *Conf. with para. 103.* Natural Conditions.

1st. Trunk drainage.—That is to say, improvements in the natural outfall, such as deepening, straightening or embanking local streams and the construction of ditches or canals to convey the water direct from the area to be drained to the outflow. Trunk Drains.

2nd. Underground drainage.—That is to say, the provision of a system of underground channels or drains intended to convey surplus water to the canal that connects with the natural outfall. The water is mechanically, as it were, drawn down through the soil in consequence of facility to escape provided by these drains. The depth of soil down to the level of the bottom of the drains has first, therefore, to be saturated before any discharge can take place, so that drains regulate sub-soil humidity. Sub-soil Drains.

107. It will be evident from these propositions that the latter without the former would be worse than useless, but that the former without the latter might under certain circumstances be quite sufficient. Drains are, in other words, artificial improvements in the sub-soil movement of water towards the outflow. The natural drainage in a plot of land may be perfect so far as the peculiarities of the soil conditions of the sub-soil are concerned. It may in fact be practically an island within a quagmire, and its fertility depends therefore on the provision of sufficient and complete trunk drainage. With a very large percentage of Indian tea gardens it may be that the former (trunk drainage) is a more pressing necessity than the latter. It is to be feared, however, that this necessity has very largely been lost sight of in the selection of land to be thrown under tea. Many Trunk Drains of Primary Importance. *Conf. with paras. 94, 95, 108.*

SUCCESSFUL DRAINAGE. gardens, especially those on grass lands, are almost on a level with the surrounding rice-fields, the annual inundation of which not only stops all outflow but raises the sub-soil level of excessive humidity to a ruinous extent. Where gardens are on higher and undulated land the *hullahs* or lower portions should be carefully surveyed and their levels ascertained in relation to the natural outflow. These should then be connected by drains sufficiently deep to act as the chief tributaries of the main current. But in many cases it would seem imperative that the outflow should be carried to some distance instead of being discharged into the nearest stream or surrounding rice land. The annual water-logging for months together of many gardens (or large portions of them) through the local streams obstructing the outflow is a fruitful source of many evils. It is generally held by chemical investigators that stagnant water in a soil checks the formation of nitrates and gives origin to several poisonous compounds. It is thus most undesirable that tea land should be water-logged even for comparatively short but annually recurring periods.

Survey of Hullahs.

Water-logged Land.

Is Deepening of Outfalls necessary? 108. In laying out a garden, therefore, it is essential to keep these conditions in view, as also when the necessity arises for draining a garden already in existence. The first operation should be to ascertain whether deepening of outfalls or even the creation of new outfalls is necessary to get a sufficient fall from all parts of the garden. This is purely surveying work. This having been ascertained, the next point is to determine the necessity or no of artificial sub-soil feeder drains, and this can usually be found by several tests.

Moisture in Sub-soil. *Conf. with paras. 94, 95, 107.* The moisture in the sub-soil, say at two to three feet deep, in December or January, should be found by taking, say, ten pounds of the soil at this depth and allowing it to dry, and then determining the loss in weight. Inasmuch as the maximum amount of water which 100 lbs. of different classes of soils (in the dry condition) can contain when saturated is approximately as follows:—

	lb.
Sandy Soil	22·5
Light Loam	30·4
Medium Loam	32·2
Heavy Loam	33·2
Clay Soil	38·5

and inasmuch as, if such a sub-soil contain more than one-third (or one-half with a sandy or light soil) of this amount in the middle of the cold weather, it will most probably be more or less water-logged in the rains, it can easily be ascertained whether the land needs sub-soil drainage or no. SUCCESSFUL DRAINAGE.

But the soil may be porous enough and yet the garden be badly in need of sub-soil drainage, and this can be ascertained by digging a hole in the land in the wettest part of the rains to find whether the sub-soil water is within four to five feet of the surface. If it is so, the presumption is that drainage is undoubtedly needed; if water is not found at such depth the presumption is that none is required, but even then only so if the soil is sandy enough to allow the penetration of any rain within an hour or two. We have therefore three tests of the need of drainage— Depth of Sub-soil Water.

(1) the moisture of the sub-soil in the cold weather,
(2) the depth of the sub-soil water in the rains,
(3) the rapidity with which heavy rain disappears through (not over) the soil on a piece of flat land.

109. It is hardly necessary here to insist on the necessity for a satisfactory outlet with a sufficient fall before any further work is done in laying out the drainage of a garden, following which the alignment of the main drain should be traced in order that the branch drains may have a definite arrangement and slope. When made they should in no case be less than from six inches to one foot deeper than the side drains running into them. Of course in some cases the natural outlet will be absolutely useless for drainage purposes. This is often the case in bheel gardens, and then the natural outlet will have to be dammed up, and the drains carried in a direction in which a better fall exists. One garden we remember in Cachar, in which the main drain was carried ten miles in order to get a satisfactory fall for the garden into a lower reach of the river: another in Upper Assam constructed a huge, almost canal-like, work 15 feet deep (more or less) for the same purpose. By some means or other the outfall must give sufficient drop to prevent flooding and backing of the drains in all ordinary rainy years. Outlet.

XXIX.—Lateral or Feeder Drains.

110. But having satisfied oneself of the existence of satisfactory natural trunk drainage, having improved the existing or created a

SUCCESSFUL DRAINAGE.

new main drainage channel, it is comparatively rare that lateral feeder drains will not be needed on Indian tea lands, but they must be of a very different character from many which have existed in the past in the various tea districts. In the olden days a system of surface drainage designed to run the water over the surface into the drains at the greatest possible rate was usual. Trenches were dug at regular distances throughout the garden and for the most part parallel with each other, running, heedless of the slope of the land, consistently over hill and dale, and finally often abutting nowhere in particular. These were on the average about 9 to 12 inches broad, and not more than 18 inches to 2 feet deep. Occasionally in the worst cases, the drains run like shallow rivers with sloping sides right through the property,—and the most extravagant example of all noticed was in one of the Kangra Valley gardens where the drains, 4 to 6 feet wide and deep, looked like secret passages constructed for some ancient strategic necessity.

Surface Drainage.

Kangra Valley.

Conf. with para. 114.

111. The difference between this type of drain and that which, if open drains at all are the best, is undoubtedly the most suitable for tea gardens is a difference not merely in degree, but in kind. It cannot be too much insisted on that the purpose of drains is to draw the water through and not over the land, that they are intended not to dry out the land but to regulate the moisture, and that perhaps their principal function is to provide against a rise in the sub-soil water owing to excessive rain which would cause stagnant water to lie among the roots of the bushes. We have, therefore, now to consider—

Correct Drains.

(1) the position of the feeder drains—and their distance apart,

(2) the slope of the drains,

(3) the shape of the drains.

Position of Feeder Drains.

112. ***Position of the Feeder Drains.***—The drains should always have a definite relationship to the main trunk drainage. This latter will of course occupy the lowest portion of the ground, and these feeder drains should follow the line of greatest ascent and run parallel to each other or converge towards the bottom as necessity may dictate. In stating that they should follow the line of greatest ascent, it is not meant to indicate that these drains should run up and down a slope if that slope is steep. In fact no drain, except under special circumstances, should have a greater slope than

Drainage of Tea Gardens.

1 in 200, or possibly a little more, and in order to obtain this it will, of course, be necessary to run the drains round rather than directly down slopes. But with this reservation the statement holds, and undulating land can never be satisfactorily drained by a fixed direction being laid down for the sub-soil drains in defiance of surface configuration. Each depression must be drained by itself and have a central receiving drain traversing the lowest portion and connected with all the other receiving drains. It is further essential also for a rapid flow of water that the sub-soil lateral drains on either side of the receiving drain should not discharge opposite one another.

SUCCESSFUL DRAINAGE.

Drain each Hollow separately.

113. ***Distance Apart and Depth.***—The distance apart will vary with every type of land. If we may trust English experience the following table will be useful as giving the depth and distance of drains which has been found to act best there in various classes of soil:—

Distance of Drains apart.

Conf. with paras. 108, 115.

Nature of Soil.	Depth of Drains.		Distance apart.
	ft.	ins.	ft.
COMPACT.			
Tenacious clay	2	6	15
Friable clay	2	9	18
Soft free clay	2	9	21
MEDIUM.			
Clayey loam	3	0	21
Gravelly	3	3	27
Friable	3	3	30
POROUS.			
Light loam	3	6	33
Sandy	3	9	39
Light gravelly sand . . .	4	0	51
Coarse	4	6	60

Three feet should be the minimum depth of lateral drains on good average tea land, and the mains or connecting drains should be correspondingly lower. The lateral drains should, if possible, not have a fall greater than 1 in 200. Some good authorities allow 1 in 100, but this gives probably rather too much slope to get the best results.

Slope of Drains.

Drainage of Tea Gardens.

SUCCESSFUL DRAINAGE.

114. ***Shape of Drain.***—As it is the object of drainage to prevent the surface flow of water into the drains, the old advice that the land should slope towards the channels is distinctly wrong in principle, and has been disastrous in practice There are gardens lying on a light sandy soil, some 8 to 10 feet deep or less, overlying clay, in which no drains of any other slope would keep open, but these are exceptions, and it should be accepted that the land should slope away from the deep drains rather than toward it, so as to *compel* the water to go through the soil, and prevent even the possibility of its going over the surface.

Drains in Sand Overlying Clay.

Narrow Drains.

Conf. with para. 110.

In addition to this, drains should be as narrow as possible. A wide drain leads to the drying out of the soil, and a drain 9 inches wide serves just the same useful purpose as one of 24 inches. Hence the ridiculous character of the Kangra drains above mentioned as 4 to 6 feet wide is at once seen, and though this, one is glad to avow, is quite unique, yet, in general, existing drains in many districts would be better if narrower.

Summary.

Necessity of Drains.

115. To summarize therefore, drains are always needed when there is not an absolutely free flow of water through the land, or when the level of the sub-soil water approaches within say 4 or 5 feet of the surface, at least, at any time of the year. The trunk drains should always follow the natural drainage channels where a sufficient fall for the water can be obtained in the rainy season. Where this is impossible they should be carried in such a manner as to ensure the greatest fall and complete drainage of the land at any time. The side or feeding drains ought to be at least 3 feet deep, to have a fall into the main drains of about 1 in 300 or a little more, and to enter these latter obliquely in the direction in which the drainage is to flow. They should further be as narrow as possible, and arranged so that the water from the surface of the land cannot flow directly over that surface into the drains, but must pass through the soil; a condition which precludes the slope of the land towards the drains which is so commonly seen in tea gardens.

Depth of Drains.

Conf. with paras. 108, 113.

Water must go through Soil.

Village Sites.

116. ***Sites of Villages, etc.***—In this connection may also be mentioned a very evident example of defective drainage. Planters are familiar with the fact that plots of land here and there, in very nearly every estate, are barren or nearly so. These may be due to two causes. On the one hand they may be caused by a spring in the

Drainage of Tea Gardens.

land, and this can only be got rid of, if got rid of at all, by careful drainage. On the other, and this is much the more common, they may be due to being the sites of old villages or coolie lines. It is a well ascertained fact that land on which human beings have resided for long is sterile, and this sterility is due partly to the compacting of the soil so that it is impervious to water and air, partly to the accumulation of poisonous organic materials, and, in the case of tea, partly to the excess of lime commonly present in such places. These soils may be repeatedly deep hoed and even richly manured, but will still take many years before the tea bushes planted on them show any luxuriance. Under these circumstances run one or two good sub-soil drains through the plot, grow repeated crops of a deep-rooted green manure like *mati-kalai*, and hoe deeply, and, in most cases, these plots will become gradually converted into good tea soil. The oxygen of the air (drawn down by the water) will convert the accumulations of organic matter from a poisonous to a highly nutritive condition. The water, both through its chemical and physical properties will open up the soil and render it arable to the needed depth, and thus drainage as a means of tillage will be demonstrated to succeed. SUCCESSFUL DRAINAGE. *Conf. with para. 105.* Village Sites.

117. ***Pipe Drainage.***—In countries where land is valuable and labour is dear, open drains, absolutely universal in the Indian tea districts, are regarded as being very wasteful of land, and as rendering mechanical cultivation next door to an impossibility. And, indeed, even in tea culture, the question has often arisen as to whether sub-soil pipe drains would not only be more effective, but would be beneficial in keeping the soil moisture in the dry weather, in enabling the land to be more evenly planted up, in saving the poverty of the bushes on the sides of open drains, and even in other ways. The authorities on the subject have, however, practically with one voice denied the feasibility of pipe drains in tea gardens. Mr. Schrottky says for instance:—"Pipe drains cannot be used, as the roots would invariably choke up the pipes, but closed stone or brushwood drains are practicable." In some districts stone drains are an impossibility owing to lack of stone, but where this is not the case, Mr. Schrottky's idea is worth serious consideration. Brushwood drains, except in the hills, would be objectionable as they would encourage the development of white-ants. But pipes, as will be seen, Mr. Schrottky emphatically condemns. Pipe Drainage. Schrottky. *Conf. with para. 103.*

Drainage of Tea Gardens.

PIPE DRAINAGE.

Bamber.

118. Mr. Bamber narrates the objections to pipe drainage in the following passage:—"The question has been raised as to the possibility of using pipe drainage for tea, and so doing away with the open drains. Several advantages would be gained by its adoption, but there are also several objections to it, the most important of which is, that in the dry season the roots of the tea bushes would certainly penetrate the joints of the pipes wherever water was to be found, and rapidly choke the drain; and it would be very difficult to discover the exact spot where the stoppage had occurred without opening the drain in several places throughout its length. Vermin, white-ants, etc., would also be liable to damage the drains, by excavating the soil below the pipes, when they would drop out of their proper level and so prevent a free flow. In the case of such an accident, the faulty spot would probably be shown by the water rising to the surface as a spring, during any very heavy rainfall."

Recent Opinion.

119. The most recent consideration of the question is contained in a paper by Mr. J. E. Aird,* himself a planter of considerable experience, who writes "I think Dr. Watt is wrong in his estimate of R750 per acre. In England draining is considered dear at £7 or R105 per acre, including everything, and I do not see why it could not be done as cheaply here as in England. As no tea bushes could be planted within 5 feet of the pipes for fear of the roots blocking them, the area of land put out of cultivation for this reason would have to be taken into account as an additional cost. As the greatest rainfall may be taken at 25 times (that is, in one day) that of England, the pipes would have to be, generally speaking, twenty-five times larger, that is, a 5-inch pipe instead of a 1-inch, which has been found quite sufficient at home. But against these extra expenses we have cheaper labour, and I believe the pipes could be made locally so as to save carriage."

Further Investigations to be made.

120. The whole matter has nevertheless not advanced beyond a suggestion, and we are not aware that a single garden has even partially adopted the system. It is still to be found (1) what would be the cost of such sub-soil pipe draining in actual practice in India; (2) what would be the increased return over the deep, narrow open drains which are now becoming the rule; (3) whether the objections raised by the older writers—Messrs. Schrottky, Bamber, Pringle,

* Journal of the Luskerpore Valley Society of Planters, 1901.

Drainage of Tea Gardens.

etc., have any foundation in fact. When an opportunity is afforded for settling these points, then and then only can the question be decided of the practicability or otherwise of this method of drainage being followed,—a method, nevertheless, which is undoubtedly preferable in principle.

PIPE DRAINS.

121. In some districts, as noted above, though pipe drains may be impracticable, there can hardly remain any doubt of the feasibility of covered drains, for stone of suitable size occurs all over the gardens. This is particularly the case in certain parts of the Terai and Dooars. A narrow drain dug in the ordinary way, and then filled to within 6 inches of the surface with large stones, soil being put on top to complete the filling, would have practically all the advantages of a pipe drain without the necessity for pipes, and with a minimum of danger of becoming blocked.

Stone Drains.

XXX.—*Burial of Prunings in Drains.*

Burial of Prunings. *Conf. with paras. 281, 282.*

122. It was formerly the practice on a good many gardens to dig new drains occasionally between the next row of bushes to those where they were already in existence, and fill up the old drains with the prunings of the bushes and with the soil from the drains newly made. This practice has, we are glad to say, practically disappeared. The mere fact that such a system has existed of periodically changing drains from between one row of bushes to another shows that it has been the existence of bushes that governed the position of drains, not the configuration of the land and nature of the soil. The pores of the soil having been so adjusted that water has found its way towards drains in particular positions; a disturbance of those positions would retard for some time the percolation and thus do positive harm. Apart, therefore, from the expense of renewing many thousand feet of open drains, with no compensating advantage, there are distinct reasons why the practice should be discontinued.

In Drains.

123. There are further trenchant reasons why not only the burial of prunings in drains but their burial at all is to be objected to. They may and in many cases do, if blighted, act as a source of further disease among the bushes, and it would be well if, in every case, they could be collected and burned. One ought to add that, in gardens badly blighted, the burning should not be delayed until

May carry Disease. *Conf. with para. 124.*

BURYING PRUNINGS.

Burning to be Preferred.

the prunings have dried. By so doing the blights contained on them mature rapidly in order to check their approaching destruction through the death of the prunings. Their germs are at once distributed and the evil it is desired to intercept is thus more widely disseminated than might otherwise have been the case. It is desirable that each day's prunings should be burned at once even should they be only charred and the leaves and the twigs alone actually burned. In that condition they are comparatively harmless and the coolies might then, if they desired, be permitted to carry off the larger portions for firewood.

Pests carried by Prunings. *Conf. with para. 193.*

124. This is the only absolutely safe course, and with prunings carrying such blight as red rust, thread blight, and grey blight it seems absolutely essential. This, we are aware, is totally at variance with the Ceylon practice and with that of a large part of the Indian Tea Districts, and it must be recognised that such burning of prunings is wasteful of a large amount of valuable manurial material which must be returned to the soil in some manner or other. The ash obtained when the prunings are carried into the roadways can and must be returned to the land, and not only this, but it must be spread round the bushes on the whole of the area from which the prunings were taken, and not on a few by the roadsides. This ash, though it may in a single season seem small in quantity, soon becomes, if removed, a most serious drain on the land, and were it not accepted as a corollary of the burning of prunings that it should be returned to the soil, the whole view of the matter might have to be revised. There is another corollary which is just as essential but is even less recognised. The prunings remove a still more valuable material than the ash,—the nitrogen, —and this is inevitably dissipated when they are burnt, and must be added to the land from another source if serious loss is not to result. There is at hand, however, in the use of green manuring crops, notably *mati-kalai*, a means of returning this nitrogen to the land almost at no expense. How this can be best done will be considered in the chapter on manuring, but if prunings are burnt as a system, *the use of such a crop at frequent intervals becomes absolutely essential.*

Ash must be Returned to Land. *Conf. with paras. 126, 261, 282, 285–286.*

Loss of Nitrogen

Green Manure must follow Burning of Prunings. *Conf. with paras. 83, 89, 126, 238–252, 282.*

125. There are some positions in which the burning of prunings is impossible, and in these cases they will have to be got rid of by burial in one form or another, however much it may be objected to

Drainage of Tea Gardens.

on principle. In order to minimise as far as possible the danger which must exist, even if the garden is practically free from blight, the following conditions must be adhered to if burial is adopted :— BURYING PRUNINGS. If buried must

(1) They must be buried deep, at least 6 inches of soil being left on top of them so that they may not be turned up by the hoe. (1) be buried deep.

(2) They should be buried immediately on pruning or as soon after as possible. In Ceylon trenches are dug to receive the prunings before the bushes are touched at all, and the prunings are put into them practically at once. Once dried up, much of the manurial value has gone, or is rendered less available. (2) be buried fresh.

(3) They should be buried with something which will destroy any latent germs or spores of fungi which are upon them. The best materials for this are Lime and Basic Slag, which not only cause the blight spores to be destroyed but also the prunings to decay more quickly. The usual way of applying the Basic Slag, which is preferable, is to dust it over the prunings of the tea in the holes where they are to be buried and immediately cover up the whole; 4 to 5 cwt. of the Basic Slag are usually applied in this manner per acre in Ceylon. 3) be buried with Lime or Basic Slag. *Conf. with paras. 281, 282.*

126. It must be understood however, that we cannot really recommend the burial of prunings even in this manner. Burning with the return of the ashes to the land, and coupled with the use of a green manuring crop of *mati-kalai* at frequent intervals, is much to be preferred. Burying not Recommended. *Conf. with para. 124.*

XXXI.—Treatment of Slopes.

127. The treatment of slopes forms a subject in itself, which we shall only be able to touch upon in this chapter. The problem manifestly in such cases has been to get rid of the excess of water beyond that required to saturate the soil at any one time, without at the same time getting rid of the surface soil itself. In places where the total rainfall is small, or even where it is great, if only it is uniform the matter is not of great difficulty, but where, as in the tea area, the rainfall is great, and a large part of it comes in bursts Treatment of Slopes. *Conf with paras. 87, 271.*

TREATMENT of SLOPES. Disastrous Effect of Neglect.

of 5 or more inches in a single day, and where, moreover, there is no crop on the ground to bind the soil together, it is evident that unless precautions are taken, the amount of surface soil washed down the slopes will be enormous. The result justifies the expectation. The earlier authors, many of them, laughed at the idea of there being any necessity for dealing with slopes in any way, judging that the water would quickly enough run off the surface. So it has, and carried surface soil away to such an extent that thousands of acres of what was once fine tea land, and bearing good tea are now abandoned, and thousands of acres more ought to be given up.

Method Varies with Soil.

128. There is however no uniform method to lay down as the only correct one in dealing with slopes. All depends on the nature of the soil, on the character of the sub-soil, and on the steepness of the land. In Ceylon a system of contour catch drains is all but universal, and would be excellent in many parts of the Indian districts. In Darjeeling terracing has become very general, and quite rightly so, for probably it is the very best method of dealing with the conditions. In Sylhet the method of "bunding" has been introduced on certain classes of land with great success, and so on. In matters of this sort the system best adapted to the conditions can only be settled on the spot, and an incorrect system may be almost worse than nothing at all. On one garden, for instance, the whole surface of the slopes looked like a chess-board—drains ran across the slopes in diagonal lines, and formed a splendid means of furnishing the streams with silt from the surface, which, very likely, fertilised rice-fields at a distance.

129. The three methods above indicated form, however, each in its proper place, the best method of dealing with the question :—

Contour Drains.

(*a*) *Contour drains*—Or drains running across the slope, laid out with a level, and banked up on the upper side, are the best system for a stiff soil and for moderate slopes. They seem to be indicated on the small undulations of many Dooars gardens lying on the great red bank of soil in that district, and also on the "hog back" formation of many of the Nowgong gardens in Assam. To be useful, however, it is essential that a level, or at least a Ceylon road-tracer, should be used in laying them out. It might be supposed that this warning would be superfluous, but we have seen

Drainage of Tea Gardens.

supposed contour drains which took a gentle slope of 1 in 30 down a hill-side! TREATMENT of SLOPES.

(*b*). *Terracing* is the method, *par excellence*, for Darjeeling, or in the plains for a district of fairly stiff soil facing in any direction but south or south-west. It must be remembered, however, that terracing increases the area of the land exposed to the sun's rays, and that where drying out of the soil by their means is to be feared, as it is on south and south-west exposures in the plains, terraces are a doubtful advantage, unless this danger can be otherwise obviated. Luckily it *can* be largely avoided by planting "*Sau*" trees (**Albizzia stipulata**) on these slopes, when the tea is young, but seeing that this tree is deciduous, and bears no leaves in the hottest part of the year, it does not answer the purpose quite as satisfactorily as could be wished. Terracing.

In all terracing, the use of the level in laying out the line of the terraces should be a *sine quâ non*, and terraces, so called, which run up and down the hills, are worse than useless.

(*c*) *Bunding* is perhaps the best system of dealing with slopes composed of light soil, where the inclination is not too great. Instead of cutting out a terrace, a bank of soil is built across the slope (laid out, of course, with a level), and the rain following causes the soil to wash in such a fashion as to make a natural wide terrace. Naturally the steeper the slope the nearer the bunds must be together, and beyond a certain steepness the method is inapplicable. In Darjeeling we have heard of the bunds being very effectively formed of bamboos and heavy prunings, and this may be admissible where white-ants are not a danger, but in the plains could hardly be recommended.

XXXII.—Irrigation in Tea Planting. IRRIGATION.

130. It is becoming increasingly necessary to recognise that in many tea districts there annually or, at any rate, often, occur periods of excessive drought through which even the best system of retaining the natural moisture in the land may prove insufficient, and the bushes at least receive a check in their growth which diminishes their yield to a great extent, and probably also renders them susceptible to blights innumerable, of which red spider, red rust, and mosquito blight (probably) are the chief. If by any means a Effect of Drought. *Conf. with paras.* 537.

Drainage of Tea Gardens.

IRRIGATION.

guarantee of soil moisture could be obtained either by rain or by some other means during the months of February, March and April, the outturn would not only be more reliable but also the gardens and bushes would be very much more healthy. The only method by which this guarantee can be obtained is that of irrigation, and the multitude of cases in which this could be carried out at a really small expense is very striking. A few feeble attempts have been made in Cachar and Sylhet to get this benefit by blocking up the drains, which always contain water, and allowing this water to rise in the soil. Such a method, we venture to think, is on totally wrong lines. If such water is left standing in the soil more than a few hours, the roots which will necessarily lie in the water are killed off, for tea roots cannot stand immersion in stagnant water, and the bushes are thus not only weakened but also rendered still more susceptible to drought in future years. On the other hand, where such blocking is feasible, it is almost always also feasible to obtain, by means of a storage tank above the plot through which the water runs, a natural fall on to the plot, and even if not so, a pulsometer pump would do all that is required. Having obtained the water above the plot it then would run over the land in channels parallel to the drains between the rows of bushes. This has practically been done in one or two cases with very striking results in diminishing the effects of drought and in lengthening the season. The exact method of carrying this out in any particular case is a matter for the agricultural engineer, but in deep light sand, in soil which is stiff and has a hard pan sub-soil, in flat lands in the droughty districts, and especially in peat bheels, there is not only an opening but urgency for the trial of such a method on an experimental scale, with almost a certainty of its paying its cost in a remarkably short time.

Bunding-up Drains Condemned.

Method of Irrigation.

CHAPTER VI.

PRINCIPLES OF PRUNING.

XXXIII.—Importance of Pruning.

IMPORTANCE of PRUNING.

131. In almost all agricultural industries which depend for their success on the continued production of a crop, whether of fruit or leaf, from a perennial plant, the cutting away of the unnecessary part of the previous growth is an important part of the system of culture. In most cases the object is to induce the continuous production of seed or of fruit, and hence the principles involved are, on the face of it, quite different from those which govern pruning for the commercial production of leaf. This does not mean, however, that pruning is any less important for the production of leaf than that of fruit, or that it can be done in any haphazard way without forethought and skill. We hold that it is the most important operation in the garden during the whole season, demanding the most skilled, careful, and constant supervision. That this is not usually given or considered to be necessary we are fully aware, but its absence may be put down as, in our opinion, one of the chief causes of the deterioration of tea gardens and hence of the lack of permanence of tea properties.

Objects of Pruning.

132. ***Objects of Pruning.***—Pruning is an operation carried on in order to induce the plant to assume a particular shape so as to facilitate cultivation and plucking of the leaf, to increase the average yield of each plant, and to retain or improve the quality of tea produced. The bush must not be allowed to grow so high that the tea is difficult to pluck, nor to spread itself so thickly that the amount of cultivation necessary—an amount varying with the position and nature of the soil—is unduly interfered with. Bushes badly pruned bear most irregularly, a year of over-bearing being followed by several of under-bearing, as a consequence of exhaustion caused by a too severe strain on the reserve forces of the plant.

Differences in Practice.

133. ***Differences in practice.***—In spite of the radical importance of the subject, differences in practice are very great. Gardens lying side by side are treated by essentially different methods, and it says much for the hardy nature of the tea bush that so many of

IMPORTANCE of PRUNING.

these seem to give very good results. It might perhaps, however, be suggested that in some cases where very good results have for a good many years been obtained, it has been *in spite of* a bad system of pruning, rather than by its aid.

Different Methods Necessary.

It must not be understood that we are prepared to recommend a uniform system of pruning for the whole of the tea districts. Nothing could be further from our purpose, and to attempt to do so would be to ignore differences in climate, in elevation, in type of plant, and in soil, which make tea planting in Darjeeling and Sylhet, in Dibrugarh and in Chittagong, in the Duars and in Chota-Nagpur, entirely different matters. But although differences in practice must exist, yet the principles underlying every system are the same, and it is to these principles we wish to draw attention in the present article.

THEORY of PRUNING.

XXXIV.– Theory of Pruning.

134. One of the ablest papers on the subject of the pruning of tea bushes was written by Sir George King as long ago as 1871 (*Journal Agri-Horticultural Society, Vol. III, Part I*). It seems desirable to give here a few passages from that paper which, it is feared, is not sufficiently well known by the planting community.

Production of Flowers.

" Now the bearing of flowers and fruit," writes Sir George, " is the natural consummation of a plant's life, and the removal of these after they have been produced does no harm to the producing plant as an individual (on the contrary often benefits it), although the act affects its possible posterity. It is true that in order to force it to bear unnatural quantities of flowers and fruit, or flowers and fruit possessing unnatural qualities, the horticulturalist often exposes a plant to treatment which is injurious to it as an individual, and which leads to premature old age; at the same time it is treatment which, as regards flowers or fruit, is the most advantageous. In contrast to this is the action of the tea grower who, by the very collection of this crop, necessarily exposes his plants to treatment which, as regards a continuation of that crop, is disadvantageous."

Leaf Crop Disadvantageous.

European Experience.

" In the cultivation of almost all kinds of fruit trees, the operation of pruning holds a prominent place. The problems respectively presented to the European grower of fruit and flowers, and to the Indian cultivator of tea being different, it is only reasonable to expect that different methods of practising that operation

Principles of Pruning.

THEORY of PRUNING.

would be advisable. The general practice of pruning as carried on by European gardeners is, however, founded, for the most part, upon a knowledge of the principles of vegetable physiology, and it is therefore also reasonable to suppose that Indian tea growers might have learnt a good deal on the general subject of pruning from European writers on gardening even although not venturing to put their plantations under the charge of practical European gardeners with full powers to do as they might see best. Until within a year or two ago, however, the only kind of pruning attempted in the tea gardens of the North-West Provinces, was the removal of wood actually dead and the application on rare occasions of a hedge-clipping scissors, which delicate implement used to be entrusted to a native gardener *(mali)* with orders to reduce by its means certain bushes to a particular height, a stick of the required length being given to him as a measure. Indiscriminating treatment like this is the kind of pruning to which a few gardens in these provinces used now and then to be submitted.

Pruning to a Fixed Height.

Rational pruning involves consideration and selection; and each bush ought to be treated according to its own individual condition, and not in accordance with a rule-of-thumb laid down for an entire field or garden. It is only certain stems and branches to which, as a rule, the knife can be applied with advantage, and these for the most part are the ones that afford the most marked examples of the natural effects of 'plucking.' Now, if we think of the matter for a little, the process of 'plucking' will be seen to be really of the nature of pruning, and to recommend pruning as a cure for the evils of plucking, may, therefore, appear paradoxical.

Pruning—Individual Necessities.

To explain the seeming paradox, let us consider briefly the appearances presented by a young shoot of tea before it has been deprived by the plucker of its tip with the three or four leaves or leaf-buds borne thereon. Such a shoot bears on its entire length, let us say, ten leaves, and at the point where each leaf springs from the stem (*i.e.*, at the axil) there lies a small bud. Each of these buds is capable of development into a lateral branchlet. In a branch bearing as we have supposed ten leaves, it is not probable that, were things left to their natural course, each of the ten axillary buds would become developed into a natural branchlet. When, however, the growing point of the shoot is removed, these axillary buds are stimulated by the ascending sap, and most of them expand into lateral branchlets; and these being in turn topped by the plucker, their axillary buds are stimulated, though in a less degree, into expansion into branchlets, and so on. The vigour with which lateral branchlets follow on 'plucking' or topping the leaders, diminishes regularly with each repetition of the process until after

Plucking a Method of Pruning.

Formation of Shoots.

Principles of Pruning.

THEORY of PRUNING.

Number of Leaves.

a few years of such treatment a period of nearly complete stagnation is reached, and the original ten-leaved shoot with which we started presents the appearance of a tough greyish-barked and often gnarled stem, bearing at its top a dense collection of small wiry twigs, which carry a quantity of small thin tough leaves totally unfitted for manufacture into good tea. These twigs, moreover, are of such low vitality that when topped they hardly respond by throwing out fresh lateral shoots or 'flushes.' This is the kind of stem of which the clumps of unpruned tea already described consist. The reason of the smallness and non-activity of the leaves upon these brush-like masses is simply that they have increased in number out of proportion to their means of nourishment. The stem, through the sap-wood layer of which their nourishment is transmitted, has not increased proportionally with the number of the leaves which have been forced into existence by the operation of plucking; and it is a physical impossibility that through the layer of sap-wood in the stem, there *can* be transmitted enough sap to support many young leaves, in addition to old ones with which its top is crowned. Were such a stem left to itself, and all plucking suspended for a time, it is probable that in some cases an equilibrium would be established between the leaves and sap-wood, and that the latter would again become extensive enough for the transmission of sap sufficient to support a natural succession of young leaves, or, in other words, to 'yield flushes.' But the process of recovery would involve time, which to the tea planter means money. A quicker way therefore of obtaining leaf must be tried, and this is found in pruning off the profitless wiry spray with which the stem is crowned, so that the sap transmitted upwards may cease to be dissipated away in the support of leaves which can never be made into tea, but which, as long as they remain on the plant, must have their needful supply of sap; and further that the sap may be directed into the new shoots which the plant may be expected to throw out after pruning."

Low Vitality of Flush-Bearing Twigs.

Weakened Stem.

Bushes Recover if not Plucked.

Dissipation of Sap.

Pruning Hurtful.

"It is thus that pruning becomes the necessary sequence of plucking, if healthy young leaves fit for tea-making are sought to be continuously produced. The end in view should never be lost sight of when using the knife, for the mere meaningless mutilation of a plant by its application is quite as likely to be hurtful as not."

Summary.

135. In summary, therefore, it may be said that pruning is a means of reducing the number of stalks on the bushes to the nourishing capacity of the remaining branches, and to ensure that the particular stalks remaining are the most capable of giving the best and most vigorous shoots the following season. This being so

THEORY of PRUNING.

there are certain botanical principles which should be kept in mind in any discussion of the subject—

Botanical Principles.

(1) In any given bush the size and vigour of shoots is, within certain limits, inversely proportional to their amount. That is to say, with a given plant the fewer shoots allowed to grow the larger each one will be, and the more strength will there be in it. *Fewer Shoots—More Vigour.*

(2) The nearer a shoot approaches the vertical the more vigorous it will be. *Vertical Shoots More Vigorous.*

(3) The more wood left of the last year's growth, the less will be the vigour of the new shoots which arise from it. To leave more wood means that a larger number of eyes from which new branches or shoots may arise exist; and *vice versâ*. If, therefore, only a short length of wood is left all the energies of the bush have to be expended on a small number of shoots, and these shoots grow with more than ordinary vigour. *Less Wood More Vigour.*

136. It seems evident therefore that in old tea at any rate it is hopeless to expect that a plot can be uniformly treated throughout, and the sooner it is recognised that the pruning should be bush by bush and not plot by plot, the better will it be for the industry at large.

XXXV.—Treatment of the Young Plant.

TREATMENT of YOUNG PLANT.

Objects in Pruning Young Plant.

137. In dealing with a fresh plant grown from seed, whether in a nursery or from seed at stake, the primary object in all pruning is recognised to be the production of a bush of the shape desired without reference to any immediate leaf production. Not only, however, should the shape produced be of primary importance, but also the permanency of that shape. Thus, it might be possible to produce a bush of splendid bearing shape for four or five years, but if, at the end of that time, it was necessary to cut so low as to spoil that shape, and cause the necessity of making a new bush, such a method would distinctly be inadvisable. And thus a second purpose becomes to produce a bush which will not need heavy or collar-pruning for many years. Thirdly, the necessity of getting the bushes to shade the soil at the earliest possible opportunity should, especially in the hotter and more droughty districts, be constantly kept in view. And lastly, so far as is

Principles of Pruning.

TREATMENT of YOUNG PLANT.

consistent with the former points, it should and will, of course, be the object of the planter to bring the bush into full bearing at the earliest possible date.

Older Opinions.

138. ***Opinions of Authors on Shape of Tea Bush.***—In the earlier days of tea planting the object in view in pruning a young plant was to obtain as long and straight a stem as possible. This was achieved by delaying the pruning for several years after planting, and in some cases by stripping off the branches which showed a tendency to form on the then much-desired single stem. Mr. Shipp, (1865) for instance, says : "Strip off to eight inches above ground, by breaking or cutting them, all the small lower branches." Mr. W. C. Muller says "Let there be fully ten inches between the surface of the earth and your lowest branches." Mr. J. F. W. Watson proposes that the seedlings should be left alone for the first two years, then pruned down to three feet, and in the third year two or three inches lower still. He then adds : "A plant thus treated has, to begin with, a stout, strong stem, and the pruning adopted leaves it ample room for side development, and it is only at the sides that real development is possible." A Cachar planter said : "An indigenous plant ought never to be touched, or have its growth checked in any way, till the end of the third year, when it should receive its first pruning by being cut back to a height of thirty-six inches."

Change of View.

139. These views are now to a large extent ancient history. Few, if any, planters would be in favour of—much less lay stress on—the existence of a thick single stem which then seemed so desirable. And as for pruning young bushes at thirty-six inches, it may be said that this is no longer heard of, and has rightly been abandoned almost everywhere. These older methods were based on an idea as to the essential importance of a primary taproot for a tea bush. But while we believe that the presence of deep and extensive roots is essential for the production of a good plant, it may fairly well be asked—"Is the formation of a long, straight taproot so very indispensable to future success?" The roots of a plant are intended to serve a three-fold purpose—(*a*) to procure plant food; (*b*) to fix the plant; and (*c*) to procure water. The plant food is almost entirely furnished by the small fine rootlets constantly growing from every portion of the root, but principally

Importance of Roots.

Principles of Pruning.

in or just below the few inches nearest the surface of the ground, and a taproot has little or nothing to do with this power of absorbing the fertilising materials from the land. The objects to be served by a taproot—the fixing of the plant, and the supply of water—can, it seems, therefore, be equally served by several deep lateral roots, provided these go to the greatest depth available.

TREATMENT of YOUNG PLANT.

Value of Taproot.

140. A taproot, proceeding directly downward as a continuation of the stem, may be therefore considered, provided deep laterals are present, as non-essential, and hence the *raison d'étre* of the high original pruning to 36 inches disappears, as well as that of the late age—three years—at which the authors cited above consider that the first pruning should be carried out. For if a taproot be unnecessary, can it be said that a seedling three years old and 6 feet high has gained any advantage in the direction of the planter's ulterior object (the production of leaf) by being allowed to attain such an extraordinary growth? It has undoubtedly been allowed to run up in precisely the way it would do if growing in its wild habitat, with a tall delicate stem with a few erect or more or less ascending lateral branches. But when the check is given by the pruner's knife, it is now commanded to make up in lateral growth what it has lost in the vain, though natural, effort to form a vertical stem. By being allowed to grow up to a long stalk it has exhausted energy in this direction which might have been employed in making lateral growth, for, afterward, the whole, or nearly the whole of the straight stem is taken away. The tall tea seedling practically contains neither branch nor bud that is not possessed by its less vigorous sapling of corresponding age. The whole question is, therefore, one of the age at which it is most advantageous to give the first check to the natural tendencies of the plant.

Advantage of Pruning Low.

141. As a result of these arguments it will readily be seen that we are inclined to believe that the planters will best be served by pruning a fresh tea seedling as low as possible, as early as possible in its life.

142. ***Height of First Pruning.***—With regard to the former point we have recently had the opportunity of comparing, in a young garden in Sylhet, where other conditions were absolutely equal, the effect of making the original cut at 2 feet 3 inches from the ground, or at 15 inches. The latter was in every way preferable: the bushes of the same age were more vigorous, there

Principles of Pruning.

TREATMENT of YOUNG PLANT.

was less hard grey coloured wood in them, and there was prospect of a far greater return in the near future. Though we say "Let the first pruning be as low as possible," definite rules as to the exact height cannot be laid down. The best part for cutting will vary with many factors, and especially with the *jat* of bush. Thus the "Assam indigenous" tends to form a straight single stem,—the Manipuri type, on the other hand, shows a much greater tendency to branch almost from the level of the ground—and hence it will be necessary to cut the former much lower than the latter to produce the best type of bush. In confirmation of this it may be said that the best practice in the Assam Valley is now to cut not higher than 6 inches from the ground, and in many cases at 4 inches: in the Surma Valley, on the other hand, where Manipuri plant is almost universal—and rightly so—it is the custom to cut at 12 to 15 inches from the surface of the soil, with the result that a bush is more quickly formed than would be the case with lower cutting. As hybrid plant is somewhat like Manipuri in respect of tendency to form low branches, it may well be treated similarly.

Difference in Method due to Jat.

Difference in Practice in Assam and Cachar.

No Single Stems Allowed.

143. The question is not, however, so much as to the exact height at which the pruning should take place, but the recognition of the fact that if a bush shows a tendency—even after pruning—to again form a single stem, it must be cut again, or removed, or not planted, as the case may be. A plant with such a tendency in a plot—unchecked—will be a source of worry and trouble in the future.

Time of First Pruning.

144. ***Time of first pruning.***—Not only should the first pruning, however, be as low as possible, it should also be as early as possible. In our opinion it should, under no circumstance, except perhaps in filling in vacancies, be deferred beyond two years from the date of germination. It would even be better if made at an earlier date so as to ensure that the stunted stem thereby produced may contain in, say, 9 inches, all the buds (possible originators of branches) of a much greater elongation of the three years' seedling.

Nursery Pruning.

Pruning after Planting out.

145. There seem two ways of carrying this out. One way—prune the seedlings in the nursery when six months old, and plant several months later when they have recovered from the shock—no plants being put out which do not show the production of lateral shoots. Or the plants may be put out as six months' seedlings at the commencement of the rains and then pruned late during the following cold

weather, or put out at one year old, and pruned the following cold weather. Between these two systems there is, on principle, perhaps little to choose. The former gives a greater power of selection of suitable plants when they are actually planted out—a selection which is very necessary even with the best nurseries and the best seed. In the latter, owing to the plants being further apart after planting, there is a greater natural tendency to branch from the base at once.

TREATMENT of YOUNG PLANT.

Exception in Darjeeling.

146. There is perhaps one notable exception to the applicability of these principles. In a less favourable climate for tea, such as that of Darjeeling or other hill districts, it seems necessary to leave the plants considerably longer before they are pruned, simply because in order to reach the same state of development they require under these conditions a considerably longer time. Therefore, whereas we have said that the original pruning in the plains districts should be carried out when the plant is not more than two years old, this time should be extended to at least two and-a-half to three years in the hill districts.

Treatment after First Pruning.

147. ***Treatment after the First Pruning.***—When the plants are pruned and planted, however, watchfulness is by no means at an end. In some types of plant the tendency even then to heal up the old cut and form a single stem bush is very great. In a case in mind this tendency was effective in ten per cent. of the plants. Under such circumstances the stem should be again headed down, and several—not less than three—lateral shoots will probably be obtained. If not, it must be replaced by another seedling. It may be said that all this involves far more care than can be given to a plot of young tea, but when it is remembered that the bushes when produced represent the capital value of the garden in large measure, it is hardly too much to believe that no amount of care can really be too great at this stage of the growth. Whatever else is neglected the pruning and growth of young seedling tea should receive the very best attention and care possible—and this not only as regards the plot as a whole, but even as regards every individual plant.

Best Attention Required.

Second Pruning.

148. ***Second pruning.***—At this stage comes the most difficult point in the pruning of a young tea bush. We will suppose a plant obtained with three, four or five branches rising from various points in the stem from two to, say, six inches from the ground. When shall the next pruning take place? Is it advisable to leave much wood, or to cut down low on the laterals thus obtained?

Principles of Pruning.

TREATMENT of YOUNG PLANT.

149. In deciding what method to adopt it is, we think, important to consider that it is at this stage that the framework of the bush for many years to come should be formed, as, unless the original prunings have been bad, collar-pruning should be out of the question for a long time. The question of immediate yield should not enter at all into consideration. This being the case, the natural conclusion would seem to be that at this stage, and at this stage only, should a considerable amount of wood be left in the bush, and this for the following reasons :—

Amount of Wood to be left.

1. It is necessary to provide somewhere for the exhaustion of the younger bearing wood, and to allow for heavy pruning. It should be possible to carry out this heavy pruning without destroying the form of the bush, and still obtain good straight non-knotted stems. If at the present stage the stems be left short, it will only be possible to cut back into them once or twice, whereas if more space be left they can be utilised for heavy cutting several times before it is necessary to go down to the ground.

Reasons Given

2. It has been laid down as an axiom that the shorter the wood left in pruning, the greater the vigour of the shoot which arises from it. It is hence advisable (see below) to leave as little wood as possible at each successive high pruning of the bush, and so at no future time will there be the chance to leave wood for a framework of the bush. At the present stage, however, the vigour of the young plant is sufficiently great (or ought to be if the land is at all suitable for tea) to render each of these main branches capable of nourishing sufficiently and vigorously the head of leaf which will form from it.

150. From every point of view therefore it seems wise to leave a considerable amount of wood at this stage; but how much? This is most difficult to answer from a theoretical point of view, but it seems that if one allows two inches to be taken off at each successive heavy pruning, it would be wise to allow for four such heavy prunings, and this leaves ten to twelve inches of new wood, or prune at fourteen to eighteen inches from the ground. There is, however, nothing absolute in these figures, and local conditions will have a great deal to do in deciding the exact point at which this critical second pruning should be made.

Principles of Pruning.

TREATMENT of YOUNG PLANT.

Leaving Bush Unpruned after Second Pruning.

One more question arises in connection with the stage now under consideration. Is it advisable to leave the bush unpruned for a year after the first cutting, say, at six inches from the ground, before that at fourteen to eighteen inches, in order that the plant may get a thorough hold on the soil, and develop for so long in a natural and ordinary fashion? We think it is. By this means the wood from the first to the second cutting becomes more mature and more capable of giving rise to new vigorous shoots.

151. Another method which avoids an original very low pruning altogether has recently been adopted by several Assam planters of experience. The bush is made to throw out lateral shoots merely by planting out at six months old in the garden,—the openness of the surroundings if the land is well hoed making the tendency to form lateral shoots predominant, and these arise almost from the base of the stem. The first pruning is therefore at fourteen to eighteen inches, but a bush is formed before this pruning is carried out. It is claimed by this means that at no time does the bush receive such a shock as the original four to six inch prune must be, and yet a plant of the desired shape and character is produced. There seems no theoretical reason why this should not be the case, but, personally, we have not seen enough of the method to be able to express a confident opinion and can, hence, not at present recommend it.

151*a*. Thus we have three alternative schemes for the treatment of the young bush, as follows, though it must be recognised that each of them may demand modification according to district, climate, and soil.

I. *a*. Prune in the nursery at, say, a year old.

b. Transplant at eighteen months old (before or in the rains), or at two years old in the cold weather.

c. Allow the plant to grow without cutting till three years from seed.

d. Prune at three years from seed 14 to 18 inches from the ground.

II. *a*. Transplant into the garden at six months or one year old.

b. Prune at one year from seed if planted at six months, or at two years if planted at one year old.

c. Allow the plant as before to grow for a season without pruning.

d. Prune at three years from seed 14 to 18 inches from the ground.

Principles of Pruning.

TREATMENT of YOUNG PLANT.

In this scheme it may perhaps be most advisable to leave pruning till two years from seed, thus giving a better chance for the plant to get a hold on the soil.

In any case if an Assam indigenous plant is being dealt with, the original pruning should be 4 to 6 inches from the ground; if a 'Manipuri' it may be considerably higher.

III. Is the method set out in paragraph 151 of which we have not seen enough to either recommend or condemn.

PRUNING of MATURE BUSHES.

XXXVI.—Pruning of Mature Bushes.

Annual Pruning Universal in India.

152. Throughout the tea districts of Northern India it may be said that an annual pruning is practically universal. The same is by no means true of Ceylon or South India, as there, we understand, it is the regular custom in the gardens at high levels to leave the tea two years without pruning, and even in some cases three and-a-half years have been allowed to elapse between successive applications of the knife. It has been and is occasionally the custom in North India, however, to leave the weak bushes on a plot unpruned for a year with the idea that by this means they would be induced to form better wood which would, in the future, produce more vigorous shoots. Such a proceeding has some very obvious advantages. There can, for instance, be no damage from over-plucking during the unpruned years, the bush has to make no new wood and is hence partially resting, and an early yield is obtained. On the other hand, such bushes always feel drought more, should it occur, than if they had been pruned; they often get red spider badly, and act, as we shall show later, as a nursery for mosquito blight; and the leaf becomes smaller and more difficult to pluck. Altogether we are inclined to think that the practice of leaving the weak, poor, bushes in a plot unpruned for a year is distinctly a good one, under ordinary circumstances, provided always that a dose of manure—preferably cattle manure—is given to the bushes so left. Without manure we doubt very much the advisability of leaving the bushes, as then the disadvantages seem to more than counterbalance the benefit which might otherwise be derived. But, given manure, the method of leaving unpruned seems the only way to ensure that the weakly bushes shall not be plucked like their vigorous neighbours, and to allow them a partial rest from the strain of not only making leaf but also making new wood. Such leaving will, as a rule, involve heavy

Leaving Bushes Unpruned.

Conf. with para. 530.

Manure Required.

pruning at a later date—generally the next year—and it would hence be wise that the weakly bushes should be left unpruned the year preceding that in which it is intended to heavy prune the plot.

PRUNING of MATURE BUSHES.

Leaving Blocks Unpruned.

153. This applies to weakly bushes, but there has been a general tendency to adopt a system of leaving whole blocks unpruned occasionally for a season. The result is said to be that a large yield is obtained from the unpruned sections in the early part of the season, and that the previous year's growth has time to mature and will become a better basis for future yield. It has even been suggested to us by a planter in Cachar that half a garden should each year be left unpruned, and so an earlier crop be obtained, and the rushes of leaf—beyond the power of the estate to cope with, so common in August and September—be largely eliminated. Without going so far as this there seem conditions under which it is distinctly advisable to leave blocks unpruned. Among these are the following :—

Advantages.

1. In Year following Heavy Pruning.

1. In the year following heavy pruning, on all except the richest lands, it appears very much to be recommended that the bushes should be left without any treatment with the knife. Of this, however, we will speak when considering heavy pruning.

2. When in Hard Unyielding Condition.

2. When, owing to exhaustion of the soil, previous bad pruning, or too hard plucking, the bushes are in a hard unyielding condition. Under these circumstances it seems perhaps the wisest plan, in the ultimate interest of the garden, to manure heavily, leave unpruned a year, and heavy prune the following season. By this means a certain amount of vigour is returned to the bush by the rest and the manure, and when cut hard it will probably respond far more quickly and strongly than it would otherwise have done.

3. For the sake of Quality.

3. Whenever, in the absence of serious danger, whether of a spring drought, or a serious dose of red spider, or other spring blight, and in the presence of a large labour force, there is great advantage in making high quality spring teas. Mr. Bamber strongly holds the close connection between the quality of tea and distance from pruning of the wood from which it is grown, and if this be so, there is strong reason why some part of the garden should be left unpruned each year, provided, of course, there is a sufficiently large labour

Principles of Pruning.

PRUNING of MATURE BUSHES.

force to deal with the leaf, which will be difficult to pluck. The decrease in the size of leaf as the bushes get further from pruning rapidly puts a limit to the possible length of time they can be left, and, in any case, only a part of the garden can by any possiblity be so dealt with each season.

Season of Annual Pruning.

154. ***Season of Annual Pruning.***—There may be said to be a consensus of opinion in favour of the annual pruning being delayed as long as the strength of the labour staff will admit. Some few writers have said, however, that pruning should be commenced immediately after the sap has ceased to ascend. This we venture to affirm is a mistake. What object could there be in needlessly exposing the cut surfaces of the branches and twigs to the drying influences of the atmosphere? Absolutely no effort will be made by the plant to cover the wounds till the sap begins in spring to carry up the food-supplies. This early ascending sap, however, has to be assimilated by the old leaves on the bush and be sent by these to the cut surfaces. This fact shows how very ill-advised the system is to direct the pruners to pluck off all the old leaves from the bushes. This should on no account be done, except in special cases, since assimilation will thereby have to be accomplished by the bark of the few young twigs still remaining on the bush, and the bursting forth of the new shoots will accordingly be greatly retarded. The special cases referred to are when the older leaves carry blight of various kinds, such as grey blight, brown blight, red rust, etc., when it may be advisable to remove these blighted leaves, but no others, at pruning. Otherwise, if it be desired to remove the old leaves, this had best be done after the new shoots have appeared, certainly never before, and better never at all. It has been said that the occasional removal of all the leaves at pruning (the so-called "stick-pruning") causes the bush to manifest greater energy the following season, and it has even been maintained that such stick-pruning was a substitute for collar-pruning in its effect on the bush. This is probably the case in some climates and soils, though it is difficult to understand, but it is a risky thing to do, and in any case must not only be restricted to Upper Assam, but even then be a very occasional operation in each block.

Early Pruning Condemned.

"Stick-pruning."

Tendency to Become Earlier.

155. In spite of the fact that on principle late pruning is recognised as correct, there is a general tendency for the pruning to become

Principles of Pruning.

PRUNING of MATURE BUSHES.

earlier rather than later as years go by. This tendency is to be discouraged for several reasons in addition to that above given, chief among which is the fact that by early pruning early growth is induced, which, supposing a drought follows, is of no value, and the bush, say in May, has to start to throw out an entirely new set of shoots, different from those which originally grew. Now, seeing that droughts, by very general testimony, seem to be becoming increasingly common in many districts, for this reason, if for no other, the pruning should be delayed so long as is feasible. A second reason in favour of late pruning is that red spider is invariably more severe on the blocks which first received the knife. A very prominent planter recently said to one of us that in his opinion the best cure for red spider was late pruning, and, partly at any rate, we are inclined to agree with him. Not only red spider but also other blights are made worse, apparently, by early pruning—mosquito blight, contrary to the idea generally received a few years ago, being one of them. This will be discussed later (see Chapter XIV), but there seems a very great body of evidence now in existence pointing to late pruning as distinctly indicated in districts liable to this most serious pest of tea.

Late Pruning Recommended.

156. ***Position and Angle of Section.***—The time of pruning having been decided upon, the most important consideration is the position and angle of the section cut. If the knife be inserted below the base of the bud and a long slanting section be made, the bud will be starved and thus produce a sickly shoot. If the section be made at a point, say from half an inch to two inches above the bud, the protruding portion will be starved and die accordingly. This is the condition known to the gardener as a "*Snag*," the evil effect of which can be found in almost every garden. When in spring the sap ascends to the shoots an accumulation takes place at a point near the topmost bud. This swells in consequence, the bud bursts into foliage, the leaves commence the process of assimilation, and had the section been properly made, the elaborated sap would have, in a comparatively short space of time, caused the bark to heal over the section and extend into the new shoot until the existence of a wound had practically disappeared. This result is most desirable, for fully matured or dead wood obstructs the circulation of the sap and retards growth. Instead of healing over, when a snag has been left, the effort made causes the swelling to grow larger and larger

Position and Angle of Section.

Snags.

Their Effects.

Principles of Pruning.

PRUNING of MATURE BUSHES.

around the base of the projecting, useless and dead apex of the old twig. The snag when it dies becomes attacked by white ants and other vermin. It is thus decomposed so that, instead of a united bark covering the wound made in pruning, a hole is formed that fills with water and sets up decay that extends far below the point of origin of the new shoot, upon which the year's (or it may be

Fig. 1.—Example of Bad Pruning.
(From a Photo. by H. H. Mann.)

several years') flushing depends. This is no imaginary picture, but is found everywhere—worse, no doubt, in some places than in others, but present in all. Figure 1 from a photograph taken in Sylhet of a typically badly pruned branch shows several snags and their effect.

Principles of Pruning.

PRUNING of MATURE BUSHES.

157. The formation of a snag may not be of very serious consequence in the year immediately preceding heavy pruning, but it is easy to find stems on which snags have been formed year after year, for ten or fifteen years, until gnarled rotten swellings, corresponding to each year's prunings, may be said to have slowly starved the plant. This fact hardly needs further illustration. The sap ascends freely within the sap-wood of the well-formed stem till it comes to a great swelling that corresponds to the position of the first pruning. Wandering round this it ultimately finds an escape, let it be supposed, to the right along a branch some 6 or 8 inches long. At the extremity of this it is a second time obstructed by swelling, which is due to a snag. We may next suppose that the current is thereby deflected to the left. It finds an outlet, however, along a more or less sickly twig. Thus, this way and that, the ascending sap is obstructed on every hand. Is it to be wondered at, therefore, that against such difficulties an insufficient supply is drawn to the growing parts of the plant? Instead of being vigorous, the flushing in each succeeding season gives distinct indications of declining activity.

Sap Circulation stopped by Bad Pruning.

158. But the full significance of retarded circulation of sap is only obtained by studying the course of the downward current. So far as is known, no portion of the ascending fluid can be utilized till it reaches the leaves to be there assimilated. While the process of assimilation is taking place, the pluckers visit the bush and the majority of the young shoots and leaves are removed. What remains of the assimilated fluid now begins to descend, but, as it has to permeate backwards and forwards through all the woody portions, the knots of dead wood formed at the snags become, not deflecting influences, but positive obstructions. It is, therefore, only natural that the lower and older portions of the stem are literally starved and often manifest immense open scars corresponding to old snags. Such bushes might, in fact, be spoken of as living at the top and rotten at the bottom to an extent beyond what words can portray. No person who has not seen a really bad tea garden can form any conception of the miserable conditions under which the tea plant will still continue to live and even give dividends to its owners. For such a state of affairs, if the obstructions are of recent growth, it may be sufficient to cut below these knots, but where the obstructions are of old standing,

Effect on Downward Current of Sap.

Principles of Pruning.

PRUNING of MATURE BUSHES.

Remedy for Bad Pruning.

collar-pruning is the only method of dealing with bushes of this sort. While saying this, however, it should be remembered that we regard the fact of the bushes being in such a condition not as a necessity in old tea, but as being the result of bad pruning, and hence of bad management, in the past, and that the necessity for collar-pruning from this cause is itself a condemnation of the previous method of dealing with the bushes.

Correct Pruning.

159. To avoid such a result the annual pruning should, for every individual twig, be conducted so that the cut leaves practically no wood above the bud from which the new shoot is to arise, and so that the cut makes an angle of about 45 degrees with the stem of the bush.

Cut out Snags as soon as possible.

160. It is often impossible to know where the bud will appear in a tea bush, and hence it is often difficult, if not impossible, to arrange that the cutting should be at the place to avoid a *snag* formation. It is only therefore the more important that the following year the snags formed in the previous season should be removed when the regular pruning is carried out.

161. ***Amount of wood to be left in pruning.***—The next point to discuss is the question how much wood, of that formed in the previous year, should be left in ordinary light pruning. It has been laid down as an axiom in the early part of this chapter that the vigour of the shoots which result after pruning is *increased* by shortening the length of wood from which they grow. Seeing that in tea pruning the object is to produce maximum vigour in the bearing shoots, it would seem to naturally follow that the less wood left, provided it contains a bud, actual or dormant, the greater would be the advantage. This would seem to have been found to be the case in practice. A few years ago four inches appears to have been the amount usually left on top of the previous pruning, but this has been reduced, and in our opinion rightly reduced, with corresponding increase in the vigour of the flushing growth. This is not the place to say exactly how much should remain of the previous wood ; this would depend on the district, the luxuriance of the plant, the probability of the existence of dormant buds in the shoots, and other influences, but we cannot see why more than two inches ("three fingers") is of any advantage as a rule.

Length of Wood to be left in Pruning.

162. And here we come to one of the most disputed points in the whole of tea pruning, and one in which we have formed an

opinion contrary to the general practice. Basing our statements primarily on theoretical grounds, we fully feel that there are perhaps reasons in practice which render it advisable to depart from the bare principle, but nevertheless we have seen most successful pruning for many years in succession carried out in accordance with the principle which follows, and hence we do not depend entirely on theoretical teaching. A very usual attempt in light pruning a tea garden is to cut the top of the bush flat, or, in other words, it is what is technically known as "table-pruning." This involves, as will at once be seen, the cutting of the central shoots in the bush at a much shorter distance from the source than those at the side. Now the result of this, according to the principles already laid down, will be that the shoots at the centre of the bush will be much more vigorous than those at the side, and this difference will increase with every successive light pruning. The result ultimately obtained after several years of upward light pruning is a small area of vigorously flushing shoots in the centre of the bush, gradually becoming less and less vigorous towards the circumference, the extreme outside producing practically nothing but a few *banjhi* twigs. That this is the case not merely in theory but also in practice is common knowledge on almost every tea garden, and the remedy is usually considered to be heavy cutting. And when this condition has been reached truly there is no other remedy. But what we would point out is that such a condition is a necessary result of a bad system of pruning, and can in large measure be avoided—and hence heavy pruning avoided—by a better system of conducting the annual light pruning.

PRUNING of MATURE BUSHES.

Table-Pruning Condemned.

Unnecessary Heavy Pruning.

163. According to the principles we have laid down, the luxuriance of the new shoot largely depends, other things being equal, on the length of wood (left by the previous cutting) from which the new growth arises, and that the shorter this length is the more luxuriant will be the growth. Now, in the system of table-pruning, so common among those who make a fetish of a broad bush, it will easily be seen that the shoots in the centre are cut the shortest, and those on the edge the longest, and that hence the maximum of luxuriance will be in the centre, and this will decrease as one proceeds outward. This effect multiplies itself with every additional light pruning, and the form of bush with a yielding centre surrounded by a ring of *banjhi* twigs is rapidly produced. Another

PRUNING of MATURE BUSHES.

cause adds to the evil effect. Table-pruning involves the retention of those nearly horizontal, more or less weakly shoots, which spring from the side of the bush and increase its area, but which when pruned are pruned long, and on account, also, of their method of growth are never luxuriant.

Broad Bushes.

164. It follows, therefore, that we do not agree with that simple form of pruning which consists in cutting the garden level, and dignifying the process by the name of "table-pruning." The object in view should be to get as great a surface of plant as possible, *provided the surface is a yielding surface.* To extend the area of the top of a bush for the sake of producing a surface of *banjhi* twigs seems to us by no means rational. It has often been said that with the labour available the only system possible is that just condemned; but we have seen some gardens in which a different method has been carried out with great success, though the labour was of precisely the same kind, and hence it hardly seems that the argument can be really a valid one.

Proper Methods of Pruning.

165. But how then should the shoots be cut in light pruning?—On principle it would seem that as the object in view is to produce an equally vigorous area all over the bush, the new wood on each shoot should be cut to approximately the same length, and that hence the pruning coolies might almost be supplied with a measure, say "two fingers," to leave on every shoot on the bush. We are aware that such pruning would not look nice, and not nearly so elegant as a fine piece of table-pruning, but we do not think it is held by anyone that pruning is carried out for appearance' sake, and if a higher yield of equal quality tea is obtained, it is full justification for an ugly looking garden at the end of the pruning season. This might be looked upon as a theoretical position, but gardens have been brought to our notice this year in which what is more or less this system has for several years been carried out, and the result has been all that one would have expected.

Vertical Shoots most Vigorous.

166. There is another point in this connection equally important with that just made. The most vigorous shoots it has been said are those which approach most nearly to the vertical position. Would it not therefore be well, on the outside of the bush where the bulk of the young shoots are horizontal or nearly so, to head these back, and so encourage the formation of vertical shoots at this part

of the plant even at the cost of a certain amount of bush surface? In other words is "cutting the sides" of the bushes advisable or no? On principle we say emphatically that such a process is not only advisable but necessary if the maximum result is to be obtained per square foot of bush area.

PRUNING of MATURE BUSHES.

Cutting the Sides.

But here again there is all the difference between cutting the sides for the purpose of inducing vertical growth, and cutting haphazard everything which the knife touches, and of course the difficulty of getting good work done with an uninstructed labour force comes very prominently into the consideration of the subject, and it is evident that such a method demands very considerable supervision. But that it can be carried out, with fairly satisfactory results, we have been convinced by our own eyes, and if it can be so done the careful and scientific cutting of the sides of the bushes, to induce vertical growth, becomes a most important part of the pruning.

Random Cutting of the Sides condemned.

167. ***Thinning out the bushes.***—It is evident that the vigour of the shoots which a single bush can support will in ordinary cases be in inverse proportion to the number present in the bush. Thus, for instance, if a bush carries, say, a hundred small shoots, none of these will be so vigorous as those on the same bush carrying twenty shoots. Further, if, say, sixty per cent. of the larger number of shoots are small and twiggy and never likely to yield any but *banjhi* leaf, it is evident that their presence in the bush will merely take away from the strength of the remaining growth without themselves yielding any return. Now at the end of every season there are always found a large number of such small twiggy shoots in every bush, which from their position and formation can never become of service for leaf production, and the question has been as to whether they should be removed during the annual pruning.

Thinning out the Bushes.

On the face of it, being no use for leaf production, these twigs should always be cut out, and cut out right at the bottom, leaving no snag behind. We have been informed that the best way of removing them is to pull them clear away, and not cut at all. Various objections have been taken to their being removed. It has heen said, for instance, that the leaves on these twigs form the lungs of the bush during the time there is no new growth. This objection will not however, hold water for a moment. The leaves which are left on the

Thin Shoots do not Form Lungs of the Bush.

Principles of Pruning.

PRUNING of MATURE BUSHES.

bush in any case, whether thinning out is done or not, are quite sufficient lungs during the dormant season of the plant. The argument would be valid against the unnecessary removal of leaves, but is certainly not so against the pruning off of useless, thieving twigs. It is said again that these twigs, with their foliage, protect the pruned bush from the sun, during the dry hot weather, and in hot districts, and we have here an important argument in favour of leaving the twigs in question on the bush. But, even here, we have the balancing of two evils—the evil of hot sun on pruned wood, and the evil of many *banjhi* twigs in the bushes. Though it needs a carefully conducted experiment to render the matter quite certain, yet we should strongly incline, even here, to thin out the bushes of the useless, non-bearing, small, twiggy, *banjhi* shoots, and just leave as many as the plant is able abundantly to nourish.

Bheels an Exception.

168. There may be cases to which these arguments do not quite apply, and where, as in a well planted bheel garden, the bushes seem capable of producing luxuriant rank growth from every shoot left in the bush; but these are exceptions, and there seems strong evidence, from observations made during the present season, of the validity under practically all conditions of the arguments just set out.

168*a*. The annual pruning then, in summary, should remove the following parts of the bush :—

Parts to be Removed in Pruning.

1. All dead branches.
2. All gnarled twigs and crows-foot clumps of imperfectly formed shoots—last year's "*banjhi*" flushings.
3. All snags which are seen to have little chance of healing over. The longer the removal is delayed the worse for the bush.
4. All "trailing" branches at the outside of the bush.
5. All the last year's horizontal shoots at the outside of the bushes should be headed back to induce them to throw out vertical shoots.
6. All small twiggy shoots throughout the bush, which will never give strong, healthy yielding material for the next year. These should be cut right back to the stem from which they arise, or pulled out.

New Wood to be left

In addition, the amount of new wood should be as little as possible consistent with this containing one bud—dormant or otherwise,

PRUNING of MATURE BUSHES.

and if possible the same length should be left on each pruned shoot throughout the bush.

HEAVY PRUNING.

XXXVII.—Heavy Pruning.

169. ***Reason for Heavy Pruning.***—Though more rational methods of annual light pruning will make heavy pruning necessary less often than it would be otherwise and has been in the past, yet just as pruning at all is necessary to remove the refuse mass of twigs which plucking, say, twenty to thirty times in the season, leaves on the bush, so heavy pruning is necessary to remove the refuse of several years of light pruning. It need hardly be repeated that the idea should be kept clearly in mind that successful flushing involves the starvation of the stem, and more especially of the stem immediately below the plucking point which cannot be fed by the large mature leaves on the higher branches. Hence it becomes less and less capable, as the bush is plucked year after year, of giving vigorous shoots again, and heavy pruning becomes the necessary sequel to light pruning.

Heavy Pruning Necessary.

170. But this should not blind one to the fact that it is an evil, though a necessary evil, and that, being so, it should never be undertaken without adequate cause, and certainly never for appearance' sake. Though it would hardly be deemed likely, yet this is often the cause which determines the heavy pruning of a section. No record of yield per plot is kept, no knowledge is in the hand of the manager as to whether the yield of the plot is stationary or declining, and it is casually decided that the plot is in need of heavy pruning, and it is pruned accordingly. We maintain that such a process is irrational in the highest degree. Heavy pruning should be determined by yield, and if records are kept they will quickly show the necessity or otherwise of the process.

Not done at Random.

171. But though sooner or later essential, there are several causes which make the heavy pruning of a block necessary sooner than it would otherwise be. Of these the first and perhaps most important is exhaustion of the soil. Given a rich soil affording abundance of nourishment to the bush, the starvation of the stem will be much retarded, and hence the heavy pruning; but given an old, possibly a washed, exhausted soil, and starvation immediately occurs, the wood acquires the greyish appearance characteristic of

Causes Hastening Heavy Pruning.

HEAVY PRUNING.

non-bearing wood, lichens grow on the stem right to the tip, and the bush is said to be "hidebound" and needs heavy pruning. We remember well a case in Upper Assam where a steep slope was planted with identically the same bushes at the same time. At the time of our visit the top of the slope was as we have described it and badly in need of heavy pruning, the bottom had magnificent bushes; and the only method of accounting for it was that the surface soil had washed from the top to the bottom of the slope, the upper bushes had been starved, especially the tips of the branches where the flushes should occur, and they would have to be removed before much improvement could be expected, while those at the bottom were still vigorous and well fed. Another example illustrating the same thing was found in a Sylhet bheel garden. No heavy pruning had taken place for twenty years and none was needed. The soil was rank enough to sustain the flushes, and the starvation of the stems, even near the tips, had been only comparatively slight. It may be said, in fact, that there is an inter-relation between the richness of the soil and the need for heavy pruning, and that if the soil be kept good and rich by manuring before the plant begins to show signs of exhaustion, the necessity for heavy pruning will be postponed without loss of yield. This inter-relation of soil and heavy pruning seems to us a most important matter not sufficiently recognised at present by the majority of planters.

Exhaustion of the Soil.

Hard Plucking Early in Season.

172. But that starvation of the tips of the stems which renders heavy pruning necessary can be more quickly produced by over-plucking in the early part of the season than by any other means. If a due amount of leaf is left in the first, second, and third flushes, these new leaves, as they mature, feed the stem: if little or none is left, the stem starves. The starved look of bushes plucked hard in May and June (as is so often seen in some gardens) is a proof that in this point practice is in agreement with the theoretical conclusions.

Stimulating Effect of Heavy Pruning.

173. But heavy pruning is not merely a method of removing the refuse non-yielding wood from a bush: it also has an effect in directly stimulating the plant to greater exertions, and this is evidenced, if by nothing else, by the greater development of small, useful feeding rootlets after the heavy cutting of the plant, provided the soil is such as to allow of their formation. This is probably one

of the principal reasons in some cases why heavy or especially collar-pruning has been such a great success. The bushes are a mass of useless wood; inadequate feeding of the root energies takes place, and hence little new root growth takes place. The bush is collar-pruned, the whole of the new growth spends its time in feeding the root, and innumerable new and valuable rootlets make their appearance, and the result is a magnificent bush, which, if dealt with properly, gives a better plant probably than has ever been in the place before.

HEAVY PRUNING.

174. ***Position for Heavy Pruning.***—Heavy pruning being accepted as a necessity, the question next arises as to how the place in the bush at which it is necessary to carry out such heavy pruning may be ascertained. And here one reaches one of the most difficult questions in the whole business—How far is it necessary to go with the knife? The whole question is so extremely difficult to decide that there is no matter on which planters are more at variance. It is extremely common to hear in one district one man declare that he never believes in taking more off the bush than can be avoided, while another declares in favour of collar-pruning under the same circumstances: and both are successful!

Position of Heavy Pruning.

It is evident that information on these points can only be obtained by experiment, and such an experiment or series of experiments was suggested in the first edition of this work, and, on the initiative of the Indian Tea Association, are now in progress in several parts of Assam—in Dibrugarh, in Jorhat, in Bishnath, and in Nowgong. The design is to take plots whose history is fairly well known but of which the yield has greatly deteriorated, manure as much as is needed, and prune in different fashions, taking careful note of the result. As these experiments have not yet been in progress for two seasons, it is impossible to give results at present, but in the near future these will be obtained—of a very interesting character we do not doubt.

Experiments in Progress.

175. In the meantime although the amount of cutting needed in any case must remain to a large extent a matter of doubt, yet there are some principles which, we think, may be looked upon as more or less certain even with our present knowledge of the question.

In the first place, heavy pruning should not disturb, where this is possible, the shape and framework of the bush, and where it is

Principles of Pruning.

HEAVY PRUNING. Framework of Bush Retained if Possible.

necessary to cut so low down that this is destroyed, collar-pruning is indicated. The random use of the knife is to be avoided. It takes several years to build up the skeleton of a good bearing bush, and it would seem to stand to reason that this skeleton should not be disturbed except in case of absolute necessity. We should not probably have insisted upon it had not such a huge amount of what might be called random pruning been carried out in the past five years.

No Knots left.

Secondly, as few knots as possible should be left below the cutting. If a bush be built up on the lines indicated in the earlier part of this chapter (*paragraphs 149—150*), there will be practically no knots below those representing the series of light pruning which it is desired to cut out, and "straight wood" will be reached with the least sacrifice of material.

Lichen and Moss removed.

Thirdly, grey lichenous growths on the bush are a sign that the wood on which they are taking place has ceased vigorously growing, and when they become thick, the inference will be that either the stems must be made more vigorous by manuring or else be cut out. This, however, hardly altogether applies to the Darjeeling and other hill districts where lichen and moss growths are commoner than anywhere else.

Manuring Necessary.

Fourthly, a necessary corollary, in nearly every case of heavy pruning is manuring. We, ourselves, prefer that this should be done the year before heavy pruning, but, whether it is done previously or at the same time, it should be an absolute rule in almost every garden that there should be no heavy pruning without manuring of the land. This is only to be expected seeing that exhaustion of the soil is one of the principal reasons why heavy pruning is necessary, and the cause of the failure of much heavy cutting to rejuvenate the bush is, beyond cavil, the absolute impossibility of the roots, new or old, finding sufficient material in the soil to build up the new shoots and branches required. If manuring is not done, heavy pruning is only a means of putting off the evil day when the plot will have to be abandoned entirely owing to exhaustion of the bushes due to previous exhaustion of the land.

Time of Heavy Pruning.

176. ***Time of Heavy Pruning.***—It seems the usual custom to do the heavy pruning on a tea garden as early in the pruning season as possible. Mr. Bamber defends this in the following words:—"It is generally acknowledged that plants, although apparently dormant

HEAVY PRUNING.

through the cold season, are slowly accumulating plant food from the soil, and storing it in their stems and branches; by early pruning, therefore, none of this reserve material is removed from the plant." If the sap circulation is stopped it is difficult to see how this storage could be accomplished, but admitting that there may be some grounds for the opinion, the whole question was a matter for experiment to decide. In Assam, at any rate, opinion, after many trials, seems to have agreed that the heavy pruning should be done before the light pruning on a garden, and not later than January. This is the conclusion in spite of the long exposure of the wood to the sun, and in spite of the likelihood that white ants may attack the dried up cut ends of the stems.

Treatment after Heavy Pruning.

177. ***Treatment of the bush after heavy pruning.***—Nothing can be more fatal than hard plucking of a bush after heavy cutting. It prevents the formation of good bearing wood; it causes the maturing of the wood, already formed, too quickly, because it is starved owing to the removal of the leaves which ought to feed it; and it brings about a stunting of the new feeding rootlets which are made to develop by the heavy pruning. In fact, we might say that we should be in favour of the easiest possible treatment after such a process,—no plucking under a very liberal measure, and even no pruning in the following season unless the heavy cutting has only been very moderate in amount. A middle pruned (*bich kalam* or *maj kalam*) bush might perhaps be light pruned again the following season, but below that it would seem far wiser to allow the bush to grow naturally for another year.

Leave Unpruned if possible.

We are well aware that this leaving unpruned after heavy pruning means the sacrifice of yield for the time being, but, though it may be impossible to prevent it, we are convinced that the sacrifice of everything, including bushes, to immediate yield has been one of the greatest curses of the industry in recent years. A place increases in crop marvellously for a season or two, and every one looks upon the management as a grand success. Ten years afterwards the garden may be all but worthless, as a result of forced growth, close pruning, etc., etc., and if recoverable at all, the place can only be brought back to condition by a systematic course of heavy and collar-pruning and nursing of the bushes for long after. While we are fully aware that, under present commercial conditions, if a garden be made to produce its maximum, yet that maximum

HEAVY PRUNING.

should be judged not by the standard of what it can do in one or two particular years, but by what it can keep on doing for a considerable number of years. Hence we argue that nursing the bushes, even to the extent of leaving them quite unpruned for a season, after heavy pruning, is wise and profitable even if it means the loss of a part of the crop which might otherwise be immediately obtained.

The question of the further treatment of the bushes will be spoken of under collar-pruning (*para. 185*).

Single Stump Pruning.

178. It has already been stated that if it is necessary to cut so low as to destroy the framework of the bush, or, in other words, to leave nothing but a single stump with or without a branch or two on top of it, then there is a good deal to be said for collar-pruning at once.

COLLAR-PRUNING.

XXXVIII.—Collar-pruning.

The Collar.

179. Theoretically the collar of a plant is the imaginary point of union between the root and stem. If the skin be peeled off a pea or bean it will be found that the contents divide into two large portions and that the halves may be seen to be hinged together by the embraced embryo. The two fat structures are the first leaves of the infant plant, greatly swollen by being made the store-houses of the food required for generation. The point of union of these seed-leaves to the embryonic axis is the true collar; the lower extremity of that axis becomes the root and the upper the stem. The most marked difference between the root and the stem lies, however, in the fact that the former (as already fully explained), has assigned to it the function of absorbing food from the soil. But it is commonly stated there is another difference, namely, that the root has no buds and cannot, therefore, be used as cuttings in the propagation of the species. Root-like structures, possessed of buds (such as the eyes of the potato), are pronounced to be underground stems, not roots. The distinction here indicated is so true of the greater number of plants, however, that when roots are found capable of independent growth they are often at once assumed to be underground stems and not roots.

The Embryo.

The Root.

Underground Stems.

180. The fear entertained, by many planters, against collar-pruning is that they run the risk of cutting below the collar, as defined botanically, and thus of killing the plant. The answer may

Principles of Pruning.

be given that a good many plants would seem to produce, below the actual collar (or point of origin of the seed-leaves), structures that we must define as roots, but which, nevertheless, can and do bear buds. The tea plant possesses this property. Let a bush, found growing on root stilts, owing to the surface soil having been washed away, be severed, so that the separate roots remain projecting out of the ground, and we venture to think a good few will shortly thereafter be seen to throw out shoots. On the faces of roadway cuttings, roots, often 3 feet below the level of the soil, may not infrequently be seen to bear shoots. From these and such like examples, it may fairly be inferred that the risk of cutting below the theoretical collar is a remote contingency. Moreover, in transplanting, seedlings are invariably placed in their new positions with a considerable portion of the stem below ground.

COLLAR-PRUNING.

Root-budding.

181. The term collar-pruning has had however a very loose signification up to the present in Assam, which is the only district in which the process has been at all common. It might mean on the one hand that the entire bush was cut away so as to leave a stump of the original stem that might be from 1 to 6, or even 12 inches above ground. The distinction between the latter and the condition designated "heavy pruning" was simply in the fact of only one instead of several stumps remaining. Collar-pruning was thus through the common stem instead of across its main branches, irrespective of position in relation to the ground or rather to the roots. It might, on the other hand, mean that the plant had been sawn off level with the ground, or it might in a few cases indicate that a hole had been dug, search made for the collar, and the cut made where this was supposed to have been.

Variations in Meaning.

182. The merits of these various processes is extremely unequal. Take the first case. The result of high "collar-pruning" (so called) is in many cases the production of a stump, rotten in the centre, and bearing whatever foliage there is from a shell not one inch thick, the whole of the remaining part of the stump having been eaten by white ants, or destroyed by fungus. It does not need very wide travel among tea gardens in Upper Assam to find such cases, and in some gardens where the process has been systematically carried out in this manner, a majority of the bushes, in spite of tarring the cut surface, are in this condition.

High Collar-pruning.

COLLAR-PRUNING.

It will be seen therefore that while we are in favour of collar-pruning in many cases, we can by no means approve of the method just described. If it is necessary to do more than heavy prune the bush across the branches without destroying the framework of the bush, there should be no question as to whether a stump, as described above, be left or whether the bush be cut right down to the ground. If the latter is done, it must be perfectly recognised that no appreciable yield ought to be expected in any case from such a collar-pruned bush for eighteen months, that in the meantime it will need the most careful attention, such as staking, very careful hoeing, it may be watering in a dry season, and even the presence of a chowkidar to keep off stray cattle, goats, etc. It must be recognised that collar-pruning is a most serious operation, demanding the expenditure of money in manure, attention and care. One often wonders how much of the collar-pruning that is done comes away at all: there is often so little care spent upon it. The most successful piece of collar-pruning we have ever seen was on the Brahmaputra Co.'s gardens, but here the plot was fenced, a chowkidar kept on the spot for months after the operation was performed, and every care was taken—a vast contrast with much that we have seen.

No yield for Eighteen Months afterwards. Attention Required

Successful Example.

Conditions of Collar-pruning

183. ***Conditions of Collar-pruning.***—The best conditions, judging from all experience, for collar-pruning, may be summarized as follows:—

Time of Pruning.

(1) Collar-pruning should be made in January or at an earlier date. There is urgent need for experiments in the time of collar-pruning best suited for various climates and conditions. This must be one of the experiments to be done at the very earliest opportunity, but in the meantime the vast majority of the tests made indicate that early collar-pruning is best.

Low Collar-pruning.

(2) The position of the section should be as low down as possible, preferably below, rather than above, the surface of the ground. It should *not* be covered with earth, as, contrary to what would have been expected, there seems under those conditions considerable difficulty in the plant forcing its new buds through the soil covering.

Collar-pruning preferred with Single Stem.

(3) Where the heavy pruning indicated involves leaving a single stem standing above the ground a few inches, collar-

pruning is usually preferable, though, as stated above, the time when this should be done in various districts urgently needs investigation. **COLLAR-PRUNING.**

(4) The exposed sections should be painted with vegetable tar (*not coal tar*) or Gondal fluid, to form a hindrance to the attack of white ants, and other insects or even fungi. The advantage of such applications is doubted, it is only fair to say, by a good many planters. **Paint Exposed Sections.**

(5) Collar-pruning *involves manuring or top-dressing as an essential part of the process.* We think this is best done with cattle manure, the year preceding the application of the saw, unless good bheel soil is available, when this might advantageously replace the cattle manure. **Manuring Essential.**

(6) The cut should be made in a slanting direction and on the lee side of the stem (to the point of greatest rainfall). The bark on its commencing to grow forms a rim around the exposed sections of wood, which must of necessity become a saucer or shallow depression to retain water, that would prove injurious were the section made on the level.

184. It must be recognised that collar-pruning should be, in a well managed garden, an exceptional occurrence. Its necessity is often the result of previous bad pruning, and though it is often necessary in old gardens, yet one should look upon it as a last resource when the wood of the bush is incapable of giving new growth of any vigour; and it becomes necessary to absolutely replace it by fresh stems and framework. **Exceptional Occurrence.**

185. ***Treatment subsequent to Collar-pruning.***—As we have said, collar-pruning involves the sacrifice of leaf for eighteen months, and even then the present yield should be sacrificed to the necessity of creating a new framework for a bush, just as with a young plant everything must be given up to make the bush. After two years we should be in favour of pruning the new growth down to a point which would allow future pruning to take place below—say 12 to 15 inches from the ground, and then light pruning could take place on top of this for a considerable number of years. These figures will vary for district and for conditions, and it would be impossible to lay down a law which would be everywhere applicable. **Treatment after Collar-pruning.**

SYSTEM of PRUNING.

XXXIX.—System of Pruning.

186. It would seem well to insist here that pruning is the most important operation in the garden during the season. It is at the pruning time to a large extent that a garden is made, or that a garden is ruined. Given the best soil, the best type of plant, and the best conditions of working, a constant change of system or a radically wrong system will so ruin the tea that a time will come when it will no longer be possible, either by pruning or by treating the soil, to bring the bushes back to anything like a reasonable yield. Such tea must be uprooted and replanted, or abandoned. But it seems a great pity that tea should be allowed to get into such a condition, and it would almost seem, if such a system were feasible—and we hardly see why it should not be—that a plan should be laid out ahead for five or ten years for pruning every plot often, and change of this, whatever manager were in charge, should only be allowed for some very special reason. The present system of going round each plot with a knife in December, and there and then deciding the year's pruning without reference to the past history of the bush is, we think, far too casual an arrangement for an industry in which the bushes represent both capital and stock-in-trade.

Pruning Plan laid out ahead.

187. We would go even further than this and say that we fancy that it would be true economy to spend more money on pruning than is at present usually the case. The unit of consideration should be the bush and not the plot, and each bush should be pruned according to its own merits as nearly as can be done under the peculiar conditions of the tea-industry. Objections are at once raised and we recognise their importance.

Should often cost more.

In the first place it is said that it is impossible to pluck a plot, variously pruned, in the early part of the season. But is not the old system of plucking to a measure now feasible? We abominate the system of pruning to a measure, but plucking variously pruned bushes to a measure is an altogether different thing. It saves the low pruned bushes; it plucks the normally pruned bushes; and it strips the unpruned bushes which can bear it. But of this more in the next chapter.

Difficulty of Plucking variously pruned tea.

The second and most vital objection to careful pruning is the

Principles of Pruning.

impossibility of getting an uninstructed labour force to prune as one would wish. Speaking as outsiders, we should have to accept this objection, were it not for the fact that gardens exist where intelligent pruning is followed out. In one, for instance, trained sirdars go through their respective portions of the garden and fasten a stake bearing a coloured string alongside of each bush that would be required to be pruned in a particular way. The manager follows and examines enough of these to see that his ideas were being carried out, and then coolies follow, each pruning his own coloured bush in his own way—a method which demands no more skill from the coolie than the ordinary system, and merely asks a number of intelligent and trained sirdars—*together with adequate supervision.* It is only fair to say that many of the most successful planters in Assam deny the possibility of getting the individual pruning well done however complete the supervision may be. In any case, in a young garden the demand for individual treatment will be very slight if the original plants were carefully selected.

SYSTEM of PRUNING.

Difficulty of Uninstructed Labour.

The impossibility of this supervision is the third objection made —and exactly its force we can perhaps hardly gauge. But if plucking can be so closely watched, as it is in many cases, that any woman plucking badly is detected almost with certainty, it seems hardly an impossibility to overlook the much more easily supervised pruning. The different pruning of different bushes in one plot will be a difficulty in an old garden, but in a young and well managed property, planted with selected seedlings, it ought to give very little difficulty as the plot will demand pruning almost exactly alike all over.

Supervision Necessary.

188. But what we want to insist upon is that pruning is a scientific operation of the utmost importance and delicacy, and one with paramount influence on the future and the permanence of the property. When this is recognised, as we believe it will be in the near future, we shall no longer see money spent in a niggardly manner on this business, and a month later be asked by managers how to employ their coolies at all; but pruning will be elevated into the most important operation of the year, demanding the all but constant presence and supervision of the planter, and all the skill of which he is capable, both in the treatment of the bush for the year in question, and in the preparation of a basis for future yield—perhaps ten years ahead.

Pruning a Scientific Operation.

APPENDIX.

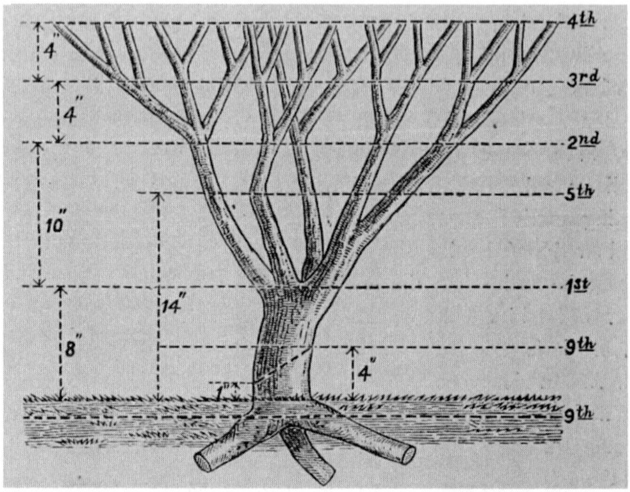

FIG. 2.—REPRESENTATION OF FIRST TO NINTH PRUNINGS.

ON MR. L. ALEXANDER'S SYSTEM.

Example of Pruning young bush. ***Conf. with paras. 142, 143.***

We include here an example of a system of pruning the tea bush in its early years which represents what has been in vogue a good deal in some parts of Upper Assam. It consisted in the following course:—

1. Bushes are cut to 8 inches when three years old. Here we prefer 6 inches or even 4 inches for Assam *jats*, and think that two years old is better than three.

2. Prune 10 inches above first pruning or 18 inches from ground.

Conf. with para. 161.

3. High prune 4 inches above the pruning No. 2. We do not see why 4 inches are left : 2 inches seem amply sufficient.

4. High prune 4 inches above the pruning No. 3. Our remarks under No. 3 apply.

5. Go back on straight wood 4 inches below No. 2. We fail to see, given good soil, why it is necessary to go back at this stage. It should be possible to go up at least three years more. Again, if it is decided to prune back, why cut off 4 inches below pruning No. 2?—2 inches should be ample.

6. High prune 4 inches above pruning No. 5.

7. High prune 4 inches above pruning No. 6.

8. High prune 4 inches above pruning No. 7. The remarks under No. 3 apply to all these cases.

Conf. with paras. 137, 175. Conf. with paras. 181, 183.

9. Cut down the bush 4 inches from the ground. We totally disagree with this pruning. First, it destroys the framework of the bush, and hence should not be necessary for a considerable number of years : and second, it leaves a single stump. If it is necessary to cut so low as this, the bush should most probably be collar-pruned, but this measure ought not to be necessary for many years ahead.

CHAPTER VII.

PLUCKING.

XL.—Continuous Production of New Shoots.

189. It has already been remarked that plucking should be looked upon as a method of pruning; further, that the planter prunes in order that he may subsequently pluck. **Plucking a Method of Pruning.**

By pruning and plucking, the tea plant is forced into the artificial condition of continually producing young shoots, and is debarred from ripening wood, with the view to the ultimate realization of the perpetuation of its species in the production of seed. It has been contended, in the foregoing chapters, that this is, of necessity, an exhausting and weakening state that predisposes the individual to disease. Consequently it has been upheld that the most hopeful and rational method of attempting the mitigation of the danger that is year by year assuming greater and more alarming proportions would be to effect such improvements in the systems of culture that may be calculated to increase the health and vigour of the plant. **Production of Seed.** **Predisposition to Disease.**

190. Plucking being the ultimate aim of the planter, it will be readily understood that around this simple act gravitate all the other injurious influences that are brought to bear on the plant. During its first three years it has to be assumed there have been produced a system of roots for the collection of food and also a framework of branches sufficient to nourish and support the flushing shoots. Future success, it has been urged, depends almost exclusively on the character of the young plant. It must possess by the end of the third year both the strength to endure and the material to allow of a systematic annual pruning for the flushings demanded, during a term of not less than nine to ten years. It is not necessary here to recapitulate our views as to the shape of bush it is desirable to obtain, but there is one point that has a distinct bearing on the question of flushing and which may, therefore, be here alluded to. By the system of allowing the seedling to grow undisturbed for three years and then cutting it down to 9, 12 or 24 inches, the shoots that originate from the stump are considerably less than one year old when they are hard plucked. This, we are convinced, is a serious mistake. These twigs **Injurious influences.** **Flushing depends on Character of Bush.** **Age of Primary Branches.**

CONTINUOUS PRODUCTION of SHOOTS.

have subsequently to become the main branches to carry the flushing shoots, and they should most certainly, if possible, be allowed more than one year to mature wood before being seriously interfered with.

Check to Growth.

191. It is the sudden check given by plucking, to the development of healthy wood, that is the chief injury the plant has to battle against. When the extremity of a shoot is nipped off, the effort to mature wood that had perhaps just then commenced is suddenly arrested, for the young leaves are, to some extent, the lungs and the mouths also of the plant. It has thus become a more imperative obligation on the plant to replace the parts removed, and in consequence return to the duty of development of wood is tardily performed. The lateral buds that may be seen nestling within the little recesses formed by the leaves at the points of their union to the twig, accordingly, burst forth and elongate into saplings to take the place of those removed. No sooner, however, have these grown to a certain extent than they are plucked, and the process of wood forming once more deferred. But the third set of flushings that must now come are, of necessity, borne upon less mature wood than the first. Time after time this is repeated, for perhaps 20 to 30 times a year, and each succeeding flush is, therefore, borne on less mature and still less mature shoots than its predecessor.

Less and still less Mature Wood.

Flushing Power.

192. This then is the state of affairs that prevails during the flushing season. For eight to nine months a year there may be said to exist a struggle on the part of the roots to cause the production of young shoots, in order to assimilate the continuous supply of nourishment which they are draining from the soil. By pruning, the balance between the proportion of root and stem has been disturbed. The roots are now rendered capable of nourishing a larger number of shoots than exist. The production of shoots is, therefore, the "flushing power" of the plant determined by the pruner's knife. But, it is needless to say, this again is but the expression above ground of the state of affairs that prevails below. A sufficiency of young and vigorous roots and a liberal supply of food materials are indispensable to the response being given by the plant to the degree of pruning to which it has been subjected.

Balance between Root and Stem Distributed.

Banjhi Buds.

193. ***"Banjhi" Buds.***—It will now be seen that it would be irrational to prune beyond the ascertained flushing capabilities of the plant. Planters in India are familiar with the condition known as

banjhi (barren) buds. Instead of elongating to the extent necessary to allow of plucking, the terminal bud of each little shoot seems to sulk, and the leaves that have already unfolded from it have become dark-coloured and matured before they are half their natural size. The bush is then spoken of as *banjhi*. Perhaps regarding few other aspects of tea-plucking could a more animated controversy be aroused than as to the proper method to treat bushes in this state. Should the buds be left on the bush or plucked off? That is the question asked on every hand. Now were the buds injured in any way and *banjhi* in consequence, the lateral buds on the shoot would sprout forth with as much vigour as if the terminal bud had been plucked. It accordingly follows that we must assume the inactivity of the buds is but the expression of a want of energy in the entire plant. To force it, therefore, into activity by plucking the terminal buds may injure it materially. It has possibly been already over-worked, the food-supply may be insufficient, or the climatic conditions unfavourable; it may be suffering from some specific disease, or its stem may be so gnarled and rotten as to be unable to support the excessive growth demanded. The cause must be sought and cured. In the majority of cases manuring and a good hoeing will suffice to cause the *banjhi* buds to once more resume activity. Many authors are of opinion that early in the plucking season all *banjhi* leaf, whether single or double, should be severely eliminated from the bushes. Mr. David Crole writes:—"I have myself tried experiments in this matter, and, to the best of my judgment, they answered my expectations." After alluding to the uncertainty of experiments not "conducted under circumstances which render a careful comparison of the results over a long period (say several seasons) at the same time easy and certain, so that a reliable average may be arrived at whereupon a fair judgment of success or failure may be based," he adds, "anyhow, I suggest the experiment as one well worthy of trial, and I am confident that it may be carried without any risk of its affecting the flushing of the bush adversely." We need hardly add to the above that we regard this recommendation, of which the quotations from Mr. Crole may be taken as an expression, as opposed to the planter's best interests.

Perhaps this opinion should be qualified by saying that we here only refer to the early part of the season. *Then* the fact of a bush

CONTINUOUS PRODUCTION of SHOOTS.

Treatment of Banjhi Bushes.

Plucking Recommended.

CONTINUOUS PRODUCTION of SHOOTS.

becoming *banjhi* is usually an expression of its weakness due to lack of manure, or of cultivation, etc., and it may be the case right through the season. Later, however, it usually merely means that the bush has satisfied its needs in the direction of leaf, and will produce no more until the *banjhi* be removed. The only way in dealing with a bush with good soil and good cultivation in the middle of the season is to pluck off the excess of leaf, *banjhi* or otherwise, which has been allowed to grow. The whole question of the best way to treat *banjhi* bushes is urgently, however, in need of carefully conducted experiments.

Abandoned Tea.

194. ***Abandoned Tea.***—It has often been stated to us that tea that has been abandoned for a few years, because of its having become so persistently *banjhi* (barren) that it was unprofitable, is found when again brought under cultivation to have vastly improved. This may be explained as due to two causes :—

Rest to Soil and lant.

(*a*) The rest given to the soil through the sort of rotation afforded to it by the unrestricted growth of weeds (fallow).

(*b*) The reparation of the defects in the bush through the rest. Being not called upon to flush it has time to mature wood to the extent necessary to sustain flushing. Moreover, the circulation of the sap becomes established by its having time to work off the obstructions caused through pruning.

Reasons for Improvement.

Both plant and soil have been brought into a healthier state. This supports in the strongest manner the argument that heavy and constant plucking weakens the bush. It causes the flushing to be made on imperfectly matured, gnarled and snagged twigs. Pruning becomes, therefore, an imperative necessity, the knife being made to go as far back as possible, in other words, on to the well formed red shoots of last year.

XLI.—Systems of Plucking.

Two Distinct Principles.

195. The problem is, therefore, how to maintain the bush in a state of health, and yet be able to gain as large a crop as possible of the highest quality tea available under the conditions. But nevertheless two distinct principles are found. In the one of these the prime object is to obtain a large crop, with comparatively little consideration of its quality: in the other the planter wishes to obtain a high quality tea, and sacrifices crop if necessary in order to obtain it.

Plucking.

These systems might be designated plucking for quantity, and plucking for quality. It is recognised that certain principles if followed will improve the quality of the tea, but we must own that the relation of quality to plucking is as yet a point on which we know extremely little. **SYSTEMS of PLUCKING.**

196. The following description may be said to be the normal **Course of First Plucking.**

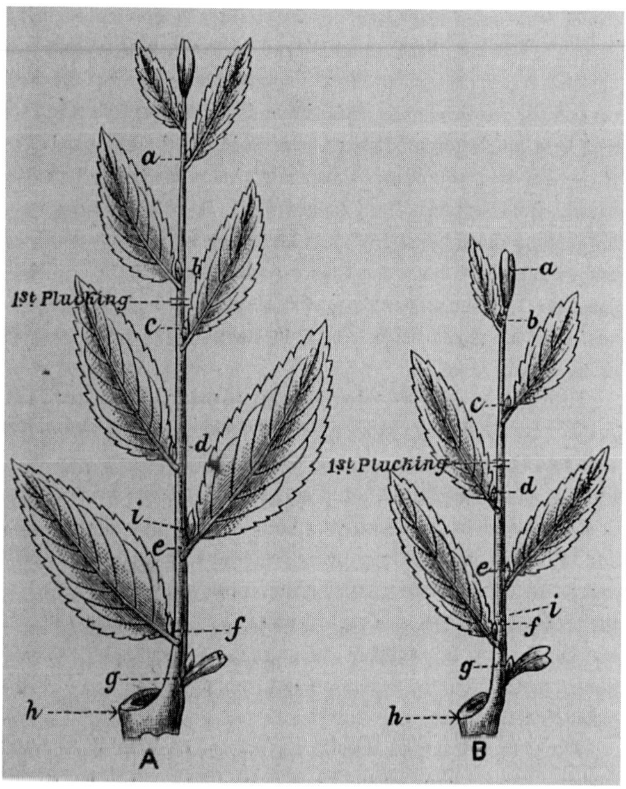

FIG. 3.—FIRST PLUCKING ON SPRING SHOOTS.

course followed in plucking during the early part of the season, and is illustrated by Fig. 3.

The normal spring shoot (A or B) has been allowed to elongate from the apex of last year's twig ("*h*" being the section of light

Plucking.

SYSTEMS of PLUCKING.

pruning made last autumn) until it has produced a number of buds, numbering in (A) eight lateral and one terminal, and in (B) six lateral and one terminal. Take first the case of (A). It is here plucked say between (*b*) and (*c*), the portion removed containing three leaves and the terminal bud. This is, of course, coarse plucking as at present understood. But putting this aside for one moment, let us look at its effect on the shoot. As a result the bud (*c*), or the buds (*c*) and (*d*), or sometimes also even (*e*) are forced to develop. It is not desirable, however, that the bud (*e*) should elongate at present, and this only exceptionally happens, the usual thing being that the buds (*c*) and (*d*) are developed. At the end of the season's plucking the next light pruning would have to be made at the point indicated by (*i*), so that one, two or three shoots might next Spring be expected, namely, from the buds (*e*), (*f*) and (*g*). It will thus be seen that the flushing shoots (*c*) and (*d*) with all their subsequent ramifications are pruned off, by the section being made into the original Spring shoot at (*i*). Much, therefore, of this season's flushing and of next year's Spring shoots depends on the method of treatment bestowed on the Spring shoot.

Normal course of First Plucking. A.

B.

Instead of this method the shoot might have been treated as in (B). In this case the Spring shoot obtained from the topmost bud at the pruning (*h*), is plucked at an earlier stage than in (A), namely, when it has at most elongated until it possesses six lateral and a terminal, or in all seven buds instead of nine. It is plucked between (*c*) and (*d*), thus leaving four buds below and removing two buds and the terminal. Subsequent flushing consists, for the most part, in the production of shoots from the buds (*d*) and (*e*), and the succeeding pruning would probably be made at (*i*), so that next year's Spring shoots might be expected from the buds (*f*) and (*g*), though generally from (*f*) only.

Difference between A and B.

These two examples represent types of two different kinds of plucking and it will be well to follow them through. So far, it will be observed, the differences between the (A) and (B) systems may be thus stated :—

1. The shoot (A) is older than (B) before the first plucking takes place.
2. Three leaves and a terminal bud in (A) are removed as against two leaves and a terminal bud in (B). This

SYSTEMS of PLUCKING.

difference is not, however, an essential one, and the argument would be precisely similar if one less leaf had been grown in (A), and two leaves with the terminal bud only plucked.

3. The portion of the original Spring shoot retained in (A) and (B) is different—three buds being left to prune on in (A) and only two in (B).

The consideration under the third head is the direct result of the first—the difference of age between (A) and (B) when the first plucking takes place. The plucking of (A) will, it stands to reason, commence later than that of (B).

Phaki or Janum Leaf.

197. ***"Phaki" or "Janum" Leaf and Bud.***—It may be here explained that the first leaf unfolded from a lateral bud is imperfectly formed. Botanically this no doubt would be designated a bud scale; by the tea planter and his garden operatives it is generally spoken of as the *phaki* (useless) or *janum* (birth) leaf. In the figures (Figs. 4 C and 4 D) this appears at (*g*), (*j*), and (*l*). It is desirable that this scale should be clearly observed, for although useless as a leaf, it still carries in its axil a bud quite as capable of future elongation as any of the buds subtended by fully formed leaves. It may also be added that the *phaki* leaf is very caducous, that is to say, it falls off the twig at an early date, so that though shown on the fairly old shoots, represented by (C) and (D), it would not usually be seen in such cases. Occasionally several *phaki* scales may be found crowded together at the very base of shoots, and it is these obscure buds that in after years mainly furnish the shoots that sprout from old branches after heavy pruning.

First Plucking causes First Flush.

198. ***First Plucking Causes First Flush.***—But to return to the subject of plucking the shoots, the portion indicated to be removed is the first plucking is made in order to cause the first flushing, so that the second plucking is designated the first flush. We understand that, in China and Japan, the first plucking is reported to yield the finest tea of the season; that is certainly not the Assam experience, and most planters say the shoots are nipped purely and simply to start the flushings, since the tea made from tipping the normal Spring shoots is very inferior. It is probable the majority of planters would agree in regarding the second and third flushes as affording the finest

Plucking.

SYSTEMS of PLUCKING.

See Fig. 4.

tea, but the Autumn flushings have a peculiar flavour of their own perfectly recognised on the market.

In Fig. 4, the flushes resulting from the second method of treatment are shown—(C) showing the first, and (D) the second flush, in each of which cases two leaves and the *janum* are retained on the bush. The letter (*h*), as before, denotes the position of last

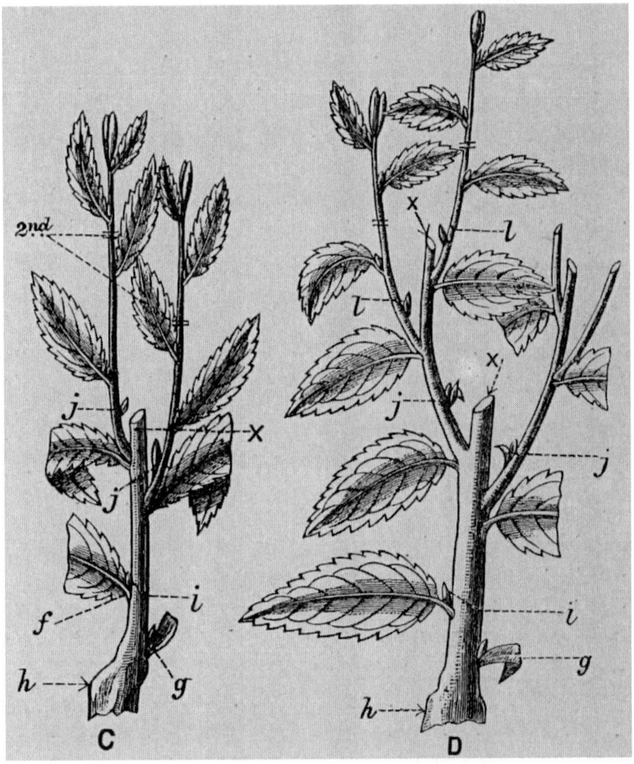

FIG. 4.—FIRST AND SECOND FLUSHES.

Autumn's pruning; (*i*) points to the position of the next pruning; (*g*), (*j*) and (*l*) indicate the *phaki* or *janum* leaves or bud-scales with their contained bud; and the projection at (*x*), beyond the bud and shoot (*x*) is a snag formed by imperfect plucking.

199. ***Number of Leaves Left in Spring Plucking.***—To return, however, to the difference represented by the systems (A)

Plucking.

and (B)—where in the one three buds are left, and in the other two. In many places it is the custom to leave more than three buds on the original shoot, but the general argument equally holds. The difference is essentially, however, that between the advocates of hard plucking in the early season, and easy plucking for the first portion of the time. Of course the advocates of such a system as that in (B) are getting very much fewer in number, but we know of cases, even yet, where plucking down to a single leaf on the original shoot is advocated.

SYSTEMS of PLUCKING.

Number of Leaves left in Spring Plucking.

Hard Plucking in Spring.

What, however, is the result of such treatment? In its favour it may be said that it causes a more rapid development of the first flush in accordance with the principle that the fewer the buds left the more quickly they respond to the cutting off of the tip of a shoot. It was formerly said that it removed danger from mosquito blight as it allowed a crop to be made in the Spring and so ensured *some* yield before the advent of the blight. This argument, as we shall show later, is, however, totally illusory. It was furthermore said that better tea could be made in the early part of the season by plucking the original shoot to one or two leaves than by leaving three or four—and this probably was so.

Supposed Advantages.

Disadvantages.

200. Against these arguments, however, there is so much to say as to entirely overshadow these small advantages, and we may say that *there has probably been more damage done to gardens by carrying out the idea of hard plucking in Spring than by anything else except by thoughtless pruning.* The reasons against such hard plucking may be stated as follows:—

Causes Stem Starvation.

1. It causes the starvation of the remainder of the bush, the rapid maturing of the old wood, and hence a quick deterioration in the capacity of the bush to bear. We have tried to indicate how the leaves feed the stems, and indeed the whole of the bush, and how, indeed, if all the leaves were constantly removed from a bush, that bush would die. If full and vigorous life is to be retained in a plant, and in every branch of that plant, including the present year's wood, it is essential that provision should be made for the retention of a sufficient number of leaves on the bush throughout the season to prevent (*a*) the starvation of the older wood—the most important consideration having in view the permanence of

Plucking.

SYSTEMS of PLUCKING.

the bush, (*b*) the starvation of the present year's wood which must bear next year's flushing shoots. This cannot be guaranteed, if less than three leaves are left below the plucking point on the original shoot, under normal garden conditions of plucking.

Causes Thin Wood.

2. It follows from (1) that the wood will be thicker the longer it is left untouched. If, therefore, good pruning wood is to be obtained, it must be kept long enough to acquire the thickness necessary. Again, three leaves behind the original plucking seems the irreducible minimum.

Only One Secondary Shoot Produced. *Conf. with para. 202.*

3. We have been furnished recently with the result of a careful experiment conducted, on our suggestion, by Mr. J. E. Aird of Deundi, Sylhet, during 1901. It will be again referred to later, but furnishes an additional reason here. In his letter dealing with the result he says that in his experiment "the great drawback" where two leaves only were left "was that it produced only one secondary shoot, and this shows that in order to make sure of the Spring shoots bearing two secondaries, *three* leaves, at least, ought to be left on it." This is perfectly evident. If at every plucking only one lateral or secondary shoot be produced, the number of flushing shoots would be the same at the end as at the beginning of the season, and truly little tea would be made, though a larger proportion might be made before the end of June.

But no further argument is needed. The system of plucking close in the early season is now all but abandoned by the best planters, and we have heard it said by one of the planters in India, renowned for the high quality of teas made on his garden, that the man whose first teas in the season are of high quality (due to close plucking), by that fact condemned his management. We perfectly agree with him.

Are Three Leaves Enough Behind First Plucking?

201. But are three leaves behind the plucking on the original shoot sufficient? This opens a question which probably varies with *jat* of plant, with district, with weather, with condition of tea, and dozens of other considerations. After heavy pruning of course it is not enough, but then heavy pruned bushes should be plucked to a measure and therefore do not come into consideration, and in all the argument here we are only considering normal high-pruned

PLATE III. (*To face Page 111.*)

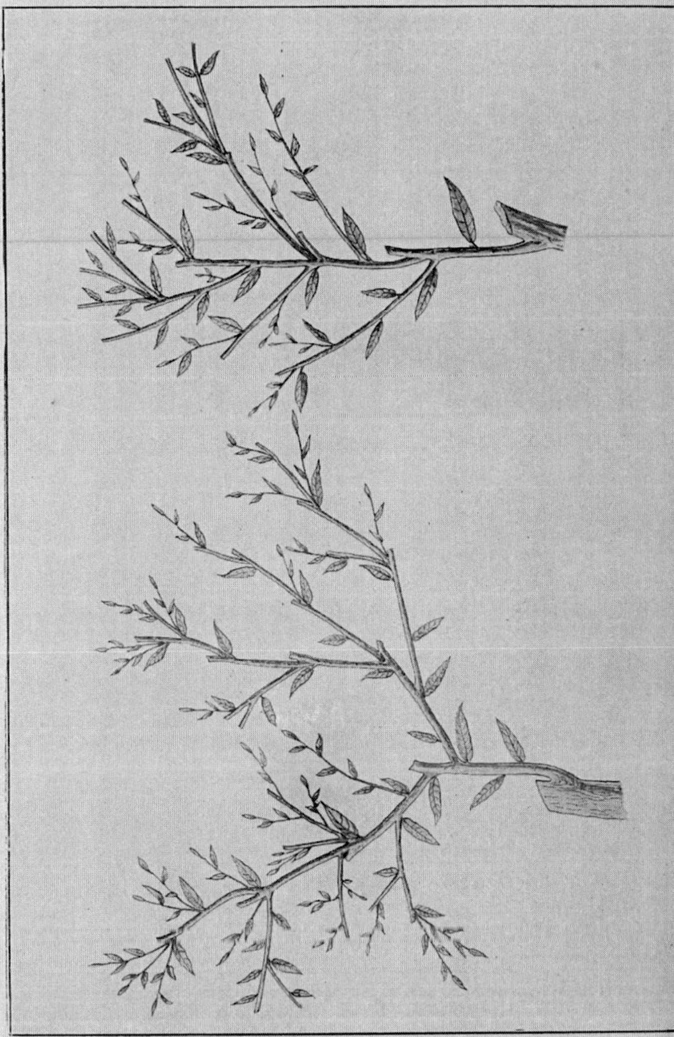

Shoots produced in Plucking Experiment described on page 111.
(From Sketch by J. E. Aird.)

Plucking.

bushes. The point raised is, therefore, one which cannot be decided without most careful experiment. If two good shoots can be produced, if leaf enough is left on the shoot, if the plucking is to be "easy" for some time afterwards, we should say that as a rule leaving three leaves is enough,—but after all there is no direct evidence in existence which gives the chance of determining the matter.

SYSTEMS of PLUCKING.

Experiment in Sylhet, 1901.

202. During a tour in Assam in 1901 the suggestion was made to us that it might be profitable, instead of leaving a good deal of shoot at the commencement of the season and then leaving little or none later on, to leave two leaves behind *every* plucking throughout the season. Theoretically the number of flushing shoots should then increase in geometrical progression, and at the end of the season they would be vastly greater in number than on a normally plucked bush. Mr. J. E. Aird was kind enough to put this to the test for us last year, and the results were very striking, proving absolutely that the theoretical conclusions were entirely wrong. *Plate 3* gives diagrammatically a picture of a shoot so plucked, and a normally treated one at the end of the season. One or two mistakes were made in dealing with the suggested type of plucking (leaving two leaves each time), but nevertheless the result is very definite. We have, as a matter of fact, the following, excluding *banjhi* shoots :—

	Normal pruning.	Suggested pruning.
In 1st generation . .	1 shoot	1 shoot
In 2nd " . .	2 shoots	2 shoots
In 3rd " . .	5 "	4 "
In 4th " . .	12 "	6 "
In 5th " . .	3 "	4 "
In 6th " . .	1 shoot	...
TOTAL .	24	17

By the suggested method, in fact, theoretically :—

the shoot	1 should	bear	2	pluckable shoots,	it has	2
" shoots	2 and 4	"	4	" "	they have	4
" "	5, 6 and 7, 8, 9, 10	"	6	" "	"	6
" "	11, 12 and 13,	"	12	" "	"	4

The great drawback is the tendency of the shoots to go *banjhi* at a comparatively early part of the season, as shown in the figure, and this vitiates the whole of the theoretical reasoning, and it is evident that such bushes as these satisfy their need of leaf growth comparatively easily. We have insisted on this case for it is one of the very few cases in which a careful record has been kept of the actual effect

SYSTEMS of PLUCKING. Number of Leaves left in Various Pluckings.

on a branch of a particular method of plucking, and illustrates well how such questions should be tackled.

E. 203. The conclusions thus far reached may perhaps be illustrated further by Figs. 5 and 6, where the effect of leaving a varying number of leaves on the remainder of the shoot in the second plucking is as shown. In (E) (*Fig. 5*) after plucking the original shoot, the buds (*c*) and (*d*) produce flushes, or perhaps (*e*) may also do so.

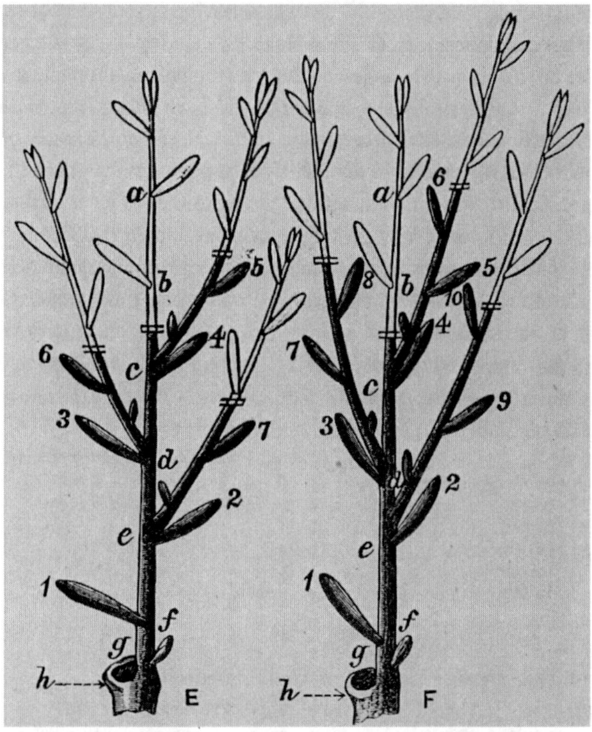

FIG. 5.—RESULTS OF SECOND PLUCKING ON QUANTITY.

These flushings are not plucked till they have each formed four leaves in addition to the *phaki*. In the two-shoot condition (*c*) and (*d*) six leaves, therefore, remain, and in the three-shoot form (*c*), (*d*), and (*e*), seven leaves.

F. By another method (F), however, the two or, it may be, three flushing shoots produced, are each retained till they carry five leaves and the *phaki*, so that with two shoots, eight leaves remain, or with three shoots ten leaves, after plucking the first flush.

Plucking.

Similarly we have (G) (*Figure 6*) in which the flushing shoots are retained till they have each formed four leaves and the *phaki*, and in (H) in which the plucking is made when the shoots have each only three leaves and the *phaki*. In (G), therefore, after the first flush has been plucked, seven leaves, and in (H) only five leaves remain.

SYSTEMS of PLUCKING. G.

H.

204. It will thus be observed that in (E) and (F) there is always the possibility of three shoots from the original stalk, and further that a larger number of leaves remain on the shoot than in (G) and (H) which

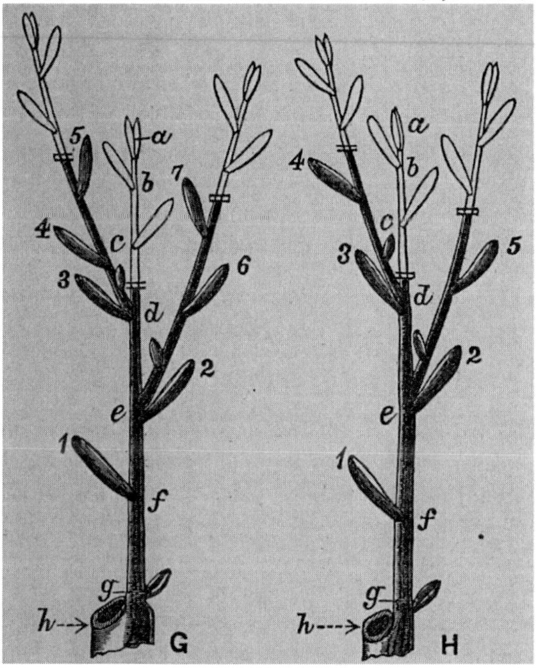

FIG. 6.—RESULTS OF SECOND PLUCKING.

are plucked somewhat harder at first. But not only are there a larger number of leaves, but the additional interspaces between the leaves open the bush up and give greater facilities to obtain light and air.

Compare this with the state of affairs in the hardest system of plucking at all in vogue in the early season, *viz.*, (H), where the shoots are plucked when they each contain three leaves and the *phaki*, and consequently at the end of the second plucking there are only five leaves left on the bush instead of the ten leaves of (F).

Plucking.

SYSTEMS of PLUCKING.

G better than H.

The system of plucking in (G) is infinitely superior to that in (H), since after the second plucking seven leaves remain instead of five, and the greater openness and additional few extra days' growth must be viewed as giving a much needed strength to the flush bearing framework.

The systems exhibited in (E) and (F) (with the variation that only two leaves and a bud are now practically ever plucked), are perhaps those most generally practised. After the second plucking the shoots will be found to have left on them six leaves, if only two shoots be produced, or seven leaves, when three shoots are formed in (E), and eight or ten leaves when two or three shoots are formed respectively in (F). It is not desirable, and rarely occurs, that more than two shoots are formed in the first flush, and so six or eight leaves may be said to be the normal amount left behind in the two cases, and for the sake of the health of the bush these should not be reduced, if possible, below this number.

FINE PLUCKING and CLOSE PLUCKING.

XLII.—"Fine" Plucking and "Close" Plucking.

205. This is in the early part of the season. Then follows a period in which the diversity of practice is about as great as it can be, and the question of the quality of tea produced by the various methods of working becomes of greatest importance. In any attempt to improve quality "fine" plucking and "close" plucking should be carefully distinguished. "Close" plucking consists, after allowing the growth which we have spoken of up to the present, in plucking off *all* or *nearly all* the growth that appears on the bush, trusting to the new leaf to be thrown out from the axil of the *janum* leaf or bud-scale. "Fine" plucking merely means that without reference so much to the amount left behind, a smaller amount of leaf is taken at each round of the garden, say one leaf and a bud, or two leaves and a bud, instead of three leaves and a bud. Though it will thus be seen that there is no really essential difference between the two methods, and as practised by planters in various districts fine plucking may approximate more or less to the really "close" plucking of the Upper Dibrugarh district, yet the distinction is practically a very convenient one. On the whole, contrasting the typical examples of really "close" and really "fine" plucking, it may be said that the former is the most exhausting method of plucking, within reason,

Difference between Fine and Close Plucking.

Plucking.

FINE PLUCKING and CLOSE PLUCKING.

that could be devised: the latter need be little more exhausting than coarse plucking, if the same amount of leaf be left behind each time as would be done in that case. The former demands perfection in climate and soil as the Upper Dibrugarh or Sadiya Road districts possess, though even there, where a garden with poor soil occurs, the damage done to the bushes is sufficiently obvious; the latter may be more or less carried out anywhere. On the other hand, the former seems to produce the finest tea and a fairly large yield; the latter produces a better tea than with coarse plucking, but hardly better in proportion to the loss in yield. Why close plucking should produce the finest tea is not at present very clear on scientific grounds, and that this is the reason for the high quality of upper Dibrugarh teas is doubted by some leading planters. But "close" plucking removes the most active agents in contributing to the plant's growth—the young leaves—and does not leave behind a sufficient number of old leaves as compensation; it allows the exposure of the youngest part of the plant to the hardening effect of the sun's rays—an effect quickly transferred to the old wood. Hence where the sun's rays are hotter than at Dibrugarh, as in Sylhet and Cachar, the Dooars, and the lower part of the Assam Valley, their injurious effect would possibly quickly render "close" Dibrugarh plucking an impossibility owing to the refusal of the plant to flush at all. And this would be doubly the case where the soil was not of the very highest quality. Perhaps plucking might become somewhat closer in gardens where there is a good soil and the slight shade of "*sau*" (Albizzia stipulata) or similar trees, but this is a matter for experiment, and it may, we think, be taken that if "close" plucking were introduced in other districts than the comparatively cool, equable climate and on the fine soil of the Upper Brahmaputra Valley or similar situations, it would have to be combined with a temporary rest to portions of the garden in rotation, say, every ten years. A suggestion has been made to us, quite recently, that if bushes were only pruned once in two years, much closer plucking would be feasible without injury to the bush than otherwise, and consequently this method seems actually to be carried out on one or two gardens. No doubt under these circumstances much closer plucking might be carried out, and a large quantity of good leaf would be obtained in the spring of the second year, but whether the

Close Plucking in Dibrugarh.

Experiment needed

Possible Results of Close Plucking.

Plucking.

FINE PLUCKING and CLOSE PLUCKING.

yielding power of the bush would, in a few years, be injured; whether the formation of hard mature stems which could not produce much leaf, would not be induced, and whether the leaf would not deteriorate after a certain length of time from pruning, are questions for trial.

206. What we have called "fine" plucking can apparently never give the same quality of teas as "close" plucking (though, as indicated above, there is some doubt on this point), nor the same quantity of them, but will give a better tea than if coarse leaf be plucked, and will become, it is generally believed, finer and finer in quality as it approximates to the "close" method. To a certain extent this may account for the superiority of October tea, for all gardens are closer plucked as the season advances. Mr. Bamber has shown that the tannic acid, which gives pungency to the tea, is in a much more stable condition in the youngest leaves than in those a little older, that is to say, there is less loss of pungency during manufacture, and this alone is sufficient to account for the increased value of the more finely-plucked teas. But it must not be supposed that fine plucking will produce high class teas on exhausted soils, or from exhausted or injudiciously treated bushes. This subject is too large to enter upon here; but it is probable that although tea will improve if bad bushes or bushes on bad soil be plucked fine, yet the difference will probably be less between the different types of plucking under such conditions than on a good garden. Then, again, fine plucking demands more careful work, a thorough control of the labour force, and plenty of pluckers if the bush is to be plucked fine, and yet prevented from "running away." How far the increased price compensates for the loss in yield, and the extra labour and supervision required, is for a practical planter to say, but it seems certain that this style of plucking may be carried out without danger to the bush, with improvement to a certain extent, varying with the fineness of plucking, to the quality of the tea, but with a loss of outturn almost proportionate to the increased fineness.

Tannic Acid in Young Leaves.

Fine Plucking means careful work.

Close study needed.

207. These are general statements, and it demands a very close chemical and botanical study of the bush before the reason for these differences in quality can be ascertained. We are convinced that much progress will be made by the careful study of the plant, and that until such study is made and more definite systems of plucking are evolved than we have at present, little more than general state-

ments will be possible. It is, however, comparatively easy to make experiments into the effect of various methods of plucking on the bush, and this, it is to be hoped, will be done in the near future on bushes of the same *jat* and character under the same climatic conditions. The effect on yield cannot be so easily ascertained, but this must and will be done at a later date when the effect of any particular method of plucking has been shown not to be an injurious one.

CURIOUS METHODS of PLUCKING.

XLIII.—*Curious Methods of Plucking.*

208. ***Two Leaves and a Bud with Portion of Third Leaf.***—It was formerly the custom along with the portion of the shoot really plucked to take a part of the third leaf, though this is not common now. This has been advocated for, perhaps, 40 years, the argument being that the bud subtended by the mutilated leaf comes away more quickly than it would do were it left entire. We accept that statement as being possibly correct. No doubt so far as the necessities of sap assimilation are concerned, the mutilated leaf would be worse than useless. Before it could be employed, the injury done to its own structure would have to be repaired, and consequently the simpler course of producing a new shoot might be resorted to, but the half leaf left on the plant might just as well have been removed entirely. It has to be viewed as non-existent, so far as assimilation is concerned, and the increased yield through plucking the portion of the leaf, as also the advantage of breaking away earlier, might have been made up, far more rationally, by giving the time to form more shoots below. By so doing the health of the plant would be secured conjointly with a high outturn.

Portion of third Leaf taken.

From the point of view, therefore, of the health of the plant, it is false economy to secure a higher yield by unnecessary mutilation, when by a more careful study of the buds, in the early plucking, the number of flushing shoots may be multiplied to almost any extent desired.

Condemned.

209. Mr. Shipp, of Cachar (1865), describes a method of plucking which for the sake of the Industry, we are glad to say, has quite died out.

Old Cachar method.

The system of plucking pursued was described as follows:—

The coolies were divided into three sets. The first gang were designated the "Pekoe pluckers." These plucked off "convoluted bud and its two expanded leaves." This then corresponded to the only

Plucking.

CURIOUS METHODS of PLUCKING.

plucking that is now-a-days made by gardens that go in for quality or medium teas. Then followed the "Souchong pluckers." These plucked off the next two leaves and were followed by the third gang, or "Congou gatherers." Now, let us see what this meant. The "two and a bud" tips were nipped off and the two subsequent collections stripped the shoots of their leaves but left them their buds intact. The coolies were instructed "to pluck onwards and leave about a quarter of an inch from the eye or bud for the reproduction of fresh shoots." This system was therefore about as absurd as could well be conceived. The plants were alone saved from complete destruction through only half the number of pluckings being taken a year as compared with the modern system. That circumstance, no doubt, allowed the shoots to grow to fully double the extent they are permitted to, at the present day.

Present Method Possibly Capable of Improvement.

210. These methods have disappeared, as indeed they were bound to do, being based on ideas which will neither bear the light of botanical principles nor the test of practice. But who can say that any of these now in vogue are the best obtainable? The questions as to the possibility of closer plucking, and its effect on the quality of the tea in the Surma Valley; the relative advisability of hard plucking with systematic renewal of stock and easier treatment with retention of the same stock; the effect of manures on the possibility of closer plucking —are among those whose solution is urgently needed. Our ultimate and final object is recognised to be the production of the largest quantity possible of the best tea, without deteriorating the garden. Only by experiment can the best method for producing this be ascertained, and hence careful experiment is a vital matter for the future of the gardens already in existence, and perhaps a still more vital matter for those which may be hereafter formed.

CHAPTER VIII.

TEA MANURING.

XLIV.—General Principles of Manures and Manuring.

GENERAL PRINCIPLES. Exhaustion of soil.

211. That every plant growing in every soil causes that soil to become poorer in some constituents at any rate, is now practically recognised as a truism wherever agricultural plants are grown. Once this has been established for an agricultural crop, manuring follows as a matter of course unless the plot is to be abandoned and new land put out under the crop. The latter has been the plan usually adopted in new countries, and it has generally been difficult to make the old agriculturists see that manuring would ever be needed. This has been precisely repeated in the case of tea. And in some few cases, the position is probably correct. There are some deep, rich alluvial sands which may probably be cultivated under tea for very many years without any fertilization being needed, but these are very few in number, and we doubt whether there are more than one or two pieces of tea land in Assam about which it could be said. But a system of abandonment and extension cannot go on indefinitely on account of the exhaustion of suitable land—a point which has been reached already in certain cases,—nor can such a system proceed for long because of its expense and because it means the removal of the best yielding land on a garden further and further from the factory. The only alternative is manuring in one form or another, and this will have to be the policy of the future.

Objections to manuring.

212. ***Objections to Manuring.***—Two objections are at once raised. "Manuring can never pay—it costs too much" is the first of these, and to this it can be replied summarily that "manuring *must* pay, or the land must become a wilderness, and the population it supports abandon it or starve." Agriculture all over the world emphasizes the fact that except in very favoured places no agriculture can be carried on on the same spot year after year without the application of manure.

Will not pay.

The second objection taken is that once manures are used it becomes a necessity to use them continually. To a certain extent

GENERAL PRINCIPLES.

this is true and necessarily so. Land which has once commenced to deteriorate will continue to do so unless by repeated applications it is kept up to the mark. And the reason which compels manuring in the first instance compels its continuance at intervals forever afterwards. This, however, can be reduced to a minimum of frequency and of cost by judicious selection of manures, leaving those as far as possible on one side whose action is purely temporary, such as Nitrate of Soda, or which themselves have a tendency to impoverish the soil for the future, as, for instance, Sulphate of Ammonia. To argue that because future manuring will be necessary therefore a garden is to be allowed at present to deteriorate beyond recall, is a policy so short-sighted that had it not been put before us on many occasions, we should not have attempted to discuss it.

Must be continued.

Manure to prevent deterioration.

213. ***General Principles of Manuring.***—As a general policy, *Firstly*, it is by no means wise to await manifest deterioration before going to manuring. A slight but continuous decrease in yield is a warning that the land is less capable of producing than it was. Collar-pruning is then often adopted and results in a temporary spurt after which the bushes only become worse again than they were before. Really what was wanted was not collar-pruning, but manure. We fancy that in nearly all parts of the tea districts, after about the tenth year of a garden some means should at least be used to retain and increase the food material in the soil, and after the fifteenth there are few cases where manure is not absolutely required, if some loss in yield and often in quality is not to be anticipated.* In some unsuitable lands put out in tea even recently, manure is required almost as soon as the tea commences to grow, but these are exceptional, and ought really never to arise.

Manures must be found on the spot.

Secondly.—The nucleus of whatever manuring is done must be found on the spot. Everything not profitably saleable that the garden produces should be returned to the land. Every morsel of cattle manure, of wood ashes, of pruning ashes, of tea refuse not sold, of sweepings of coolie lines, of road sweepings, of jungle cut round the tea, etc., etc., should be put on the tea if a really economical manurial policy is to be carried out. If all these were collected

* An exception to this is found in some of the peat bheels of Cachar and Sylhet, but they quite form exceptions.

GENERAL PRINCIPLES.

and composted with soil during the whole season and then put on the land, much less manure would be required from outside. To have such products and allow them to rot about the place, unless for some trenchant reason, is wasteful in the extreme.

Little manure bought from Calcutta.

Thirdly.—As little should be bought outside the district as possible. Artificial manures should be reduced to the lowest quantity especially in view of the enormous cost of their importation. There are occasions in which it may be necessary to use them, but the less they are needed the better. Assam, as a province, is extremely rich, and this applies to the other sections of the tea districts of India, so that while there is so much unoccupied land, it seems almost inconceivable that nearly all the materials required for fertilising the tea cannot be produced on the spot, and it should be the aim to obtain all that is possible in this way.

Mixed manures condemned.

Fourthly.—If artificial manures be required, it should be regarded as essential just to supply the constituents which are deficient, and no more. Complete mixed manures for new districts like those under tea in India, as sold ready-made under the name of "Tea manure," are not only generally very dear for what they contain, but also contain several constituents of no value under the special circumstances.

Permanent manures preferred.

Fifthly.—Manures of lasting character should be chosen rather than those which, while more powerful for a short time, are soon used up. Of the latter class are Nitrate of Soda, or Nitrate of Potash, and Sulphate of Ammonia, and, in general, those easily soluble manures, which are apt in large measure to be soon washed out of the land if not immediately taken up by the tea.

Constituents removed by Tea.

214. ***Soil Constituents removed by Crops.***—Tea itself is not an exhausting crop for the soil, compared with many others. It is rarely that more than ten maunds of tea are taken away from the garden, and the ashes of the prunings should be returned to the soil, so that the Nitrogen in the prunings when these are burnt is the only manurial matter which forms a dead loss. Now ten maunds of tea roughly contains :—

Nitrogen	36 lbs.
Phosphoric Acid	8 „
Potash	20 „
Lime	1 „

Tea Manuring.

GENERAL PRINCIPLES.

Constituents removed by crops.

Compare this with the quantity of these constituents removed by other crops of which some are given below :—

	Wheat 40 bushels.	Sugar Beets 18·19 tons.	Cotton $1\frac{1}{3}$ tons.	Tobacco 720 lbs.
Nitrogen	48 lbs.	121 lbs.	$58\frac{1}{3}$ lbs,	$28\frac{3}{4}$ lbs.
Phosphoric Acid .	24 "	72 "	45 "	$6\frac{3}{4}$ "
Potash	16 "	304 "	$70\frac{1}{3}$ "	$41\frac{3}{4}$ "
Lime	1 lb.	32 "	88 "	$51\frac{3}{4}$ "

Even if the above quantity of Nitrogen be doubled to represent the loss in burning the prunings, it will still be far and away below the amount needed for many crops, and the quantity of other constituents removed is much less than with most agricultural products. Tea does not, therefore, make very excessive demands on the soil, and both from a consideration of these figures, and from analyses of old and new tea soils, one may, we think, say that usually in India only Nitrogenous and Phosphatic manures will usually be needed at present, and only the latter will be required from purely artificial sources.

XLV.—Local Manures Available.

Top-dressing soil as manure.

215. ***Top-dressing Soil Manure.***—But let us consider the manures locally available. The first and most important of these, both for the extent to which it has been used, and for the extension which its use is likely to take in the future, is top-dressing soil material. It is not in many climates and countries that the extremely rich deposits which can be used are available, and their presence arises from the low character of the land, from the fact that the excessive rainfall causes it to be cut up in every direction, and from the extreme rankness of the vegetation which causes the low uncultivable tracts thus produced to be immediately covered with plants, which by constant growth and decay give a topsoil of exceeding richness. On the other hand, it must be remembered that after all, it is a very clumsy method of manuring, as it often involves the removal of 100 tons of soil to get 5 tons of valuable material, and that it is only in a country where labour is extremely cheap that it could even be thought of. The success which has followed its application has tended to make it somewhat of a fetish, and we have seen many hundred tons of

Clumsy method.

material put on the land which, except for some slight mechanical improvement of the soil to which it was applied, could have little or no manurial value. When it is remembered that the usual dressing of 6 inches deep (equal to 2 to $2\frac{1}{2}$ inches when settled down) means the application of 400 tons of material per acre, it will be seen how extremely wasteful it is of labour, strength and money if the material be not of the best. It has also been objected that "bheel soiling" lowers the quality of the tea obtained. In this connection it must be remembered that there are various kinds of top-dressing; real peat bheel might lower quality, but even this question is still *sub judice*, while it would be difficult to conceive that forest surface soil could do so. It is quite possible that the supposed lowering of quality is as much due to the sappy growth after cutting down, for the time of heavy pruning has usually been chosen for top-dressing, as to the top-dressing itself. LOCAL MANURES. Quality said to be affected.

216. ***Peat Bheel Soil as top-dressing.***—The various kinds of top-dressing have however very different properties and are of very different value. Best of all, as producing luxuriance, is real peat bheel soil. A real peat is formed by the decay of many generations of rank growing plants, the principal part of this decay occurring under water. Where this has occurred, naturally drainage, and hence wastage of material, has been at a minimum, especially as under these conditions practically no nitrates are formed. It implies long years of formation, for the particular deposit termed peat is of very slow formation. These deposits occur sometimes on the surface, sometimes at some depth under the soil, especially in the Tezpur and Nowgong districts of Assam. The Nitrogen and organic matter in these is usually very high, as the following analyses both from the Tezpur district show:— Peat bheel soil.

	Organic Matter, etc.	Nitrogen.
1	30·29 per cent.	·60 per cent.
2	21·78 " "	·68 " "

Another bheel soil of the same character from Chittagong, which came into our hands, is even richer.

3	50·85 per cent.	1·15 per cent.

217. These peats are eminently valuable, and wherever found, should be undoubtedly used for manure, as they will assuredly pay

Tea Manuring.

LOCAL MANURES.

Experiment on effect of bheel soil on quality.

for putting on the land. It has been said, as noted above, that they lower the quality of the tea. We have recently had the opportunity, through the kindness of Mr. M. Chamney of the British Assam Tea Company's gardens at Tezpur, of comparing the quality of tea produced by two similarly light-pruned plots lying side by side on the Tezpur bank, one of which was treated with the very rich bheel material marked "2" above, at the rate of 100 tons to the acre, while the other received none at all. The top-dressing was carried out in February, March and April, 1901, and the yield of the plots was as follows (up to September 26th), in 1900 and 1901, weighed as green leaf:—

		Maunds.
Plot top-dressed in 1901 (34 acres)	1900	481
	1901	543
Plot unmanured in either year (35·7 acres)	1900	458½
	1901	358¾

The increase in yield is therefore enormous. Messrs. W. S. Cresswell & Co., of Calcutta, who were good enough to report on the quality of these teas, say that in each case the plots treated with top-dressing give a tea with a slightly brighter liquor than that obtained from the unmanured section, but in other respects not differing in value.

218. This experiment, the only one carried through under exact conditions which is on record, affords decided evidence that such top-dressing does not cause a loss of quality: the impression is, however, very strong among planters that deterioration is produced by this means. At present we have no reason to suppose that the leaf is poorer after top-dressing with bheel soil than before. Material so rich as this should, however, never be applied in greater quantity than 100—120 tons to the acre, or an entirely different state of affairs might result.

Black sub-soil of Assam, etc.

219. Often in the same districts as these peat bheels, and in many other places besides, both in Assam and the Duars, there exists a black sub-soil which, at first sight, seems to possess the character of peat. It consists of a very finely divided, greasy, slimy material, containing no vegetable remains, which, when damp, cuts like cheese and which contracts very much on drying. It will write on a white surface like graphite. Wherever this material occurs near the surface,

LOCAL MANURES.

the tea is invariably not luxuriant, and we have never seen it penetrated by the roots of the tea bush. By itself it therefore is certainly not suitable for tea. On the other hand, it is rich in plant food, as the following analyses show:—

Analyses.

	1	2	3
Organic Matter, etc.	6·69	8·58	9·19
Oxide of Iron	5·90	4·66	7·25
Alumina	5·60	6·39	3·79
Lime	·34	·21	·67
Magnesia	1·07	1·19	·52
Potash	·52	·63	·33
Soda	·45	·26	·27
Phosphoric Acid	·15	·14	·11
Sulphuric Acid	·18	·02	·62
Insoluble Silicates (Sand)	79·10	77·92	77·25
TOTAL	100·00	100·00	100·00
*Containing Nitrogen	·15	·21	·16

Other samples, in which only the Organic Matter and Nitrogen were determined, gave in percentages—

	1.	2.
Organic matter, etc.	13·68	13·65
Nitrogen	·30	·18

Assam black sub-soil of doubtful value.

220. This material, which will, we think, be everywhere recognised from the above description, is of very doubtful value as a manure. On no account should it be put on soil which is already somewhat stiff, as it will tend to puddle the surface. Further, it contains always a certain quantity of Sulphur as Sulphides, which forms Sulphuretted Hydrogen (a plant poison) under certain conditions. In the first of the above samples this sulphur amounted to ·22 per cent., equal to ·42 per cent. of iron pyrites, and when moistened the soil smelt distinctly of the above-named sulphuretted Hydrogen. This, however, would soon pass off on exposure to the air; and it is well worthwhile to try this material on a small scale, on light land only, as it is quite possible that it may turn out very valuable, and in some places it occurs in inexhaustible quantities. In such a case it would be wise to keep it, so far as possible, from actually touching the stems of the bushes when first placed on the land.

Tea Manuring.

LOCAL MANURES.

221. ***Hullah soil as manure.***—The most common material applied as top-dressing is however hullah soil—a material as variable in composition as can well be imagined. In some cases where rank vegetation has existed for many years it approaches bheel soil in character : in others it is little else than sand from the bed of a running stream.

Hullah soil.

For a hullah soil to be really valuable, it should, we think, fulfil the following conditions :—

Conditions when it is valuable.

(1) It should carry a rank vegetation ; wild cardamoms are often a feature of suitable situations.

(2) It should be black in colour, at any rate when wetted, and contain plant refuse, rootlets, etc.

(3) It should not be taken from running water.

(4) In cases where the soil to which it is to be applied is heavy or close in texture, it should at least be of a lighter character than that on which it is to be placed.

If it answers to these characters, it may fairly be assumed that the material is good enough to safely apply to most of the land in India under tea. Such are some of the soils in which the following determinations of Nitrogen and Organic matter have been made :—

Examples.

Garden.	Organic Matter, etc.	Nitrogen.
	Per cent.	Per cent.
Cinnamara	6·05	·25
Sangsua (6" deep)	8·62	·23
Samaguri (6" deep)	9·73	·30
Gotoonga (7" deep)	8·40	·23
Suntok	7·45	·15

Waste in top-dressing twice from same hullah.

222. In this connection there is one practice, which, from an economical point of view, one cannot condemn too strongly. This is that of top-dressing from a hullah, and then again using the material of the same hullah for top-dressing again three or four years later. In the meanwhile there has not been sufficient time for a new layer of vegetable soil to form, and the practice merely consists of putting on little more than a layer of sub-soil of little manurial value, and certainly not worth the thirty to forty rupees per acre, which is the

least that the application would cost. The following are the partial analyses of some of these hullahs, which it was suggested to use for top-dressing but which had been used three or four years before :— **LOCAL MANURES.** Examples of hullah sub soil.

District.	Organic Matter, etc.	Nitrogen.
	Per cent.	Per cent.
Tezpur	4·89	·06
Jorhat	4·23	·13
Do.	4·00	·09
Do.	4·03	·12

In each of the above cases the soil was poorer than that on which it was intended to put it, and so money spent on this business would have been almost entirely lost. Even under the most favourable conditions, such as those of the Brahmaputra Company, in Assam, where the hullahs are fed annually with rich river silt, as well as the refuse of an exceedingly rank vegetation, it is considered that the same hullah cannot furnish top-dressing material again before ten years have elapsed, and this estimate is much too low for the average garden. In certain cases, however, practical experience seems to indicate that mere sub-soil from hullahs may be of some service. This has apparently been the case on some of the Assam Company's gardens. At present the only explanation is that it has some beneficial effect on the texture of the land, but if so, it can only be in rare cases that it will repay the cost of application.

223. ***Forest surface soil as Manure.***—In the absence of peat or good hullah soil, the surface of the forest has often been used, and, provided it has not to be carried more than a few yards, this has been distinctly an economical success. Only about the top six inches is usually however valuable, and the depth at which the removal should stop can generally be seen by a change of colour in the land. This material is useful exactly in proportion to its richness in Organic Matter and Nitrogen, and no more. Its effect on the texture of the soil to which it is applied can be practically neglected. If, therefore, it is richer in the above constituents, as it presumably is, than the soil to which it is to be applied, it is useful, but an analysis of both **Forest surface soil.**

Tea Manuring.

LOCAL MANURES.

will be necessary (in regard to these constituents) before one can say whether it will be profitable or not. Thus the material used at Salonah, Nowgong, taken from the surface of *Korkani* Jungle, contained 9·53 per cent. of organic matter and ·18 per cent. of Nitrogen, the soil on which it was put contained 5·13 and ·08 per cent., respectively, hence the material did very great good. Another forest surface soil which came into my hands from Golaghat (Assam) contained 4·97 per cent. organic matter and ·13 per cent. of Nitrogen. As the soil was a light one, it would probably be of advantage, but it will not usually pay, even on light land, to put on material containing a much less amount of valuable matter than this.

224. In these cases it becomes a very grave question as to whether other less cumbrous methods would not give better results. The method is costly, from 30 to 100 rupees per acre being spent on one application, but the usual justification seems to be that this is expended in labour, and the labour must in any case be paid. Therefore, as the process of putting it on the land comes in the slack months, the expense is not entirely an out-of-pocket one, but represents money, a large part of which would have to be expended in any case. This opens up an aspect of the question which we are hardly competent to discuss; but would it not be possible for coolies to be more profitably employed? In certain cases, at any rate, would it not be feasible to plant up some of the waste land of the grant with a crop in the cold weather which would yield an equal amount of manure, and a valuable product as well? Such a crop would be mustard, which would entirely be produced with comparatively little labour in the slack time of the year, and would give a valuable manure cake, and also a large quantity of oil needed by the employés of the garden. We throw this out merely as a suggetion, but it certainly seems hardly the most profitable and economical method of manuring to remove, say, 200 tons of material per acre, only 5 per cent. of which is in any way valuable to the tea plant.

Mustard cake as substitute.

Conf. with para. 265.

Garden sub-soil as manure.

225. ***Garden Sub-soil as Manure.***—There remains to consider one type of top-dressing which one cannot condemn sufficiently as unprofitable, namely, that of putting on ordinary garden sub-soil as manure. In several cases canals have been cut through the garden at the sacrifice of one or two rows of tea, and then the material down to 4 feet deep put on the surrounding land. This can be justifiable

only in the special case where excessive wash has taken place, the bushes are standing right out of the ground, and it is essential to replace the soil lost, anything being better than nothing for the purpose. In other cases, however, such a process is all but absolutely devoid of advantage, save very occasionally to improve the texture of the land. In some cases the application of sub-soil has even resulted in material injury to the bush, and we cannot recommend it on economic grounds in any but those places where the sub-soil is itself a black peaty material. To show the average extreme poverty of the sub-soil, the following figures are given :— LOCAL MANURES.

Analyses of garden sub-soil.

No.	Percentage in Sub-soil of		Percentage in Soil of	
	Organic Matter, etc.	Nitrogen.	Organic Matter, etc.	Nitrogen.
1	4·94	·07	4·69	·09
2	3·75	·09	4·81	·13
3	...	·07	3·59	·09

226. In every case the sub-soil to be applied as manure is poorer than the soil on which it is to be placed. Can it therefore be worth applying as manure? It might perhaps be answered that these sub-soils may contain stores of mineral food apart from the above-named constituents and that these are rendered useful to the plant by putting the material on the surface. This may be the case to a small extent, but from my analysis of the Assam sub-soils, they are never so rich as to make it worthwhile applying it to the tea at an enormous cost. A top-dressing soil should therefore be analysed in respect of Nitrogen and Organic Matter before application. The whole process only takes a very few days, and it would save the absurd waste of labour which has taken place recently. Any sample sent should be accompanied by a description (sandy, heavy, red clay, etc., etc.) of the soil to which it is intended to apply the material, and thus a vast amount of waste expense would be saved. Need for analyses.

227. ***Summary as to Top-dressing Soil as Manure.***—In summary, therefore, relative to material for top-dressing, peat will always increase the luxuriance of tea, but there exist some doubts whether the quality is not deteriorated by it: hullah soil is the most Summary.

LOCAL MANURES.

variable material possible, but to be valuable should be (1) black; (2) covered with rank vegetation; (3) not from running water; (4) lighter in texture than the land to which it is to be applied. Once scraped, a hullah cannot usually be profitably again used for top-dressing purposes, even under the most favourable conditions, for ten years. Forest jungle soil may occasionally be profitably applied but no general rule can be laid down, and garden sub-soil is only worth using either to replace the soil taken away by wash, or to improve the texture of the land. It is emphatically advisable that a partial analysis should be made of any material suggested for top-dressing before this latter is applied.

Summary re Top-dressing Soil.

Cattle Manure.

228. ***Cattle Manure.***—Next in importance to top-dressing soil as a fertilising agency in India is cattle manure. Nothing is more astonishing to an outsider visiting Indian tea gardens than the little use which is made of this material. Always present, generally in enormous quantity, it is indeed rare to find any place where any systematic attempt is made to utilise it. On the average garden of 500 acres there are usually at least 500 cattle, and each of these may be estimated to produce at least 2 tons of dung per annum, or, allowing 25 per cent. to be inevitably lost during the grazing in the day time, about 750 tons per annum for the property. Now ten tons per acre is a very fair dressing, and hence with care from 50 to 75 acres could be treated per annum, or the whole garden, at the least, once in ten years.

Amount Available.

Collection of Manure.

229. Such a proceeding, simple though it appears, involves care in the collection and preservation of the dung which is rarely seen at present. First in its collection. The most feasible and satisfactory way of collecting the manure is to have the whole of the cattle driven at night into an enclosed space or yard, part of which might be roughly covered over or not, as most convenient, and from which they were allowed to go to graze during the day. Adjoining such a yard should be the manure pit, and it would seem hardly too much work for a man to remove and put in the pit daily the dung voided by the cattle during the night time. Such a yard is in operation at some of the gardens we have visited and is a great success, as the coolies have the satisfaction of knowing their cattle safe, and yet the manure is retained and saved without much trouble for the garden. If another man were retained to sweep up

all material from the coolie lines daily and put in the manure pit, another source of dung—goats, fowls, etc.—would not be lost. As to the preservation of the manure, the pit, which we suggest should be a necessary accessory to every garden, may be formed by digging several feet into the ground, and covering over the hole thus made with the roughest of thatch roofs, say, 12 feet from the ground at the lower eaves. Into this every piece of dung, wheresoever picked up, would be placed, and so gradually rot during the season, and be ready for application after pruning is done in the cold weather just before the first spring hoeing. Without such a method of covering up the dung from the weather an enormous loss takes place from washing out of the valuable matter by the rain, and although a large loss is unavoidable in keeping manure under the best conditions, yet there is no reason for making this loss greater than it really is. In some recent experiments in Canada, where the rainfall is much less than here, when the loss of manurial matter in exposed and protected was compared, it was found that while the exposed lost 540 lbs. of organic matter, the protected only lost 288 lbs.; while the exposed lost 14 lbs. of Nitrogen, the covered only lost 8 lbs; while the uncovered lost 4 lbs. of Phosphoric Acid, the covered lost none, and while the open manure lost 22 lbs. of Potash, the Potash in the protected remained absolutely intact. In India the loss would probably have been far greater proportionately in the manure left open to the weather. As a conclusion to the above quoted experiment, it is pointed out that the best conditions of rotting necessitate (*a*) protection from rain, sun and wind; (*b*) a water-tight floor; (*c*) that the mass of manure should be kept as compact as possible, and there is little doubt that the nearer one gets to these conditions, the more valuable the cattle manure will become.

LOCAL MANURES.

Coolie Line Sweepings.

Loss on exposure of cattle manure.

Needs in manure shed.

230. At present there seems no simple way of retaining the urine, but if this could be done a great point would be gained, as the urine contains the most valuable and also the most easily assimilable part of the material voided by the cattle.

Urine should be retained.

231. But is Indian cattle manure worth all this trouble? Is its composition such as to make it worthwhile to adopt all these means of retaining it? The following figures show the composition of dung from Indian cows grazing just as Assam cattle do, and where

Tea Manuring.

LOCAL MANURES.

the urine is not retained (Dr. Leather, *Agricultural Ledger, 1897, No. 8*):—

Value of Indian cattle manure.

	1	2	3	4
Moisture . . .	76·05	78·84	75·61	73·95
Organic matter . .	14·90	13·43	14·69	15·95
Siliceous matter . .	7·24	6·67	8·46	8·24
Phosphoric acid . .	·182	·167	·192	·126
Nitrogen . . .	·273	·237	·269	·251

Amount to Apply.

A certain amount of drying would take place during the rotting of the manure, and hence there would be far less moisture in the finally rotted product than appears from these analyses, but an application of 10 tons of even such moist material as that shown would mean the addition of 1½ tons of organic matter, of 56 lbs. of Nitrogen, and of 30 to 40 lbs. of Phosphoric Acid to the resources of each acre of land, an amount by no means to be despised, especially when it is gained at merely the cost of collection.

Loss of quality from cattle manure doubted.

232. It has been again and again suggested that this manure deteriorates the quality of the tea, even when applied in reasonable quantity. We think it may be said that there is absolutely no evidence of this being the case, and such reasonable quantity would be not much more than 10 tons per acre. Of course if an enormous quantity were added, one could not guarantee that an unnatural growth would not be produced (as has, indeed, been shown to be the case with many fruit trees), but the amount named could, we are sure, be applied with perfect safety.

Will suit all soils.

233. Cattle manure will suit almost any Indian tea soil, but it is specially indicated on those which are heavier than the average, and its addition would much benefit such land. Very light sand also, especially such as lies over clay, would also derive very great advantage from the application. The manure, as stated above, should be applied, when well rotted, before the early spring hoe, and immediately buried by the hoeing. Its effect should be visible in May and continue throughout the season.

Said to encourage Orange Beetle.

234. One objection has been raised against the use of cattle manure, that it encourages the orange beetle in the garden. We have been, however, unable to trace any connection, and fancy that

the prevalence of jungle and especially of *ulu* grass has more to do with the presence of the beetle than the manure application.

LOCAL MANURES.

Filling in vacancies.

235. In one matter one may regard cattle manure as all but indispensable, namely, the filling in of vacancies. There still remain men who deny that it is profitable to fill in the vacant parts of old tea. In some cases we own it would be better to uproot and replant, but where this is not necessary, vacancy filling should be regarded as an essential, and a garden with a large percentage of unoccupied soil should be its own condemnation. For it has now been definitely proved by numerous examples that land *can* be filled in with perfect success if only care be taken. It is decidedly not sufficient to take a seedling from the nursery, plant it as one would in a fresh clearance, and expect success. It would be a wonder if a plant put out thus *did* prove a good one. But that such plants cannot be made to flourish where old tea is flourishing has, we think, by many planters been shown to be a fallacy.

Best method of filling vacancies.

236. A mature tea plant is worth about 6 annas. A planter very successful in filling in vacancies informed us that each plant filled in cost him 2 annas at the time of planting, and he did not expect success without spending this amount. His method was as follows: A hole 2 feet deep and 18 inches wide is dug and the soil removed. The bottom is then filled with jungle soil and a 2-year old plant with a very large block of earth attached is put in, hand-pressed down *hard* round it, the remainder of the hole filled with cattle manure and the whole well compacted by treading down. Then straw is put round the plant to prevent the direct rays of the sun striking the plant's own soil. One year after planting (3 years from seed) the new bush is pruned at 6 inches from the ground (not more), and in order to avoid injury from plucking when not ready to pluck, it is generally arranged, if possible, that the plot should be heavy pruned as a whole when these infillings are cut down. The method has been a splendid success, and we can recommend none better. The only point is that jungle soil is not always obtainable, but a substitute could well be made during the previous season by making a compost with soil and cattle manure on the plot itself. To do this the cattle manure should be taken on to a vacant place, if possible under shade, on the plot to be treated, and made into a layer 4 inches thick, and then

Substitute for jungle soil.

LOCAL MANURES.

covered with 6 inches of ordinary garden soil; on top of this another 4 inches of manure should be placed and then soil as before, alternating layers thus until enough has been produced for the purpose. This will unite into a rich black mass by the following cold weather, and may be used instead of jungle soil with equal confidence of success.

Summary *re* cattle manure.

237. ***Summary re Cattle Manure.***—As a whole then cattle manure is capable of being used far more than it has been, and, properly collected and preserved, should form on most Indian gardens the nucleus of the manure required. It is valuable for all kinds of land, but especially for those with stiff soil, and for the extremely light sands. It should be applied in the spring and immediately hoed in. For filling in vacancies it is almost indispensable.

Green manuring.

238. ***Green Manuring.***—Only second in importance to cattle manure, and probably likely to take enormous extension in the future, is green manuring or the growing of green crops among the tea, to be hoed in entirely so that, by their decay in the soil, the land may be improved and food added to the soil. It is long since they were first recommended, but in spite of very successful experiments their use until the past two years has not been at all general. Mr. Bamber in 1893 indicated several plants which might be useful for this purpose, and in the former edition of this work, the value of the method was repeatedly insisted on, and the plant was pointed out which has hitherto been most successfully employed, the *Mati Kalai*—(**Phaseolus aconitifolius** or **Phaseolus mungo**).

Mati Kalai.

Conditions for Green manure to fulfil.

239. A plant to be used as a green manure should fulfil the following conditions:—

(1) It should be one which develops rapidly, so as to occupy the land as short a time as possible.

(2) It should give the largest mass of green vegetation possible, for hoeing in.

(3) It should be as deep-rooting a plant as possible.

(4) It ought to be sufficiently hardy to itself flourish under fairly unfavourable conditions of climate and soil.

(5) It ought, also, to return more to the land than it has extracted for its own growth.

(6) It should be grown at a time when it may retain manurial constituents in the soil, which would otherwise be washed out.

LOCAL MANURES.

(7) It should easily rot when hoed into the land.

(8) It ought to be grown without in any way interfering with the tea or with the plucking of it.

Grasses not suitable.

240. The conditions (1), (2) and (3) at once condemn the grasses for green manuring. Neither rice, grass, wheat, maize, nor buckwheat are the *most* suitable plants for they all possess very shallow roots (*see Plate III*), and except for maize, the amount of vegetable matter to be hoed in is small in proportion to the land covered by the crop. Maize might, however, be valuable in some hill districts. In some measure this objection applies to a very large proportion of the weeds of tea gardens. The Ageratum, known as "cold weather weed" in Assam or "*ilami*" in the Dooars, and which forms perhaps the most common weed in tea culture, though succulent in the extreme, yet possesses a most meagre root development (*see Plate III*), so that although it is usually a sign of well cultivated land it could hardly be recommended for special planting as a green manure. The same may be said of most other weeds which are not objectionable in themselves.

Maize.

Ageratum.

Weeds.

Weedy gardens objectionable.

241. In fact we can hardly say that we believe in the theory of a garden being allowed to become weedy for the sake of the green manure these weeds supply. When a miscellaneous collection of plants like the usual crop of weeds are allowed to grow in a garden, some may be valuable, some may be neither valuable nor harmful, and some may very likely be distinctly injurious inasmuch as they may form refuges for the pests and blights of the tea, and further they, at some seasons, abstract water from the soil that the tea-plants need. Perhaps there is not much objection to a few weeds in September and October, but even then, as first suggested to us by Mr. Henderson of Salonah, it is surely far better to have a definite crop known to be valuable on the ground than a mixture of useless, and, it may be, injurious plants.

Better Definite crop than useless weeds.

Mustards and Leguminous Plants.

242. It will be found that the plants which answer most of the conditions laid down only belong to two classes: the mustards on the one hand, and leguminous plants on the other. The former answer every condition admirably, except that of returning more to the land than they have extracted, but the latter answer this as well as all the others. This condition does not exclude the use of the mustards for green manuring though they have been hardly

LOCAL MANURES.

found to be profitable in other countries. Land, however, which grows leguminous crops too often is apt to become "sick" of them, and under these circumstances mustard might replace them with great advantage.

243. ***Leguminous Plants as Green Manure.***—To the leguminous crops, however, one has to turn to supply the really most valuable green manures, and this because they return to the soil more Nitrogen than they take from it, owing to the growth of a bacterium on the root which fixes the Nitrogen of the air and passes it on to the plant—a bacterium which seems exclusively to grow on the roots of this order of plants, on whose roots it forms nodules nearly always visible to the naked eye.

Mati Kalai.

The only plant of this order hitherto used to any great extent in Indian Tea culture is *Mati Kalai* (Phaseolus aconitifolius or Phaseolus mungo) and its growth has been very successful. It has been most systematically tried perhaps by Mr. Hutchison of Dooria, Golaghat (Assam), and in a recent letter he says:—

Conditions of using.

"I have sown *kalai* in various months with varied success, as good growth is much dependent on moisture, and not too hot and dry a time. April is a good month for sowing, provided you take advantage of a wet period, and it is not followed by a hot, dry April sun just after the seedlings are a few inches high, or the whole crop may be ruined. The same remarks apply to May. Both these months are good for sowing *kalai* in low pruned tea, as it is beneficial in keeping off or lessening the effects of blight. In June the growth is very rank, and I don't think so beneficial.

"The best time of all, I think, is September. During October the *kalai* can be hoed in, and a deep hoe given for the cold weather. I also believe there is $1\frac{1}{2}$ to 2 per cent. more Nitrogen in the root nodules during the time the plant is forming seed in October. The result is very perceptible at the commencement of the following season; although the bushes are having a rest, the roots I believe are active during the cold weather, and during the first flush the bushes have a healthy oily green colour, so that in walking over a plot you can pick out the line treated with *kalai* from the line not so treated.

"As regards the actual increase in outturn, I have never set apart a plot to test the increase in pounds, but a healthy plant is more capable, I take it, of giving more quantity and better quality than an unhealthy one. * * * * * I am planting now (August 1901) 70 acres with seed for deep hoeing in October."

No use sown in November.

244. When first suggested, it was put on to the land at the same time as is done in local native cultivation, that is to say in November. The result was a very small plant which quickly went to flower and seed, and which when hoed in did little good, and we doubt not, in many cases, considerable harm. This was only to be expected as

Tea Manuring.

it contradicted all principles of green manuring—only a small amount of vegetable matter was produced, and this was growing and abstracting moisture from the soil just at the time when it was most important to preserve it. If, on the other hand, it be sown from April to August, a rank growing plant is produced, which gives much vegetable matter, occupies the land when there is always, or nearly always, excess of moisture, and fulfils every condition required.

LOCAL MANURES.

Sow April to August.

245. In successful culture it has been usually applied in April and May, and certainly has in several cases been very successful. Mr. Wylde at Bamgaon, Tezpur, estimated the increase in yield in 1900 of about three quarters of a maund per acre on the plots treated, and the cost was practically *nil.* At Cinnamara it has now been applied for several seasons to sections of the garden, and one of the principal advantages there noticed was that green fly did not appear to attack the tea all the time the *Mati Kalai* was on the ground. During 1901 it was used on several gardens in Nowgong with much benefit to the condition of the soil, and also to the health of the bushes.

Bamgaon experiment.

246. On evidence in hand at present, therefore, we are inclined to think that we have in the *Mati Kalai* an exceedingly valuable green manuring crop. It may be planted at any time from April to August, though we ourselves prefer April and May, and is hoed in about six weeks after, when it forms a mass of green foliage at least two feet high. Some planters have had difficulty in growing this crop owing to the extreme poverty of the land. Mr. Buckingham particularly notes in a letter to me the difficulty of getting the crop to grow on poor land. In this case it would be wise to put on a slight dressing, say one ton per acre, of farmyard manure before sowing the seed of the *Mati Kalai*, when probably a very luxuriant growth will occur. Another trouble seems to have been the difficulty of hoeing in the crop when grown, but this is overcome by giving an extra deep hoe for the time of year, when the crop goes on very satisfactorily. To quote Mr. Hutchison again :—

Summary.

Manure added in Poor Land.

"Its application is comparatively cheap and easy. During its growth you can dispense with one round of the hoe, which about pays for the *kalai*. In fact if you hoe the *kalai* in six weeks after sowing, the extra deep hoe then given will do for another six weeks. Thus we have one hoe in the three months and benefit derived. These remarks apply more to the sowings in the early part of the year."

Avoids One Round of Hoeing

Tea Manuring.

LOCAL MANURES.

Cost of seed.

247. The cost of application is very small. *Mati Kalai* seed rarely costs more than five rupees per maund, and half a maund is about sufficient for one acre. The seed is broadcasted after rain and left. It is said, however, to possess deeper roots if covered up at the time of sowing. The plant is not appreciably injured by the coolies walking it for plucking purposes.

Use in uprooting and replanting.

248. There are two or three cases in which such a green manuring crop as we are discussing seems particularly useful. The first of these is in connection with uprooting and replanting. After uprooting the land should be ploughed and at the earliest opportunity *Mati Kalai* seed put in—say in May and hoed in in June. A second crop is sown in August and hoed in at the commencement of October, and the land is ready for planting again the following cold weather. If replanting be then carried out with liberal use of farmyard or cattle manure, we have very little fear of failure of plant. Of course two-year old plant should be used, and allowed to grow a year after planting before being pruned to six inches. *Mati Kalai* is also useful on land which has been cleared and is not yet planted. Such land deteriorates very quickly if left bare, but a crop of *Mati Kalai** in the rains, will keep a large amount of the valuable material in the soil which would otherwise escape.

Land cleared but not planted.

Sensitive Plant.

Crotalaria striata, etc.

Conf. with para. 250.

French Beans.

249. There are probably other crops which would answer for green manuring quite as well as *Mati Kalai*.† **Dr. Watt** mentions several. The sensitive plant **(Mimosa pudica)** he points out would be valuable, but for its thorns. He also names **Crotalaria striata, Desmodium polycarpum,** and **Uraria crinita** among others. The first of these three has been strongly recommended by **Mr. Bamber** to the Ceylon planters, but **Mr. Buckingham's** experiments with the plant have not up to date been very promising. In addition to these, **Mr. Hulbert** has used French Beans as a green manure on the Assam Company's gardens, but no apparent good effect was produced and the treatment was discontinued.

* Sensitive plant **(Mimosa pudica)** has also been recommended under these circumstances, but seems hardly to have as much advantage as the *Mati Kalai*, owing to the comparatively meagre vegetable growth it shows.

† I have recently noticed the enormous number of root nodules possessed by **Sesbania aculeata.** It would hence very likely be an extremely valuable plant for this purpose, and experiments are in progress on the subject.

Tea Manuring.

250. In all that precedes it has been assumed that the green manuring crop was an occasional crop on any particular plot. We think, however, that there seem distinct arguments in favour of making it an annual and regular matter on many soils, and having a green crop on the land during the greater part of the rains. The object secured by this means would be-- LOCAL MANURES. Mati Kalai as regular crop.

(1) The prevention of a great amount of nitrates being washed out of the soil, because they would be used up by either the tea or the green manuring crop as soon as formed. Advantages.

(2) The avoidance of much destructive wash.

(3) The reduction in the number of hoeings, although at the same time each hoe would be deeper.

Under such a system we might have the following scheme:— Scheme.

(*a*) Sow *Mati Kalai* in May with the spring rains on the top of a recent hoeing.

(*b*) Hoe in the crop about the end of June.

(*c*) Give an ordinary hoe in August, and on top of this,

(*d*) Put in a crop of mustard (or even *Mati Kalai* again if the land will stand it) to be hoed in at the commencement of October.

251. This would, under such a scheme, be applied, with modification as to time and to crop, to a large part of the cultivated area each year. We are sure it is worth experiment. It would avoid two hoeings per annum, and although two of these given would have to be deeper than is usual, yet the total labour would probably be less than before, and a large amount of valuable matter, otherwise washed out, would be retained in the soil. Modification necessary.

252. ***Summary re Green Manure.*** Summing up therefore, green manuring has already proved a success where it had been tried, but the crops used up to date with success have only been Mustard and *Mati Kalai*. The latter is usually the best, and has been used the most. It (1) gives more healthy bushes; (2) increases the crop; (3) improves the texture of heavy soil; (4) is said to keep off green fly while it occupies the ground; and (5) acts as a direct manure by fixing the Nitrogen of the air. It is best sown at the rate of half a Summary on green manure.

TREES AMONG TEA.

maund of seed per acre either in May or at the end of August, and in each case should be hoed in after about six weeks. Other crops have been suggested for green manuring, but have as yet received no adequate trial. Finally, there seem distinct arguments in favour of regularly having the ground covered with a green manuring crop during a great part of nearly every rains, and thus making it a normal part of tea culture instead of a special occasional means of manuring.

XLVI.—Leguminous Trees among the Tea.

Sau Tree.

253. In connection with this subject of green manuring, that of the use of leguminous and other trees among the tea must be considered, and the question of their value or otherwise has formed one of the vexed questions of tea culture for many years. We cannot do better perhaps than reprint Mr. Hooper's summary, in the former edition of this work, of the history of the use of the *sau* tree (Albizzia stipulata) for the purpose of fertilising tea gardens. He writes:—

Mr. Hooper's Summary.

"Several years ago Colonel Hannay (in Dibrugarh, Assam) called attention to the value of the *sau* tree, and gave it the name of the tea fertilising tree. * * * * To Mr. J. Buckingham belongs the honour of having prominently drawn attention to the value of the *sau* tree. Several experiments were made by him which went to prove that *sau* possessed peculiar properties in bringing round exhausted soils and causing the bushes to flush vigorously, while imparting a vitality of which old tea was deficient. On the 2nd October, 1884, Mr. Buckingham published, for the benefit of the Indian Tea Association, a little pamphlet on this subject, which gave his own experience and that of several planters regarding the *sau* tree. Shade is not usually the cause of an increase in yield, and is in fact condemned by the generality of planters, as it tends to make the bush throw out long stalky shoots, and thus to produce poor and woody flushes; such, however, can hardly be said to be the case where *sau* is employed. The tea bushes under that tree have been reported by those who believe in it to yield a considerably higher amount in a given area than in any other part of the garden, under similar conditions of soil and age of bush. It has been observed that tea grown under *sau* enjoys a considerable immunity from blights and pests while the surrounding trees are suffering badly.

"The action of the *sau* was attributed by some to the beneficial shade which it casts over the plants; others considered that it was the manure furnished by the dead leaves; a few thought that the advantage of interplanting the trees was the fact that the roots went to a greater depth than the tea roots, and drained the superabundant moisture from the surface soil, while, on the other hand, they brought up from the sub-soil food material for the tea plants. Mr. Buckingham remarks:—I do not wish to contend that *sau* is capable of improving tea plants where the soil contains

Tea Manuring.

elements which in some instances nature has abundantly supplied for the support of a bush, but I do assert that the vitality of the tea bush is limited, probably in a great measure depending on the character of the soil, and unless we restore some of these essential parts we are yearly, I may say weekly, abstracting, the tea planter in a few more years may be surrounded by tea which the very best cultivation and the most scientific pruning can never bring round. **TREES AMONG TEA.**

"The immediate benefit which Albizzia confers upon the soil and the tea plants where it grows is not due to some chemical ingredient imparted to the soil, as was once supposed, but to the presence of tubercles which are attached to the roots. The discovery * of these tubercular bodies on the roots of the *sau* tree was made by Dr. Watt during his tour in Assam in 1895."

254. It will thus be seen that the *sau* tree (**Albizzia stipulata**) was the first tree which was supposed to have fertilising properties. Others have been since used with nearly as much, if not with equal, success. But all of them belonged to the same family of leguminosæ, and all have had nodules on the roots which fix the Nitrogen of the air. Such are the *medeloa* (**Dalbergia Assamica**), the *koroi* (**Albizzia odoratissima**), and still other species of **Albizzia** have been used, as well as **Erythrina indica.** **Sau Tree first Introduced.** **Medeloa.** **Koroi.**

The advantages claimed for these trees are as follows :—

(1) They give a slight shade to the tea which is itself an advantage. The value of shade, however, has been very much doubted, but probably this is only another instance of general conclusions drawn from particular districts being quite fallacious in others. In the lower part of the Brahmaputra valley, except where mosquito blight is abundant, slight shade will be found of distinct advantage. This will probably be especially the case in Nowgong. And it will be of advantage here because it will, to a certain extent, prevent evaporation from the soil by the exceedingly hot sun in a district rather deficient in rainfall. On the other hand, we hardly think that the shade itself will be a sufficient cause to warrant the planting of the above trees in Dibrugarh, Sibsagar, or North Lakhimpur. It might be noticed, in passing, that Mr. Bamber has expressed himself recently in favour of slight shade for tea in Ceylon. **Slight shade an advantage in some Districts.**

* We believe the nodules or tubercles on the roots of the *sau* tree were observed long ago by Mr. Bamber, but he did not publish his observations.

Tea Manuring.

TREES AMONG TEA.

Leaf of manurial Value.

Mr. Bamber on Grevillea.

(2) The continual dropping of leaves, flowers, etc., from the trees are a distinct manurial gain to the soil round about, as the material of which they are formed is obtained from a different layer of soil from that in which the tea bush feeds. Mr. Bamber has laid stress on their utility in this respect in connection with the Grevillea tree (*Report on Ceylon Tea Soils, 1900*). He writes :—

> "One of the means by which lime has been preserved in Ceylon soils has been the general growth of grevilleas (**Grevillea robusta**) as shade or for wind belts. As a rule, the roots of the Grevillea descend into the soil to considerable depths, * * * bringing up stores of plant food, including a large proportion of lime, which the tea plant could not have reached. This plant food after being utilised in building up the grevillea, is largely returned to the soil on the fall of the leaf."

Quantity of Leaf very Small.

On the other hand, the quantity of leaf falling from one tree could hardly be greater than 15 pounds, and with these planted at 40 feet apart, the total quantity of leaf per acre would be 180 pounds or thereabouts. It is difficult to see what great effect this quantity of material could have on the land; as it amounts to little more than $1\frac{1}{2}$ cwt. per acre of what is confessedly only a poor material. In some experiments made at Amgoorie, Mr. Buckingham found the leaves, spread on the land, produce no visible effect, and this would agree with expectation. We think that the amount of manurial matter added through the leaves in the single season is hardly worth consideration.

Root penetration.

(3) The penetration of the soil by the roots makes the soil more porous, and hence in better condition for tea culture. This is no doubt the case, and for this reason alone these trees are highly to be recommended in heavy soils, as they quickly improve the texture considerably.

Nitrogen fixed in root nodules.

(4) The nodules on the roots contain bacteria which fix the nitrogen of the air, and thus enrich the soil in this most desirable constituent. Under these circumstances it would have been thought that near the trees, or at any rate near the roots, the soil would be decidedly richer. Mr. Buckingham has been kind enough to supply one of

<table>
<tr><td>Sikkim.
1800 ft
July 1896
G, C. Dudgeon</td><td>Sikkim.
1800 ft
July 1896
G, C. Dudgeon</td><td>Sikkim.
1800 ft
July 1896
G, C. Dudgeon</td><td>Sikkim.
1800 ft
July 1896
G, C. Dudgeon</td><td>Sikkim.
1800 ft
July 1896
G, C. Dudgeon</td><td>Sikkim.
1800 ft
July 1896
G, C. Dudgeon</td><td>Sikkim.
1800 ft
July 1896
G, C. Dudgeon</td><td>Sikkim.
1800 ft
July 1896
G, C. Dudgeon</td><td>Sikkim.
1800 ft
July 1896
G, C. Dudgeon</td><td>Sikkim.
1800 ft
July 1896
G, C. Dudgeon</td></tr>
<tr><td>Sikkim.
1800 ft
July 1896
G, C. Dudgeon</td><td>Sikkim.
1800 ft
July 1896
G, C. Dudgeon</td><td>Sikkim.
1800 ft
July 1896
G, C. Dudgeon</td><td>Sikkim.
1800 ft
July 1896
G, C. Dudgeon</td><td>Sikkim.
1800 ft
July 1896
G, C. Dudgeon</td><td>Sikkim.
1800 ft
July 1896
G, C. Dudgeon</td><td>Sikkim.
1800 ft
July 1896
G, C. Dudgeon</td><td>Sikkim.
1800 ft
July 1896
G, C. Dudgeon</td><td>Sikkim.
1800 ft
July 1896
G, C. Dudgeon</td><td>Sikkim.
1800 ft
July 1896
G, C. Dudgeon</td></tr>
<tr><td>Sikkim.
1800 ft,
Aug. 1896
G. C. Dudgeon</td><td>Sikkim.
1800 ft,
Aug. 1896
G. C. Dudgeon</td><td>Sikkim.
1800 ft,
Aug. 1896
G. C. Dudgeon</td><td>Sikkim.
1800 ft,
Aug. 1896
G. C. Dudgeon</td><td>Sikkim.
1800 ft,
Aug. 1896
G. C. Dudgeon</td><td>Sikkim.
1800 ft,
Aug. 1896
G. C. Dudgeon</td><td>Sikkim.
1800 ft,
Aug. 1896
G. C. Dudgeon</td><td>Sikkim.
1800 ft,
Aug. 1896
G. C. Dudgeon</td><td>Sikkim.
1800 ft,
Aug. 1896
G. C. Dudgeon</td><td>Sikkim.
1800 ft,
Aug. 1896
G. C. Dudgeon</td></tr>
<tr><td>Sikkim.
1800 ft,
Aug. 1896
G. C. Dudgeon</td><td>Sikkim.
1800 ft,
Aug. 1896
G. C. Dudgeon</td><td>Sikkim.
1800 ft,
Aug. 1896
G. C. Ludgeon</td><td>Sikkim.
1800 ft,
Aug. 1896
G. C. Dudgeon</td><td>Sikkim.
1800 ft,
Aug. 1896
G. C. Dudgeon</td><td>Sikkim.
1800 ft,
Aug. 1896
G. C. Dudgeon</td><td>Sikkim.
1800 ft,
Aug. 1896
G. C. Dudgeon</td><td>Sikkim
1800 ft,
Aug. 1896
G. C. Dudgeon</td><td>Sikkim.
1800 ft,
Aug. 1896
G. C. Dudgeon</td><td>Sikkim.
1800 ft,
Aug. 1896
G. C. Dudgeon</td></tr>
<tr><td>Sikkim.
1800 ft.
Sept. 1896
G, C. Dudgeon</td><td>Sikkim.
1800 ft.
Sept. 1896
G, C. Dudgeon</td><td>Sikkim.
1800 ft.
Sept. 1896
G, C. Dudgeon</td><td>Sikkim.
1800 ft.
Sept. 1896
G, C. Dudgeon</td><td>Sikkim.
1800 ft.
Sept. 1896
G, C. Dudgeon</td><td>Sikkim.
1800 ft.
Sept. 1896
G, C. Dudgeon</td><td>Sikkim.
1800 ft.
Sept. 1896
G, C. Dudgeon</td><td>Sikkim.
1800 ft.
Sept. 1896
G, C. Dudgeon</td><td>Sikkim.
1800 ft.
Sept. 1896
G, C. Dudgeon</td><td>Sikkim.
1800 ft.
Sept. 1896
G, C. Dudgeon</td></tr>
<tr><td>Sikkim.
1800 ft.
Sept. 1896
G, C. Dudgeon</td><td>Sikkim.
1800 ft.
Sept. 1896
G, C. Dudgeon</td><td>Sikkim.
1800 ft.
Sept. 1896
G, C. Dudgeon</td><td>Sikkim.
1800 ft.
Sept. 1896
G, C. Dudgeon</td><td>Sikkim.
1800 ft.
Sept. 1896
G, C. Dudgeon</td><td>Sikkim.
1800 ft,
Oct, 1896
G. C. Dudgeon</td><td>Sikkim.
1800 ft,
Oct, 1896
G. C. Dudgeon</td><td>Sikkim.
1800 ft,
Oct, 1896
G. C. Dudgeon</td><td>Sikkim.
1800 ft,
Oct, 1896
G. C. Dudgeon</td><td>Sikkim.
1800 ft,
Oct, 1896
G. C. Dudgeon</td></tr>
<tr><td>Sikkim
1800 ft,
Oct, 1896
G. C. Dudgeon</td><td>Sikkim.
1800 ft,
Oct, 1896
G. C. Dudgeon</td><td>Sikkim.
1800 ft,
Oct, 1896
G. C. Dudgeon</td><td>Sikkim.
1800 ft,
Oct, 1896
G. C. Dudgeon</td><td>Sikkim.
1800 ft,
Oct, 1896
G. C. Dudgeon</td><td>Sikkim.
1800 ft.
Nov, 1896
G, C. Dudgeon</td><td>Sikkim.
1800 ft.
Nov, 1896
G, C. Dudgeon</td><td>Sikkim.
1800 ft.
Nov, 1896
G, C. Dudgeon</td><td>Sikkim.
1800 ft.
Nov, 1896
G, C. Dudgeon</td><td>Sikkim.
1800 ft.
Nov 1896
G, C. Dudgeon</td></tr>
</table>

TREES AMONG TEA.

us (H. H. M.) with samples of soil taken from these positions, but we have as yet been unable to find any marked improvement in that taken from near the roots. The following are the figures of the analyses * :—

Analyses of sau-tree soil.

	Surface Soil.		Soil 10 inches deep.	
	Nitrogen.	Organic matter.	Nitrogen.	Organic matter.
Near roots of *Sau* tree .	·106	4·25	·089	3·82
Away from root of *Sau* tree	·100	4·13	·091	4·30
Near root of *Medeloa* tree	·085	3·92	·113	5·26
Away from root of *Medeloa* tree	·105	4·46	·093	4·29

Results Irregular.

256. The numbers are wholly irregular, and no result can be deduced from them. Nevertheless, in spite of this, there is little doubt that the marked benefit resulting from these trees is due largely to their fixation of atmospheric Nitrogen, which they pass on, in part, for the use of the tea bush. Whether the fact that it cannot be detected in the soil indicates that it leaves the leguminous plant in such a soluble form as to be washed quickly from the soil, or whether the tea plant is fed only by contact with the Albizzia or other root, and the nitrogenous body never exudes into the soil, we do not know at present. The benefit is, however, undoubted, and can only rationally in chief part be attributed to the fixation of Nitrogen by the roots.

Suggested Reasons.

257. ***Objections to trees in tea gardens.***—Several objections have been raised against these trees in tea gardens. The first and most common is that they induce a long stalky growth and hence give a lower quality of tea than would otherwise be obtained. This objection is just, as we have been informed in a very large number of cases, but depends, we think, on the trees being planted too thickly. On Mr. Buckingham's garden they are planted 40 feet apart

Objections to trees.

Lower quality.

* Mr. Buckingham has later supplied us with samples of the soil round the fine rootlets of these trees. The determination of the amount of Nitrogen in these has given results just as inconclusive as those here set out.

TREES AMONG TEA.

throughout the best part of the tea, and this is quite close enough, and probably 60 feet would be better. That a proper proportion of *sau* trees is not injurious to quality may be regarded as certain. Badulipar, the garden producing about the best tea in the Golaghat district, is largely covered with them, at 60 feet apart, we believe. But this objection may be entirely removed by cutting down the trees to a moderate size as they grow up, and so preventing them ever casting an appreciable amount of shade. They may even be entirely cut down after three years' growth, if only a new lot are growing up to replace them. It has again and again been found that their beneficial action remains after the tree has been removed. Such was found to be markedly the case on the Seleng garden of the Jhanzie Tea Company, and I am likewise informed that this continuance of benefit after removal of the trees has been noticed on the Moran Tea Company's gardens. It would, therefore, appear to be good policy to have a regular rotation of trees, none more than three years old, at 15 feet apart in the rows, the various lots being newly planted seedlings, one year old plants, two year old plants, and three year old plants ready for removal. At any rate, this would be a simple method of obtaining the benefit of the *sau* tree in situations where shade would be harmful.

Tree can be cut down periodically.

Effect on blights.

A second objection is that these trees, as well as any shade, encourage various pests and blights of which the chief are mosquito, faggot worms and similar caterpillars, and blister blight (**Exobasidium Vexans**). With regard to faggot worms I have never been able to trace a connection. If mosquitoes are systematically caught as they ought to be in an affected district, these should little more trouble under trees of this character than elsewhere. But all these pests would be prevented from benefiting by the shade, if only the trees were cut down in rotation as above suggested.

Selection of trees.

258. ***Selection of trees to be used.***—Among the trees recommended I think there is little to choose between the *sau* (**Albizzia stipulata**) and the *medeloa* (**Dalbergia assamica**). The *koroi* (**Albizzia odoratissima**) is distinctly inferior to these two, as its form is quite different and not nearly so suitable. From what we have seen, we prefer the *sau* itself, because the foliage gives a slighter shade than the *medeloa*, but really both are so equally valuable that there should be no hesitation in putting in either.

Tea Manuring.

Another species of **Albizzia**, the **Albizzia procera** (one of the "*siris*" family) seems better in the hill districts than the *sau* itself. Other trees than the leguminosæ cannot be recommended as a rule, as they have practically no manurial value. The Silver Oak (**Grevillea robusta**) has been shown to do no harm to tea,* and makes a good wind belt, but we have never seen any benefit accrue from its presence. Several other local trees have no harmful effect, but nevertheless do no good, and their shade is usually objectionable. Others should at all costs be removed. Such are the India-rubber tree (**Ficus elastica**), the *Simul* (**Bombax malabaricum**, the *Nahor* or *Nagassa* (**Mesua ferrea**) (unless this last is preserved for show at the cost of the tea bushes) and several others.

TREES AMONG TEA.

Unsuitable trees.

259. ***Leguminous bushes for planting among tea.***—We have often been asked by those who object to shade, whether there is any bush which answers the purpose of the *sau* tree, and yet would not have the supposed harmful effect of a large tree. In this connection Mr. Buckingham, who has experimented on the subject, has supplied us with the following note :—

Leguminous bushes.

"You ask if I have ever experimented with leguminous plants as manurial agents for tea, which have, instead of the tree form like *sau* or *medeloa*, a bush shape, so that the manurial benefit of the *sau* may be obtained without the shade, as you are constantly asked whether the effect cannot be obtained without the shade.

Note by Mr. Buckingham.

"To say nothing of *kalai*, I have experimented with the following leguminous plants that are of the bush type :—

(1) **Crotalaria striata.**

(2) **Tephrosia candida.**

(3) **Desmodium polycarpum.**

"The first named is an annual growing very much like a lupin and possessing a considerable number of nitrogenous tubercles on the roots. This I experimented on in young tea, and I must confess that I could not see that the results were in any way remarkable. The plants were allowed to grow to their full height (about 5 feet), and then hoed in, and also some were hoed in when a couple of feet high.

Crotalaria striata.

* We have been recently informed by Mr. C. T. Dunlop, of Monobarie, and have seen cases on his garden, that tea is apt to die out round the decaying stumps of Grevillea. This is a serious objection to these trees.

Tea Manuring.

TREES AMONG TEA.

Tephrosia candida.

"I next tried the **Tephrosia candida** and I am still carrying on my experiments with this bush. The advantage of this plant is that it is a perennial, has a goodly number of root tubercles, and will grow in almost any soil. My plan is to let it grow some 3 or 4 feet high, and then prune it down to about a foot; some three prunings can be done in the year. This leguminous plant will grow in almost any soil. I have seen it come on well in hard barren land, where certainly *sau*, *medeloa*, **Erythrina indica**, **Crotolaria striata**, and others would die out in a month. I am pleased with the result accruing from this plant, and intend this cold weather (1900-1901) to sow the seed over, I hope, from 50 to 60 acres of the garden in spots where the soil is hard and stiff, and the tea poor.

"In small patches I have already planted, I certainly notice an improvement in the tea which I attribute not only to the Nitrogen assimilated by the bacteria, but also to the enrichment of the soil by leaves, contributing to the amount of organic matter and acting eventually as plant food.

Desmodium polycarpum.

"With regard to No. 3, the **Desmodium polycarpum,** this is a trailer * * * * and does not grow over a foot high. The roots possess a larger number of tubercles than I have seen in any other leguminous plant * * * * I have not perhaps given the plant the attention it deserves, as it is of such a straggling nature, that the hoes were always cutting it out. My opinion is that to be of any practical use, it should be allowed to run wild in poor tea for a year or so, and the land not touched with the hoe; any other jungle growing might be hand weeded. No. 2 (**Tephrosia candida**), however, is the shrub I shall call particular attention to for the present."

Tephrosia candida.

This plant (No. 2) recommended by **Mr. Buckingham** and locally named the *bogga medeloa*, is still in the experimental stage. It should be tried among the tea in districts like Bishnauth which have had mosquito to such an extent as to render it inadvisable to plant the *sau* or *medeloa* trees.

Adhatoda Vasica.

260. One other plant has been several times highly recommended for planting among tea—the **Adhatoda Vasica**—on the expectation that it acted as a manure. This plant does not belong to the Leguminosæ and, so far as we know, does not fix Nitrogen, and we have failed to note any improvement in the bushes round

about it. The leaves are, however, very rich in Nitrogen, and their dropping may be of some value if not of much. At the same time while we do not think it worth while to plant among the tea, yet the leaves form such a valuable insecticide (giving off alkaline vapours on crushing) that it would be worthwhile to grow a few square yards, by putting in cuttings one foot apart on any waste land, when a supply would be obtained for use against some of the pests of the gardens.

BONES and OIL-CAKE.

XLVII.—Bones and Oil-cakes as Manure.

261. ***Bones as Manure.***—Such are the manures actually produced or producible on the tea gardens themselves. To them might be added the wood ashes which, on all gardens burning wood, are produced in enormous quantity. We will, however, deal with those later. But there are locally produced other manures which ought to be put to the utmost use. The first of these is Bones, which in certain districts, notably on the grass plains of the north bank in Assam and in the Dooars, could easily be collected in large quantities for use. At present we believe there is an export of bones from the Brahmaputra valley, and a certain import of the same bones crushed for use on tea gardens. If bones are valuable they should never be allowed to leave the province and be re-imported, but rather be bought in the collecting districts by the planter and crushed on the spot by means of small Devil Disintegrator, the cost of which would be recovered, if much bones were used, in the first season. More than one planter has come under our notice who buys up local bones and crushes them in this manner, and is eminently satisfied with the result.

Wood ashes.

Conf. with para. 285.

Bones could be collected and ground.

262. But are bones of great advantage as a manure? On the basis of their composition they should be eminently so. The analysis of a typical Indian bone meal is as follows:—

Advantage of bones.

Analysis.

Moisture	7·50
Nitrogen	4·05
Phosphoric Acid	23·25
Equal to Phosphate of Lime	50·68

But the actual value of the application in this form has everywhere proved much less than would be anticipated on the basis of the analysis. In fact, according to recent experiments in

Value of bone phosphates.

BONES and OIL-CAKE.

Germany,* the phosphate of lime, though it forms half of the weight of manure, may be almost ignored in determining its manurial worth, and the whole value calculated at little more than that of the Nitrogen and Organic Matter. This being so, the benefit accruing from the application of bone meal or steamed bones is much less than has hitherto been assumed. In fact we doubt whether bone meal is ever worth importing to Assam in this form at a price at Calcutta higher than Rs. 2 per maund, at which it at present stands.

Value on garden of bones.

263. On the spot, bones are, however, very valuable, and worth probably on the garden in Assam, about one rupee per maund before crushing. Their limitations must, however, be recognised. They are an exceedingly slow manure. In the first year no benefit will be seen, only possibly some advantage in the second. In a recently published report on one of the Darjeeling Tea Gardens † it is stated that the beneficial effect of bone applied in 1897 was visible in 1900. In fact it may be said that bone meal is an excellent manure to apply to a good garden in order to keep it from deteriorating, but is not sufficiently active alone to bring back a garden already deteriorated into good condition.

It has been said that bone meal causes the production of seed, but of this we have not been able to obtain any evidence.

Effect on quality.

264. Bone meal may be relied upon not to affect the quality of the tea. It should be applied at the rate of 5 to 10 cwts. per acre, ground so as to pass through a sieve of $\frac{1}{8}$ inch holes at least though even more finely ground bones are preferable, and would be best applied buried round the bushes in a small trench made for the purpose a foot away from the stem, at the end of the rains while the ground is still moist. For a consideration of the use and value of dissolved bones, see paragraph 278.

Conf. with para. 278.

Oil-cake.

265. ***Oil-cake as Manure.***—Another valuable manure which is to a certain, and can be to a greater, extent produced locally, is oil-cake. The local production is limited almost entirely in the tea districts to that from mustard seed, and the imported almost entirely to castor cake. In his book Mr. Bamber mentions various

Various cakes.

* "On the effects of bone meal as a source of phosphoric acid to crops" by Maeroker and Steffek, Berlin, 1895.

† Kurseong and Darjeeling Tea Company, 1901.

other of these materials which might be used, including margosa cake, cocoanut cake, poppy cake, niger cake, cotton cake, sesamum cake, mahua cake and linseed cake. But in order that a manure of this type should be valuable, it must either be produced locally, or else be so rich as to pay the expense of transit to the place where it is to be used. Of all this list the only ones which could, in any way, be worthwhile importing would be cotton cake and linseed cake. Both of these are fairly rich in manurial matter, and, together with the cake obtained from castor, form the only ones which it would pay to carry to Assam or even the Dooars, and which are obtainable in sufficient quantity. We had at one time some hopes of mahua cake (from **Bassia latifolia**) but the analysis made showed it to be hardly worth the cost of importation.* **BONES and OIL-CAKE.** **Mahua cake.**

266. Local supplies should, however, here again form the chief source from which the manure is derived. Mustard is grown in large quantities practically throughout the province of Assam for the production of oil. In some cases the seeds are exported direct to Calcutta as such; in many others, they are pressed locally by native presses. We wish to insist here on the necessity of increasing, so far as is possible, this local pressing of mustard seed, in order that the oil may be saved for local consumption and the manure for the tea. Why, for instance, should a small bonus over and above the price obtainable in the market not be offered for all mustard seed brought to the factory, when the oil would be expressed and sold to the coolies on the garden (where the demand is always great), and the cake applied as manure? Or, alternatively, there seems no objection to encouraging the growth of native local presses, by giving a slightly higher price for the cake? Or, even as was suggested to me by one of the leading Assam planters, why not grow mustard on some of the waste land attached to the grant, and press the crop, which should amount to twenty bushels per acre, at the factory, by means of an oil press—which is not very expensive? This would only require labour about November, and when the seed was ripe in March—two periods at which labour can be to a certain extent spared. One cannot go into the details of such a scheme, but there are few grants where twenty acres could not be given up for this **Local supplies.** **Growing mustard on waste land.**

* The sample in hand contained only Nitrogen 3·11 per cent., Phosphoric Acid 1·44 per cent., and Lime ·20 per cent.

Tea Manuring.

BONES and OIL-CAKE.

purpose, and on this land ought to be produced about 400 bushels or 300 maunds of seed, giving 200 maunds of cake, or sufficient to give a moderate dressing to twenty acres. Such land would be allowed to revert to jungle after gathering the crop, and the herbage grown up in the meantime would be ploughed in before again sowing the next November; or better still, the same land might only be used once in, say, three years for mustard growing, being allowed to revert to jungle in the meantime. The oil produced would, by sale on the garden, nearly recoup the cost of the crop, and the tea would be manured almost for nothing. At any rate, to send out of the province for oil-cake, when so much land (not suitable for tea, but quite suitable for mustard) exists even on the tea grants, seems hardly economical.

Sale of oil.

Value of oil-cake as manure.

267. But is oil-cake of value for tea? Luckily on this question we have definite figures of recently carried out experiments. The first here reported was carried out at the Harchurah garden of the Borelli Tea Company by Mr. J. C. H. Mitchell. Taking three very even one-acre plots similarly pruned in the previous year—

No. 1 was left without manure.

No. 2 was treated with $15\frac{1}{2}$ maunds castor cake and $15\frac{1}{2}$ maunds bone meal per acre.

No. 3 was treated with $15\frac{1}{2}$ maunds castor cake only.

The soil was on the Tezpur bank. The following table gives the results for 1899 and 1900:—

Experiment at Harchurah.

	Plot 1.	Plot 2.	Plot 3.
	Mds. Srs.	Mds. Srs.	Mds. Srs.
Total Tea in 1899	3 $38\frac{1}{4}$	5 $26\frac{1}{2}$	6 $24\frac{1}{2}$
Do. in 1900	4 16	5 $26\frac{3}{4}$	6 $9\frac{3}{4}$
Increase in 1899	...	1 $28\frac{1}{4}$	2 $26\frac{1}{4}$
Do. in 1900	...	1 $10\frac{3}{4}$	1 $33\frac{3}{4}$
Total increase in 2 years	...	2 39	4 20
		Per cent.	Per cent.
Percentage increase in 2 years	...	26·2	35·0
		R a. p.	R a. p.
Total cost of manure	...	76 0 0	44 9 0
Cost per lb. of increased crop	...	0 5 1	0 2 0

The mixture of bone meal and castor cake was therefore somewhat profitable on the first two years' yield, and further it left the bushes much more healthy than it found them, but the castor cake alone gave an immediately profitable return. **BONES and OIL-CAKE.**

268. A similar experiment was carried out in 1900 on the Bindukuri garden of the Bengal United Tea Company, on the low flat land between the Tezpur bank and the river. The soil by analysis was shown to be more or less exhausted.

Experiment at Bindukuri.

Plot 1 was again unmanured.

Plot 2 received 15 maunds 9 seers of castor cake.

Plot 3 received 15 maunds 20 seers castor cake and 5 maunds of bone meal.

Tabulating the results as before, we have :—

	Plot 1.		Plot 2.			Plot 3.		
	Mds.	Srs.	Mds.	Srs.		Mds.	Srs.	
Total Tea in 1900	10	17	12	14		12	30	
Increase in 1900	...		1	37		2	13	
			Per cent.			Per cent.		
Percentage increase in 1900	...		18·53			21·2		
			R	a.	p.	R	a.	p.
Total cost of manure	...		69	1	6	82	14	9
Cost per lb. of increased crop	...		0	7	2	0	7	2

These figures only refer to one year's crop. It is probable that the effect will be felt for at least two years further, and, if so, the whole increase for those two years will be obtained at no out-of-pocket cost whatever. The acting manager (Mr. C. B. Taylor) reported at the end of 1900 that "the strong growth and healthy condition of the manured section is remarkable, and there is very little doubt that these sections will give increased yields next year, and probably the year after."

Oil-cake is profitable manure.

269. It may thereafter be taken that oil-cake, whether applied as castor cake, as in the above instance, or as mustard cake or other locally produced material, increases the crop to an extent which, even with castor cake costing nearly 3 rupees per maund on the garden, would form a profitable application. Its effect on quality certainly was not a deteriorating one, and we look on castor or mustard cakes

Tea Manuring.

BONES and OIL-CAKE.

as the manures for tea, obtainable from sources outside the gardens themselves, which have the greatest future before them. They supply all the constituents which the tea bush needs, and if imported, should be bought on a guaranteed analysis, not to contain, in the case of castor cake, less than 5·5 per cent. Nitrogen and 4 per cent. Phosphate of Lime; in the case of mustard cake, less than 4·5 per cent. Nitrogen and 5 per cent. Phosphate of Lime; in the case of cotton cake, less than 4 per cent. Nitrogen and 5 per cent. Phosphate of Lime; and finally, in the case of linseed cake, less than 4·5 per cent. Nitrogen and 5 per cent. Phosphate of Lime. The following are some analyses made recently of good quality oil-cakes used recently in the tea districts. Of the item marked "alkalies, etc.," about half in each case will consist of Potash.

Guarantee for oil-cake.

Analyses of oil-cake.

	Castor cake Imported.	Mustard cake local (Dibrugarh).	Mustard cake local (Bishnauth).	Mustard cake local (Nowgong).
Moisture	7·67	8·44	9·04	19·33
* Organic matter	82·78	82·92	80·90	72·39
Lime	·83	·90	·81	·91
† Phosphoric Acid	3·07	2·97	2·81	2·66
Alkalies, etc.	3·31	2·93	3·05	3·41
Sand	2·34	1·84	3·39	1·30
	100·00	100·00	100·00	100·00
* Containing Nitrogen	6·46	5·17	4·61	4·78
† Equal to Phosphate of Lime	6·70	6·48	6·13	5·80

Apply in Spring.

270. Oil-cake is best applied before the first hoeing, in Spring (when it is mixed with the soil by that hoeing), at the rate of 10 to 15 maunds per acre. It may roughly be said that mustard cake is from three-quarters to four-fifths as valuable as castor cake, and linseed cake slightly more valuable than the former. The best way to apply it is in a trench round each bush a foot away from the stem, but broad-casting and then hoeing in is almost as good.

Treatment of washed slopes.

271. Some things, however, castor or other oil-cake cannot do. It cannot, for instance, bring back a washed slope, consisting of little else than sand, to a highly fertile condition. In such a case it is a question for bheel soil or cattle manure, and practically

nothing else will answer. Further, it will not make tea luxuriant on a stiff clay. Here the condition of the soil is at fault, and must be remedied prior to any manuring by means of the methods given in Chapter IV. But with exceptions like this, oil-cake bids fair to be the most important of manures, outside actual garden sources, in the future.

ARTIFICIAL MANURES.

Treatment of stiff clays.

XLVII.—Artificial and Chemical Manures.

272. Apart from the fertilisers so far dealt with, we are limited to imported chemical manures. These have, of course, the immense advantage that they are far more concentrated than the locally produced materials can ever hope to be, are susceptible of much more exact application, and can be imported to fill any particular defect in the soil without adding a large amount of unnecessary material. Nevertheless, we cannot consider that at present they can have, except as regards phosphates, any but a very subsidiary position in the Indian Tea Districts which are almost virgin lands teeming with waste products not produced from tea land, but well capable of replacing much of the loss caused by tea culture. We will, however, consider briefly some of those most likely to be useful.

Only subsidiary position as manures.

273. ***Nitrogenous Fertilisers.***—And first for Nitrogenous fertilisers. The artificial manures, specially supplying Nitrogen, are almost limited to the Nitrates of Soda and Potash, and to Sulphate of Ammonia. The first is imported from South America, the second is a local Indian product, while the third is a necessary bye-product in a well conducted gas works. They all three have a fundamental objection, that in a rainy climate they are quickly washed out of the soil. In 1900 Nitrate of Soda was used on several of the Assam Company's gardens, and the general result showed that six weeks after application, the effect of the manure began to disappear, and the treated plots were soon reduced almost, if not entirely, to the level of the untreated plots. A contradictory result was obtained by Mr. F. H. Edwards at Heeleaka (Jorhat), where the improvement was manifested right through the season, and the bushes appeared better at the end and have since maintained the improvement. In this case, however, it is probable that for some reason or other, not the exhaustion of the soil, the roots had ceased developing, and the Nitrate of Soda gave the necessary stimulus to make

Nitrogenous manures.

Nitrate of soda experiments.

Tea Manuring.

ARTIFICIAL MANURES.

Nitrate of soda washes quickly from soil.

them start again. In such cases Nitrate of Soda may be of value, but they are comparatively rare. As a rule, it will give an abnormal growth for two or three months, and then, if the soil be poor previously, there is a tendency for the bush to fall back to its previous position, unless in the meantime manuring with oil-cake has been carried out. There is another reason against its use. It is an extremely soluble salt, and the soil does not retain it in the slightest. A few inches of rain after application would wash nearly all the application into the drains in a day or two. At any rate, if applied at all, it should be used in very small quantity, say 5 per cent. of an application containing some more permanently useful material like oil-cake. As an application before collar-pruning, or even heavy-pruning, it is absolutely out of place.

Nitrate of potash.

274. Nitrate of Potash is very similar in its action. It has the valuable Potash, instead of the all but useless Soda, but as Potash is not usually required in Indian Tea Soils, this is not usually of very material advantage.

Sulphate of ammonia.

275. The third typical manure is Sulphate of Ammonia, and it contains more Nitrogen than any other manure which could be used. We cannot advise it in practically any case, although it has, in time past, been very extensively advised as a constituent of mixtures. It would appear to be objectionable because :—

Objections.

Removes lime and potash.

(1) It causes incidentally the removal of a large amount of other valuable constituents from the soil, the chief being the Lime and the Potash. In order to ascertain to what extent this might go on, we shook two typical Assam tea soils with a one per cent. solution of Sulphate of Ammonia for two days, allowed to settle, and analysed the liquid. There were extracted in the two cases as follows, calculated on the air dry soil —

	Soil No. I.	Soil No. II.
Lime . .	·037 per cent.	·018 per cent.
Potash . .	·052 „ „	·056 „ „

That is to say, one application of Sulphate of Ammonia might remove more Potash than the tea bush would do in ten years, and a large quantity of Lime. Now the latter is present in very small quantity in Assam soils, and though it could be replaced, yet there are other means of manuring tea which have not this objection, and do not necessitate a further expensive and really unnecessary application. **ARTIFICIAL MANURES.**

(2) It is easily washed out of the soil, almost as easily as Nitrate of Soda, and is hence not suited for a rainy climate where the rains form the cropping season. **Easily washes from soil.**

(3) It has only a very temporary action on the bush, and after the year of application the soil is poorer than it originally was. **Temporary action.**

276. In 1900 an extensive correspondence took place as to its use for tea in Ceylon. The late Sir John Lawes, perhaps the greatest authority in the world on manuring, wrote:—"My objection to Sulphate of Ammonia does not arise because it is a highly nitrogenous and soluble manure, but because it removes Lime from the soil, and I understand that the Ceylon soils are poor in Lime." If it is to be condemned in Ceylon because the soils are poor in Lime, it is much more so in India, where the tea soils are generally poorer. **Opinion of Sir J. Lawes.**

277. There are grave suspicions that large quantities of these soluble concentrated nitrogenous manures injure the quality of the tea, but this requires confirmation. We cannot, however, think, for the reasons above given, that any of them should be used, except rarely, and then only in combination in small quantity with permanent feeding manures, as a slight stimulant to bushes which, for an unknown reason, have become stationary and refuse to yield, and in these cases we should much prefer the Nitrates of Soda and Potash to Sulphate of Ammonia. **May injure quality.**

278. ***Phosphatic Manures.***—We come now to Phosphatic manures, that is to say, to those which have the closest relation of any to quality in tea. Though bones, as such, hardly act at all as a source of Phosphates for the plants, yet they may be prepared in such a way that they do this very effectively. The Phosphate in bones is present as Tribasic Phosphate of Lime, which the plants are almost unable to take up. If, however, Sulphuric Acid be added to the bones, a different Phosphate is produced—the Mono-Phosphate of Lime—which the plants are perfectly capable of assimilating. Under this form the manure is known in commerce as dissolved or vitriolized bones, and would probably be very useful, both as a source of Nitrogen and Phosphates. Actual field experiments are not, however, to hand, and any attempt to utilise this material would **Phosphatic manures.** **Dissolved bones.**

ARTIFICIAL MANURES.

be more or less of an experiment—an experiment however very likely to yield successful results. If put on, it should be used at the rate of 5 to 8 cwt. per acre, and put in a trench round the bushes at about one foot from the trunk. It should be guaranteed to contain 2 to 2½ per cent. of Nitrogen and 12 per cent. of soluble Phosphate of Lime.

Mineral superphosphate.

Superphosphate of Lime, prepared from mineral Phosphate deposits, now chiefly in Carolina and Florida, will also supply Phosphates to the plants. It is obtained from these sources in a precisely similar fashion to that in which the last named manure is prepared from bones. Alone it should not usually be applied, but mixed with oil-cake it forms a very effective manure, or indeed it might be added along with Cattle Manure to soil deficient in Phosphates.

May exhaust Lime.

279. The objection to all these manures made by treatment of some raw product with Sulphuric Acid, is that it is apt to exhaust the Lime already rather deficient in the soil, and hence, though one could recommend small quantities in mixtures, they are not materials to be added in large quantity.

Basic slag.

280. ***Basic Slag.***—The Phosphatic manure which has been the most successful up to date is probably Basic Slag, and in Ceylon its use has had a very great extension. It has practically only been on the market ten or eleven years, being a bye-product of the manufacture of steel by the Basic Bessemer Process, and consists, it is supposed, of a Tetra-Basic Phosphate of Lime, together with Iron compounds.

Preparation of Basic slag.

It varies very much in value, and should always be bought on a guarantee of at least the equivalent of 35 to 40 per cent. of Phosphate of Lime, and a fineness of 70 to 80 per cent. (that is to say, this percentage will pass through a sieve of 10,000 meshes to the square inch).

Analysis of Basic slag.

As it contains an excess of Lime, it cannot be mixed with or stored with most other manures, and further, it is of little or no value applied alone.

Ceylon method of using Basic slag.

The greatest success in Ceylon has been obtained by burying light prunings in trenches with this manure, when the rotting mass becomes quickly interlaced with a mass of the feeding rootlets of tea. We have seen some of these trenches opened after six months, when the prunings had fairly well rotted, and found this to be the case.

Burial of prunings.

281. ***Burial of Prunings.***—This, however, raises the whole question of the advisability of burying prunings, a practice which, on the recommendation of Mr. Bamber, is in vogue in almost all the best tea culture in Ceylon.

Tea Manuring.

282. There is no doubt, however, that the advice given in the former edition of this book to burn all prunings, is far and away the safest in every case. It may be perhaps that more spores of grey blight are blown about and alight on other bushes by carrying off the plot to burn than by sweeping them immediately into a trench and covering up, but such cases are isolated in the extreme, and under all conditions the burning of prunings is very much the safest way, always making a point of returning the ashes to the land. This returning the ashes to the land is always a difficulty. On one of the best managed gardens in Upper Assam, last year, we found the ashes from several acres spread over a strip a few yards wide. If this is done serious depletion of the land takes place, and it surely is comparatively little trouble to see that the ashes are effectively distributed over the land from which they were taken. Burning, therefore, is the ideal way of disposing of prunings, especially if the Nitrogen thus dissipated be returned to the land by means of a leguminous green manuring crop the following spring. In heavy pruning this green manuring should always be carried out, as the amount of Nitrogen removed by the pruning is considerable.

ARTIFICIAL MANURES.

Safest method to burn prunings.

Ashes must be put on land.

Green manuring in connection with burning of prunings.

Burning should in every case be resorted to to get rid of prunings if blights are prevalent in the garden. The most dangerous in this connection are red rust and thread blight, but one does not know how many others are carried by means of their burial. To leave prunings lying about in a garden with these blights on them is suicidal, and to bury them is dangerous. If the garden is, however, free from blight there does not seem any absolute reason against burying the light prunings—and these only—provided the following conditions are adhered to:—

Blights and burial of prunings.

(1) They must be buried deep. At least six inches of soil should be left on top of them, so that they will not be turned up by the hoe.

Conditions of burial.

(2) They should be buried immediately on pruning or as soon after as possible. In Ceylon trenches are dug to receive the prunings before the bushes are touched at all, and the prunings are put into them practically at once. Once dried up much of the manurial value has gone, or is rendered less available.

(3) They should be buried with something which will destroy any latent germs or spores of fungi which are upon them. The best materials for this are Lime and Basic Slag, which not only cause

ARTIFICIAL MANURES.

the blight spores to be destroyed but also allow the prunings to rot more quickly. The usual way of applying the Basic Slag, which is preferable, is to dust it over the buried prunings from a tin in which holes have been made, and immediately cover up the hole. In this way 4 to 5 cwts. would be applied per acre, and in Ceylon the method, coupled with a more complete manure on the surface the following spring, has been said to be eminently successful.

Burial of jungle.

283. If conveniently situated, the burial of jungle, provided it does not contain thread blight, would be advantageous on heavy soils. It should be put in in trenches, and Lime or Basic Slag added as suggested in the cases in which burial of prunings is admissible.

Basic slag with green manuring.

284. ***Basic Slag in Combination with Green Manuring.***—The above course can only be recommended in blight-free gardens, and in general, the method which follows would probably be a better way of applying Basic Slag. Instead of burying this with prunings, broadcast it on the surface, either at the Autumn deep hoe (which is preferable) or with the first Spring hoe, and then follow with a crop of *Mati Kalai* in April or May, to be hoed in in June. The green manuring crop is rendered more vigorous by the Basic Slag, absorbs a large portion of its Phosphoric Acid, and when it decays passes it on to the bush. This method was carried in the Spring of 1901 in several gardens on our recommendation. It is too early yet to judge its ultimate effect (as at the rate of 8 cwt. per acre it would last for several years, and several green manuring crops), but we think there is distinct promise of this combination proving a very effective manure. We should recommend its trial with much more confidence as a quality manure than either the dissolved bones or the superphosphate previously mentioned. It must again be insisted, however, that *alone* Basic Slag is almost useless, as it has no faculty of diffusing itself in the soil, and hence the roots have no chance to come in contact with it.

Basic slag useless alone.

Wood ashes.

285. ***Wood Ashes.***—Another Phosphate manure of great value now often largely wasted, but produced on the great majority of gardens is wood ash. This is of course usually put on the land, but only when three-quarters of the virtue has gone. If it is advisable to put cattle manure under cover, it is ten times more so to protect wood ashes from the rain. May we suggest that the wood ashes

Tea Manuring.

produced should be put on the covered manure heap, which we hope henceforth will be a necessity on every garden. It was formerly supposed that any alkali, such as wood ashes are, would increase the evolution of ammonia from a dung heap and hence bring about deterioration of the cattle manure under such conditions, but that idea has now been abandoned and probably manure keeps better somewhat alkaline than otherwise. It would then be applied with the cattle manure. Alone it would be valuable (1) before green manuring at the rate of 5 cwt. per acre; (2) for burying with prunings (if this be done), or (3) as a mixture with oil-cake, but it is of little use in any case if it has stood exposed to the rain for months.

ARTIFICIAL MANURES.

Put on manure heap.

Methods of applying wood ashes.

286. Wood ashes form not only a Phosphate manure, but also even more essentially a source of Potash. The analysis of samples of fresh ashes, and ashes exposed to the rain, has given the following figures. Of course, they vary much for every tree and wood :—

Wood ashes a source of potash.

	Fresh Ashes.	Washed Ashes.
Moisture	12·0	12·0
Potash	5·5	1·4
Phosphoric Acid	1·9	1·7
Lime	34·1	35·9

As a source of Potash, however, they should be used in an exactly similar manner to that just described.

287. ***Potash manures***—Will probably be rarely specially required for tea in the Indian Districts. If analysis of the soil indicates that Potash is deficient and wood ashes are not available in sufficient quantity, the only two manures which would be worth carrying to Assam are the Sulphate of Potash (containing 50 per cent of Potash) and the Muriate of Potash, containing a little more. They can form components of mixtures, but should never be applied alone to the bushes.

Potash manures.

287. ***Lime as Manure.***—We now come to the use of Lime. Very little of the tea soil of India is in need of Lime, or is likely to be for a good many years, if manures like Sulphate of Ammonia be avoided, although at present it contains far less of this constituent than the average agricultural soil. Lime has its functions, however, and should not be totally neglected.

Lime as manure.

(1) It is often useful to apply to a garden affected with fungous and insect blights, not so much as a manure (though this may in

Applied to kill blights.

ARTIFICIAL MANURES.

the future be found to be of advantage in connection with blights), but as a means of destroying the insects, caterpillars, and fungus spores in the soil round the bushes. For this purpose it should be freshly slaked—if possible, slaked just before use. Slaked lime bought and imported ready slaked is of little value for the purpose, as usually 50 per cent. has reverted to the state of Carbonate of Lime, and is useless.

Lime a substitute for Basic slag.

(2) It forms a good substitute for Basic Slag as an addition when burying prunings, and has the same effect in increasing the rapidity of rotting, but not the advantage of adding Phosphoric Acid.

Lime, to mix with Cattle manure.

(3) It is useful also in keeping cattle manure. By adding a layer of Lime to a manure heap occasionally, a sort of compost is formed, the manure rots more quickly, and the Lime becomes entirely incorporated with the manure.

Further than this Lime seems to possess no immediate use in manuring tea in India.

Sulphates of Iron and Manganese.

289. ***Other Manures.***—Various other more or less rare salts have been suggested as additions to tea. Sulphate of Iron and Sulphate of Manganese have been suggested as manures for quality in Ceylon. As at present they are expensive—in the latter case very expensive—and of no present proved value, we cannot recommend them.

List of useful manures.

290. We therefore limit the possibly profitable manures in India for the present to the following :—

(1) Bheel Soil and Top-dressing material of all kinds.
(2) Cattle Manure.
(3) Green Manuring.
(4) Fertilising Trees and Bushes.
(5) Bones.
(6) Oil-cakes, chiefly those of castor and mustard.

These are all more or less complete manures. Of those useful for special constituents, we have—

(7) Nitrate of Soda, or Potash, in rare cases, for Nitrogen.
(8) Superphosphate from Bones or from Mineral Phosphate for Phosphoric Acid.
(9) Basic Slag for Phosphoric Acid and Lime.
(10) Wood Ashes for Phosphoric Acid and Potash.
(11) Sulphate or Muriate of Potash, in rare cases, for Potash.
(12) Lime.

XLVIII.—Systems of Manuring.

SYSTEMS of MANURING.

We have already, under each heading, pointed out the utility of each of the manures just mentioned, but it remains now to submit certain general considerations on the methods in which it should be carried out.

Carried out before Heavy Pruning.

291. We are strongly of opinion that manuring should always be carried out the year before heavy pruning a plot. Thus, if a section is to be cut down in December 1903 it should be manured with whatever it needs in the winter of 1902-1903. This is on the principle that before a serious operation is undertaken, the general health of the bush should be as great as possible, and the manure should be so incorporated with the soil that without undue stimulation the bush recovers from the serious cutting.

Rotation of Crops.

292. In the previous edition of this work it was stated in several places that rotation of crops in some form or other was imperatively needed in tea gardens. There is equal need of rotation of manuring, and we would suggest here some rotations which might be profitably carried out. As far as manuring is concerned, I do not think that a period of more than seven years should go by on any plot of established tea without at least one application of manure. Ten years might occasionally pass on some lands and some gardens, but this is, we fancy, quite the limit. Take, for instance, a garden of 500 acres, soil light and fairly deep, top dressing soil easily available and cattle manure well kept. Such a garden would be divided into seven sections, of seventy acres each, and a method of dealing with it might be:—

Rotation of Manures.

Suggested Rotation for Light Land.

1st Section.—*1st year.*—Bheel soil, light dressing not more than 4 inches thick when put on.

2nd year.—Crop of mustard in May and June to be hoed in as green manure.

3rd year.—Nothing in growing season. Basic Slag (8 cwt. per acre) in November.

4th year.—Crop of *mati kalai* in May and June to be hoed in as green manure.

5th year.—Nothing.

6th year.—Dressing of 7 tons per acre of cattle manure in March.

7th year.—Nothing.

Tea Manuring.

SYSTEMS of MANURING.

When the first 70 acres received the bheel soil, the second would be having the second year's treatment, so that every year would see one section under some kind of treatment coupled with rotation of crop. The total expense outside the garden for the seven years would be thus limited to the 8 cwt. per acre of Basic Slag in the 4th year, which would probably not be needed in the next seven years' series on the same plot. Of course endless variations could be introduced. If bheel soil were not available, a dressing of 1c cwt. per acre of castor or 12 cwt. per acre of mustard cake would more or less replace it, and cost no more, but in most cases rather less. The Basic Slag might be replaced by Lime, or a smaller dressing, say 4 cwt. per acre, might be put on and added to each rotation instead of once in 14 years. The cattle manure might be found not to be needed or finally the Basic Slag might be altogether omitted and superphosphate (2 cwt. per acre) be added with the farmyard manure. The cost roughly would be as follows :—

Cost of Foregoing Rotation.

	Say. R	a.
1. Bheel soiling	30	0
2. Mustard seed	2	8
(The hoeing in would be paid for by missing a regular hoe.)		
3. Basic Slag, 8 cwt.	30	0
4. *Mati kalai* seed	2	0
6. Cattle manure, including carting and application	10	0
TOTAL .	74	8

Seven Years' System.

or a cost of 10 rupees 10 annas per annum for the first seven years, and 6 rupees 8 annas per annum for the second seven years. Even if an increase of tea were kept going of thirty pounds per annum, this expense would be doubly wiped out, for the treatment suggested would certainly not lower the quality.

293. The rotation suggested might be extended to ten on some gardens, as we said above, by the introduction of a year without treatment after the first, fourth, and sixth years, and so the cost would be reduced to $7\frac{1}{2}$ rupees for the first period, and $4\frac{1}{2}$ rupees per acre for the second. We have placed the bheel soiling at 30 rupees per acre, a rather low figure perhaps, but the dressing we suggest is only a light one. If the material were very good, even a less dressing

would suffice, if there was any prospect of a repetition at the end of seven years.

SYSTEMS of MANURING.

294. Another rotation based on entirely different lines, say for a heavy soil, might be—

Suggested Rotation for Heavy Soil.

1st Section.—*1st year.*—Deep trench the soil between alternate rows (*see para.* 77) and put in the trenches 2 tons cattle manure per acre, another 3 tons being applied on the surface of the plot.

2nd year.—Grow *mati kalai* over the whole plot in May, and hoe in in June.

3rd year.—Nothing.

4th year.—Deep trench the other rows, and add jungle in the trenches with Basic Slag, 4 cwt. per acre.

5th year.—Grow mustard over the whole plot in May, and hoe in in June.

6th year.—Nothing.

7th year.—Grow *mati kalai* as in the 2nd year.

295. In the next rotation of seven years, the section would be deep trenched in the corresponding years across the former lines of trenching between the other rows. The cost of such a system would be:—

Cost of Rotation.

	R	a.
1. Deep trenching, say	8	0
2. Cattle manure, 5 tons, say	7	0
3. *Mati kalai* seed, say	2	0
4. Deep trenching, say	8	0
5. Carrying jungle, say	5	0
6. Basic Slag, 4 cwt., say	15	0
7. Mustard seed, say	2	8
8. *Mati kalai* seed, say	2	0
TOTAL .	49	8

or a cost of 7 rupees 1 anna per acre per annum, and all, except that for Basic Slag and the various seeds, would be paid for labour, which would in any case have to be employed. Oil cake can always replace cattle manure, at the rate of 2 cwt. of the former to one ton of the latter, but with a stiff soil the improvement of condition with the cattle dung renders it preferable.

SYSTEMS of MANURING.

296. We are confident that rotations of this character, the above being only offered as suggestions in which the cost of the operations would vary in every district, will have to be regular things in the future. They, to a certain extent, prevent the land getting so one-sidedly exhausted as it would by growing tea constantly, and above all, would, we believe, retain the quality of the tea. For this last reason specially, we have introduced a Phosphatic manure in each example given. The whole, however, in each instance, should be based on an analysis of the garden soil, the value of any artificial manures bought should be checked by analysis, and a most rigorous control instituted in every part of the system.

CHAPTER IX.

THE INSECT PESTS OF TEA.

PESTS and BLIGHTS.

XLIX.—Introductory observations.

297. In now proceeding to consider the Tea Pests and Blights themselves, in detail, it may be pointed out that as a matter of convenience we have accepted the word "Pest" to denote Insect and other Animal Enemies, and the word "Blight" to refer to Fungal and other Vegetable Parasites of the Tea Plant. While convenient, the restrictions indicated for these words are, of course, open to criticism.

Constitutional Diseases.

Predisposition to Pests.

298. In the former chapters we have endeavoured to discuss the principles underlying certain aspects of the cultivation of the plant in order to form a sound basis for reform in the future. To our mind there exists sufficient presumptive evidence to justify the opinion that certain misapprehensions and defective methods of procedure have originated constitutional weaknesses that may be said to constantly predispose the plant to actual disease, or, in other words, to render the depredations of its enemies and parasites more alarming than they might be otherwise. We have therefore advocated such reforms as, from our theoretical standpoint, seem desirable, and which we believe will be found useful in practice, and feel that these should necessarily accompany more specific efforts to battle with the pests and blights.

Scientific Report.

299. It may be remarked that there are about perhaps a dozen enemies at present of serious moment. The others, while occasionally doing considerable injury, are nevertheless of a local and accidental character. But to solve the life histories of even these dozen would take probably several years' patient study, and to discover methods of dealing with them would occupy much time and necessitate detailed and elaborate experiments. This study has been little more than commenced as yet, but is developing as the years go by.

Experiment Indispensable.

300. A slight difference will be noticed in the arrangement of what follows from that adopted in the first edition. To indicate the relative importance of pests two kinds of type have been employed.

The Coleoptera or Beetles.

INTRODUCTORY OBSERVATIONS. Arrangement adopted.

Those dealt with in full-sized type may be considered as actual serious pests, or dangerous menaces for the future; those in smaller type are of less importance and in some cases have only any interest because they have at one time or another been found on the tea bush. Thus, although the numbering of the species is consecutive, their relative importance can be at once recognised from a practical tea planter's point of view. In the case of each of the important pests, the districts in which it has been found will be indicated, and then will follow in succession an account of the history of the attacks, a description of the pest itself, a statement of its effect on the bush and of its depredations, and finally the remedies either actually used or likely to be of use in combating the evil.

301. Though the arrangement is not strictly a scientific one, it will be convenient to take the pests belonging to the great natural orders of insects as follows:—

Classification.

1. **Coleoptera** or Beetles.
2. **Lepidoptera** or Moths and Butterflies, with the corresponding Caterpillars.
3. **Diptera** or Flies.
4. **Hymenoptera** or Ants, Wasps, and Bees.
5. **Orthoptera** or Crickets and Locusts.
6. **Hemiptera** or Bugs, including the Tea-Mosquito, Green-fly, Scale-Insects, etc.
7. **Pseudoneuroptera**, where White Ants are the only species of importance for our purpose.

And beyond this, as not belonging to, but closely related to the insects, we have—

8. **Arachnoidea** or Mites and Spiders, including the Red Spider and analogous pests.

COLEOPTERA.

COLEOPTERA.

The Beetles.

I.—*The Beetles.*

Larvæ of Beetles known as Grubs.

302. In this Order of insects there are several stages of growth, two of which, the grub and the mature beetle, may attack tea. The maggots or grubs are sometimes devoid of legs, but more frequently have three pairs of jointed legs,—one pair on each of the three segments of the body near the head, and a pair of sucker-feet near the

PLATE IV. (*To face Page 167.*)

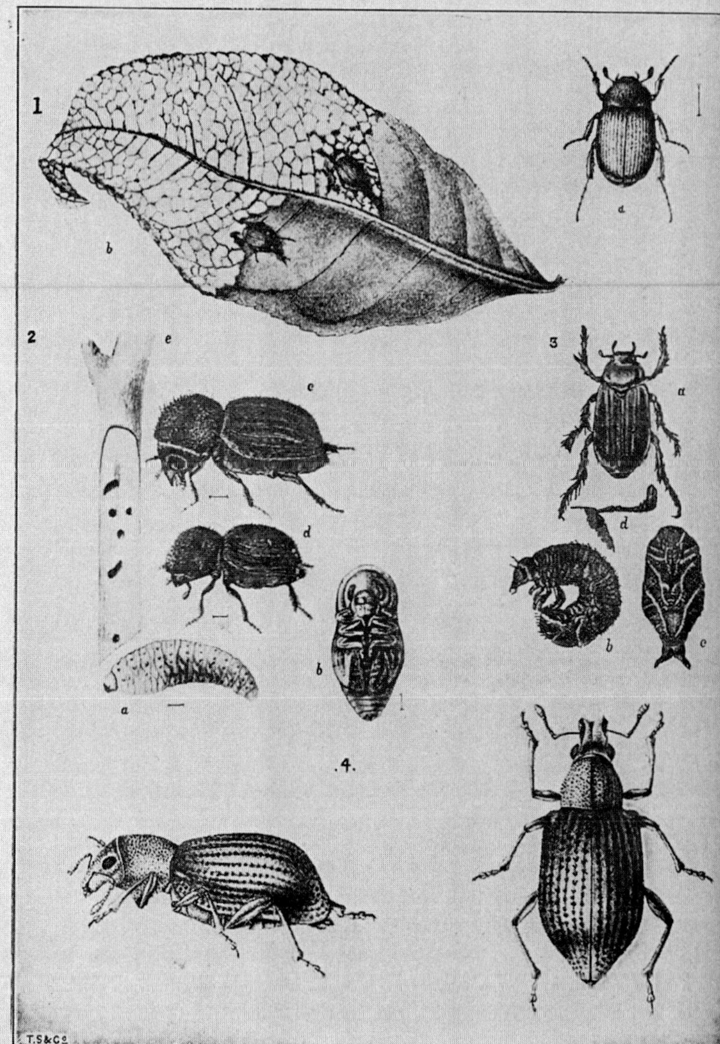

1. Serica assamensis (p. 169).

a. Beetle, enlarged; *b.* Beetle, at work, natural size.

(From Indian Museum Notes.)

2. Xyleborus fornicatus (p. 174).

a. Larva; *b.* Pupa; *c.* and *d.* Female and Male Beetles; *e.* Shoot, showing injury.

(From Indian Museum Notes.)

3. Lachnosterna impressa (p. 167).

a. Mature Beetle; *b.* Grub; *c.* Pupa; *d.* Antenna magnified.

(After Cotes.)

4. Brachyaspistes tibialis (p. 178).

Back and Side View of Beetle, much enlarged.

(From Indian Museum Notes.)

The White Grub.

hind or anal extremity. The chrysalis looks like a deformed beetle curled up and motionless. The perfect insect or beetle has an upper pair of hard wing-cases, called the *elytra*, and below these a pair of large membraneous wings which fold underneath the wing-cases. **LACHNOSTERNA IMPRESSA.**

303. There seem to be three serious pests of tea belonging to this group of insects, and several others which attack the plant and might become serious under favourable circumstances. Of these the Cockchafer or White Grub in its grub or larval stage eats the roots of the plant, and in its mature form would appear to possibly devour the leaves as well; the Orange Beetle is only injurious in the mature stage, then feeding on the young leaf; while the Ceylon Wood-Boring Beetle has only recently been found in India, and its spread should receive careful attention.

Family SCARABÆIDÆ.

1. Lachnosterna impressa, *Burm.*

THE COCKCHAFER OR WHITE GRUB.

SEE PLATE IV, No. 3.

References.—*Tea Cyclopedia, 44; Notes on Tea in Darjeeling, 54; Tea Planter's Vade Mecum, 105; Bamber, Chem. and Agri. Tea, 242; Indian Museum Notes, Vol. I, 59; II, 149; III, 3, 122; IV, 186, 261; Cotes, Tea Insects, 5—7; Tropical Agriculturist, 1892. 257.*

Found in all districts in India.

304. ***History.***—The first mention of this beetle, as an enemy to the tea plant, is contained in the letter from a Darjeeling Planter published in 1874. The author of *Notes on Tea in Darjeeling* (1888) gives it the local name of *Kumla;* and Mr. Bamber says that it occurs in all the tea districts. Mr. Cotes remarks that it appeared in vast numbers in Darjeeling in 1891. "Its prevalence in other years," Mr. Cotes adds, "is shown by the fact that in 1883 no less than 2,695,000 individuals were collected and destroyed in the public gardens of Darjeeling." It was collected by the authors in Assam in the Sibsagar district in 1895, and again in Tezpur in 1900. **Darjeeling Pest.** **Discovery in Assam.**

305. ***Description.***—The eggs of this beetle are laid in the ground and about a month afterwards the larvæ escape, and form white, soft, **Grubs Live on Roots.**

The Coleoptera or Beetles.

LACHNOSTERNA IMPRESSA.

fleshy, maggot-like grubs (*see Plate IV, No. 3 b*), which probably, in the first instance, attack the roots of weeds. At any rate, the whole of this, the really dangerous stage of its life, the insect remains in the ground, feeding on roots of all kinds including that of tea when it gets an opportunity. How long it remains before changing into the mature beetle, we do not know, but from analogy with similar ones it may be two or three years. At all events, these grubs never come to the surface until after they have passed the pupal stage (*figured in Plate IV, No. 3 c*), when in due course they emerge as a large copper-brown-coloured beetle, which is shown in *Plate IV, No. 3 a*, the antenna enlarged being shown at *d*. The mature beetle, from one of the authors' (G. W.) observations at Khumtai, appears to emerge from the ground in the spring (April), and then seems to attack the leaves of the plant.

Period of Larval Existence.

It is very probable that this is not the only beetle of a similar kind attacking the roots of tea.

Probably other Grubs attack Tea. *Conf. with para. 322.*

306. ***Depredations.***—Though the most important damage is done to seedlings, yet the bush appears to be injured at all stages by the attack of the beetle. In the case of seedlings, the plants rapidly die off, and this is often most marked in the richest land, and especially where cattle manure is employed in planting out, at any rate in the Darjeeling district. The reason for this is that the grub feeds on decaying as well as living vegetation, and is hence found most abundantly when this is in greatest amount.

Seedlings attacked.

When first attacked, the tea plant, of whatever age, appears to have lost its vigour. The buds often become *banjhi*, and as the ravages of the beetle advance, the leaves droop, turn brown, and finally the bush appears as if killed, and it may actually be so. The appearance in fact is very similar to that when a wood-borer is at work (such as **Zeuzera coffeæ**), with this difference, that the whole bush appears to be suffering instead of one portion of it only, as is generally the case with borers. From what has already been said of this beetle it will be understood there may be very little evidence of its ravages for months, while the grubs are steadily sapping the life of the plants, for as a rule the grub, if present, invades a considerable area, so that a whole plot of tea may be seen to be injured, and clumps of bushes killed. When this occurs, the bushes, if dug up, will very often be found to have the roots invaded by fungi, and the inference is some-

Appearance of Bush.

Conf. with para. 382.

The White Grub.

times drawn, though incorrectly, that the fungus is the cause of the destruction when bushes are seen to die in the manner indicated. It would, in such cases, be a good plan to have a healthy bush, near to those killed, dug up and carefully examined. It may then be seen that the fungus does not attack the roots till the bush has previously been killed, and the grubs may be found feeding on the living roots not yet affected by the fungus. LACHNOSTERNA IMPRESSA.

307. ***Remedy.***—So far no cure has been discovered except to dig up the grubs and kill them, and, even more effectively, to collect and destroy the mature beetles. By giving a pice for every thirty grubs collected to his coolies when hoeing the land, the planter who first reported the pest obtained two lakhs of grubs (filling two hogsheads) from 15 acres. He also found burying jungle in holes very effective as a trap, the grubs leaving the tea to attack the rotting vegetation which could then be removed and burnt—grubs and all. Wherever young plants die off after the use of cattle manure in planting out, the presence of this grub may be suspected and it should be sought for and removed before the seedlings are replaced by fresh ones. Collection of Grubs. Quantity collected. Burying Weeds. Effect of Manure.

2. **Serica assamensis,** *Brenske.* SERICA ASSAMENSIS.

SEE PLATE IV, NO. 1.

References.—*Indian Museum Notes, Vol. IV, 176; V, 14.*

Found in the Duars.

308. In April 1899 samples of this beetle were received at the Indian Museum as having been destructive to tea in the Duars. The mature beetle fed at night and apparently did a good deal of damage for a day or two by eating off the surface of the leaf (*See Plate IV, No. 1 b*), and then disappeared. The Manager wrote at the time as follows:—"I am disposed to think the beetles were flying over the garden, and dropped down on different parts of it, and ate the tea leaves, but found they were not to their liking, and so did not eat them a second time." Seeing that nothing has since been heard of the matter, we are inclined to agree with him. Duars Pest. Has disappeared.

In the previous year the same beetle attacked the tea leaf in the withering sheds at the same garden at a corresponding part of the season. Ate withered Leaf.

The beetle is of a yellowish brown colour, and about $\frac{1}{4}$ inch long and $\frac{1}{8}$ inch broad. (See *Plate IV, No. 1 a*, where it is shown much enlarged.) There seems no present danger of the spread of this pest, but if it did appear, catching and destroying the beetles is the only remedy.

The Coleoptera or Beetles.

Family ELATERIDÆ.

ELATER SP.

3. Elater sp.

THE WIREWORM.

Found in Assam and Darjeeling.

Assam and Darjeeling.

309. The wireworm, or larva of the click beetle, is among the most destructive of the pests of crops, and recently serious damage on a small scale has been reported from both Assam and Darjeeling. The larvæ do not usually attack the roots of perennial plants, but in the present instance seem to go for the finer rootlets of the plant, ultimately resulting in the death of the attacked individuals. In form, they are bright yellow, polished, hard grubs, with six legs near the head and no more, about an inch or more long. In England almost every method of eradicating them has been tried without much success. Salt (10 cwt. to the acre) acts fairly well, but it would be impossible to apply this where tea bushes are growing. Mustard cake (*not castor cake*) is thought by many English farmers to attract the grubs from the roots, when they are supposed to die of over-feeding. It might be applied here, as a manure as well, at the rate of 5 cwt. to the acre, but if the wireworms become serious, the English method of employing boys to dig them out is probably the best.

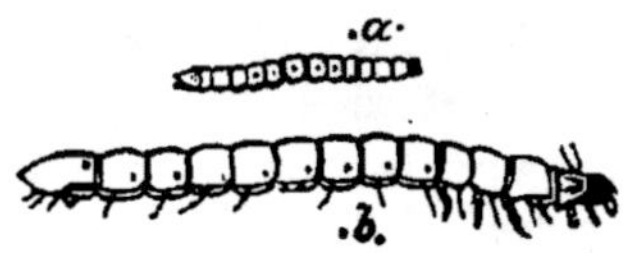

FIG. 7.—THE WIREWORM.
a. Natural size. *b*. Enlarged.
(After Miss Ormerod.)

Salt as Remedy.
Mustard cake as remedy.
Digging out.

Family CHRYSOMELIDÆ.

DIAPROMORPHA MELANOPUS.

4. Diapromorpha melanopus, *Lacord.*

THE ORANGE BEETLE: PEAL'S BEETLE.

References.—*Journ. Agri.-Horti. Soc. Ind., Vol. II, Proc. Nov. 17 (1869); Vol. IV, Proc. Sept. 19 (1872); Feb. 27 (1873); April 24 (1873); Vol. V, Proc. Aug. 27 (1874); Vol. VI, Proc. July 24 (1879); Sept. 25 (1879); S. E. Peal, in Tea Cyclopædia, 35; Notes on Tea in Darjeeling, 52; Bamber, Chem. and Agri. Tea, 242; Indian Museum Notes, Vol. I, 106; II, 154; IV, 121; V; Cotes—Tea Insects, 7; Planter, June 20, 1896; Oct. 28, 1899; Nov. 18, 1899; Crole, Tea Textbook, 222.*

Found in all districts.

310. ***History.***—It would appear that Mr. E. L. Edgar, of the Cossipore Tea Estate, Cachar, was the first to draw attention to this beetle. He then wrote, "It has only appeared this year (1869), in any numbers." We next hear of it in 1872 from the Moran Tea

The Orange Beetle.

DIAPROMORPHA MELANOPUS.

Early Records.

Estate in the Sibsagar district, Assam, and both these samples were identified with the **Diapromorpha melanopus** of Lacordaire. Mr. S. E. Peal contributed some very interesting particulars in the form of an article on Tea Pests which will be found in the *Tea Cyclopædia*. It has since been reported from Darjeeling by many writers, and also from Kumaon, and is probably more or less common in almost every tea garden.

Small Orange-coloured Beetle.

311. ***Description.***—In spite of the numerous observations made, the life-history of this insect has not been followed. The mature beetle is the only form ever seen on the tea bush, and can be found there from the beginning of April to the middle of October at least and probably later. The insect does not lay its eggs on tea, nor do the larvæ feed on tea. Mr. S. E. Peal, who watched it more carefully than probably any other observer up to date, was of opinion that it lived its early life in *Ulu* or *Sunn* grass **(Imperata arundinacea)**. "From what is known of other species of the same family," writes Mr. Cotes, "it may be expected that the eggs are laid upon the leaves, that the larvæ are active little creatures that feed upon the foliage, eventually transforming, in some sheltered corner, into stationary pupæ from which the beetles ultimately emerge." "These points, however," he adds, "require corroboration."

Eggs laid on Leaves.

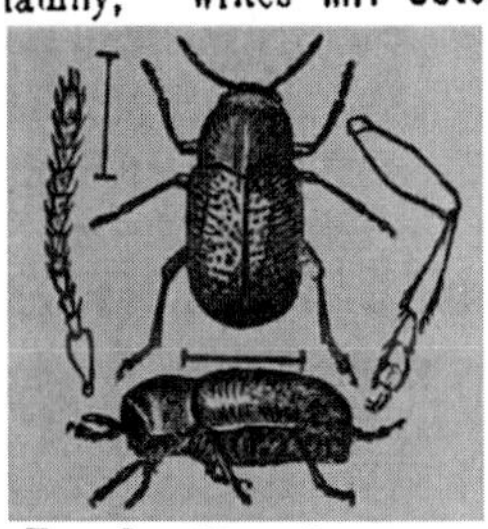

FIG 8.—THE ORANGE BEETLE.

(Showing back and side view of insect, the antenna to the left, and leg to right,—all much enlarged.)

(After Cotes.)

Description of Insect.

The mature beetle is a small oval orange-coloured insect with hard pitted wing cases, with the head slightly darker coloured than the body, and the belly pale coloured. Size—about ⅜th inch in length. (*See Fig. 8.*) It apparently feeds at all hours of the day.

Appearance of eaten shoots.

312. ***Depredations.***—Regarding the manner of its depredations there can be no doubt. Mr. Edgar, the original discoverer, says, "These insects scrape the green stem below the Pekoe or Pekoe Souchong leaf, sometimes below the Souchong leaf, if the flush is quick grown and the stem soft. They scrape or eat a place on it from half an inch to one and a quarter inches in length and from just touching it to three-fourths through. According to the depth they

The Coleoptera or Beetles.

DIAPROMORPHA MELANOPUS.

go, so soon do the two or three leaves tumble over and wither." The Assistant Manager of Moran Company, Assam, in his letter even goes more fully into the subject. He says, "So serious is it that I estimate a loss of at least a maund of tea from this flush alone, which I am now plucking, and the loss on the entire year must be very serious." "The insect eats or gnaws only a small portion of the stem of the young shoot, which, whenever the sun touches it, withers, droops, and in about a day falls off and then the shoot looks just as if it had been plucked; so that to discover the entire depredations of this little pest, the bushes have to be examined once or twice every day." Mr. S. E. Peal's original account of this pest is also worthy of being quoted, since it throws some additional light on the methods of procedure adopted by this insect. "Naturally," he says, "it is grass-eater, and may be found in considerable numbers where larger grasses abound in the open. It has a habit of alighting on the tips and flies rather slowly, resting under the curved-over tips of the *ulu* grass. These insects are at times found in threes or fours, and rest there in the little shade afforded. In attacking tea, they generally eat away portions of the green stem of the shoot that is just fit to pluck; the shoot falls over, withers, dies and turns black and dry. If this beetle is at all common, considerable damage is done, and a garden or patch of tea presents a brown, withered appearance. As the portion eaten out of each stem is not large, a single beetle may ruin half a dozen shoots as one morning's work."

Loss sustained.

Presence of Ulu Grass dangerous.

The author of *Notes on Tea in Darjeeling* says, "This is a small reddish-yellow insect, which always runs up if cow-dung has been put down, and sometimes on new extensions, probably from the same cause. This beetle seems to attack heavy pruning or young tea more than other pieces. It bites the shoot low down, and the shoot then withers and rots away. If there is *sunn-grass* near the tea, the beetle goes to the grass, instead of the tea."

Attack Young Tea.

A Darjeeling correspondent in *The Planter* says, "Often when reading articles on tea blights I have been surprised never to have seen the 'orange beetle' mentioned. I have often seen a dozen or more of these beetles on one bush and every bud lying over dry and making the bush look almost as though withering up at first sight. Another peculiarity about them is, that they only seem to go for the Assam *jats*, and are scarcely ever seen on a China bush,

Prefers Assam Jats.

The Orange Beetle.

DIAPROMORPHA MELANOPUS.

evidently preferring the more succulent shoots of the Assam bush to the less juicy one of the China." The fact of this insect showing a decided preference for the Assam tea is a point of considerable interest. This has also been noticed by Mr. Peal and others, as well as by ourselves.

Early History not known.

313. ***Remedy.***—In consequence of our ignorance of the early history of this insect, only one cure is open for consideration, namely, to collect and destroy the beetle. This Mr. F. Moore recommended over twenty years ago, and nothing further has been brought to light. A planter whose letter originally appeared in the *Tea Gazette* says, "I have had thousands of bushes damaged by this insect, and find it pays 'hand over fist' to give coolies so much for catching the little pests, say a pice for fifty. By so doing I have succeeded in destroying as many as twenty thousand in the day." Mr. Peal says, "eight or ten well-made butterfly nets, depth say 18 inches, and diameter at mouth one foot, ring and hook of stout brass wire, bent, soldered, and inserted in four feet high bamboo handles. These in the hands of as many smart boys will bring down the numbers very rapidly. If at all plentiful, a boy can easily 'bag' 300 beetles per hour, and where not much of a pest, I have taken several times myself at the rate of 250 per hour. A few days of this and the nuisance will abate perceptibly."

Method of catching.

We should like to insist, however, upon the connection between this pest and the "jungly" nature of the garden. Where weeds, especially *ulu* or *sunn* grass, are allowed to grow up in the tea, or the garden is cut up by weedy *hullahs*, there the pest is almost invariably at its worst. Mr. Peal agreed with us in this, and was of opinion that far from *ulu* grass being a protection (as suggested by the author of *Notes on Tea in Darjeeling*), it is the chief cause of the mischief, and there is now no question of the close relationship of grass jungle to the prevalence of the Orange Beetle. As cultivation becomes more careful, as jungle becomes less prevalent in and about the tea, the pest is gradually becoming of less importance.

Connection with Jungle in Garden.

314. ***Ladybirds mistaken for the Orange Beetle.***—A warning is perhaps advisable, in passing, to those who, unfamiliar with the appearance of the Orange Beetle, might be too hasty in coming to the conclusion that any small orange-coloured or red beetle, found

LADYBIRDS.

on tea, is the pest here dealt with or "at all events has no business" on the tea, and had therefore better be removed. That such confusion has often occurred is undoubted, and yet the true ladybird is one of the planters' best friends. The ladybird beetle usually met with on tea is almost circular in outline and of a bright red colour with a few spots on the wing cases. The Orange Beetle is a narrow elongated insect with a somewhat large and curiously truncated head, as if cut off abruptly. The wing cases are of one uniform orange yellow colour throughout, and seem as if they had been dabbed all over with the point of a needle—the surface of the wing cases being pitted. Those of the ladybird, on the other hand, are perfectly smooth and polished.

Planters' Best Friend.

Carnivorous.

Conf. with paras. 572, 578.

The larvæ and even the mature insect of the ladybird beetle are carnivorous and feed for the most part on the black aphis (**Ceylonia theæcola,** which see), and possibly also on the larvæ of the tea-mosquito and tea green fly. It does not injure the tea in any way, and should most certainly be encouraged, and on no account destroyed through the mistaken notion that it is the Orange Beetle. The value and utility of encouraging, and even introducing, ladybirds and similar insects for the purpose of preying on any pests of tea will be discussed when dealing with the scale insects.

Conf. with paras. 581 and 889.

Family SCOLYTIDÆ.

XYLEBORUS FORNICATUS.

5. Xyleborus fornicatus, *Eichhoff*.

THE WOOD-BORING BEETLE. "THE SHOT HOLE BORER."

SEE PLATE IV, No. 2.

References.—*Indian Museum Notes, Vol. IV, 57. Planting opinion, 1899, p. 339. Report, Roy. Bot. Gardens, Ceylon, 1899, p. 14, Indian Tea Association Circular No. 58, 1900. Tropical Agriculturist, 1901, p. 177.*

Found in Ceylon and Upper Assam.

Appeared in Ceylon.

315. ***History.***—This curious little beetle has been found, ever since the year 1897, in Ceylon, to riddle the tea stems. It was first discovered there by Mr. E. E. Green, and has apparently been extend-

ing its depredations ever since. Till the autumn of 1900 it was unknown in India, but then suddenly appeared and did very considerable damage on a garden in the Upper Dibrugarh district, before its nature was discovered and measures were taken to deal with it. One of the authors has since found it in a second place in Upper Assam, again doing considerable damage. **XYLEBORUS FORNICATUS.** **Now in Upper Assam.**

316. ***Description and Depredations.***—As will be seen from the figure (*Plate IV, No. 2* where *a.* represents the grub, *b.* the pupa, and *c.* and *d.* the female and male beetles respectively, all much enlarged,—the natural size being represented by hair lines), this insect is a small beetle rarely more than one-eighth of an inch in length which is found riddling the branches and stems of the bushes, both as a grub and in the mature condition. The extremely small size of the beetle often prevents its recognition until a very large patch of tea has been attacked and seriously affected. **Size and Description.**

When first reported in India, the Manager of the estate on which it occurred described the plot affected as a piece of pure Assam indigenous Tea, and then went on to say, "The affected part looked at first as though it had been struck by lightning, a number of bushes turning red and then dying off completely. No notice was taken of it until it was seen to be spreading, when, on close examination, powdered wood was noticed round the affected bushes, and small holes in the stems a few inches above the ground. On the stems being split open, a number of beetles and grubs were found to be inside, and to have tunnelled the stem in all directions (see *Plate IV, No. 2, e.*), but only for about six inches in height, and in every case just above the ground." **Appearance of Tea.**

Though in this case only the stems just above the ground were affected, this is not by any means generally the case. Regarding the pest in Ceylon Mr. Green writes to us: "Another habit of this insect has been recently observed, namely, that of girdling the strong red wood branches. Such branches snap off when handled or often die back. An examination of affected branches shows that a tunnel has been run down the centre of a branch for several inches, terminating in a horizontal circular or spiral gallery that practically girdles the stem. In this gallery are usually found the larvæ of the insect. The galleries of the insect are laid with a short but dense growth of fungus, upon which the beetles and their larvæ are supposed to feed. **Girdles Branches.**

The Coleoptera or Beetles.

XYLEBORUS FORNICATUS.

An American Entomologist, Mr. H. G. Hubbard, is of opinion that the galleries are constructed by these insects solely for the purpose of growing these minute fungi. Whatever the purpose may be, the result upon the plant is equally injurious. The presence of the fungus seems sometimes to irritate the surrounding tissues; and produces a purple discoloration extending for some distance beyond the borings, and often resulting in the death of the parts attacked."

Grevillea said to attract Insect.

It has been suggested that Grevillea trees attract the insect, and undoubtedly it is present in these trees to a considerable extent in Ceylon, but the connection does not seem by any means necessary, and one planter writes, "My worst attacked fields have been those where Grevilleas practically do not exist."

Remedy.

317. ***Remedy.***—As this pest has hitherto appeared in India in small well-defined plots, and has been dealt with when first noticed, the methods which follow have been successful in treating it. The bushes were at once cut down to the ground, burnt on the spot, and a trench about six inches wide and at least six inches deep was dug round the affected plot and filled with quick lime in order to prevent the pest spreading with impunity. This last precaution has since been found, on the basis of Ceylon experience, to be of little or no value, as the pest is spread by the winged females, which fly from bush to bush, and do not creep along the ground. It was further suggested at the time, that it would be wise to paint the stems of all the adjacent bushes with Stockholm (*wood*) tar so as to render them objectionable to the beetle. Mr. Green, who has tried quite a number of applications of this sort, including Lime white wash, Bordeaux mixture, Cowdung, Macdougall's Insecticide wash, Gondal fluid, Arsenate of Lead and Lime, and Coal Tar, has recently written us that none of these produced any apparently beneficial results. "Females that had tried to penetrate the young stems of Albizzia moluccana trees, were found to have been caught and killed by the natural exudation of gum. This suggests the use of some viscid fluid as an application to the tea stems." (*Green.*) It further indicates that an application of wood tar, while not a cure, may do something to prevent the attack of a bush by the beetles.

Burn all Prunings.

Where the pest affects larger areas than those dealt with in India up to date, all the prunings should be religiously burnt as was

The Green Beetle.

originally recommended by Mr. Green, and the cut surfaces of the stems may be painted with some greasy mixture which will suffocate many of the insects in the galleries. Gradually the methods here detailed appear to have the effect of keeping the pest within bounds even in Ceylon, but under conditions of extensive development it is practically impossible to exterminate it. XYLEBORUS FORNICATUS.

Family CURCULIONIDÆ.

6. Astycus chrysochlorus, *Wied.* ASTYCUS CHRYSOCHLORUS.

THE GREEN BEETLE.

References.—*Indian Museum Notes, Vol. III, 99, 126; Cotes, Tea Insects, 8.*

Found in Cachar and Upper Assam.

318. This insect has been reported as doing some injury to teas in several districts, notably Cachar, North Lakhimpur, and Sibsagar. It is said to strip the young leaves off the tea shoots. The beetle, which is about ¾ inch long, is covered with small scales which give it a bright pale green colour. Green Beetle. Eats Leaves.

As to remedy, nothing further can be said than has already been mentioned in connection with the Orange Beetle. The insect should be collected and destroyed whenever seen, and the sooner a pest like this is attacked the better.

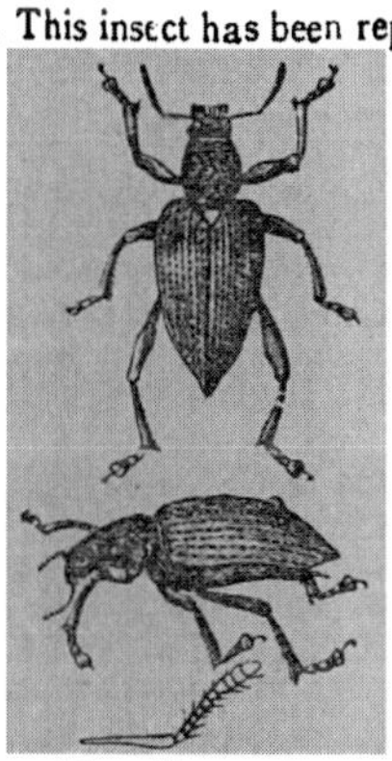

FIG. 9.—THE GREEN BEETLE.
(Showing back and side view of insect, natural size, and the antenna, much enlarged.)
(After Cotes.)

7. Astycus lateralis, *Fabr.* ASTYCUS LATERALIS.

THE SMALLER GREEN BEETLE.

Reference.—*Indian Museum Notes, Vol. IV, 184.*

Found in Upper Assam.

319. This is a much smaller beetle (half an inch long) than the last mentioned, but otherwise very similar in appearance, except that it is of Green Beetle.

The Coleoptera or Beetles.

ASTYCUS LATERALIS.

a dark brownish black ground colour, with a distinctly green metallic tinge. It appeared in 1897 on the Hukanpukri Division of the Jokai Tea Co., and was said to come by night in thousands and simply strip the bushes. There is nothing to add to the remarks on Astycus chrysochlorus as to the methods of dealing with this pest.

ASTYCUS.

8. **Astycus (?),** *Watt.*

Found in Assam.

Green Beetle.

320. A third species of beetle belonging to this group has caused occasional anxiety in the Amgoorie district, and was also found in North Lakhimpur. It is intermediate in size between the last two described, and closely approximates in colour to **Astycus lateralis.** In the late Mr. Barlow's opinion it was, however, a species distinct from either. It should be dealt with in the same manner as the other beetles of this genus.

BRACHYASPISTES TIBIALIS.

9. **Brachyaspistes tibialis,** *Jekel.*

SEE PLATE IV, No. 4.

References.—*Administration Report, Roy. Bot. Gardens, Ceylon, 1899, 14; Indian Museum Notes, Vol. V, 52.*

Found in Ceylon: not known in India.

Found in Ceylon.

321. In November 1899, young tea plants, 3 months from planting, were badly attacked by this weevil in the Bogawantalawa district of Ceylon. The weevils were said to eat off all the young shoots; leaving the stumps quite bare. They persisted for several months, but were kept in check by close planting. Mr. E. E. Green kept some of the beetles under observation, and found that they fed freely on young tea leaves, and remained alive for more than two months; small batches of eggs were laid by the beetles just below the surface of the ground, which hatched out as minute yellowish grubs, which soon died. It is probable that in nature the grubs feed upon the rootlets of plants, either of the tea itself or of some weed. The figures given in *Plate IV* of the beetle are much enlarged, the average sample being about half an inch in length. The insect is not at present known in India.

Ate off young shoots.

322. Several other grubs and beetles have been sent as attacking tea, but nothing more than the names and localities can be recorded:—

Curculio tanymecus (*Journal, Agri.-Horti. Soc., India, Vol. VI, 1879*), from Mangaldai.

Crioceris impressa, **Oides bipunctata** } Sent from Nowgong by Mr. W. J. Fleet, in 1897, as eating the leaf of tea.

A Longicorn (**Cerambycid**) boring beetle, probably belonging to the genus "**Prionus.**"

A Lagriid beetle, sent in 1896 as attacking tea in Burma.

LEPIDOPTERA.

CHAPTER X.

THE INSECT PESTS OF TEA—continued.

LEPIDOPTERA.

LI.—The Butterflies and Moths, and their Caterpillars.

Moths and Butterflies.

323. It is perhaps hardly necessary to explain that the insects of this order pass through three complete phases. In the early part of their life they emerge from the eggs as caterpillars, and it is in this stage that they are destructive to crops, the perfect insect being always quite harmless. The caterpillar or larva of a moth or butterfly is at once distinguished from the grub of a beetle by the possession of one to four pairs of sucker feet (or prolegs) placed near the middle or toward the hinder part of the body. When full fed the caterpillars moult and pass into the second phase or chrysalis, the resting stage during the life of the insect. From this the perfect insect—butterfly or moth as the case may be—emerges, and alone has the power of laying eggs and hence of reproduction. It is quite harmless to any plant.

Caterpillars of moths.

324. Butterflies may generally be recognised from moths by the antennæ resembling little drum sticks. They may be said to be day-loving insects, whereas the majority, though not by any means all, of the moths, come out during twilight or at night. So far the larva of only one butterfly—**Pareba vesta**, *Fabr.*—fairly common in Assam and Darjeeling tea gardens — has been found feeding on tea, and its damage is not of much moment. The series of moth caterpillars, however, which attack the plant, is extensive, and the damage they do is in several cases serious.

Butterflies.

325. The most successful method of dealing with caterpillars hitherto practised has been to hand pick them. They are easily seen, and their depredations for the most part at once visible. But it would be a more successful plan still to collect the harmless looking chrysalides or even train a gang of children to capture the winged insects. This latter has been done in at least one case—by **Mr. E. Ramsden** of the Pabbojan Tea Company, who had one boy with a butterfly net to so many acres—and the estate has not suffered so seriously from caterpillars since as previously, though this may of

Collection of Caterpillars.

Of Moths.

LEPIDOPTERA.

course be a coincidence. In the winged state the moths are harmless, yet it must be remembered that they are then flying about to deposit numerous eggs which give origin to new generations of caterpillars.

Family SATURNIIDÆ.

ATTACUS ATLAS.

10. **Attacus atlas**, *Linn.*

THE ATLAS MOTH.

References.—*Hampson, Fauna Brit. Ind.* (*Moths*), *Vol. I*, *15. Circular Royal Bot. Gardens, Ceylon. Series I, No. 19* (*1900*), *265.*

Found in Ceylon attacking Tea.

326. We have no record that the huge caterpillars of the Atlas Moth, have been noticed to feed on tea in India. In Ceylon, however, Mr. Green records having had them sent to him as defoliating tea bushes. In this connection he remarks, "Fortunately this insect may at present be looked upon more as a curiosity than as a tea pest. But every caterpillar that can exist on a diet of tea leaves must be considered as a potential tea pest. Some unrecognised factor may completely upset the balance of nature as concerns this particular insect, and it may suddenly assert itself as a formidable enemy. And a formidable enemy indeed would be the caterpillars of the 'Atlas Moth' if it should gain an ascendancy." The caterpillar is pale green in colour with brownish speckles, with spines both on the back and side of many sections (somites) of the body, and an oval red ring on the hind section of the body next to the claspers. The larva is found 2 to 3 inches long.

CRICULA TRIFENESTRATA.

11. **Cricula trifenestrata**, *Helfer.*

THE CRICULA SILK-WORM.

References.—*Hampson, Fauna Brit. Ind.* (*Moths*), *Vol. I, 28 ; Dict. Econ. Prod. Ind., Vol. VI, Pt. III, 88-93 ; Ind. Mus. Notes, Vol. II, 153.*

Found in Assam attacking Tea.

327. This silk moth caterpillar was sent as feeding on tea from the Borsillah Tea Estate, Assam. The caterpillar is blackish brown with a crimson pair of claspers at the hind or anal extremity, and the cocoon is composed of bright golden yellow silk firmly united into a network. Its occurrence on tea is exceptional, and no fear need be anticipated from it.

Family BOMBYCIDÆ.

ANDRACA BIPUNCTATA.

12. Andraca bipunctata, *Wlk.*

THE BUNCH CATERPILLAR.

THE BROWN OR "BUNCH CATERPILLAR." A PEST OFTEN DESIGNATED MERELY "CATERPILLAR."

SEE PLATE V, No. 1.

The Bunch Caterpillar.

THE BUNCH CATERPILLAR.

References.—*Hampson, Fauna Brit. Ind. (Moths), Vol. I, 40; Jour. Agri.-Horti. Soc., Ind, IV (1872); V (1877); Peal, Tea Cyclopedia, 35; Tea Planter's Vade Mecum, 105; Baildon, Tea in Assam, 46; Ind. Mus. Notes, III, 2 and 58; IV, 41; Cotes, Tea Insects, 22-23.*

Found in nearly all Indian districts.

328. ***History.***—This was one of the pests of tea noticed early in the history of the industry, attention having been drawn to it by a Cachar planter in 1872, but Mr. Peal's description of its depredations in the *Tea Cyclopedia* under the name "Caterpillar" is the first detailed account of its ravages. Mr. Bamber makes no reference to it, and Mr. Cotes only speaks of it as received from Cachar and the Jorhat division of Assam. **Caterpillar.**

As a matter of fact, it is a very widespread pest found in practically every garden on the south of the Brahmaputra in Assam, and becoming really most serious in Dibrugarh. In Cachar it is common, and recently the authors have found it in Darjeeling at an elevation of over four thousand feet. It is said to do much damage to wild tea in the Lushai country. **Distribution.**

329. ***Description.***—The caterpillar in question is very well known, and is called the "bunch caterpillar" from the circumstance that during the day the larvæ live in a compact mass. (*See Plate V, No. 1.*) They hold on by the hind or anal legs, and when disturbed, simultaneously extend their bodies in a threatening manner. When full grown, they become two and a half inches long and a quarter to three-eighths thick. They are smooth and hairless, of a grey colour with lateral brown patches on each segment of the body, and three faint whitish lines drawn parallel to each other lengthwise and across the other markings. Over the prolegs there are small red patches or streaks. **Live in compact masses.**

The life history of the insect has been worked out most completely by Mr. J. A. Thomson, late of Ligri Pukri. He says the moth "lays its eggs on the underside of the leaves. These are arranged very methodically, and each female deposits from fifty to two hundred eggs. Each such deposit becomes afterwards a colony of caterpillars which remain together. In about a week the eggs hatch and the caterpillars take nearly a month to reach maturity The insect breeds all the year round, but it is most prevalent in May, **Life history.**

The Lepidoptera (Bombycidæ).

THE BUNCH CATER-PILLAR.

June, and July. The cocoons are formed, one might say, below ground or rather on upturned corners of clods and near the base of the stem." This latter is a curious fact with this family of insects, but the cocoons in hand are certainly silken structures showing no sign of attachment to twigs as would be usual. The cocoons are usually aggregated together in threes and fours, the united structure showing a flat face such as might be formed by attachment to upturned clods of earth.*

Cocoons on the Ground.

The moth (*see Fig. 10*) is brown in colour and by no means a very striking one. It flies, and lays its eggs, at night.

FIG. 10.—THE BUNCH CATERPILLAR, COCOON, AND MOTH.
(After Cotes.)

Caterpillars collected daily.

330. ***Depredations.***—The caterpillars of this moth feed at night and often defoliate the bushes over a large patch of garden before the morning. "They strip the bushes," says Mr. Baildon, "of every vestige of green, leaving nothing but hard stalks. From six to eight weeks are generally required for the bush to recover itself, for the most minute buds are taken off as well as the large leaves." Mr. Cotes mentions a case in Cachar where in "six months, ending May 1893, it was found worth while to spend fifteen hundred rupees in employing coolies to pick the insects off the bushes. In this case no less than sixty-nine and a half maunds of caterpillars were said to have been destroyed." In gardens seriously affected it is not unusual for the daily catch to amount to 8 to 10 maunds in one day, and in many gardens in Sibsagar and Dibrugarh

* According to this, the illustration, derived from Mr. Cotes, though correct in form, is certainly wrong in showing the cocoon attached to a twig.

PLATE V. (*To face Page 182.*)

1. The Bunch Caterpillar on Tea Stem (p. 180).
(From Photograph by T. H. Hall.)

2. The Bag Worm (p. 191).
(From Photograph by T. H. Hall.)

half a maund, as Mr. Peal says, can be daily collected by five or six children.

THE BUNCH CATERPILLAR.

Collect Caterpillars and Cocoons.

331. ***Remedy.***—There is but one cure,—hand-collecting,—in other words, to pick the caterpillars off the bush; to see that the cocoons met with during hoeing are carefully gathered and destroyed, and to train children to recognise and capture the moths, thus checking the deposit of eggs. Mr. J. A. Thomson was in the habit of sending specially trained men in autumn to mark down the bushes on which the caterpillar had been feeding. These can at once be recognised by the large quantity of their droppings that may be seen on the surface of the soil. On the bushes being so marked, a few coolies were told off to remove soil round the stem with their kodallies. They have little difficulty in picking up the cocoons from the soil thus turned over.

Fortunately the pest is not a difficult one to deal with, since during the day (as already mentioned) the caterpillars crowd together in vast numbers, and a handful may therefore be lifted at once.

Family SPHINGIDÆ.

13. Chærocampa alecto, *Linn.*

CHÆROCAMPA ALECTO.

THE SPHINX MOTH.

References.—*Hampson, Fauna Brit. Ind. (Moths), Vol. I, 85.*

Green Caterpillars.

332. It is indeed rare that the larva of this Sphinx moth does any damage to tea. One case only is on record, on the garden of Mr. J. Begg, of Moriani, Assam. It is occasionally found, however, all over the districts, and is a pale green smooth hairless caterpillar, about 2 inches long, with an erect horn (so-called) on the tail and with circular spots on each section of the body. When found, it should certainly be removed and destroyed.

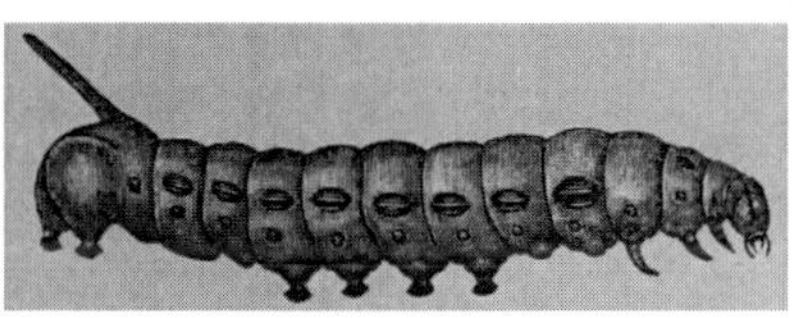

FIG. 11.—CATERPILLAR OF CHÆROCAMPA ALECTO.

(From drawing by G. Watt.)

Family NOTODONTIDÆ.

14. Stauropus alternus, *Wlk.*

STAUROPUS ALTERNUS.

THE LOBSTER CATERPILLAR.

THE LOBSTER CATERPILLAR.

Found in Assam, Darjeeling, and Ceylon.

References.—*Hampson, Fauna Brit. Ind. (Moths), Vol. I, 149; Green, Insect Pests of Tea Plant, 25; Bamber, Chem. Agri. Tea, 244; Indian Mus. Notes, Vol. II, 153; Cotes, Tea Insects, 10; Circular, Roy. Bot. Gardens, Ceylon, Series I, No. 19, p. 265.*

The Lepidoptera (Notodontidæ).

THE LOBSTER CATERPILLAR.

333. ***History.***—Although it cannot be said that this insect has hitherto been a really serious pest of Indian Tea it has been noticed a sufficient number of times feeding on the leaves of the tea bush to make it advisable to draw attention to it and occasionally has done very considerable damage. Mr. Bamber remarks, for instance, that it is "said to attack the foliage of tea and cocoa in Ceylon, also seen in Darjeeling." In 1895 one of the authors (G. W.) found it at Moabund and Amguri in Assam,—and it was there said to do a considerable amount of mischief,—but since that time little or nothing has been heard of it as a tea pest till the present year (1902), when it has again appeared badly at Moabund. This species may therefore be accepted as one of those curious cases of spasmodic development that are of so frequent occurrence. An insect suddenly assumes alarming proportions, and as mysteriously disappears again, for a number of years.

Sudden Development.

334. ***Description.****—The caterpillar is of a dark red brown colour with a pale line along the back, and streaks of grey on several of the sections (somites). The hind section (somite) is swollen and carried over the back, and has two processes which look like antennæ from the end, but which are really prolegs. In general colour the creature may be said to have the tint of a fallen leaf, except for the rich deep chestnut velvety patches and

Leaf Mimicry.

FIG. 12.—THE LOBSTER CATERPILLAR, COCOON, AND MOTH. (After Cotes.)

* The figure given of the caterpillars, taken from a drawing by Mr. F. Moore, does not seem to be quite correct as applied to all the Assam caterpillars, but very closely resembles them.

The Lobster Caterpillar.

bands of white, which are not unlike openings or perforations in such a leaf. This appearance probably acts as a great protection from caterpillar-feeding birds. During the day it sits perfectly still and it feeds in the evening, when the leaves from the apex down to the base are eaten, and large curiously formed excreta are deposited on the leaves. By this means the presence of the caterpillar may be detected.

THE LOBSTER CATER-PILLAR.

Coloration and Altitude.

335. ***Remedy.***—Hand-picking off a large caterpillar like this should be a comparatively simple matter, and unless the pest takes a great extension, will probably be quite sufficient to keep it in check.

Family SYNTOMIDÆ.

15. Syntomis cyssea, *Cram.*

SYNTOMIS CYSSEA.

References.—*Hampson, Fauna Brit. Ind. (Moths), Vol. I, 213.*

336. The caterpillar of this very plentiful Indian moth have occasionally been found eating the leaves of the tea plant. It can hardly be called a pest.

Family ZYGÆNIDÆ.

16. Pintea ferrea, *Wlk.*

PINTEA FERREA.

References.—*Hampson, Fauna Brit. Ind. (Moths), Vol. I, 213.*

337. This is also a common moth, the larva of which has occasionally been found to feed on tea. Practically no importance need be attached to it.

17. Heterusia cingala, *Moore.*

HETERUSIA CINGALA.

THE "RED SLUG."

THE RED SLUG.

SEE PLATE VI, No. 3.

References.—*Hampson, Fauna Brit. Ind. (Moths), Vol. I, p. 262; Report by E. E. Green, Planting Opinion, 1899, p. 339; Indian Museum Notes, Vol. IV, 279; Vol. V, 16; Circular, Roy. Bot. Gardens, Ceylon, Series I, No. 19 (100).*

Found in Assam, Cachar, Darjeeling, and Ceylon.

338. ***History.***—In the first edition of this work a note was made (*para. 414*) of a caterpillar collected at Ligri Pukri, and at Nigriting, which at that time could not be named. Since that report was written, the insect in question has multiplied so considerably in Ceylon as to amount to a serious pest, and has been reported as doing considerable damage both in the Nowgong and Jorhat districts of Assam, in Cachar, and in Darjeeling. The following description is reproduced from Mr. Green's circular on the pest in Ceylon.

The Lepidoptera (Zygænidæ).

THE RED SLUG.

Mr. Green's Description.

339. ***Description.***—"Caterpillar broad and comparatively short. Brownish red to bright brick red. With six longitudinal series of small tubercles (*see Plate VI, No. 3 c*), on the summits of which are two or three short hairs and one or two pores which secrete a globule of clear viscid fluid, giving a dewy appearance to the living caterpillar. There are the normal number of legs, six on the front and ten on the hinder part of the body. Length of full-grown caterpillar slightly over one inch."

Cocoon.

"The cocoon is formed in the fold of a leaf. It is tough and closely woven, of a pinkish straw colour. (*See Plate VI, No. 3, d.*) It contains a creamy white chrysalis. Caterpillars that formed their cocoons in my breeding cage on January 2nd emerged as moths on the 22nd of the same month."

Moth.

"Moth: fore-wing black with metallic green reflections, with a creamy white patch at the base, a broad creamy white bar just before the middle, and some creamy white spots towards the extremity. Hind-wing, peacock blue suffused with black, with a very broad pale primrose-yellow band across the middle, and some yellowish spots towards the extremity. Anterior half of the body peacock blue and black, posterior half bright yellow. In the male the antennæ are broadly, in the female narrowly, feathered. The expanded wings measure $1\frac{1}{8}$ inch in the male and $1\frac{1}{2}$ inch in the female. (*See Plate VI, No. 3, a and b.*)

Moth flies by day.

"The moth flies in the daytime, and might easily be mistaken for a butterfly on account of its bright colours. When handled, it emits some frothy matter which has a strong pungent smell (very like that of the English lady-bird beetle), which is thought to afford the insect protection by making it distasteful to birds, etc.

"The caterpillars were observed in large numbers in November, in the following January, and again in April.* I have been unable to determine the exact length of the caterpillar stage, but the complete life-history of the insect appears to occupy about ten weeks.

"These caterpillars have no stinging hairs, and may be handled without any unpleasant results."

340. ***Depredations.***—"On some estates" in Ceylon "the attack appears to have been very severe. Acres of tea bushes were com-

* It must be remembered that these dates refer to Ceylon. In Assam the caterpillar is at its worst early in July and in September.

PLATE VI. (*To face Page 186.*)

1. Euproctis latifascia (p. 218).
a. Caterpillar; *b.* Male, *c.* Female Moth.

2. Prodenia littoralis (p. 222).
a. Caterpillar; *b.* Moth; *c.* Chrysalis.
(From Indian Museum Notes.)

3. Heterusia cingala (p. 185).
a. Female, *b.* Male Moth; *c.* Caterpillar; *d.* Chrysalis.
(From Indian Museum Notes.)

pletely defoliated, and the affected fields were said to have looked as if they had been burnt." * THE RED SLUG.

341. ***Remedy.***—"The caterpillars should be collected and destroyed whenever seen, together with cocoons and even more especially the moths, which are brilliant and easily seen. And all dead leaves should be swept up from below the bushes and burned. The caterpillars are fortunately subject to the attacks of a parasitic fly (**Exorista heterusiæ**, *Coquillet*). This fly fastens its eggs upon the back of the caterpillar, the young maggots penetrate the body of their host and feed on its contents, taking care not to touch any vital spot until they are ready to undergo their own transformations. The diseased caterpillar has usually sufficient strength to spin its cocoon but collapses without turning into a chrysalis. The sudden disappearance of this pest, after reaching its climax, is usually due to the work of this useful parasite, though sometimes a bacterial disease is still more effectual in the work of extermination." Parasitic Fly.

LII.—Bag-worms, Faggot-worms, etc. BAG WORMS.

Family PSYCHIDÆ.

342. This family of moths gives, in the caterpillar stage, perhaps the most dangerous of all lepidopterous pests. There are many species found in every Indian district, and also in Ceylon. Most of these have been identified. Identification.

The bag-worms differ from all the other moths already described, in that the caterpillar forms around itself a small house by fastening together fragments of leaves, twigs or other portions of the tea plant. It thus, snail-like, carries its house on its back and pops inside on the slightest alarm. When it has reached its full growth, the bag or bundle of faggots is tied up to a branch. The worm then inverts itself so as to bring its head where its tail was formerly, and there remains till the time comes for it to escape as a winged moth. But as a rule, only the males become winged, and the females continue within their little houses. The males come and mate with them and the eggs are laid within the house, and thereafter the female dies. Peculiarities. Females have no wings.

* While the foregoing was in the press, a good deal more has been seen of the caterpillar and moth than hitherto in Assam, where thousands of the former were caught daily on some estates, and the moth was found flying in very large numbers from 4 to 6 P.M.

BAG-WORMS.

As a rule, there are only a few males and many females, so that insects of this family are rarely seen on the wing. Perhaps of a hundred cocoons that may be preserved in a breeding cage, so as to procure the males, only two or three will be obtained.

Eggs.

343. It is therefore most important not to regard the dead-looking old bags or faggot-houses as past any danger. They may be literally packed full of eggs from which a large progeny of young caterpillars would most certainly come forth. We have just recently found a whole colony of caterpillars just hatched in one of these bags in November in Sylhet. All should be collected and destroyed. Mr. Green, in a letter to hand, remarks what will be seen, from the description below, to be our experience also, that the smaller and more obscure members of this family are the most destructive as tea pests. He also says, "From the fact that the females are wingless, it is evident that these pests can only spread in the caterpillar stage. It is probable that the very young larvæ are distributed by attaching themselves to the coolies' clothing, or they may be carried for some distance by the wind. Otherwise it would require a very considerable time before a large field could be affected from a given centre."

CLANIA CRAMERI. THE FAGGOT-WORM.

18. Clania (Eumeta) crameri, *Westw.*

THE FAGGOT-WORM. "THE STICK INSECT."

SEE PLATE VII, No. 4.

References.—*Hampson, Fauna British India (Moths), Vol. I, 291; Jour. Agri.-Horti. Soc. Ind., IV. n. s. Proc., 29th May 1873, XXV; June 26th, XXXI; 21st August, XXXIV; Vol. V, Proc., 30th July 1874, XXXVI; Peal, in Tea Cyclopædia, 36; Green, Insect Pests of tea, 3—8, Figure 5; Bamber, Chem. and Agri Tea, 243; Indian Museum Notes, Vol. I, 204; II, 157; III, 133; IV, 17—18, 41; Cotes, Ins. and Mites. etc., 14; Planting Opinion. 1809, p. 623; Green, Circular Roy. Bot. Gard., Ceylon, Vol. I, (900), p. 260.*

Found in all districts.

344. ***History.***—This insect has been known since the very early days of tea, and was actually recorded in 1873 both from Assam and the Darjeeling Terai. In Ceylon it was common on coffee before the introduction of tea, and it must be remembered that it is an exceedingly common species in the Indian jungles.

345. ***Description.***—It seems hardly necessary to say more than that this is the common faggot-worm of the tea districts. The

THE FAGGOT-WORM.

caterpillar nips off short lengths of young twigs and fastens these together parallel to each other, each usually extending the whole length of the house. They vary considerably in size, and run from $1\frac{1}{2}$ to 3 inches in length and $\frac{1}{2}$ to 1 inch in diameter. (*See Plate VII, No. 4, a, b.*) As with other psychids, when feeding the caterpillar protrudes the head and thorax from the case, but on the slightest alarm it withdraws into its house and closes the mouth of the faggot case with an operculum-like lid, which is hinged to the top. The grub itself has no protecting mantle, as seen when extended out of the faggot house in walking or while feeding. We have often bred out the male moth, which is an inconspicuous brown one, about 1 inch in span across the wings. (*See Plate VII, No. 4, d.*)

Lid to close Faggot House.

346. ***Depredations.***—This caterpillar, so long as it confined itself to eating the tea leaf, or even cutting off the young twigs to make its house, might not be considered to do much harm, but when it attacks the bark its damage is much more serious. This is, however, usually its habit and we have seen bushes in which every stem was barked almost from top to bottom by this pest. Luckily it does not spread fast. Like most of the psychid caterpillars, it does most damage in India in the early season, say from January to May.

Eats Bark.

347. ***Remedy.***—The only cure is to collect the faggot-cases and burn them. It should be recollected that the female is a wingless creature that never leaves her house, so that old and dead-looking cases, as well as those seen moving about, should be collected, since the former may contain the eggs. Mr. Cotes very properly remarks that "the most remarkable feature about the caterpillars is their extraordinary vitality. Indeed, they will withstand an amount of rough handling which would be fatal to the larvæ of almost any other group of moths. The point is an important one in considering how best to dispose of what are brought in by coolies." All bags collected should in fact be burnt in the boiler fire.

Collection of Faggot-cases.

19. Clania (?) holmesi, *Watt.*

CLANIA HOLMESI.

THE SPIRAL FAGGOT-WORM.

THE SPIRAL FAGGOT-WORM.

348. ***History.***—This insect, closely allied to that last discussed, seems first to have been recorded by one of the Authors (G. W.) in the former edition of this work. It had then been noticed in Assam:

Wide distribution.

THE SPIRAL FAGGOT-WORM.

we have since collected it in Cachar, Sylhet, and the Terai—and to show that it is by no means confined to the tea districts, it has been sent to us growing on a totally different plant (**Flacourtia sp.**) from the Bankura district of Bengal.

349. ***Description.***—The largest samples do not as a rule exceed $1\frac{1}{2}$ by $\frac{1}{2}$ inch in size. The little sticks of which the case is built are cut uniformly to lengths of from $\frac{3}{8}$ to $\frac{1}{4}$ inch. The longer ones are used at the lower extremity and the shorter at the upper, placed parallel to each other, but slightly sloping. They are across the main axis of the larval case, so that they form a complete spiral of four coils. When extended out of its spirally constructed house, the little yellow caterpillar with one brown spot on each of the body segments is seen to be surrounded by a large open mantle. This consists of a dull grey silken membrane, studded with chestnut-coloured minute specks. There seems to be one brood per annum, though this is doubtful.

Short twigs used.

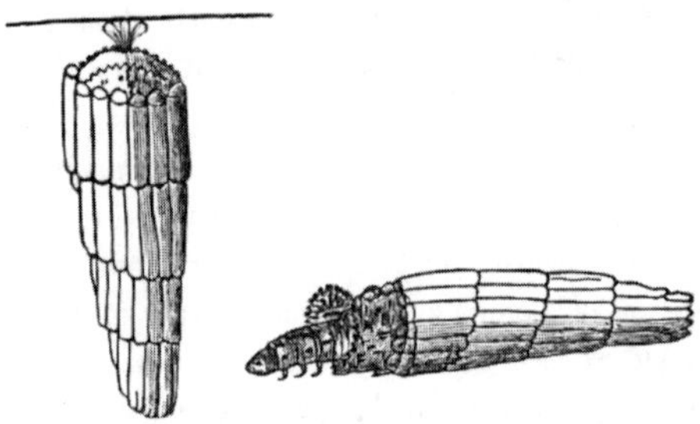

FIG. 13.—THE SPIRAL FAGGOT-WORM.
(From drawing by G. Watt.)

Though we have repeatedly attempted to obtain the moth of this caterpillar, all efforts have failed to date, probably owing to the fact that we do not certainly know the breeding season in India.

Collection and Destruction.

350. ***Depredations and Remedy.***—Nothing can be added to what was said under the previous species. It works similarly and should be dealt with in like manner.

CLANIA VARIEGATA. THE BAG-WORM.

20. Clania variegata, *Snell.*

THE BAG-WORM.

SEE PLATE VII, NOS. 2 AND 3.

References.—*Hampson, Fauna Brit. Ind. (Moths), Vol. I, 291; Dudgeon, Indian Mus. Notes, Vol. II, 63—67, 157; III (pt. 3), 111—112; IV, 41; Cotes, Tea Insects, 15; Planting Opinion, 1899, 623.*

PLATE VII. (*To face Page 191.*)

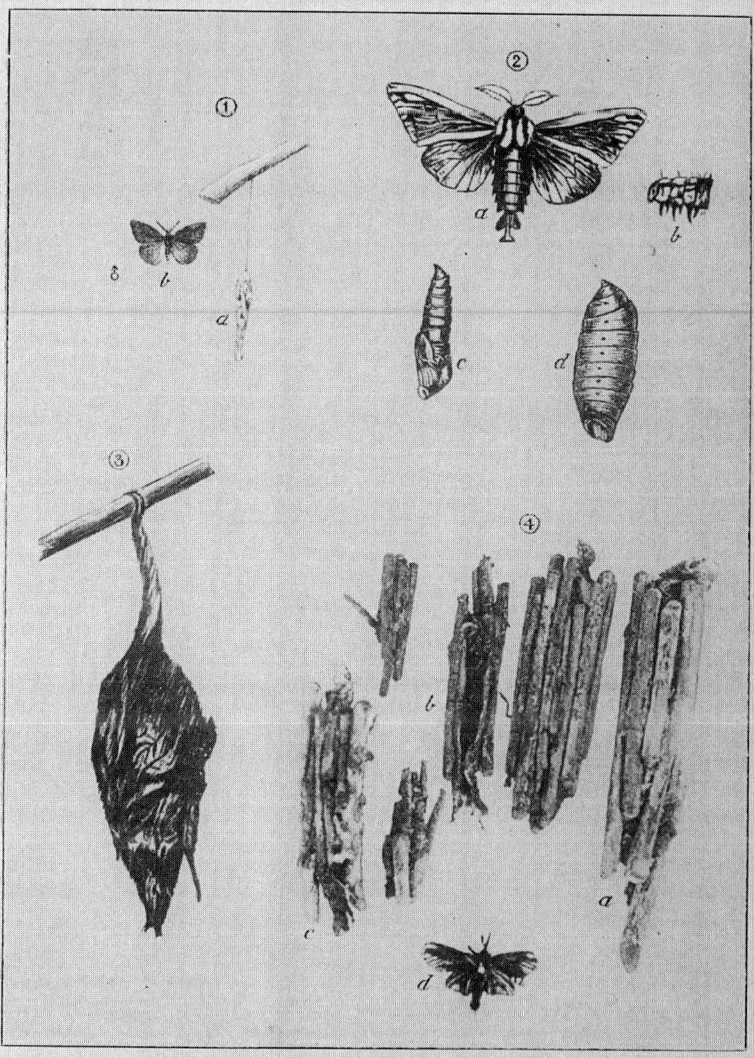

1. Acanthopsyche subteralbata (p. 196).
a. Larval Case; *b.* Moth.
(From Indian Museum Notes.)

2 & 3. Clania variegata (p. 190). The Bag Worm.
2. *a.* Moth; *b.* Head of Caterpillar; *c.* Chrysalis; *d.* Female Moth.
(After Dudgeon.)

4. Clania crameri (p. 188). The Faggot Worm.
a. Larval Cases; *b.* Larval Case, split open; *c.* Case, after emergence of Moth; *d.* Moth.
(From Photograph by H. H. Mann.)

The Bag-worm.

THE BAG-WORM

Found in all districts.

351. ***History.***—This species of psychid is a common one in India, and repeatedly in the older days of tea, the presence of what was apparently this pest was put on record (see Peal, *Tea Cyclopædia,* 36). Mr. Dudgeon, however, in a most admirable paper published in 1891, fully described the life-history of the insect as it occurs on *sal* (Shorea robusta) trees, and since that time little more has been discovered, save that it has been found to exist on almost every garden in the tea districts.

Description

352. ***Description.***—During the caterpillar stage this insect has generally one or two entire leaves, and perhaps a twig or two loosely attached to it *throughout their length* and thus resting flat on the surface of the bag. (*See Plate VII, No. 3.*) The caterpillars usually leave the egg about the end of March or the beginning of April in the hills or a little earlier in the plains. "This is the first brood of the year, but the others do not follow in any regularity, and it has been impossible to ascertain how many broods there are, as the larvæ and pupæ are found in all stages throughout the rains." (*Dudgeon.*) When they first come out, they are only $\frac{1}{16}$ inch long, reddish brown in colour. When mature, the larval case is usually about $2\frac{1}{2}$ to 3 inches long, and when the caterpillar is walking or feeding, it is seen to have a protecting silken mantle within which it withdraws on being disturbed, the mantle being gathered together around the mouth of the bag. It has no lid such as is possessed by the Faggot-worm. The head of the caterpillar is shown in *Plate VII, No. 2, b.* to the extent it is protended from the case. The same plate shows the winged male (*a*), the male chrysalis (*c*), and the mature female (*d*), the last of which is practically nothing more than a bag of eggs.

Eggs laid in March

353. ***Depredations.***—The work of this insect is quite similar to that of the faggot-worm, and it shows just as great a tendency to go for the bark as that insect, and is hence just as dangerous.

Collection of Bag-worms

354. ***Remedy.***—There is but one thing that can be done, namely to collect all the bag-worms found and to destroy them. If this be systematically accomplished, there need be little fear of the occasion ever arising when more severe measures would be indicated, but it requires careful and close watching, especially in the spring, to prevent them doing considerable damage.

The Lepidoptera (Psychidæ).

AMATISSA CONSORTA.

THE BASKET WORM

21. Amatissa consorta, *Templ.*

THE BASKET WORM, *Barota* (KANGRA). *Batea banda puk* (HOUSE-FORMING CATERPILLAR) ASSAM.

SEE PLATE VIII, No. 1.

References.—*Hampson, Fauna Brit. Ind. (Moths), Vol. I, 292; Jour. Agri.-Horti. Soc. Ind., Vol. V (1877) xxxi; Tea Cyclopedia, 55; Ind. Mus. Notes, Vol. III, 111; Cotes, Tea Insects, 16; Planter's Gazette, 1900, 235.*

Found in practically all districts.

Found in Assam and Kangra.

355. ***History.***—Certain vague references probably to this insect occur in the early literature of tea, but it was not till 1893 that definite records of its occurrence as a tea pest in Darjeeling were made by Mr. Cotes. It is, however, by no means confined to Darjeeling, but was found in Kangra by one of the authors (G. W.) during November 1894 in the young active stage, and in Assam during 1895, especially in the Sibsagar district. It is in fact an extremely common species.

Caterpillars.

356. ***Description.***—The larval cases will readily be recognised from the photograph on *Plate VIII*, the figure given by Mr. Cotes certainly not representing the usual form. The caterpillar commences its career, after emerging from the eggs, by covering itself with a few minute pieces of tea leaf, attached by one end to the leaf. (*Plate VIII, a.*) They are at first conical little houses standing on a flattened base and not more than ¼ inch in size. At this stage they are very dangerous and spread all over the bushes in such numbers that they may be said to ultimately ruin the entire foliage of a bush, and then take to the bark. As they grow larger they seem to be less voracious, and the bulk of them disappear by some means or other. The full-grown case is about 1½ inches long and nearly as broad, and is clothed with tea leaves each united by its lower extremity, the upper end being free and spreading or curling outwards from the bag (*Plate VIII, b.*).

Cocoons covered with leaves.

Appears at isolated places.

357. ***Depredations.***—It is somewhat striking to see how often this insect suddenly appears at isolated points over a good part of the area of an estate. The chrysalid cases hung up in the bushes give birth to a visitation of caterpillars in very large numbers. These completely destroy every leaf of that and of the next one or two bushes and then disappear for a time, the nucleus of a future generation being carried to some little distance before being hung up in the way indicated.

PLATE VIII. (*To face Page 192.*)

1. Amatissa consorta (p. 192). The Basket Worm.
a Young Larval Cases; *b*. Full-sized Larval Cases.
(From Photograph by H. H. Mann.)

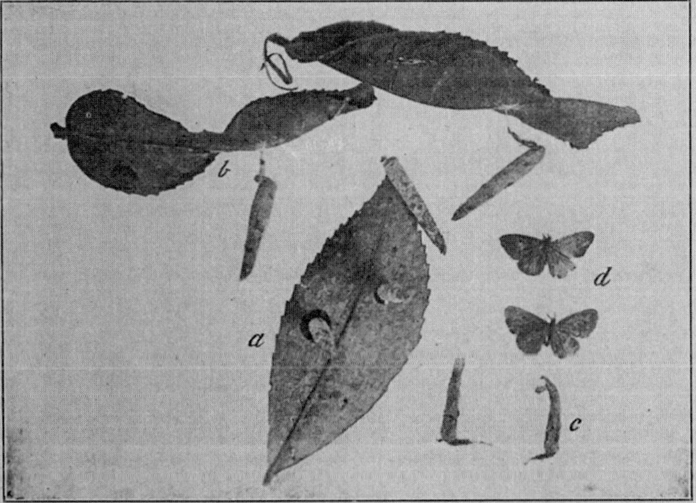

2. Acanthopsyche snelleni (p. 195). The Leaf Perforating Psychid.
a. Larval Cases on Leaf; *b*. Chrysalids; *c*. Cases, after emergence of Moth; *d*. Moth.
(From Photograph by H. H. Mann.)

The Basket Worm.

It has been supposed by some that the bite of the caterpillar is poisonous to the plant. One writer says, "His bite must be very poisonous, as I have seen a stem about 9 inches in length and from which he had only taken a very small piece of bark, rot completely off." The evidence on this point is not, however, in any sense sufficient to render this poisonous bite certain, or even probable. Occasionally the insect multiplies to such an extent as to seriously damage a plantation. One writer states that to his knowledge, for instance (see *Tea Cyclopedia*), "several hundreds of bushes had been killed and many thousands attacked. All hands were called out and work stopped, and these little cages or cocoons containing the caterpillars picked off." "The insect is generally seen hard at work in April."

THE BASKET WORM.

Bite said to be poisonous.

358. ***Remedy.***—Should the insect here dealt with appear in a garden, the proper way to deal with it is to at once get dry straw and fire the one or two bushes seen to be invaded with the countless hordes of the minute caterpillars. Having done this, a careful search within a radius of, say, 20 to 30 feet all round should be made for any of the large leaf-encased basket worms. These should be systematically picked off and destroyed. Burning the bushes in this way, when only a few plants are badly affected, is probably the quickest and safest method of dealing with the pest, as it is extremely difficult to get all the multitude of small larvæ picked off by hand in the case of a bad attack. This hand-picking is, however, the only other alternative.

A spring pest.

Prompt treatment necessary.

22. Acanthopsyche reidi, *Watt.*

ACANTHOPSYCHE REIDI.

THE LIMPET CATERPILLAR.

THE LIMPET CATERPILLAR.

References.—*Jour. Agri.-Horti. Soc. Ind., Vol. V (1878), p. xxxvi; Bamber, Chem. Agri. Tea, p. 243* (?).

Found seriously in Upper Assam; occasionally in Cachar.

359. ***History.***—This is the most serious of the psychid pests of tea in India, but except for the above references, which are only doubtfully applicable, it seems to have never been described until one of the authors (G. W.) found it on some gardens in Sibsagar in 1895. Since that time the extent of its ravages has apparently extended considerably, and now includes several places in the Dibrugarh district, as well as in Sibsagar.

In Upper Assam.

The Lepidoptera (Psychidæ).

THE LIMPET CATER-PILLAR.

360. ***Description.***—The larval cases of this species might almost be described as small thorns considerably under an inch long, of a dull grey colour, pointed at the apex and slightly and suddenly widened below into a circular sucker-like mouth. They do not carry fragments of leaves or sticks attached to them, but are perfectly smooth. These caterpillars attack the upper surface of the leaf and eat circular spots about an eighth of an inch in diameter, each of which has a tiny speck of epidermis left in the centre. They move from place to place until they reduce the leaf to a mass of thin brown membraneous blotches that correspond to the dead under epidermis. But the leaf is not perforated right through. The time occupied to eat the tissue of the leaf from each circular spot is about five minutes. After the leaves and the buds have all been destroyed, they attack the bark and similarly eat away circular spots all over it. When seen on the twigs and branches, they can hardly be recognised since they are of the identical colour and shape of abortive twigs. Indeed the bush, when invaded with this pest, looks like a thorny plant; it has a countless multitude of these most destructive creatures all over it, and within a few weeks it is damaged almost beyond repair without

Description.

Method of attack.

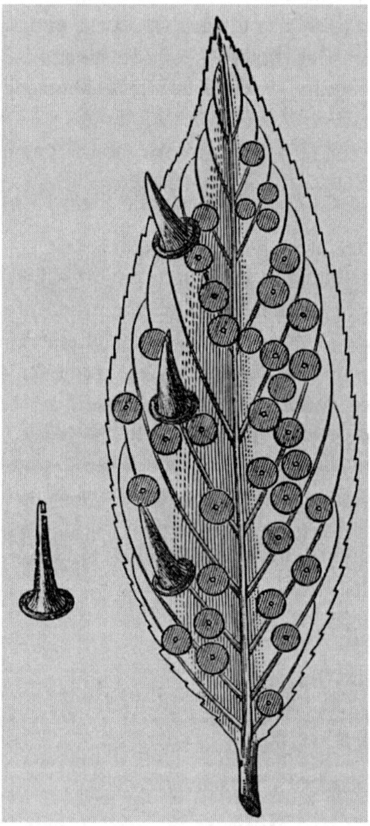

FIG. 14.—THE LIMPET CATERPILLAR ATTACKING THE *upper surface* OF THE LEAF.

(From sketch by G. Watt.)

very heavy pruning. We have not as yet succeeded in breeding the moth of this species. THE LIMPET CATER-PILLAR.

361. ***Depredations.***—Occasionally when this pest is allowed to spread, it becomes exceedingly serious. An attack is on record where on a garden in Sibsagar every leaf and twig on a block of 30 acres was destroyed in the manner described above. Often there are as many as 20 or 30 of the thorn-like cases on a single leaf. At a garden in the Dibrugarh District it made its appearance in January 1901, and continued practically to the end of April,—and then we were informed that no less than 4,000 "*haziris*" had been expended in getting rid of it by picking off the insects and affected leaves. In bad cases the bushes are literally grey coloured through the multitude of larval cases distributed over everywhere on leaf, twig, and stem. Depredation in Spring.

362. ***Remedy.***—Where the amount of the insect present is small, it is possible to employ children to pick off the larval cases; where they get beyond this stage—and they are never to be allowed to do so—there is little else to do than to fire the bushes affected, and if necessary the plot. Remedies.

23. Acanthopsyche snelleni, *Heyl.*

ACANTHOPSYCHE SNELLENI.

THE LEAF-PERFORATING PSYCHID.

THE LEAF-PERFORATING PSYCHID.

SEE PLATE VIII, No. 2.

References.—*Hampson, Fauna Brit. Ind. (Moths), Vol. I, 296; Bamber, Chem. Agri. of Tea, 243; Indian Mus. Notes, Vol. II, 12-13, 157; III, 25; Cotes, Tea Insects, 17.*

Found in all Indian plains districts.

363. ***History.***—It is very probable that Mr. Bamber alluded to this insect as "Babula sp.," but we cannot be certain, as he says it "builds for itself a *conical case* from the epidermis of the leaves on which it lives." This would also be applicable to the limpet caterpillar above mentioned, but, at any rate, the present species is common enough over all the plains districts of Assam and Bengal where tea is grown. Very frequent in Assam.

364. ***Description.***—The insect forms a nearly cylindrical larval case, which does not widen at the mouth (*Plate VII, a*). This case, when full grown, is an inch long, coarse in texture with a few irregular patches or fragments of leaf firmly woven into it. When passing into the cocoon, it draws out of the inside of the case a silken thread

THE LEAF-PERFORATING PSYCHID.

about ¾ inch in length and sufficiently rigid that the cocoon is suspended in a slightly slanting manner (*Plate VIII, b*). The male moth (*Plate VIII, d*) is dark brown or almost black, and has no distinctive colour markings.

Operates on the under-side of Leaf.

365. ***Depredations.***—The insect nowhere occurs at present in such abundance as to cause anxiety. It operates on the under-side of the leaf, and eats circular holes that are gradually widened until they may be ¾ inch in diameter. It is by no means confined to tea as a food, and feeds on many jungle plants in Assam.

366. ***Remedy.***—Hand-picking the caterpillar-cases and cocoons seems the only cure; this should, however, be done systematically, as the insect might become a serious pest.

Other less important species of psychid caterpillars attacking tea, closely related to the foregoing, are as follows :—

ACANTHOPSYCHE BIPARS.

24. Acanthopsyche bipars, *Wlk.*

References.—*Indian Mus. Notes, Vol. II, 157; Vol. III, Pt. IV, 17; Hampson, Fauna Brit. Ind. (Moths), Vol. I, 293.*

Found in Darjeeling.

367. This insect was found in Darjeeling by Mr. Dudgeon. He noticed "that it completely strips the bushes it feeds on, and often kills them by taking off the bark to make its case." It has not been recorded from any other district, and we have never collected it.

ACANTHOPSYCHE SUBTERALBATA.

25. Acanthopsyche subteralbata, *Hmpsn.*

SEE PLATE VII, NO. 1.

References.—*Ind. Agriculturist, Dec. 1, 1896; Journ. Agri.-Horti. Soc. Ind., 1896, 465; Indian Museum Notes, Vol. IV (1899), 118.*

Found in Chittagong, Cachar, and Ceylon.

368. This insect has been recorded to do a good deal of damage in Chittagong where it first appeared on *gold-mohur* trees (**Poinciana regia**), and afterwards systematically defoliated the tea bushes. It also does damage in Ceylon. We have recently noticed a *gold-mohur* tree all but completely cleared of leaves in Cachar. The plate shows the case which it forms, as well as the moth, both natural size. The moth has a bluish grey tinge on the under-sides of the wings.

ACANTHOPSYCHE PLAGIOPHLEPS.

26. Acanthopsyche plagiophleps, *Hmpsn.*

Found in Ceylon and Kangra.

369. Found in the Kangra Valley (Dudgeon) and in Ceylon (Green). It occasionally does considerable damage. The larval case is suspended by a long silken thread, and is covered with minute fragments of tea leaves, and is about ⅓ to ¾ inch long.

The Conical Psychid.

27. Acanthopsyche rhabdophora, *Hmpsn.* ACANTHOPSYCHE RHABDOPHORA.

Found in Ceylon.

370. This species is found in Ceylon and possibly also in the Kangra Valley, and sometimes injures the tea bushes. The larval case is ½ inch long, and is formed of "comminuted fragments of vegetable matter, that of the male rougher and suspended by a long thread, whilst the case of the female is smoother and without a thread." (*Hmpsn.*)

28. Acanthopsyche alstoni (?) *n. sp.* ACANTHOPSYCHE ALSTONI.

Found in the Duars.

371. This is the smallest species of all, found doing damage at Sylee, Duars, in November 1900. The larval case is less than ¼ inch long, suspended by a thread. The insect acts on the under-side of the leaf and perforates it into a mass of minute perforations like shot. It has not been noticed elsewhere. We have not yet succeeded in obtaining the moth of this species.

29. Acanthopsyche sp. ACANTHOPSYCHE SP.

Found in Assam.

372. Found in Jaipur, Assam, in 1895. It might be considered as a much larger form of **Acanthopsyche snelleni,** the larval case being 1½ inches long, and bearing a few short twigs loosely attached. The caterpillar, when feeding, is seen to have a double mantle, one part within the other. Whether it is a form of one of the species previously named or a separate one has not yet been determined, as we have so far failed to breed out the moth.

30. Acanthopsyche sp. ACANTHOPSYCHE SP.

Found in Assam.

373. This is a still larger species than the last one named, being often 2 inches long, and having a few fragments of leaves and flower-buds attached to the cases. The caterpillar, when feeding, is seen to have only one protecting mantle, and that very irregular in form. It was found at Moabund, Nigriting, and in Golaghat (Assam).

31. Psyche assamica (?) *Watt.* PSYCHE ASSAMICA.

THE CONICAL PSYCHID. THE CONICAL PSYCHID.

References.—*Hampson, Fauna Brit. Ind. (Moths), Vol. I (account of genus),* 297—300.

Found in Assam, Cachar, and the Terai.

374. ***History.***—Previous to the visit of one of the authors (G. W.) to Assam in 1895, there is no record of this species having been found there. It was then, however, found in almost every part of the Brahmaputra Valley. We have since found it in other districts, notably in the Terai.

The Lepidoptera (Psychidæ).

THE CONICAL PSYCHID.

375. ***Description.***—The case of this insect might be described as an example of a very short and greatly dilated limpet caterpillar case with a few fragments of leaf and bark adhering. It attaches itself in the same sucker-like fashion and has for this purpose a soft disc-like rim surrounding the mouth. Within this a diaphragm stretches across which is perforated near the middle by a small opening through which the head of the caterpillar escapes when feeding. The accompanying rough sketch, natural size, represents a leaf showing two of the caterpillars feeding on one side of the leaf; several patches representing portions of the leaf already devoured, on the other; also a pupal case from which the moth has escaped appears suspended from the leaf. On the margin have been given a larval-case (*a*) to show the sucker-like rim, the diaphragm across the mouth, and the little hole through which the caterpillar comes when feeding; (*b*) the chrysalis-case showing the manner in which the diaphragm is drawn out making the structure biconic when hung up in

Similar to Limpet Caterpillar.

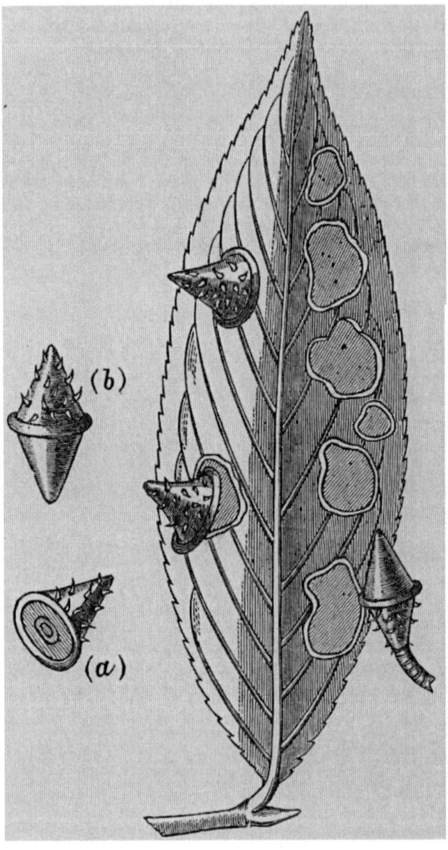

FIG 15.—THE CONICAL PSYCHID ATTACKING THE *under-surface* OF THE LEAF.
(From sketch by G. Watt.)

Attacks under-side of Leaf.

The Conical Psychid.

the resting stage. The insect is very closely similar to **Psyche albipes** found in Ceylon and Cachar, and when the moth is obtained, it may prove to be identical with it. **THE CONICAL PSYCHID.**

376. ***Depredations.***—The effect of this caterpillar on the bush is very similar to that of the Limpet Caterpillar. But there is one curiously dissimilar feature. While the limpet caterpillar operates on the upper surface and eats the tissue down to the under epidermis, this insect (which for convenience has been called the Conical Psychid) acts in the opposite direction. It eats the *under epidermis and tissue of the leaf* through to the upper epidermis. By neither of these insects, however, is the leaf perforated through. There is also another point of difference. By the limpet caterpillar perfectly circular holes are eaten, each independent of the other; by the conical caterpillar the portion eaten is gradually widened into irregularly shaped patches—in other words, the insect eats its way forward instead of moving from spot to spot. **Effect on Bush.**

This then is a more difficult pest to recognise than even the limpet caterpillar, since it can only be seen on the under-side of the leaves. But in both these instances pale yellow spots all over the leaf, corresponding to remaining epidermis, are visible enough, and should instantly suggest the presence of either of these Psychids. **Difficult to recognise.**

377. ***Remedy.***—The moment this or any of the smaller psychid caterpillars are seen, children should be at once sent to the affected bushes, and every specimen met with carefully picked off and destroyed. If they get beyond this method, the bushes must be fired, but if this becomes a necessity, it is due to neglect to check the advance of these enemies in the earlier stages. **Remedies.**

32. Psyche albipes, *Moore.* **PSYCHE ALBIPES.**

THE "SMALL BAG-WORM." **THE SMALL BAG WORM.**

References.—*Hampson, Fauna Brit. Ind. (Moths), Vol. I, 298; Green, Circ. Roy. Bot. Gard., Ceylon, 1900, 262.*

378. This is the Ceylon representative of the last-mentioned and is possibly identical with it. Mr. Green says with regard to it, "It is this species that gives most trouble on tea estates. The caterpillar lives in a conical greyish case with a few fragments of bark or leaves attached to the outside. The male moth is dark brown with white feet . . . It has a wing expanse of ¾ inch. The female moth is a whitish fleshy grub-like insect, merely a bag of eggs. It remains concealed within the larval case. This insect has frequently been reported as destructive to tea plants in new clearings in the Kelani Valley districts. After defoliating the plants, it does still further mischief by gnawing off the bark.

The Lepidoptera (Cossidæ).

PSYCHE VITREA.

Hand-picking is the only practical remedy. Plants in which the bark has been eaten away must be cut back below the injured part."

33. **Psyche vitrea**, *Hmpsn.*

References.—*Hampson, Fauna Brit. Ind. (Moths), Vol. I, 299.*

379. This species, which forms a shiny grey long narrow larval case, about one inch by ⅛ inch in size, has been reported as eating tea in the Kelani Valley, Ceylon. It was not known in India until recently, but has been found in 1902 by Mr. C. B. Antram in Cachar.

CHALIA DOUBLEDAYI.

34. **Chalia doubledayi**, *Westw.*

References.—*Moore, Lepid. Ceylon, Plate 118.*

379*a*. This species, which forms a larval case of longitudinally arranged twigs, has done considerable damage as a defoliator of tea in the Kelani Valley, Ceylon.

LIII. Wood-boring Caterpillar.

Family COSSIDÆ.

ZEUZERA COFFEÆ.

35. **Zeuzera coffeæ**, *Nietner.*

THE RED BORER.

THE RED BORER.

SEE PLATE IX, No. 1.

References.—*Hampson, Fauna Brit. Ind. (Moths), Vol. I, 312; Jour. Agri.-Horti. Soc. Ind., IV (1873), XV (1874) X; S. E. Peal, Tea Cyclopedia, 35; Nietner, Enemies of the Coffee Tree, 14; Bidie, report on the ravages of the coffee-borer; E. E. Green, Insect Pests of the Tea Plant, 8—12; Bamber, Chem. and Agri. Tea, 243; Ind. Mus. Notes, Vol. I, 198; II, 157; III, 1; IV, 41; Cotes, Ins. and Mites, etc., Tea Plant in Ind, pp. 8-10; Agricultural Ledger No. 27, 1896, p. 3; Circular, Roy. Bot. Gard., Ceylon (1900), No. 19, 265.*

Found in all districts.

380. ***History***.—It would appear that of Indian writers Mr. E. L. Edgar, of Cossipore Tea Garden, Cachar, was the first to draw attention to this tea pest (1873). Mr. S. E. Peal (Sibsagar district, Assam) seems to have next come forward with useful particulars. Mr. E. E. Green (*Insect Pests of the Tea Plant*), of Ceylon, furnished a long and instructive description of the insect and its ravages. Mr. Bamber mentions it as tunnelling "the stems of tea bushes in Ceylon and Cachar." Mr. Cotes (*Insects and Mites, etc.*) mentions that samples had been furnished to the Museum by tea gardens in Darjeeling. It was collected by the authors in Sibsagar, Dibrugarh, and North Lakhimpur and Sylhet. It also occurs in the wild tea of the Shan States, Burma.

Occurs throughout District.

It may thus be accepted that this pest occurs practically throughout the Indian and Ceylon tea districts.

Boring Caterpillar.

381. ***Description***.—The boring caterpillar, when cut out of the branches, is found to be of a red or orange colour and to be from 1

PLATE IX. (*To face Page 201.*)

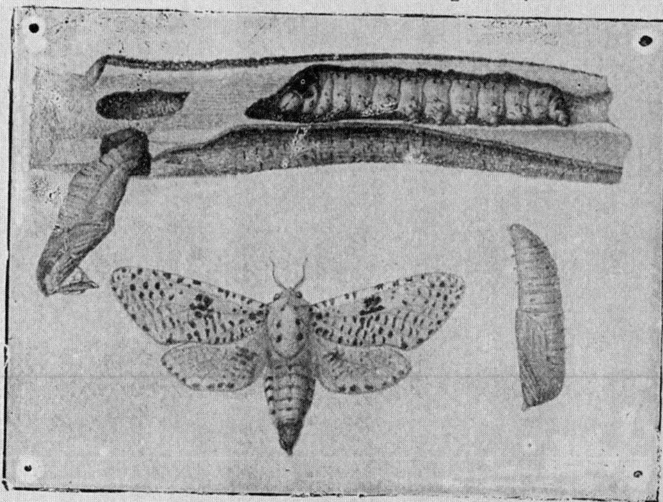

1. Zenzera coffeæ (p. 200). The Red Tea Borer.
Showing Caterpillar, Cocoon and Moth.
(After Cotes.)

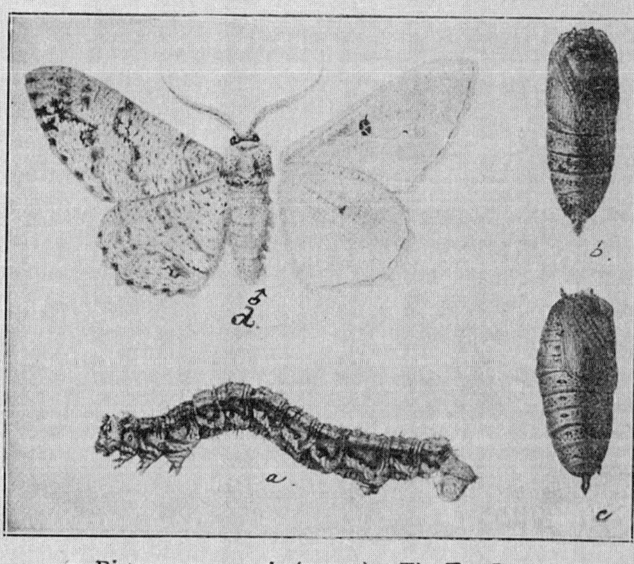

2. Biston suppressaria (p. 224). The Tea Looper.
a. Caterpillar ; *b.* and *c.* Chrysalis ; *d.* Moth.
(From Indian Museum Notes.)

to 2 inches long. The head is small and horny. The adjoining segment is swollen and protected by a blackish-coloured plate : there is also a similar plate at the anal extremity. On attaining maturity, it constructs within its tunnel a small chamber, and there it changes into the chrysalis. "The moth is a remarkably pretty insect with translucent white wings, the upper pair marked with numerous metallic steel-blue spots and bars. The legs are deep shining blue while the body is thickly clothed with white hair looking like fine cotton wool" (*Green*). Mr. Bamber says that "the full-grown caterpillar can be found about December, after which it changes to a moth which appears in March. The period actually spent in the larval stage has not, however, been satisfactorily made out. It is more than likely that it lives for over one year. Mr. Green tells us that he has seen the moths at several different times of the year. The eggs are deposited in ropy masses, and look like strings of minute amber beads. Each egg is broadly oval and of an opaque waxy appearance. They are usually joined end to end, but sometimes side by side" (*Green*). They are laid in crevices of the stems.

THE RED BORER.

Moth appears in March.

Eggs laid in Crevices of Stem.

382. ***Depredations.***—"The young caterpillar gnaws its way into the wood, choosing at first small shoots adapted to its size and bores a tunnel along the inside. It completely devours the pith and inner wood, leaving a thin outer shell just sufficiently strong to support the branch. From the small shoots the borer, as it grows, eats into the larger branches and stems. I have seen a two-year old tea plant with the stem completely hollowed out from about three inches above ground to the ends of the shoots. The presence of the grub may generally be detected by the small round pellets, like conglomerated saw-dust, the excreta of the insect, which accumulate at the foot of the tree."

Presence detected.

"Young plants are killed down to the ground and may or may not throw out fresh shoots. In older bushes, one or more of the main stems only will be affected ; the dead leaves on such stems will show where the borer is at work, for they do not fall off as in some other diseases, but dry up and remain fixed in their original positions." (*Green.*)

Mr. Peal remarks that "it causes more damage than caterpillar,* each individual, ere killed, generally destroying a plant or branch.

* The Bunch caterpillar, **Andraca bipunctata**, is meant by Mr. Peal.

THE RED BORER.

It is fortunate that they are not found in larger numbers." It does not necessarily commence near the ground. Often a branch will show no trace of injury for even two feet from the soil,—and it usually works downward. It apparently attacks indiscriminately old and young tea, boring down, sometimes into the roots, so that even collar-pruning hardly removes it. Its prevalence can generally be seen at the pruning season, and its borings often form the point of entrance for white ants—a far more destructive pest.

Borings form Entrance for White Ants.

Pruning off Affected Branches.

383. ***Remedy.***—Every sign of borer should at once be cut out, and not only this, but the insect should be destroyed. In pruning orders should be given when the section is seen to be rotten with a boring to cut lower and still lower till entire wood is found. In this way the young larvæ will be prevented from continuing their ravages. The coolies should be offered a reward in hoeing for every tree they detect with the characteristic heaps of excreta round the stems. In America the use of lights to attract the very similar moth **Zeuzera pyrina** has been attended with some success, and might be useful in the present case, as the moth is undoubtedly strongly attracted by light.

LIV.—Slug-like stinging caterpillars.

Family LIMACODIDÆ.

LIMACODIDÆ.

384. The caterpillars belonging to this family are greenish yellow thick slug-like grubs. Some of them would seem at first sight to possess neither mouth nor feet since these are often retractile, and hence, being more or less elliptic in outline, look like little patches of jelly on the tea leaves. Others are more active and have a series of warts arranged on the back and sides which bear stinging hairs, and for this reason alone are extremely objectionable. Occasionally they have appeared in such vast numbers as not only to defoliate many acres of tea, but as to render it impossible for the work-people to enter the invaded portions of the estates. The caterpillars of certain species drop to the ground in order to form their chrysalis, and the people treading on them with their naked feet, get sores sufficiently painful to incapacitate them for a few days or even invalid them for considerable periods. Sores on the sole of the foot are by no means easily cured, and it may be that a good many of the ulcers on the feet so common in the latter half of the rains among

the coolies are caused, in the first instance, by the stings of this group of caterpillars. THOSEA CERVINA.

This is, therefore, a family of pests to be by no means ignored, especially as they have recently shown a considerable tendency to increase in various localities where a few years ago they were hardly known.

36. Thosea cervina, *Moore.*

THE ASSAM TEA SEED MOTH: THE ASSAM NETTLE-GRUB.

THE ASSAM TEA SEED MOTH.

SEE PLATE X, No. 2.

References.—*Hampson, Fauna Brit. Ind. (Moths), Vol. I, 379; Indian Museum Notes, Vol. IV, No. 4.*

Found in Assam, Sylhet, Duars, and Darjeeling.

385. ***History.***—A good deal of confusion has crept into the naming of this family of caterpillars as found on tea, but contrary to what was at one time believed, little doubt remains that this species is that most commonly seen. It was found in 1894 in the Dam Dim district of the Duars. It has since been noticed as doing a good deal of damage in the Doom Dooma and Nowgong districts of Assam, and certainly it is one of the very objectionable pests in Darjeeling. Extended Range.

386. ***Description.***—The larva or caterpillar is a rather active (for this group) green caterpillar with a brownish purple, yellow-bordered, irregular band on the back, rather widened in the middle. There are groups of stinging spines (tubercles) at the front and back slightly to each side, and on the side itself two further series of spines set the whole length of the body. (*See Plate X, No. 2 a and b.*) This caterpillar appears in June in the plains, in August or September in the hills, and the pest is at its height during the next two or three months and often on into the cold weather in November and even later. So far as we can make out, there is only one brood per annum. One Brood per annum.

The cocoon is exactly like a tea seed both in shape and size, and is *buried in the ground about an inch deep* under the bushes. So much do these resemble tea seeds that they have been taken for them by old planters. So far as we know, they are never formed on the bush, always beneath the surface of the soil, where they remain for some months, usually till the following March, when the moths appear. Cocoon like Tea Seed.

The moth [*see Plate X, No. 2 d (male) and e (female)*] is a brownish inconspicuous creature. The fore-wing is a silky grey brown colour with one dark spot. The striking point is, however, the Moth.

THE ASSAM TEA SEED MOTH.

light coloured line across the front wings of both male and female. The figures are drawn natural size.

387. ***Depredations.***—To show the serious nature of this pest, it is only necessary to quote from several managers' letters. One from the Duars says, under date 27th August 1899, "About 100 acres of our best Tea have been attacked by the 'slug-like stinging caterpillars' to such an extent that it is with great difficulty I can get the pluckers to enter the invaded portions. Last time we plucked it, half of our usual force remained in the lines or rather hid in the jungle. Yesterday I put on all the people I could spare off the leaf (75) and gathered thousands, enough to fill one of our wheelbarrows (gathered off 20 acres)." The same manager writes a little later (7th September 1899), "In our last round of plucking, we got the men to wrap bags round their legs, and hope thus to manage this year."

Accounts of effect.

Again Mr. John Henderson wrote from Nowgong (18th August 1900)—

Effect in Nowgong.

"For some time I had noticed that the piece of tea attacked by the caterpillars looked most unhealthy and gave little or no leaf while the balance of the block looked well, and flushed well. I was unable to account for this in any way, excepting that the lay of the land was lower than the healthy piece and I decided to increase the number of drains in it. Early in June, while marking out where the new drains were to go, I and the coolies, who were with me, got stung considerably by the caterpillars. . . . . There did not appear to be very many about, and no notice was taken of them, but as they increased I, early in July, put coolies on to collect them. It was then the cocoons were noticed, and I had them collected too. I got large numbers of both caterpillars and cocoons—maunds of the latter and as many as 12 to 18 at one tea root. They were generally found buried in the ground to the depth of an inch to an inch and a half. The caterpillars devoured the old leaves. . . . They did not touch the bark—only took a lump out of the side or end of the leaf."

The last statement in the above letter illustrates the characteristic way in which this caterpillar eats the tea. It simply eats a lump from the side or end of an old leaf (*Plate X, No. 2 a*) and makes no discrimination as to veins or anything else.

Collect cocoons.

388. ***Remedy.***—The one remedy is to collect the caterpillar and the cocoons—especially the latter. This is very simple when it is known where to look for the latter. Where done, this method has been very successful. One manager writes, "I am glad to be able to say that we have not seen a single sign of its (the slug pest's) presence

PLATE X. (*To face Page 204.*)

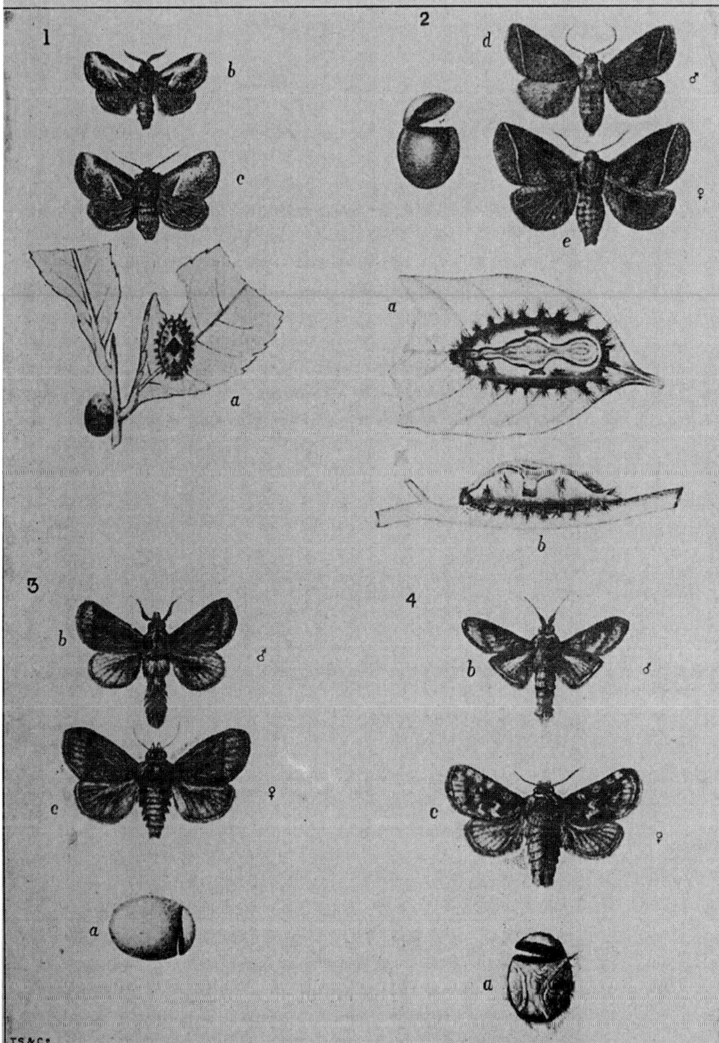

1. Thosea recta (p. 205).
Caterpillar and Cocoon ; *b.* and *c.* Male and Female Moths.

2. Thosea cervina (p. 203).
a. and *b.* Caterpillar ; *c.* Cocoon ; *d.* and *e.* Male and Female Moths.

3. Thosea divergens (p. 207).
a. Cocoon ; *b.* and *c.* Male and Female Moths.

4. Belippa lohor (p. 209).
a. Cocoon ; *b.* and *c.* Male and Female Moths.

(From Indian Museum Notes.)

this season, so I am in hopes we thoroughly cleared them out last cold weather when we gathered *tons* of cocoons—8 to 10 maunds daily, for some days" (*4th September 1900*). Therefore, where it is known that the caterpillars have appeared badly, the ground all over the affected part should be carefully hoed, and the tea-seed-like cocoons collected and destroyed. The collection of the caterpillars themselves is somewhat difficult, but the children who do the work soon learn to manipulate them with two pieces of stick, and hardly ever get seriously stung.

THE ASSAM TEA SEED MOTH.

37. Thosea recta, *Hmpsn.*

THOSEA RECTA.

THE "MOROWAK-KORALE" NETTLE-GRUB. (*Green.*)

SEE PLATE X, NO. 1.

References.—*Hampson, Fauna Brit. Ind.* (*Moths*), *Vol. I, 378; Indian Museum Notes, Vol. IV, 56; Planting Opinion, 1899, p. 574; Tropical Agriculturist, Sept. 1899; Aministr. Rep. Roy. Bot. Gard., Ceylon, 1899, p. 13; Circ. Roy. Bot. Gard., 1900, p. 251.*

THE CEYLON NETTLE-GRUB.

Found in Ceylon.

389. ***History.***—Just as the stinging caterpillar last mentioned has caused a good deal of trouble in several of the Indian tea districts, so that now under discussion has caused consternation in Ceylon. It apparently was first heard of there in 1885, and then at different times reports were received of its presence in the Ambagamuwa district, at Balagoda, and finally the outbreak at Morowak-Korale in 1899 " seems to have caused quite an unprecedented scare." (*Green.*)

Discovered in 1885.

390. ***Description.***—The following account of the species is due to Mr. E. E. Green.

"The eggs of this species have not yet been observed, but they are probably laid upon the surface of the leaves."

Caterpillar: lozenge shaped, slug-like, of an apple green or yellowish green colour, often with a series of irregular red patches on the back. Stinging spines arranged on small tubercles in a marginal and two dorsal series. Head concealed on the under surface. The insect has no legs but progresses in a slug-like fashion. The fully grown caterpillar measures from ½ to ¾ inch in length." (*Plate X, No. 1 a.*) " Cocoon—dark brown, egg-shaped, compact and smooth,

Caterpillar.

THE CEYLON NETTLE-GRUB.

attached either to the under surface of a tea leaf or in the angles of the twigs and stems. . . . Specimens kept in captivity remained as cocoons for from 17 to 21 days. Moth—grayish brown, with a rather furry body. The female has a blackish spot in the centre of the fore wing and two faint lines, one near the base and the other near the tip. . . . The male has a darker patch at the base of the wing bounded by a short white streak . . . The male moth has an expanse of ¾ inch. The female is rather larger, measuring slightly more than an inch across the expanded wings." [*Plate X, No. 1 b* (*male*), *c* (*female*).]

Cocoon.

Moth.

391. ***Depredations.***—The Ceylon planter, where the worst attack occurred, wrote with reference to it:—

Effect in Ceylon.

"I first noticed it on July 15; it was seen on about half an acre of tea. After two days it had spread over about 3 acres, and then at the rate of about five acres a day over 25 acres of tea. The damage done was not of a permanent nature; but the caterpillars eat out almost every vestige of green leaf, and the whole 25 acres was stripped almost bare. When I found I could not prune quick enough to overtake its spread, I pruned broad belts round the area attacked, burning the prunings and sweeping the ground. I found the insects seemed unable to cross these belts, and as I pruned out all the tea inside, it died fast, exposure to the sun and want of sustenance apparently combining to kill it. In about five weeks from its first appearance, it had disappeared almost entirely, although I found a few insects here and there in other parts of the estate. When, however, the young flush grew (about five weeks after pruning), I found it covered with a minute form of the same insect. I stripped all the young flush off for about four rounds, and after that it again disappeared, and I have not been troubled with it since."

392. ***Remedy.***—With regard to remedy, Mr. Green says, "Before this outbreak could have assumed the proportions described in the above correspondence, there must have been at least two earlier and smaller broods. I can only repeat my warning to keep a good look-out for these preliminary broods, and destroy them before they have time to gain ground. When the pest is at its height, if the attacked field is nearing the proper time, pruning will be the best remedy, care being taken to effectually destroy all the prunings, and to search for and remove all cocoons attached to the stems of the trees. If the field is only just coming into bearing, the foliage may be thoroughly sprayed with arsenate of lead, or other similar insecticide, which will poison the leaves and the caterpillars feeding upon them. No leaf should be plucked from such trees for at least 14 days. The actual leaves that will then be taken will have been disclosed since the application of the poison."

Collect Preliminary Broods.

Collect Cocoons.

We have nothing to add to these recommendations. THOSEA DIVERGENS.

38. **Thosea divergens,** *Moore.*

THE ASSAM BROWN AND GREEN STRIPED NETTLE-GRUB. THE BROWN AND GREEN STRIPED NETTLE-GRUB.

SEE PLATE X, No. 3.

References.—*Hampson, Fauna Brit. Ind. (Moths), Vol. I, 380; Indian Museum Notes, Vol. IV, No. 4.*

Found in Assam and Cachar.

393. The caterpillars of this moth were formerly thought to be the chief species of stinging caterpillars in Assam. Now this is found to be those of **Thosea cervina** (*vid. sup.*). **Thosea divergens** does occasionally occur and do damage, being reported from Bishnauth by Mr. W. J. Fleet, and from Silcuri, Cachar, by Mr. Moore. We have recently bred it out at Moabund, Sibsagar. Mr. Fleet obtained cocoons and perfect insects as follows:—*Cocoon* very similar to **Thosea cervina**: ovate, ⅜ths inch long, opening by a circular lid, smooth, brownish coloured, formed underground. *Perfect insect.*—A little over an inch across the expanded wings, of a rich pale chestnut brown colour. Fore wings with two dark lines that extend from the costal margin (starting at a point about ⅛ inch within the apex) and passing across while they diverge toward the inner margin. *Conf. with paras, 385–388.*

The pest should be dealt with like **Thosea cervina,** the caterpillar being extremely similar to that species.

39. **Thosea cotesi,** *Swinh.* THOSEA COTESI.

References.—*Hampson, Fauna Brit. Ind. (Moths), Vol. I, 380; Ind. Mus. Notes, II, 36; IV, 41; Cotes, Tea Insects, 11.*

Found in Darrang, Assam.

FIG. 16.—THOSEA COTESI.
(Showing the male and female moths, and cocoon.)
(After Cotes.)

394. This insect was discovered in 1891 in Darrang, and reported to be defoliating tea bushes. It is a stinging caterpillar, and forms a cocoon just like **Thosea recta** above mentioned. The moth is here figured, the smaller example being the male, the larger the female. If found, it should be dealt with as described for **Thosea cervina,** but being smaller there is somewhat more difficulty attached to eradicating it. Assam.

The Lepidoptera (Limacodidæ).

THOSEA CANA.

40. **Thosea cana**, *Wlk.*

THE GREEN NETTLE-GRUB.

References.—*Hampson, Fauna Brit. Ind. (Moths), Vol. I, 378; Circular, Roy. Bot. Gard., Ceylon, 1900, p. 254.*

Found in Ceylon.

Ceylon.

395. This is another Ceylon pest, very similar in character and effect to **Thosea recta** above described. The caterpillar is, as a matter of fact, practically indistinguishable. (*Green.*) The moth "may be distinguished by its more uniform grayish brown colour and by the absence of the short white streak which marks the fore wing of **Thosea recta**. **Thosea cana** has two indistinct brownish lines across the wing, with a small brown speck in the space between them" (*Green*). The pest should be dealt with in a manner precisely similar to that described for **Thosea recta**.

What appears to be this caterpillar has recently (1902) appeared in Chittagong, and also in the Dooars, and done very considerable damage.

NATADA NARRARIA.

41. **Natada narraria**, *Moore.*

THE FRINGED NETTLE-GRUB.

References.—*Hampson, Fauna Brit. Ind. (Moths), Vol. I, 380; Circular, Roy. Bot. Gardens, Ceylon, 1900, p. 256.*

Found in Ceylon.

Ceylon.

396. This is still another Ceylon pest, which has luckily not yet appeared in India on tea. In Ceylon Mr. Green writes that the caterpillars have been recently responsible for considerable injury to the tea in several districts (Uva and Rangalla). The eggs are inconspicuous oval, flat, very pale green objects laid singly on the upper surface of a tea leaf; the caterpillar varies in colour from a yellowish to a whitish green with a purplish stripe on the back. "All round the margin is a fringe of long pointed tubercles bearing tufts of stinging spines, and a row of smaller spiniferous tubercles on each side of the dorsal stripe. . . When full grown, it is little more than half an inch in length. It rests on the under surface of the leaves." (*Green.*) The cocoon is oval, smooth, and brown, and the moth escapes by a lid at one end. They are attached to twigs or leaves, or to fallen leaves and rubbish. The male moth is "pale, ochreous, the middle of the fore wing covered by a reddish brown patch in the centre of which is a black spot. . . Expanse $\frac{3}{4}$ inch. The female is a little larger.

Cocoons attached to Twigs.

The caterpillar works in a similar fashion to the other members of this family, attacking the old leaves of the tea, and not touching the bark. It should be dealt with in the same manner.

NATADA VELUTINA.

42. **Natada velutina**, *Koll.* ?

References.—*Hampson, Fauna Brit. Ind. (Moths), Vol. I, 383.*

397. What the late Mr. de Niceville thought to be the larva of this moth was sent to us from Cachar in 1901 as doing considerable damage to tea in the Eastern part of that district. It is a very large caterpillar, two inches long, and with huge spines both at the front and hind ends of the body. It can hardly as yet be called a pest.

The Gelatine Grub.

44. **Parasa lepida,** *Cram.* PARASA LEPIDA.

THE BLUE-STRIPED NETTLE GRUB.

References.—*Hampson, Fauna Brit. Ind. (Moths), Vol. I., 388; Green, Insect Pests of the Tea Plant, 66—71; Bamber; Chem. and Agri. of Tea, 244; Ind. Mus. Notes, Vol. I., 197; II., 158; Cotes, Tea Insects, 13; Circular, Roy. Bot. Gard., Ceylon, 1900, No. 19, p. 250.*

Found in Ceylon and Assam.

398. "This caterpillar, which has occasionally done considerable damage in Ceylon, is broad and comparatively short, rounded in front and behind, and bright yellow green, with a rich lilac stripe along the middle of the back and a bright blue stripe on each side, each stripe bordered by a darker line of the same tint." (*Green.*) The poisonous spines are green in colour, and there are four tufts near the head, and another pair near the tail; there are four large black spots at the hinder end of the body. It has only rudimentary legs. The cocoon is similar to other members of this family, and placed on the stems. The moth is a pretty insect, the fore wings being chocolate brown with a green stripe. Ceylon.

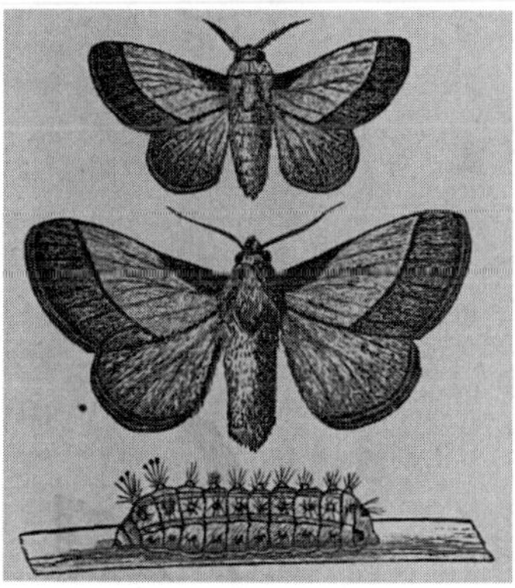

FIG. 17.—THE BLUE STRIPED NETTLE GRUB.
(Showing male and female moths, and caterpillar.)
(After Cotes.)

In India it has not been found till recently upon tea, but has appeared lately in Assam, and can be dealt with like the other members of the family.

45. **Belippa lohor,** *Moore.* BELIPPA LOHOR. THE GELATINE GRUB.

THE LEAF-ENVELOPED TEA SEED MOTH: THE GELATINE GRUB.

SEE PLATE X, No. 4.

References.—*Hampson, Fauna Brit. Ind. (Moths), Vol. I., 400; Indian Mus. Notes, Vol. IV., 183.*

Found in most Indian districts.

399. ***History.***—The "gelatine grub" has been long known to the industry. Indeed the lumps of jelly, as they look like, adhering to the leaves of the tea bush and stinging when touched could hardly have been missed. It is, however, perhaps only in the Sadya road districts of Upper Assam that it can be regarded as a troublesome Lumps of Jelly.

THE GELATINE GRUB.

pest, but here, for the last half of the season, it causes considerable trouble.

400. ***Description.***—The larvæ of this moth appear about September on the bushes as small legless caterpillars which resemble nothing more than green or brownish semi-transparent bulbs of jelly

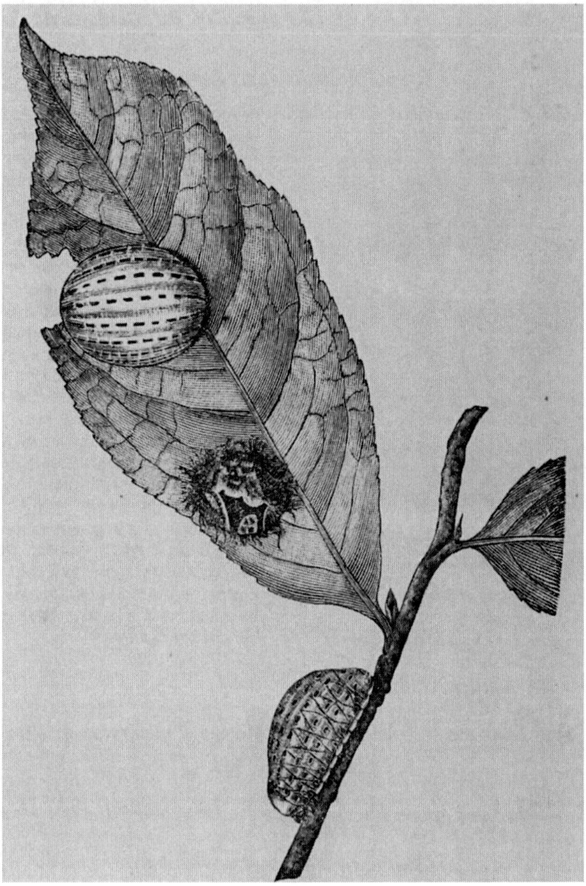

FIG. 18.—GELATINE GRUBS AND COCOON.

(After Moore.)

with thin skins. "They are quite round on the back, but have prickles all over them which sting badly if touched." (*Kirwan.*) In this state

The Gelatine Grub.

the attached figure—(modified from Mr. Moore's figure of **Belippa laleana,** which species, however, does not sting) accurately represent their appearance. In this state they live for about two months (a time which varies considerably), and then change into hard tea-seed-like cocoons. These differ from the otherwise similar cocoons of **Thosea cervina** in that the surface is whitish brown coloured and never smooth, always bearing traces of having been stuck between leaves or twigs (*see Plate X, No. 4 a*). It is, in our experience, never buried in the ground.

THE GELATINE GRUB.

Cocoon never smooth and never buried.

From this cocoon about March or April (according to our experience of breeding them in captivity) moths emerge (*see Plate X, No. 4 b and c*), the female being considerably larger than the male, the latter being about one inch across the forewings when fully expanded. The female has head, thorax, abdomen and wings of a light fulvous colour, and undulating markings of a dark colour on the forewings; near the apex of the forewing on the outer margin there are two minute black spots, and beyond these and projecting from the costal margin a small white band; also two pale coloured spots on the apex of the wing-cell. The hind wings are of a paler and more uniform colour, but with a small black marginal spot at the apex, and a still more indistinct one at the anal angle. The male is much darker (nearly chestnut) in colour, but with similar markings.

Moth.

401. ***Depredations.***—In Upper Assam the larvæ of this moth do considerable injury at the end of the season. They luckily attack only the old leaves, and as they progress slowly, it is only their enormous numbers which give them importance. They disappear about the end of January.

Only attack old leaves.

402. ***Remedy.***—Little can be added to what has been said relative to the methods of dealing with the class of caterpillar. Collecting the grubs and cocoons is in every case indicated, and with this particular species the latter will be found at pruning either on the bushes, or on the rubbish beneath them. In a recent communication from Mr. C. P. Cumming, of the Budla Beta Tea Co., he states that he has bred a fly from the cocoons, so that it is evident that the natural attacks of parasites are aiding any efforts made to keep down the pest. This fly lays its eggs in the caterpillar, and its larvæ breed therein and ultimately destroy it.

Remedy.

LV.—Hairy Caterpillars.

Family LASIOCAMPIDÆ.

LASIOCAMPIDÆ.

403. This family of caterpillars has not yet caused much trouble on tea. They are, however, quite capable of doing so, and they form serious pests of certain trees and perennial plants. **Gastropacha pini**, for instance, attacks pine forests in Germany. **Gastropacha quercifolia** is a serious pest on apple trees in England. The caterpillars are usually hairy, "with lateral downwardly directed tufts of hair, and often subdorsal tufts or dorsal humps on the anterior somites (sections) thickly clothed with hair." *(Hampson.)*

Pests in Europe.

Two or three of this group have been noticed on tea in India, and a note is therefore made of them.

GASTROPACHA SP.

THE LAPPET CATERPILLAR.

46. **Gastropacha** *sp.?*

THE LAPPET CATERPILLAR.

Reference.—*Hampson, Fauna Brit. Ind. (Moths), I., 428—29.*

Found in Sibsagar and North Lakhimpur, Assam.

404. This caterpillar was found at Nahorhabi, Seleng, and Moabund in Sibsagar, and at Patalipam in North Lakhimpur. It was very large, being fully four inches long and nearly half an inch thick, and was found adhering to dry exposed pruned twigs which, in colour, it closely resembled. The examples were clearly the larvæ of a lappet moth, and were in colour a beautifully mottled grey brown with pink markings. The prolegs were incased by heavy tufts of downwardly directed hairs, looking like trousers round the feet. The third, fourth and tenth sections (somites) had these trouser-like tufts with abortive prolegs. On the first and third sections there were black bands on the back which may be hid from view by the movements of the body. The ninth section has a hump projecting above, and the tenth one below. The fourth to eighth sections have pink spots arranged in a single row along the side. The cocoon is a large, loosely formed grey structure arranged on the upper surface of a leaf with one or two leaves brought down on the top of it and with fragments of leaves nipped off and fastened at both extremities of the enclosure thus formed. The material was of a felted texture with many grey and black hairs, similar to those on the caterpillar dispersed through it.

Description.

Cocoon.

405. It is probable that this caterpillar is the food of a parasitic fly, as in two cases in which it was attempted to breed the moth a fly emerged from the cocoon. This would seem to be probably the principal security against the spread of the caterpillar. While not a great cause for anxiety at present, this species might easily become so, and in view of the serious nature of the attacks of several similar caterpillars in Europe, on no account should the pest be allowed to become established, and every carterpillar seen should be collected and destroyed.

Parasitic Fly.

406. The next three species belonging to this family of moths were found feeding on tea by Mr. J. A. Thomson at Ligri Pukri. They are not pests at present, but their occurrence on tea should be recorded. TARAGAMA SP.

47. **Taragama** *sp.*

48. **Trabala vishnu,** *Lef.* TRABALA VISHNU.

49. **Estigena pardalis,** *Wlk.*—This one may be a distinct and new species. ESTIGENA PARDALIS.

50. **Suana concolor,** *Wlk.*—is also another occasional defoliator of tea plants in Ceylon. Mr. Green informs us that the injury, however, is usually confined to one or two bushes, and is of a temporary character only. SUANA CONCOLOR.

Family LYMANTRIIDÆ.

LYMANTRIIDÆ.

407. One of the most striking features of this family and the next is that they have large hairy caterpillars. The hairs are utilized in forming the cocoon. In many cases some of the hairs are poisonous (though this is by no means universal), so that under this family in all probability should be grouped the letters and reports by planters that mention "hairy poisonous caterpillars" as distinct from the short, thick, slug-like caterpillars, already dealt with as belonging to the family of **Limacodidæ**. Hairy Caterpillars.

It is a group, moreover, of some importance, and a considerable amount of damage is done by several members, while others are occasionally found on tea all over the districts.

51. **Orygia postica,*** *Wlk.* ORYGIA POSTICA.

The Small Tussock Moth.

THE SMALL TUSSOCK MOTH.

References.—*Hampson, Fauna Brit. Ind. (Moths), Vol. I., 436; Indian Mus. Notes, II., 159; E. E. Green, Ann. Rep., 1898.*

Found in Ceylon.

408. This is a "small hairy caterpillar with brushlike tuft, projecting forward on each side of the head, a similar tuft on the tail, two shorter tufts on each side, and four very compact tufts on the back. The female moth is wingless—merely a bag of eggs, which she deposits on the surface of her cocoon. The male moth is a sober coloured insect with brown wings marbled in darker shades. As all the eggs—and they are very numerous—are deposited in one spot, the resulting brood of caterpillars is at first confined to one bush. This is the time to attack them, and they can easily be exterminated before they have wandered further afield and started fresh broods." (*Green.*)

* This insect is the same as **Orygia ceylanica,** Nietn., reported previously as attacking tea in Ceylon.

The Lepidoptera (Lymantriidæ).

DASYCHIRA MENDOSA. THE INDIAN TEA TUSSOCK MOTH.

52. Dasychira mendosa, *Hübn.*

THE INDIAN TEA TUSSOCK MOTH.

References.—*Hampson, Fauna Brit. Ind. (Moths), I., 452; Bamber, Chem. Agri. Tea, 244; Ind. Mus. Notes, II., 43, 159; III.* (v), *11, 15, 42; Cotes, Tea Insects, 21.*

Found in Assam and Darjeeling.

Wide distribution.

409. ***History.***—Though first found in Darjeeling feeding on tea, it is very probable that this caterpillar occurs throughout the Indian tea districts. At any rate, it has been found by the authors in almost every Assam district, and, after **Andraca bipunctata** (the Bunch Caterpillar), may be regarded as the most abundant and most widely distinguished of all Assam caterpillar tea pests, although only occasionally prevalent to such an extent as to occasion much anxiety.

Caterpillar.

410. ***Description.***—There are apparently several forms of the caterpillar. In one place the prevailing colour is a steel-grey with darker coloured tufts of hair: at another, pale yellowish brown, with the head and first section (somite) scarlet, the dorsal tufts grey. The latter is perhaps the most abundant and dangerous form. In every case, however, it is an extremely active little caterpillar, and makes off from the bush on the slightest alarm being given. The figure while not good, as applied to the Assam insect, will serve well for identification. The moth is a pale brown creature, the figure being drawn natural size, and representing the male. The cocoon is formed of grey brown spinose hairs, and is deposited on the under surface of two leaves drawn together. The hairs forming the cocoon are feathered, and some of them end in tufts exactly similar to those on the back of the caterpillar, only twice as long or more. It would thus appear that the creature produces

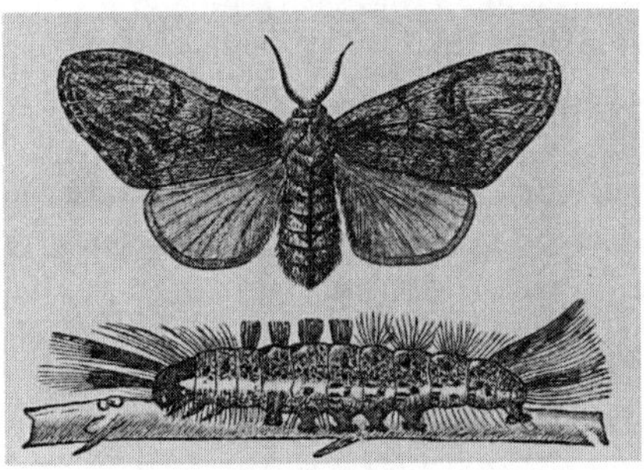

FIG. 19.—DASYCHIRA MENDOSA. Showing moth and caterpillar. (After Cotes.)

Moth.

Hairs used for making cocoon.

THE INDIAN TEA TUSSOCK MOTH.

greatly elongated hairs on its back just before the time of passing into the stage of a chrysalis.

Feeds at night.

411. ***Depredations.***—The insect, like most of the members of the family to which it belongs, feeds for the most part during the night. In the daytime the caterpillars hide below projecting corners of clods, in drains, or in rotten portions of the stems. They show a special liking for newly planted out tea, both in young garden and in vacancies. It is this feature of the insect which constitutes its chief danger. No person could walk through a garden in Assam without being struck with the remarkable fact that, along road-sides where there may be young tea bushes, in vacancies all over the estate, or in new extensions, all the old mature leaves of the seedlings have been riddled to pieces. The entire inter-cellular tissue of the leaf has been eaten away, and only a skeleton remains, corresponding to the midrib and veins. The young shoots and tender leaves are rarely attacked.

Skeletonises the leaves.

This state of affairs may be found for a long time without the depredator being discovered, for it feeds almost entirely at night. At Tiphook, in 1895, one of the authors (G. W.) looked vainly for the cause of the skeletonised appearance of the leaves on young tea during the day, but on returning at 5-30 P.M. the cause of the destruction was obvious. The bushes were then at once seen to have each one, two, or more of the caterpillars of **Dasychira mendosa** on them. These were carefully watched for a time, and it was fully established that they were the insects causing the depredations. On hearing voices, the insects stopped feeding, and turned up their heads in a threatening attitude as if both on the defensive and offensive. It was then discovered that this remarkably active insect hides in the ground and crawls up the bushes late in the afternoon so as to feed at night.

Remedy.

412. ***Remedy.*** Collect and destroy the caterpillars and cocoons. When the insect is found to be doing serious damage, it would be a good plan to give the surface soil a good dressing with quicklime and immediately after to hoe the ground. Were this done in the early part of the day, a very large percentage of the caterpillars would be destroyed. With closely similar caterpillars in Europe and America, good results have been obtained by girdling the tree with a band of grease which prevents the caterpillars from ascending

The Lepidoptera (Lymantriidæ).

THE INDIAN TEA TUSSOCK MOTH.

Girdling the trees with a band of grease.

Conf. with para. 419.

the stem. The best substance for this purpose is what is known as "dendrolene" in America (which is a petroleum product), as it cannot be washed off by rain, and remains sticky for months, but any sticky or greasy materials with similar properties will do almost as well. It would seem therefore that if done before the hatching of the eggs this would prevent the ascent of the young caterpillars, and later on check the mature ones from reaching the ground. The method seems worth trying with seedling tea plants, as the caterpillar is accustomed to descend to the ground every day, and as the eggs seem often to be laid and the caterpillars bred on other plants than tea

DYSCHIRA THWAITESI.

53. **Dyschira thwaitesi,** *Moore.*

References.—*Cotes, Tea Insects, p. 18 ; Bamber ; Chem. and Agri. Tea, p. 244 ; Ind. Mus. Notes, Vol. I., 29, 203 ; II., 158 ; III. (pt. 4), 18, (pt. 5), 11, 14, 42 ; IV., 42.*

413. Mr. Cotes tells us that caterpillars identified as belonging to this genus were found on a tea garden in the Duars in 1886, where they were said to have caused serious damage by feeding on the leaves of the tea plant. Mr. Bamber, alluding apparently to the same fact under the name **Dasychira Thwaitesi,** *Moore,* says that the insect had been "reported as doing much damage by defoliating tea and *sal* (**Shorea robusta**). The *sal* trees throughout 200 square miles of forest in Assam are said to have been defoliated by it in 1878. Since the time above referred to its presence on tea has not been noted. It is only fair to state, moreover, that the moth of this caterpillar has never been seen in India, and is only recorded as occurring in Ceylon. Hence it is probable that the above reports really refer to the much more widely spread **Dasychira horsfieldi,** No. 55 below.

DASYCHIRA SECURIS.

54. **Dasychira securis,** *Hübn.*

Reference.—*Hampson Fauna Brit. Ind. (Moths), I., 453.*

414. The caterpillars of this moth were found by Mr. J. A. Thomson feeding on tea at Ligri Pukri, Assam. Nothing further is known of it as a pest.

DASYCHIRA HORSFIELDI.

55. **Dasychira horsfieldi,** *Saund.*

References.—*Hampson, Fauna Brit. Ind. (Moths), I., 448 ; Cir., Roy. Bot. Gard., Ceylon, Series I. (1900), p. 265.*

415. This species has been recorded by Mr. Green as occasionally a tea pest in Ceylon, and it is probable that it was collected by one of the authors at Tiphook in 1895. The larva is yellow with tufts of long yellow hairs, shorter tufts on several sections, and one black patch on the back. It can hardly be called a pest.

EUPROCTIS DIVISA.

THE NOWGONG HAIRY TEA CATERPILLAR.

56. Euproctis divisa, *Wlk.*

THE NOWGONG HAIRY TEA CATERPILLAR.

Reference.—*Hampson, Fauna Brit. Ind. (Moths), Vol. I., 471.*

The Nowgong Hairy Tea Caterpillar.

THE NOWGONG HAIRY TEA CATERPILLAR.

Found in Nowgong and in Sylhet.

In Nowgong since 1890.

416. ***History.***—We now come to a caterpillar which has long been known and dreaded both in Nowgong and in the Chargola Valley (Sylhet), but whose name has only recently been made out. It appeared in Nowgong in 1890, and in several years since in the spring, coming on usually in May and remaining till July, and has been an annual visitor in the Chargola Valley for several years.

Moth bred out in 1902.

417. ***Description.***—The caterpillar (which in general appearance closely resembles the species which is dealt with next in order, figured in *Plate VI, No. 1*) is a black creature with two yellow stripes, and hairy all over. It is about one inch in length when full grown. The moth is white in colour, the abdomen dark, with a tuft of orange hairs on the anal or hinder end. The moth was bred from the caterpillars by Mr. F. D. Ballantyne, of Chargola, and identified as above by the kindness of Mr. H. W. Peal, of the Indian Museum (July 1902). It apparently has only one brood per annum, and invariably disappears in July.

Show special attack on red-rusted shoots.

Conf. with paras. 802-829.

418. ***Depredations.***—The caterpillars seem to invade the gardens from the jungle, and may be seen crossing the roads in vast numbers, and covering almost every bush. During a bad attack thousands may be killed or collected every day by any children who may be employed for the purpose. They attack the less vigorous plants by preference, and seem to eat the bark even more readily than the leaves. It is further said that they show a special favour for "red-rusted" shoots. The pest is a serious one, being at its height in June when the new season's wood is being made. This they strip of its bark, as well as eat the leaves, and the result to the bush is disastrous.

Collect Caterpillars.

419. ***Remedy.***—Up to the present nothing has been done but to catch and kill the caterpillars, and until we know whether the insect lays its eggs on the tea bush or in the jungle, nothing more can be done. If they are laid on the tea bush, then the moths, which can easily be seen (being quite white fluffy creatures), should be caught at all hazards: if, as we think, in the jungle, then a more effective way would be to prevent the caterpillars ascending the tea bushes by putting a band of grease round the stems on the patches affected or likely to be affected. The best material for this purpose is an impure low grade vaseline known as "dendrolene" in America

EUPROCTIS LATIFASCIA.

Put grease on stem.

Conf. with para. 418.

which absolutely resists wash by rain. It should be applied three-sixteenths of an inch thick and will then last a whole season. It is probable some of the Indian petroleum companies could supply a similar product. The whole efficacy of such an application depends on the home of the eggs from which the caterpillar arises, a point not yet quite made out.

57. Euproctis latifascia, *Wlk.*

THE DARJEELING HAIRY TEA CATERPILLAR.

THE DARJEELING HAIRY TEA CATERPILLAR.

SEE PLATE VI, No. 1.

References.—*Hampson, Fauna Brit. Ind. (Moths), Vol. I., 472; Notes on Tea in Darjeeling, p. 53; Indian Mus. Notes, Vol. IV., 180, 185.*

Found in Darjeeling.

Found in the Hills.

420. ***History.***—While the last species seems to confine itself, as a tea pest, to the plains, the present one, very closely allied to it, has been exclusively found up to the present in the higher districts. What appears to be this species was long ago noticed by the author of "Notes on Tea in Darjeeling." In 1897, however, there appears to have been an epidemic, and complaints were numerous from several gardens in the Darjeeling district. Since that time it always does a certain amount of damage, but has never caused serious alarm.

Epidemic in 1897.

421. ***Description.***—The character of the caterpillar can be seen from the Plate, where it is drawn natural size. It is a creature about an inch long when fully grown, blackish brown in colour and hairy, which eats principally the old leaves and bark from the bushes. The moth, in which the difference in size between the male (*Plate VI, No. 1 b*) and the female (*Plate VI, No. 1 c*) is considerable, is a white fluffy insect, which can often be seen hovering about the tea bushes in the months of May and June. It has been given the local name of "Cabbage Fluffy" in one of the Darjeeling valleys on account of its appearance. The wings, head and thorax are dull white in colour, the abdomen dark with an orange tuft at the anus. Except in size, there are no marked features different in the appearance of the sexes.

Eats old Leaves and Back.

422. ***Depredations.***—In 1897 Mr. Harrison, of the Lebong Tea Estate, wrote with reference to this caterpillar: "It attacks the old leaves and strips the trees. It performs all its ravages at night, and

The Darjeeling Hairy Tea Caterpillar.

THE DARJEELING HAIRY TEA CATERPILLAR.

Conf. with para. 419.

hides itself under clods and stones during day. . . . They appear on the dry ridges and are not found in any damp hollows. They have stripped the leaves from some 50 to 60 acres of an adjoining garden, and are now attacking the bark." Another writer says: "During the night (it) comes out in swarms, and has eaten up every old leaf on the bush. In the day it burrows under clods. . . . On one garden near Darjeeling and not a very large one, no less than 5,000 or thereabouts of the vermin caterpillars were caught by 12 *chokras.*"

423. ***Remedy.***—Nothing can be added to what has been said under the previous species. It will be seen that the method of attack and other particulars of this pest correspond in every particular, and the treatment should thus be the same.

424. The three following species have been noticed as feeding on tea, and their names should therefore be put on record. They are hardly however naturally tea-feeders and hence not tea pests.

NEUMENES SILETTI.

58. **Neumenes siletti,** *Wlk.* [See *Hampson, Fauna Brit. Ind.* (*Moths*), *Vol I.*, *456.*]—Found in Assam.

LEUCOMA SUBMARGINATA.

59. **Leucoma submarginata,** *Wlk.* [See *Hampson, Fauna Brit. Ind.* (*Moths*), *Vol. I.*, *487.*] Found in Upper Assam.

60. **Porthesia xanthorrhæa,** *Koll.* [*See Hampson, Fauna. Brit. Ind.* (*Moths*), *Vol. I*, *485.*]—The larvæ of this insect are found in Ceylon frequently on tea bushes, feeding on young leaves and blossoms. It does no appreciable damage.

Family HYPSIDÆ.

HYPSA ALCIPHRON.

61. **Hypsa alciphron,** *Cram.*

Reference.—*Hampson, Fauna Brit. Ind.* (*Moths*), *Vol. I.*, *502.*

425. This very common moth was found feeding on tea in one or two places in Assam. The caterpillars were reared by **Mr. J. A. Thomson** at Ligri Pukri. It can hardly be said to be a pest.

Family ARCTIIDÆ.

426. This family of nocturnal moths is, like the last, characterised by having fairly large hairy caterpillars. It is probable that some half a dozen or more species are occasionally found on the tea plant, but none of them have as yet assumed a very definite position as tea pests. The following have, however, been noticed attacking the tea plant.

ARCTIA RICINI.

62. **Arctia ricini,** *Fabr.*

References.—*Hampson, Fauna Brit. Ind.* (*Moths*), *Vol. II.*, *17*; *Ind. Mus. Notes, III.* (*6*), *14*; *Jour., Agri.-Horti. Soc. Ind.* (*1897*), *Vol. XI.*, *603.*

The Lepidoptera (Noctuidæ).

ARCTIA RICINI.

Found in Darjeeling.

427. In 1897 the caterpillar of this moth is said to have done considerable damage on the Singtom Tea Estate, Darjeeling. The manager then wrote: "The caterpillars are in millions here and are quite stripping the bushes of their old leaves." The caterpillar in question is "dark brown, speckled with white, and with dorsal and lateral tufts of long dark hair." (*Hampson.*) It has not been heard of since as a tea pest.

CREATONOTUS LACTINEUS.

63. Creatonotus lactineus, *Cram.*

References.—*Hampson, Fauna Brit. Ind. (Moths), II., 27; Ind. Mus. Notes, I., 55; II., 158; III. (pt. 5) 57—58; Cotes, Tea Insects, 22 (?)*

Found in Jorhat and Ligri Pukri.

428. This well-known defoliator has only once or twice been found on tea. It is probably the insect referred to by Mr. Cotes (*loc. cit.*) as damaging a garden in Jorhat in 1891, and was found and reared from Tea by Mr. J. A. Thomson, of Ligri Pukri, in 1895. The caterpillar is black with tufts of red brown hair along the sides, and a scarlet spot on each side of the back on each section of the body, and two spots on several sections. The moth is pure white with a scarlet band along the margin of the upper pair of wings and has four black spots on the lower wings.

Though, as said above, this insect has never got serious hold of tea, it is a serious pest of agricultural crops, for it attacks cotton, sesamum, pulses, brinjal, and other plants in India,—and coffee in Ceylon. It is hardly necessary to say that every effort should be made to prevent this caterpillar getting a foothold on tea plantations.

CREATONOTUS EMITTENS.

64. Creatonotus emittens, *Wlk.*

429. This insect has been found on tea in Assam, but, fortunately, only very rarely.

LVI.—Moths with Mostly Naked Caterpillars.

Family NOCTUIDÆ.

430. This very large family of moths are with few exceptions nocturnal. The larvæ are naked; in most cases they go underground for the chrysalis stage, and only exceptionally from a cocoon. They form very serious pests of agriculture in almost all parts of the world. Fortunately tea has not been seriously attacked by them in the past except in sporadic instances.

AGROTIS YPSILON. THE CUT-WORM OR BLACK GRUB.

65. Agrotis ypsilon, *Rott.*

THE CUTWORM OR BLACK GRUB.

References.—*Hampson, Fauna Brit. Ind. (Moths), Vol. II., 182; Green, Insect Pests of the Tea Plant, 57—62; Bamber, Chem. and Agri. of Tea, 244; Ind. Mus. Notes, Vol. I., 95, 103, 108, 206; Vol. II., 6, 161; III, 1698; Cotes, Tea Insects, 24; Circ., Roy. Bot. Gard., Ceylon, 1900, p. 265.*

Found in Ceylon.

Found in Ceylon.

431. ***History.***—Mr. Green says: "This caterpillar and its allies are well-known agricultural pests all over the world; in Ceylon they

The Cutworm.

THE CUTWORM.

are most destructive in tea nurseries and to young plants growing from seed-at-stake. In the latter case the pest is even more annoying, as, owing to the extended area, little can be done to check it." Though many planters have spoken to us of the destruction of seedlings in such a way as to lead us to suspect this was the enemy, the insect has always, where we have been able to investigate personally, been the cricket, and not the cutworm. There is little doubt the cutworm does attack tea in India, but we have no positive information on the point. We owe therefore the following account of the insect and its ravages in Ceylon to Mr. Green.

Caterpillar.

432. ***Description.***—"The eggs are usually laid upon the leaves and twigs of small plants." "The full grown caterpillar is a smooth dull brown grub, about an inch and three quarters in length; its head is hard and horny, and there is a horny plate on the back of the second segment; there are several rows of small shining black spots along its body, but these are inconspicuous against its general dark colour; the legs are short, and more suitable for burrowing than climbing. When ready to undergo its transformation, it forms a rough earthen cocoon underground, within which it changes to a bright red chrysalis. The moth flies only at night, resting during the day under leaves and rubbish; it is a dull-coloured insect, the front wings dull brown mottled and barred with darker markings, the hind wings white with faint brown veins. The female is a darker insect than the male, and the markings on its front wings are not so conspicuous."

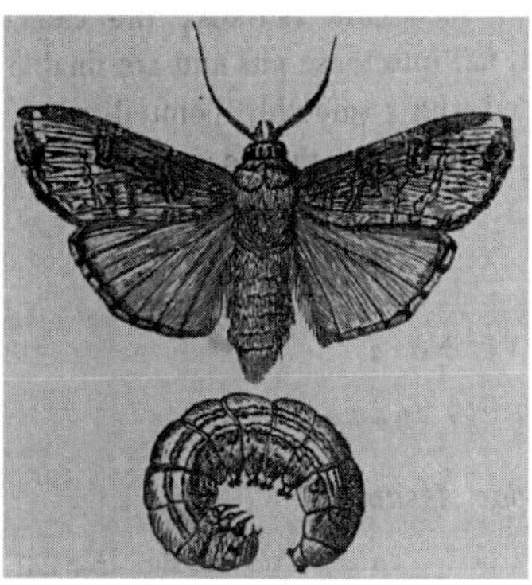

FIG. 20.—THE TEA CUTWORM.
Showing moth and caterpillar.
(After Cotes.)

Cocoon underground.

Moth.

Hide in ground in day time.

433. ***Depredations.***—"The caterpillars hide themselves in the ground during day time, and are particularly fond of the loose earth of nursery beds; at night they come to feed, and then the work of destruction commences. The animal wastes very much more than it consumes, for it will eat only the succulent part of the

THE CUTWORM.

Each Caterpillar attacks many seedlings.

stem where it joins on to the root. While the caterpillar is young, it may perhaps be content with sacrificing one plant each night, but as it grows larger it increases the number until the full-grown larva may very possibly shear off ten or twelve plants at each meal: in the morning the severed plants will be found lying where they fell, looking just as if they had been cut off with a knife, and the perpetrator of the outrage will have taken refuge again underground."

Remedy.

434. ***Remedy.***—"The only remedy for this pest is, collecting the grubs each morning and destroying them before they can do any more mischief. With a little practice, the burrow of the caterpillar can generally be found near one of the decapitated plants: sometimes it is indicated by few green eaves partially drawn into the opening. The grub will be found about an inch below the surface, generally coiled up." "Smooth conical holes sunk in the beds have sometimes been found successful as traps; the caterpillars, wandering about at night, fall into these pits and are unable to climb out: they should be formed with a smoothly pointed stake, pressed into the moist earth and rotated until the sides of the holes are smooth and firm." (*Green.*)

Traps for Caterpillars.

PRODENIA LITTORALIS.

66. **Prodenia littoralis,** *Boisd.*

SEE PLATE VI, NO. 2.

Reference.—*Hampson, Fauna Brit. Ind. (Moths), II., 247.*

Found in Upper Assam.

Found in Sadya Road in 1900.

435. This, one of the most destructive caterpillars in the tropical countries of the old world, suddenly in 1900 turned its attention to tea in one or two gardens in Upper Assam (Sadya Road District). and by the completeness of the destruction it caused for the time being, fully maintained its reputation as an agricultural pest. The caterpillar, which is about $1\frac{1}{2}$ inches long and pale violet brown in colour with a row of yellow and of white spots on each side, suddenly appeared in August of that year and ate everything across which it came, stripping bushes, eating jungle and grass, and doing enormous damage whenever it went. The caterpillars were caught by thousands, but it was not until almost the end of the season they were brought under hand, and have since not done serious damage. Figures of the moth, caterpillar and pupa are shown on *Plate VI, No. 2.*

OPHIUSA MELICERTE.

67. **Ophiusa melicerte,** *Drury.*

References.—*Hampson, Fauna Brit. Ind. (Moths), Vol. II., 494; (as Achæa melicerte) Ind. Mus. Notes, III., 112; Cotes, Tea Insects, 26,*

PLATE XI. (*To face Page 223.*)

1. The silken case of the Bark Eating Borer.
(From Photograph by H. H. Mann.)

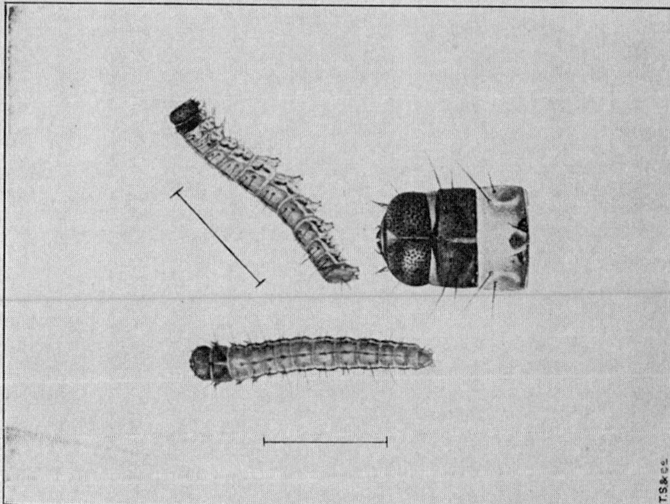

2. The Bark Eating Borer.
(From drawing made at the Indian Museum.)

Found in Dehra Dun.

OPHIOSA MELICERTE.

Found in Dehra Dun.

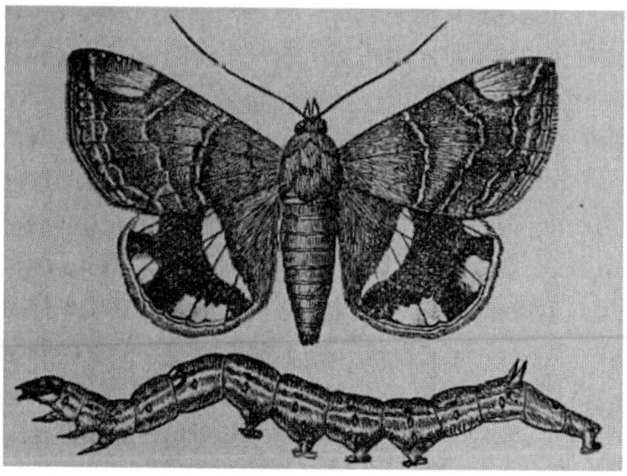

FIG. 21.—OPHIUSA MELICERTE.
Showing moth and caterpillar.
(After Cotes.)

436. Mr. Cotes informs us that the caterpillar of this moth was reported from Dehra Dun to have done considerable damage to tea in 1892. It has not been found in Assam. The Figure, reproduced from Cotes, will show its appearance, and that of its moth. Nothing can be done against it except to catch the depredator.

68. **Ophideres fullonica**, *Linn.*

OPHIDERES FULLONICA.

Reference.—*Hampson, Fauna Brit. Ind. (Moths), II., 560.*

Found in Assam.

437. The caterpillars of this very common moth have been collected on one or two occasions on tea in Assam, and reared until the perfect insect was produced. It can hardly as yet be regarded as a tea pest. A doubt has indeed been raised recently as to whether the caterpillars have really been feeding on the tea when caught, because caterpillars of this genus, as a rule, feed only on plants of the natural order **Menispermaceæ**, some of which are common on tea estates, even among the tea bushes. The observation recorded here has not been repeated recently.

69. THE BARK-EATING BORER.

THE BARK-EATING BORER.

SEE PLATE XI, NOS. 1 & 2.

Found in Assam, Sylhet, and Cachar.

South Sylhet, Assam and Cachar.

438. During a tour in South Sylhet in 1900 the work of a peculiar caterpillar was pointed out by Mr. Sanderson, of Chundeecherra, which weaves a sort of web of small bits of bark, hung together with silk, round the stem of the plant. It appears to belong to this family, but all efforts to breed out the moth have up to the present been unsuccessful. The same caterpillar was afterwards found by Mr. George Moore at Moabund, where the damage done was considerable. As a matter of fact, it seems spread in small quantity over a considerable part of the two districts named, as well as Cachar, not only attacking tea but also several other trees of which the most common is the peepul (**Ficus religiosa**).

The Lepidoptera (Noctuidæ).

THE BARK-EATING BORER.

Method of attack.

The method of attack is as follows :—In the first place, a hole, is bored in the stem generally through a knot or snag, or piece of old wood, but this hole seems to be simply used as a home to which the caterpillar can retire, and not as a place for feeding. Out of this hole it then comes and feeds on the bark. As it works on the bark, a kind of spiral cell is built round the stem (*see Plate XI, No. 2*), and in this it travels and feeds, the cell being made, as stated above, of particles of half-eaten bark fastened together with silk. The caterpillars are evidently hatched out in the early spring, as those found at that time of the year are all very small, say half inch, whereas they ultimately attain double that length, and even more. They are light greyish brown in colour with a black head (*see Plate*), and grow much larger than the hair-lines in the drawing would indicate, as large, in fact, as the drawings themselves. All attempts to obtain the cocoon or moth have hitherto failed, but they are probably formed in the ground.

Attack hide-bound bushes.

They seem to attack, principally, the old hide-bound tea bushes, and there do a very considerable amount of harm. Mr. George Moore even said to us : " It is far and away the worst form of caterpillar I have seen." As to remedy, until we know the life history of the caterpillar there seems nothing to do but to remove all the web-like runs at the pruning season, cutting out at the same time all pieces into which the insect has bored, as otherwise even after they have been abandoned they are bound to become foci for various other, even more serious, pests, such as White Ants.

70. Simplicia robustalis, *Green.* [*See Hampson, Faun. Brit. Ind. (Moths), Vol. III, 36.*]

438*a*. " Caterpillars of this species have recently been sent with the report that they were swarming upon the dead prunings, and from thence attacking the living tea, though not, as yet, to any serious extent. The caterpillar is of a dull purplish brown colour, and looks more like that of some Pyralid." (*Green, December 1902.*)

GEOMETRIDÆ.

Family GEOMETRIDÆ.

439. This family has been designated that of the Loopers or Measuring Worms, because of the peculiar mode of progression of the caterpillars. These lack all save one or two pairs of abdominal legs, and so in moving they first extend the body to its full length,

then bring the posterior end close to the front legs, looping the body in the centre, then stretch out again depending on the hind anal legs, and repeat the procedure. There is never any difficulty in recognising the caterpillars on this account. The moths can generally be known by their slender bodies, small heads, and very broad wings which are as a rule frail and thin. Samples of loopers were collected attacking tea at Ligri Pukri (green, $2\frac{1}{2}$ inches long), and at Nigriting (grey, 3—4 inches long) in 1895, but nothing more has been heard of them at these places. Two geometrids, however, one in India and the other in Ceylon, have recently become locally of great importance and have done considerable damage.

THE LOOPER CATERPILLARS.

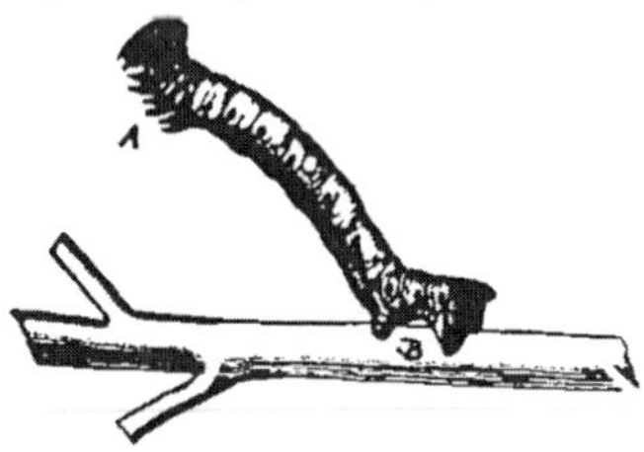

FIG. 22.—A LOOPER CATERPILLAR. (After Cotes.)

70. Biston suprессaria, *Guen.*

THE INDIAN TEA LOOPER.

SEE PLATE IX No. 2.

BISTON SUPRESSARIA.

THE INDIAN TEA LOOPER.

References.—*Hampson, Fauna Brit. Ind. (Moths), III., 247; Ind. Mus. Notes, V. (1902), 51.*

Found in Cachar, Duars, and Darjeeling.

440. ***History.***—Looper caterpillars seem occasionally to have attacked tea all over the Indian Tea Districts without anyone being able to identify exactly the caterpillar to which the damage was due. In 1900 and 1901, however, three specific attacks by that named at the head of this article occurred, and in two of these (Duars and Cachar) the damage done was considerable.

Serious attacks in the Duars and Cachar.

441. ***Description.***—The eggs of the moth seem to be laid on the leaves of various food trees, including tea, principally at night, whence they come out in a time varying at different parts of the season, but amounting to about fourteen days during the rains, as small brownish green loopers with very rapid motion, which immediately begin to feed on the leaves. The caterpillars thus produced are very inconspicuous, being remarkably like a branch of the tea plant, and it is with great difficulty that they can be detected on the bush. They grow to 2 inches in length. The chrysalis is buried in the ground and is dark brown in colour (*see Plate IX, No. 2 b & c*).

Eggs.

Caterpillars.

Chrysalis.

The moth is grey, irrorated with black, the head brown, and the thorax and abdomen have yellow bars. The habits of the moth

Moth.

The Lepidoptera (Geometridæ).

THE INDIAN TEA LOOPER.

Sits on trees in the day time.

are peculiar. During the day-time it sits with outstretched wings flat against the trunk of any tree which may be around its feeding ground, leguminous trees like the *sau* (Albizzia) being apparently preferred. On these the moths congregate in crowds, and thousands can thus, during a severe attack, be killed by simply smiting them while in this position. The moth is $2\frac{1}{4}$ to $3\frac{1}{4}$ inches in span across the wings.

Three broods per annum.

There are at least three broods per annum in Cachar, the caterpillars being active respectively in June, August, and October, with lulls in between, though of course at all times some caterpillars could be found.

442. ***Depredations.***—When a serious attack commences, as in the cases previously named, the whole of the leaves of the bushes are eaten off, and so ravenous are the caterpillars that Mr. Sproull, the planter on whose garden the Cachar attack above referred to occurred, wrote saying that he thought "about ten caterpillars would strip a fair sized bush in a couple of days." They can in fact be heard feeding, when one is standing near, when a bad attack is on the way.

Ten maunds in one day collected.

They increase so fast that during the third brood in 1901 as many as ten maunds of caterpillars were collected on one garden in Cachar in one day.

Remedy.

443. ***Remedy.***—The habits of the moth, described above, render it comparatively easy to kill an enormous number and so prevent the deposition of a very large quantity of eggs. This it is most important to do, since the destruction of one moth may mean the

Kill moths.

removal of a hundred caterpillars of the next brood. None the less, however, should the caterpillars be collected and destroyed, and the many pupæ from the ground below the bushes should be carefully dug up.

Is attacked by an Ichneumon Fly.

There is, in addition, a natural enemy—an ichneumon fly which lays its eggs in the living caterpillars, when they die either without forming its chrysalis or just after forming it. This parasitism was very marked in many of the samples obtained from Cachar last year, and it may be due to this that it is rare that the pest attacks a garden seriously two years in succession.

BOARMIA BHURMITRA.

THE TWIG CATERPILLAR.

71. **Boarmia bhurmitra,** *Wlk.*

THE "TWIG CATERPILLAR" (*Green*).

References.—*Hampson, Fauna Brit. Ind.* (*Moths*), *Vol. III.*, *260*; *Circ., Roy. Bot. Gard., Ceylon, Vol. I,* (*1900*), *p. 263.*

The Twig Caterpillar.

Found in Ceylon.

THE TWIG CATERPILLAR. Found in Ceylon.

444. Mr. Green has recently (Sept. 1900) given the following account of this new tea pest in Ceylon :—

"Although this insect has been observed commonly in Ceylon for a great number of years, it is only within the last month that it has been brought to my notice as an insect pest. Its work on an estate in the Kandy district has now well earned for it this reputation. I was able to pay a personal visit to the place, and found the caterpillars simply swarming on the tea, which they were rapidly defoliating. I was shown a large **Grevillea** clearing, across half of which the plague of caterpillars had swept. They had stripped these trees bare, together with the young Cardamon plants growing below them, and had treated several Iron-bark Gums in the same manner. On turning up the ground underneath the **Grevilleas**, the chrysalides were found in large numbers just below the surface. The manager of the property has given me the following history of the pest, as observed by himself. It has been noticed on this particular **Grevillea** clearing for the previous three years, but to a smaller extent, increasing its area of attack each consecutive year. It usually appears in February and disappears during the rainy season. The pest always starts at the top of the ridge and works downhill, directly against the prevailing wind. In the present year the plague of caterpillars continued well into August, at which time the moths were appearing in thousands, coolies being employed to catch them as they were resting on the bark of the trees. Over 50,000 were said to have been destroyed in this manner in the space of one week, a single cooly bringing in sometimes nearly a thousand moths. The showery weather greatly assisted in the success of this work, as the moths are sluggish at such times and do not readily take wing. The manager was advised to prune the zone of tea upon which the caterpillars were then feeding and to fork lime into the soil with a view to the destruction of the chrysalides. All prunings were to be burned or buried. At the time of my visit it was noticed that large numbers of the caterpillars were dying, attacked by some fungal diseases that had an extraordinarily rapid action. Apparently healthy specimens collected that morning were dead and covered with fungus ten hours later.

Attacks Grevilleas.

Is attacked by Fungus.

Remedy.

"The fact that this pest makes its first appearance, each year, on full-grown **Grevillea** trees will make it difficult to stamp it out at its commencement without sacrificing such trees. The spread of the pest is not due to an actual migration of the caterpillars, but to the fact that the moths move onwards and lay their eggs where there is food for the future larvæ. Between the months of February and July, the period when the pest is usually prevalent, there have probably been three or four distinct generations. It has not yet been determined what becomes of the insects during the rest of the year. This is a point that requires investigation. It is possible that a few individuals carry on the breed. Or it is again possible that eggs laid in July and August may remain dormant until the following January."

Caterpillar.

445. The colour of this caterpillar is not at all dissimilar to that last described, being mottled and streaked in different shades of brown so that it equally resembles a tea twig. "A full grown caterpillar measures $1\frac{1}{2}$ inch. The chrysalis is formed just below the surface of the ground. It is of a reddish colour, smooth and glossy. It remains in this stage about 14 days. The moth is very pale brown, minutely specked and spotted with darker markings which form wavy lines across the wings. Expanse from $1\frac{1}{3}$ to $1\frac{3}{4}$ inch. The moths rest during the daytime flattened against a tree trunk or rock, with wings expanded,

Chrysalis.

Moth.

The Lepidoptera (Tortricidæ and Tineidæ).

THE TWIG CATERPILLAR.

in which position their colour harmonizes remarkably with their surroundings." (*Green.*)

HYPOSIDRA SP.

72. Hyposidra, *sp.*

References.—*Hampson, Fauna Brit. Ind., Vol. III., 212; Ind. Mus. Notes, IV., 120.*

446. A looper caterpillar attacking tea was found by Mr. W. J. Fleet in Nowgong, from which he reared moths named as above. It was attacked by a parasitic (Chalcidid) fly. Nothing has been heard of it since.

EUSCHEMA MILITARIS.

73. Euschema militaris, *Linn.*

Reference.—*Hampson, Fauna Brit. Ind. (Moths), III., 468.*

Found at Ligri Pukri on Tea.

447. The caterpillar of this extremely abundant moth was picked off tea bushes by Mr. J. A. Thomson, and reared until the perfect insect had been obtained. It is fortunate that so far this moth has shown no very decided liking for tea, since it is perhaps one of the most plentiful in Assam. Unlike the majority of the family to which it belongs, it is to be seen on wing during the day time, and in shape of wing and flight is more like a butterfly than a moth. It is a large insect, the prevailing colour being golden yellow with deep purple spots especially near the outer half of the wings.

LEAF ROLLERS AND LEAF TIERS.

LVII.—Leaf-Rollers and Leaf-Tiers.

Families TORTRICIDÆ AND TINEIDÆ.

448. The very large assemblage of moths, most of them small, that have to be assigned to these and perhaps one or two other families may be dealt with conjointly. This is the more necessary since comparatively few of this group of moths found in India have as yet been identified and named. They may be very destructive, and three or four species are plentiful tea pests.

GRACILARIA THEIVORA.

74. Gracilaria theivora, *Wlsm.*

THE TEA LEAF ROLLER.

THE TEA LEAF ROLLER.

References.—*Green, Pests of the Tea Plant, 62—66; Ind. Mus. Notes, II., 49, 164; Cotes, Tea Insects, 27.*

Found in all districts.

Found in all districts.

449. ***History.***—This tea pest was discovered by Mr. Green in Ceylon, where he published an account of it, and it was long before its presence was even recognised in the Indian Tea Districts. It is however very common in North East India, and the authors have found few gardens in Assam free from it, while more recently it has been noticed in the Darjeeling district to an elevation of 4,500 feet. There is a little doubt whether the examples found of similar work in the Kangra Valley are caused by the same insect, but for present purposes they may be considered as identical.

Egg.

450. ***Description.***—The egg is deposited near the midrib and on the under surface of the leaf. On hatching, the minute caterpillar is at first a leaf-miner. It eats along, in a somewhat

The Tea Leaf Roller.

THE TEA LEAF ROLLER.

tortuous course, toward the margin. It then escapes and becomes a leaf-roller, and subsequently causes the margin of the leaf, for half an inch to an inch in length and perhaps less than one-eigth of an inch breadth, to turn over itself. Within that enclosure it commences to eat the epidermis of the enclosed portion. Shortly after, however, it migrates to a fresh leaf and now commences its more vigorous action. The overturned margin dies, and gives to the leaf a withered, discoloured and torn appearance. Few gardens exist in which leaves, that would answer to this description, are unusual, though their wretched condition is generally attributed to hail or rough handling on the part of coolies.

Caterpillar.

It requires very little skill to recognise the winding slightly discoloured passage within the texture of the leaf and the overturned margin described above [*Fig. 23* (*a*)]; all such leaves should be instantly removed in order to check further depredations.

Leaf Miner and Leaf Roller.

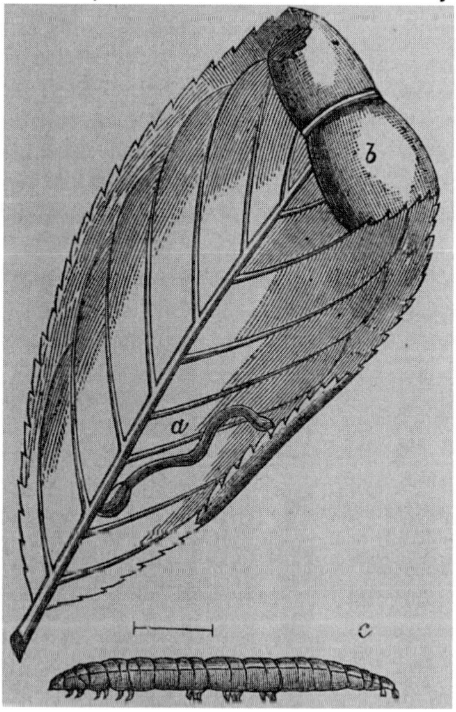

FIG. 23.—THE TEA LEAF ROLLER.
a. Leaf-mining stage. *b.* Leaf-rolling stage. *c.* Caterpillar much enlarged.
(From a sketch by G. Watt.)

In the rough sketch of a leaf taken possession of by this pest we have (*Fig. 23*) shown both the leaf-mining stage (*a*) and the leaf-rolling (*b*) on the same leaf. This may be taken as rarely happening. The insect in fact, during its larval existence, repeatedly changes its house, and thus destroys a large number of leaves. The caterpillar (*c*) is shown greatly enlarged. It is a minute yellow-white creature which, when full grown, is little more than half an inch in length. It will be observed to possess only three pairs of prolegs in the middle of its body.

The Lepidoptera (Tortricidæ, etc.).

THE TEA LEAF ROLLER.

The caterpillar and moth are also shown in *Fig. 24*, from specimens occurring in Ceylon, and drawn by Mr. Green.

Experiments.

451. On the leaf-houses being plucked, the caterpillars come out, since the leaves soon thereafter begin to wither. If given fresh leaves they refuse them. To overcome this Mr. J. A. Thomson undertook to carry out a series of experiments. Six muslin bags, each 3 to 6 inches in size, had two of those caterpillars placed within, and then inverted over and tied round a healthy twig. The object was to get them to attack the enclosed leaves, eat and form cocoons, and in time come out as perfect insects. To make certain of obtaining this object, six twigs were also selected, each found to contain a rolled-up leaf. These were with the utmost care tied within muslin bags and were to have been left undisturbed in order to allow the insects to be formed. But both experiments failed completely, since next day the caterpillars in each case, finding themselves prisoners, cut holes through the muslin bags and made off. To rear the insect, therefore, it is necessary to enclose a seedling within a fine zinc gauze cage.

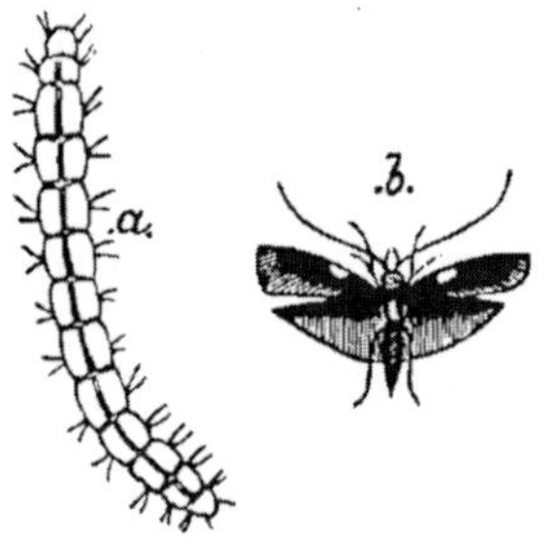

FIG. 24.—CATERPILLAR AND MOTH OF TEA LEAF ROLLER.
a. Caterpillar. *b.* Moth.
(After E. E. Green.)

Cocoons.

The cocoons may easily be discovered, however, and the perfect insect obtained from them. When mature, the caterpillar spins a small silken cocoon about one-quarter of an inch long and little more than one-sixteenth in breadth. This will be found within depressions of the leaf or under the lee of the midrib. It opens by a circular mouth, to allow of the escape of the perfect insect.

Moth.

The moth when its wings are expanded is a very small pretty insect with deeply fringed wings, the front pair shining with iridescent tints and being crossed by a yellow band.

452. ***Depredations.***—The insect commences its ravages by carefully sewing up the leaf as it rolls it round (see *Fig. 23*) and when the conch-shell-like structure, thus formed, has been completely wound up and firmly bound together at both ends, the caterpillar proceeds to eat the leaf from the tip downwards. As it progresses

the excretory matter is carefully packed on one side, and partitioned off by a fold off the margin of the leaf brought down for that purpose. When the contained portions of the leaf have been devoured, the operation of winding up the leaf still further is renewed. Coil after coil is made, but usually not more than half the leaf is eaten. The insect then migrates and commences once more to roll a leaf around itself.

THE TEA LEAF ROLLER.

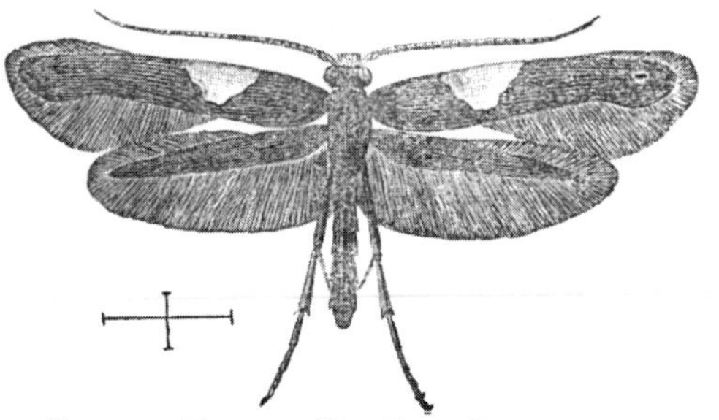

FIG. 25.—MOTH OF TEA LEAF ROLLER, MUCH ENLARGED.
(From a drawing by Lord Walsingham.)

It never, however, severs its house in any way from the rest of the leaf, but, on the contrary, the shattered leaf again uncoils when the caterpillar leaves it. In fact, to allow of its free egress, it methodically forms a door. It seems, moreover, to always leave its feeding house when the time arrives for its changing into the condition of a chrysalis.

Method of work.

453. During his study of this caterpillar one of the authors (G. W.) uncoiled a leaf house and placed it on his table. "The caterpillar at once proceeded to coil the leaf round itself once more, and in 20 minutes it had completely accomplished that object. Raising itself to its full height, it applied its mouth to a distant part of the leaf, the head was then swept rapidly to the opposite margin and a thread attached there. Backwards and forwards the head moved for three or four seconds in the same direction, then it was carried down to the bottom across the strands, and up through them again carrying as it were cross threads that tightened the former ones and thus brought the fold of the leaf over itself. While engaged in this cross binding operations, the caterpillar held on by its anal prolegs and made the whole of the rest of its body swing backwards and forwards with great rapidity. In another leaf unfolded, two caterpillars were found, and it was interesting to watch how they acted in concert, the heads flying backwards and forwards in the exact same direction for a time, then changing to the opposite action simultaneously."

The Lepidoptera (Tortricidæ, etc.).

THE TEA LEAF ROLLER.

454. In causing the leaf to coil this insect seems to nip the midrib, and at the points of reversion, too, it often cuts it nearly through. The surface of the leaf within the coiled-up portion is also seen to be pitted more or less all over. These portions soon turn brownish, and to the naked eye resemble minute scales. These were at first taken for eggs of some kind, but under the microscope were found to be actual injuries inflicted by the caterpillar, hence it would appear the caterpillar feeds on the sap of the leaf and eats a layer of the cellular tissue as well. Within the coiled-up portion there is always a little watery fluid. This seems to decompose the leaf, since the coiled-up portions are often observed to be quite brown and membranous in addition to the fact that the soft pulpy under-surface has been completely eaten away.

Attacks second, third and fourth leaves on shoot.

455. It was also noted that the insect destroys its silken cords before emerging from its conch-shell house, and in consequence the leaves, as already remarked, uncoil to a certain extent. They then constitute a large percentage of the leaves that are seen to have rotten and fungoid-attacked tips. In this respect, however, the final action of the leaf-roller is not so objectionable as the sandwich caterpillar described below, since it destroys, as a rule, only one leaf at a time and but the top half of that, whereas the sandwich insect unites together a large number of leaves, destroys the middle and lower portions of them and leaves behind it a putrid and decomposing mass, the nursery-bed doubtless of many other pests. This caterpillar appears specially bad in the Sibsagar District of Assam. In one garden, during April and May, every bush might have three or four leaf-rollers upon it. It does not go for the old and comparatively useless leaves of the plant, but for the second, third, and fourth leaves of the young shoots, so that it interferes directly with the yield. It is therefore a dangerous pest, and should not be looked upon merely as a curiosity, and hence should be kept strictly in hand.

Pick off rolled up leaves.

456. ***Remedy.***—There is but one cure. Put on all hands necessary and pick off the rolled up leaves, but more especially the tunnelled leaves, with reflexed margins. If these contain the larvæ, every leaf so plucked means the saving of perhaps a dozen leaves that would be otherwise subsequently rolled up and destroyed.

75. Capua coffearia, *Nietn.*

CAPUA COFFEARIA: THE TEA TORTRIX.

THE TEA TORTRIX.

References.—*Green, Pests of the Tea Plant, 89—93; Bamber, Chem., and Agri. Tea, 295; Cotes, Tea Insects, 28; Ind. Mus. Notes, II., 163; Planter, Sept. 26, 1896; Administ. Report, Roy. Bot. Gard., Ceylon, 1899, p. 13; Circ., Roy. Bot. Gard., Ceylon, Vol. I. (1900), 244; Vol. II. (1903).*

Found in Ceylon, Darjeeling, Cachar, and Assam.

457. ***History.***—This pest has never been severe in India, but in the Dikoya and Dimbula districts of Ceylon, and in South India (under the name of the "flush-worm") it seems to have been of considerable importance. It has been supposed that there were two or three species involved but, according to recent study, all the Ceylon forms are identical, and too little is known about those of India to warrant them being placed under a separate heading. The work they do is closely similar. Most severe in Ceylon.

Even in Ceylon, where the attacks of this caterpillar have been more serious than anywhere else, it produced at first only spasmodic attacks, but "during the last three years it has assumed a more permanent character, and is responsible for a considerable annual loss of yield in certain localities." (*Green.*) The loss through this single pest has been estimated in places as ten rupees per acre in one year, and there are signs that the pest is extending its ravages in several districts of the island.

458. ***Description.***—Mr. Green has carefully studied this pest, and has kindly placed his results at our service. We are, in fact, dependent almost entirely on his account for what follows. The eggs are deposited in dense flat clusters (overlapping like the scales of a fish) on the upper surface of the tea leaves. As they are of a pale greenish yellow colour, and are flattened and disc-shaped in appearance, they are conspicuous objects on the dark green leaves, and can be easily seen and collected. Two native boys, who were put on to the work, collected in a couple of days 1,075 clusters. Each cluster measures about $\frac{5}{8}$ inch by $\frac{1}{4}$ inch, and contains, on an average, a little over 300 eggs. At an expenditure of about R1, therefore, 322,500 individuals were accounted for. Eggs. Collection.

The Lepidoptera (Tortricidæ, etc.).

THE TEA TORTRIX.

Caterpillar. "Caterpillar: dull green or greenish white, with a shining black head and a black horny patch on the back of the second segment. (*See Fig. 25 b.*) There are about 12 minute tubercles on each division of the body, from each of which springs a fine bristle. When full-grown the caterpillar is about ¾ inch long. (*See Fig. 25 a.*)

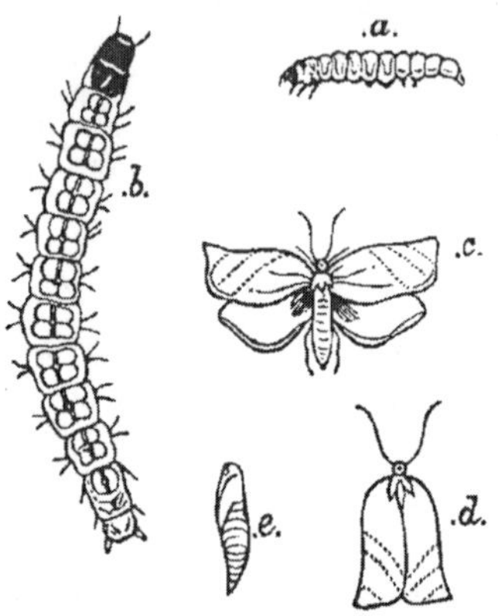

FIG. 25.—THE TEA TORTRIX.
a. Caterpillar, natural size; *b.* caterpillar, enlarged; *c.* and *d.* moth; *e* caterpillar.
(From a drawing by E. E. Green.)

"Until the first moult the caterpillars are more or less gregarious. They fasten two leaves together and live beneath that shelter, feeding on the enclosed surfaces of the leaves. After the next moult they distribute themselves over the tea-bush, and each individual forms a separate shelter for itself by spinning one or two leaves together—often enclosing a young shoot—within which they live and feed."

Chrysalis. The larval stage occupies from three to four weeks, after which the caterpillar fastens two leaves firmly together and turns to a dark mahogany-coloured chrysalis. (*See Fig. 25 c.*)

Moth. The moth usually appears in from seven to ten days' time, though twenty days have been known to elapse before its emergence. It is an inconspicuous insect. The fore-wings of a pale reddish-ochreous colour, with some indefinite diagonal lines. The hind-wings are straw-coloured, without markings. The expanded wings of the female measure nearly one inch. The male is somewhat smaller and of a darker tint. When at rest the wings are folded so that their outline is like that of the section of a bell. They fly at night, and it is at this time that the egg masses are deposited. They are attracted by light.

459. ***Depredations.***—The caterpillar under discussion is serious because of its habit of spinning together two or three leaves *including the flush*, and feeding on the enclosed parts. "When the

PLATE XII. (*To face Page 235.*)

2. The Moth of Sandwich Caterpillar.—See page 235.
(From Photograph by T. H. Hall.)

3. The Sandwich Caterpillar at Work.—See page 236.
(From Photograph by T. H. Hall.)

pest is at its worst the leaf may be destroyed over whole fields of tea, resulting in a very serious loss of flush" (*Green*). It appears that in Ceylon the fields attacked are generally three to six months from pruning, just when the best flushes are coming on. The tea plant is not by any means the only one affected by the insect. It also attacks Grevilleas, Albizzias (*Sau*), and even Eucalyptus trees. THE SANDWICH CATER-PILLAR.

460. ***Remedy.***—The observations of Mr. Green relative to the eggs seem to afford a simple, inexpensive, and radical cure, if only the eggs can be once recognised. There seems little doubt that these means will be quite effective in controlling the pest, and it is at least the most important of the methods hitherto suggested. Remedy.

Measures should also be taken to destroy the caterpillars by plucking off the folded leaves and burning them. The use of Paris Green, an arsenical mixture, has been recommended for spraying the bushes, and it has been stated that leaf could be plucked ten or twelve days later without danger of any arsenic getting into the tea. We should be glad, however, to avoid the method if possible.

The moths being attracted by light can be caught by means of lamps at night, but the practical value of the method is still doubtful.

76. The Sandwich Caterpillar.

See Plate XII, Nos. 1 and 2.

Reference.—*Indian Mus. Notes, IV., 61.*

Found in Sibsagar, Lakhimpur, and in Cachar.

461. ***History.***—Very closely allied to the two insects mentioned above, comes the one to which the fanciful name of the Sandwich Caterpillar has been given. It is the larva of one of the larger tortricid moths, but its strict identification has not yet been made out. Though it can be found on tea in Cachar, it is confined, so far as one can be certain, as a serious tea pest to a comparatively small area in Sibsagar, Assam, and a still smaller area in Dibrugarh and North Lakhimpur, but here it is a very serious enemy. As an example of its possible importance, it may be said that Mr. Ferguson (of the Hunwal Tea Co., Moriani) informed us he had spent over 2,000 rupees in 1900 in dealing with this blight alone. The "House forming Tineid" of the previous edition of this work, obtained from Borsillah, is almost certainly a somewhat modified form of the same caterpillar. Found in Upper Assam.

The Lepidoptera (Tortricidæ, etc.).

THE SANDWICH CATERPILLAR.

Eggs not known.

462. ***Description.***—The eggs are not known. They are probably laid on the older leaves of the plant.

Caterpillars.

Caterpillars.—These are generally ½ to 1 inch in length and a tenth to an eighth of an inch or thereabouts in thickness. They are long, narrow, quick-moving creatures, of a dirty brownish colour above, and yellow or orange colour below, smooth, shining and hairless, except one or two long white hairs, which spring from the bottom one of an inverted triangle of three spots on the sides of each segment of the body. In older insects hairs may also be seen springing from the top spots as well, so that in that case three spreading hairs occur on the sides of the somites which otherwise are smooth and naked. The terminal segment and the head are dark brown, and the last two anal segments have retractile portions, which are possibly used to enable the worm to wriggle and jump when disturbed. An important difference between this caterpillar and the leaf-roller already described exists in the fact that it has four pairs of prolegs in the middle of the body instead of three pairs.

Chrysalis.

The chrysalis is a naked, black brown little structure with a polished shining surface. It has the power of moving when disturbed, and is deposited either in the sandwich houses or in the soil at the foot of the tea bush. During the season this stage lasts about three weeks, but later on it appears to be the form in which the insect hibernates and is found in the ground in the late autumn.

Moth.

The moth is a dirty white, small creature with fringed wings. The forewings have a row of small black spots near to and parallel with the edge. (*See Plate XII, No. 1.*)

Method of work.

463. ***Depredations.***—The work of the caterpillar may be described as follows. It brings down a few leaves flat on the top of each other and ties them in that position by silken threads. Two, three or more form its house, but it adds a fresh leaf with dew on it day after day until it has fastened together a fairly conspicuous mass, the bottom leaves of which become rotten. Bushes with this pest upon them consequently appear very untidy. When opened up the older leaves of the sandwich masses are seen to be eaten about the middle and lower half, and according to age manifest brown portions and numerous perforations. On tearing the topmost leaf off a little water will generally be found within, together with a large quantity of excretory matter and fragments of leaves. The agent

of this destruction will readily be recognized as a small, very active little caterpillar, one or two of which will often be found within each of these bundles of leaves sewn together. In spinning its nest within the sandwich mass of leaves, the insect turns over the margin of one or two leaves, and takes about half an hour to accomplish this task. THE SANDWICH CATERPILLAR.

Large consolidated slabs of decomposing leaves drawn together from all the neighbouring twigs are not only unsightly and destructive to a distinct proportion of the flushing power of the bush, but positively dangerous. We cannot say that thread blight is a fungus that has been demonstrated by us as being in direct association with the sandwich caterpillar, but it is within the bounds of possibility that the decomposing structure and the contained manure left by that insect might become the nidus in which thread blight and other blights originate. Many fungi are purely saprophytic in the first half of their lives, and parasitic during the second. That is to say, they live for a time on decomposing vegetable matter before they are able to attack living plants. In the sandwich masses of leaves and excretory matter, a fertile bed for the propagation of many such germs, would no doubt exist. May act as Nidus for Fungi.

464. ***Remedy.***—Fortunately this curious little pest is one easily seen, and the nimble hands and the quick eyes of the children should be at once utilized in removing and bringing the patches with their contained caterpillars to the factory to be there destroyed. There is no other treatment simpler, nor more likely to be successful, than systematic and persistent plucking. When the sandwich structures are found fresh and green they will contain the active caterpillar, or when withered they most probably may each have one or more chrysalides. In both cases, therefore, it is desirable to remove and destroy them, even should it be found that there is little ground for the suggestion that these decomposing masses of leaves become the breeding for other pests and blights. Remedy.

CHAPTER XI.

THE INSECT PESTS OF TEA–continued.

DIPTERA.

DIPTERA.

LVIII.—The Flies, Gnats, Gad-Flies, etc.

465. The maggots or larvæ of a large number of the two-winged flies **(Diptera)** are dangerous pests to agriculture in various parts of the world. These maggots are, with few exceptions, footless, and in many instances hardly possess what may be called a head. There is only one tea parasite, so far as is known, that belongs to this order of insects, *viz.*:—**Oscinis theæ.** There are, however, a very large number of friendly Dipterous flies parasitic upon the larvæ and chrysalides of many of the moths described in the preceding chapter.

OSCINIS THEÆ.

LEAF-MINING FLY.

Conf. with para. 488.

76. Oscinis theæ, *Bigot.*

THE TEA LEAF-MINING FLY.

References.—*Green, Insect Pests of the Tea Plant, 66, Bamber; Chem. Agri. Tea, 245, 255; Ind. Mus. Notes, I., 204; II., 166; III., 138; Cotes, Tea Insects.*

Found in all districts.

466. ***History.***—This is perhaps the most common insect to be found on the tea bushes in India and Ceylon. **Mr. Green** was the first to draw attention to it in Ceylon, and though **Mr. Bamber** mentions the existence of a leaf-mining insect, **Mr. Cotes** declared in his book (1895) that it "had not yet been recorded from India." It can, however, be found in almost every garden, and where no other parasite of the bush is present on a garden, the silvery white runs where the insect has fed cannot fail to attract the eye on the older leaves.

Common in Assam.

467. ***Description.***—The rough sketch opposite gives the appearance of a leaf, burrowed by this insect. After wandering about to a considerable extent and devouring the tissue, below the upper epidermis, the larva moves towards the margin and there pupates. The letter (*a*), *Figure 27*, indicates the pupal case. In Ceylon the larvæ seem to form sinuous tunnels instead of burrowing and eating over a more or less compact space—the more usual habit of the

The Tea Leaf Mining Fly.

Indian insect. The sinuous tunnels of the Ceylon insect are, however, found commonly enough in India. **OSCINIS THEÆ.**

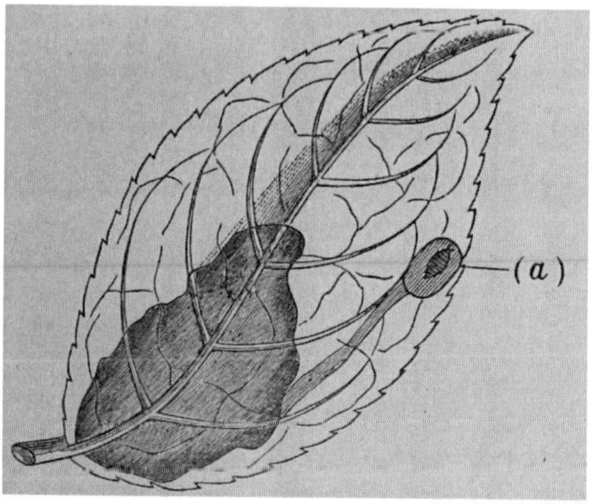

FIG. 27.—THE TEA LEAF-MINING FLY.
Showing (*a*) the pupal case.
(From a sketch by G. Watt.)

468. ***Depredations.***—Fortunately this interesting little fly seems to prefer last year's leaves, and not more than one affected leaf here and there can be said to be met with, so that at present it has to be viewed as a curiosity more than a pest. At the same time we have found some gardens sufficiently attacked to suggest the undesirability of this fly being allowed to increase. Mr. Green tells us that the larvæ lie from first to last in the single leaf upon which the egg was deposited. "The action," he remarks, "of the little miner, while at work, can be distinctly seen through the thin cuticle of the leaf. It moves its head—which contains a sharp-cutting instrument—in regular sweeps, like a mower with his scythe. At each sweep a portion of the cuticle is separated from the leaf and (presumably) a portion of the leaf is taken into the animal's body. It is a very rapid worker: a specimen under examination cleared a space more than twice its own size within half an hour's time." **Found on last year's leaves.**

It may be here added, however, that several allied insects, such as the Hessian Fly on wheat, the Frit Fly on oats, the Turnip leaf-miner, the Rice Fly, are serious agricultural pests, and this shows that mining flies cannot be despised. There can be no doubt that every leaf invaded is destroyed to the plant, and the study of pests is beset with sudden and unexpected expansions, so that it would be unsafe to say that this minute parasite is incapable of ever becoming a source of anxiety to the tea planter.

CHAPTER XII.

THE INSECT PESTS OF TEA—continued.

HYMENOPTERA.

HYMENOPTERA.

LIX.—The Saw-flies, Gall-flies, Ichneumon-flies, Bees, Wasps and Ants.

469. This order of insects embraces a good few forms that are destructive to plants such as the Saw-flies and Gall-flies, but many others that are parasitic on plant pests, such as the Ichneumon-flies. It is somewhat curious that no species of Saw-fly nor Gall-fly has, so far, been recorded as met with on the tea.

The members of this order are all characterised by the possession of mandibles; wings, when present, in two pairs which, during flight, are often linked together so as to act as one pair; and by the first segment of the abdomen being separated from the remaining segments and united to the thorax, the attachment of the remainder of the abdomen being by a flexible joint.

Two species of ants are commonly found on the tea plant. Some planters regard these as friendly. They are as follows:

CREMASTOGASTER ROGENHOFERI.

RED AND BLACK ANT.

78. Cremastogaster rogenhoferi, *Mayr.*

THE RED AND BLACK ANT OF THE TEA BUSHES.

SEE PLATE XIII, No. 1.

470. This insect which had not been, prior to 1898, apparently recorded as a pest of tea cultivation, is closely allied to **Cremastogaster Dohrni**, *Mayr.*, which in Ceylon has been found to injure Cinchona, Coffee and Tea. It forms small, black-looking, mud enclosures around the twigs, mostly near the bifurcations of the shoots. These may at first be only an inch in length, and contain perhaps not more than a dozen ants. In course of time, however, they gradually increase in size, until they become from a foot to a foot and a half in diameter, and then contain many thousand ants. The hive is constructed of a black-papier-maché looking material, in which no doubt

Hives on tea bushes.

The Red and Black Ant.

there is a large proportion of mud. It is formed more or less in layers, so it would appear when viewed from the outside, but, on being cut open, it is seen to be composed of a vast number of galleries of cells in every direction. There is no outer protecting membrane, and it is of one material throughout. **THE RED AND BLACK ANT.**

471. It was formerly the idea among a considerable number of planters that these ants building in the tea bushes was the means of protecting an estate from other insect pests. Needless to say the idea is altogether false, and is exploded practically all over the tea districts at present. **Ants are not beneficial.**

472. The head and thorax of the ant are of a bright brick-red colour: it has two sharp spurs on either side of the middle portion of the "alitrunk" or first abdominal section attached to the thorax. The abdomen proper is of a somewhat triangular shape, pointed at the anal extremity, and during the act of running is carried in a strikingly erect and threatening attitude. A very large number of small nests of this ant may generally be found constructed on bushes badly affected by the Tea Aphis (**Ceylonia theæcola**). Up and down the shoots these clever little ants may be seen running while paying their attention to the aphis. Far, however, from eating that particular tea pest, they protect and even imprison it; for this purpose they carry up some of the material of which their hives are formed and cement the leaves of the shoot around the aphis. It seems probable, therefore, that new ant nests are formed around colonies of that insect, and it is the sweet sugary exudation which the aphis produces that they are after, so that they are careful to protect, rather than kill, the aphis. The Ceylon ant, according to **Mr. Green**, imprisons scale insects (**Lecanium, etc.**) for the same purpose, but we have not noticed this in India. *Conf. with paras. 572–578.* **Imprison the Tea-aphis.**

473. The ants, however, become pests themselves of a serious nature. They injure the bark on the portion of the branches within their hives to such an extent that the circulation of sap is checked, and the parts projecting above the hive are accordingly starved and rapidly die. On no account, therefore, should these ants be allowed to get established in tea-gardens. The injury they do to the tea plant far outweighs any possible help they may render, and their hives should accordingly be cleared off every bush upon which they are found.

The Hymenoptera.

ŒCOPHYLLA SMARAGDINA. RED ANT.

80. Œcophylla smaragdina, *Fabr.*

THE RED ANT OF ASSAM.

474. This is the common ant seen on trees all over the province. It draws together a mass of leaves and unites them by a fine white silken web into a hive. It is capable of biting with considerable severity on being disturbed, and is accordingly a source of great annoyance to the women while picking tea leaf. It is no doubt a carnivorous insect, and might do good, but is distinctly objectionable. Besides this, it cannot be healthy for the tea bush to have a clump of its twigs and leaves, perhaps 2 feet in length and breadth, tied up in the manner indicated. There is also evidence from experiments by Dr. Butler that it carries "red rust" about the trees on which it builds its nest. Flushing with that portion of the bush, on which the nest is placed, is quite out of the question, and we are much disposed to think that the two or three bushes adjoining a red ant's nest are very likely to be neglected by the pluckers and the hoers.

Source of annoyance and loss.

Remedy.

475. ***Remedy.***—The best way to get rid of both the above species of ants is to place a small box over the hive and light a basin of flour of sulphur below. The majority of the ants will be killed, and in the morning the hive may then be cleared off or the branch bearing it may be cut off.

THE SMALL BLACK ANT.

81. The Small Black Ant.

476. A small black ant, whose scientific name we have not yet been able to ascertain, appears in a considerable number of places about the roots of the tea bush, even penetrating it where a hole exists. This is found both in Assam (Koliabar) and Darjeeling. At first sight it was supposed the insects were after a scaley bug of some sort, and occasionally this is found to be the case. At other times neither the cause of their presence nor their work has yet been made out, but the enormous numbers present occasionally have given a good deal of anxiety in several of the estates where they occur. The best method of dealing with them is probably to spray them and the hole where they enter with kerosene emulsion. Two or three applications of this kind will soon clear them out.

Conf. with Appendix.

WASPS.

82. Wasps.

477. Various species of Wasps are occasionally found on the tea bushes, and should be killed and their hives removed in the manner described for ants. A small nest of red ants, lopped off and placed at night against a wasp's hive, will, we are told, be found an excellent method of dealing with wasps. Two or three ants attack each wasp, and in a few hours' time the entire swarm will be found dead.

LOCUSTS.

CHAPTER XIII.

THE INSECT PESTS OF TEA—continued.

ORTHOPTERA.

LX.—The Grasshoppers, Crickets, Locusts.

478. The insects belonging to this order are so called because the wings are folded lengthwise, the lower wings being closed fan-like beneath the upper pair. The body is more or less cylindrical, and the forelegs very often formed for burrowing in the ground. They accordingly dig holes, many of them living very largely on larvæ and worms, others on roots, fruits and leaves. The Locust is, perhaps, the best known defoliator of this assemblage of insects, but to the tea planter the Cricket is the most serious pest of the order. It would seem probable that there may be two or three species of Cricket, though we have only met with one in Assam.

83. **Acridium peregrinum,** *Oliver.* ACRIDIUM PEREGRINUM.

84. **Acridium flavicorne,** *Fabr.*

85. **Catantops indicus,** *Saussure.*

LOCUSTS. LOCUSTS.

References.—*Cotes, Tea Insects, 43 ; Peal, Tea Gazette.*

479. Particulars are given by Mr. Cotes of the above species. Mr. Peal

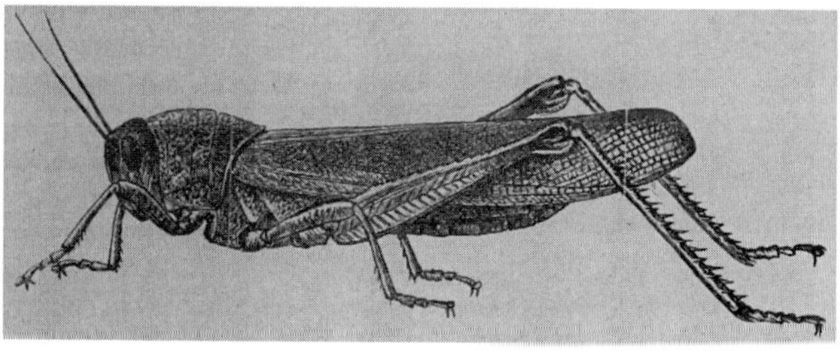

FIG. 28.—LOCUST ATTACKING TEA.
(After Cotes.)

in a letter to the *Tea Gazette*, says: "Lately part of my garden was taken possession of by many thousands of locusts, apparently the same as those I have seen in flights in the hills of the North West." "These insects did not feed on the tea, but they seemed to prefer the bushes to live on, and did a considerable amount of damage by walking over and

The Orthoptera.

THE CRICKET.

apparently mouthing the young leaves, which, whenever the locusts touched them, turned black and curled up." We have not met them on our tours through the Indian Tea Districts.

Larvæ.

480. Mr. Cotes concludes his account of locusts thus: "Acridiæ of this kind are likely to lay their eggs in the ground. The larvæ are active grasshoppers, which differ from the adult chiefly in being smaller in size and wingless. They are active throughout their entire existence, and devour the leaves of plants in large quantities."

BRACHYTRYPES ACHATINUS. THE CRICKET.

86. Brachytrypes achatinus, *Stoll.*

THE CRICKET.

References.—*Journ. Agri.-Horti. Soc. Ind., I., (1869) xiii; Tea Cyclopedia, 40; Money, Tea Cultivation, 89; Baildon, Tea in Assam, 46; Notes on Tea in Darjeeling, 55; Ind. Mus. Notes, III (5), 77; Cotes, Tea Insects, 45; Crole, (1897).*

Found in all districts probably.

History.

481. ***History.***—The earliest mention of the Cricket as a tea pest occurs in a letter of Mr. Peal's to the *Agri-Horticultural Society of India, dated 1869.* A little later Mr. Peal wrote a paper on tea pests (that will be found in the *Tea Cyclopædia*), but omitted to mention the Cricket. Whereupon a Cachar planter wrote to the *Tea Gazette* drawing attention to this as a serious omission. Colonel Money devotes only a few lines to the subject of pests under the heading of "White-ants, Cricket and Blight." The fourth edition of his work appeared in 1883, so that even nineteen years ago the subject of pests and blights was regarded by the author of the Prize Essay on tea as practically of no moment.

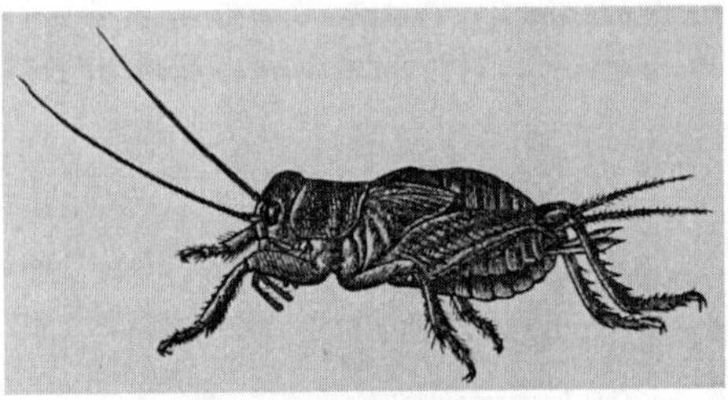

FIG. 28.—THE TEA CRICKET.
Young Larva.
(After Cotes.)

He, however, tells us that the Cricket was very destructive to seedlings. The same opinion has been given by Baildon and by the author of *Notes on Tea in Darjeeling (1888).* Mr. Cotes mentions that the only occasion on which representatives of the insect had been sent to the Indian Museum was in July 1893 and from Jorhat in Assam. The figure (at page 45 of his book), given by Mr. Cotes, is of the immature insect, and is little more than one-half size of the full

The Cricket.

grown Cricket. Mr. Bamber makes no mention of the Cricket, and Mr. Crole (1897) confuses it with Lachnosterna impressa. THE CRICKET.

From our own observations it can be found in practically every district in Northern India, and is hence very widely spread. It may be, however, that some of the damage attributed to the Cricket may be the work of the cut worm (Agrotis ypsilon) (which see), but in the cases we have been able to personally examine the damage there has remained little doubt that the Cricket was primarily responsible for the effect noticed. *Conf. with paras. 431-434.* Very widely distributed.

482. ***Depredations.***—Both the cut worm and the cricket have the same vicious habit of living in nurseries or new plantations. During the night they emerge from their burrows to eat off the young stems. The seedling, in the majority of cases, is thereby killed. The Cachar planter, to whom reference has been made above, wrote that "the Cricket is both common and very destructive in Cachar. It is about 1½ inch in length when full grown, and lives in small burrows, sometimes singly, sometimes two or three in one hole. The burrows frequently penetrate to a great depth, and where the Crickets are so numerous that it becomes necessary to dig them out (which sometimes happens), the tunnels are followed a foot and a half or two feet, and even then not uncommonly without avail. The Cricket feeds on the young leaves of the young plants; and to obtain these, it cuts through the stem of the plant, about three quarters of an inch from the ground, and then carries off the top to his hole, so that each meal which the insect makes causes a vacancy; where they appear in any number the destruction may be imagined. They will cut through a stem as thick as a pencil without difficulty, and amongst small plants in a nursery they sometimes do incalculable mischief. We have seen them attack an old plant, where they eat off the young shoots, and thus did a great deal of harm to the succeeding flushes; but this only rarely occurs." Kills seedlings. Sometimes do enormous damage.

The following passage may be taken from the *Indian Museum Notes* in amplification of the above letter from Cachar:—"The creature was observed to be specially abundant on sandy soil. It makes burrows from 9 to 18 inches deep in the ground, where it conceals itself during the day-time. In the evening it sits at the mouth of the hole, and may be recognised by its shrill piping." The

THE CRICKET.

only addition to make to these records perhaps is to note that the cricket does not always cut off the plant so near the ground as here stated. When the seedling has become older, and the lower wood too hard for his taste, he will climb some few inches from the ground in order to get a shoot in suitable condition to be gnawed off and carried away.

Method of capture.

483. ***Remedy.***—The usual remedy, and perhaps the only one, is that generally pursued in Assam, namely, to reward children for catching the insect. And they do this very cleverly. Armed with a straw or long flexible twig and a piece of bamboo, by way of a spade, they proceed to the nursery or new plantation. Having found a likely hole, they insert the straw as far as it can go, and then proceed to dig down (following the straw) till they come on the Cricket. It might be desirable to substitute a soft copper wire for the straw, and, if properly used, the wire might even kill the Cricket. Its use would not in any case necessitate such care to avoid cutting the guide, as is the case with a straw or twig. Poisonous fluids poured down the holes might also be effectual. In Europe the mole-cricket is captured by burying in the ground flower pots or other vessels with smooth sides, mouth upwards. The Crickets fall into these at night-time and cannot escape.

Traps.

Poisonous baits.

Another method used in similar cases elsewhere might be very effective, namely, the use of poisonous baits. Soak some bran, or even freshly cut grass in sugar solution containing an arsenic compound like Paris green (which can be bought in Calcutta), and put balls of this under stones at various places on the plot affected. The Crickets will eat the poisoned bait during the night and so be destroyed in a comparatively wholesale manner.

Desirable to know breeding season.

484. The life history of the Indian species has not been worked out, so that we do not know when the breeding season occurs. The eggs are laid in small caverns underground no doubt, as is the case with the English mole-cricket. It would be an effectual method of dealing with the pest to have every hole traced out and the eggs discovered and destroyed at the breeding season. The female generally keeps watch at the mouth of the tunnel leading to the eggs, and the larvæ very possibly take more than one season to reach maturity.

Destroy the eggs.

It is most desirable that we should obtain full particulars of the life history of the Indian Cricket, in order to be able to suggest methods of treatment.

PLATE XIII. (*To face Page 247.*)

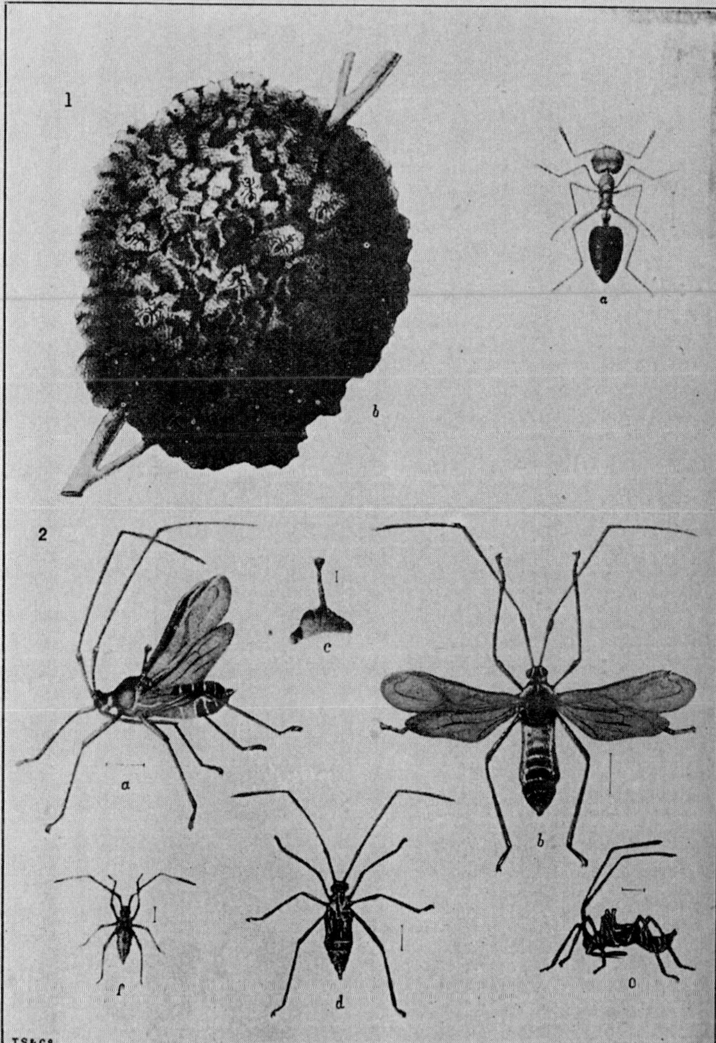

1. Cremastogaster rogenhoferi (p. 240). The Red and Black Ant of Tea Bushes and its nest.

a. Ant (enlarged); *b.* Nest of Ant.

2. Helopeltis theivora (p. 247). The Tea Mosquito Blight.

a. Mature female, side view; *b.* Ditto, back view; *c.* Drumstick on back of insect, enlarged; *d.* Larva, about 6 days old, enlarged; *e.* Side view of ditto; *f.* Larva, about 2 days old.

(From Indian Museum Notes.)

THE TEA MOSQUITO.

CHAPTER XIV.

THE INSECT PESTS OF TEA—continued.

HEMIPTERA.

LXI.—The Tea-Mosquito, Tea Green-Fly, The Tea Aphis, Plant-Lice, Scale-Insects, Plant-Bugs.

485. Under the order HEMIPTERA are comprised what are far and away the most alarming and serious insect pests of tea. Of these the damage done by the Tea-Mosquito and the Tea Green-Fly alone probably equals that of all other pests taken together, while the scale insects, in certain districts, are of very serious moment. The term Bug is often applied to the members of this order, which is divided by entomologists into two sections, the true plant bugs forming the HETEROPTERA, and to this belongs the Tea-Mosquito; and the aphidae, scale-insects, etc., forming the HOMOPTERA. It is not proposed here to make more than a popular distinction between these two sub-orders.

Family CAPSIDÆ.

HELOPELTIS. SP.

87. **Helopeltis theivora,** *Waterhouse.*

88. **Helopeltis febriculosa,** *Bergroth.*

89. **Helopeltis antonii,** *Sign.*

[The above apparently distinct species of Tea-Mosquito have been said to attack the plant. How far they are distinct is at present somewhat doubtful, and the species will be here considered together, as, from a planters' point of view, they are practically identical in effect.]

The "TEA-MOSQUITO," The "TEA-BUG," "BLIGHT."

THE TEA MOSQUITO.

SEE PLATE XIII, NO. 2, AND PLATE XIV.

References.—*Report, Commissioners appointed to enquire into State and Prospects of Tea Cultivation in Assam, Cachar and Sylhet, 1868, p. 3. Peal in "Englishman," 18th September 1872; 20th March 1873; 12th September 1873: Journ. Agri.-Horti. Soc. Ind., n. s., Vol. I., Proc., Jan. 20th, 1869 (Blight in Cachar), p. vii; Vol. III., p. 221; Vol. IV. Peal, the Tea-Bug of Assam, pp. 126—132, with coloured plates; Proc., 27th February 1873, p. vii; Proc., 20th November 1873, pp. xlv—xlvii; Vol. V.; Dr. C. Aleyboom, "Roest" (Rust) on Tea Plant, pp. 55—61; Proc., 15th April 1874, pp. xvii—xix; Proc., 25th June 1874, pp. xxvii—xxix; Proc., 30th July 1874, p. xxxvii; Proc., Aug. 27th, 1874,*

The Hemiptera (Capsidæ).

THE TEA MOSQUITO.

pp. xlv—xlvi; Proc., 24th Aug. 1876, p. xxvi; Vol. VI., Proc., 18th December 1879, p. xli; 22nd July 1880, p. xxi; Vol. VII., Proc., 28th October 1885, p. clxxxv; Proc., 30th December 1885, p. cxcv; Vol. IX., 24th November 1893, pp. cdvii—cdx; Tea Cylcopædia, pp. 36, 37, 46, 47—49, 50—54; Stoker, Notes on the Management of Tea in Cachar (1874), p. 19. Money, Tea Cultivation, fourth edition, July 1883; (Also original Prise Essay, Agri.-Horti. Soc. Journ., Vol. III., 1871, p. 221); Baildon, Tea in Assam (1871), p. 45; Official Correspondence on the Deputation of Wood-Mason to Assam, 1880-1881; Wood-Mason. Report on Tea-Bug in Assam (1884), pp. 12—20; Trimen, Nature, Vol. XXX. (1884), p. 634; Tea Planter's Vade Mecum (1885), Tea-Bug, pp. 100—102, Mosquito 103—104; Notes on Tea in Darjeeling (1888), p. 51; Green, Insect Pests of the Tea (1890), pp. 71—81; E. T. Atkinson (? 1890) (Rhynchota) in Indian Museum Notes, Vol. I., (pt. 4), pp. 175—186, plate XII.; L. de Niceville, l. c. pp. 197—198; Bamber, Chem. and Agri. of Tea (1893), pp. 245—248, Ind. Mus. Notes, Vol. II., pp. 43, 166; Vol. IV., p. 42; G. C. Dudgeon in Ind. Mus. Notes, Vol. III., (pt. 5), pp. 33—38; Miles, Bulletin Micro. Soc., Calcutta, Vol. IV., July 1895, pp. 40—44; Christison, Home and Colonial Mail, 1st Jan. 1897; Crole, Tea Text-Book, pp. 82, 223; Planter, July 23, 1898; Sept. 3, 1898; Sept. 23, 1899; May 19, 1900; Indian Gardening, May 13, 1899; Planting Opinion, May 6, 1899; May 20, 1899; Indian Planters' Gazette, April 21st, 1900; Green, Circ. Roy. Bot. Gard., Ceylon, 1901, Series 1, No. 21; 1902, Vol. II., No. 2; H. H. Mann. Journ. Asiat. Soc., Bengal, 1902; H. H. Mann, Indian Tea Association, Circ. 1902.

Found in all important Districts.

History.

First mention in Cachar.

486. ***First Mention of Blight.***—The facts regarding the appearance of this, the most alarming of all Indian tea pests, may be said to be fully indicated by the above citation of papers, reports, and letters that have appeared. It seems to have been first noticed in Cachar about 1865. The Report of the Commissioners appointed by Government to enquire into the state and prospects of Tea Cultivation, informs us that "heavy losses from blight in 1865 and again in 1867" had been sustained. "It is said to show itself," wrote the Commissioner, "in the end of June or July, and to continue more or less to the close of the season. The circumstances of its appearance and progress have not been noted with the accuracy necessary to enable us to form an opinion of its nature." "The loss from this cause in the gardens of one company in 1867 was estimated as high as 50,000 lbs. of tea. It is a singular fact that blight is almost, if not entirely, confined to that part of Cachar which lies to the south of he Barak River."

The Tea Mosquito.

487. The next historic incident to which attention may be drawn is the almost simultaneous discovery of the pest in Assam and Darjeeling. In 1869 **Mr. S. E. Peal** sent samples of the blighted leaves from the Brahmaputra Valley to **Dr. T. Anderson,** the Superintendent, Royal Botanic Gardens, Calcutta, and the latter gentleman stated that he had himself observed the disease called "Blight" by Cachar planters on some tea plants in Darjeeling. At this time the idea prevailed that we had here to deal with a fungus blight, but this was rendered improbable by the failure of **Mr. Berkeley** (to whom **Anderson** had sent **Peal's** samples) to find any fungus, except perhaps a species of **Asterina** unlikely to cause the disease. **Dr. Anderson** also soon added his testimony and said that "he had carefully examined the bushes and could find no diseased leaves in any other stage of the disease, but that forwarded to **Mr. Berkeley.** He, however, found several leaves with a small insect lying under the epidermis of the leaf, and he supposed that this insect must have devoured the parenchyma, and caused the transparent spots (blight) with which the leaf was covered. **Dr. Anderson** exhibited some of these leaves with the insect in position; also a few leaves with minute eggs of an insect, collected in patches on the surface of the leaf. He further said that he found many of the indigenous plants in the forests, adjoining those tea estates in which blight had been observed, were also affected. He particularly noticed **Gordonia Wallichii,*** a Ternstrœmiaceous plant nearly allied to tea, a **Polygonum,** an **Osbeckia** and **Mæsa montana** as suffering much from the blight. **Dr. Anderson** shewed young leaves of **Cinchona succirubra** from a tea estate at Darjeeling; these leaves were covered with the blight spots."

THE TEA MOSQUITO. — **Early mistake.** — **Cachar Blight not a Fungus.** — **Found in Darjeeling, 1869.** — **Mæsa indica.** *Conf. with paras. 528, 599.*

488. **Dr. Anderson** had, in fact, come correctly to the conclusion that the disease was caused by an insect, but was totally in error as to the nature of that insect. His small insect lying under the epidermis of the leaf was probably the tea leaf-mining fly (**Oscinis theæ**) and his eggs were, so far as one can judge, the white scales of **Chionaspis theæ**—a scale insect, of which an account is given later. Furthermore, the fungus found by **Mr. Berkeley** and named

First suggestion of Insect origin. — *Conf. with para. 605.*

* **Schima Wallichii,** *Choisy,* as it is now called.

THE TEA MOSQUITO.

as a species of Asterina (*vide supra*) was probably nothing more than the black soot so commonly associated with scale insects all over the tea area, and had nothing to do with the blight at all. The interesting point is, however, that in 1869 Mr. S. E. Peal found the blight in Assam, and Dr. Anderson noticed Tea, Cinchona and several other plants punctured by Mosquito blight in Darjeeling. It is thus probable that it appeared at various points of the tea area in India all but simultaneously, and the points on which it originally appeared have remained to the present the centres of distribution of the pest.

Discovery in Java.

489. It had evidently appeared at approximately the same time in Java, and had there caused a good deal of consternation. Dr. Aleyboom, of that colony, investigated the matter, and after testing every aspect of the disease that seemed to suggest a fungal origin, he arrived at the same conclusion as the Indian workers that it was caused by an insect, which, however, he neither named nor described.

Discovery in Ceylon.

It was not till long after that mention was made of blight in Ceylon. In 1884 only was its presence recorded as a serious pest on Cocoa and Cinchona by Dr. Trimen, and this was at a period when the nature of the insect had been made out with considerable detail.

Discovery in Assam.

490. ***Identification of insect.***—To Mr. S. E. Peal belongs both the credit of having awakened interest in this insect and of having himself written perhaps the best account of the methods of depredation effected by it, that exists even to the present day. "*The Tea-Bug of Assam,*" with seven coloured plates, will be found in the fourth volume of the Agri.-Horticultural Society's Journal. Ten years later Mr. J. Wood-Mason paid Mr. Peal the compliment of saying that in his opinion the Society " did not spend as much money as the beauty of the drawings and the importance of the subject demanded." Mr. Peal did not give the insect its scientific name and he did not discover its method of depositing its eggs on the tea shoots, but in every other respect his paper contains very nearly all that we at present know of a practical nature regarding the pest.

Insect named.

Mr. Peal further furnished the entomological experts in England with examples of the insect, and Mr. Moore was able from his samples finally to identify it as a new species of Helopeltis (a genus of Capsidæ) of which four species were then known—one from Ceylon and two from th Malay Archipelago. The Assam

The Tea Mosquito.

THE TEA MOSQUITO.

form was thus the fourth and much resembled the species from New Guinea. From its feeding on the juice of the tea plant, Mr. Moore named it Helopeltis theivora.

Professor Westwood's Paper.

491. From this date (1874) the journals devoted to the interests of tea teem with articles and letters on the subject of blight, but little more was discovered relating to it. Professor Westwood, for instance, wrote a paper on it, the only point of historic interest in which being the fact that the Java insect had been identified and named in 1871. In the meantime, with occasional fluctuations, the disease was rapidly extending the area of its attack. In 1874 Mr. Peal, for instance, who had been asked for a further supply of specimens, rashly reported, "curiously enough the bug is not here this year, the early and exceptionally heavy wet may have something to do with it." He soon had cause to recall his statement, for on August 27 of the same year he again wrote: "I now find I was rather premature in this, as they are again causing damage. This year they seem to have shown later than usual." In 1872 the bug appeared seriously in the Darjeeling Terai in the group of gardens lying at the foot of the Himalayas, of which Pankhabari is one.

Scientific investigations.

492. ***Scientific investigations required.***—So serious in fact had the blight now become that the Calcutta Tea Agents appealed to Government to send an Entomologist to the tea districts to study the insect on the spot. In their letter to the Government of India they asked for the services of both a Botanist and an Entomologist. They stated that information was desired on the following points:—

Subjects of information desired.

1st.—The nature of the insect.

2nd.—Its manner of propagation.

3rd.—Its time of propagation.

4th.—Its place of propagation.

5th.—The stages of its existence.

6th.—The stage in which most easily destroyed.

7th.—The most effectual modes of its destruction.

8th.—Whether modes of pruning, plucking and cultivating the bushes, etc., are not at fault, and what changes in these directions would be likely to have a beneficial effect.

493. As a result of these representations, the late Mr. J. Wood-Mason was deputed to visit Cachar, in order to study the "Tea-Bug"

The Hemiptera (Capsidæ).

THE TEA MOSQUITO.

and to suggest the best means for destroying the pest. His explorations took place from March to November 1881, and his "*Report on the Tea-Mite and the Tea-Bug of Assam*" appeared in 1884. It must be frankly confessed that his report is a disappointment.

494. Indeed, it seems somewhat unfortunate that it did not occur to Mr. Wood-Mason that it would be desirable to attempt to trace out the history of the pest. He does not mention the gardens where he found it, nor those in which he did not find it. He makes no reference to the annual date of appearance and disappearance. He disposes in a few words of the suggestion of its possible association with particular soils, with shade, or with methods of cultivation. These, he says, are not singly nor collectively causes of the disease.

Method of depositing eggs.

He discovered its method of depositing its eggs on the young shoots —a practical fact of great importance—but he does not venture on a suggestion, even, as to its method of hibernation,—the period when in all probability it could be most easily assailed. In the official correspondence prior to his deputation to Cachar Mr. J. Wood-Mason laid before the Government of India a paper of Professor Ray Lankester's (which had appeared in *Nature*) on the subject of the possibility of attacking the insect pests of crops by communicating to them the spores of destructive (parasitic) fungi.

Natural enemies.

But in the report of his investigations Mr. Wood-Mason makes no further allusion to this subject, nor to his having discovered any of the natural enemies of the mosquito.

Various species of Helopeltis.

495. This carries us to the year 1884, and in this state the question remained for several years. Except for the discovery of Helopeltis in Ceylon on Cocoa and Cinchona in 1884, and of various other species on different plants, nothing was done. In 1891 Mr. E. T. Atkinson published a review of the known species of Helopeltis, which had by this time grown in number to ten—four of which feed on tea, of which Helopeltis antonii was obtained from Ceylon, Helopeltis romundei from Java, and Helopeltis theivora from the Indian Tea Districts. *Plate XIII, No. 2,* is a reproduction of the very beautiful figure* of Helopeltis theivora with which Mr. Atkinson's paper is illustrated.

---

* This figure is incorrect in one particular. The antennæ are figured with three joints: they always have four, but the terminal one is very easily broken off.

The Tea Mosquito.

THE TEA MOSQUITO.

Dudgeon's paper.

496. ***More recent investigations.***—Perhaps the next Indian papers of importance are those by Mr. C. N. Harcourt (*Ind. Mus. Notes, Vol. II., 43*) and by Mr. G. C. Dudgeon (*Ind. Mus. Notes, Vol. III., (pl. 5), pp. 33—38*). Both these writers deal with the method of depositing eggs on the young shoots. But Mr. Dudgeon adds several interesting additional details. A point of special value may be here alluded to in Mr. Dudgeon's paper, *viz.*, where he tells us that the abdomen in fresh specimens of both sexes *is invariably bright emerald green*, marked dorsally, on the third to ninth segments, with shiny dark brown. So again, he continues, the larvæ are greenish with deep ochreous or orange legs and antennæ. He further discusses the question of the puncturings, similar to those on tea, that are to be seen on jungle plants, such as on **Mæsa indica**, and adds that so far none of these have proved to be caused by **Helopeltis theivora.**

Cotes's account.

497. Lastly, Mr. Cotes' account of this insect, in *Insects and Mites of the Tea Plant in India (pp. 29 –33)*, may be characterised as a useful review of the literature of this pest, but one which furnishes no additional information. Since that time few, if any, investigations have been done in connection with the insect in question till Mr. Green's work in Ceylon during the past two years, and that of the authors in the Indian tea districts.

498. ***Conclusions.***—To conclude this brief historic review of the early literature of the subject, it may be said that it is significant that a form of the so-called Tea-Mosquito should have simultaneously appeared in Cachar, Assam and Java from 1865 to 1868, and if Dr. Anderson's observations can be accepted as pointing to mosquito blight, in Darjeeling also at the same period. We only hear of it in Ceylon at a much later period.

Description.

Totally different from ordinary Mosquito.

499. In order to prevent a confusion which has frequently arisen among planters and which still arises, it will be advisable to preface our account of the life history of the Tea-Mosquito by saying that it bears absolutely no relationship to the insect which attacks human beings and animals. The term mosquito-blight is in fact a most unfortunate one. The true mosquito belongs to the natural order **Diptera**: the Tea-Mosquito to the **Hemiptera**. The former in its young stages lives in water as a grub totally different in character

The Hemiptera (Capsidæ).

THE TEA MOSQUITO.

from the adult insect: the latter does not change, except for the growth of wings, essentially, in its appearance throughout its life, the whole of which is passed on the plant on which it lives. Again, the former insect has two wings: the Tea-Mosquito four. There is in fact absolutely no relationship, beyond a very superficial resemblance, between the two insects.

Life history.

500. This being made clear, we can consider the life history of an individual Tea-Mosquito, so far as it is known, at the height of the season. In all varieties it appears to agree in essential particulars.

Eggs.

The eggs are laid generally in groups of two or more in the succulent stem of the tea shoot. The discovery of their position we owe to Mr. Wood-Mason, and the figures 29 and 30 show their appearance when embedded in the tissue. Mr. Wood-Mason's original statement of his discovery is as follows:—

Wood-Mason's discovery.

"*Tea-Bug.*—Have discovered, by observation of specimens of this formidable pest kept in confinement, that the female deposits her eggs singly in the substance of the tenderest shoots of the plant, in the *internodes* or portions of the stem between the pekoe and the two or three leaves succeeding from above downwards, and in the buds developed in the axils of plucked leaves and in the parts thereabout; that the presence and position of each egg is from the first indicated on the exterior by two unequally long, glistening, white, bristle-like prolongation of its shell, and later by discoloration of the point pierced. . . . These observations have been verified in the field upon numerous blighted bushes; but though eggs have readily been found by the unaided eye on blighted portions of bushes, not a single one has yet been seen on any perfectly uninjured shoot."

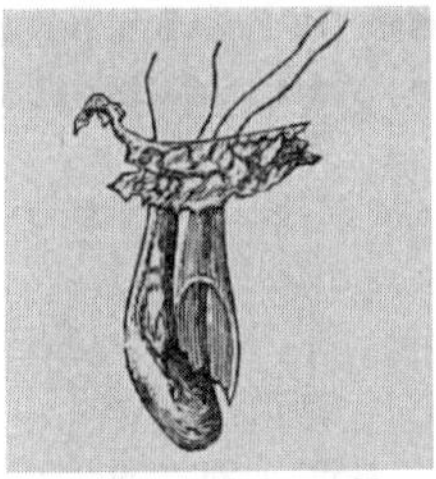

FIG. 29.—EGG OF TEA MOSQUITO IN SHOOT.

(After Dudgeon.)

501. The Tea-Mosquito, however, lays its eggs in many more places than the extremely succulent shoots below the pekoe leaf. Mr. Dudgeon says for instance:—

Egg in stem below shoot plucked.

"The eggs . . . are generally found in the green stems of tea which has been passed over by the leaf pluckers as being too hard for manufacture. Did the insect content itself with laying in the soft green stems, doubtless it would soon be exterminated on tea gardens where leaf is not allowed to run out much. But apparently nature has provided against man, and the eggs are laid in the unpicked slightly hardened stems."

The Tea Mosquito.

THE TEA MOSQUITO.

But even this does not give the entire range in which the egg may be deposited. One of the authors (H. H. M.) has recently found them embedded in the midrib of a large mature leaf of the tea plant. In general, one may say they are laid in the green stalk of the bush—by preference in the young succulent, newly developed shoots,—but sometimes in any green stalk on the bush which has not hardened sufficiently to prevent the introduction of the ovipositor of the female insect.

Description of Eggs.

502. "The eggs are at first pure white . . . just previous to the larvæ emerging the eggs become yellowish, the inner or more spherical end being streaked with orange red (representing the legs and antennæ of the larvæ)." (*Dudgeon.*) "The eggs *are about* $\frac{1}{32}$ *inch in length and very* slender." (*Harcourt.*) "The knobbed ends and also the sides of the two tubular processes of the mouth of the egg-shell, to a greater or less extent, are studded with button shaped elevations, each of which has a minute pit in its centre. These pits are probably the ends of minute tubules which place the lumens of the processes in direct communication with the exterior, and thus serve to carry air to the developing ovum. The eggs are provided with deep saucer-shaped lids, perforated, sieve-like, with holes which are large enough to admit the spermatozoa." (*Wood-Mason.*)

Hairlike Protuberances.

503. As Mr. Wood-Mason states, the eggs can be discovered on the shoots by means of two hairlike protuberances at one end which stick out from the surface of the shoot. It was formerly supposed that these were produced in the act of deposition by the stretching of a drop of viscous liquid accompanying the egg, and then spontaneous drying. Mr. Dudgeon has, however, shown that this is not the case. The eggs already bear the threads in the abdomen of the female, and they are probably there in order to keep open the aperture in the stalk, and so provide that air should be supplied to the growing larva in the egg.

Length of time before hatching.

504. The time which elapses between the laying of the egg and the exit of the larva probably varies very much with the season and hence with the temperature. At the height of the season, Mr. Green gives it as ten days in Ceylon. In India, according to experiments made by Mr. Graham, of Tarrapore, Cachar, in 1899, the eggs deposited by a female which coupled on the 16th October, gave rise to larvæ on the 25th—a period again of ten days.

The Hemiptera (Capsidæ).

THE TEA MOSQUITO.

505. It might be expected that the larva would emerge from the stalk by the aperture formed by the introduction of the egg and kept open by the hairlike process. According to Mr. Dudgeon, this is, however, by no means the case. He says that the larva actually comes out "from the lower or interior end. Moreover, the stems in which empty eggshells are found will be seen to be hollowed out and brownish in colour; the core of the stalk having been eaten away, a small amount of gelatinous-looking matter alone remaining, which probably represents the digested portions of the stalk excreted by the larvæ." (*Dudgeon.*) This last statement must, as Mr. Green points out, be a mistake. The young insect has no mouth parts capable of biting, and the death of the tissues round the base of the egg is more probably due to the wound and the irritation of the egg. "My observations lead me to believe that the larva *does* emerge through the upper extremity by bursting the cap." (*Green.*) The exact method of emergence therefore remains doubtful for the moment.

Larva.

506. ***Larvæ.***—The young larva as it emerges on to the tea shoot is a small insect either reddish or greenish in colour according to the species to which it belongs (*vide infra*), with longish legs and antennæ, "looking not unlike one of the slender ants that frequent the tea blossoms." (*Green.*) Whatever the colour of the larva, the legs and antennæ are a deep orange brown colour. In this stage of their existence they are usually found on the small very succulent leaves, on which, so soon as they emerge from the egg, they commence to feed. They grow with great rapidity, but the length of time taken to become winged and mature is not known very closely. This is owing to the difficulty of rearing the insect in captivity, and we have never succeeded in bringing up one from the egg to the adult stage, nor do we know anyone who has.

Colour.

Length of time to become mature.

507. At any rate, the minute larva, the body of which is at the commencement from $\frac{1}{16}$ to $\frac{1}{8}$ inch long, increase rapidly in size, the form and colour remaining approximately the same. During this period they moult at least three times, and probably more.* A very

* Dr. L. Zehntner, in Java, has recently found that the insect found on Cacao in that country moults five times during the larval stage at intervals of two days. It is not certain whether he was dealing with the same insect as our Indian Tea-Mosquito, but the observation agrees exactly with the few cases noticed in India, as to the time spent by the mosquito in the larval condition.

The Tea Mosquito.

early writer (in the *Tea Gazette*) describes the growth very clearly as follows. The sudden changes which he points out of course represent the times of moulting :— THE TEA MOSQUITO.

Early description of growth of Larva.

"When very young, they are difficult to see and really can only be found by searching closely among the small Pekoe buds that have been punctured . . . They are extremely like little spiders, are of a brownish red colour, and retain this colour until the wings are developed, when they become black as described by Mr. Peal. The rapidity with which the wings are developed is something wonderful: with one specimen which I had imprisoned for about seven days, no wings were visible; then two little embryo ones like minute quills showed themselves; and after these had remained about three days, the full four wings were developed apparently at once; certainly late one evening no wings were visible, only the little stumps of quills, and in the morning the four wings were fully developed, and the insect had changed from brown to black, the spidery look had quite disappeared, and our unwelcome pest, the mosquito, stood developed. Another, which I put into a bottle one evening as a three-quarter grown "spider:" appeared in the morning with its wings—a full blown mosquito. While in the "spider" stage, they are all alike, except in regard to size."

Larval stage lasts 10 days.

508. According to this, therefore, the larval stage would take about ten days at the height of the breeding season. Even in this stage, as well as in the adult condition, each individual possesses the curious and characteristic drumstick-shaped horn (*see Plate XIII, No. 2 c.*) on the back, rising from the part known to entomologists as the "scutellum."

Adult Mosquito.

509. ***The Adult Mosquito.***—Having gone through the various moults during the larval stage, the insect on its last change of skin appears with wings, and the male and female can be differentiated. Not only this but what we have considered up to the present point as one species now stands revealed as possibly two or three, differing in colour of the abdomen and in the shape of the "scutellar horn" on the back. The male and female of these species can in each case be distinguished by the appearance. One of the earliest writers on the subject noted this and wrote as follows :—

Male and Female.

"When fully developed, two different kinds appear: one a slim, delicate sort of fellow, all black; the other with an orange hump between his shoulders, and with a dirty white abdomen.* The former I take to be the male, and the latter the female: certainly the black one appears always to keep the same size, after he has once got his wings; but the other gets much enlarged about the abdomen, and I believe lays either eggs or young ones. . . . The two anterior wings are not hard at any point, but are smaller at the point of insertion: they are in shape

* The colour of the abdomen may vary.

THE TEA MOSQUITO.

somewhat like a lawn tennis bat, and when closed, the bladder of one overlies the other, but they do not cross: all four wings are transparent, both when observed with the naked eye and through a magnifying glass."

Eggs in abdomen.

510. This description is an excellent one, and the mark here pointed out—the orange hump between the shoulders—is the most striking mark of the female insect. If, however, the abdomen of one of these orange-humped insects be gently crushed and the material examined with a lens, a confirmation will generally be obtained, because eggs will be found in greater or less number, looking like very minute sausages and each with its two hairlike protuberances attached. The female can further be identified by the structure of the abdomen, and the attached ovipositor (*see Fig. 30*, which we owe to Mr. Dudgeon). The latter can, however, only be seen with some difficulty.

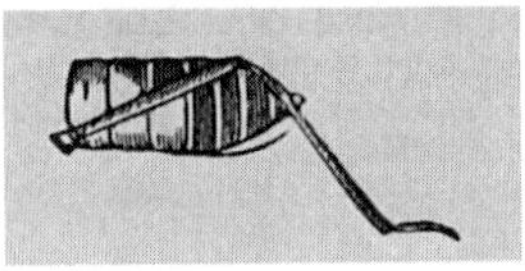

FIG. 30.—THE ABDOMEN, HIND LEG, AND OVIPOSITOR OF TEA MOSQUITO.

(After Dudgeon.)

In Fig. 31 the male of the Ceylon species is shown,* and in Fig. 32, the female. *Plate XIII, No. 2* shows the female only of the Indian species.

511. How long the insect lives in the adult condition we do not yet know. The time probably varies much with the season, and it is very possible that some individual may pass through the time when they disappear from the tea bush in this condition (*vide infra*). The difficulty in any attempt to ascertain the length of time taken consists in the impossibility of keeping the insects in captivity—they almost always die within a short time of their incarceration.

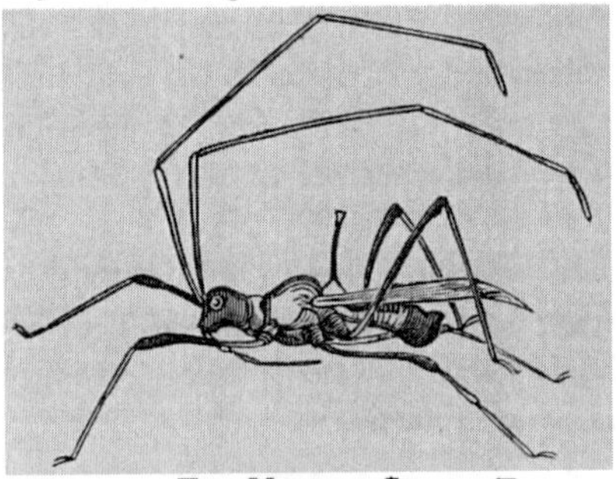

FIG. 31.—THE MALE OF CEYLON TEA MOSQUITO.

(From a sketch by E. E. Green.)

* Mr. Green was kind enough to draw this figure from a living sample expressly for this work.

The Tea Mosquito.

THE TEA MOSQUITO.

512. ***Species of Tea Mosquito.***—Until 1895 it had always been supposed that the insect attacking tea in India consisted of a single species slightly differing from that in Ceylon but similar throughout the tea districts. In his tour in Assam in that year one of the authors (G. W.) however found considerable difference in the appearance of the insect, and slight difference in the method of attack of the bush, in various parts of the Brahmaputra Valley. Starting a tour on the south bank of the river for weeks on end many thousand insects almost daily were seen and examined. "They were all of a bright orange-red colour, almost pink in the very young larval stage, but deepening with age, the males becoming almost black in general colour. Mr. Peal's plates are, if anything, too yellow for the insect as seen by me; Mr. Wood-Mason gives no description of the insect he investigated in Cachar." (*Watt.*)

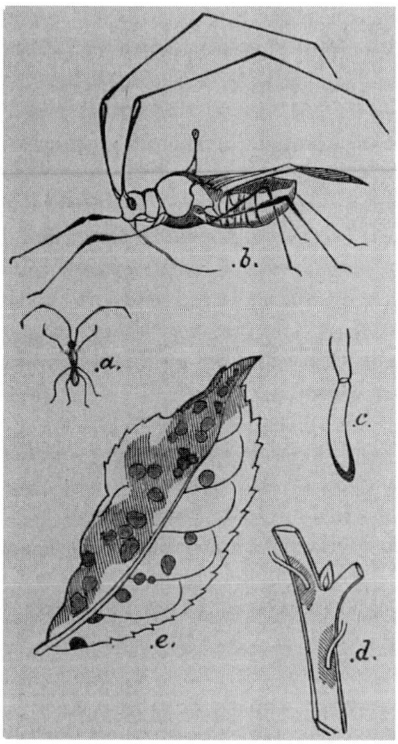

FIG. 32.—THE CEYLON TEA MOSQUITO.
(*a.* Adult female, natural size; *b.* Adult female, enlarged; *c.* Egg of mosquito, much enlarged; *d.* Eggs in position in shoots; *e.* Leaf with punctures.)
(After E. E. Green.)

513. ***Green colour of Mosquito.***—"Prior to my visit to Assam I had read the passages . . . where the mosquito is said to turn green on its absorbing the tea sap. As I had failed to find any

THE TEA MOSQUITO.

examples of that colour, I was surprised and mentioned the fact to Mr. Peal. He at once said it was a mistake, that the colour deepens with age, but does not change on its sucking the tea juice. To make quite sure I had some insects placed on a tea bush enclosed with mosquito-curtain cloth, and watched them puncture the leaves, saw the brown spots gradually form on these, but never witnessed any change of colour in the insect itself before, nor after its meal. I never came across a green mosquito in any of the gardens of Sibsagar or Dibrugarh." (*Watt.*)

Green insect.

514. "But I was greatly surprised on my crossing to North Lakhimpur (that is to say, to the gardens on the north bank of the Brahmaputra) to find the young insects of a pale emerald colour, and yellowish green with faint brown markings in the adult condition. At Patalipam, visited in July 1895, I could not find an orange-red mosquito on the tea, though I was told a red insect was occasionally met with. This led me to compare my collections of red mosquito with the live green ones. They differed in several respects.

Orange insect description.

"The orange-red insect, in its mature state, was seen to be larger than the straw-coloured form. It was observed to be very nearly glabrous (that is to say, had few, if any, hairs on the body, legs, or antennæ), and the abdomen was of a bright shining dark orange-red with black bands on the five terminal segments. These bands, at least the last three, could hardly be called dorsal, however, since they were seen to be nearly as deep in colour on the belly as on the back of the segments.

Green insect description.

"The green and straw-coloured insect, on the other hand, was noted to be considerably smaller and very much more hairy, than the red form, especially on the lower portions of the legs, and on the antennæ, while the drumstick-like spine on the scutellum was observed to be almost bristly, both on the shaft and on the knob. A pale-coloured lateral line was also noted as extending across the dark dorsal bands of the last three segments, and the belly was pale straw-coloured. The males seem to turn quite black and the wings to become nearly twice the length of the body.

"These characters may not of course suffice to justify their separation as two species, but I still further observed that the effects on the plant, of the puncturings of the green insect, were very different from those of the red." (*Watt.*)

The Tea Mosquito.

THE TEA MOSQUITO.

515. On careful comparison with the type samples identified by Bergroth in the Indian Museum, Calcutta, it appears, in fact, that the green, straw-coloured, north bank insect may be considered as identical with **Helopeltis febriculosa,** and the name **Helopeltis theivora** should be retained only for the orange coloured larger south bank form.

Distribution of species.

516. Now as to the distribution of these species. This cannot be stated very definitely, as their relative proportion in any one district varies considerably. In Patalipam, for instance, the very garden in which the green mosquito was collected in 1895, the superintendent informed us (in July 1897) that the green insect was getting more scarce every year, and the red one taking its place and samples furnished consisted of quite 50 per cent. of the red subglabrous insect with black or rather brown black abdominal segments. It might be suggested that the green insect was being driven out by the red, but this is not supported by the evidence of other districts at present.

517. The distribution in the current year (1902) may be roughly said to be as follows:—

Assam—South Bank—Red mosquito principally, but not exclusively.

North Bank—Both mosquitoes occur in variable proportion.

Cachar—Green mosquito practically alone.

Sylhet—As in Cachar.

Terai and *Dooars*—Chiefly green insect, but a very few red ones occur.

Darjeeling—At low elevations green mosquitoes usual: at higher elevations red is found.

Terai insect.

In connection with this it might be noted that Mr. Dudgeon, who worked in the Terai, described the abdomen in fresh specimens of both sexes as invariably bright emerald *green* by transparency, marked dorsally on the third to ninth segments with shiny dark brown. "The extent of brown on the third segment is limited to a small dorsal patch or is altogether absent; on the fourth it extends over the whole dorsal region; on the fifth partially lateral and wholly dorsal; the remaining segments are all dark brown; the segmental divisions are greenish. The male differs from the female in having the pronotum very slightly tinged with yellow; the abdomen more slender and the absence of the ovipositor. The larvæ are *greenish* with deep ochreous or orange legs and antennæ; in some the abdomen is distinctly yellowish, although the same become green after having fed." (*Dudgeon.*)

Except for the last statement (the correctness of which we venture to doubt), this description agrees with what we have ourselves almost exclusively observed in the Terai.

518. This discussion of the various species of the insect may be considered to have only an academic interest. The method of attack is closely similar, and so far as we know at present, the life history is practically the same. In what follows therefore we shall speak as if dealing with one species of insect only, though, of course, future research may indicate that the difference in species may be of radical importance. For the present, from a practical point of view, they can hardly be distinguished in effect.

Depredations.

Method of puncturing leaves.

519. ***Method of Puncturing the Leaves.***—No one has better described the effect of the tea mosquito on the shoots and leaves of the tea-bush than Mr. Peal in his original description of the insect, which we still can quote as authoritative. He thus describes the ravages caused by the pest:—

"The general view of the tea is that the shoots are all brown, withered, and, in fact, dead, and the tea presents a generally brown look instead of the bright healthy green that is usual.

"On examining a tree so affected, if the blight has only recently affected it, the appearance is very different from that of a tree which has suffered some time. In the former case the general growth and the look is normal, but the youngest shoots and tips are more or less spotted with brown, the size of the spots varying with the age of the insect. If the bug is very young, the punctures are close and minute and the discolorations coalescent; but if it is full grown, the spots are larger, say an eighth of an inch in diameter. Again, if the punctures are recent, the colour is pale brown and darkest at the edges; but if one or two or more days old, the spots are dark brown verging on black, the entire leaf curling up and withering completely if they are close.

Peal's account.

"In the case of a tree that has suffered some time and severely, the symptoms are often less visible at first glance; the dead leaves

PLATE XIV. (*To face Page 263.*)

1. Shoot just attacked by the Tea Mosquito.
(From Photograph by H. H. Mann.)

1. Bush badly attacked by the Tea Mosquito.
(From Photograph by H. H. Mann.)

The Tea Mosquito.

have mostly fallen off, and the minute shoots at the leaf axils alone show the damage, and all are dry and dead ; there is less dead leaf showing and in its place we find dead "tips" everywhere. (*See Plate XIV, No. 1.*)

THE TEA MOSQUITO.

"A more careful study will often show a still more unpleasant fact—*i.e.*, that ere it ceased entirely to shoot out, the tree has made many efforts to grow, all of which had been rendered abortive; and a branch that has not yielded one single leaf or tip will present all the appearance of having been very severely and persistently plucked.

Peal's description of effect.

520. "On the tips of the young vigorous shoot being punctured, it has died as certainly as if nipped off, and the eyes below in the leaf-axils shoot out vigorously; and ere the bug can do serious damage, one or two shoots have attained some size and carry several leaves; but as the insects increase in size, these tips again are attacked and other shoots start from other eyes, though attaining a less vigorous growth, and in a short time we have a regular "broom" where not one leaf or tip has been taken by us, but has been killed off or sucked dry by the bug alone. . . . . When this is the case, growth will have come to a complete standstill, as every shoot requires from (say) forty to fifty days to mature from an eye to be fit to pluck. We may say the trees shut up for about two entire months at least; and it is specially unfortunate that this takes place usually about mid-season and when we should be doing our very best."

Size of punctures varies with age of insect.

521. This description holds to this day almost to the very letter. One point in it has, however, been called in question, and it is desirable to confirm the accuracy of Mr. Peal's description. It will be noticed that he says that the size of the spots varies with the age of the insect causing them. In our own experience this correspondence has been most striking, and it has been possible to detect the bushes which have been attacked by a winged mosquito which has flown on to the plant from those where the damage has been done by young larvæ which have bred on the bush. In the former case the spots are not only larger but irregular in outline, are generally in medium sized leaves or at any rate not in the tip, and in the spring when the blight is beginning to appear, are generally on the surface leaves of the bush, whereas the larvæ can be found only on the slightly shaded foliage. It has, in fact, been possible in experiments conducted by one of us (H. H. M.) to ascertain the proportion of the

THE TEA MOSQUITO.

bushes attacked from the outside as against those on which the pest had actually developed. Recent observations in Ceylon also fully confirm the accuracy of Mr. Peal's statement.

Feeding period.

522. The insects principally feed at night and in the early morning, very little puncturing being done during the hot parts of the day. Provided the weather is suitable however—damp, dull days without rain—their feeding period extends far into the morning. It has been somewhat of a mystery where the insects conceal themselves during the daytime, and experiments have been made to test whether they leave the bush and go into the ground by putting a broad band of sticky substance round the stems of some bushes at midday. All punctured leaves were removed from these bushes, but fresh punctures, evidently made by wingless insects, appeared during the following night, proving that they had been resting somewhere above the sticky line. Mr. Bamber rather indicates that they fall to the ground when disturbed, but this is certainly not usually the case. The boys who are employed to catch the insects, and who become very expert at the work, have shown us several times the immature larvæ resting on the underside of the young leaves in the interior of the bush, whence they scurry down the branches when disturbed.

Do not fall to the ground.

Time of attack in India.

523. ***Time of Attack.***—In the first description of the insect it was said to commence its ravages in February and go on till the end of August. If this was true at that time, it cannot be said to be so now in India, and as a matter of fact the height of the attack is now usually from August to October in the Indian Tea Districts. The progress throughout the year may be taken to be approximately as follows:—

January.

January.—The mosquito is for all practical purposes absent from the tea bush, and this is the case to such an extent that many planters have affirmed that it really is not present. This point has been investigated recently by one of us (H. H. M.), and we will return to the subject later.

February.

February.—During the whole of this month mosquitoes are rarely seen except in districts in which the blight is very serious. In any case, they are difficult to find and seem to largely restrict themselves to the shoots in the interior of the bush shaded by the young foliage on the surface.

***March* and *April*.**—The same remarks apply to these months as to February, but by the end of April the blight becomes more obvious in badly affected districts. THE TEA MOSQUITO. March and April.

***May*.**—When mosquito blight begins to affect the *crop* in May, the outlook is considered to be very serious. Nevertheless by this time it can always be seen in affected gardens, and it is largely a question of the suitability of the weather as to whether it is able to attack the plucking shoots on the surface of the plant. May.

During ***June*** and ***July*** the blight increases in amount, and always becomes very obvious, being favoured by dull, damp days without heavy rain. It is at this time that planters often declare that a garden was shut up in a week, being converted from a waving mass of leaf to a brown bare mass of withered foliage. The true explanation of such an attack is that conditions have been favourable to the development of the larvæ and eggs already in the bushes, and they have come to the surface shoots, which they have been prevented from touching previously by excessive sun or rain. June and July.

In ***August, September*** and ***October*** the pest is at its height. Given favourable weather, the flushing leaf often comes through at the beginning of October, and by the end of that month this is very general. During ***November*** the blight is decreasing in amount, and in ***December*** little can be seen, and the insects have to be sought for with a good deal of care. August to October.

524. In Ceylon, as would be expected, a very different cycle takes place. As described by Mr. Green in the Kelani Valley (and the cycle in the Morowak-Korale district does not appear to be very different) it appears that "the worst attack takes place in July and August. After September there is a rapid drop, reaching its lowest level in November, followed by a tendency to gradual (fluctuating) increase up till February or March, when there is another rapid fall. In April and May the pest practically disappears. The recrudescence commences towards the end of June, and reaches its height in July or August. There thus appear to be two periods of increase and decrease during the year, a major and a minor period. The major period is represented by the zero point in April and May, followed by a maximum in July and August. The minor period consists of the fall in September, October, and November, followed by the increase up to March. The March attack never approaches Time of attack in Ceylon.

THE TEA MOSQUITO.

the gigantic proportion of the July-August attack, the figures being approximately as 4 to 9." (*Green.*)

Connection with rainfall.

525. ***Connection with Rainfall.***—An attempt has been made to trace a connection between the rainfall and the prevalence of the tea mosquito. On the face of it, it would appear that both in Ceylon and India the pest was worst in the rainy months, and the conclusion might be drawn that excessive rainfall favours the development of the insect. But why then the attack in Ceylon in January, February and March,—the months of lowest rainfall? Why also is it that in India the worst years for blight are not those with heaviest rainfall, but often rather the reverse? In fact, in spite of the apparent connection at first sight between the rainfall and the blight, any simple relationship is not only unproved, but very unlikely. Between the *distribution* of the rainfall and the blight there is, however, a much more probable connection, but even this is by no means proved. (*Vide infra under "Remedy."*)

Effect of distribution of rainfall.

Conf. with para. 537.

Hibernation.

526. ***Hibernation.***—This brings us however to the point which has been most discussed in the habits of the Helopeltis,—a point which it is, furthermore, essential to know if a rational method of dealing with the blight is to be devised. Perhaps the earliest idea, and one which prevails to some extent even at the present day, is that the pest hibernates in water. This suggestion has been made probably from a mistaken idea that the insect was an actual mosquito. It would serve no useful purpose to give a review of the repeated occasions on which this statement has been made. As expressive of all, we may give the following:—"I believe the blight hibernates in water or swampy ground. Tea in the neighbourhood of such surroundings is invariably first attacked." It cannot, of course, be said, off-hand, that hibernation in water is impossible, but in view of both old and recent observations it is not only highly improbable, but practically excluded.

Not in water.

527. ***Hibernation in the Soil.****—Another opinion, very commonly held among planters, is that the insect hibernates in the soil

* We understood from reading Mr. Dudgeon's paper on the tea mosquito that he was of opinion that the insect hibernated in the soil. While this volume was going through the press, he informed us, however, that this was not his meaning, and that he always held the opinion that the tea mosquito would be found in the lower part of the bush in the adult stage, and that he has recently been able to prove himself correct by direct observation.

round the base of the tree. It is, however, merely a conclusion to which some men have come from the apparent impossibility of finding the insect in the bush at certain periods of the year, and hence, by a process of exclusion, it is supposed to be in the soil. There has never been a scrap of direct evidence in favour of the theory, and it may be said to be all but abandoned by all who have made any serious observations on the insect.

THE TEA MOSQUITO.

Hibernation in soil.

Though many of the experiments made have been open to this explanation, they would be equally well accounted for by the hibernation of the mosquito on the tea bush itself.

Supposed Hibernation in Jungle.

528. ***Hibernation in Jungle.***—One of the most generally believed theories has been that the insect retired on the approach of the cold weather, when there were no young succulent leaves on the tea bushes, to the jungle where it spent its time on a variety of plants, of which Bamboo, "*Tun*" (Cedrela toona), "*Tita-phul*" (Phlogocanthus thyrsiflorus), and Mæsa indica may be taken as samples. On some of these plants (and others also) the tea mosquito has been observed during the ordinary breeding season, but it may as well be stated at once that the theory of their hibernating on these trees or on jungle at all is based on no evidence whatsoever. One of us (H. H. M.) has searched jungle of very mixed kind during the hibernating period (January), in a district where the insect was extremely abundant, without finding a single sample of the insect, and the same may be said for all others who have made similar search.

Based on no positive evidence.

529. As regards its occurrence on other plants during the ordinary season, it may be well to take one by one those on which it has been said to live.

Supposed occurrence on Bamboo.

Bamboo never is attacked by mosquito so far as we are aware. The idea that it encouraged the pest is simply and solely due to the persistence of the insects under the shade which it yields.

On Tun.

Tun (Cedrela toona) has often been accused of harbouring the tea mosquito, and it is undoubtedly often found especially bad under the shade of tun trees. It has never been seen, however, to puncture the leaves of this tree.

Rubber (Ficus elastica) has been reported to be attacked by the Helopeltis antonii of Java. The mosquito insect in India is commonly more serious under the rubber trees than on the rest of

THE TEA MOSQUITO.

Supposed occurrence on rubber.

an estate, but we have never observed the insect actually attacking this tree in India.

On a Polygonum.

Polygonum sp.—During a tour through the Nambar Forest in 1895, one of us (G. W.) noticed a **Polygonum** punctured very similarly to tea, but the insect was not discovered. As the puncturings were very different in shape to those on the tea plant, it was inferred that they were probably not caused by Helopeltis.

On Mæsa indica.

Mæsa indica (called *Malmuriya* in Sylhet, *Bilauni* in Nepalese).—This tree is common all over Assam, etc., and is punctured in a manner very similar to tea, and moreover the insect lays its eggs, in a manner very similar to **Helopeltis theivora.** The insect is, however, not the tea mosquito, as **Dudgeon** showed, and has not the characteristic scutellar horn of **Helopeltis.** The attack is in fact caused by another closely allied capsid bug **(Disphinctus dudgeoni** *Kirkaldy*), and a very similar bug attacks Mæsa and other trees in Ceylon **(Disphinctus founosus).**

FIG. 33.—PUNCTURE IN MÆSA INDICA.

On pan.

Wild Pan **(Piper)** has often been said to be attacked by mosquito, and one writer goes so far as to say, "It is very fond of the pan plant." There is, however, no really authentic evidence of its being found actually feeding in this plant.

On Cocoa. On Cinchona.

Cocoa and *Cinchona* have been attacked by **Helopeltis antonii** in Ceylon, and the latter by **Helopeltis febriculosa** in India.

On Phlogocanthus.

Tita-phul **(Phlogocanthus thyrsiflorus)** has been attacked by what appears to be the mosquito insect. It was collected by one of us (H. H. M.) in the larval condition from this plant in October 1901.

On Eugenia. On Garden plants.

Eugenia sp. has, according to Mr. Green, been attacked in Ceylon. Occasionally in flower gardens the insect is seen to attack cultivated plants. Mr. Ilbert, of Moran, Sibsagar, reports having had Hibiscus plants injured by it: Mr. Harcourt found it on **Schima Wallichii** (*chilauni*) and on fuchsias: Mr. Nosworthy (Ging, Darjeeling) pointed it out on geraniums.

On Chilauni.

Hibernation on tea bush.

530. ***Hibernation on the Tea Bush.***—That the insect hibernates in the tea-bush itself has been put almost beyond doubt by

investigation during the past year by Mr. Green in Ceylon and by one of the authors (H. H. M.) in India.* In both cases careful search at any time of the year, even when the planters said that none could be obtained, revealed the presence of a few mature mosquitoes, and also eggs in the bushes—though the latter were few in number when compared with the number present in the middle of the breeding season. They could, however, be found, and in many cases in such a position that neither plucking nor pruning would have removed them. Some were even laid embedded in the midrib of large more or less mature leaves on the bush. A curious point noticed both in Ceylon and India is that females examined at this period contain many more eggs than is usually the case in the season. As Mr. Green expresses it, speaking of the Kelani Valley, "The paucity of recently deposited eggs was the more remarkable when it was found that the insects that were being captured at the same time . . . . . . contained in their bodies a larger number of fully formed eggs than I had previously found in insects examined, during the period of greater activity. The day's catch . . . was critically examined. It contained twenty-one female Helopeltis insects and twenty-six males. Dissection of the females showed eggs ranging in number from seven to twenty and giving an average of 12·25 per insect. My previous record had been eight eggs per insect." **Eggs found in body of female at different seasons.**

In another district the same thing was noticed, for "nine females were dissected, resulting in an average of 13·22 eggs per insect."

Our own observations in India confirm this, for while during the season 7 to 10 is about the usual number of eggs to obtain from one female, in February fourteen was common, and as many as twenty-three have been obtained in November.

531. Direct experiments agree with the results of observation that hibernation takes place on the tea bush itself. On our suggestion, Mr. Langmore, of Panighata, covered some bushes with wire gauze during the hibernating season. It will be easily seen that, if even only one of the bushes so covered are attacked, it is proof positive that in some cases there are mosquitoes there, and hence the insect hibernates on the bush or possibly in the soil round the base. **Result of enclosing bushes in wire gauze.**

* Mr. Dudgeon, we recently learnt, is quite in agreement with us on this point, and has actually seen the hibernating insect *in situ* on the lower part of the bush during the so-called hibernating period.

THE TEA MOSQUITO.

This is precisely what happened. In a certain proportion of cases the bushes were attacked earlier than the tea surrounding and more severely. The remaining bushes were not attacked plainly because no insects were hibernating in those particular bushes.

Proportion of larvæ and adults at various seasons.

532. In the Indian Tea Districts in January it is only rare that a young larval mosquito is found. On January 9, 1902, in the Terai every insect caught was an adult, two days later only 5 larvæ were found out of 200 insects caught. A month later in Cachar, however, the larvæ were coming out vigorously, and instead of 2½ per cent. of the catch they formed 88 per cent., or in some cases even more. From this point the larvæ go down in proportion, and May and June the young ones form about 50 per cent. of the insects caught. In October, on the other hand, the proportion of larvæ is very small certainly in our experience, not usually above fifteen per cent. Later than this the number is still smaller, till by the end of November not more than 6 to 7 per cent. of the insects are usually larvæ if shade is absent. We have thus adult insects practically alone in the cold weather, an immense proportion of larvæ in spring being reduced to 50 per cent. of insects by May, and gradually decreasing from September to the end of the season.

Distribution.

533. ***Distribution.***—It may serve a useful purpose if we indicate the extent to which this blight has spread in the Indian and Ceylon districts. There is little doubt that, even yet, it is spreading fast and will be found in future years where it is never thought of now. This being the case, every precaution should be taken in those districts where it has not yet become established. To take first the Indian districts.

(*a*) *Districts where the crop is often reduced by 25 per cent. and over.*—Darjeeling Terai; Extreme West of Duars; Bishnath district, Assam; one or two districts in Cachar.

(*b*) *Districts where it is less serious than the above, but a very serious pest.*—Golaghat and North Lakhimpur districts, Assam; Remainder of Cachar; Darjeeling district in many parts; Chargola Valley, Sylhet.

(*c*) *Districts where effect is seriously noticeable.*—Dibrugarh; Sibsagar; Nowgong districts, Assam; Longai and Juri Valleys, Sylhet; Many parts of Duars; Remainder of Darjeeling.

THE TEA MOSQUITO.

(*d*) *Districts where it is known, but has never yet done serious damage.*—Tezpur District, Assam; Lungla Valley, Sylhet; Remainder of Duars.

(*e*) *Districts where it is practically unknown.*—Mangaldai district, Assam; Sylhet to the West of the Lungla Valley; Chittagong; Kangra Valley; Dehra Dun; Kumaon; Chota Nagpur, etc., etc.

Distribution in Ceylon.

In Ceylon, according to Mr. Green, it is extending its range. "It formerly confined its ravages . . . . to estates in the low-country, *e.g.*, Kelani Valley, Kalutara, Udagana, Morawak-Korale. I have recently investigated an undoubted case in the neighbourhood of Nawalapitiya, at an elevation of 2,000 feet, and I hear of other affected estates in the same district." (*Green, 1902.*)

Remedy.

Effect of local circumstances.

534. ***Physical and Geographical Conditions.***—We are not yet in a position to gauge entirely or even approximately the effect of various physical and geographical conditions on the growth and development of the tea mosquito, but considerable progress has been made since the first edition of this work was published, and it would seem well to summarize and examine the statements made on the subject and to add the results of our new observations. There are many points still, however, absolutely unexplained. The appearance of the insect in one garden, its disappearance from another only a mile or two distant, and its re-appearance in a third, are local circumstances that possibly may be accounted for by external influences that favour the growth of the insect in the one, and are inimical to it in the other. Such things cannot surely be accidental and they are likely to be governed by conditions on the one hand favourable, on the other unfavourable to the life of the insect. To be able to contest the ground held by this terrible pest, therefore, we must fully understand such influences, and steps should be taken to obtain something more than personal opinions and speculations. An annual census of gardens with blight and of its time of appearance and disappearance, would be of great use in this connection.

Effect of Geographical position.

535. ***Effect of Geographical Position.***—Up to the present all observations made have discounted the effect of mere geographical position. Undoubtedly the worst attacks of all have been at the base

THE TEA MOSQUITO.

of hills on the north of the garden. But this is by no means universally the case, and attacks are often met with entirely apart from hills of any sort. It is not, furthermore, only on flat land *or* hilly land that the pest abounds, and although above 4,000 feet it is rarely serious, yet we have collected specimens in a healthy, vigorous condition as high as 5,000 feet above sea level. The effect of mere geographical position may therefore, on present information, be ignored.

Effect of soil.

536. ***Effect of Soil.***—In 1884 Mr. Wood-Mason wrote as follows:—

> "After an exhaustive examination of every case in which the quality of the soil, or shade, or want of cultivation, and the Bug-disease seemed to be connected as cause and effect, I have arrived at the conclusion that neither of these separately, nor all three in combination, can be considered to be the cause of, although they may, when combined, possibly promote the disease."

Wood-Mason's dictum.

The idea that the character of the soil has something to do with the prevalence of the blight has nevertheless been a very favourite theory, and there are some striking examples in which it appears. For instance, in a garden in the Bishnath district of Assam there are two classes of soil: one a low level greyish loam with a hard pan at a depth of under one foot, the other a high red bank soil, somewhat similar to that of the red bank at Tezpur. The two lie side by side, the bushes on the former are badly attacked by mosquito, so much so, indeed, that some has been abandoned on this account; on the other the blight is rarely seen. The same takes place in the Duars, on several gardens we have seen—high, good land has no mosquito; low, shallow soil is badly affected. In general it would almost appear that soils subject to drought were also liable to mosquito, and *vice versâ;* and though there are some very striking exceptions to this rule, yet, in spite of Mr. Wood-Mason's dictum, there may be found in the future some connection between soil and blight. The matter is worthy of further investigation.

Exceptions.

Effect of Climate.

537. ***Effect of Climate.***—In considering the effect of climate one is met at the outset by the difficulty of differentiating between those cases in which the blight has got a hold in a garden and is merely maintaining it,—and any climatic conditions which caused it to get that hold. To eliminate either factor entirely seems impossible, but it may be said that the years in India in which the greatest extension into new grounds occurs are those in which there is a long spring

Effect of drought.

drought, and hence in which spring growth is retarded. And in confirmation it be pointed out that most of the districts in which the blight is worst are those in which this spring drought often happens, and in which the soil is such as to feel the effect very badly.

Irrigation suggested.

So much is this the case that one of us (H. H. M.) has suggested during the present season the trial of spring irrigation as a means of fighting the blight,—more especially in gardens in which only a little blight occurs, for where it is well-established the effect would hardly be seen for a number of years. While this is a possible method of dealing with the blight, it cannot be said to have been tried as yet.

Effect of shade.

538. ***Effect of Shade.***—It is well known that the tea mosquito has a preference for the shade of certain trees like the '*tun*," the species of "Ficus," the bamboo, etc., but it cannot be said to love shade of all kinds. In fact, writers on the subject have made far too general statements on the subject. One writer in the *Tea Cyclopædia* says definitely: "It is worst under tree shade." On the other hand, in Ceylon we are informed by Mr. Green that "the bushes in the immediate shelter of windbelts (Grevillea and other trees) showed a remarkable freedom from attack." It seems therefore not to be wise to condemn shade altogether and to be the best plan to ascertain which trees have a bad effect like Ficus and "*tun*" and eradicate these.

Objectionable trees.

Effect of cleaning out bushes.

Conf. with para. 167.

539. ***Effect of Ventilation in Bushes.***—Under this head we can discuss the effect on the blight of various methods of pruning, resulting in a bush concentrating its attention on a few strong healthy shoots, or spreading its energies on a badly ventilated bush containing a mass of scrubby shoots. Direct experiments on the prevalence of mosquito in land pruned by both methods have not been carried out, and it would be very difficult to carry them out, but this we can say that those districts like Dibrugarh where what one may call a "clean" system of pruning is followed are precisely those in which the amount of blight has decreased, while it has been extending its ravages elsewhere. This may or may not be due to the clean open pruning, but now it is almost certain that hibernation takes place in the tea bush itself, it will be readily seen that the presence of a large number of twiggy shoots would give just the position for the insect to shelter and to lay its eggs in the cold weather in preparation for an early attack the following season. While recognising that we have not

THE TEA MOSQUITO.

here a matter on which one can speak very definitely, we think that a method of minimising the pest may probably be found in "clean" open, well-ventilated bushes.

Cultivation.

540. ***Effect of Cultivation.***—One of the favourite ideas of those whose gardens have never been really seriously affected is that good deep, thorough hoeing will bring the bushes through an attack and eradicate the blight. In a slight attack the whole evidence seems to point in this direction,—but we regard this as the direct result of the stimulating action on the bush of the thorough hoeing enabling it to grow faster than the mosquito can keep pace with it. In districts really badly affected opinion is quite the reverse, and it has often been said to us that heavy cultivation on a badly affected block is a waste of labour, for the more the leaf tries to grow the more effectually is it choked by the insect. Thus in the Terai and part of the Duars it is customary to abandon cultivation on a piece of tea that is so badly affected as to be shut up. From the dozens of experiments in the subject it may be concluded that in a slight attack cultivation as thorough as possible will probably enable the bushes to outgrow the mosquito quickly, while in bad attacks it is useless.

Cultivation no use in serious cases.

Cutting Surrounding Jungle.

541. ***Effect of Cutting Surrounding Jungle.***—It may be said that in Cachar it is absolutely universal to cut the jungle round the tea where mosquito blight is likely to occur, partially to allow light and air to thoroughly penetrate to the bushes, and partly in pursuance of the old idea that the insect hibernated in the jungle. We now know that its effect from the latter point of view will be extremely small, and indeed all it can do is, to a small extent, to prevent a fresh invasion of wild insects. It does seem wise to keep the tea as open as possible especially where bamboo jungle is the rule, and the method should be followed, not with the hope of thus preventing an attack, but simply to reduce the conditions favourable to the growth and extension of the blight.

Liming soil.

542. ***Effect of Liming the Soil.***—On the assumption that the resting stage of the mosquito occurred in the ground, it has been suggested that a liberal top-dressing of lime, worked into the soil in a dry state, might have a beneficial result. Though this is not likely on the basis of what we now know, yet we should like to see a plot badly affected with mosquito treated in this manner, and another plot "middle pruned" and every shoot, twig, and branch on the

Experiment required.

bush whitewashed or limewashed completly immediately after the pruning. The latter would probably have great effect if the plot was not re-infected from the outside.

THE TEA MOSQUITO.

Burning prunings.

543. ***Effect of Destroying Prunings.***—In almost all methods for dealing with the blight the burning of the prunings is an essential part, and as a safeguard it should always be done. There is distinct evidence, however, that on the withering of the green shoots in which the eggs are laid these latter never develop, and hence die. The question is one of importance, and needs further investigation. In the meantime it will be well to at least clear all the prunings from mosquito-blighted blocks in every case.

Time of pruning.

544. ***Effect of Time of Pruning.***—In the earlier days of the blight it was often reasoned,—and the reasoning is used to a considerable extent to the present day,—that inasmuch as the pest become serious in July or August, it would be a good plan to prune the garden so as to ensure an early crop before the blight shut up the garden. An unforeseen result occurred, however, to vitiate the reasoning. If early pruning is adopted, it means that the first shoots which appear in the spring are, especially in times of drought, not vigorous, and hence not capable of resisting the attacks of the insect, and under these conditions the pest became serious at an earlier date each year. The idea is, in fact, abandoned in most places now, and though a careful experiment on the point is needed under strictly defined conditions, yet practically all the evidence at present is in favour not of earlier, *but rather of later pruning* than usual in a garden affected with mosquito blight. Succulent vigorous growth is in fact the great enemy of the Helopeltis.

Late pruning advised on mosquito blocks.

Hard plucking.

545. ***Effect of Hard Plucking.***—After having found that the eggs of the insect were laid in the young green shoot, Mr. Wood-Mason suggested that, as this was the case, the plucking of these shoots as soon as possible would probably be a means of dealing with the pest. He says, in fact, that "the vigorous and unremitting plucking of the blighted portions of bushes might remedy the evil." Mr. Cotes repeats the recommendation and says, "This treatment would no doubt tend to be beneficial, but cannot be looked upon as complete in itself.

Wood-Mason's recommendation.

Fatal result.

It may, at once, be said however that we consider the recommendation as one of the *worst ever made in the interests of the tea*

THE TEA MOSQUITO.

industry. In the first place, Mr. Dudgeon, and, since, Mr. Green have shown that the eggs are laid quite as much in that part of the green shoot which would not be plucked, as in that which would be removed. Mr. Green, in a letter to one of the authors, says, for instance :

> "My Ceylon experience leads me to think that the eggs are—in by far the majority of cases—laid in the soft green stems. They are very frequently deposited in the internode between the bud-scale and the first leaf, and it is this fact that allows so many of them to escape destruction in the ordinary course of plucking."

Mr. Green's opinion.

In the second place, the close plucking recommended by Mr. Wood-Mason results in a broom-like mass of shoots on the bush, precisely the arrangement which gives the pest the best chance of feeding and laying eggs. To quote Mr. Green again. "For the present, I must recommend the abandonment of close plucking. There is no doubt that this system tends to produce a brush-like formation of small shoots specially suited to the tastes of the Helopeltis. A free succulent growth should be encouraged, just as anything that tends to reduce the vitality of the Indigenous variety lays it open to attack, so any extra vitality in the hybrid and china "Jats," producing a character approaching that of the indigenous plant, will incline to make it distasteful to the pest."

There is no doubt that Indian experience tells in the same direction, and close plucking has, there is little doubt, led to the extension and encouragement of the pest,—and should be abandoned as a method of dealing with it, especially when applied to the early months of the season.

Stimulation of bush.

546. ***Effect of Stimulating the Bush.***—It has been suggested that extremely forcing manures should be added to the plots affected with the blight in order to make the growth more succulent, and hence unfavourable to the mosquito, during the critical period in June and July. Though this can only be looked upon as a palliative, yet there seemed a reasonable chance of success, and one of the authors (H. H. M.) has conducted an experiment in the Terai during 1902 applying nitrate of soda to the bushes at the rate of 1 cwt. to the acre. The results are to hand, and seem to indicate that we have here a very successful method. The block to which the nitrate of soda was applied early in June, was free from mosquito blight up to the middle of September, while the other end of the same piece of

tea was black and producing no leaf long before. Further experiments in this direction will be carried out later. THE TEA MOSQUITO.

547. Up to the present we have dealt with remedies which have been suggested, but have not been proved to be satisfactory, at any rate alone. The attacks can, it seems, be somewhat modified by variations in the methods of pruning, of plucking, of cultivating, and possibly of stimulating the bush by other means, but none of the methods set out up to this point have been more than the merest palliatives. Some of those which follow must be placed in the same category, but they have either been greater successes or have greater promise for the future. All previous methods are useless or only palliatives.

And here we may frankly say that the attempt to find a cure for mosquito when it is in full vigour at the middle of the season is likely to remain quite futile. The insect belongs to a group very difficult to reach with insecticides, which are not attacked by many other insects (though they are by a few), and even were it possible financially to syringe the bushes in mid-season it would be impossible to do so without ruining the crop, and it would not be in the least likely to be effective against a flying insect like the mosquito. We firmly believe that any method likely to be of use must be largely if not entirely of a preventive and not a curative character,—and in this line there seems at least a possibility of success.

548. ***Collection of the Mosquito.***—This is perhaps the most common method by which it is attempted to deal with the pest, and it was introduced very early in the story of the blight. One writer in the *Tea Gazette* wrote before 1880 as follows:— Collection of mosquito.

"After long observation I found that I could catch without much trouble a large number of the pests in all the different stages, and after a while I put on a batch of women under an experienced sirdar, to whom I had previously shown the mosquito in all its forms, to catch all the insects they could, and pluck off all the punctured leaves and buds: this latter is necessary, as the injury done to the leaves by the insect has some poisonous influence on the shoots, and they blacken and die off, effectually stopping any further flushes for a considerable time. Hopeless as the work appeared at first, yet after the women once got into the way of it, I found that they could catch about an average of 60 to 100 insects per diem, and this sufficed to clear about 55 acres of tea in a week. Of course once going over Old opinion.

THE TEA MOSQUITO.

will not be sufficient, as a number of the more minute youngsters will be left, and these will have to be searched for afterwards: but even one clearing has been of immense benefit."

It is evident that the author of this article had never had his garden badly attacked!

Since the time at which this letter was written the employment of children to catch the mosquito has been practically the only method of dealing with the pest that has been generally employed,—and with few exceptions it is still more or less employed on nearly all gardens badly affected with the insect. The opinions of planters as to value are, however, very different. Some hold that this and this alone will suffice, if done thoroughly and at the proper time, to clear a garden: others after many years' experience with the blight are inclined to believe it is almost useless—a difference of opinion which re-appears on all matters connected with the blight, and which forms one of the great difficulties of the subject. The truth of the matter appears to be that on gardens where the method has been successful the blight has never been allowed to become very serious, or, if it has, the catching has been of a most thorough kind, and done at the most suitable time. It may be said that, if catching the insects is to be effective, (1) it must be done early in the season. We have seen mosquitoes being caught in February, and it is evident that one caught then is worth hundreds caught in July. We doubt, in fact, whether catching after the garden is "black" with blight is worth much for that season;—to be useful it is in spring, when the blight first appears, that it should be carried out. (2) It must be done thoroughly. Once going over a plot and then passing off to another will do little good: the children who catch the insects should be kept on one plot till not another puncture is found—all punctured leaves being plucked off each round. This may mean a very heavy force at work, but thorough work is essential if any good is to follow.

Catching must be early in season, and must be thorough.

549. Other methods of catching the mosquitoes have been tried. The use of lights among the tea bushes was thought likely to be of great use in the early days of the industry, but it was found that while the lights attracted hundreds of other species, the mosquitoes did not seem to take any notice of the lights at all. In an experiment by Mr. Green an acetylene lamp of 50 candle power was employed, and though representatives of almost every order of insects

Lights among bushes a failure.

The Tea Mosquito.

were caught, not a single mosquito came near, though the bushes round about were badly affected with blight. THE TEA MOSQUITO.

Still another method has been suggested, though I am not aware that it has been tried, based on the use of the hopper-dozers employed for catching locusts in America. We are afraid we have not much faith in the method. Hopper-dozers probably useless.

Another method which has universally proved a failure is the attempt to catch the insects by sticky bamboos, or sticks, or cloths. The insects simply refuse to be caught by any such contrivance. Sticky Bamboos, etc., useless.

550. ***Selection of Resistant Stocks.***– It has been noticed long ago that the blight preferred the China *jat* of tea, liked Hybrid, but Assam indigenous hardly at all. Mr. Wood-Mason went into great detail on the subject. He says:— Resistant stocks.

"The species which affords the strong and rasping liquor, when pure, enjoys an almost complete immunity from attack; but the species which affords the milder liquor suffers most severely. I have no doubt that the more powerful juices of the Indigenous tree serve to protect it from its enemies, and that the milder juices of the China bush render it liable to attack."

To a certain extent this holds good still, we have never seen a dark-leaved Manipuri jat of tea suffer very severely: but there is no doubt that the insect is gradually accustoming itself to the Assam plant, and even the jats resistant at present will probably be badly attacked in the future. We have seen practically every plant in a nursery of indigenous tea badly affected with the blight, and so it cannot be said that "indigenous" plant is now by any means unattacked.

Nevertheless the replacement of China or Hybrid plant by Manipuri or even, to a less extent, by Assam indigenous has been found a great protection. Unluckily it is not possible to replace tea in full bearing, and though this method may be occasionally useful, say on the side of a badly affected garden adjoining another patch seriously attacked, it cannot be considered as practical in the majority of cases. Impossible to replace old tea.

In putting out new gardens in blighted districts, however, there can be no excuse for choosing susceptible jats, as we have seen done during the past year. Only the best and most resistant stocks should be used, and advice should be sought as to the susceptibility of the *jats* suggested before seed is bought.

But a wider question is raised in connection with this subject. In a garden it is by no means an unusual occurrence to find here Breeding resistant stocks.

THE TEA MOSQUITO.

and there bushes not attacked by the mosquito, while all others around are black and every shoot killed. Surely the selection of a mosquito-proof stock would be by no means impossible. So again such instances as, in conversation, were related to one of us (G. W.) by Mr. Peal are not unusual, *viz.*, of certain bushes attacked year after year when the rest of the garden has escaped or practically escaped the pest. Examples of this nature point very possibly to a class of bush that should be eradicated as early as possible.

Conf. with paras. 37—40.

The subject of a more careful selection of stock is one of immense potentialities.

Natural enemies.

551. ***Encouragement of the Natural Enemies of the Mosquito.***—Many years ago Mr. W. L. Distant found, among some samples of Helopeltis from Ceylon, a few examples of a Reduviid insect which he thought might be parasitic on the mosquito. During the explorations of one of us (G. W.) in Assam in 1895 a Reduviid insect was likewise found which was undoubtedly parasitic on the red variety of tea mosquito. This is an insect perhaps half as large again as the male mosquito, has its legs mottled orange and brown, also very hairy. The thorax is of a brown tint, and the abdomen orange coloured. It is thus remarkably like the mosquito, only a little larger and stouter built, but may instantly be distinguished by *not possessing the drumstick-like protuberance on its back* so characteristic of the tea mosquito. The insect was watched in the act of capturing the mosquitoes and transfixing them with its powerful proboscis.

Reduviid insect.

Since that time it has been frequently seen in several parts of Assam. It is, there is little doubt, the natural enemy of the mosquito and the planters' greatest friend. If the collections brought in by the children are carefully examined, there will be no difficulty often in picking out a few of these insects, for they are, we fear, regularly gathered with the idea that they are mosquitoes. In fact, we have seen a catch of supposed mosquitoes in which the bulk of the insects consisted of this Reduviid.

To be encouraged and bred.

We would suggest that the greatest care be expended on the encouragement and the multiplication of this insect. A few might be placed in a cage, consisting of a tub with growing tea bush enclosed by mosquito-curtain cloth and live mosquitoes daily given them to eat. If the children employed to catch mosquitoes were made to feed these insects with live mosquito, they would soon be recognised, and their

THE TEA MOSQUITO.

destruction discontinued. At the same time, the life history of the **Reduviid** should be studied, with a view to discovering a method of artificially increasing their number, by breeding them in captivity and liberating large swarms on the estate.

Bugs feeding on tea mosquito.

552. This insect is apparently only found to attack the red mosquito. In North Lakhimpur two much larger plant bugs were pointed out as feeding on the mosquito—one belonging to the Genus **Melamphaus** and the other to the Genus **Sycanus**. Nothing further is, however, known as to their value.

Spider feeding on tea mosquito.

Mr. C. H. Harcourt, of Ging, Darjeeling, mentioned a small spider which attacked the tea mosquito, but though spiders are practically all friendly, yet we have never seen a case in which they have done any good against the tea mosquito. Mr. G. Peter has finally noticed dragon flies feeding on the blight in Cachar.

Ladybird beetles unlikely to be of use.

Ladybird beetles do not attack the pest in question so far as we have seen. The most likely insect to be of advantage is the **Reduviid** above mentioned, and it should receive very careful attention, as it may be of great advantage. Of course, seeing that the use of **Vedalia** (Ladybird) beetles in California to attack the fluted scale of the orange has been such a great success and that that pest practically disappeared in less than two years, it has been thought probable that other pests might be dealt with similarly. It must be remembered, however, that the conditions were very special. The **Vedalia** beetle was first an insect introduced from a foreign country (Australia), where it was on the whole rather scarce and kept in check by natural enemies; secondly, it was introduced in America where these natural enemies did not exist, and where the insect found favourable opportunity for multiplying; and lastly, and most important of all, the Australian ladybird recognised no other insect among those found in California as proper food, and naturally confined itself entirely to these scales. That similar success should be attained where these special conditions are absent is not to be expected, but nevertheless the **Reduviid** above mentioned is likely to do good service.

Fungi parasitic on mosquito.

553. ***Parasitic Fungi as a Cure for Mosquito.***—In the introductory review of the historic facts that bear on the study of mosquito blight, a suggestion made by Mr. J. Wood-Mason has been alluded to, namely, that an effort should be made to discover some

The Hemiptera (Capsidæ).

THE TEA MOSQUITO.

parasitic fungus that might be employed in the eradication of mosquito. The idea is a most admirable one, and since this method has recently made considerable progress in other countries and in connection with other industries, we commend it as worthy of the most careful enquiry. So far as investigations have gone, we have failed to find any tea mosquito that give evidence of being parasitised. That, however, cannot be looked upon as in any way detracting from the value of the proposal. To bring about the result indicated would necessitate the formation of a laboratory for advanced microscopic research, and the discovery of the desired fungus might be protracted for years.

It ought, however, to be stated that the insect at present under consideration is a most unlikely pest to be attacked by a fungus. Mr. Green, whose experince on the subject is very great, recently wrote to us as follows :—"Of all hexapod insects the Hemiptera (excluding coccidæ, aleurodidæ, etc.) seem to be least subject to diseases of this nature. I do not recollect having ever seen any of the Heteroptera (to which tea-mosquito belongs—H. H. M.) attacked by parasitic fungi."

Firing tea estates.

554. ***Firing estates as a Remedy.***—Seeing that it has now been rendered almost certain that the insect hibernates in the tea bush, the idea of firing whole plots has a rational basis, provided of course the garden or plot is sufficiently isolated from other gardens or plots attacked by the pest. Under these conditions, the method has been adopted in several places with success. In one Dibrugarh garden in 1886 the owner, after trying every measure that could be suggested to check the wholesale destruction that was being effected by mosquito, decided to fire the entire plot. The bushes recovered the shock rapidly, the garden was improved, rather than injured, the pest was entirely eradicated, and up to 1895 it had not returned. The cure seemed complete. In a Nowgong garden (Koliabar) the same story was told. In 1899, the affected plots were fired, and the blight, to date, has not returned. In this latter case, however, the garden is quite isolated from all others. Under the conditions named, the method seems worthy of more attention than it has yet received.

Successful results.

Insecticides.

555. ***Preventive Measures with Insecticides.***—The idea of using insecticides has been scouted by most of the writers on the subject, and if it is intended to kill the insect during the season, we are quite at one with them. Since the discovery of the hibernation

of the mosquito in the bush, the whole matter takes another aspect, considered as a preventive measure. In fact, we would point out that if one applies such treatment to a bush shortly after pruning so as to prevent further eggs being laid in the bush, and so as to hinder the eggs hatching out, it will very much moderate the attack, and after similar treatment for several years the pest should be practically eradicated. Working from this point, an experiment has been conducted for one of us (H. H. M.) by Mr. A. D. Browne, of the Longview Tea Estate, on an isolated piece of tea on that estate during the present season (1902). The plot of tea pruned so as to remove two years' growth was divided into two halves. On one-half the tea was sprayed, about a month after pruning, with Chiswick soap (25 lbs. to 200 gallons of water), and on the other with Kerosene Emulsion,* in each case at the rate of about 150 to 200 gallons per acre. Observation in May in comparison with a check block usually affected similarly by mosquito, showed 2 per cent. of the bushes affected on the treated plots (both being equally free) as against 75 per cent. of affected bushes on the untreated block. Further than this, many which were affected had been attacked by flying insects from the outside, as was witnessed by the form and position of the punctures. A later letter from Mr. Browne read as follows:—

THE TEA MOSQUITO.

Successful experiment.

"I find now that the majority of the bushes show signs of mosquito, but the bushes are still flushing freely, which cannot be said of the other blocks you saw when here. The bushes on the experimental block have quite a vigorous growth by comparison with the other blocks, and I am of opinion that they will be able to throw off the blight shortly, and when the non-sprayed blocks are completely shut up, the experimental block will be giving us leaf" (Aug. 1, 1902).

The result as thus reported was far beyond our expectation, and certainly we should have been very well pleased if the blight had been kept off for a month. By the end of the season it was actually estimated that there had been an increased yield of about a maund an acre. After initiating these experiments, we have heard of the

* This is prepared as follows:—Dissolve $1\frac{1}{2}$ lbs. of soap in one gallon of water, and while the mixture is practically boiling add two gallon of kerosene and thoroughly mix, if necessary by passing through a spraying-machine until the whole forms a white creamy mixture. This mixture should keep for several days. When wanted for use, dilute the above quantity to 30 gallons.

THE TEA MOSQUITO.

partial success with Chiswick compound on several gardens in Cachar and Sylhet. The discovery of the hibernation on the bush is, however, the basis on which the rational development of this method lies. The matter is in a very tentative position at present, and it will only be after another year of experiment that one will be able to say very definitely the chances of success at present. If any one takes up this matter during the coming cold weather, we would urge that it should on no account be used unless carried out absolutely, thoroughly and unless a proper spraying machine is used and not a garden syringe. The latter would probably be useless and very wasteful in addition. It should also be remembered that the enemy is a flying insect, and so, if any results are to be obtained, the experiments should be done on an isolated block. Otherwise the plots will be invaded from the outside before the experiment is completed. We have up to date experimented on an isolated block, and in dealing with mosquito by any similar method it would be of immense advantage if only the blocks were separated by a narrow piece of jungle. Mr. Green, in this matter, says: "I am strongly advocating the isolation of fields by subdividing the larger areas into smaller blocks (of, say, 10 acres) by close belts of other trees (*vide Royal Botanic Gardens, Ceylon, Circular, Series II., No. 2. 'Further observations on Helopeltis,' page 30*). Such a system would lead itself admirably to kerosene emulsion treatment." The Terai planters are beginning, by bitter experience, to recognise the value of isolating blocks, but the idea that jungle-favoured mosquito has led to the opening out of every hindrance to the free circulation of the insect, and hence where the blight might have been restricted to a corner, it has now in many cases spread over whole estates.

Conclusions.

556. ***Conclusions as to Remedial Measures.***—The methods of remedy we have discussed lead us to the belief that really we can only rely on three or four methods as possible in dealing with this serious blight. No doubt, modification of "cultivation," of pruning, and, even more, of plucking will palliate an attack if it be not serious, but these alone will not get rid of a bad attack. For this purpose, we still believe in catching the insect, but we think the most important month in the year is February, and then March and April. A failure in July or August is to be expected. The use of insect enemies has not progressed much, but we believe that artificial

The Tea Mosquito.

extension of the "Reduviid" insect mentioned above could do much good. Beyond this there is the preventive method by insecticides like "kerosene and soap," or "Chiswick compound," both of which have been equally successful in the experiments to date, though these experiments have hardly passed the preliminary stages. THE TEA MOSQUITO.

In fact, we must not and cannot look to cures. What will be of use is the proper utilization of the measures in our hand to prevent each season, by every means in our power, the spreading of the pest, and the regaining of what has already been conquered by the pest.

89. Hyalopeplus rama, ***Kerly.*** HYALOPEPLUS RAMA.

Found in Ceylon.

557. This pest has not appeared in India. Mr. Green has been good enough to give a description of the insect as it occurs in Ceylon. A Ceylon pest like tea mosquito.

"This Capsid bug seems to be responsible for almost as much damage as is caused by **Helopeltis** in some of the low country districts, although it is very commonly present at higher elevations without attracting any attention as a pest. It is frequently found in association with the **Helopeltis.** The coolies bring in about equal numbers of each species. The eggs are embedded in the same manner and in similar situations, but they may be recognised from those of **Helopeltis** by a prominent conical, white process that takes the place of the hair-like horns found in the eggs of the Mosquito blight."

More recent observations by Mr. Green in Ceylon have thrown considerable doubt as to whether this bug is really the depredator it has been supposed to be. Isolated individuals, in captivity, will not feed on tea, and all attempts to make them do so have given quite negative results. Whether this insect really does the damage attributed to it must therefore be left to future experiment to decide. In the meantime it should be looked upon with grave suspicion, and the insects collected wherever they are found.

90. **Another capsid bug,** whose name is at present undetermined, has recently attracted attention in Ceylon as a tea-pest. "It is a small uniformly pale green insect about one-fifth of an inch long. The egg is embedded in the succulent shoots. It is without the hairlike processes found in eggs of **Helopeltis** and **Disphinctus,** and is consequently very difficult to detect. My correspondent reports as follows :—"The small bug is seriously injuring my tea, and attacks also **verbena** plants in my garden. There are thousands of them of all sizes, some with wings and some without. Tea, badly attacked, shuts up completely for some time. On a previous occasion a bed of nasturtium in my garden was completely ruined by the insects. A few years ago they temporarily spoiled some 20 acres of tea." The punctures of this insect do not produce the conspicuous brown spots noticed in Helopeltis attacks; but the punctured shoots flag and wither or curl up.

Family PENTATOMIDÆ.

91. Pæcilocoris hardwickii, ***Moore.***

References.—*Journ. Agri.-Horti. Soc. Ind. Vol. II. Proc. Nov. 1869, p. ix. Proc., Dec., 1870, p. lxxxvi.*

The Hemiptera (Pentatomidæ).

PÆCILOCORIS HARDWICKII.

Found in all Indian districts.

Large bug.

558. This large bug is found in clusters of five or ten low down underneath the shade of the bush. They are most inactive creatures and never seem to be doing anything. They are between half to three quarters of an inch in length and a little less in breadth and are pale yellow coloured with curious finger-nail-shaped orange-red patches round the thin margin. The head is bright metallic blue. The thorax scarlet, and behind the thorax there are three metallic blue patches, the centre one of the three forming the outline of a triangle. Along the back are three orange-red bands and right over the anal extremity other two metallic blue bands. Though often found infesting tea plants, it has been no very easy job to find out exactly what it does to the bushes. Mr. Fleet wrote that having placed the insects under observation he could not find that they were injurious. On the contrary, he wrote: "The original ones that I first noticed on a bush . . . have not even moved from the leaves on which I found them." Mr. Green, to whom further samples were sent, replied: "This is apparently immature, and would eventually develop into one of the large Pentatomid bugs. It belongs to a plant-sucking family; but some of them are known to vary their diet by transfixing and sucking caterpillars. The habit of this large species should be watched. It may prove to be a friend."

Sucks tea-seed.

Quite recently, Mr. Lytle, of the Alyne Tea Estate, Cachar, caught one of these bugs sucking an unripe tea-seed, and showed it to one of us (H. H. M.) with the beak still embedded in the tea seed. Later information has since been received which seems to indicate that this is one of its common methods of feeding.

Family JASSIDÆ.

CHLORITA FLAVESCENS. THE GREEN FLY OF TEA.

88. Chlorita flavescens, *Fabr.*

GREEN FLY: STUNTED BLIGHT: CRINKLY BLIGHT.

SEE PLATE XV, No. 1.

References.—*Peal, Tea Cyclopædia, 37-38; Correspondence* re *Green Fly.—loc. cit. 43—49: Journ. Agri.-Horti. Soc. Ind., VII. (1884), xcv; Tea Planter's Vade Mecum, 104; Notes on Tea in Darjeeling, 49; Bamber, Chem. and Agri. Tea, 248-251; Bamber, Annual Report, 1893, p. 92; Ind. Mus. Notes II., 167; III., 9-12: pt. 3, 140; IV., 42; Cotes, Tea Insects, 34-36; Miles, Journ. Micro. Soc. Ind., V., 45; Crole, Tea Text-Book, 83, 223; Planter, May 19, 1900.*

Found in nearly all districts in India.

Very serious pest.

559. ***History.***—If mosquito blight be excluded, the pest now under consideration does probably more damage than any of the insects attacking tea. Originally discovered on the tea bush in 1874 in Assam, samples were not carefully examined till 1884, and then Mr. Wood-Mason identified them as a homopterous insect closely allied to "the little green flies which are such a pest in the rains in Calcutta." He added that he had met with them frequently on tea-bushes, but could never satisfy himself that they did any harm. Then followed a period of confusion. Mr. Peal mixed up the insect with the tea aphis; Mr. Bamber confused it with "blister blight," and made some

The Tea Green Fly.

insecticide experiments against it, which from knowledge of the nature of the insect might have been expected to prove unsuccessful; Mr. Crole was even more in a fog on the subject. In the former edition of this work it was held that the connection between the insect and the blight was not proved. We can say little more than this even now, though considerable information is to hand which seems to render it more probable. One thing seems certain, many attacks of what has been called "green fly" or "stunted flush" are probably due to totally different causes, and many things—such as a considerable number of cases of so-called "thrip" as well as mere stunted leaf from bad pruning or other causes—have been called green fly merely from lack of knowledge of its real nature.

THE TEA GREEN FLY.

Confusion about this pest.

560. ***Description.***—The insect which goes by the name of green fly, belongs to the family known as leaf-hoppers "which are small slender insects with the wing covers (*i.e.* forewings) narrow and slightly thicker than the broad hind wings, which are the only effective organs of flight. The thorax is broad and square, the head usually short and very broad, in most cases somewhat crescent shaped, with prominent eyes occupying a large part of the sides. If we examine the insects on the under side, it appears as if the beak or rostrum came out from the breast between the front legs, so much is the head curved under. The antennæ are very short and bristle-like*: the legs are well developed, the hind pair especially being long and powerful set with spines on the tibiæ, somewhat as in the grasshoppers, and like them the insects are powerful leapers. This they are in all stages, but as adults they are also ready fliers, and hence difficult to capture." (*J. B. Smith.*)

A leaf hopper.

Description.

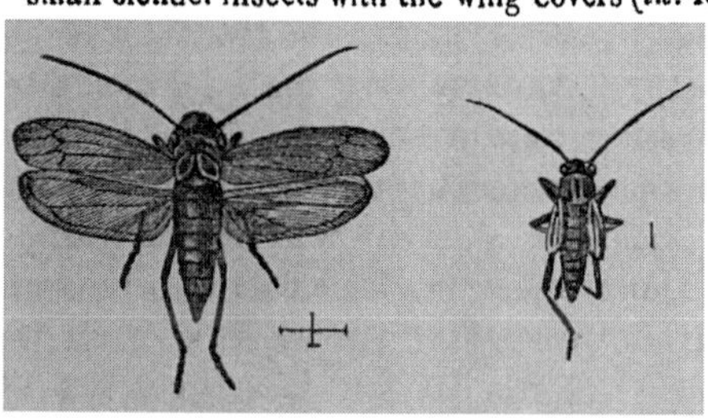

FIG. 34.—THE TEA GREEN FLY.
No. 1. Mature; No. 2. Immature Insects.
(After Cotes.)

561. The life history of the particular species under discussion is not made out. It is probable, though we have not been able to make

Life history unknown.

* The illustration given in Fig. 34, taken from Mr. Cotes, is incorrect in this particular. The antennæ should be much shorter.

The Hemiptera (Jassidæ).

THE TEA GREEN FLY.

certain of it yet by breeding, that the eggs are laid in the yet unfolded tip leaf, and that during the season the young larvæ come out in about four days. They spend their larval stage on the young leaves of the plant, being then often mistaken for Thrips. We have recently observed punctures on the stunted shoots of gardens badly affected with the blight, not on the leaves, but on the young green growing shoots. If the epidermis be carefully removed, underneath will be found a large number of small (almost microscopic) brown punctures. It would therefore seem that the lancets in the mouth organs of the insect are pushed right through the skin, the juice being obtained from the inside without apparent spotting of the surface layer. It is only fair to state, however, that we have not always been able to see these punctures during an attack of green fly, but they are certainly often present. The length of the life of any individual is unknown: they can be seen in all stages in the months of May and June more especially, and the insect can be detected easily by its peculiar crablike way of running sideways round the shoot when observed. The hibernating stage is unknown. Other members of the family which are injurious generally pass the winter as the full-grown insect, hiding in all sorts of rubbish or in crevices, wherever they find opportunity. In the spring they leave their winter quarters, attack their host plant, and lay eggs. "The number of hibernating individuals is usually not very great, but they lay a large number of eggs, and the young and future broods become troublesome." (*J. B. Smith.*) The figure (34) shows the full grown insect, and the last stage before becoming adult. The hair-lines give the natural size.

Conf. with para. 637.

Punctures found.

Hibernating stage unknown.

Depredations.

562. ***Depredations.***—Mr. Peal says that "in attacking tea, the young leaves and stems alone are punctured: growth becomes remarkably arrested" (*see Plate XV, No. 1*); "the internodes or stem between the eyes become shortened; the leaves present a paler dwarfed appearance, and after a time they fall off and the stunted bare little shoots proclaim the blight at once. There is less mark left than by the bug (mosquito), and the effect is mainly to dwarf the growth and shrivel up the young shoots. I do not think the question of 'soil, manure etc.,' have very much to do with either the cause or cure of these insect blights, though it probably has with fungoid ones." A writer, who signs himself "Green-fly," will be found in the *Tea Planter's Vade Mecum* to say of green-fly that it "is becom-

PLATE XV. (*To face Page 289.*)

1. Twig attacked by the Tea Aphis.
(From Photograph by J. L. Alexander.)

2. Twig attacked by the Tea Green Fly.
(From Photograph by H. H. Mann.)

The Tea Green Fly.

THE TEA GREEN FLY.

ing most common in the Darjeeling hill gardens, the effect of which is to deprive the leaf of its ordinary amount of sap. The leaf is small and stunted, as is the length of the flush, which would not weigh one-fourth of its ordinary weight: and this takes more than twice the ordinary time to come on, and, if left, the bushes shrivel up, and the buds or tips die off." The author of *Notes on Tea in Darjeeling* gives even a more gloomy account. "It used not to come, until well on in the second flush, but last year it was in the bushes nearly all the cold weather, and came out in swarms during pruning." "The effect on the bushes is that the shoots stop growing, leaves shrivel up, and only grow to 2 inches long, showing little eyes at every 4 inches, the length of shoots being perhaps 2 inches and having six or seven eyes breaking on each shoot."

Effect in Darjeeling.

563. **Mr. Cotes** gives a series of wood engravings, which are reproduced here, to show the effect, or supposed effect, of the insect. These are very instructive and denote clearly the state of affairs that exist in "stunted blight" whatever be its cause. In the one twig (shown half life size) the parts are healthy and fully developed. Those alongside are stunted and perhaps less than a third the size of the healthy shoot. Commenting on the samples from which these drawings were made, **Mr. Cotes** tells us that a garden of $199\frac{1}{2}$ acres so affected, gave less leaf on being plucked than from another patch of 17 acres. "To bring the state of things before you," wrote the manager, "in the most comprehensive manner, I have pressed some shoots and send them by to-day's post,

Loss in yield.

FIG. 35.—THE EFFECT OF GREEN FLY BLIGHT.
a. Normal Tea shoot; *b*. Shoots affected by Green Fly. (After Cotes.)

THE TEA GREEN FLY.

together with a little bottle containing about 100 of the insects which do, or are supposed to do, the damage. They are so active and difficult to catch that it took a boy a day and half to procure the specimens sent." "In no case," says Mr. Cotes, "do its habits seem to have been observed with any minuteness. It was generally supposed in the tea districts, however, to be responsible for the injury caused to the tea bushes, and as this was of a kind that it would be quite capable of inflicting, the probabilities are that it was rightly accused."

Doubt as to cause of blight.

564. From what has been said it may have been inferred that we are by no means satisfied that it has been proved that **Chlorita flavescens** is responsible for *all* the injury attributed to it. Since the discovery of the punctures there seems little doubt that it is the cause of the typical green-fly blight, but this is a very different thing to putting down as the evil effect of every case of "stunt" to this insect. We have often seen "stunted" and "crinkly" blight without any green-fly visible.

The blight is most frequently seen and most serious on heavily-pruned tea. The shoots are stunted, succulent, very hairy, and the space between the leaves (internodes) deflected right and left in a zig-zag fashion. But they are in no way discoloured and there are no markings or puncturings visible on the surface. As they advance in age the leaves rise on end (or stand in a vertical attitude) and become curiously closed up, face to face as it were, along the upper surface, while the midrib in time becomes curled backward, or even twisted spirally, to a slight extent. *(See Plate XV, No. 1.)*

Commences attack in May.

565. Green-fly usually commences its attack on the tea plant during May—about the time of the second flush. This means, however, that it becomes serious at this period—it has probably been there some considerable time before this time. It is checked, according to Mr. Steele, often by unduly hot weather, of even a week's duration. On the light pruned tea it comes and goes, rarely staying more than three weeks or a month. On heavy pruned tea it stays much longer, and often does damage throughout the remainder of the plucking season from May.

Experiments.

566. Experiments were undertaken in 1895 by one of the authors (G. W.) and by Mr. A. T. Wright, of Noakachari, to try and obtain artificial infection by enclosing insects with bushes under wire gauze,

The Tea Green Fly.

THE TEA GREEN FLY.

During the whole time of the investigations the bushes showed no signs of stunting or crinkling, but it is recognised that they were not carried on long enough to justify any definite conclusions being formed. The matter requires further investigation at once, as there is little doubt that the blight is increasing. One of us (H. H. M.) has commenced a series of observations on this insect during the present season, and it is much to be hoped that there will be opportunity to carry them to a definite result.

Remedy.

567. ***Remedy.***—Little attempt has been made to deal with green-fly,—and until we have decided whether the insect is the offender or no we are not disposed to definitely propose any treatment. The more natural course is to suggest treatment when we have discovered that we are dealing with the actual cause of the disease, and have learned at least a few particulars of the life of the pest concerned. We would therefore urge on tea planters the desirability of performing some practical experiments with the object of proving whether or not this insect is the cause of the diseased conditions complained of. All that would be necessary would be to have a few healthy bushes enclosed so as to prevent external influences, except green-fly purposely placed within the enclosure. If the bushes become stunted after, say, a couple of months, while a couple of bushes treated in every respect similarly except that no green-fly was placed within their enclosures, the inference might be admissible that green-fly was the cause of the disease. Another method might be to clean very carefully a bush in the middle of an affected plot, and enclose it with a fine wire gauze house having, perhaps, a couple of glass windows on the sides to admit light. A test bush alongside, with green-fly within its enclosure, would afford a useful comparison. If the bush from which green-fly had been rigorously excluded improved, while the other bush continued stunted and even got more stunted than the surrounding bushes in the open, it would be fair to assume that the exclusion of the insect very possibly had something to do with the recovery. Of course the act of enclosing bushes excludes light and air to a large extent, and these circumstances may have a beneficial or injurious influence. The experiments undertaken would accordingly have to be repeated once or twice, and varied in such a way as to remove the possibility of a wrong conclusion being formed.

Cannot propose remedies till sure what insect causes blight.

Experiments proposed.

The Hemiptera (Jassidæ).

THE TEA GREEN FLY.

Hard-plucking as remedy.

568. ***Hard-plucking.***—Some few attempts have been made to deal with the insect, of which the most common is the hard-plucking of the stunted shoots, when it is maintained that the new generation of shoots are of normal size and luxuriance. We are not able to say whether this is really always the case, but it seems to be held to by many planters in the worst districts that an attack can be considerably minimised by this means.

Insecticides as remedy.

569. We have further reports in hand of good results from syringing with Adhatoda Vasica, but have not personally seen the garden on which the experiments have been carried out. Ten years ago Mr. Bamber experimented with insecticides (mostly solutions containing arsenic) in the treatment of the insect. For a time the plot of bushes syringed was freed from green-fly, but, after the first shower of rain the insects again returned, and it was found that the foliage was injured by the fluid used. When it is considered that a sucking insect cannot be poisoned in this way by a solid stomach poison, and when also one is dealing with a winged insect, the result would have been expected to be a failure, as indeed it was.

570. This is the present position of the subject. We do not know for certain whether the insect is the cause of the stunted shoots on the bushes, nor, if so, what is its life history and what will be the best time to attack it. With regard to the entomological aspect of the study of tea, there is no question demanding more immediate attention than this. If the insect is the real offender, then there are a dozen methods of dealing with it. For instance, light attracts them in enormous numbers: cloths or paper rendered sticky with tar or bird lime have been used to catch very similar insects with good success; kerosene emulsion has likewise been of service in analogous cases. It is essential, however, first to settle the nature of the blight which will, we hope, be done in the near future.

Attracted by light.

Other possible methods.

Family FULGORIDÆ.

PHROMNIA MARGINELLA

92. **Phromnia marginella,** *Oliv.*

THE GHOST BUG.

THE GHOST BUG.

References.—*Journ. Agri.-Horti. Soc. Ind., Vol. VI., (1879) p. xix, VI. (1879), p. xli, Ind. Mus. Notes, II., 39, 92, 95, 166; IV., 42; Cotes, Tea Insects, 36.*

The Tea Aphis.

Found in North-East India.

THE TEA APHIS.

Under Grevillea and Rubber trees.

571. This insect is very common in the jungles of Assam and Northern and Eastern Bengal, and probably when found in a tea garden it is an invader from the jungle. It is very conspicuous owing to the coating of white wax with which the larvæ cover themselves. These larvæ jump with great vigour, leaving a good part of the wax behind them when they are disturbed. In our own observations it has been in greatest abundance under and on Grevillea and Rubber trees. The perfect winged insect is shown in the figure. It has a pink line round the margin of the wing, hence its name.

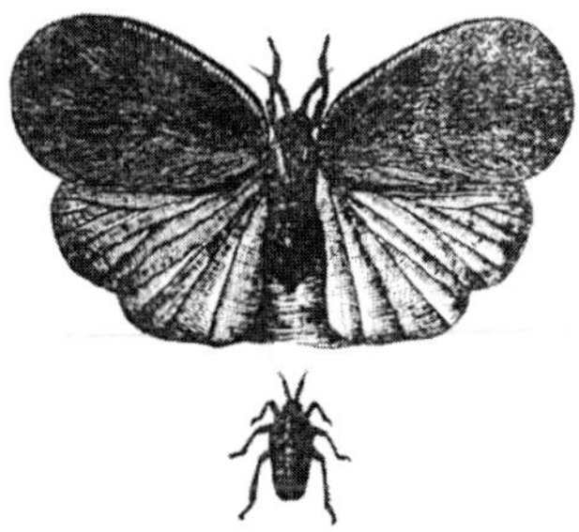

FIG. 36.—PHROMNIA MARGINELLA.
(1) Adult, (2) Larva.
(After Cotes.)

It is on record that this insect at one time did considerable damage in the Mangaldai district when it was said to have been found feeding on the tea and stopping the flushing. We doubt whether it can be classed as a pest, but we have collected it in Sibsagar, Dibrugarh, North Lakhimpur, and Bishnath districts. If ever serious, it can easily be dealt with by means of kerosene emulsion.

Family APHIDÆ.

93. Ceylonia theæcola, *Buckton.*

CEYLONIA THEÆCOLA.

THE TEA APHIS.

THE TEA APHIS. THE BLACK BUG OR BLACK FLY OF MOST ASSAM PLANTERS.

(SEE PLATE XV, No. 2.)

References.—*Journ. Agri.-Horti. Soc. Ind., Vol. IV., Proc., 18th Sept. 1873, p. xli. (Assam); Vol. VII. Proc., 24th June 1885 (Kumaon); Tea Cyclopædia (Darjeeling Planter), pp. 44—45; Green, Insect Pests of Tea, pp. 45—45; Bamber, Chem. and Agri. Tea, p. 251; Ind. Mus. Notes, Vol. II. (pt. 1), 34—35; Vol. III. (pt. 4), p. 60; (pt. 5) 54; Cotes, Insects and Mites, etc., pp. 38—39.*

Found in all districts.

572. ***History.***—This is probably as common and widespread an insect as any occurring on tea, but luckily the damage which it does has not up to the present been found to be serious. It was originally noticed on tea in Jorhat, Assam, in 1873, then in Kumaon in 1885, and shortly afterwards in Darjeeling, and described as a small black bug and fly which appeared immediately after pruning. Mr. Green, of Ceylon, however, gave the first careful description of the insect, and from samples supplied by him it was given the above scientific name by Mr. Buokton. It has now been collected by us from

Jorhat.

Kumaon.

Ceylon.

The Hemiptera (Aphidæ).

THE TEA APHIS. Other districts.

Cachar and the Terai in addition to the above mentioned localities, and curiously enough it appeared on a tea bush kept in Calcutta for experimental purposes.

Life history and description.

573. ***Description.***—This aphis lives in colonies, crowded together on the topmost leaf or two and the terminal bud of the flushing shoots, or on seedlings in the nursery. As already remarked, it is most prevalent in Spring, but may occasionally be seen throughout the year. The insects of each colony are of a dark brown to almost black colour, and in size not larger than the head of a pin. If examined under the lens, they will be seen to be either all wingless, or there may be a few winged individuals, crawling about among the wingless ones, or a whole colony may be winged. It will be found that the majority of colonies consist of the wingless form, with a few winged individuals scattered about.

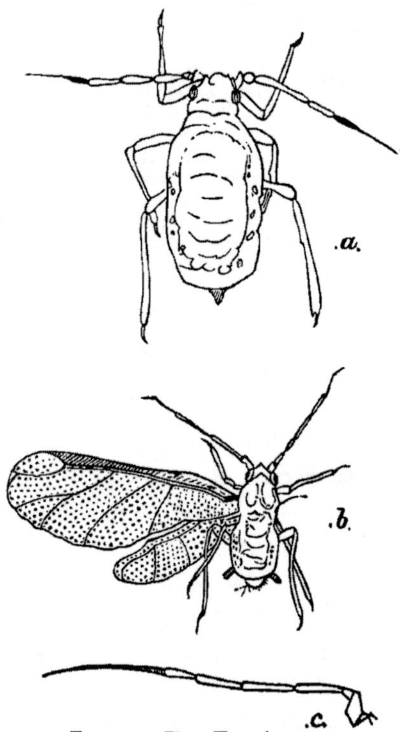

FIG. 37.—THE TEA APHIS.
a. Wingless form; *b.* Winged insect, one wing being removed; *c.* Antenna—all much enlarged.
(After Cotes.)

The figure given by Mr. Cotes, and here reproduced, represents both the wingless and winged insects much enlarged. The wingless form will be found to have two teats (not shown in the illustration) and a pointed anal extremity, looking like a third teat. The body of the winged insect is also larger relatively to the other than represented, and it has only two teats in all, the anal projection shown in the figure is not present so far as we could find in the Assam insect. THE TEA APHIS.

According to Mr. Green, the male insect would not appear to have as yet been discovered, and the winged and wingless females have both the power of reproduction without the intervention of any male. They "are viviparous, and are capable of producing fresh colonies of the pest by their own unaided efforts." "I have frequently watched," continues Mr. Green, "the formation of one of these colonies. The female, either a winged or wingless individual, flies or crawls on to a new leaf, and commences to produce living young ones which settle themselves by her side and immediately plunge their beaks into the tissue of the leaf. Within ten or twelve days these new arrivals will be full grown and actively engaged in increasing their numbers until every available shoot is populated. Emigrants, meanwhile, will have wandered off to form new colonies on other bushes. In this manner the increase is so rapid that it has been calculated that a single aphis, if unchecked, could be ancestor of ten thousand million of millions (10,000,000,000,000,000) in three months' time. But most fortunately the many natural enemies of the insect are able to prevent this excessive increase. In England and other northern countries, a brood of males and oviparous females is developed at the approach of winter. Eggs are deposited, which remain dormant during the cold weather, hatching out in the following spring into a sexual viviparous females." Male not yet discovered. Rapidity of increase. Natural enemies.

"In Ceylon," adds Mr. Green (and this may be true of India also), "where vegetation continues throughout the year, there is no limit to the reproduction without sexes. We have given this subject some attention, but have failed to find a male insect, although the reproduction of a generation from eggs would seem essential to provide for the complete disappearance of the aphis for many months together, and its sudden and almost simultaneous re-appearance on the spring shoots all over the province."

574. ***Depredations.*** From the remarks already offered this pest can hardly be regarded as of no consequence. It occasionally occurs to a distinctly injurious extent, and might multiply, without any warning, to a degree previously unknown, and become then positively alarming. The women in gardens, where this aphis exists abundantly, often complain of the fingers being poisoned from the Depredations. Poisons pluckers' fingers.

THE TEA APHIS.

brown-staining fluid produced from crushing the aphis in the act of plucking tea. But it must be borne in mind that this pest chiefly occurs in the nursery or on the early spring shoots. In both cases it does more injury than at first sight appears. The young seedling can ill-afford to have the sap sucked from its terminal leaves and bud. It stops growing in consequence, becomes bark-bound and *banjhi*. It is not killed in most cases, and the injury done is disregarded, though it has received a severe check that may alter its shape by forcing out buds that may not be desired, and retard its growth so materially as to represent several months' delay in its reaching the flushing state. Insignificant though the depredations of the aphis may appear at the time, it has effected a permanent injury to the life of the plant. So in a like manner the spring buds, especially upon a plant that has been severely pruned, or is otherwise unhealthy, may be so materially checked by the aphis that fresh shoots may have to come away from the wood before any progress can be made. The appearance of a bush badly affected is shown in *Plate XV*, from a photograph by Mr. J. Lindsay Alexander.

Method of attack.

575. The method of its attack has often been observed. It is generally present both in the winged and wingless states in separate colonies on adjoining leaves. They are arranged in lines along the leaf midribs and twigs, and suck the juices of the tea suddenly and altogether as if under command, then repose for a little and again simultaneously swing to one side, seemingly in the effort of straining. The proboscis can easily be observed to be deeply inserted. The arrangement on the leaf and the synchronous movements are very peculiar, but the young ones do not get fixed in the same manner till nearly mature, probably on the opening out of the next leaf above, which is to be their feeding ground.

Natural enemies.

Conf. with para. 314.

576. ***Remedy.***—Under the subject of ladybird beetles above, we have already alluded to the larvæ of these insects being, perhaps, the most valuable of the Assam natural enemies of this pest. Other carnivorous larvæ will also be found to prey on it. In Ceylon Mr. Green tells us that "the larvæ of several hovering flies, belonging to the family SYRPHIDÆ, subsist entirely upon aphides and are fortunately very abundant. They are leech-like grubs. One kind sets to work without any disguise, another conceals itself under a canopy of its slain victims. They are very voracious and exterminate

THE TEA APHIS.

whole colonies of the pest. The small pear-shaped pupa is fixed to the stem of the plant. The perfect flies, with banded bodies, like diminutive wasps, may generally be seen hovering over the diseased plants, depositing their eggs upon the leaf amongst the aphides. Another little creature, the Aphis lion, assists in the war of extermination. This grub also piles up the skins of its victims upon its back, leaving only its head and long sickle-shaped jaws exposed. It is the larva of one of the delicate lace-winged flies. The eggs are deposited in clusters on the leaves, each at the summit of a long thin hair. The larvæ of several "ladybird" beetles materially help to thin the numbers of the pest. And a small shining black wasp (**Rhopalum?** *sp.*), after paralysing them with its sting, carries off the young aphides to store them in cells excavated in pith of mana grass as food for its own young." Natural enemies in Ceylon.

"But the most insidious of its many enemies is a minute ichneumon fly, that lays its egg within the body of the living aphis. This egg developes into a tiny grub that gradually consumes the vitals of its host. Whole colonies of defunct aphides may sometimes be observed, each with a circular trap door cut in its back from which the parasite has escaped." Ichneumon fly.

So far as we have been enabled to learn, the larvæ of the ladybird beetle is the chief enemy of the aphis in Assam, but we repeatedly came across other larvæ devouring the aphides, so that with sufficient time for study no doubt it would be found the pest is kept in check in India by as complete an assemblage of enemies as in Ceylon. Natural enemies in Assam.

577. Many planters have been in the habit of regarding the red and black ant as feeding on the aphis and hence as friendly. This is, however, absolutely a misapprehension. The ants do not feed on the aphis at all, but protect them in order to feed on the honey-dew which they secrete. On this account they sometimes enclose them within a wall of leaves joined together by a black earthy substance, so that they can always have the honey-dew on tap. Ants should hence be always looked upon with suspicion on a tea bush. Red and black ant is not an enemy to insect.

578. The most interesting part of Mr. Green's investigations, in connection with this pest, may be said to be his study of the insecticides that may be used in its destruction. He found that wood ashes, powdered sulphur, and dry carbolic powder were unavailing, but that the aphis readily succumbs to kerosene emulsion or phenyle. On Insecticides.

THE TEA APHIS.

this subject he says, "A weak wash of kerosene emulsion or phenyle applied with a brush will instantly kill every aphis. It should be applied either in the evening or on a cloudy day. Hot sunshine upon leaves freshly drenched with kerosene is apt to scorch them. One part of kerosene emulsion to eighty parts of water will make a mixture strong enough to kill every aphis with which it comes in contact, while a still weaker mixture of phenyle, one part to two hundred and forty of water, is sufficient for the same purpose." "Watering the nurseries with a weak phenyle wash is a very simple cure. The phenyle should be applied in the evening and followed the next morning by a liberal supply of pure water."

Kerosene emulsion.

Phenyle.

COCCIDÆ.

Family COCCIDÆ.

THE SCALE INSECTS.

THE SCALE INSECTS, SCALEY BUGS, ETC.

579. Though up to the present the Scale Insects have not been among the most serious of pests preying on the tea plant, yet they have become sufficiently important in certain districts to lead to a suspicion that they may become at any moment of prime danger. This is especially the case as they have, in tropical and subtropical districts, proved among the most serious pests of most cultivated plants, though a few species afford valuable economic products. To take a few examples. The Green-Bug (**Lecanium viride**) proved almost calamitous to the coffee industry of Ceylon, assisted as it was by the Black-Bug (**Lecanium nigrum**) and by the Brown-Bug (**Lecanium coffeæ**). So again the fluted scale (**Icerya purchasi**), and the red scale (**Aspidiotus aurantii**) of the orange in California, and the closely allied scale (**Aspidiotus ficus**) of Florida are perhaps the most serious pests of the orange trees in America; while the Egyptian Cottony Cushion Scale (**Icerya aegyptiacum**), the Mussel-Scale (**Mytilaspis pomorum**), the Purple Scale (**Mytilaspis citricola**), the Long-Scale (**Mytilaspis gloveri**), the Mealy-Bug (**Dactylopius destructor**), and others are among the most serious pests of crops under cultivation. It is of the greatest importance therefore that these insignificant looking insects should be clearly recognised and their injurious action fully understood, not merely because of the present injury they are effecting, but, to a far greater extent, because of their possibilities of infinite mischief in the future.

Pests of coffee.

Pest of orange trees.

The Scale Insects.

580. Mr. Green, of Ceylon, who has studied this class of insect in the East to a greater extent than any living authority, remarks that "it is a curious fact in connection with scale insects, that particular species are liable—under certain circumstances, such as the accidental extermination or reduction of some natural enemy—to suddenly spring into prominence. Another great source of danger is the introduction of new species from other countries." Some of the most alarming scale and other insect scourges hitherto recorded have been in consequence of the introduction of a species from one country to another. In its original home the insect may have been comparatively harmless, because of its being kept under by its natural enemies. On getting to a new country, where these enemies do not exist, its facilities of multiplication, and thus its possibilities in the path of crop destruction, are limitless. A good example of this may be mentioned in the case of the Phylloxera of the vine. In its original home, in the Eastern United States, it was comparatively harmless, but in Europe and other countries into which it had unfortunately been introduced, it very rapidly threatened the very existence of vine culture.

THE SCALE INSECTS.

May suddenly increase abnormally.

On the other hand, a new pest of this type may suddenly appear and disappear again apparently without reason. A local manifestation of the sudden appearance and as sudden disappearance of what was possibly a scale insect, we might refer to the experience in Coonor and Kotagiri. Some four years ago, in an issue of *Planting Opinion*, the following passage occurs: "In one case a young extension at Kotagiri was dreadfully damaged, over 2,000 young trees being actually killed out by it, and many more being left very shaky. Curiously enough, since last December, the bug seems to be going off as rapidly as it came on, and this without any application whatever." It is to be feared that many useless methods of dealing with pests have obtained a fictitious reputation from their having been employed at the period of the natural disappearance of a pest.

Example in South India.

581. It has long been known that the various species of ladybird beetle are the most formidable of enemies to scale insects. But the ladybird has its own enemies, and, in consequence, often cannot increase in number beyond an established balance. Taking advantage of the fact indicated above, that an introduced insect may suddenly multiply to an almost limitless extent, the very best results

Ladybird beetles

THE SCALE INSECTS.

have been obtained by the introduction of the ladybirds from one country to another, in the hope that these may be able to successfully attack a plague of scale insect before they are themselves discovered and destroyed. A case in point may be mentioned in the marvellous results obtained by the introduction of the "**Vedalia** beetle" into California, which resulted, in a remarkably short time, in the extirpation of the fluted scale from the orange plantations of that country. For particulars regarding the Australian ladybird (**Vedalia cardinalis**) and its effect on the fluted scale of the orange, see the *Indian Museum Notes, Vol. III. (pt. 3), pp. 29—30.*

Vedalia Beetles in California.

Useful scale insects.

582. But as a set-off against the long list of destructive scale-bugs, the useful species may be here mentioned briefly:—The cochineal insect (**Cocus cacti**); the lac (*lakh*) insect (**Tachardia lacca**); the Chinese Wax insect (**Ericerus pela**).

Description.

583. ***Description***.—This group of insects differ from all others by several characters which render them very easily distinguishable. In the first place the females have never any wings, and spend their whole life from a few minutes after leaving the egg, glued to one spot without visible boundary between the head and thorax. During its immature life the male insect is likewise stuck to the plant as a scale, but when full grown it creeps from underneath as a two winged insect, the second (hind) pair of wings usually present in this order of insects being represented by hooks which are used to strengthen the wings in flight. The scales of the male and female insects of the same species are often very different in character. Those of the most common of tea-pests—**Chionaspis theæ**—would certainly be taken, at first sight, to belong to different species.

Additional characters

584. In addition to these characters Mr. Green gives the following which may be of use in identifying these insects. The legs of both sexes (when present) terminate in single claw: there is normally only one joint to the tarsus (or terminus of the leg); there is no mouth or feeding part to the adult male: the female has the mouth (rostrum) far back on the under-surface of the scale, and it is formed for sucking; the insect usually secretes a waxy, fibrous, or resinous cover or protection for itself at an early stage of its existence.

'Coccidæ of Ceylon" by Mr. E. E. Green.

585. Very little is known, however, about the Indian Coccidæ. The authoritative work on the "Coccidæ of Ceylon"—admirably conceived and beautifully illustrated as it is—by Mr. E. Ernest Green, now in course of publication will, when completed, cover nearly all the ground yet worked. It will describe all the species met with on tea, coffee, and other crops and hence has a practical value, besides its very high scientific merit. Unfortunately only the first two parts have been issued as yet, but we commend it to all planters who may wish to look into the matter of

scale bugs,—and no study needs more attention in India than this. It is published by Messrs. Dulau & Co. at £5 for the complete work, and the two parts now available contain sixty full-page coloured plates. Beyond this the Indian Museum Notes contain many valuable articles on scale insects, and we should be delighted to give further information as to sources of information to any planters who are anxious to take up the subject. THE SCALE INSECTS.

586. ***Remedies.***—There are four methods, differing in principle, which have been successful in different cases in dealing with these pests. These are :— Remedies.

(1) The method of gassing.
(2) The method of spraying.
(3) The method of insect enemies.
(4) The method of burning.

587. ***Gassing Method.***—Where isolated bushes are affected, perhaps this method, which has been found very effective in fruit-culture, is the best. It consists in covering the affected bush with a tent made of "cotton drill" sewn together and painted. Underneath this a dish is put containing $\frac{1}{3}$ oz. of Cyanide of Potassium (a rank poison) and $\frac{2}{3}$ oz. water, and when all is ready $\frac{1}{3}$ oz. Sulphuric Acid is added and the tent dropped at once and left for an hour. The tent should then be carefully removed, as the gas is Prussic Acid and is excessively poisonous. The quantities given will be sufficient for any tea bush, but we could not recommend this method unless there would be European supervision from beginning to end without intermission. With this it would be probably the best system in good many Darjeeling gardens, and it will penetrate almost any scale and destroy it. Gassing.

588. ***Spraying Method.***—Where the pest is too widely spread for gassing, the method of spraying should be adopted. This, however, is not so effective, and should be done as early in the season as possible as, especially with the armoured scales, it is difficult to touch the older scales with any spray. Whatever is applied should be put on as a very fine spray—a garden syringe is no use at all unless it has a proper spray ("Cyclone" or "Vermorel") nozzle—and then it is best with a force pump. Two sprays can be used with good effect. The first is merely a soap and water solution at the rate of one lb. of fish oil soap to one gallon of water. It acts by asphyxiating the insects. The second is the "kerosene emulsion" made by boiling up one to two pounds of soap with one gallon of water, and then adding the hot mixture to two gallons of kerosene Spraying.

Conf. with page 283, Footnote.

THE SCALE INSECTS.

and churning until a creamy liquid results which thickens on cooling. The three gallons is then diluted to thirty gallons at the time of using, when the oil ought not to separate. This acts by poisoning and asphyxiating at the same time.

The finer the spray used the better,—and the whole of the bush should be wetted. It should be applied after pruning and then again if necessary at the beginning of the season.

Natural insect enemies.

589. ***The use of Insect Enemies.***—The use of **Vedalia cardinalis**, a ladybird beetle, against the fluted scale in California has led to many attempts to use insects against other scales, but, as yet, not with very great success except in two or three cases. Ladybirds are, however, responsible for devouring a very large number of scale insects in India. "It was at one time supposed by planters that the ants, which are so constantly in attendance upon scale-bugs, were preying upon them, and the formidable "Red ant" (**Œcophylla samaragdina**) was actually imported into some estates with a view to exterminating black-bug on the coffee trees. This is now known to be quite a mistaken idea. The ants are attracted by a viscid sugary liquid emitted by the bugs, and which consists of, in fact, their excreta. This substance is being constantly shed upon the surrounding leaves, and proves very attractive not only to ants but to flies of all kinds and even to bees and wasps. It is of the same nature as the "honey-dew," so abundantly produced by aphides. Far from feeding upon the bugs, we believe the ants actually transport them from place to place to found fresh colonies of them in convenient situations. "It is certain that the small black nest-building ant (**Cremastogaster dohrni**), that is such a nuisance on some of our estates, invariably includes in its nests colonies of mealy-bugs (**Dactylopius**) and one or more species of **Lecanium**." (*Green.*) In the Assam gardens we have already said the red and black ant (**Cremastogaster rogenhoferi** above) encloses the black aphis within its nest. Although we have not come across an instance, we have no doubt it uses also several species of scale-bug in the manner Mr. Green describes with the similar ant of Ceylon.

Red Ant not an enemy.

Conf. with para. 471.

Conf. with para. 470.

Parasitic Fungi.

Conf. with para. 848.

590. In many cases a fungus will be found in association with scale-bugs. This subsists on the sugary exudation and is not itself directly harmful to the plant. Under the account given above of the tea mosquito (**Helopeltis**), we have alluded to this as being

in all probability the "Sooty Bug" of the early writers, who apparently associated it with mosquito. The fungus will be found to grow on the upper surface of the leaf, the part upon which the sugary deposit would naturally accumulate. While distinctly very untidy-looking, it cannot interfere with the respiration of the plant very materially, since the stomata or breathing mouths are on the under-surface. It must, however, largely exclude light, and therefore cannot be said to be altogether harmless. Still its chief interest lies in the fact of its pointing the way to the existence of a dangerous scale-bug on the leaves and twigs of the plant, where the sooty fungus exists.

THE SCALE INSECTS.

Sooty blight.

591. Occasionally, however, the scale insect itself is parasitised with a fungus and is killed by it. The green bug of coffee is, for instance, often killed off wholesale by a greyish fungus. The male scale of Chionaspis theæ are destroyed by a red fungus. These have not been utilised up to date, but they might be of great value in the future.

592. ***Burning the Bushes.***—When a large area is affected, perhaps burning the bushes is the best way of dealing with the pests. At any rate it is effective. Straw is put under the bushes and the whole set on fire, the charred parts being afterwards removed. This method has the advantage over cutting out and removal of the affected parts, that there is not the same chance of spreading the disease in carrying the prunings off the land.

Burning bushes.

94. Aspidiotus camelliæ, *Signoret.*

ASPIDIOTUS CAMELLIÆ.

THE YELLOW BARK LOUSE.

THE YELLOW BARK LOUSE.

References.—*Green, Coccidæ of Ceylon, 60, Pl. XIII; also Insect Pests of Tea Plant, 21; Bamber, Chem. and Agri. Tea, 252; Ind. Mus. Notes, II., 59, 168; III., 52; IV., 187; V., 2; Cotes, Tea Insects 41: Howard, Yearbook, U. S. A. Dept. Agri. (1894), 261.*

Found in Assam, Darjeeling, South India, and Ceylon.

593. ***History.***—This pest was first discovered by Mr. Green in Ceylon on tea, and it has since been repeatedly found in Assam and Darjeeling. It is really a very abundant and wide-spread species, having been recorded from England, Portugal, New Zealand, Australia, and the United States, in addition to Ceylon and India.

History.

THE YELLOW BARK LOUSE.

Description.

594. ***Description.***—The scales of this species are of a pale-yellow colour, with a reddish or brown central mark, and they are somewhat hairy. These hairs, however, "really belong to the plant, and are incorporated in the scale during its formation. If the scale were found on a glabrous stem or leaf, no hairs will be found on it." (*Green.*) The scales resemble minute oyster-shells, with the younger scales clustering around and often overlapping the older ones. They are crowded together near the axils of the leaves, extend along the leaf stalk, and to some extent up the midrib. In consequence they are fairly conspicuous objects, and should be easily enough recognised.

Rarely entirely recover.

595. ***Depredations and Remedy.***—Mr. Green says of this species: "Badly infected plants seldom recover their vitality, the stems become thin and wiry, and seem very reluctant to throw out fresh shoots. There is nothing to be done, but to take out the plant and supply another in its place. The diseased plant should on no account be allowed to remain beside the new one, or this latter also will speedily become infected." So far as we have been able to judge, firing bushes or plots of tea affected by this pest is fairly successful. The plants receive a severe shock, no doubt, and those that were nearly dead in any case die outright, but a large percentage of the bushes are saved which, as Mr. Green very properly remarks, would certainly be killed, when once this pest becomes fairly established.

Fire bushes.

ASPIDIOTUS THEÆ.

THE KANGRA BARK LOUSE.

95. Aspidiotus theæ, *Mask.*

THE KANGRA BARK LOUSE.

References.—*Maskell, Ind. Mus. Notes, II., (pt. 1), 59; Journ. Agri.-Horti. Soc. Ind., VIII., Report ending Dec. 1889, 435; Green, Ind. Mus. Notes, V., 3.*

Found in the Kangra Valley.

Kangra pest.

596. ***History.***—This insect was first described by Mr. A. Maskell, as above, from specimens furnished from India, and, as a matter of fact, authentic samples are only in existence from the Kangra Valley, while it does not appear to occur in Celyon. It is incorrectly known to the Kangra planters as a Lecanium.

The Kangra Bark Louse.

THE KANGRA BARK LOUSE.

Description.

597. ***Description.***—In appearance the insect is very like that last described—practically a small oyster shell in appearance,—but more widely distributed along the twigs and more crowded at the points of branching than within the leaf axils. The figure shows it (to the left) natural size on a tea twig; and to the right is an enormously enlarged diagram of the newly hatched larva to show its legs and antennæ, also the long coiled proboscis which it eventually inserts into the tissue of the plant.

FIG. 38.—THE KANGRA BARK LOUSE.
Left-hand, natural size, on tea twig; *Right-hand*, under side of newly hatched larva, much enlarged.
(After Cotes.)

One of the serious pests in Kangra Valley.

598. ***Depredations and Remedy.***—This appears to be a more severe pest than the closely similar one met with in Assam and Darjeeling. Kangra may be said to have but two pests of any consequence, the present one and the *barota* or basket-worm (**Amatissa consorta**). Neither should be viewed lightly, since it is possibly an accident, more than anything else, that they have not as yet assumed gigantic proportions.

In the Journal, *Agri.-Horticultual Society* (*loc. cit.*), particulars are found of a treatment with kerosene emulsion that seems to have been successful. It should be used at the first onset.

ASPIDIOTUS CYANO-PHYLLI.

96. Aspidiotus cyanophylli, *Sign.*

References.—*Green, Coccidæ of Ceylon, p. 51, Pl. IX.*

Found in Ceylon.

599. This scale is found on the under-surface of the leaves of tea and cinchona plants in Ceylon. It has not yet been met with in India, but it is a very widely distributed species.

ASPIDIOTUS DICTYOS-PERMI.

97. Aspidiotus dictyospermi, *Morg.* var. **arecæ,** *Newst.*

References.—*Ind. Mus. Notes, IV., 119; V., 2; Journ., Bombay. Nat. Hist. Soc., XIII., 68.*

The Hemiptera (Coccidæ).

ASPIDIOTUS DESTRUCTOR.

Found in Kangra.

600. Among some samples obtained from Holta, in the Kangra Valley, were leaves—apparently—of tea which were completely covered with this scale insect. It is widely distributed on the stems of roses, ivy, and **Cycas revoluta**. It has not been found elsewhere on tea, and cannot be regarded as a pest.

98. **Aspidiotus destructor**, *Sign.*

References.—*Ind. Mus. Notes, II., 168 ; III (5), 52 ; IV. Green, Insect Pests of Tea Plant (as Aspidiotus transparens) 1890, p. 20 ; Bamber, Chem. and Agri. Tea, p. 253 ; Journ., Agri.-Horti. Soc. Ind., X. (1894), 37 ; Cotes, Tea Insects, 41 ; Agri. Ledger, No. 27 of 1896, p. 3.*

Found in Ceylon and Duars(?).

Ceylon. 601. The full grown female scale is only one-thirtieth of an inch in length. Nevertheless it occurs to a considerable extent, and does a good deal of damage on many plants including Tea, Pepper, Ceara Rubber, **Loranthus**, **Mæsa indica**, etc. "Altogether a very widespread species, almost omnivorous." (Green.) It was noticed by Mr. Cotes on tea from Jalpaiguri, and by one of the authors (G. W.) on Letpet Tea from Burma.

Duars.

Burma.

602. Nothing more than the names of the following members of this genus of insects can be recorded as having been found on tea.

ASPIDIOTUS NERII.

99. **Aspidiotus nerii**, *Bauchi.* (See *Trop. Agriculturist*, 1898, p. 516.) It is said to be common on tea in Ceylon.

ASPIDIOTUS CYDONIÆ.

100. **Aspidiotus cydoniæ**, *Comst.* (**Aspidiotus lataniæ**, *Sign.*) is found on the stems of tea plants in Ceylon. (See *Green Coccidæ of Ceylon, Part I, p. 62, Pl XIV.*)

FIORINIA THEÆ.

101. **Fiorinia theæ**, *Green.*

(See Plate XVI, No. 3.)

Reference.—*Ind. Mus. Notes, Vol. V., 3.*

Found in Assam and Kangra.

Assam and Kangra. 603. This insect was found constantly by one of the authors (G. W.) both in Assam and Kangra, and it is undoubtedly the most prevalent of all forms of scale bug in Assam. It is not confined to low jat bushes, but the bushes affected with it always have a dusty unkempt appearance—the leaves being invariably coated with dust, especially on the under-surfaces. The long, narrow, and brown scale-louse might in fact be said to be buried in the mud adhering to the leaf. It lives on the under-surfaces of the leaves and may sometimes be seen in hundreds on the same leaf, sufficiently numerous to give it

Lives under leaves.

PLATE XVI. (*To face Page 306.*)

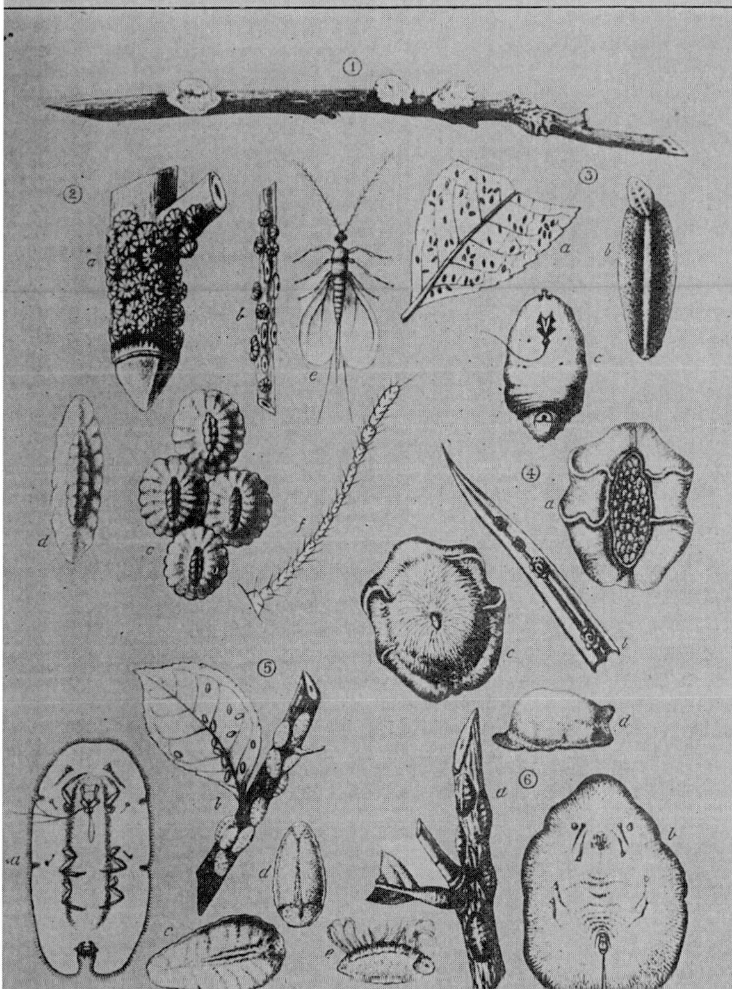

1. Ceroplastes ceriferns (p. 316).
2. Carteria decorella (p. 317).
3. Fiorinia theæ (p. 306).
4. Ceroplastes myricæ (p. 314).
5. Eriochiton theæ (p. 310).
6. Lecanium watti (p. 314).

(*For description see List of Plates, page viii.*)

(From Indian Museum Notes.)

FIORINIA THEÆ.

a dirty brown appearance. This genus does not produce any sugary exudation or one would have thought the mud would adhere on this account, but whatever be the explanation of the circumstance mentioned, it is so invariably the rule as to hardly escape notice, and must greatly interfere with the respiration of the leaves The plants are sickly and unproductive. The insect may be described popularly as a long narrow chestnut-coloured scale, with a ridge down the middle (*see Plate XVI, No. 3*). It shows very frequently smaller scales escaping, as it were, from the top or near one extremity.

After what has been said, it need hardly be added that this pest (insignificant though it may appear to the planter who may find here an affected bush and there another), is a dangerous insect to neglect. Mr. Green has kindly furnished us with a specimen showing the scale parasitised by a fungus. His remark on the same may be here quoted: "If this Coccid should become troublesome in the Indian tea districts, it would be easy to introduce this fungus if it does not already exist." The fungus is not at present found in India so far as our experience goes, and it certainly would be worth while to obtain a supply if the blight becomes serious.

Attacked by fungus.

102. Fiorinia fioriniæ, *Targ.*

FIORINIA FIORINIÆ.

References.—*Green, Coccidæ of Ceylon, p. 94; Journ., Bombay Nat. Hist. Soc., Vol. XIII., 256.*

604. This is the Ceylon counterpart of the last-mentioned species. It is, however, not at all common, being only found on low jat tea in the up-country districts. It is also subject to a fungal disease which keeps it in check. "The diseased insects are easily recognised by the fringe of bright orange-coloured matter projecting from beneath the scale."

103. Chionaspis theæ, *Maskell.* (Chionaspis exercitata, *Green.*)

CHIONASPIS THEÆ.

The White Tea-leaf Louse.

THE WHITE TEA-LEAF LOUSE.

References.—*Maskell, Ind. Mus. Notes, Vol. II. (pt. 1), 59—60; Ind. Mus. Notes, also I., 188; II., 168; III., 25; (pt. 4), 60; IV., 42; V., 4; Green, Insect Pests of the Tea Plant, 12; Journ., Agri.-Horti. Soc. Ind., X., (1895), 328; Bamber, Chem. Agri. Tea. 252; Cotes, Tea Insects, 39; Green (Coccidæ of Ceylon), 113.*

Found in all districts.

605. ***History.***—This is undoubtedly the most frequently found scale insect of Indian Tea, and occurs commonly in Ceylon. It was

Serious pest in Darjeeling.

THE WHITE TEA LEAF LOUSE. originally examined and named from samples taken from the Kangra Valley, but can be found practically everywhere. Little harm seems to be done, however, except in the Darjeeling district, but here, especially in the neighbourhood of Kurseong, the bushes are often white with it both on the lower and upper shoots.

Male scale. 606. ***Description.***—The male scales will be recognised as forming little patches or colonies of white waxy flakes, neatly arranged on the leaves of the tea plant. The very natural difficulty is at once suggested, on viewing these colonies, of the improbability of the female being able to reach the leaves in order to deposit the eggs of these male scales. As a matter of fact, however, the covering scale of both sexes are to be seen on the leaves. The male scale may be described as a small yellow pellicle placed at the extremity of a structure that consists of three white waxy ridges, parallel to each other. The

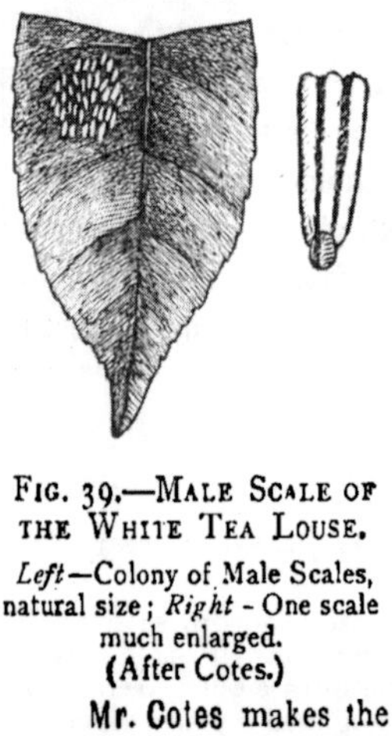

FIG. 39.—MALE SCALE OF THE WHITE TEA LOUSE. *Left*—Colony of Male Scales, natural size; *Right* - One scale much enlarged. (After Cotes.)

Female. female scale is much larger ($\frac{1}{10}$ inch long), is of a brown colour, in shape pyriform, flat, with a brownish pellicle at the narrow extremity. The scales of both insects are common when the pest is in serious amount. Otherwise there are very few females.

Dispersion. Mr. Cotes makes the very practical remark under this species that " In all scale insects the question of dispersion is an important one for, owing to the adult female being stationary, it is only the newly hatched larvæ which are able to travel from bush to bush, and thus spread the evil. It is important, therefore, to ascertain at what period of the year the larvæ emerge and the extent to which they are liable to be carried by the winds."

Confined to leaves. 607. ***Depredations.***—So far as is known, this species is confined to the leaves, the colonies of male scales (or puparia) being on the upper surface, and the female very often below. They must, of course, abstract a large amount of sap from the plant, but, so far as we have been able to discover, this insect, though common here and there in Assam, nowhere exists so abundantly as to cause material injury. There is, however, a very different state of things in Darjeel-

The Ceylon Tea Bark Louse.

ing, in certain of the valleys, where the damage is great. A letter from a planter in the district reads as follows:— THE CEYLON TEA BARK LOUSE.

"These scales do a large amount of damage to young plants either in extensions or nurseries in the district. I have this year from young extensions had several hundred plants brought in in a day as evidence of the destruction caused and the coolies did not by any means bring in all the plants, as some that had previously been destroyed were dead and withered up. What they brought in were with fresh leaves on them."

608. ***Remedy.***—Luckily the scale insect—both male and female—is usually badly attacked with one, and we think two, parasitic fungi, and this probably prevents its extension to a ruinous extent. More than this, it might be greatly mitigated by sending out children to strip the leaves seen to bear white colonies of the male scale through the fingers. This would, no doubt, kill the males and very often the females also. In serious cases the bushes should be treated as described above for other scale insects. Parasitic fungi.

104 Chionaspis biclavis, *Comst.* CHIONASPIS BICLAVIS.

THE CEYLON TEA BARK LOUSE.

References.—*Green, Insect Pests of the Tea Plant, 12 (in part refers to this); Ind. Mus. Notes, IV., 2; Trop. Agri. (1898), 515; Green, Coccidæ of Ceylon, 152.*

Found in Ceylon.

609. This is a very inconspicuous species—the female scales looking like small blisters on the bark. "Often present in large numbers and responsible for hard wood and short flushes." (Green.) The male is unknown. This insect has been found to resist the action of hyrocyanic acid gas—a most deadly poison, and could probably best be dealt with by scrubbing "the affected stems with a pad made of coir yarn or cocoanut matting which will dislodge the scales and crush the insects. This treatment has the further advantage of removing accumulation of lichen and moss, which particularly affect such hide-bound trees." (Green.) This pest has not been found in India. Scrub stems.

105. Chionaspis separata, *Green.* CHIONASPIS SEPARATA.

References.—*Ind. Mus. Notes, V., 5.*

610. This is a quite new scale insect from a single garden in Darjeeling. It forms numerous conspicuous, white, pyriform scales about $\frac{1}{18}$ inch long. The male is considerably smaller.

106. Chionaspis manni, *Green.* CHIONASPIS MANNI.

Found in Darjeeling.

611. This insect has been recently named from material supplied by the authors and is found on tea bushes in nearly every valley in Darjeeling.

The Hemiptera (Coccidæ).

HIONASPIS MANNI.

The male scale forms groups of long scales which are attached "end on" to the twigs, and where present in large quantity this pest quite stops the flushing of the bushes, and in old standing cases the branch on which it occurs is practically ruined, becoming very reduced in size and starved below the groups of scale insects. The female scale is very inconspicuous, almost as much so as that of **Chionaspis biclavis.** Mr. Green proposes to publish a scientific description in an early number of Indian Museum Notes.

CHIONASPIS PRUNICOLA.

107. **Chionaspis prunicola,** *Mask* var **theæ.**

Reference.—*Ind. Mus. Notes, IV., 60.*

612. This has been described as a tea pest, but no locality is given for it. This is very possibly identical with **Chionaspis manni,** but as no examples are available for study, it cannot be stated with certainty.

ORTHEZIA INSIGNIS.

108. **Orthezia insignis,** *Dougl.*

THE LANTANA BUG.

References.—*Green, Trop. Agri., (1895), Jan., 437; (1898), Feb. 517; Journ., Bomb. Nat. Hist. Soc., XII., 537; Circ., Roy. Bot. Gard., Series I, No. 10, (1899); Administ. Rep. Bot. Gard., Ceylon, 1899, p. 14.*

Found in Ceylon.

Ceylon pest.

613. This very troublesome pest seems to have been introduced into Ceylon on ornamental plants, and now it occurs plentifully on **Lantana** (a plant plentiful in some parts of Assam). It spreads to the neighbouring tea, though it luckily does not seem to relish it. To the naked eye a colony looks like a group of little particles of white wax. It might become a dreadful scourge, and must be dealt with promptly should it appear in India. Mr. Green writes that he has met with the pest crowding on young tea shoots, and that the method being adopted is to fire the plot or poison the insect with Hydrocyanic Acid Gas as described above.

PULVINARIA PSIDI.

109. **Pulvinaria psidi,** *Mask.*

Found in Ceylon.

Reference.—*Green, Trop. Agriculturist, 1898, p. 517.*

614. This has not, so far as we are aware, occurred in India, but sometimes occurs in enormous numbers in certain Ceylon districts, and does considerable injury to infested plants. "The female is at first just like **Lecanium viride** (*vide infra*). It afterwards secretes a dense white cottony ovisac, while the insect itself shrivels up and appears as a brownish scale at one end of a smear of what looks like white paint ⅛ inch long." (*Green.*)

ERIOCHITON THEÆ.

110. **Eriochiton theæ,** *Green.*

(SEE PLATE XVI, No. 5.)

References.—*Ind. Mus. Notes, II., 60; IV., 188 (under the name Ceronesera sp.) V., 10.*

Found in Darjeeling

Serious in Darjeeling.

615. ***History*** and ***Description.***—The first sample of this scale insect was received from the Thurbo garden, Darjeeling, in

1897, and since that time it has been found on a considerable number of estates. The leaves on the upper surfaces were densely coated with a black sooty fungus, and on the under surfaces, more especially near the midrib, bore numerous long pure white scales that had a tuft of waxy hairs arranged along a medial ridge. (*See Plate XVI, No. 5, e.*) ERIOCHITON THEÆ.

The twigs likewise bore these very characteristic scales and also the larger female scales ($\frac{1}{8}$ inch long).

Though the black fungus on the upper surface of the leaf gives its name to the general term "Soot Blight" applied by planters to the disease, yet the fungus has really nothing to do with the attack and only feeds on the sugary exudation of the scale insect. There are several fungi which grow on this sugary liquid, but that which has been found most common in this instance was **Capnodium Footii**, *Berkl.* and *Desmaz.*, a well-known fungus on insect-infested Camellias in cultivation, and one which blackens lime trees (**Tilias**), in Europe, appearing in association with the honey-dew aphis. Soot Blight.

It seems probable that the author of *Notes on tea in Darjeeling* (p. 53) may be alluding to this blight under the heading "Soot Blight." He says: "It is a small insect with a sooty covering, which makes the trees look fearful and stops all flushing. Luckily this is not common, and, as a rule, only one or two trees will be found on a garden."

616. ***Depredations*** and ***Remedy.***—In the original correspondence on this subject it was stated that spraying the bushes with kerosene emulsion might stop the pest, but, if only a few bushes are affected, we would recommend, as more effectual, that they should be at once fired. If below each bush and amongst its branches a few handfuls of dry straw are placed and then ignited, the sudden flame produced will char all the leaves and twigs and completely eradicate the blight. Only the very sickly bushes will be thereby killed. The flushing will be retarded for a month or two, but the cure will be complete. As a rule, it is not wise to fire bushes much after March. If later than that, the shock is very much more severe, and the flushing may not be resumed before six or eight or, perhaps, eighteen months. But even a delay, such as I have indicated, would be preferable to the bushes being killed and the disease extended Kerosene emulsion. Firing bushes.

ERIOCHITON THEÆ.

over the estate. Diseased bushes of course suffer more severely from being treated in the manner proposed than healthy ones accidentally fired, but if even 50 per cent. are saved and a troublesome disease eradicated, the gain is distinct. Other less severe methods of treatment may possibly give a higher percentage of bushes saved, but they involve the risk of the disease spreading or even being artificially distributed in the act of cutting down or of constantly visiting and handling the bushes. In a letter Mr. Sproull, of Thurbo, who carried out experiments on the subject in 1897, wrote: "There were about a dozen bushes attacked, the leaves of which were all black and appearing as if they had been dusted with soot."

A later letter informed us that a fair percentage of the bushes, that had been burned, were again under leaf. Many of the bushes seemed to have been so badly attacked with the scale that they were nearly dead before being fired. Speaking of the advantages of firing circumscribed plots of tea, badly affected by blights, Mr. Sproull added: "I do not think anything better than fire. It is cheap, handy, always available. One knows from experience how great a quantity of fire it takes to kill a bush, as seen when abandoned portions are again reclaimed or along the edge of cultivation after being scorched by jungle fires."

Kerosene Emulsion. *Conf. with para. 588.*

More recent efforts with the kerosene emulsion spray above described have been equally successful, so that, though this would be an excessively serious visitation if it became general, and on certain garden has already been serious, it can be dealt with without great difficulty.

LECANIUM VIRIDE. THE GREEN BUG.

111. Lecanium viride, *Green.*

THE GREEN-BUG.

References.—*Green, Observations on the Green Scale Bug, Ceylon, 1886; Bamber, Chem. and Agri. Tea, 252; Ind. Mus. Notes, I., 49, 113; II., 168; III. (6), 18; Trop. Agri., (1898), 507.*

Found in Ceylon and South India.

LECANIUM NIGRUM. THE BLACK BUG.

112. Lecanium nigrum, *Nietner.*

THE BLACK-BUG.

References.—*Anderson, Journ. Agri.-Horti. Soc. Ind., 1869, vii; Ind. Mus, Notes, I., 113; II., 168.*

THE BROWN BUG.

Found in Ceylon.

113. Lecanium hemisphericum, *Targ.* var. coffeæ.

LECANIUM HEMISPHERICUM.

THE BROWN-BUG.

THE BROWN BUG.

References.—*Green, Insect Pests of the Tea Plant, 81 ; Bamber, Chem. and Agri. Tea, 252 ; Ind. Mus. Notes, I., 113 ; II., 168 ; III, (iv), 41 ; IV., 8 ; V., 7.*

Found in India and Ceylon.

617. Of these three insects, with which we propose to deal jointly, only the last has hitherto been found in India on tea, while all have been most serious in Ceylon. "Green-bug," though it killed out the coffee in whole districts there, has fortunately not, even in the same districts, seriously attacked the tea. "Black-bug" is now rarely found on coffee, its earliest noticed host plant.

Grows under shelter in Ceylon.

618. None of these bugs appear to have been discovered in India till 1895 when the "Brown-bug" was noticed by one of the authors (G. W.) in North Lakhimpur. Subsequently it has been found on several occasions on the north bank of the Brahmaputra, in Assam, and also in the Duars. Mr. Green, who identified the earlier samples, says that in Ceylon this insect is only dangerous under shelter from rain: the samples obtained in India were, however, obtained in open flats of tea without any shelter whatever, though some of them were attacked by a parasitic fungus. The following details apply to "Brown-bug" only.

Description.

619. ***Description.***—The full grown female scale is almost spherical, and of a pale chestnut brown colour and somewhat polished. When younger, it is an oval scale with a strongly marked longitudinal ridge, and two transverse bands. The larvæ are active pale canary yellow or almost lemon yellow creatures that move fairly actively for a time. As in other members of the genus, they have an anal sinus with two short hairs arising within it. The male has a smaller more elongated or linear scale, never becoming spherical, and when mature is almost transparent revealing the pink chrysalis which in time gives forth its minute winged insect.

Black Fungus.

620. ***Depredations.***—On all occasions where the brown bug has been met with in Assam, attention was attracted to the bushes by their black sooty appearance due to the upper surfaces of the leaves being coated with a black fungus,—apparently the same species

THE BROWN BUG.

as occurs in association with the bug in Ceylon. The bug lives on the under-surfaces of the leaves and on the twigs and shoots. The female insect, on its becoming fixed, inserts its delicate hair-like proboscis and sucks the juices of the tea. The plant is thus gradually impoverished and soon shows the extent to which it is suffering by discontinuing to produce flushing shoots.

Remedy.

621. ***Remedy.***—This pest must be treated in exactly the same manner as with all other scale insects. Whenever seen, the bushes should be carefully brushed with kerosene emulsion. Should the disease be found securely established and be giving indications of expanding, rather than risk the larvæ being blown by the wind or carried by the clothes of the coolies far and wide, fire the plot. It is more economical to lose the bushes than to risk a wide distribution of this or any other scale bug.

LECANIUM FORMICARII.

114. **Lecanium formicarii,** *Green.*

References.—*Ind. Mus. Notes, IV., 10; Trop. Agri., (1898), 515.*

Found in Ceylon.

622. Found on stems of tea and other shrubs, always sheltered by nests of a small brown ant (**Cremastogastor dohrni**). Highly convex, almost globular; dull brown. (Green.)

LECANIUM SIMILANS.

115. **Lecanium similans,** *Green.*

622*a*. "This is a species superficially resembling and having the same habits as **Lecanium formicarii**, with which it has hitherto been confounded; but differing in microscopical characters. It is not solely confined to ants' nests, but may be occasionally found uncovered." (*Green.*)

LECANIUM WATTI.

116. **Lecanium watti,** *Green.*

(SEE PLATE XVI, No. 6.)

Reference.—*Green, Indian Museum Notes, Vol. V., 1.*

623. This very large species of scale insect has been sent to us from the Sibsagar district and also from the Dehing Valley in Assam. The scales are about ¼ inch long and are of an oval shape, and a thin cartilaginous texture. They are found attached to the shoots and completely encase the twigs, while the leaves are covered with the soot-like fungus that accompanies most species of the genus. This could be a formidable pest, but as yet appears to be rare. It should be treated like other scale insects allied to it.

CEROPLASTES MYRICÆ.

117. **Ceroplastes myricæ,** *Linn.*

(SEE PLATE XVI, No. 4.)

Reference.—*Indian Museum Notes, Vol. V., 1.* (*Green.*)

The Scale Insects.

Found in Assam.

CERO-PLASTES MYRICÆ. Like lac insect.

624. On the north (and also, as has been more recently discovered, on the south) bank of the Brahmaputra in Assam there occurs a scale, similar in general appearance to the lac insect. In fact, it was shown to one of us (G. W.) as the lac insect itself in 1895, and although on careful observation it shows very considerable differences, yet the resemblance is, at first sight, very close. The insect was identified by Mr. Green under the above name.

Association with other scales.

625. It occurs in constant association with other scale insects—sometimes with the Brown-bug (**Lecanium coffeæ**), and sometimes (on "**Cycas**" and not on Tea) with **Aspidiotus orientalis**, *Newst.* "This association of species has nothing of the nature of symbiosis. It is an accidental circumstance due probably to the fact that a weakly or unhealthy plant is more readily seized upon by insect parasites of all kinds." (*Green.*)

Description.

These waxy-looking bugs may be said to be pale-pink, sea-anemone-like creatures that have on either side of their waxy encasement two waxy-like folds. The encasement may be spoken of as comprising an outer more or less flattened rim, with a central globular portion, so that in main shape the waxy structure is not unlike a Parsi felt-hat. (*See Plate XVI, No. 4.*) At one extremity, and situate on the outer rim, there are three circular bodies, two right and left, and one in the middle—the latter being the anal orifice. This anal orifice opens every now and again, and a deep purple structure protrudes. From this a little fluid is first blown into a miniature bubble, then bursts and is dispersed as dew, after which the organ is withdrawn. A longitudinal section through the insect would show the body completely encased by a waxy deposit. . . After gestation the ventral parts of the body shrivel up and the cavity becomes filled with the eggs which in due time hatch out, the larvæ escaping from beneath the dead body of the parent.

Very serious if it became general.

626. ***Depredations*** and ***Remedy.***—Were this large scale bug to become general, it might threaten the very existence of the tea plant. Hitherto it has appeared spasmodically, a clump of two or three bushes being killed, before it had been recognised. Fortunately it is easily seen and fire is the best means of stamping out the disease when discovered in a few bushes.

CEROPLASTES MYRICÆ.

Badly parasitised.

It is also a fortunate matter that the insect seems badly parasitised, since the waxy encasements are often perforated, no doubt owing to the escape of some ichneumon-fly that during its larval existence had lived on the scale-bug. The larvæ of a very small orange-red-coloured ladybird beetle (without any markings on its wing-cases) are also seen to be actively at work. These were very energetic little creatures and from the formidable-looking hairs with which they are clothed on the back seemed as if they might also be poisonous (*Conf. with Ind. Mus. Notes, Vol. IV, 27—28*).

Black Fungus.

After the scale-bugs are killed or have died on one part of the bush, the black fungus invades the shoots as well as the leaves, so that the advance of the pest from branch to branch and twig to twig may be traced by the black coating on the portions of the stem that have been abandoned.

CEROPLASTES CERIFERA.

THE INDIAN WAX INSECT.

118. **Ceroplastes cerifera,** *Anderson.*

(See Plate XVI, No. 1.)

The Indian wax insect.

References.—*Ind. Mus. Notes, I., 188 ; II, (3) ; III., (1) ; V., 8.*

Found in India and Ceylon.

627. The large irregularly shaped, white, waxy tubercles of this insect, often one-fourth inch in diameter, are occasionally seen on tea scattered here and there along the branches. They are so unlike an insect that, unless the wax be dissolved off their bodies, they can hardly be recognised as such. The species nowhere occurs in sufficient abundance to justify its being classed as a tea pest, but it is fairly common in Assam, the Terai and Darjeeling at least, and probably elsewhere.

CEROPLASTES FLORIDENSIS.

119. **Ceroplastes floridensis,** *Comst.*

Reference.—*Indian Museum Notes, Vol. IV., 40.*

Found in India and Ceylon.

628. This curiously shaped pink-coloured wax insect is fairly common on tea in Assam and Darjeeling, and according to Mr. Green it is frequent in Ceylon, "but not in injurious numbers." It will be generally seen on the upper surface of the leaves and in its young state, when not much larger than the head of a pin, is a very pretty star-shaped object.

CEROCOCCUS FICOIDES.

120. **Cerococcus ficoides,** *Green.*

References.—*Green, " On a new tea pest from India," 1899.*

CEROCOCCUS FICOIDES.

Found in Duars.

629. This, which is the first sample of the genus **Cerococcus** in India was received from the Duars in the early part of 1899, and was described by **Mr. Green**. The waxy scale of the female is dull reddish brown about $\frac{1}{20}$ inch in diameter. No further reports of damage have been since received.

CARTERIA DECORELLA.

121. Carteria decorella, ***Mask.***

(SEE PLATE XVI, NO. 2.)

Reference.—*Indian Museum Notes, Vol. IV., 58.*

Found in Darjeeling and Assam.

630. This insect has been known for a considerable time to attack tea and forest trees in North India. One of us has recently found it doing considerable damage in Upper Assam.* Its appearance can be judged from *Plate XVI, No. 2.* It should be dealt with like other scale insects. **Assam.**

DACTYLOPIUS THEÆCOLA.

122. Dactylopius theæcola, *Green. Mss.*

THE MEALY BUG OF TEA.

631. Considerable anxiety has been caused on several of the spurs in the Darjeeling hills during the past two years, owing to the discovery of a large number of the roots of the bushes affected by a louse-like mealy bug. **Mr. Green** has been good enough to inform us that it is a previously unknown species which he proposes to describe shortly in the Indian Museum Notes. **Darjeeling.**

One of the planters on whose garden the insect is found writes as follows:—

"It is found clinging to the bark of the stem, just under the surface of the ground. Some people say that it burrows into or eats the bark, causing great damage. I have watched the insect for the past year and a half, but have not yet been able to trace *any* damage actually done by it. It comes and goes at different seasons, and when it disappears it leaves a little white mark of wool from its body, but when this is brushed away there is no evidence left. It comes only on hybrid or indigenous tea *with single stem,* on the strongest bushes as well as the weakest indiscriminately. I have not seen it upon the leaves or any part of the bush but the collar." **Description of effect.**

A later letter from the same planter gives further information—

I have found a bush with mealy bug on the main branches. This is a bush by the side of a road, where soil has been thrown down and the bush earthed up to some extent. White ants had also carried soil up the branches and the bug had crept up under this soil . . . There are always ants present where the bugs are : tiny black ones, also sometimes

* Still more recently it has been sent to us from the Bishnath District, where it had done serious damage.

The Hemiptera (Coccidæ).

THE TEA MEALY BUG.

red . . . For years past I have often seen the mealy bug on the root of a weed which the Nepalese call "*manipat,*" but only within the past two years have I seen it on tea."

Ants associated.

632. One of us (H. H. M.) has had the chance of personally examining the mealy-bug on the roots of the tea plant, and certainly there does not seem to be any injury to the plants. In the beginning of the rains when the soil becomes wet the insects descend lower in the ground, and this probably accounts for their apparent disappearance at certain seasons. The ants spoken of above are always present, and, of course, feed on the sugary excreta of the bug. Mr. Green confirms our opinion as to the damage likely to be done by this coccid as follows :—"I do not fancy it will cause any serious injury to the plants, unless present in enormous numbers. It will certainly not injure the bark sufficiently to lead the way for white-ants, as suggested by one of your correspondents."

633. If it increases to such numbers as to be injurious to the plants, removal of the soil round the collar and spraying with kerosene emulsion will almost certainly be a cure, as the bugs have no protective covering against the emulsion.

Conclusion.

634. It may here be added by way of conclusion to the description of scale insects as pests of tea, that there is no group which is more capable of becoming a serious menace to the industry than this. It is the duty of the tea planter, therefore, to avoid the dangerous attitude of smiling at the idea of a bush which shows scale-bugs being viewed as serious. The larvæ of these pests are so minute that they can be blown far and wide by the wind, or carried on the wings and feet of insects that come to feed on the sugary exudation. In one night from a nucleus of two or three bushes, acres of tea might be invaded and the life sapped out of the bushes before the evil is recognised. The story of the Ceylon coffee-bug must never be lost sight of, nor its warning neglected. Many of the scale insects are so protected by their waxy coating, or the hard shell-like structure of the scale, that insecticides cannot reach them. They may be mitigated or even killed by insecticides, however, after a careful study of their life histories has been made, as in many cases where the adults cannot be touched the larvæ are easily killed. The

Danger of scale insects.

The Mealy Bug of Tea.

THE TEA MEALY BUG.

larvæ, for instance, rapidly succumb to kerosene emulsion and a washing or spraying with the fluid, repeated at the periods of each brood of larvæ, would in time no doubt eradicate the pest. The danger is that in the intervals of the insecticide treatment, swarms of the larvæ may have been allowed to escape. In cutting down the bushes the stroke of the axe may distribute the larvæ, and they may be shed over a large number of healthy bushes by the prunings being carried away by the coolies. Unless the life history of one of these insects is known, firing the bushes has much to be said in its favour, but if the life of the scale is known, as it ought to be in each case, it ought rarely to be necessary, and less drastic methods should be perfectly satisfactory.

CHAPTER XV.

THE INSECT PESTS OF TEA—continued.

THYSANOPTERA.

LXII.—The Thrips.

THRIPS.

123. Thrips sp.*

References.—*Green, Insect Pests of the Tea Plant, 98; Ind. Mus. Notes, II., 172; Cotes, Tea Insects, 43.*

Effect in other Industries.

635. The question of the serious nature, or otherwise, of several species of Thrips as pests of tea is one which has been very much discussed, but never thoroughly investigated. This group of insects nevertheless do a considerable amount of injury to other crops. Thus for instance they sometimes attack onions with fatal effect—"the rich green colour of a normal onion field being changed to a peculiar sickly yellow." (*Smith*) Cabbages are likewise seriously attacked, and more serious than either, the crop of grass in farming is often seriously reduced by their means. On the other hand, many injuries have been attributed to them for which they are not accountable, and the well known "Thrip" of grapes is due to a totally different

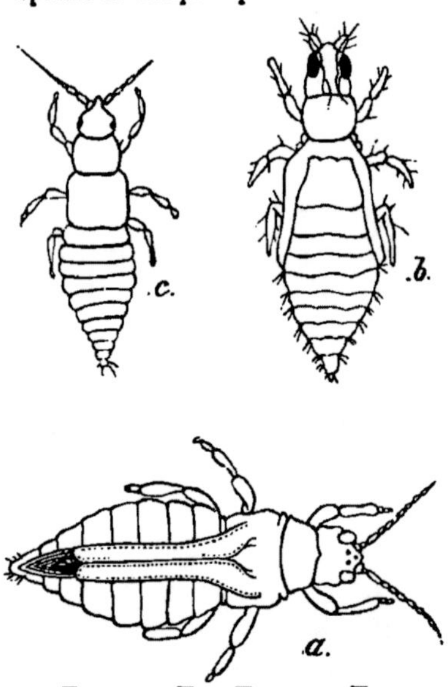

FIG. 39.—THE THRIP OF TEA.
c. Larva, enlarged: b. Pupa, enlarged: a. perfect insect, enlarged.
(After Green.)

* The correct name of these thrips is probably "Heliothrips hœmonhoidalis," *Bouché*, but a certain determination has not as yet reached us.

The Thrips.

insect, belonging to the same class as the green-fly (Chlorita flavescens) of tea. THRIPS.

636. The thrips are very small black red or yellowish insects. "They are so small that it would take a dozen or more, placed end to end, to measure an inch, and when disturbed they are apt to thrust the end of their bodies up in the air as if they meant to sting, looking as ferocious as such small insects can look. They are extremely lively, leaping and taking flight with great agility. Under a microscope their four narrow wings, delicately fringed all around with long hairs, may be seen: these wings are laid flat down the back when at rest. The red or yellow ones are wingless, and are the young of the black species." (*Comstock.*) Description.

637. Occasionally insects of this type are seen on the under-sides of tea leaves—specially on bushes overcrowded or under shade. In this case the larvæ are pale greenish yellow in colour, and are less than $\frac{1}{16}$ inch in size. Occasionally they may be seen to have formed a minute web below which they repose. The antennæ are thrown back over the head and between the large crimson coloured eyes. The mouth might be described as a short sharp rigid proboscis in which are two pairs of long lancets which are used for perforating the leaf, in order to suck the juice. When they pierce the leaf, they cause irregular patches to become discoloured, and these sometimes even show through to the upper surface. Found on Tea.

638. Exactly what is the extent of damage for which they are responsible, one cannot say at present. To do this would require a special enquiry. But a great deal of what is called "thrip" in Cachar, for instance, has no relation to these minute insects, but is almost certainly due to the young of the tea "green-fly." Many times what was called thrip has been pointed out to us, and in almost every case the green-fly was that referred to. On the other hand, the true tea thrip does probably do considerable harm, and we have seen them in the Duars and in Cachar certainly injuring the plants. It may be that they are responsible in part for the damage attributed to green-fly, but investigation is urgently needed on the point. Till one knows whether the damage is of any moment, it is distinctly too previous to recommend methods of treatment. Amount of damage doubtful.

CHAPTER XVI.

THE INSECT PESTS OF TEA—continued.

PSEUDONEUROPTERA.

LXIII.—Termites or White-ants.

Damage done in tropics.

639. Among all the classes of insects there are few the study of which has been more neglected than that of White-ants, and this in spite of the fact that in tropical countries they are of exceedingly great economic importance. The cause of this may be their lack of beauty, the fact they always work in hiding, and their restriction as serious enemies to tropical and sub-tropical countries, but the result has been to introduce an amount of confusion and contradiction into the information with regard to them, and the methods to be adopted against them, greater than with almost any group of pests. If it is recognised, however, as was found by one of the authors (G. W.) in 1895-98, and as has been confirmed since by numerous observers, that there are several totally distinct species of White-ant, some of which attack dead wood of one kind, some dead wood of another kind, and some living wood only, a great deal of the confusion and contradiction will disappear.

Distinct species.

640. The three or four forms recognised differ, in fact, in structure, in habits, and in food. Unfortunately the state of the collections in the Indian Museum has prevented the comparison of the specimens collected with standard types, and of assigning to them their scientific names if such exist. For the present, therefore, we must content ourselves with such popular descriptions as we have been able to make. It is, nevertheless, of vital importance to any progress in the study of White-ants with a view to their eradication, that it be recognised that we have in India many forms of Termites, some of which will ordinarily only eat dead vegetable matter, and others that will attack and kill plants.

641. The three or four forms to which notice is now to be directed, as met with on tea-gardens, may, however, as a matter of convenience, be discussed under the only scientific name hitherto applied to them in India :—

TERMES TAPROBANES.

124. **Termes taprobanes,** *Wlk.*

THE CASTELLATED WHITE-ANT OF INDIA,

The White-ants.

WHITE-ANTS.

References.—*Report of Committee of Enquiry on the Ravages of White-ants in St. Helena, 1864; Scott in Journ. Agri.-Hort. Soc. Ind., Vol. III. (1871), pp. 42-47; Col. Money, Essay on Tea l.c., p. 219; D. D. Cunningham, Fungi in White-ant Hills, Journ. Agri.-Hort. Soc. Ind., IV., pp. 51-53, also Proc., 20th May 1875, xvii; Vol. IV, Ravages of, on Tea, Proc., 25th Nov. 1880, p. xxxvii; 22nd Dec. 1881, p. lxiii; Vol. VII., Proc., Woodrow on Corrosive Sublimate as a cure, 5th Jan. 1883; Proc. 31st Oct. 1884, p. cxi; Proc., 25th Nov. 1885, p. clxxxvii; Vol. VIII., Proc., 15th Sept. 1886, (Liotard on Neem Leaves as a cure), p. lx: Cleghorn on White-ants, Vol. X, Proc., 29th May 1896, pp. 526-533; Tea Cyclopædia, 52-53; Green, Insect Pest of the Tea Plant, 93-98; Ind. Mus. Notes, Vol. I., 63-66 (Chutia Nagpur White-ants eat the roots), II., 172; III., 23; IV., 36, 102-104; Cotes, Insects and Mites, 46-48; Gollan, (reprinted) Indian Agriculturist, Mar. 1, 1897; Administ. Rep., Bot. Gardens, Ceylon, 1899, p. 14; Indian Gardening, Feb. 23, 1899; Agri. Journ., Cape of Good Hope, XV. (1899), 53; Planters' Gazette, 1900, p. 191; Indian Gardening, Mar. 1, 1900.*

Found in all districts.

642. ***Different Forms.***—The common species of Bengal, we are told, bears the name of **Termes taprobanes**, *Wlk.* Viewed from a popular standpoint, and having regard more to their modes of life and methods of effecting destruction, than to their structural peculiarities, the ants found would seem to be widely diversified. This will at once be exemplified by the mention of one circumstance. The castellated mud nests (often 5 to 10 feet in height) so commonly formed by the white-ants in Bengal, are not apparently constructed by the white-ants of several other provinces in India, and this fact is possibly accountable for by the supposition that some forms of white-ants live in cavernous excavations below, others in superficial structures above ground. Be that as it may, white-ants are known to abound in localities and positions where readily recognizable White-ant nests are not found. In some cases they exist in vast colonies, in others as very small and isolated communities. How far these may be but stages in the life of one species is one of the obscure points that urgently demand solution. **Various forms.**

643. According to our observations, there are in Assam, for example, at least three, if not four, different forms of White-ants :— **Insect constructing round hills.**

1st.—A large species that constructs the immense (non-castellated) rounded ant-hills which, when levelled and brought under cultivation in the garden, have been said to constitute barren patches. This might be regarded as the species that abounds in the jungles and forests, more particularly in association with the bamboo. It is

The Pseudoneuroptera.

WHITE-ANTS.

often found in aggregations of hillocks, covering a more or less extensive area, and giving to the clearances of such tracts a curious undulated appearance. This species does not appreciate association with man and dislikes the direct action of the sun. It consequently abandons its hillocks very rapidly on the forest being cleared for tea estates. It seems to live exclusively upon dead timber.

Castellated white-ant.

2nd.—There is the village and cultivation-loving species that forms large castellated hillocks of mud. This will generally be found on somewhat clayey soils, but only when above inundation level, hence it chooses the strips of high land around cultivation or on the homestead lands. This very possibly originates by a pair of winged ants (male and female) finding their way into the ground and existing for some time in subterranean caverns. But as the workers and soldiers of the new community (born from the eggs laid by the young queen) increase in number, the clayey ingredients of the soil are carried above ground, and the castellated hillock gradually formed. Passages under-ground, that extend for marvellous distances, are also formed, but the combs and queen cells of the hive are, as a rule, placed above water level.

White-ant of houses.

There would, however, appear grounds for suspecting that the very similar-looking termite that invades human dwellings is in reality a distinct species from the castellated white-ant of cultivation. If they be the same, then it belongs to a species that possesses the power of living under widely different conditions. For the present we accept the usual opinion that they are the same, and therefore this species may be said to live on dead wood, furniture, leather, paper, cloth—in fact any dry animal or vegetable matter. But by encasing dead portions of plants with mud it not only eats these, but extends the destruction to living tissues.

Football white-ant.

3rd.—A rather long and very thin species of white-ant that constructs hives not larger, as a rule, than an ordinary foot-ball. These occur over grass lands, the hives or nests being found half under-ground. They may be kicked out, and, while full of white-ants, will be found to have no deeper connection in the soil. Sometimes these hives may be seen to consist of reeds * cut to a desired

* The fact of reeds being occasionally used shows that this is not the comb of the castellated white-ant, carried or washed to the surface of the ground.

length, assorted parallel, then cemented together. At other times the hive consists throughout of a black vegetable (non-earthy) substance, extremely hard, and so firmly compacted that the hives may be dashed on the ground with great force and still remain entire, or nearly so. The material of which they are constructed, it may be added, is very combustible. In one garden, hives of this nature were collected in scores daily, piled up in heaps and ignited—an excellent mèthod of disposing of them. WHITE-ANTS.

Lives on green matter.

When cut open, they may contain male and female ants in the imperfect winged state, and neuters that are clearly the warriors and workers of the community. But though we broke open many hives, we never came across what could be regarded as the queen of the community. So far as has been ascertainable, this species lives very largely on green vegetable matter.

Raider white-ant.

4th.—Lastly, there is a small white-ant that lives under-ground and particularly among the roots of bushes or within the decomposed branches above ground. This excavates oblong caverns that might be said to range from less than 1 foot to 2 or 3 feet in size. One might say that it would be next to impossible to dig a trench anywhere in Assam in suitable land without exposing several of these remarkable excavations, the interiors of which always contain a curiously reticulated structure that might be compared with the combs of a bee-hive in pieces about as large as a wall-nut. Similar combs exist in the castellated hives.

The form that we desire to draw attention to in this paragraph might be designated the White-ant of Agriculture. Mr. Whigham has suggested for it the expressive name of the "Raider White-ant." It lives on the roots and lower shoots of living plants (on the tea, sugar-cane, dall, gram, etc.) and, having made an entrance through the bark, it tunnels the roots and stems, unobserved for the most part, until by storms these are blown over and the existence of the pest revealed.

Ceylon species.

644. Mr. E. E. Green, in his interesting little book *The Insect Pests of the Tea Plant*, makes the remark: "I have recently received from different planting districts, several specimens of full-grown tea-stems completely hollowed out by a kind of white-ant. It is quite a distinct species from the common white-ant that attacks dead wood and sawn timber, being fully twice as large as the latter, and feeding upon green, instead of dead, wood. Of the species at present under

WHITE-ANTS.

notice, I have seen only the worker and soldier ants which were taken from the galleries excavated in the tea-stems."

It thus seems probable there may be many species of white-ant that would fall under the section of those that directly attack living plants, and are thus pests to agriculture. They appear to agree on the main point of commencing their depredations, for the most part, on the roots or low down on the stem, or, at times, higher up, and by entering the stem through any openings in the bark that may be afforded them.

Conditions of an ant community.

645. ***Conditions of an Ant Community.***—Each nest of white-ants is supposed to consist of a Queen-ant—an unwieldy creature that lays all the eggs of the community; Ant-neuters—the workers and soldiers; and wingless Larvæ, both male and female, as well as several other classes of no importance to the point at issue. The larvæ become adult and winged at a certain season of the year, and escaping from the nest in countless numbers and late in the afternoon, migrate from the ancestral dwelling. After a time these lose their wings and crawl away, in pairs (one male and one female), when certain, but very few, of the females in time may become queen-ants and give origin to new colonies. After impregnation, the abdomen increases vastly in size. An ordinary sized queen may be put at from 2 to 4 inches in length and fully half an inch in thickness. Mr. Green says that the queen may attain a length of 6 inches, and that she lives for several years.

Eggs laid by queen.

Mr. J. Scott (quoting from Dallas) remarks that 80,000 eggs are sometimes laid by the queen in the course of twenty-four hours. There are often two or sometimes even three queens, as also several masked (reserve) or "neoteinic" queen to each white-ant hive. The latter remain inactive within the nest until the queen dies, out of season or from some unforeseen circumstance. The reserve queens seem to be derived, though this is doubtful, from the annual swarm of winged insects, one being purposely carried to a special cell for that purpose. It is not enough, therefore, to remove the queen, for, if one of the masked or reserve queens be left behind, she will immediately take the place of the queen, and continue the production of eggs. But if all the queens are destroyed, the ant-hill is said to be abandoned, but doubt on this point has by no means been set at rest by the observations made up to date.

The White-ants.

WHITE-ANTS. Distribution.

646. ***Distribution.***—There is hardly a situation from Cape Comorin to Kabul or from the tropical swamps of the plains to the temperate slopes of the Himálaya, where some species of termite is not met with. They may not be very abundant, but they are there. Afford them favourable conditions of food and leave them unmolested for a short time,—an inconceivably short time,—and they will multiply to a perfectly appalling extent and effect destruction in the least suspected positions. Most persons who have been stationed in districts badly affected by white-ants have witnessed beams, rafters, tables and other articles of household furniture suddenly collapse, owing to the interiors of certain portions having been eaten away to a shell,—only just sufficient to carry the varnish or paint and to leave the article the external semblance of unimpaired strength. All unsuspected, these minute workers have carried destruction forward, devouring the drier and more central wood first, working, in other words, from the centre towards the circumference as they ascend from the damper to the drier extremity.

Mud round the stem.

647. ***Mud Encasements.***—Residents in the East are also familiar with the way white-ants encase with mud the stems and branches of trees, forming for themselves thereby covered ways that extend from the level of the ground often to the topmost bough. On these encrustations being removed, the bark is seen to be pale-coloured, because of the superficial and drier layer having been eaten away. The white-ants do not, at first sight, appear to do any more serious injury to the barks of the trees, though it would be hard to believe that they are not injured by these coatings of mud. But if the white-ants do not eat the bark, the very natural question arises,—for what purpose do they form these mud-protected passages?

Conf. with para. 648.

It has been a very generally accepted opinion that white-ants will not eat living and growing wood, and consequently that they do not kill, though perhaps they injure, living plants to some extent. This opinion, we feel satisfied, may be true of certain forms of white-ants, but is wholly untrue of others.

Effect of white-ants on soil.

648. ***Influence on the Soil and Roots.***—There surely can be no doubt that white-ants, if permitted to take up their abode for some time in and among the roots of a plant, do incalculable harm. During their subterranean operations they remove the earth from below to form the mud encasements above ground and around the

WHITE-ANTS. stem. Speaking of the tea bush, it is by no means an unusual state of affairs to find the plant growing as it were on the summit of a dome of hardened earth that surrounds the cavernous dwellings of its colony of termites. A section made by means of digging a trench, for 3 or 4 feet deep, across the space occupied by the bush and hard against the main stem, will reveal a most unhealthy state of affairs. At a depth varying from 1 to 3 feet a large central cavern will be found and fringing this numerous smaller ones. In fact, an elaborate system of excavations will be revealed, and found to be occupied, like the Roman catacombs of old, by both the living and the dead. The roots that stretch across the larger caverns will be seen to have formed bark and to have assumed, to all intents and purposes, the condition of branches. The delicate absorbing fibrils will, moreover, be observed to have all disappeared, so that it needs little explanation to enforce the opinion that there has been a useless accumulation of plant energy below ground at the expense of leaf production above. But this is not all. A serious disturbance to the drainage of the soil and to its powers of retaining moisture has been effected by these unbidden colonists. When white-ants infest a neighbourhood, to any great extent, the soil is hardened, caked and dried to a degree that in hot weather is sure to prove disastrous to the crop and may ultimately even endanger the life of the older plants. On the other hand, during the rains, a surface wash takes place and an uneven percolation that may be noted to cause the subsidence of certain bushes. This necessarily means that the roots are torn from their positions and killed, food being thus provided for the white-ants and an entrance afforded them to the older woody portions. The presence of white-ant encasements on tea bushes should at once be regarded by the planter as giving warning of the necessity for immediate attention to that part of his estate.

Hardening of soil by white-ants.

Living wood affected.

649. ***They devour Living as well as Dead Wood.***—It is freely admitted that white-ants will attack the timber of very nearly every species of tree. Occasionally one hears of the great merit of this wood and that (particularly teak wood) as being proof against white-ants. And in some few instances this is doubtless true, though it would perhaps be safer to say that the merit is but relative. In some cases life has hardly left the plant when it becomes attacked

WHITE-ANTS.

by these destructive creatures. In others, the timber has to be fairly well seasoned, and in still another sort has to be so old that its protective resin or other substance that the white-ants have an aversion to, has been dissipated. But whether such immunity is only comparative or complete, the main principle remains the same that white-ants will attack and devour practically any dead wood wherever it is left exposed to them and undisturbed for a short period.

650. But there are many directions in which these generalisations regarding white-ants and their depredations may be entirely upset. It is not uncommon to find the opinion advanced that white-ants can and do attack living plants. With that opinion we entirely concur. Let the mud encrustations of the bark be carefully removed and the ant road-ways followed upwards, until the stump of a withered branch or the scar from which a branch has been wrenched is reached, and the observer will witness how white-ants ultimately devour as they gradually kill plants. They will be seen to have eaten, or nearly so, the whole of the severed portions, but having found a passage through the external zone of living and growing structures, have begun to attack the fully-formed wood. They have deposited a dense coating of mud within the gaping wound and splintered timber with *a two-fold object of preventing the process of healing and of supplying an absorbent plaster that will suck the moisture from the wound and transmit it to the air.* In a very short time a layer of the wood will be thus killed and rapidly devoured. Layer upon layer follows until the stem is cut into very seriously, if not entirely severed. The circulation of the sap having been thus intercepted, these mining engineers turn upwards into the dead and dying wood. Operating below ground and thereby diminishing the supply of moisture, while availing themselves at the same time of every abrasion or injury to the stem or its branches above ground, is it not to be wondered at that the process of destruction, though it may be almost imperceptible, is nevertheless certain in its ultimate result!

Manner of killing wood.

But let it be clearly observed that most white-ants live mainly on wood, not on green vegetable matter. The majority will not, as a rule, kill the green sapling, nor attempt to eat their way though the external zone of green wood on healthy plants. They will preferentially attack plants that contain a central axis of fairly well-formed wood, and may require even then the aid of some accidental agent

Attack mature wood chiefly.

WHITE-ANTS.

to give them access to the wood. By their action below ground they dry the roots, the bark of which is much thinner and not permeated to the same extent by sap as the bark of the stem and its branches. The species that attack seedlings or small woody shrubs generally commence operations from below. Those that live on trees, on the other hand, start their depredations, as a rule, above. The result is the same in both cases, the wood is first dried and killed, then devoured.

Effect of Borers.

651. ***Practical Considerations.***—The story of the manner in which white-ants can and do attack and kill plants and thereafter eat the woody portions of their stems and branches, is true in a thousand and one modifications. Let a boring insect make an entrance into the stem, branch or root, and white-ants will soon follow. Let the planter prune ruthlessly, leaving large surfaces, or snags, or torn portions of wood exposed to the action of the air, and if white-ants are about they will rapidly cover up his slovenly work with a shroud of mud. The vigorous efforts of the living bark may, however, more or less completely embrace and enclose the scar, but sooner or later the plant will give clear indications of its cankerous state by ceasing to be productive. The bark may appear quite entire and comparatively healthy. On being probed, however, it will suddenly snap asunder and reveal a mass of mud within a shell of living tissue.

Effect of bad pruning.

Conf. with para. 156.

652. These are no imaginary pictures. We have already alluded to this subject under Pruning. Hardly a tea garden exists in which the evil effects of careless pruning followed, it may be, by the depredations of white-ants cannot be seen. Bushes will be found here and there all over most estates, in which the lower half of the stem is a portion of an old shell, perhaps not more than half an inch in thickness which carries on its apex a sickly and distorted dome of useless and unproductive branches. In other words, it is no uncommon occurrence to find the lower half of the stem gnarled and rotten with numerous mud stumps representing abortive branches or having one side only alive, the place of the other being taken by a great open scar, perhaps mud encased and infested with white-ants.

Personal experiences.

653. This is what might be described as the normal condition of a large percentage of the bushes in many old gardens. But one not infrequently hears of wholesale destruction where both young and old tea have suffered, more especially the former. During our

WHITE-ANTS.

tours in Assam not a few gardens have been visited where a high percentage of young tea had the stems encased with white-ant mud and where very many plants were being directly attacked by the insects. Through the kindness of Mr. W. H. C. Whigham, we have received samples of tea three to four years old, well formed and healthy looking, and which had attained a height of 6 to 8 feet. In many of these samples the stems have been cut almost square across, at a height of about 3 to 6 inches above ground. In other cases the stems have been furrowed and excavated to such an extent as of necessity to kill the plants. And this has beyond doubt been accomplished by white-ants upon otherwise healthy plants.

Mr. Whigham has described very clearly the manner in which in many cases the white-ants had effected an entrance into the well-formed central wood of his samples, and his views corroborate our own observations. He says:—

Manner of action on young seedlings.

"The lowest branch of the tree, some 2 or 3 inches above the ground and frequently springing from the surface of the soil, is injured in some way at the point it leaves the main stem, by some borer or other pest. It then drops, withers and finally falls off from the tree. White-ants (or what we commonly accept as being white-ants) have by this time effected an entrance into the tea bush, working upwards, eating out the centre, and leaving the stem hollow. The first storm of wind breaks off the tree just above the ground."

Time of most serious effect.

Further on Mr. Whigham adds: "I am unable to state what causes the low lateral branches first to droop and then fall off from the tree. I can discover no borer or other insect, but it is possible some such pest may, in the first instance, show the way for the white-ants to follow. The damage is most apparent from August to December, when, usully speaking, white-ants are most abundant and visible. . . . . I have never seen any clearance so devastated as this one has been from what, after a long experience of Assam and Cachar, I should name to be white-ants." Speaking on the subject of the season of the year when ants are worst, Colonel Money (*Cultivation and Manufacture of Tea, p. 90*) says: "From the close of the rains to the cold weather is the worst time for white-ants, and the time the planter should guard particularly against their ravages. At that time if he examines his trees closely, he will very likely find white-ants on a quarter of the whole."

WHITE-ANTS.

Tea Cyclopœdia.

654. ***Opinions of Authors and Practical Planters.***—A writer in the *Tea Cyclopædia* says: "I had a belief that white-ants only attack old gardens which are not kept clean, and where dead wood is allowed to rot; but it is not so. I see that the white-ants will infest young and old gardens equally, though every care be taken to keep them free from decayed timber. Our garden is only 2⅛ years old, and the best block is suffering from the depredations of the white-ants. It is heart-rending to see a young thriving bush, which showed no symptoms of decay in the evening, lying prostrate on the ground next morning, with a hole in the trunk an inch long and ¼ inch in diameter. I consulted several of my brother planters, old and experienced, in Chittagong, and they all advised me to keep up constant hoeing, but it had no effect. I next tried kerosene oil, and painted every bush in the block with a brush, but it was of no avail.

Mr. Whigham's opinion.

655. During our Assam explorations we became satisfied that, although the common white-ant usually attacks the upper parts of the stem, in the manner already detailed, another form—a smaller insect—attacks the roots of recently transplanted seedlings and the plants in nursery. The external mud encasement around the lower portion of the stem (seen in the latter case) is intended very possibly to suck the sap from the bark and dry the wood, thus preparing the way for an advance from the roots to the stem. That a system of sucking moisture, both from the plant and the soil, is a governing principle, so to speak, in their methods of destruction, must be evident to every person who has given this subject any degree of consideration. Mr. Whigham put this matter pointedly during a march through some portions of the Hautley Estate. We went to a castellated hillock, and he said that every second or third day he had ordered the top to be knocked off. Time after time it had been replaced. The soil for months past, Mr. Whigham explained, had been parched, not a drop of moisture to be had anywhere for the poor tea bushes, and yet these little pests seem to find the moisture necessary for their building operations. The explanation no doubt is, that they gradually suck the moisture from the roots, from the soil, and even from the moist bark, below their mud encasements, and also utilise the dew found on the leaves. Wherever obtained, water is employed in the repairs or construction of the castellated hillocks or mud encasements, and this being exposed to the air is soon dis-

WHITE-ANTS.

sipated with the not unnatural result that the soil is gradually parched to an injurious extent, and in time the plants are killed.

Mr. Hall's opinion.

656. In a letter to us, Mr. James Hall, late of the South Sylhet Tea Company, wrote: "I am certain that the mound-forming ant does little or no harm to tea. There are in this valley gardens covered with ant-hills, and these gardens, as a rule, have not suffered from the ravages of the white-ants. There are other gardens where there are almost no ant-hills, and on these gardens the bushes were, for the first year or two, cut down by thousands. The amount of damage done by white-ants depends entirely on the nature of the soil. On light soils, more especially if *teela* or plateau, they are usually most destructive. The ant-hills on these soils seem to me to be different from those made by the jungly or larger white-ant. They are usually not so high. If Dr. Watt cares to visit Sylhet, he will see gardens almost without ant-hills, that have lost 10 per cent. plants from the ravages of white-ants, and others, where ant-hills are very plentiful, that have hardly lost a plant."

Mr. Scarth's opinion.

657. In another letter Mr. E. Scarth, the late Superintendent of Attaree Khat Tea Company, says: "The ant which, so far as my experience goes, is to be feared as doing damage to tea plants, is the small species that lives under ground in oblong caverns: the large white-ant that raises large hillocks does comparatively little damage, and if the queen ant is dug out from the hillocks, the rest of the ants leave it. I have levelled many of these deserted hillocks and planted them out with fair success." "It is the small white-ant which is our enemy, and a good trench hoeing or forking in autumn should, I consider, be the best remedy."

658. Having furnished in the above paragraphs information to hand, corroborative in certain directions of the remarks offered, in the first part of this chapter, it may be as well if we give here certain opinions that are opposed to our views:—

Mr. J. Scott's opinion.

659. The late Mr. J. Scott, formerly Curator of the Calcutta Botanic Gardens, in a most instructive and thoughtful paper entitled "*Notes on Horticulture in Bengal,*" says of white-ants: "There is a prevalent, but certainly a mistaken, notion, that they also devour the living parts of plants. Cuttings of sugar-cane, as also those of many of our garden plants, are said to be especially liable to their attacks, and I have thus been induced to bestow considerable attention on

The Pseudoneuroptera.

WHITE-ANTS.

their habits. In sugar-cane cuttings, I find that diseased portions are very quickly attacked by the white-ants, and scooped clearly out to the very surface of the living part: further gnawing then ceases, though the insects remain to sip the exuding juices and this, as frequently happens—when the diseased surface is large—so weakens the cutting that it is unable to afford the necessary nourishment for the young offshoots, until they are self-sustaining, and thus all die, and of course become the prey of the white-ants. It is doubtless from examination of the cuttings of these stages only that they have been falsely accredited with their complete destruction. Though I am thus certainly of opinion that the white-ants do not eat the living parts of the cane-cuttings, I nevertheless believe that they cause a certain amount of damage to them. This they effect by gnawing off the dead and dry parts, thereby exposing a fresh and living surface, from which they continue to draw the thin freely exuding sap, and thus weaken and intensify the disease in a manner which might have occurred naturally. I thus think that of two similarly and partially diseased canes, of which one is free from, the other attacked by, white-ants, the latter will be less liable to resist the further inroads of the disease than the former. For the same reasons they are likely to cause injury to cuttings of our ordinary flowering plants; but this can only occur through the neglect of the *mali*. To attract the white-ants, there must needs be a partially dead cutting in the pot on which they, in the first instance, ensconced themselves; thence extending their excavations they come in contact with, and perhaps remove the soil from the cicatrising base of other cuttings, thereby checking and may-hap killing them, in thus withdrawing their supply of moisture. In these respects, then, I admit that white-ants may, and I believe do, cause mischief to cultivators; but that they really devour the living parts of plants is, I believe, wholly unfounded."

Secondary Agents.

Kills wood before feeding on it.

660. If the opening sentence and the concluding expression of personal opinion were removed from the above passage, we should have no objection to its appearing as an opinion supporting powerfully our contention that white-ants kill tissues and, in time, whole plants, and, when so killed, devour them. It seems to us to beg the question to say that they do not eat living and growing tissues. If they possess the power of slowly killing plants, the practical result is the same to the tea cultivator as if they ate them alive.

The White-ants.

661. So, in the same way, much has been said on the theme that white-ants are only secondary agents, following on the path of a grub that eats the roots, or of a borer that works in the stem. That contention (which is doubtless true in some instances) is probably inadmissible as a general guiding principle in the practical consideration of white-ants as a pest to crops. Dysentery may be a disease that very frequently follows some other ailment, but it is an aspect of the patient's case that must be dealt with promptly. To argue that white-ants may have been unjustly accused of being a primary pest, is dangerous. WHITE-ANTS.

662. Mr. J. B., of . . . , in a private letter to one of us (G. W.), dated May 25th, 1896, in this connection writes: "White-ants will not attack a healthy tea bush; if they did, I am afraid there would not be a tea bush left in Assam. I have seen healthy tea bushes thriving in the middle of an ant's nest." Further opinion.

"You have a very strong case, I own, at Hautley garden, but the general opinion is that there must be some other cause, the bushes being sickly. White-ants then come in for the final destruction. I do not suppose a single old tea bush is pruned down, or what we now call collar pruned, without being found to be attacked by white-ants in the centre of the old and decayed stump. You pointed this out yourself to me, and my experience is that in all cases of collar pruning the centre of the original stump gradually decays, and is eaten away by white-ants; while from the outside of the stump (very often under ground) new shoots start, the nucleus of fine and healthy bushes. In collar pruned tea, one is fortunate if one does not lose more than from 5 to 10 per cent. of the bushes, but we are well rid of these, for they are usually the sickly ones that cannot stand a pruning of such a drastic nature, and the only remedy is to fill the vacancies up with young plants." Hautley.

"I mention this simply to show what a chance we give to white-ants to destroy our tea wholesale, but they cannot do it."

Mr. B. then concludes his letter by the following sentences: "I would ask a simple question and it is this: Has any planter, by the application of any of the emulsions you name, brought a sickly bush round (*i.e.*, a bush to all appearance being destroyed by ants); the ants may be destroyed, but has that bush ultimately recovered and become vigorous?"

The Pseudoneuroptera.

WHITE-ANTS.

Several species.

663. One might venture to point out that the above criticism has overlooked a point on which we have laid stress, namely, that there are several forms or species of white-ant, one that will distinctly attack young seedlings, and another that has not the power to do so, but commences its operations on dead wood. We could mention a score of gardens in Assam where the former white-ant can be found attacking seedlings direct, and our correspondent may certainly congratulate himself that it has not so far been his misfortune to make their acquaintance. The other form may, however, ascend the stem of old plants, and, if it finds wood anywhere exposed, will devour that, and, having thus found its way into the stem, will eat down the centre until in time it produces the condition Mr. B. has so vigorously described. The answer to the question put above has certainly to be given in the negative, for, if badly attacked, there is no cure but collar pruning. It may be that white-ants find sickly plants more easily preyed upon than healthy ones. The diseases they were suffering from, however, were possibly curable, whereas, once the centre of the stem has been eaten out, there is no cure. It is not cure, therefore, that we have advocated, but improvements in cultivation as methods of prevention and also the eradication of the pest if that be possible. But we should like to ask if the decomposition of the centre of the stem is a necessary and unavoidable consequence of age and whether only old trees have their stems so decomposed? If that be so, then white-ants are doubtless fulfilling a provision of nature in destroying what is useless. In our opinion, however, white-ants are very much more frequently a cause, than a consequence of the decomposition of the stem.

Collar pruning.

Mango seedlings attacked.

664. ***White-ants attacking Mango Seedlings.***—Speaking of the form of white-ant that attacks the root of seedlings (though this is a digression somewhat from a report on the pests of the tea plant), we may illustrate our contention by a passage or two from a most instructive paper from the Settlement Officer, Balaghat, in the Central Provinces:—"White-ants," that Officer writes, "are especially fond of young mango trees. In some villages repeated efforts to make a mango grove have failed, on account of the roots of the young trees being attacked by white-ants. I once doubted this fact, and was disposed to believe that in these villages the people were unusually negligent in watering the sapling." He then goes on to

WHITE-ANTS.

narrate how he tried to raise some mangoes near his own bungalow, but "a number of the saplings died, they being in most cases attacked by white-ants. I have dug up three of the trees in different stages of the white-ant disease. One of the plants was almost dead, and it would have been difficult to prove that the white-ants were not innocent scavengers removing useless dry wood. Another tree was half-dead, and the theory that exonerates the white-ant from the charge of devouring living timber, could only be maintained by crediting the termite with a marvellously accurate prophetic instinct, that told the scavenger which of the trees were already doomed to die, and might be removed as useless, for the tree was not yet dead, but only likely to die shortly. In the third case, the tree still looked quite green save for a suspicion of unhealthiness about some of its leaves. On digging it up I found that its roots have been eaten through in places by white-ants, and that a detachment of the voracious termites was actually pushing its way up the heart of the sapling eating its path through perfectly good juicy wood. . . I have found fields of *tur* **(Cajanus indicus)** in which a number of the plants have withered owing to the roots being eaten by white-ants, and in gram fields I have had similar damage pointed out to me."

Cajanus Indicus attacked.

665. ***Death of Twigs Low Down on the Stem.***—As already stated, there is no doubt Mr. Whigham's specimens have been cut across and furrowed by white ants, and although, he says, he has been unable to solve the problem of how the lower lateral branches have been killed, he is very possibly correct in believing that it was through the death of such lateral branches that the white-ants found an entrance to the wood of the main stem provided they did not enter by the roots. Where the destruction has not been preceded by a borer or other parasite, nor has been caused by defective pruning, it may be due to the branches being broken, or simply by being imbedded during deep hoeing. But there are many circumstances that might each contribute to injure the lower branches. The point of importance, that it is here desired to urge, is that, without some external abrasion or injury, giving access to the central wood, white-ants are, as a rule, unable to accomplish their mission of destruction. The risk the lower branches are exposed to during heavy hoeing is, however, very great, and *where white-ants are known to abound*, it should be a point for careful study whether it would not be the wiser course to remove all

Death of low twigs allows white-ants to enter.

WHITE-ANTS.

the lower branches at an early stage and encourage the formation of only one or at most two or three main stems with no branches for some distance above ground.

First pruning as affected by white-ants.

666. ***Best Time for First Pruning.***—A question raised by Mr. Whigham has been partly disposed of by the remarks already made, but it may be emphasised here. He says:—

> "The full-grown bushes appear to be selected in preference to the younger and smaller plants. Do you suppose, as the bushes grow older, they develop something peculiarly favourable in the wood or sap for the pests to feed on? Would earlier pruning, say after the plants have been a year in position (cutting down to 6 or 9 inches), strengthen the plants?"

Absence of sap desired by insect.

667. The answer to the former question must of course be that it is not a sap favourable or otherwise that white-ants desire, but the absence of sap. The central wood of a growing plant after a certain age, might almost be described as dead. It is not at any rate actively living and growing, but is timber more or less completely formed, and the older it becomes the more true is this observation. Fully developed wood is the food that white-ants are partial to, and such has only to be exposed to them to be devoured. The best protection to the stem, far and away superior to all insecticides, is a healthy and entire bark with a vigorous sap-wood.

Present state of affairs preventable.

668. The answer to Mr. Whigham's second question might be in the affirmative, but the point is one that should be carefully determined by practical tests. There would seem to us no doubt that the process of pruning, when seedlings are three or four years old, exposes them, in certain districts at all events, to a far greater extent to the attacks of white-ants, than pruning accomplished at an earlier stage. But on general principles of tea cultivation, we have already recommended a fairly early period being fixed for the first heavy pruning, say, not later than two years. Our views on the subject of pruning have been so fully expressed, that it would be superfluous to repeat them here. We believe bad pruning to be the chief reason why the centre wood of old bushes is so very frequently rotten and white-ant infested. Far from being prepared to accept the state of affairs that prevails, as a necessary condition of age, it is almost certainly largely preventable.

Conf. with paras. 142-143.

669. But the first step in that direction is the recognition of white-ants, each and every form of them, as injurious to tea. We have already stated that we do not believe the castellated form ever

directly attacks and kills bushes, but we are abundantly satisfied that it is capable of the greatest possible mischief. It will at once attack any dead wood that may be on a tea bush. Once any species of white-ant deposits its mud encasement on dead wood, it eats slowly, and, as it progresses, the mud sucks out the moisture and disseminates that to the air, so that, deprived of its sap, layer upon layer, is killed and eaten. White-ants thus work into the very heart-wood and run up or down the stems and even along the roots, with a natural enough result. The bush becomes unproductive, and is pronounced old and diseased. White-ants are an ever-present danger that have aged prematurely many gardens, and are to a perfectly alarming extent lowering the productive capabilities, of most gardens in India. All the while they are but too frequently looked upon as necessary evils, harmless little creatures that have by some misguided people been falsely accused of eating living plants, while they only kill them first and eat them afterwards. WHITE-ANTS.

670. ***Harbouring White-ants.***—Having thus briefly dealt with the manner in which white-ants attack living plants and the destruction they are capable of effecting, we turn now to the circumstances that may be regarded as harbouring these undoubtedly dangerous pests. The very foremost consideration should be given to the removal, as far as possible, of all ant-hills or nests. Many planters prefer, so they told us, to leave these alone, because of the all but universally admitted opinion that tea will not grow on the top of ant-hills, and that the area of sterility is greatly extended by levelling them down and scattering the earth over the surrounding land. We have examined many large rounded mounds (some of them with tea growing on the top) which in every case we were told were "old ant-hills," but did not come across one in which ants were found nor one of this class described as a new ant-hill. While not questioning the accuracy of the opinion given regarding these mounds, nor even that it might be possible to find many that contained countless myriads of ants, we simply affirm that we did not come across one *within the limits of a tea garden* that was inhabited, or seemed inhabited, by ants. Many similar round ant-hillocks in the forest and jungles were found, all inhabited by the ant. So again, the castellated ant-hillock is by no means common in tea gardens, though occasionally one may be seen on the Removal of ant hills.

The Pseudoneuroptera.

WHITE-ANTS.

roadsides or commencing to grow up around a bush, though this is generally an indication that the hoeing of the garden has been neglected. The contradictory opinions that one obtains as to the sterility or fertility of ant-hillocks may, as it seems to us, proceed from the two kinds of mounds, above indicated, being widely different. At all events, our observations have led us distinctly to the conclusion that the white-ants of the jungles love neither the jungle clearances, accomplished by the planter, nor the object of his solicitude.

Further investigation required.

671. This is, however, a point regarding which there should be no uncertainty. Very little study would suffice to remove all doubts Clearly if the rounded mound-forming ant be a distinct species, and one that is comparatively not injurious to the tea, but dies out after it has been exposed for a few years to the full action of light, there would be little or nothing gained by levelling the mounds. Better leave them alone for a few years until, by the growth of weeds, they had been shown to be converted into fertile soil. But if we are wrong in this suggestion and they are, as some planters believe, great fatherlands of this tea pest, the sooner they are levelled and dug out the better. Whatever present expense this may entail, that would be preferable to increasing the danger hereafter of white-ants.

Effect of burying wood, etc.

672. ***Burying Wood, Prunings, etc.***—During the clearance of new land nothing seems more pernicious than the habit of burying stumps of trees, branches, roots, etc., in the soil. Food is thereby provided all over the future estate for great colonies of white-ants which, when their store of food, thus provided by the planter, gets exhausted, it may be, will lose no opportunity to attack the tea. This argument holds good with even greater force to the habit of burying the prunings from the tea plant itself. This subject will be found fully dealt with in another chapter, and it is only here alluded to as having a direct bearing on the question of white-ants.

Conf. with paras. 281, 282.

All woody structures to be burned.

673. All woody structures, whether from the jungle clearances or the subsequent tea prunings, should be burned. In the form of ashes they are valuable, while as wood they are dangerous. It has been asked whether the stakes employed in planting out tea tend to introduce and distribute the pest of white-ants. The answer is that they most undoubtedly may do so. It would seem a great safeguard if these were all dipped in tar or Gondal Fluid before being used,

The White-ants.

as their presence seems essential where tea is being planted out, or where vacancies are being filled up. WHITE-ANTS

No dry wood of any kind should be left lying about in gardens that are addicted to white ants, and the very first principle of pruning should be to remove all dead and dying, and therefore useless wood from the bushes.

Effect of cultivation.

674. ***Remedies.***—As already briefly indicated, the very foremost consideration should be given to the subject of eradication of white-ants. When and where possible they should be dug out, not merely by hand cleaning the stems and branches of the mud encasements —a sure indication of the presence of this pest—but by digging out and destroying the nest if this be possible. Colonel Money says:—

"Digging round the plant where they are, disturbs their runs, and does much good. At the same time they should be brushed off any part of the tree they have attacked, and the tree should be well shaken. All this, however, only does temporary good, for they often are found as thick as ever on the plant a week later.

Kerosene oil.

"Tobacco water is beneficial, but in wet weather it is soon washed off. Kerosene oil is *very* efficient. A little is put round the stem; but it is expensive. The next best thing I know of is the earth-oil from Burma, and this is cheap enough. It is thick, but used from a bottle it gets heated by the sun and is then quite liquid.

"When white-ants are found on a tree, a little petroleum applied with a brush is put on the part they have attacked. They are also well shaken off, and a ring of oil is placed round the stem. My experience is that they will not attack that tree again for a long time. I was at first fearful that both it and the kerosene . . . . would injure the trees, but both are safe."

Earth-oil damages bark.

675. This view is, however, directly contradicted by the more recent experiments of Mr. Whigham, until recently an Assam planter. He says: "Earth-oil and tar damage the bark of the trees and cannot be used." "In the middle of the rains in 1895 I painted about 50 Bazaloni tea bushes on the stem, a little below and above the ground with earth-oil, and the same number with tar. The result was identical in each case.

"During the remainder of the rainy season the ants were kept away, but as the cold weather came on, the bark in nearly all

The Pseudoneuroptera.

WHITE-ANTS. instances was found to be eaten through by the tar and oil. The stem of the bushes were charred and burned looking as if a tight bandage of, say, 6 inches wide, had strangled the growth of the tree Soon after this they lost vitality, and had to be collar pruned down to the ground."

676. We have heard other planters also speak unfavourably of the use of kerosene. Mr. Bamber recommends a dressing with petroleum earth-oil. He adds :—

"It is most important that all ant-hills should be destroyed, especially when near a nursery or young plantation, as if the plants are attacked at an early stage, and the main stem at all damaged, they will never recover, and yield the same as an uninjured plant.

Mr. Bamber's recommendations.

"It might be possible to destroy the ants before they take flight by burning sulphur or other material in such a manner, that the gases and smoke would penetrate the numerous passages of the hill, and either cause the ants to emerge or smother them inside. Such a remedy could be easily tried, and would be far less laborious and expensive than cutting away the mounds, some of which are of great size.

"Fires of brush wood could be lighted on the windward side, and either sprinkled with sulphur or covered with damp jungle or straw and old bamboo mats, to assist in forcing the smoke into the interior.

"Small quantities of heavy earth-oil poured into holes bored in the mounds in a sloping direction would also, when burning with a limited supply of air, cause a heavy smoke to penetrate throughout."

The above recommendations have been before the planters now for some few years, and it would be interesting to know if they have been tried, and if so, what degree of success has been attained. Personally we should prefer to remove ant-hills, at all costs, as being the more direct way of dealing with the pest, and the sooner this is accomplished the better; and there seems sufficient evidence against the measure to make one feel that kerosene should never be used as a dressing for the bark, and if tar is employed, it should not be coal tar, but the vegetable (Stockholm) product.

Adhatoda vasica.

677. We have been informed that the cold infusion of the leaves of **Adhatoda vasica** has been found an effectual cure for white-ants. In another part of this report the properties of that insecticide have been alluded to and we need not enlarge on the subject here.

The White-ants.

The contents of a kerosene oil-can of the infusion, poured into the holes of a fairly well-established nest, is said to have sufficed. Shortly after being treated in this manner, the nest was dug out and the queen ant and all the others were found dead. This result seems, therefore, fairly hopeful. It might be tried on a more extended scale and the results reported. We are not, however, very sanguine of the value of this insecticide in the eradication of the pest. Thorough and cleanly agriculture should in the long run prove both more economical and more effectual. Where possible, white-ants should, in other words, be dug out, the roots of the bushes freed from their excavations and hives, and the stems and branches at the same have all mud encrustations removed. WHITE-ANTS.

678. In the *Journal of the Agri-Horticultural Society* Mr. Liotard announced that he found a few leaves of the *neem* tree buried in the ground, and drove away white-ants from his rose bushes. The Assam *bukhain* cannot be used as a substitute for it, for it does not seem to contain the active properties of the *neem*. From experiments performed some years ago we should be disposed to believe the insect may have an aversion to the latter substance. Many writers have affirmed that the fresh juice of the leaves of the American Aloe, poured on to a badly affected plot of land, will drive away white-ants. Neem tree.

679. The Commissioners in St. Helena to enquire into the subject of white-ants, experimented with some sixteen different substances sent to them from all parts of the tropical world, as being useful preventions or cures against the depredations of white-ants. Some of these may be here alluded to:—Mr. Robertson, of Ceylon, recommended sugar mixed with arsenic; another Ceylon correspondent mentioned arsenic, creosote, and bichloride of mercury; Mr. Davies, of Madras, recommended arsenic, aloes and chunam soap. Many writers spoke favourably of tobacco juice and common salt mixed, but the report may be said to have pronounced that each and every method had been tried, and none proved effectual either to check the ravages of the scourge or to protect woodwork from destruction. St. Helena experience.

680. ***Useful Preventive.***—While travelling in Kattiawar some short time ago, the attention of one of the authors was directed to a habit that prevailed in the Gondal State of painting the stems of trees to a height of 3 feet above ground with a red-looking substance. It Gondal fluid.

WHITE-ANTS. was impossible to march through the State and not be struck with these red bands. On enquiring the reason, it was asked whether white-ants could be noticed attacking the trees so painted. Throughout the States of Kattiawar white-ants are a positive calamity, as they attack and practically destroy whole avenues of trees. The red paint, whatever it consisted of, was found to be an effectual protection. In no instance were trees discovered encased with mud where the red ring was fairly visible.

681. On enquiry into the nature of the preparation used, the information was given that the red colour was due to the refuse of *Al Dye* (**Morinda citrifolia**) works or to red Ochre, but that on these its value did not really depend at all. The useful ingredients were said to be as follows:—

1 part *dekamali* gum (the resin of **Gardenia gummifera** or **G. ludica**).
2 parts asafœtida or *hingra.*
2 parts bazar aloes or *musubar.*
2 parts castor-oil cake.

Constituents. These are well pounded, mixed and kept in water for about a fortnight. When thoroughly united, and what may be called decomposed, into a thickened compound, water is added in order to bring to the consistency of paint, and the colouring matter then added.* The mixture is now ready for use, and, if thoroughly applied for about 2 feet, will check the attacks of white-ants, and many other insect pests. Its effect has been said to last for two years or more. The cost of the preparation comes to about 4 to 5 rupees per 100 trees.

From other parts of India the reputation is very general that this preparation is of great value, and the red ochre added to the above preparation may not only be useful as indicating the trees that have been painted, but give a needful consistency, if it does not serve to mechanically hold the other ingredients.

682. Since the time at which the above observations were made, a good many experiments have been carried out as to the value of the

* It is not wise for a planter to attempt to make this material himself. It will cause considerable trouble to get the first-named constituent in the tea districts, and the preparation of the mixture does not always proceed easily. The fluid can, in fact, now be bought ready made in Calcutta.

paint thus prepared against the pest we are considering, not only on tea, but also on orchard and avenue trees.

WHITE-ANTS.

Experiment at Saharanpur.

In the latter part of 1895 it was applied by the Superintendent of the Botanical Gardens, Saharanpur, to mango, *shisham*, and *siris* trees on the road side. Before applying the paint, the coating of earthy matter was removed, and up to April 1896 no further white-ants had attacked the trees. These were full size, and it cost at the rate of 3 annas 10 pies per tree, an amount which could easily, of course, be much reduced. A similar experiment in the Calcutta Botanical Gardens was equally successful.

Tea Garden results.

In the few cases in which the Gondal Fluid has been applied in tea gardens, the records have been very contradictory as to its effect. This is, of course, very probably due to its not being applied quite thoroughly, but making every deduction it seems certain that by its means bushes can be protected for at least six months after the application. In very bad cases, such as occur on the raised banks and plateaux of medium loam soil both in Assam, Cachar, and the Duars, we think that a very thorough trial is worth the attention of the planters. It is at least as effective as tar, and has not the risk of injuring the bushes which that substance undoubtedly possesses.

Bisulphide of carbon.

683. A great deal of attention has been given to this subject by Mr. Green in Ceylon, and he has there obtained the most promising results from treatment with bisulphide of carbon. The fumes of this liquid are very heavy and when pieces of tow soaked in this substance are placed at the entrances of the ant-hills and all the holes blocked up, they would sink into the ground and kill all animal life. Unfortunately being an inflammable liquid it is difficult to obtain in Ceylon at a reasonable cost,—but this should cause comparatively little difficulty here, as it is, we think, manufactured in the neighbourhood of Calcutta. Recent experiments on this insecticide, which has been often used elsewhere, with some success, for destroying phylloxera on the vine, for instance, have shown it to be very effective against white-ants. It can be recommended for trial in the Indian Tea Districts.

Summary.

684. In summary as to remedies, therefore, we believe that the most rational cure for white-ants will be found to be—

(*a*) Thorough cleanliness; by which we mean all mud deposits systematically removed, accompanied with deep and repeated hoeing.

WHITE-ANTS.

(*b*) When the bushes have been severely injured, collar-prune, though the exact point at which this is necessary, is a difficult one to decide.

(*c*) When collar-pruning has to be resorted to, it should not be above the surface of the ground.

(*d*) Heavy pruning, or collar-pruning, should be at once followed by painting all the wood, and even the exposed portions of stems and large branches with the "Gondal *Paint*," above described. Coal-tar has a strong tendency to kill the bark, a ring being formed where the tar was applied, that looks as if a rope had been tied tightly around. The tar would possibly partly protect the wood from white-ants, but it cannot be said to have no injurious effects of its own. The Gondal Paint is perfectly harmless.

(*e*) It may be possible that future experiments will show that not only is Carbon Bisulphide effective, but also that it is cheap enough to practically apply.

685. The objects of the above recommendations are based upon certain well-established facts. White-ants will not live long in localities where they are repeatedly disturbed. It is on this account that they are most destructive on young gardens and old nurseries: the natural operations of cultivation driving them from the ground. But if left alone for four or five years, they produce results that affect the whole after-life of the plant, so that they should not be regarded as a temporary plague. Exposed wood dries up, and is thus prepared for the depredations of the white-ant. By not collar pruning above ground and by the cut surface being immediately covered over with a protection the wood is not exposed to the withering and drying effects of the open atmosphere. If, further, all cut surfaces be completely coated with the Gondal Paint, the white-ants will not look at them for a considerable time.

686 The subject of white-ants has been very little studied in the past, and it would be of extreme advantage if samples of the insects, their combs and the results of their devastations could be forwarded to the Reporter on Economic Products to the Government of India, at the Indian Museum, Calcutta. For a complete examination the manager of a badly affected estate should proceed as nearly as possible in the following fashion. Let him get a small bottle, to be used for each tea bush.

The White-ants.

WHITE-ANTS.

He should proceed by carefully breaking down the earth from the branches and stems, and having 100 or so of all the insects seen in these collected and put in the bottle. He will pick the insects up without injuring them by means of a twig dipped in the spirits of wine and applied to the insects. He should then carefully remove the earth and cut a trench across the face of the ground in which the bush stands for a depth of, say, 3 feet. The trench should form a perpendicular face so as to reveal all the subterranean workings of the ant. The vertical face should then be advanced on to the bush, by cutting away a slice of 2 inches at a time. If combs are found, these should be carefully removed (or large pieces of them) and laid out on the ground to harden in the sun. Samples of the combs are necessary for a complete examination of the species. As the section is advanced, a series of all the insects found should be picked up, more especially the queens, soldiers, and others that seem different in shape, size, or colour found above ground and within the branches and stems of the tea plant as also below ground and within the combs. We have suggested that two or three affected plants should be examined, so as to make sure that all the peculiarities are examined, recorded, and specimens collected. When this has been done if the whole of the samples can be furnished, and a description of the observations be also sent, it is pretty certain that our knowledge of the Indian Termites will become rapidly more complete, and the possibility be much greater that they will be brought under complete control as agricultural pests.

Method of collecting.

CHAPTER XVII.

SPIDERS and MITES.

ARACHNOIDEA.

LXIV.—The Spiders, Mites, etc.

Difference between insects, spiders and mites.

687. We have so far dealt with those pests of tea which belong to the class **Insecta** or are true insects. The Spiders and Mites, to which the bulk of the remaining animal pests belong, differ from those so far dealt with in possessing either four (Gall-mites) or eight (**Acarinæ**) legs in the adult stage (while the true insects always have six), and by the head and thorax being fused completely together into one portion of the body. In the spiders proper, this is separated from the abdomen by a constricted portion very similar to the jointed process in wasps, but in the mites (the **Acarinæ**, to which class the so-called Red Spider belongs) this separation does not exist.

Red spider.

688. Until very recently the mite which has come to be known as "Red Spider" was the only member of the class supposed to exist on tea. The late **Mr. Wood-Mason** devoted nine months in Cachar during 1881 to the study of the Mosquito Blight and Red Spider, and in his report makes no mention of having come across any other mites, and it may perhaps be that at that time there were no others which had attacked the tea bush. In 1890, however, in his *Insect Pests of the Tea Plant* **Mr. E. E. Green** described two other species of mite (in addition to Red Spider) as met with in Ceylon. During the explorations of one of the authors (**G. W.**) in Assam in 1895, all **Mr. Green's** forms were met with, and one or two in addition. It would thus appear probable that the past 15 years or so has witnessed a great increase in the number of species of Tea Mites, as it has seen a wider distribution of the losses attributable to this series of pests.

Other mites.

TETRANYCHUS BIOCULATUS.

THE TEA RED SPIDER.

125. Tetranychus bioculatus, *Wood-Mason.*

THE TEA RED-MITE: THE RED-SPIDER.

References.—*Wood-Mason, the Tea-mite of Assam, 1884, Journ. Agri. Horti. Soc. Ind., Vol. I., n. s. Proc., 9th Sept. 1868, p. lxix (Letter by S. E. Peal forwarding specimens and drawings of "Red-Spider"); Samples were examined by Dr. Stolicska, who said it was a species of Acarina and possibly a species of Thyroglypus, Peal,*

THE RED SPIDER.

Vol. IV., p. 126; Tukvar Tea Company, Vol. VI., Proc., 19th Sept. 1878, p. xxxix; Vol. VI., p. 85; Treatment of Red Spider in Cachar in 1878; H. C. Sproull in Vol. VII., Proc., 27th Sept. 1882, p. xxiv; Proc., 30th Dec. 1885, p. cxciv; Indian Tea Association Report, 1892, p. 31; Schrottky's Articles on Agriculture (Tea Planting), 1878, pp. 31—35; Tea Cyclopædia, pp. 38–39 40, 56–66; Notes on Tea in Darjeeling, pp. 45—49; Tea Planter's Vade Mecum, pp. 100—101; Green, Insect Pests of the Tea Plant, 30—35; Baildon, Tea in Assam, p. 46; Bamber, Chemistry and Agri. of Tea, pp. 253—254; Voelcker, Report on Improvement of Indian Agriculture, p. 267; Indian Museum Notes, Vol. I., 169; II., 173; III., 26, 46—50; IV., 42; Cotes, Insects and Mites, etc., 49—56; Miles, Joun. Micro. Soc., Calcutta, Vol. IV., (1895), pp. 36–41; Christison, Darjeeling News, April 11th, 1893; Some comparative trials of Insecticide Pumps . . and Experiments in the Treatment of Red Spider-Fleet, Ind. Mus. Notes, IV., 3; Administ. Rep., Bot. Gard., Ceylon, 1899; Circ., Roy. Bot. Gardens, Ceylon, Series I., No. 17; Ind. Gardening, Mar. 8, 1900; also Vol. XX. (1901), 388.

Found in all districts.

689. ***History.***—It would seem that the presence of Red Spider on tea was discovered in Assam in 1868 by Mr. Peal shortly after his discovery of the Tea Mosquito, and he furnished specimens and drawings of the little depredator, to which he gave the name, now universally used, of Red Spider. It appeared shortly afterwards in Cachar, and a little later again in Darjeeling. Mr. Peal, in a paper which will be found in the *Tea Cyclopædia*, says that he had found it on the *kadam*, or *roghu-kadam* tree (Anthocephalus Cadamba), but whether it had gone from this to tea, or *vice versâ*, he was not able to establish. In a further passage Mr. Peal alludes to the fact that the disease may sometimes be found on one or two bushes, in the middle of an expanse of tea not affected, and from that circumstance he assumed that it was possibly carried by insects. Mr. Wood-Mason, in his scientific monograph, fully disposes of that idea. It does not belong to the groups of mites that are carried by insects.

Discovery in Assam.

Occurs on the Kadam tree.

690. In 1880 the pest had become so serious that a general request was made that an expert should be sent to the tea districts to investigate this pest, along with mosquito blight. Mr. Wood-Mason therefore spent the best part of 1881 in Cachar working at these subjects. His report did not appear till 1884, and from a scientific point of view is very valuable as definitely identifying and describing the species. Unfortunately Mr. Wood-Mason did not attempt to study the number of generations a year, nor the condition and place

Mr. Wood-Mason's mission.

The Arachnoidea.

THE RED SPIDER.

of hibernation, nor did he propose any remedial measures. From the planter's point of view his researches were, therefore, singularly devoid of practical results. And what is more surprising, we know still as little of the life history of the species during the year as at the end of Mr. Wood-Mason's deputation to Cachar twenty years ago.

Hibernation.

691. We do not know, for instance, if it hibernates in the form of an egg or in a pupal stage; we are ignorant as to where the hibernating germs are located during the inactive period; we do not know how many days the individual lives, nor the number of generations that take place in a year. Is it, therefore, to be wondered at that no progress has been made with its eradication? The European species of Red Spider, M. Duges informs us, from experiments in a garden near Paris, hibernates under stones and in shady corners within walls, and it rests in what might be called a pupal stage, not in the egg condition.

European experience.

692. ***Description.***—After the very exhaustive account of the mite published by Mr. Wood-Mason, and republished by Mr. Cotes and others, it is hardly necessary that much space should be devoted to the discussion of even the leading characteristics of this remarkable pest. To the naked eye it appears like a red speck, but under the microscope it is seen to have certain parts of different shades, the prevailing tint being scarlet. The eggs are laid in little sheltered spots on the upper surface of the leaf, such as near the mid rib or alongside of the veins. They are small spherical bodies of various shades of colour until ultimately they become red as the young are about to be hatched.

Naked eye appearance.

693. The young red spiders are at first six-footed, and Mr. Wood-Mason tells us they "do not attach themselves as parasites to the bodies of insects and spiders, as do their distant relations the Trombidiidæ, nor undergo any of these strange changes which many other mites pass through, in the course of their development, but attain to the adult condition by a simple change of skin that usually, though not perhaps invariably, is made on the same leaf as that on which they emerged as larvæ from the egg. The shells of the hatched eggs remain glued to the leaf for some time as microscopically small objects resembling porcelain saucers."

Young red spider.

694. The skins thrown off by the larvæ also remain attached to the leaf as white specks dispersed over the surface of the invaded leaf.

Larval skins.

The Red Spider.

695. The males are considerably smaller than the females, and pointed at the anal extremity. They live together in colonies, the vast majority of each colony being females. The upper surface of the leaf is enveloped in a fine web that is rendered visible in the early morning, through the coating of dew upon it. This, as Mr. Wood-Mason originally suggested, is formed as a protection against slight showers of rain. When destroyed by heavy rain, the mites are doubtless swept away and killed, but the pest reappears again with the first bright warm day, owing to the eggs not being destroved by rain, however severe. Time after time the mites may be killed by rain and still the pest returns, and this will continue until all the eggs that exist have been hatched. But should the intervals between the showers not suffice to allow of a new supply of eggs being laid, the pest will in time be entirely destroyed. It is on this account that, with the establishment of the monsoons, the pest, as a rule, gradually disappears, but with insufficient rain or long intervals of dry weather the mites may be enabled to exist practically throughout the year.

THE RED SPIDER.

Effect of rain.

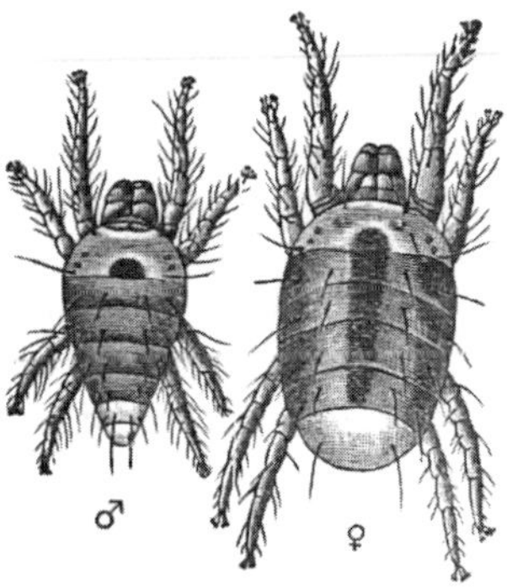

FIG. 40.—THE RED SPIDER.
Left.—male, right.—female, both much enlarged.
(After Cotes.)

696. We have learnt nothing as yet about the methods of hibernation of the Indian species of Red Spider. Whether like the European species it spends its resting stage in a so-called pupal condition, or whether there always remain sufficient individuals left in the active condition to pass on enough to originate the attack of another year we do not know. All experience seems to indicate that their hiding place is in the bark of the bushes, from which they come out when conditions are favourable.

Hibernation.

697. ***Depredations.***—The mite injures the tea by withdrawing the sap, by means of its "pharyngeal pump with which it, like all other arachnids, is provided." At first the leaves look mottled light and dark green, but in time the punctured portions turn brown and

Sucks out the sap.

The Arachnoidea.

THE RED SPIDER.

the leaves assume a bronzed, dry, crumpled appearance and, when badly injured, fall off the bushes.

A spring pest.

698. Red spider is essentially a pest of the spring, in other words, of the dry hot months. It appears, first of all, on the old mature leaves on the lower and outer circumference of the bush. In time it gradually ascends and invades the whole bush, and thus checks completely the flushing. As already remarked, it very often commences near the coolie lines, and spreads along the roadsides, or accompanies the direction of the main open and dry drains, and in such a manner as to suggest that it may possibly be distributed from its point of seasonal origin by the clothes of the coolies. Mr. Wood-Mason says: "The tea mite, so far as I have been able to make out, usually first affects small patches consisting of a few bushes, whence it rapidly extends over the whole or a large part of a garden. It always seemed to consist of numerically larger and more active societies on the bushes of very old gardens, from which it never appeared to be entirely absent, as vigorous societies were to be obtained therefrom as often as I wanted fresh material for my observation."* Mr. Bamber remarks that, though the bushes near the coolie lines are almost certain to be first attacked, these bushes are rarely seen to suffer much from the effects of the blight, as the soil is always in good condition, and they are accordingly able to throw off the effects of the attack. "Where the soil is in poorer condition, the bushes are far more affected, the older leaves assuming a dry hard appearance and character, by which absorption of atmospheric food is largely prevented, and the bushes cease to flush." Mr. Green remarks: "An attack of red spider does not immediately affect the existing flush. The insect feeds only upon the older leaves. But from the continued visitation, and the loss of sap imbibed by the insects, the leaves become dry and curled; cease to perform their proper functions; and in bad cases fall off, thus weakening the whole tree." "The pest is most injurious during the dry weather. Although light showers do not interfere with its habits, it seems unable to withstand continued and heavy rain, and at such times can only

May be distributed by coolies' clothes.

Effect of soil.

* That remark may be accepted as having reference to the term of Mr. Wood-Mason's residence in Cachar, *viz.*, from March to November 1881.

exist in sheltered spots. Trees growing under overhanging rocks afford strongholds for the pest during the rainy season."

Prepares for grey-blight.

699. In one respect the attack of the red spider itself on a garden is the least of its injurious effects, for there remains little doubt that it hardens the leaves which it attacks to such an extent as to bring them just into the condition most suitable for the development of grey blight—an attack of which almost invariably follows a bad dose of red spider. We noticed this especially in the Darjeeling district, but the close connection of these two blights can be traced almost everywhere.

Remedies.

700. ***Remedies.***—There have been two recognised methods of palliating, if not of thoroughly dealing with this pest. The first of these is by varying the season and manner of pruning, the second by the use of insecticides. The influence of *jat* is recognised, but it cannot be regarded as a method of dealing with the blight, because, once planted, it is out of the range of practical politics to think about the uprooting and replanting of a garden on account of red spider. But in planting out a new property the susceptibility or otherwise of a jat is a matter which ought to be considered in choosing seed, and in this respect probably "Manipuri" and the allied types are the least attacked, "Assam" indigenous the next, while "Hybrid" and "China" bushes are most affected.

Influence of Jat.

Effect of heavy pruning.

701. ***Influence of Pruning-Heavy pruning.***—The most diverse opinions have been recorded as following heavy pruning. Thus, for example Mr. Green writes: "A well-known planter of great experience tells me that he has repeatedly noticed that a bad attack of red-spider follows a few months after heavy pruning. In one case it was particularly noticeable, when a small patch in the middle of a field was pruned, while the rest was allowed to run up. A few months after, this very patch looked quite purple against the rich green of the surrounding tea, the boundary being abruptly marked by the difference of tint." A planter whose opinions are published by Mr. Cotes (in *Insects and Mites, etc., p. 56*) says: "Red-spider does not attack heavy-pruned tea as a rule." *The Tea Cyclopædia* says: "It has been noticed that, in cases where plants were cut down almost to the ground, and the prunings burnt, and buried in the form of ash, the pest appeared on the new growth. Heavy or light pruning seems to make little difference."

Contradictory results.

The Arachnoidea.

THE RED SPIDER.

Season of pruning.

702. The season of the year at which pruning is accomplished would appear, however, to exercise a distinct influence. The following passages from letters by planters in the *Tea Cyclopædia* may be taken as expressive of the usually accepted views: "I noticed the spider commenced on the garden first pruned, and seemed to attack each garden in the order it was pruned." Another planter says: "If planters would only delay their pruning for a few weeks longer after the flush has stopped, they would find that the blight does not make its appearance so rapidly as usual." Here is another excellent example: "About the middle of December 1876 a section of the garden was pruned, and about the middle of February 1877, the adjoining field was pruned; the former was red with spider in 1877, while the latter was quite green. I attribute the attack of these spiders to early plucking as much as to early pruning. In 1878 both these patches were pruned about the end of January, and both were well covered with spiders." The Cachar planter, whose views were published by Mr. Cotes, speaks of red-spider appearing first upon the early pruned tea. An Assam planter (*l. c., p. 56*) says: "In connection with red-spider, it may be of interest to you to note that this blight rarely, if ever, attacks bushes pruned after the last week in March. For three years I have kept small plots of bushes unpruned till the last week of March, and this year I have kept some 30 acres unpruned till after the third week of March, the difference of the plots so treated being now very marked; that portion of same plot, early pruned, being more or less covered with blight, and the later pruned throwing out shoots without a sign of blight." Still another writer says: "I am of opinion that late pruning—not before the first week in April preferably—will be found the best remedy or rather preventive for this blight; the bushes liable to it will probably get the blight on them before they are pruned, but the pruning will remove a good deal, and the bush will throw out shoots straight away without a check."

Late pruning keeps off the blight.

Experiments in Ceylon.

Experiments on the effect of varying the time of pruning are being carried out in Ceylon, and though the results, we understand, are most promising, they are not yet published. Mr. Green has informed us, however, that they tend to show that April pruning gives the best results as regards freedom from Tea Mites of all kinds. In India there remains little doubt that if it is wished to avoid the pest in

THE RED SPIDER.

question pruning should be delayed as long as possible. It may be that by this method the hibernating mites become fixed on the very parts which are removed, and distribution by shaking off the bushes in pruning when the active mite is upon them is avoided.

Explanation of effect of late pruning.

703. The effect of late pruning in reducing the pest may also be explained in another way if it be accepted as correct that the pest is mainly distribued by the clothes of the coolies. Late pruned tea (*i.e.*, pruned in March or April) would not begin to flush, until the period of chief distribution of the pest had been passed. Not being much visited by the pluckers before June, late pruned tea would stand a chance of escaping contamination, and if contaminated at the time of first plucking, the pest would soon thereafter be checked by the establishment of the monsoons. But this explanation of necessity almost presupposes that the pest does not hibernate on the bushes of plots that are annually invaded, and that it has to be brought to them. Finding in the plots annually invaded more favourable conditions than in the other portions of the estate, the pest annually develops there first and spreads to the other portions of the estate later. If the pest hibernates on the bushes, we should have to look for another explanation to account for its not at once starting on the unpruned tea in March and April. Pruning with the pest in activity should only more thoroughly distribute the germs over the later pruned plot itself, and possibly also carry the pest over the remaining portions of the estate.

Plant sap and red spider.

704. Still another explanation has been offered for the palliating result of late pruning. The impetus to renewed activity on the part of the pest may be dependent on the ascent of the plant sap. This would presuppose that the insect hibernates on the plant. But if this statement can be demonstrated as a fact, then it would not be difficult to believe that pruning is a direct agent in originating or rather expediting the ascent of the sap, so that late pruning would mean a delay in the date of commencement of the ascending current. Were that so, it would be easy to account for the advantage observable, for the plant would be carried nearer the date of the bursting of the monsoon before being dangerously invaded. It may on this line of reasoning be stated that the later date of the ascending sap in the higher jat Assam and Manipuri Indigenous teas accounts partially, at any rate, for their comparative immunity from the pest.

The Arachnoidea.

THE RED SPIDER.

705. Whatever theory be the correct one, there is now such a body of opinion that a very large amount of reduction in the seriousness of this blight can be made by late pruning, that one may consider the matter as almost beyond doubt. This being the case, every advantage should be taken of the discovery, especially as, for other reasons, we have shown (Chapter VI) that late pruning is much to be preferred.

Conf. with para. 155.

Insecticides.

706. ***Use of Insecticides.***—The honour of having effectively introduced the use of insecticides as methods of dealing with Red Spider belongs undoubtedly to Mr. G. W. Christison, the Superintendent, until lately, of the Lebong Tea Company, Darjeeling, who first utilised "Sulphur" as a dressing on the gardens under his management. In the early days such methods as covering the bushes with muddy water were used, but it was found that, though it killed the mature spiders, it was altogether useless against the eggs. Lime also dusted or whitewashed over the branches and the stems, shortly after pruning, has been strongly advocated by many Assam planters, but this, as a method actually in use, has also disappeared. Though an infusion of **Adhatoda vasica** is instantly fatal to red spider, it has also had the disadvantage that the eggs are not injured, and to a certain extent the same remark applies to the infusion of wild fern used in Dibrugarh. It should always be remembered in connection with this class of pests, that they are far less sensitive to chemicals than other insects. The eggs especially have a very dense cuticle, so as to render them quite impervious to the chemical action of insecticides.

Sulphur Lime.

Adhatoda Vasica.

Sulphur the most valuable.

707. The use of Sulphur stands on an altogether different level from the methods just reviewed. Mr. Christison originally described his method as follows: "My process of application is simple and inexpensive. We put sulphur in gauze bags of open texture, and after wetting the bushes thoroughly over and under the leaves, and the branches and stem, the sulphur is dusted over the whole bush by shaking the bag with its contents over it. With a dry spell of weather and no wind the garden will remain yellow for weeks, which is most desirable."

Expense.

708. The objection to the sulphur treatment, as recommended by Mr. Christison, is its needless expense. He estimated the cost as about R20 to R25 per acre, a large part of which was incurred

THE RED SPIDER.

for wetting the bushes. Others, however, have put the cost much lower. Mr. Cotes quotes a Cachar planter who only spent R8-4 per acre and got an increased yield of 11 lbs. made tea per acre per month as a result.

Economies.

Since then further economies have been introduced, and now the cost should not much exceed R5 per acre. These economies consist in—

(1) No need to damp bush.

(1) avoiding the costly damping of the bushes by utilising the dew which is almost always present in the early morning. The sulphuring coolies are sent out at daybreak when the bushes are more thoroughly wet than by any damping they could get artificially, and the sulphur sprinkled on as Mr. Christison recommends, the process being continued until the dew begins to rise and leave the leaves dry.

(2) Sulphur can be reduced in quantity.

(2) reduction in the amount of sulphur. We believe that originally 1½ maunds per acre were used,—now half a maund is considered ample, and a good many planters use less. Half a maund per acre may be considered as a standard dressing in a flat district, if only the sulphur is in good condition and finely enough divided, for the lightest dusting seems as effective as a heavy coating of the leaves. Taking 150 rupees per ton as the price of sulphur *on the garden* in Assam, we have thus about R3 per acre as cost of material, which allows R2 as the cost of labour.

(3) Only spray alternate rows.

(3) only spraying alternate rows. Thus modification was, we believe, introduced by Mr. G. Grant Gordon at the Teesta Valley Company's gardens, and from what we have seen of it the effect seems almost, if not quite, as good as if all the bushes had been treated. The reason for this is probably that there is sufficient sulphur blown on to the untreated rows during the operation of sulphuring to kill the red-spider.

Must stay on leaves three days.

709. It is usually put on as soon as the blight appears. Fine weather is essential and the sulphur should remain on the bush for at least three days to secure the best results. The reason for this is that although the adult red spider is killed within 24 hours of the application, the eggs are quite unaffected, and it is only when they hatch out that the sulphur has a chance to exert its poisonous action.

The Arachnoidea.

THE RED SPIDER.

It was suggested some time ago to use the sulphur immediately after pruning so as to destroy the mites in its hibernating stage when they are probably few in number. This was tried in 1900 on a garden in Assam, but the effect was not satisfactory and did not prevent the pest to anything like the extent obtained by the more usual method. It is, however, worthy of further trial.

Effect of sulphur.

710. And now as to the effect. Mr. Christison, in a letter in the Colonial and Indian Mail, wrote as follows:—

> "In regard to red spider I have had at least fifteen years' sad experience in battling against it. The soil of the gardens I managed seemed predisposed to this blight and favourable to its propagation, and I could not imagine any gardens to be worse with it than they were for years. From 1880 to 1885 this pest was in fact a dreadful scourge; but it has been practically overcome by sulphur. After having applied sulphur in quantities of 3 to 20 tons annually since 1880, the effectual cure of red spider, at a moderate cost per acre, is with me no longer a matter of opinion, but something that has in my own experience been successfully achieved. It has also to be taken into account that the sulphur not only proves a remedy for the Red-spider, but for many soils a valuable manure."

One of the largest users of Sulphur in Assam wrote to us last year,—"It is very rare that a recrudescence of the disease takes place after one application of sulphur,"—and many more similar remarks might be quoted.

Treatment with sulphur in Europe.

The treatment of red spider and other mites with sulphur has been pursued in Europe and America for a very long time, and it may be said that sulphur is a specific against nearly all mites. Now that the cost has been reduced to practical limits, we think that its use is indicated wherever red spider is a serious pest; at any rate until careful study of the life history of the spider has revealed a more satisfactory method of dealing with it.

Supposed manurial value.

711. A great deal (*vide* Mr. Christison's letter above quoted) has been made of the supposed manurial value of the sulphur. There is no doubt, apart from the removal of the blight, apparently a great increase in vigour of sulphur-treated bushes, and this has led to the idea that in adding it, one was adding a valuable plant food. This is, however, quite false, and the manurial effect merely consists of a stimulating action on the bush, probably working through the leaves—which though very valuable can in no sense replace proper manuring when the soil is exhausted.

The Scarlet Mite.

712. Chiswick Soap, which we understand is a combination of Sulphur and Soap, syringed on the bushes was introduced some years ago to try and get the well known insecticide effect of soap along with that of sulphur. It has been much used in Cachar, and with good effect,—clearing the red spider as well as sulphur does. It is, however, somewhat more expensive, and unless further experiments show, as seems probable, that it will be effective against mosquito blight, it possesses no advantages over sulphur. **THE SCARLET MITE. Chiswick soap.**

713. It may perhaps be understood that it is the expense and difficulty to deal with a million or more bushes simultaneously that is the chief drawback to insecticide treatment, when once a pest, such as red-spider, has taken a firm hold of an estate. But it has no right to be allowed to obtain that supremacy. The insecticide materials and appliances should be at hand and used promptly on first appearance. Accidental visitations would thereby be at once checked. But until we are in possession of the full facts of the life of each pest, as also of the physical, chemical and vital influences that check or foster that development, we are not in a position to deal with them satisfactorily. **Drawbacks to insectiside treatment.**

126. Brevipalpus obovatus, *Donnadieu.*

THE NEW RED SPIDER; THE SCARLET MITE.

References.—*Donnadieu—Recherches pour servir a l' Hist. des Tetranyques, Paris, 1875; Circ., Roy. Bot. Gardens, Ceylon, 1900, No. 17.*

Found in Assam and Ceylon.

714. This mite, as a pest of tea, was discovered by one of the authors (G. W.) at Borpukhuri in 1895, and has been identified under the above name. It was afterwards found at several other gardens in Bishnauth and Nowgong, and since that time has done considerable damage in Ceylon. **Found in Assam.**

It is in many respects very similar to the common Red Spider only considerably smaller and of a more uniform scarlet colour with a soft woolly appearance. It was universally found feeding on the *under* surface of the leaf (instead of the upper), and it spun a small web near the base of the leaf to which it ran for protection. The larva, which was presumed to belong to this form, was seen to be at first quite transparent, but gradually to obtain two circular red spots one on either side of the rounded and swollen **Compared with red spider. Larva.**

THE SCARLET MITE.

body,—otherwise the larva was quite colourless. They had six legs, while the adult form had, like the ordinary red-spider, eight.

On high jat plants.

715. This form lives on the finer *jat* plants and on the young leaves, the third to the fifth (from the bud) never upon the old lower leaves. Instead of becoming bronzed, the leaves turn at first pale-coloured, almost white, but in time the base and margin, corresponding approximately to the portion over which the web is spread, withers, changes colour, and finally turns dark brown. The flushing stops entirely, and a very unhealthy appearance of bush supervenes.

In Ceylon, Mr. Green says of its effect :—

In Ceylon.

"Apparently a very injurious pest. The branches and whole bushes are almost denuded of leaves, the bark shrivelled and hidebound. The terminal buds have ceased growing. In some instances the trees have been actually killed. The mites are crowded on the under surface of the leaves, and their attack results in a brownish scurfy discolouration extending along the midrib and on each side of it, causing its premature detachment."

The pest has not yet spread far in the Indian Tea Districts, but is still causing considerable damage on one at least of the gardens on which it was originally observed. From samples received it seems likely that this pest has also appeared in Sibsagar.

Remedies.

716. ***Remedy.***—This is not a pest to be overlooked, and every effect should be made to stamp it out. Syringe the bushes with infusion of **Adhatoda vasica** or weak soap and kerosene emulsion, or better than either, treat with sulphur when the dew is on the bush as for red spider. In a recent note **Mr. Green** makes the following valuable remark : "If the mite passes its resting stage in crevices of the bark, the kerosene emulsion treatment, as suggested for **Helopeltis**, immediately after pruning, ought to be successful in eradicating this pest also."

TARSONYMUS TRANSLUCENS. THE YELLOW MITE.

127. Tarsonymus translucens, *Green.*

THE YELLOW-MITE ; "THE APPLE-FOLIAGE BLIGHT."

References.—*Tea Cyclopædia, 41 (?) ; Green, Insect Pests of the Tea Plant (with figure), p. 40 ; Ind. Mus. Notes, II., 173 ; III. (pt. 4), 57 ; Madras Weekly Mail, Aug. 3, 1899 ; Green, Report for 1898 ; Green, Circ., Roy. Bot. Gardens, Ceylon, March, 1900, p. 200.*

Found probably in all districts.

Serious pest in Ceylon.

717. ***History.***—This part of tea, a mite very much smaller than the red spider, and, indeed, microscopic in character, was discovered by Mr. Green on those gardens in Ceylon in which the bushes were

The Yellow Mite.

known as sulky. So struck was he by the damage which it is capable of doing that he considered it as one of the worst tea pests present in the island. **THE YELLOW MITE.**

Its discovery in India dates from the visit of one of the authors (G. W.) to Assam in 1895, and though the proof of the identity of the cause of the affection in Assam and Ceylon is not complete, yet there is no longer any room for doubt as to the Assam plants being destroyed by a very closely allied mite to that met with in Ceylon. Since that time the same condition of the bushes has been met with in several other Indian districts. **Discovery in Assam.**

718. ***Description.***—The following descriptive account of the form met with in Ceylon will be of interest to Indian planters:— **Description in Ceylon.**

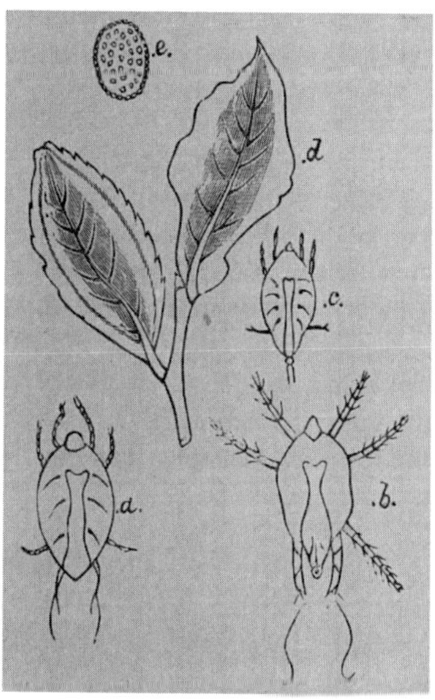

FIG. 41.—THE YELLOW MITE.

a. Yellow mite, female, magnified; *b.* Male, magnified; *c.* Larva, magnified: *d* Tea leaves, underside, showing injury, from mite; *e.* Egg, highly magnified.

(After Green.)

"This species," says Mr. Green, "feeds on the flush: the living insects can be found only upon the bud and the under sides of the two following leaves. As each bud opens, the colony moves higher up, deserting the older leaves. But these latter are permanently injured, and always retain the marks of the disease. The distinguishing sign is a roughened surface and brown stain extending for some way on each side of the midrib; sometimes covering the whole of the under side of the leaf, but generally confined to the central portion. Sometimes again, these is a brown crease between the margin of the leaf and the central diseased part looking like a supplementary rib on each side of the median one. This crease results from the attacks of the mite upon the unopened bud, while then edges of the leaf are still folded inwards. The diseased leaves never attain their full size; they lose their natural gloss, become hard and puckered, and give an unhealthy appearance to the whole bush that is very noticeable. After a prolonged attack, the bush becomes smaller and smaller with little spaces between the leaves; and finally the tree refuses to put out flushing shoots." **Appearance of leaves.**

The Arachnoidea.

THE YELLOW MITE.

"The individual insects are so minute as to be invisible without the aid of a magnifying glass. Under a good microscope they may be distinguished, in all stages, crowded upon the youngest leaves at the tip of the shoot."

Young mite.

"The young mite has only six legs and is of a sluggish disposition. It is of a very pale-yellow colour with clouded whitish stripe along the middle of the back. It seems to undergo only one moult before assuming the perfect stage."

Adult female.

"The adult female is of a clear amber colour, with a smooth glistening skin, and with a clouded dorsal stripe, as in its larval stage. It has now an additional pair of legs, but this fourth pair is carried, apparently, more for show than use. They are much thinner than the others, and terminate in two bristles of unequal length."

Male.

"The male is so unlike both the young and the adult females that I should have thought it to be a distinct species had I not myself witnessed its transformation from the larval stage. It is of the same colour as the female, with the same clouded dorsal stripe, but it is of a very different build. Its legs are more powerfully developed. The hindermost pair, though not used in locomotion, are stouter than the others, and probably act as clasping organs. They are armed with a strong curved tooth on the inner margin, and a long whip-like bristle on the foot.

Appearance of bush.

719. ***Depredations.***—Owing to its microscopic nature, few planters probably ever see the pest which does the damage. This latter is, however, sufficiently obvious. A bush, for instance, will be seen here and there in April and May which presents a contrast to the rest of the plot by being covered with dark green foliage through not having started to grow from the time of being pruned, while the others round about are covered with their new spring shoots. Closer attention will show the leaves crumpled on the upper surface, while on the under surface, near the midrib and for some distance on either side, they are coated with a brownish red tomentum that gives them the soft woolly appearance of the spring foliage of the apple-tree. The general appearance of the bush cannot be better expressed than by the Ceylon term "Sulky."

Such a bush usually makes no attempt to flush till July at the earliest, or perhaps not till August or September and even then the quantity of leaf obtained is very small. It is probable that bushes once affected never recover, but get worse and worse until finally they are killed; and it seems possible that the blight is responsible for a large number of the vacancies occurring over most gardens. One very striking peculiarity, which has been noticed both in Assam and Ceylon, is the fact that the disease does not originate from a common centre. A bush here and another there may be affected without apparently having anything in common. It is certainly more prevalent in old, than in

Increasing in amount.

The Yellow Mite.

new, gardens, and unhealthy, rather than healthy, bushes; but is found on seedlings in the nursery, on China bushes, on hybrid bushes, and on the finest Assam indigenous. All alike are liable to this visitation without there being afforded the slightest indication of any means of communication from the one to the other. **THE YELLOW MITE.**

720. ***Remedy.***—Mr. Green says: "I consider this 'Yellow Tea-mite' to be one of the most serious pests we have to deal with. Protected as it is by the downy hair that clothes the under surface of the young leaves, it is unaffected by heavy rain and continues its ravages uninterruptedly throughout the year. As it is confined to the flush, the persistent plucking of every shoot on such diseased trees, ought to remove the cause of the disease. The flush is usually so hard and *banjhi* that it is apt to be passed over by the pluckers. After pruning one of these "Sulky" trees, the prunings should be at once removed and destroyed. In fact, I think the systematic destruction of all prunings *while still green*,—either by burning them *in situ*,—or by removing and burning them, would of itself prove an immense check to the insect pests of all kinds." **Most serious in Ceylon.** **Burning. Prunings when green.**

721. In the Indian tea districts, the mite does not seem to be active during the whole year. It has not been likely that we shall be able to treat it by altering the time of pruning, as is possible in Ceylon, for this would mean very possibly delaying that operation till August, and it might then prove fatal to the bush. The recommendation of Mr. Green to carry off and burn on the spot all the prunings should be rigorously carried out on all affected bushes.

722. Two methods of treatment have been recommended in the past. The first is to collar prune the bushes and at once burn the prunings, the second to fire the affected bushes not later than March. The latter method has been most used, and where the bushes had not been too much damaged by the blight, or the burning had not been done at an unsuitable time, the effect has been very satisfactory, and the mite is certainly removed entirely. Such burning should never be done when the sap is circulating freely. **Collar pruning.** **Burning bushes.**

723. A comparative test of burning and collar pruning was carried out some years ago at Ligri Pukri by Mr. J. A. Thomson. His report on the result was as follows:—

"The apple-foliage blight experiments are going on all right. The plants that were burnt sprouted away much faster than those collar pruned, **Experiment.**

The Arachnoidea.

THE YELLOW MITE.

and the shoots are strong and show no signs of disease, but if the plant required collar pruning at any rate, I would prefer to use the saw and only burn those that had been collar pruned already. I burnt bushes that had been collar pruned some years ago all over the garden, here and there, and the result is very satisfactory, I fancy that the ashes from the stuff for burning acts as a manure. The bushes neither pruned nor burned, are just managing to live, but have not given a single leaf fit to make tea."

On the other hand, information to hand from Assam recently seems to indicate that collar-pruning is not very satisfactory after all. A planter writes : "Dr. Watt suggested collar-pruning. This I did last season, but many bushes have thrown up with the leaves showing the blight."

Sulphur.

724. These methods, even if successful, are very drastic, and we should be glad if a method involving less destruction could be found. Sulphur is a specific for mites if only it can come in contact with the offender. Whether it is, as a matter of practice, effective in this case, can only be determined by experiments, but it is certainly worth a trial, applied in the same manner as for red spider.

THE CACHAR STALK-KILLING MITE.

Occurrence.

128. The Cachar Stalk-killing Mite.

725. During the past two years, and apparently on some occasions before, there appeared in Cachar a blight which has caused considerable anxiety, and which has received, unfortunately, the local name of "Sulky Blight." In 1901, when it was brought to our notice, it was almost confined to the North Bank of the Barak, but extended from North Cachar on the west to the extreme east of the Lakhipur district. It has been much confused with green-fly (or thrip, as it is incorrectly called in the district), but is really quite distinct.

Destroys green shoots.

726. The cause of the affection appears to be a microscopic mite of the same type as the red spider, but colourless and much smaller. It seemed to abound in 1901 in immense numbers in April to July owing to the dry spring of that year, and then lived on the leaves, chiefly on the undersides, and a sure accompaniment of its presence consists in injury to the leaf in two (or more) streaks, one (or more) of which was found on each side of the midrib, and parallel to it. It is not, however, on the leaf that the serious damage is done. At some stage of its life (though at what stage, we are at present ignorant) it leaves the leaf and goes down either to its base or to the junction of two green shoots, and there causes a deep depression in

the shoot. The result is that, in self-defence, the stalk develops a mass of corky tissue at this point, the free circulation of the sap is prevented, and the shoot dies down to the point where it is injured by the mite, which is usually found in the hole which it has made. Our knowledge is, however, very imperfect on the subject, and this description is made from an examination of an insufficient number of specimens for us to be sure on many points. The mite is in many respects very similar to the "Sulky" Blight last described, but is of a much more epidemic character than the latter when conditions are favourable, and its shape and action are not by any means the same. THE CACHAR STALK-KILLING MITE.

727. Our knowledge of the mite and its effect is too fragmentary as yet to allow remedies to be more than suggested. There are, however, two points of importance in dealing with all mites. First, they never flourish in wet weather, and it seems they are all destroyed by sulphur, if they can only be reached by this substance. The danger of the blight is therefore almost entirely in the spring before the rains, and in actual practice it quickly disappears with the onset of the monsoon. Further, if the sulphur treatment for red spider be adopted in March and April, at a cost of not more than 5 rupees per acre, it is very probable, though not yet certain, that it will also destroy the activity of the blight in question. Experiment on this point and indeed on the whole history of this pest is, however, much needed. Knowledge fragmentary.

129. Phytoptus carinatus, *Green.* PHYTOPTUS CARINATUS.

THE FIVE-RIBBED TEA MITE; THE PURPLE AND WHITE MITE. THE FIVE-RIBBED TEA MITE.

References.—*Green, Insect Pests of the Tea Plant, 35; Ind. Mus. Notes II., 173; III (4), 56; Circ., Roy. Bot. Gardens, Ceylon, March, 1900, p. 199.*

Found in Assam, Darjeeling, Duars, and Ceylon.

728. ***History.***—This mite like so many other pests was first discovered in Ceylon by Mr. Green, and he met with it in the nursery as well as on the plants in the tea estate generally. One of the authors (G. W.) first noticed it in Assam in 1895, and since that time it has been found doing very considerable damage in India, more especially in the Duars.

The Arachnoides.

THE PURPLE MITE.

Smaller than red spider.

729. ***Description.***—This mite is very much smaller than red-spider, and can only be seen by the aid of a lens. It feeds on the upper and under surface of the leaf, and there appears to be some evidence that it is more common on the under surface in the resting stage, and on the upper surface in the active or dangerous stage,—at any rate in Darjeeling. It is found more especially along the ribs and margins of the leaf.

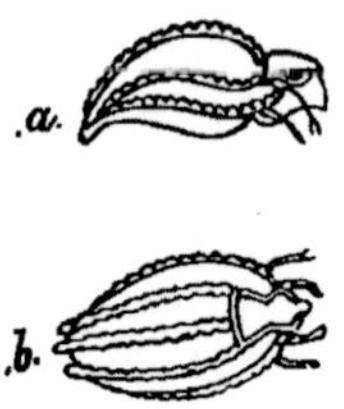

FIG. 42.—THE PURPLE MITE.

a. Side view; *b.* Back view.

(After Green.)

Description.

"The eggs are unknown.* The young mites are greenish, semi-transparent, pear shaped, tapering to a point behind. The white ridges which characterize the full grown insect are hardly perceptible in the young stage, but become more prominent after each successive moult. The adult mite is a dull purple-coloured insect with five white ridges of a waxy material running along the back; and a similar ridge surrounds an hour-glass shaped space in the front of the body. These waxy ridges are secreted by the insect, and are soluble in spirits of wine. . . . There is a sucker at the extremity of the body which assists in locomotion and acts as a prehensile organ. The insect can erect itself until its body stands upright, using the caudal sucker only to retain its hold on the leaf." (*Green.*)

* One of the authors (G. W.) has made observations which may indicate the position and nature of the eggs. The following is his description (from the first edition of this work) of what was noticed by him: "Certain leaves seem to be especially set apart for the purpose of breeding. On the under surface of these leaves will be found numerous thickened patches like little warts. On looking through the leaf, these are seen as transparent, pale coloured spots. . . On careful examination they will be found to be cavernous formations within the tissue, just below the epidermis, and contain what I take to be the eggs of the purple mite. Apparently the mites on escaping from these blisters or wart like houses wander off to other leaves to feed; and it would seem that on moulting they congregate under the shelter of the veins on the upper surface. As a consequence the upper surface of the leaves, even to the naked eye, appear as if dusted along the line of the veins with very minute particles of pure white powder. These are the cast-off skins, which, in badly affected leaves, may be seen in thousands upon thousands. But I never came across, though I looked carefully over many samples, a warted or blistered leaf bearing also the powdery deposit of cast-off skins. In the supply sent me from the Duars, there might be perhaps one in ten of the leaves warted and devoid of the powdery deposit."

The Purple Mite.

THE PURPLE MITE.

Conf. with paras. 733-739.

730. ***Depredations.***—The effect of this blight is to give a bronze appearance to the leaves as if sunburnt, but they retain their shape. From appearance of the leaf alone it is often difficult to distinguish the attack from that of "pink-mite" (*q. v.*) which indeed often occur with it. "If closely examined, the leaves are seen to be thickly dashed with very minute white specks, the cast-off skins of the insects." (*Green.*)

Assam Jat most attacked.

In the Duars, where the attack has been most serious, it has attacked every type and age of plant. But the Manipuri jat seems less affected than the Assam indigenous. Though hindered by the advent of the rains, it is by no means removed as red spider is, and its effect more or less continues throughout the plucking season, though June seems the worst month. At this time the affected leaves fall off the bushes wholesale, and give the bushes a thin appearance which is the very opposite of luxuriance. The result is an immediate decrease of leaf, and what is even more important, the bush itself is injured by the absence of its feeding organs, and a so-called hide-bound condition results, causing heavy pruning to be necessary at an earlier date than otherwise. In the Chulsa district of the Duars it has obtained, quite wrongly, the common name of "Blister Blight," to which it really has no resemblance whatever.

Worse in June.

Makes the bush hide-bound.

Conf. with paras. 779-787.

It has been suggested that the mite was imported from Assam to the Duars in the soil used to pack seed. This is unlikely, but may possibly have been the case.

Treatment with kerosene or phenyle.

731. ***Remedy.***—All mites succumb very rapidly to a treatment with kerosene or phenyle. Mr. Green recommends "one part of kerosene emulsion to eighty parts of water, or one of phenyle to two hundred and forty parts of water." "The nurseries should be watered with the mixture in the evening and with pure water in the following morning, unless rain should have fallen during the night. This treatment would not altogether exterminate the insects, as some of them are sheltered beneath the leaves, but it would probably prove a wholesome check to many insect pests in the nursery. But after being pulled for planting the plants might be dipped in buckets of the mixture, which would certainly free them and give a fair start in the field. The stem and leaves only should be dipped, not the roots."

The Arachnoidea.

THE PURPLE MITE.

Treat at commencement of attack.

732. A dangerous visitation, such as has appeared in the Duars, should at the commencement of the outbreak be treated with kerosene emulsion and water, or an infusion of **Adhatoda vasica.** Every bush should be thoroughly syringed two or three times at intervals say of one week. At the pruning season all withered leaves should be carefully cleared off the bushes, and the whole plant thoroughly painted over with the emulsion and water. In this way it seems likely the return of the pest during the ensuing spring would be averted.

Sulphur should be tried.

As an alternative, and, if successful, a much simpler, method we should suggest the application of sulphur at the same manner and time as for red-spider.

PHYTOPTUS THEÆ. THE PINK MITE.

130. Phytoptus theæ, *Watt.*

THE PINK-MITE.

Reference—*Circ., Roy. Bot. Gardens, Ceylon, March, 1900, P. 203.*

Found in Assam, Cachar, Darjeeling, and Duars.

733. The pink mite was discovered in Assam in 1895. The following is the description of the conditions which led to its detection, as published by one of the authors (G. W.).

Dr. Watt's description of discovery.

"During my explorations in 1895, through the chief tea districts of Assam, I was taken to a clump of tea supposed to be badly attacked by green fly. Instead, however, of the leaves being dark green, erect and folded or crinkled in the peculiar manner said to be characteristic of green fly, they were very pale coloured, almost white, dry, convex above, with the margins and veins of a pink colour. In what could at once be seen as an advanced stage, the leaves were almost bronzed, from the extension of the pink tinge over larger portions of the leaves, but they did not appear to wither and fall off the bush.

"A little examination sufficed to reveal these plants as suffering from a pest with which I was then unfamiliar, but which was clearly quite distinct from green-fly. Under the lens the leaves were observed to be covered with thousands of a very minute mite which, in the adult state, was of a pink colour, hence the pink tinge to the leaves. These mites were further noted to be most abundant on the margin and along the lines of the veins. Though very abundant on the upper surface of the leaves, they were also found below. But it was curious to observe that about one in every hundred or so was of an entirely different shape, and of a purple colour. The latter I subsequently identified as a distinct species,* though met with in association with the pink mite. The association of two or more minute pests together is one of those extremely difficult problems that seem almost incomprehensible. This is peculiarly

* **Phytoptus carinatus,** *Green. See para. 728.*

The Pink Mite.

THE PINK MITE.

troublesome in the study of scale insects and mites, in which very nearly invariably two species are found in intimate association and have repeatedly been mistaken as the males and females of one species instead of being two entirely distinct forms."

In Cachar, Duars and Darjeeling.

Since this time it has been found as a serious pest in Cachar and the Duars, and to certain extent in Darjeeling, where we have seen one of the finest slopes in the district seriously affected by it.

Description.

Only two pairs of legs.

734. ***Description.***—Seen under a fairly powerful lens, the adult pink-mite is a linear oblong creature, broadest near the head, and gradually tapering to the tail. It may be described as being about 100th part of an inch in length. It walks about in a curious attitude, with the head carried at a higher level than the tail. In moving it also twists its body, being apparently aided in progression by a sucker-like process at the anal extremity. The legs are two pairs, placed in the front of the head and directed forward. They are three pointed and have two minute hairs at the joints. Under the microscope the body seems to consist of four sections, one a somewhat triangular terminal portion that we may designate the head. The next two are sections of the body proper, and the fourth the anal extremity. This is furnished with what appears to be a retractile sucker by which the mite can fasten to the leaf and raise the other portions of its body jerking and propelling itself about. Down the centre of the body a faint line is discernible, which near the middle of the two central divisions swells to a circular spot. The mouth seems to consist of two mandibulate processes with antennæ-like feelers in front. The sketch, shown above, was made from the live insect.

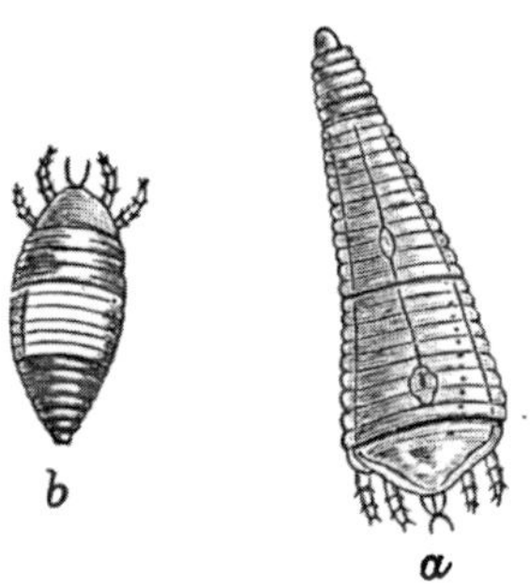

FIG. 43.—THE PINK MITE.
a. Adult Mite; *b*. Larva of Mite.
(From a sketch by G. Watt)

Larvæ.

735. The immature mites or larvæ (*b*) are more elliptic in shape and tapered at both extremities. At first they are almost pure white and hyaline. With age they become coloured, the second and fourth sections of the body being darker coloured than the first (or head) and the third or central section. They moult in the usual

The Arachnoidea.

THE PINK MITE.

manner by throwing off one or two skins before they attain the adult condition.

Absence of eggs.

736. A striking peculiarity of the colonies of this mite is the entire absence of eggs, a state of affairs so different from what occurs with the red-spider, and its work. But the margins of the leaf are thickened and even warted for some distance inwards. These are probably the breeding chambers within which the eggs are deposited, and also the shelters of the young larvæ, but this has not been certainly made out. The mite is, however, all but certainly a felt-gall forming mite not very remote from **Phytoptus pyri, Phytoptus ribis,**—the blister mites which attack the pear tree and the blackberry bush respectively.

Probably eggs are laid in Gall.

Causes loss in yield.

737. *Depredations.*—This blight is one of the least easy to be detected of all the serious blights of tea. The plot affected looks pale and sickly, but the leaves do not fall off, the mite itself is by no means obvious, and the only effect to mark the presence of such a serious enemy is the loss in yield. This is, however, sufficiently marked. We have, for instance, been favoured with the following figures showing the loss in yield in a Cachar garden, a loss attributed principally, if not entirely, to this pest :—

YIELD TO THE 22ND JULY.

	No. 6. 16 acres.	No. 7. 29 acres.	No. 12. 30 acres.
	lbs.	lbs.	lbs.
1895 . . .	15,400	24,200	(1899) 18,040
1900 . . .	9,460	16,080	10,600
Loss .	5,940	8,120	7,440

Not found on China plant.

738. The Pink mite is hardly, if at all, found on the China plant, and less on the Manipuri jat than on the Assam indigenous. It occurs on rich plateau lands and, like other mites, prevails to a greater extent during dry seasons than in wet weather, but is not washed off the bushes by rain at all easily, as if a fortnight's dry weather occurs in the middle of the rains it is again present and doing damage. The light colour which it gives to the bush is often put down by planters as an evidence of the high class character of

the jat of plant, while all the time the yield is dropping off year by year without any one being able to account for it. THE PINK MITE.

739. ***Remedy.***—We are indebted to Mr. H. Weir, of Kalline, Cachar, for an account of a series of experiments which he has carefully carried out now for some years. He writes: "Cutting down the bushes is a cure for about two years, but it seems to come on again the third year. I am satisfied that only thorough spraying in the cold weather will stop it, and probably the 'lime and sulphate of copper mixture' would be the best, and most thoroughly get into the crevices of the bark.

Experiments at Kalline.

"I have had different plots staked off and tried Chiswick compound, lime, lime and sulphate of copper, Adhatoda Vasica, and 'green sulphur.' All of the first three were most efficacious and seemed to have stopped the blight. . . . The others were almost equal. With the sulphur it is difficult to get the powder to hit the underside of the leaves, otherwise I am inclined to think it almost the best; wherever it does fall it destroys the mite instantly."

Bordeaux mixture apparently best.

Later experience has convinced Mr. Weir that the lime and sulphate of copper mixture (Bordeaux mixture) is the best, and that the bushes should be sprayed immediately after pruning. He finds the cost is amply repaid in a single season.

We think that there is still room for further trials with sulphur, which Mr. Weir has not found as permanent a preventive as Bordeaux mixture, but in the meantime the experiments at Kalline have shown a satisfactory method of dealing with a serious, and, we are afraid, rapidly extending blight.

ANIMAL PESTS.

CHAPTER XVIII.

OTHER ANIMAL PESTS.

Elephants. Cattle. Land rats. Hares.

740. Having dealt with chief insect pests of the tea garden, there remain to be mentioned a few animal pests that do not belong to the Class Insecta, or to the Spiders and Mites. It need hardly be remarked that wild elephants often do considerable damage both by trampling down the tea bushes and by pulling them out of the ground. Stray cattle also harm the bushes by breaking off the branches. Occasionally land rats are present to such an extent as to be positively hurtful. A letter in the Journal of Agri.-Horticultural Society of India (*Vol. V., Proc. 27th January 1876*), submitted by Messrs. W. Moran & Co. from one of their managers in Cachar, states that rats "are very destructive in gnawing off young plants level to the ground and eating the roots." A similar case was recently brought to our notice in Upper Assam. In the Duars hares are a cause of much anxiety, especially with young plantations and on grass land. They eat the leaves, shoots, etc., and kill the plants.

Land crabs.

741. In the Darjeeling district and the Nilgiris it has been said that land crabs are sometimes injurious especially in perforating drainage embankments. But passing over all the higher forms of animal life that may occasionally or indirectly injure the tea bush, there may be said to be three classes of animal pests in addition to those already dealt with. These are the **Anguillulidæ** or Eelworms, the **Myriapoda** or Julus-worms or Millepedes, and the **Molusca** or Snails and Slugs.

ANGUILLULIDÆ.

LXV.—Nematode Worms or Eelworms.

HETERODORA RADICICOLA. THE TEA EELWORM.

131. Heterodora radicicola, *Muell.*

THE TEA EELWORM.

SEE PLATE XVI.

References.—*E. E. Green.—Report for 1898, reprinted in Planting Opinion, May 6, 1899; Indian Gardening, June 14, 1900; Madras Mail, July 19, 1900; August 9, 1900; Indian Gardening, August 9, 1900; August 23, 1900; C. A. Barber, A Tea Eelworm Disease in S. India, Bull, Dept. Agri., Madras, Vol. II., Bull. 45.*

PLATE XVII. (*To face Page 373.*)

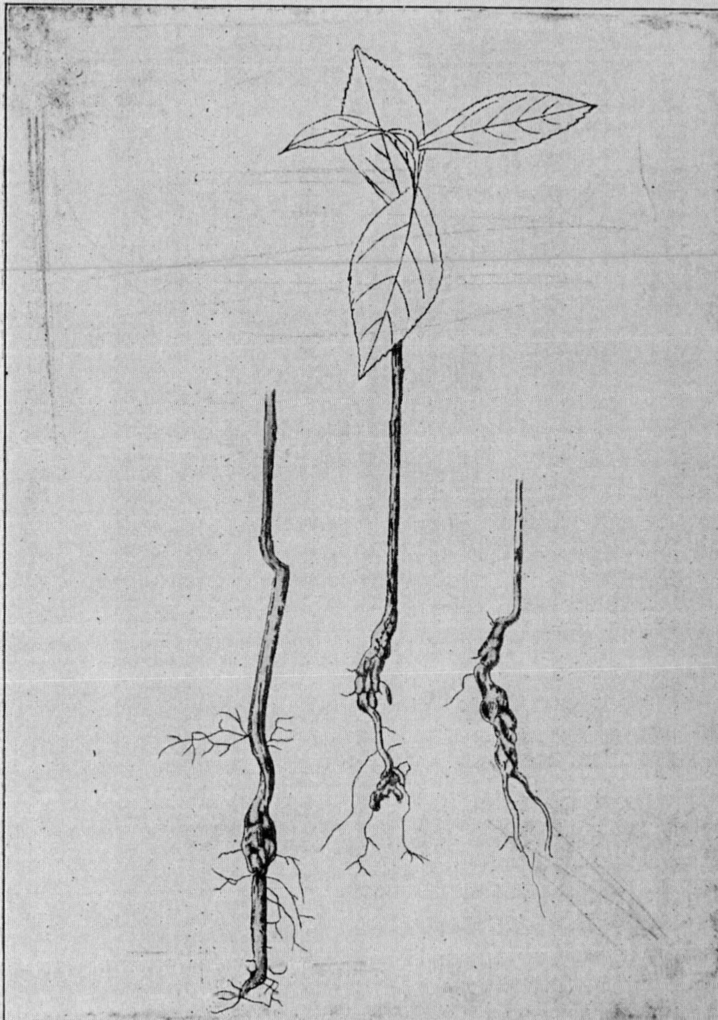

The Effect of the Tea Eelworm on Seedlings.
(From Sketch by C. A. Barber.)

The Tea Eelworm.

Found in Ceylon, Madras, Darjeeling, and Assam.

THE TEA EELWORM.

Discovery in Ceylon.

Discovery in South India.

742. ***History.***—Though Mr. Green was the first to draw public attention to the occurrence of an eelworm as a pest of seedling tea plants,* it was not till a visit of one of the authors (G. W.) to South India that general interest was felt in it as an enemy to tea. At that time Mr. A. Brown, of the Glenfruen Tea Estate, Devala, sent a parcel of dead tea seedlings, which after some delay, were found to be attacked by the pest in question. So serious was it that in 1900 no less than 75,000 seedlings were killed on the one estate. Great anxiety was felt, and the whole question was carefully investigated by Mr. Barber, the Government Botanist of Madras, who, while confirming the serious and widespread nature of the attack, allayed in a certain measure the somewhat wild alarm which had prevailed. Since this time it has been noticed, and done serious damage in a restricted area, in Darjeeling, and has been found also in Assam.

Description.

743. ***Description.***—The attack of this minute worm shows itself as a swollen, gall-like formation on the collar and upper roots of the plant. (*See Plate XVI.*) "If a piece of swollen root be cut in two, its tissue will be seen to have scattered through it a series of small holes about the size of a pin's head. Upon applying a needle, a whitish pulp can be extracted. This, when looked at through the microscope, is seen to consist of a sac containing a multitude of minute kidney like eggs, in many of which small worms may be detected coiled up or commencing to wriggle. These masses of eggs and the membranous coating around them are all that is left of the much swollen and altered adult female of the eelworm."

Life history.

744. "The minute worms escape from the decaying root and for a short time wander in the soil around the rootlets. They then enter the tissues of the plant piercing the cells with a minute stylet which they bear in their gullet. The male, at any rate, undergoes a kind of

* The pest investigated by Mr. Green in Ceylon seems not to be the eelworm with which we are here dealing. Though the latter is common enough in many flower and vegetable gardens, it has never, in Ceylon, attacked seedling tea-plants. The nematode noticed on young tea seedlings some years ago was a very distinct species, and is a comparatively large worm, nearly $\frac{1}{3}$ inch long, and could be readily seen with the naked eye when the diseased roots were macerated in water. It seems to have been successfully dealt with by allowing the land to lie without a crop and yet cultivated for a year.

Other Animal Pests.

THE TEA EELWORM.

moult inside the plant. Its inner organs shrink to a mass of protoplasm in the centre, leaving the skin as a loose protecting layer. From this develops later a larger worm which, rupturing the old skin, is prepared to fertilise the growing female. The latter process probably takes place outside the plant tissues, and when the fertile female re-enters the rootlet she does so for life. Her shape at that time is more or less worm-like, but as she absorbs the juice of the

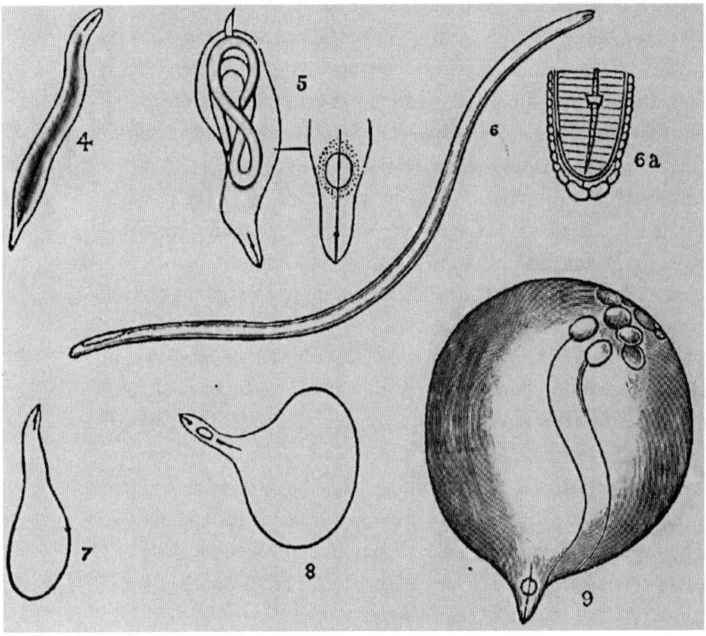

FIG. 44.—THE TEA EELWORM.

4. Male Worm, before encystment; 5. do., undergoing transformations; 6. do., after emerging from cyst; 6*a*. do., sucking end, enlarged; 7, 8, and 9. Different stages of female.

(From a sketch by C. A. Barber.)

plant she swells to a pear like body of comparatively enormous size, and in the later stages the hinder part is a mass of young, and her form is so altered that it took many years for observers properly to make out what these so-called "Cysts" were. A little care with the tea seedlings will, however, show all the stages." (*Barber.*)

The Tea Eelworm.

745. At all times the actual pest cannot be observed with the naked eye owing to its minute microscopic character, but its effect on the roots of the seedling can easily be seen. This, as shown in the plate, consists in the production, just below the collar, of an abnormal swelling of all the soft root tissues: "The upper part of the root is much thickened . . . . The whole strength of the plant seems to be taken up in the formation of a parenchymatous mass of tissue in which the various stages of the parasite are to be found. The rest of the root system is poor and stunted. The plant ceases to grow. A few leaves are formed which, in spite of careful watering, soon fall off, and the plant, after struggling on for some time, dies completely away." (*Barber.*) **THE TEA EELWORM. Effect on root and on plant.**

746. ***Depredations.***—Up to the present time the disease has only done any damage when attacking seedling plants. It has, however, been observed in mature tea bushes, and though no damage has been traceable to it as yet, it is not at all impossible that it might develop the power of seriously attacking the roots of the mature tea plant. The question of getting rid of the pests at once is therefore of more importance than appears at the onset. **Only seedlings attacked hitherto.**

One of the most serious points about the eelworm is the fact that in affected areas it attacks nearly all the weeds as well as the tea. Mr. Barber mentions the following plants, common on tea gardens as attacked:—**Ageratum conysoides**, the cold weather weed or "*ilami*" of North India gardens, **Sida rhombifolia**, one of the commonest weeds of roadsides and round buildings; **Desmodium**—a common procumbent leguminous plant. Beyond these the less common **Mollugo stricta**, **Impatiens kleinii**, **Triumfetta rhomboidea**, **Centrantherum reticulatum**, **Lycopersicum esculentum** (tomato), and others were attacked among the tea. **Found on weeds.**

It appears to be especially prevalent where villages and village gardens have previously existed. Thus, for instance, in the case investigated in Darjeeling, the land had been under village cultivation for a long period. Dirty land and neglected clearances are also just the places in which those weeds which are peculiarly susceptible to the disease will be likely to grow, and pass on the eelworm to the tea. **Found in village land.**

747. ***Remedies.***—The first point indicated in dealing with eelworm is to totally rid the land of all weed herbage, and this must **Remove weeds.**

THE TEA EELWORM.

be done by pulling up, and not by hoeing in the plants,—the latter process will of course spread the disease. This having been done, there are two processes which have been used more or less successfully in Europe to clear the land.

Trapping worms.

748. The first consists in trapping the worms by plants which are particularly liable to it, and then removing the plants and the worms with them. It is found in Germany that two crops are usually sufficient to carry away practically all the worms from the soil. In the Indian tea districts the best crop for this purpose would be mustard, of which the worm is very fond, and after this has been growing for six weeks to two months in the early rains, pull it up, and destroy it. A second crop is grown in August, and this will be similarly removed in October, and the land should be ready for seedling tea plants, which after such exhaustion should be planted with manure such as oil cake.

Starving out the worms.

749. The second method is to starve out the eelworm by either allowing the land to lie without a crop and yet cultivated for a year, or by growing an insusceptible crop, well-cultivated, for, say, two seasons, and then plant tea. In the hills Buckwheat would be a suitable crop for this purpose. By merely allowing the thorough drying out of the surface soil by constant cultivation in the dry weather for a season, it has also been claimed that complete success was attained.

No curative method.

750. It is necessary to recognise however that the tea eelworm belongs to a class of internal parasites with which it is very difficult to deal. It has even been suggested to burn the surface soil of land where they occur, and of course, this would be a radical cure, though we think it unnecessary in the majority of cases, and, it would be long before the soil would again be capable of agricultural development. It should however be recognised that a diseased plant must be removed. It is, on the basis of our present knowledge, hopeless to attempt to kill the pest in the plant; and hence an attempt at cure of plants once affected is obviously most unlikely to succeed.

MOLUSCA.

LXVI.—The Snails and Slugs.

Slugs.

751. Two or possibly three species of slugs (**Limacidæ**) are

common on tea, and do considerable injury occasionally to the older leaves. They have never been carefully examined and named. The presence of sulphur, applied as a treatment for red spider, will probably keep them off while it remains, but it is not worth while adopting a special treatment. THE SNAILS AND SLUGS.

Of the snails, one species is fairly plentiful, especially in seed gardens. Colonel H. Beddome has been kind enough to identify this as **Helicarion salius**, *Benson.* Snails.

The treatment usually pursued in Europe, when slugs or snails assume the proportions of pests, is to scatter lime over the crop. The first dressing may not kill the slugs owing to their slimy exudation throwing off any substances that may adhere to them. After one or two applications, the lime finally takes effect and the slugs are killed. It is in the seed garden or on tea under shade, where the slugs and snails are most prevalent. They have been mentioned here mainly as denoting a possible danger when there is too much moisture in the soil or injurious shade. Lime dressing.

MYRIAPODA.

MILLIPEDES

LXVII.—The Julus-worms or Millipedes.

752. It would be difficult to find a neglected and untidy tea bush in Assam that did not contain a few large dark-red Millipede worms, perhaps from one and a half to 3 inches long. On being touched, these roll themselves up and fall from the bush to the ground. They are well known to the planter and his labourers, but are universally regarded as harmless. European writers usually speak of the Julu-worms as living upon decaying vegetable matter, but occasionally as attacking living plants as well, and thus becoming pests. Many species are found in the tea garden and may be friendly. This is a point that deserves to be investigated.

753. Another Myriapod has recently been charged with doing serious damage to tea plants in Ceylon. Relative to this Mr. Green writes:—"I have recently received specimens of a remarkable Myriapod (**Polyzonium picteti**, *Humbert*) which were found at the roots of sickly tea plants in the Bandarawella district. There is no convincing evidence, however, that these animals were the real cause of injury. **Polyzonium** is remarkable as having the mouth parts modified in the form of a suctorial beak-like organ."

VEGETABLE PARASITES.

CHAPTER XIX.

VEGETABLE PARASITES OF THE TEA PLANT. THE BLIGHTS.

Distinction between pests and blights.

754. It will be recollected that we have imposed a somewhat arbitrary restriction on the words "Pests" and "Blights." The former has been assigned to all the parasitic manifestations of an animal origin, and the latter will be employed in the following chapters as denoting the depredations effected by parasitic plants—whether ferns, lichens, mosses, fungi, or belonging to other classes. The list of these is probably by no means complete. The more important vegetable parasites may be said to be two or three fungi found on the leaves: a fungus and an alga on the stem ; and two, at least, species of fungi on the roots. These blights, at least, demand careful study, since nearly all of them might become quite as dangerous as any of the pests already dealt with. But before taking them up it may be as well to mention one or two unimportant enemies of tea cultivation that naturally fall within this chapter.

LORANTHUS.

132. **Loranthus** *sp.*—"ROGAMULLA."

755. It is often found, especially in a seed garden, that many of the tea plants bear parasites closely resembling the mistletoe of apple and oak trees in England. They are, like the mistletoe itself, destructive parasites that sap the life of the plant. Fortunately they are easily recognised and should instantly be removed. We have seen some seed gardens with every alternate bush or so bearing two or three great clumps of **Loranthus.** It is a serious mistake to allow these to grow, since they must weaken the plants and injure the seed.

Found in Burma.

The tea plant is peculiarly liable to this class of parasites. In a correspondence regarding tea in Burma (published in *The Agricultural Ledger No. 27 of 1893*) it will be found that a species of Loranthus, then known as *chibaung*, is spoken of as killing the tea. This no doubt would be the final result with any **Loranthus** if left to itself.

Conf. with paras. 680-682.

Remedy.—Saw off the branch bearing the Loranthus, and coat the wound at once with the Gondal paint.

133. FERNS AND OTHER PLANTS IN THE BUSHES. **FERNS, ETC.**

756. In Kangra a species of **Euphorbia** introduced from America (**Euphorbia heterophylla**, *Linn.*) has proved troublesome as a weed growing within and around the tea bushes. This is not met with in other districts, but several species of ferns, and occasionally one or two other plants, growing in the bushes, do them considerable injury. *Ulu* grass ("*sunn,*" "*ciru*") is specially destructive to tea when it gets a footing in a garden. These and such like should, however, be rather viewed as indications of neglect than as pests and blights, but there can be no two opinions as to the fact that weeds within the bushes themselves are most injurious. They rise up and choke the tea, and their roots interfere with those of the tea plant. **Euphorbia** **'Ulu' grass.**

Remedy.—Handpick and remove every plant found within the tea bush.

134. LICHENS AND MOSSES. **LICHENS AND MOSSES.**

757. Old bushes and those growing in localities with too much shade and imperfect ventilation or defective drainage, or a moist temperate climate like that of the higher Darjeeling districts, become coated with lichens and mosses. Their presence is one of the most striking indications of a "hide bound" bush, but they are in reality the consequence, and not the cause of the condition complained of. In the majority of cases it will be found that age is the chief cause of the hide bound condition as also of the coating of lichens, mosses and other similar growths. So long as a plant is vigorous and its stem constantly expanding in circumference, lichens will make little headway. Let its activity decline from age, unfavorable surroundings, or disease, and it will immediately harbour lichens and mosses. The chief insect pests that favour the growth of these epiphytes are the scale insects. When plant-lice infest the bush, insignificant though they appear, they instantly commence to check its activity. The bush becomes unkempt and untidy. Its leaves are rapidly besprinkled with sand and mud, and turn black through the growth of fungi ("soot blight") that feed on the sugary exudations of the insects, or they may be seen to support a botanic garden of beautiful and varied forms of mosses, lichens, liver-worts, fungi and algæ. The bark is seen to split in all directions, to be dry and useless, and to bear a copious coating of lichens and mosses, **Found especially in higher Darjeeling district.** **Favoured by scale insects.** ***Conf. with para. 615.***

Vegetable Parasites of the Tea Plant.

LICHENS AND MOSSES.

or to protect the female scale insects that nestle beneath and are in fact the cause of the bark being split and torn from the stem.

Not true parasites.

758. Lichens are not parasites. They attach themselves to plants, stones or other objects in order that they may secure certain advantages of exposure to the air and protection from unfavourable circumstances. Thus, for example, the stems of palms growing in open positions will be found lichen-coated on the lee side to the point of greatest rainfall of the locality. Lichens are epiphytes, that is, they live on the air and attach themselves to the surface of plants, without materially abstracting anything from them.

759. ***Remedy.***—To cure the plants so infested, the cause must be discovered and the treatment regulated accordingly. If the land be imperfectly drained, that must be corrected. If the jungle be too near, or the ventilation defective, a clearance must be made by cutting openings in the forest to allow of a freer circulation of air. If age be the cause, collar-pruning would very possibly renew the garden, and for a time allow of enhanced returns, but ultimately a point would be reached, when, in our opinion, nothing further can be done except to uproot and replant. But should the cause be a severe outbreak of bark or leaf-louse, the surest and most effectual remedy will be found in firing the plot. This should be accomplished early in spring, then light prune a fortnight later, and, while pruning, wash or brush the stems and branches with lime to remove all the charred lichens, mosses, and other adhering matter.

Drainage.

Clearing jungle.

Conf. with para. 592.

760. Needless to say that, in any case, at every pruning season an effort should be made to get rid of these suffocating growths, either by picking and rubbing them off the branches, or as is done in Ceylon, by dusting the bushes with freshly slaked lime. Bordeaux mixture would likewise answer the purpose.

Rub moss from branches.

Dust branches with lime.

LXVIII.—Parasites and Blights on the Leaves.

PESTALOZZIA GUEPINI.

THE GREY BLIGHT.

135. Pestalozzia Guepini, *Desmaz.*

GREY BLIGHT.

(SEE PLATE XVIII.)

References.—*Desmazieres in Ann. Sc. Nat. Ser. II. p. 183; Diseases of Plants—von Tubeuf trans. by W. G. Smith, p. 494; Cooke—Journ. Agri.-Horti. Soc. Ind., Vol. IV. Proc. Feb. 27, 1873 (?); Massee, Kew Bulletin, June 1898, p. 106; Planter's Gazette, Nov. 12, 1898; Massee—Diseases of Plants, 1899; Planting*

PLATE XVIII. *(To face page 380.)*

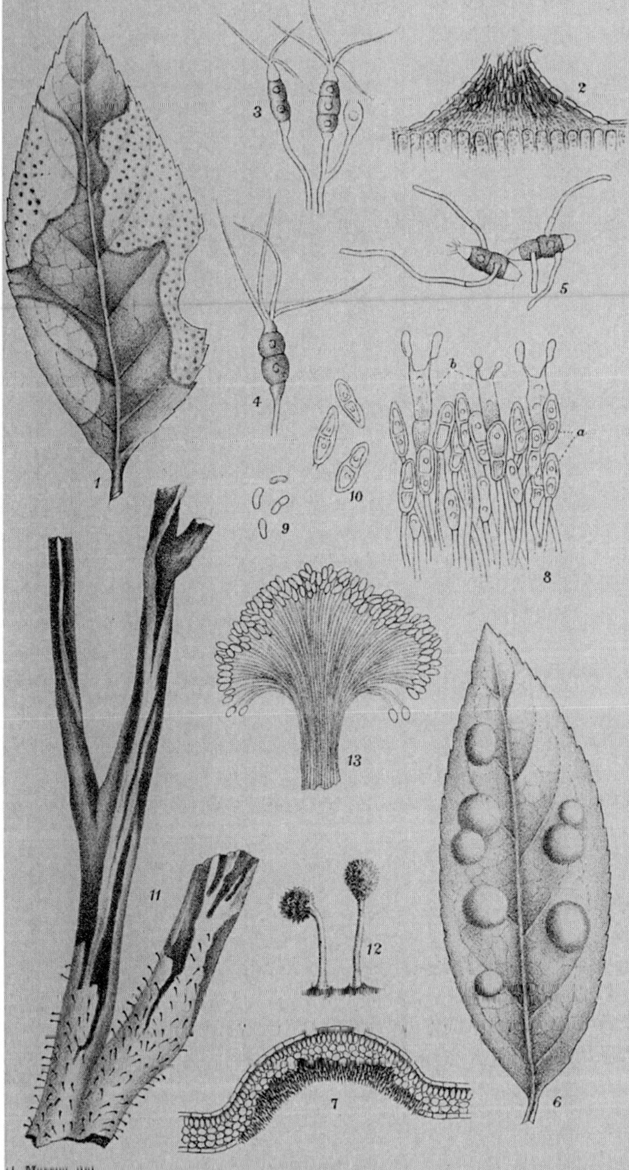

G. Massee, del.

TEA BLIGHTS.

Reprinted by permission of the Director, Royal Gardens, Kew, from Kew Bulletin of June 1898.

The Grey Blight.

THE GREY BLIGHT.

Opinion, Aug. 19, 1890; Aug. 26, 1899; Other planting papers in 1899; Circ., Roy. Bot. Gard., Ceylon. 1899; Trop. Agri., Nov. 1, 1890; Feb. 1900; Ind. Plant. Gaz., April 28, 1900; Circ., Roy. Bot. Gard., Ceylon, II., p. 1 (1902).

Found in all districts.

Found in 1873.

761. ***History.***—This, the most common fungus blight of tea, has been long known, though little notice was formerly taken of it. In 1873, for instance, samples of a blight from Cachar were examined by Mr. M. C. Cooke, and from his description of it there is no doubt that he had this blight in his hands. How it has spread we have no information, but now there is not a district, not even new ones like the Wynaad and Travancore, in which it is not present. It is met with on all jats of plant, and shows little preference for one over another.

Now universal.

762. In Europe it is a well-known blight on **Camellia, Citrus, Magnolia, Rhododendron**, but till found on tea was not known to occur in India, and even now it has not been noticed on other plants than tea either in India or Ceylon, though it is almost certain that it does occur in the jungle of most parts of the tea area.

Method of growth.

763. ***Description.***—This blight appears at first on the upper surface of the older and harder leaves as minute brownish grey spots. These increase in number and coalesce into large patches, which thus come to have an undulating outline. The individual patches will be seen to manifest a slightly thickened rim of a pale greenish brown colour, and near this may be observed a series of very small black spots or warts (perithœcia). As the rim widens, zone upon zone of these perithœcia are formed until the whole surface of the affected area becomes spotted with minute black dots over the otherwise smooth and ultimately whitish grey surface. These dots or perithœcia are not, however, universally present, many of the leaves being simply covered with numerous variously shaped brown and grey patches,—sometimes extending right across the leaves. On the under surface of the leaf a corresponding portion to that invaded by the grey patch on the upper surface will be seen to be discoloured, but to manifest no external formations.

Spores.

Appearance of under surface.

764. It very often happens that these brown and grey patches commence near the base of the leaf, and this is one of the most alarming forms of the disease, for then the leaf will turn brown and

Vegetable Parasites of the Tea Plant.

THE GREY BLIGHT.

Form on leaf stalk.

drop off apparently without visible blight,—for the fungus has only attacked the leaf stalk and extreme base of the leaf. The attack may commence, however, on the apex, or on the margin, or two or three patches may form at once and extend till they unite, when the entire leaf may assume a dirty whitish grey colour.

Carried by wind.

765. The fungus itself is propagated by means of spores which are carried about by the wind in all probability. Being blown on to a tea leaf they there germinate, and their mycelium penetrates under the epidermis or outer skin of the leaf. There it absorbs the sap and grows at the expense of the plant, whose tissue is thereby completely transformed and the leaf killed. Here and there as described above it throws out fresh groups of spores which form the dots, warts or perithœcia visible on the affected leaves. (*See Plate XVIII, Nos. 1—5.*) These spores shaped as shown in the figure (*Plate XVIII, Nos. 3 & 4*) are then blown on to fresh bushes or leaves to continue the spread of the blight. The grey colour of the blighted leaves is due to the epidermis being raised up from the rest of the leaf tissue like the loose skin over a blister. There is no blister or swelling however, the leaf is of normal thickness, and far from being blistered, it will be found that the tissue of the leaf has been dried up, so that on handling it crumbles to pieces.

Cause of grey colour.

Very protean inform.

766. But, in appearance, this is one of the most protean of blights. We have described the normal form, but there are many which it is impossible to identify without the microscope, and several other blights formerly separately described have been now found to be nothing but other forms of Grey Blight. This has proved to be the case, for instance, in the "*Chestnut Patches built up of Concentric Zones*" mentioned in the first edition of this work.

Possible second form.

767. It seems possible that a second form of the fungus reproducing by a different method without the intervention of spores, may exist. A diseased leaf drops into contact with a healthy leaf below, and where they touch become cemented by a tuft of fungus filaments, which are the basis for a new attack. This appearance has not yet been thoroughly investigated. It is, however, known that Grey-Blight is what is called a 'form-genus,' that is to say, another and higher form of the fungus may exist, most probably living on dead leaves. The fact that such a form probably exists renders it absolutely essential that dead and dying leaves, whether on the bush or on the ground, should be destroyed.

The Grey Blight.

THE GREY BLIGHT.

768. ***Depredations.***—As has been already indicated, this is the most widespread of the parasitic fungi to which the tea plant is liable. It commences for the most part on one side of a bush, very often on the same side of all the bushes over an affected plot,—a circumstance that may be taken as indicative of the germs having been wind-conveyed. It then may work round or over the bush until every leaf is killed. It appears occasionally to become epidemic, and then as the disease advances the leaves fall off, and lie on the top of the bush, and then the disèase will pass from bush to bush until in large plots nearly every bush will be injured.

Epidemic form.

769. In other cases it seems to just attack odd bushes,—generally the weaker ones—in a plot, and go no further. One may say, in fact, that the bulk of the sporadic grey blight seen almost on every garden in India, is of this type, and is the result of weakness of the bushes attacked. It has been said that bushes were killed outright by this fungus; but we have personally never seen any case in which this has occurred. It is by no means an unusual occurrence, however, to find bushes with holes eaten out of them, as it were, on one side, or with the circumference reduced artificially, and often, at any rate, such occurrences were the work of grey blight. It can well be understood, therefore, that where this blight has appeared to any serious extent, it gives very great anxiety.

Attacks weak bushes.

770. Though the immediate and effective cause of the disease is the fungus mentioned, yet there are several causes which render the plant liable to the disease. Of these, the first is the presence of water-logged, sour, undrained land, where we have seen as bad epidemic grey blight as anywhere; a second, curiously enough, is the fact of the tea being planted on dry, droughty land. On some of the dry ridges in the Darjeeling district grey blight occurs very badly. A third cause of a serious attack of grey blight is a previous visitation of Red Spider. This latter hardens the leaves before their time and renders them peculiarly susceptible. In fact everything which makes the plant weak brings on grey blight, and it should be recognised that the best means of combating the disease is to render the bushes as healthy and vigorous as possible.

Encouraged (1) by water-logged land; (2) by land subject to drought; (3) by preceding attack of red spider.

Very many other reasons have been given especially in Ceylon for the prevalence of the blight. It has been attributed to infected Indian seed—a most unlikely supposition. Imported Castor Cake

Other supposed causes

Vegetable Parasites of the Tea Plant.

THE GREY BLIGHT.

has also been blamed for the blight, which is equally, if not still more unlikely. But essentially the primary cause is weakness, and whether this be due to soil conditions or to previous blights like Red Spider or Red Rust, it is equally likely to cause an attack of Grey Blight.

Remedies.

771. ***Remedies.*** The method which is the simplest in application (provided the causes of weakness have been as far as possible removed) and which has proved very effective when systematically carried out is the removal by plucking of the diseased leaves. To carry out this effectively all diseased leaves should be plucked, swept up, and burned at the pruning season together with the prunings. After this the plot should be watched, and every blighted leaf plucked and burned as it appears. On Tingri (Dibrugarh) where a very bad attack has been successfully dealt with, all pluckers were supplied with a second bag in which blighted leaf was put as they went round the garden, and this blighted leaf was paid for at the same rate as the leaf for manufacture, and it could then be burnt. By a somewhat similar method an epidemic attack was successfully dealt with on another garden in Dibrugarh recently. The only need is systematic and thorough removal of the blighted leaves in the spring and burning them. If this is left till the bushes become seriously affected in the middle of the season, more drastic measures may have to be adopted if anything is to be done at all.

Plucking leaves.

Successful examples.

Burn all prunings.

772. In a garden badly affected all the prunings should be religiously burnt, and this alone has been reported as having had some effect in moderating the blight. High cultivation has also been stated to materially reduce the susceptibility of bushes, and this is only to be expected if carefully done so as not to cut the bigger roots, as it renders the bushes more vigorous and healthy. Firing the bushes has not been very successful, as in the case of a serious attack spores floating in the air almost always cause the new growth to be attacked. It might be worth while, however, to burn badly attacked bushes before pruning, as this avoids the possible spread of the blight by carrying off the prunings to burn. The charred wood can then be pruned off in the regular course of pruning.

Fungicides not indicated.

773. We cannot think, now that the life-history of the fungus is known, that there is much field for the use of fungicides. A spraying with Bordeaux Mixture in spring would, however, protect the old leaves from attack, and so perhaps render the bushes healthier and

more vigorous. This will be only used in serious epidemic cases of grey blight. The removal of affected leaves in the spring, starting soon after pruning, has proved such a success where thoroughly tried that if this (together with an effort to make the bushes more vigorous by high cultivation, possibly manuring, and careful pruning), be carried out systematically, we think there is little fear of the blight getting or retaining a serious hold on a garden.

THE BROWN BLIGHT.

136. Colletotrichum cameliiæ, *Massee.*

COLLETOTRICHUM CAMELLIÆ.

THE BROWN BLIGHT.

(SEE PLATE XIX, No. 1.)

References.—*Massee—Kew Bulletin, July and Aug., 1899; Indian Agri., Sept., 1899, p. 286; O Collett—Ind. Plant. Gas., April 28, 1900 (copied from Ceylon papers), and various references in Ceylon planting publications.*

Found in Ceylon, Assam, and South India.

774. ***History.***—A blight which answers exactly to the description of Brown Blight was collected by one of the authors in Assam in 1895 here and there all over the Assam valley, but curiously enough it was especially prevalent in the seed gardens. Another form of what appears to be the same fungus was also found and described as "*Brown Rings within one another*" and occurred at a few odd places,—Ligri Pukri, Hautley and Doom Dooma for instance. Three years later the same blight caused widespread alarm in Ceylon, where it was stated by many authorities to be worse than Grey Blight. It still occurs there, but has not been so serious since 1899 as it was in that year.

Found in Assam in 1895.

In Ceylon later.

775. ***Description.***—The blight first appears on the upper side of the leaf as a yellowish brown patch with an expanding border which is the actual seat of the growing disease. This expands to the edge of the leaf, often causes a constriction there and the affected portion of the leaf turns over and shrivels up. "When the leaf is held up to the light, a yellowish hand is seen round the affected area due to the spreading of the mycelium into the still unattacked area of the leaf which loses its green colour." (*Willis.*) As the range of attack extends, the central portions of the leaf often fall out, leaving leaves with large perforations in them.

Description.

Vegetable Parasites of the Tea Plant.

THE BROWN BLIGHT.

The fungus causing the disease is spread by means of spores. The figure in *Plate XIX, No. 1*, shows a section through the growing fungus, the sausage-shaped tips to nearly all the mycelia representing the spores by which the disease is spread. They are, like those of grey blight, blown about with the wind either attached to small fragments of diseased withered leaf, or else alone.

Very serious in Ceylon.

776. ***Depredations.***—In Ceylon it has been thought that this is a more serious disease than grey blight, as it apparently is even more common, and attacks the younger growth (though not the flush itself) while the other blight restricts itself to the older leaves. It is also much more continuous in the damage it does, lasting throughout the year, while grey blight is essentially a blight of the monsoon. It seems also able to reproduce itself with greater rapidity. In India it is probable that very many attacks have been confused with grey blight, and there are few cases on record of its having been a serious depredator.

Treat as with grey blight.

777. ***Remedy.***—The methods of attacking this blight are similar to those for Grey Blight, and there is a just as great reason in this case for the collection and burning of the leaves, as **Colletotrichum** is also what is called a "form-genus," that is to say, a lower stage of a fungus which exists in the decaying leaves in a higher form (an ascigerous fungus)—and if this is allowed to grow in the dead leaves it will inoculate the new leaves again the following season.

Bordeaux mixture suggested.

Mr. Massee, who first described the fungus, suggests spraying with Bordeaux Mixture, and adds: "In spraying plants like the tea having glabrous leaves, success mainly depends on the fineness of the spray; which should hang like a fog. A coarse spray causes the solution to form drops which roll off the polished surface of the leaves." Spraying, however, will rarely be necessary if systematic removal of the leaves, right from the pruning season, be carried out as suggested under Grey Blight.

137. Pestalozzia Guepini, *Desmaz.* and Colletotrichum camelliæ, *Massee* } combined.

RIM BLIGHT; MARGINAL CORROSION.

RIM BLIGHT.

Found in Assam.

778. More serious than either the Grey Blight or Brown Blight alone is, where it occurs, the disease formed by a combination of the

two. It was described in the former edition as "Marginal Corrosion," but its nature was not known, and has only recently been made out by Dr. Butler, Cryptogamic Botanist to the Government of India. Since that time it has spread extensively, and now has done a good deal of damage in Dibrugarh, Nowgong, and other Assam districts.

THE RIM BLIGHT.

Found in Assam.

The leaf simply begins to shrivel round the edge, and the shrivelling increases until the whole leaf decays,—the portion decayed being deep chocolate brown in colour and quite brittle. It spreads faster than either Grey or Brown Blights, and in one garden in Nowgong its spread could be almost daily watched. It seems rather a special blight of Bazaloni and similar jats of tea.

Attacks high jat tea.

It can best be dealt with by the same method of plucking the leaves recommended with Grey and Brown Blights, but if this is to be done successfully it demands even closer watchfulness than in either of these cases, for once the disease gets a head it is extremely difficult to stop its progress.

More difficult to deal with than grey blight.

138. Exobasidium vexans, *Massee.*

EXOBASIDIUM VEXANS.

BLISTER BLIGHT.

Blister Blight, White-Blister.

(See Plates XVIII and XIX.)

References.—*Peal, Journ. Agri.-Horti Soc. Ind., Vol. I., Proc., June 17, 1868; IV., 1873, p. 126; Baildon, Tea in Assam, 45; Massee, Kew Bulletin, June, 1898, p. 109; Trop. Agri., Sept., 1899; Massee, Diseases of Plants, p. 168.*

Found in Upper Assam only.

779. ***History.***—The earliest mention of this blight takes us as far back as 1868, where the late Mr. S. E. Peal gave a description of it and expressed the opinion that it was caused by a fungus. As he stated that he had known it ten years before, it is probably one of the oldest enemies of the tea bush. Mr. Baildon (1877) is the only author of a book on tea who makes mention of blister blight. He says: "I think this is worse than mosquito blight. I do not know whether it has been really ascertained what causes 'Blister Blight.' A leaf gets a small speck upon it at first, which, as it enlarges, assumes the appearance of a blister, and ruins the leaf entirely. An old belief was, that when a drop of rain or dew remained on a leaf, the sun coming out acted as a magnifying glass upon it, and burnt a hole. Others believed the blight to be caused by a bug. I think this most probable." The sun theory of blister is constantly brought up to account, not only for the present disease, but for the minute blister-

Described in 1868.

Magnifying glass theory.

THE BLISTER BLIGHT.

ings of the mites. We have never seen a case of sun blistering, and suspect there may be some mistake. If it does occur, excessive evaporation, and not the magnifying glass theory, would have to be accepted as the explanation.

The blight was next noticed in 1895, and then, on the basis of samples collected by one of the authors (G. W.), Mr. Massee, of the Botanic Gardens at Kew, definitely ascertained that the cause of the disease was a fungus and suggested methods for its treatment.

Found in Upper Assam only.

780. So far as we have been able to observe, this blight is, and has always hitherto been, exclusively confined to Upper Assam. It has never been definitely reported below the Jorhat district on the South, and the North Lakhimpur district on the North Bank. It has never visited either Cachar, Sylhet, Darjeeling or the Duars,—and any blight locally called blister blight in those districts has always been found to belong to an entirely different fungus or even to a mite attack.

Peal's account.

781. ***Description.***—The following is Mr. Peal's account of this blight. We make no apology for giving it in full since it practically tells all that we know to the present day, and shows that the chief peculiarities of the blight have not been modified in any essential, during the past forty years or so:—

"I take the liberty of enclosing some leaves of tea that have been attacked by a kind of white-blister. This disease is so common about here just now, that it might be called an epidemic. It attacks young leaf, and is injurious, inasmuch as it stops the bush to a great extent in giving leaf. I have noticed it, sparingly, for some years, and have not been able to ascertain the cause, but I apprehend it is a fungus 'smut or rust,' and not caused by any insect.

Chiefly but not entirely on leaves.

"It is chiefly confined to the leaves, but it is also seen occasionally on the green part of a stem, or the green husk of the seed. When fresh, it presents the appearance of a pale green spot (usually pitted) on the upper surface of the leaf, and on the lower surface is seen as a raised white blister-like spot with a floury or mealy texture usually circular. The diseased portion eventually turns a brownish colour, and the leaf, wholly or in part, dies.

"So far it seems peculiar to tea. I have searched for it in vain on other plants, as it seems to attack it under all circumstances alike, equally so in the open as under shade, in jungle or in clear and highly cultivated patches; this, at least, is my experience so far;

PLATE XIX. (*To face Page 388.*)

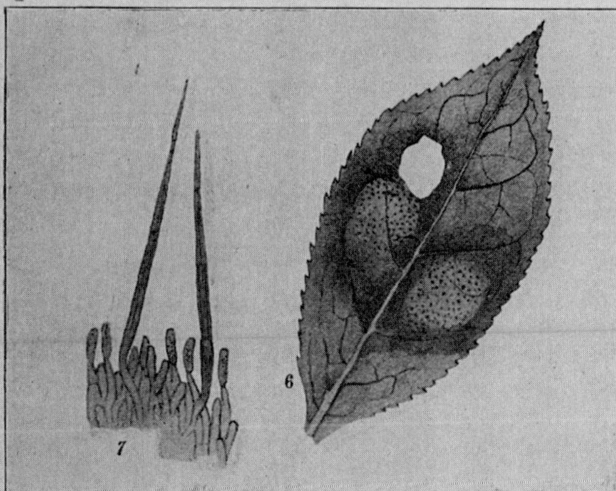

1. The Brown Blight of Tea.
6. Affected leaf, natural size. 7. Section through spore bearing part of fungus.
(From the Kew Bulletin.)

2. Blister Blight—Upper Surface of Leaf.
(From Photograph by T. H. Hall.)

3. Blister Blight—Under Surface of Leaf.
(From Photograph by T. H. Hall.)

THE BLISTER BLIGHT.

varieties of tea, including the 'China,' seem to suffer less than those more nearly allied to Assam. I have reason to believe that this disease shows chiefly after long heavy rain. I had heard so before and this year would seem to confirm the supposition, the rainfall during April having been very heavy. A patch of tea near here, of 20 acres or more, has been so generally attacked by this disease, that I have ceased to pluck it, and the garden in places presents quite a withered appearance. Other gardens around are also suffering, the disease being, if anything, on the increase. I have heard that, about ten years ago, the tea suffered severely from this same blight, but that the following season it all but disappeared. It will certainly have a marked effect on all the estimates of 'crop,' as it seems to check leaf coming out."

Chiefly on Assam Jat.

Description in 1895.

782. By way of comparison with Mr. Peal's description it may be useful, if we record here a description of the blight as met with by us. It first appears as a minute pale brown or pinkish spot on the upper surface of the leaf. This enlarges in size, mostly in a perfectly circular manner, gradually becomes depressed into a pit about the size to admit the tip of the little finger, is smooth, polished and glistening, as if coated with honey-dew. On the under-side of the leaf there is a corresponding swelling which is pure white, woolly and soft, but quite dry. As it advances, numerous blisters appear on the same leaf and even coalesce into large patches. They also occur on the young shoots, and cause much destructions of the stalk. In time the blisters change colour, become brown, and ultimately black. The shoots next wither, and the entire block of tea may then look, in May and June, as if the blast from a furnace had passed over it and killed every shoot and leaf.

Technical description of growth.

783. The fungus as described by Mr. Massee is illustrated in Plate XVIII, Nos. 6 to 10. (No. 7 is drawn incorrectly by mistake. The convex side of the blister should be represented on the underside of the leaf, and the fungus on it there.) The spore (or seed) of the fungus having alighted on the leaf begins to grow and to push its mycelium between the cells. There is then a rapid disappearance of starch and chlorophyll grains; this is followed by a rapid increase in the number of cells constituting the spongy tissue of the leaf and situated within the area to which the fungus mycelium spreads. The bulging of the blisters is caused by this increase in

Vegetable Parasites of the Tea Plant.

THE BLISTER BLIGHT.

the cells over a limited area of the leaf being resisted by the healthy remaining tissues. Finally, the fungus mycelium ruptures the epidermis of the leaf, and forms two kinds of spores shown in Plate *XVIII*, Fig. 8—where *a* represents the conidio spores,—which are first formed, and *b* the basidio spores formed later. These are shown separately in Figs. 10 and 9, respectively. In some blisters we collected in December 1900 (a most unusual time) only the first form spores (conidia) was found in any case.

Alarming nature of blight.

784. ***Depredations.***—This is truly one of the most alarming of maladies, but up to the present has been prevented from extending its ravages by some influence which we do not yet know. For instance, it is very serious one year,—and then may hardly be seen for several seasons. In 1895, for instance, it was serious; in 1896 there was a mild attack only; and then till 1900 little more was said about it. In that year, however, it did immense damage on quite a number of gardens especially in the Dibrugarh and Sadya Road districts. In 1901 and 1902 it has not done serious damage.

Occurs in spring.

785. But when it comes in large amount it is one of the most destructive of blights. It usually appears on the young shoots in spring and spreads like wild fire over a block. Attempts have been made to keep it in check by plucking off the leaves, but it gets ahead of the pluckers almost at once, and this method of dealing with it is useless. It attacks the young leaves and shoots, and continues its ravages into May when, on the arrival of the really hot weather, it begins to die down, the blisters dry up,—and the shoots and the bushes, having had all their first shoots destroyed, now begin to put out fresh growth. The result is that the bushes are weakened, and two months of the season may be lost.

Starts on unpruned tea.

786. This very remarkable blight attacks chiefly the higher *jat* indigenous (Assam) teas, neither hybrid nor Manipuri being seriously affected up to date. It almost always starts either on unpruned or on lightly pruned tea. Plants heavy pruned the previous year, and left unpruned to make wood, are particularly susceptible. This may be due to the fungus being in the bush for a considerable time before the attack, or it may be merely a result of these bushes being the only ones with young and succulent leaves at the time the attack occurs. From these centres it may spread over the whole of a garden. It is (contrary to Mr. Peal's opinion) very fond of shade, and

could only be found in December 1900 where the shade was fairly dense. It has never been certainly seen up to the present on jungle trees or plants. **THE BLISTER BLIGHT. Fond of shade.**

787. ***Remedy.***—Few successful efforts have been made yet to combat the blight. Mr. Lindsay Alexander found dusting with lime, when the blight appeared, an effectual cure. The most likely method appears to be to spray the whole block on which it is found when it first comes on with Bordeaux Mixture, but even this is, as Dr. Butler has pointed out to us, open to the objection that the plant may absorb copper from the Bordeaux Mixture through the leaves. In any case, to be safe, the Bordeaux Mixture should be applied early in the season before plucking commences. This method will involve loss of a few weeks' leaf, but if the shoots can be saved this is of little importance. Every effort should be made to spray the underside of the leaves since it is there that the fungus lies and grows. A stock of fungicide and sprayers should be kept in hand wherever the blight is likely to occur. **Suggested remedies.**

139. **Cercosporia sp.**

THE SHOT HOLE FUNGUS.

788. Almost all over the tea districts the older leaves of the plants will occasionally be found to bear small brown circular spots—looking at first sight like the punctures of mosquito blight. They are, however, caused by a fungus, and will be noticed to differ from the punctures mentioned by being perfectly circular and to grow if kept in a damp place. They are of little importance as blights, but this class of fungi have done considerable harm in some agricultural industries, and hence they should be carefully kept under observation. **THE SHOT HOLE FUNGUS.**

140. BLACK FUNGI ON THE LEAVES.

789. Under the account of "Red-rust" mention will be found of a black fungus that is often seen on the tea leaves, in association with the orange-red patches of the alga (**Cephaleuros mycoidea**). It not infrequently happens that in a damp situation, or near the jungles, this fungus is very prevalent, without being accompanied, in any very special manner, with the foliar patches of red-rust. The fungus to which we allude is, however, purely epiphyllous, and further than possibly harbouring other pests does not appear to be injurious. **BLACK FUNGI ON LEAVES.** *Conf. with para. 807.*

790. In connection with the account of scale insects, mention has also been made of another black fungus found on the tea leaves, which has generally been given the name of 'Soot Blight' on tea gardens. This, which has all sorts of methods of growth and fruiting, has been found to be a **Meliola** by Dr. Butler who examined our samples. One form of it is known as **Capnodium Footii,** *Berk.* & *Desmas.*, which is common in Europe on the Camellia in cultivation, and is the species which blackens lime trees, appearing there as a growth on the secretion of the honey-dew aphis. These have only interest as being associated with, and a sign of attack by scale insects, and are not in themselves blights of the tea plant. *Conf. with para. 6 6.*

THE THREAD BLIGHT.

CHAPTER XX.

VEGETABLE PARASITES OF THE TEA PLANT—continued.

LXIX.—Blights on the Stem.

STILBUM NANUM.

141. Stilbum nanum, *Massee.*

THREAD BLIGHT; WITHER BLIGHT.

(SEE PLATES XVIII AND XX.)

References.—*Journ. Agri.-Hort. Soc. Ind. Vol. I. (n. S.) Proc., 15th July, 1868, p. liii; Vol. VI., Proc., 27th Feb., 1873, p. ix; Proc., 19th March, 1874, p. xiii; Jour., VII., pp. 258-262; Vol. X., Proc., 27th March, 1896, p. 470; Vol. XI, 26th March, 1897, p. 601; Tea Planters Vade Mecum, 104—105; Bamber, Chem. and Agri. Tea, p. 257; Christison (White Thread Fungus), Home and Colonial Mail, Jan. 1st, 1897; Dr. D. D. Cunningham, Scientific Mem. Med. Officers of the Army of India, Pt X., pp. 20—22; Massee, Kew Bulletin, June, 1898; Massee, Diseases of Plants, 1899, p. 326; Mann, Ind. Tea Association, Report, 1900, p. 220.*

Found in all Indian districts.

Difficulties in studying blight.

791. ***History.***—This very destructive blight has been known to the industry for many years, and has again and again been sent to experts on fungi. Unusual difficulties have presented themselves, however, in the attempt to examine it and determine the class to which it belonged, for the reason that it was rare indeed for it to produce fruit and spores. It is well known, however, that many fungi do exist indefinitely without producing spores,—and when this occurs the species can only be propagated by a piece of the mycelium (or stalk of the fungus) being carried from one place to another. Under certain circumstances it does, however, appear to form spores, and from samples furnished by one of us (G. W.) from Assam its character and its position among fungi have been determined.

Occurs in all Indian districts.

792. It now occurs in every Indian district, and in some of them has done a great amount of damage. It is found everywhere in the jungle on a very large number of widely dissimilar plants, of which may be mentioned,—bamboo, the *utengah* of Assam (**Dillenia Indica**), and the "*gaekwa*" or *wild tamul* of Assam—on each of

PLATE XX. (*To face Page 392.*)

1. Healthy Tea Bush.
(From Photograph by T. H. Hall.)

2. Results of Thread Blight.
(From Photograph by T. H. Hall.)

3. Thread Blight on Twig.
(From Photograph by T. H. Hall.)

The Thread Blight.

which it is especially plentiful. The "*Loquat*" (**Eriobotrya japonica**) and the Sapodilla Plum (**Achras Sapota**) are trees which are often affected,—as well as the Mango. **Daranta** hedges are often destroyed by this blight, and it is a question to what extent any jungle plant can be considered absolutely free. **THE THREAD BLIGHT.**

793. ***Description.***—In the early parts of the season this blight may often be seen on the branches of a bush, and the white thread (from which it gets its name) often appears to originate at the junction of two branches and to run both up and down the stem. This thread is soft and woolly. Very often it only occurs in one of the smaller branches, and then grows down that branch till it comes to a fork when one part of it runs up the second branch thereby rendered accessible. **Method of growth.**

On reaching the leaf the fungal thread thickens on the leaf stalk, twists round and runs up the midrib on the lower side where it expands into a soft felted layer that ultimately covers the whole under side of the leaf. We have never come across an instance where it ran up the upper side of the leaf; occasionally after covering the under side it spreads over the margin on to the upper surface, but never extends very far there. **Growth on leaf.**

Once the under surface has been coated, the leaf begins to fade and gradually turns brown (hence the name "Wither Blight"). But as it changes colour and decays, it falls down and usually becomes attached to the stalk by a mass of fungus filaments. Held in that position the final decomposition of the leaf is accomplished, and the somewhat curious appearance is presented of a tuft of brown rotten leaves adhering round the base of the branches. The bush looks green on top and for a time may even be vigorous, but as the thread advances leaf after leaf drops, and ultimately the whole bush is rendered brown and barren. (*See Plate XX, Nos. 1 and 2.*) **Causes leaf to wither.**

794. The fungus itself, in the ordinary thread-like form in the woody parts of the bush, consists in a number of very thin strands which are attached to and draw their nutriment from the stem. Wherever they go there is an internal mycelium just under the bark and the branches are ultimately killed by the choking of the vessels in the exterior of the "cambium zone" (that is, just under the bark) by the mycelium of the fungus. "So far as can be observed," says Mr. Massee, "the fruit of the fungus is only produced after the **Condition of threads.**

Vegetable Parasites of the Tea Plant.

THE THREAD BLIGHT.

branch on which it occurs is dead, when it appears on the surface of the bark under the form of miniature pins about half a line high, and of a pale yellowish colour. These fruits generally occur in large numbers, giving to the branch a minutely velvety or hairy appearance as seen with the naked eye. When on the under surface of the leaf on the other hand it sends down a multitude of what are apparently suckers— and by their means quickly kills the leaf by abstracting nutriment.

Very common.

795. ***Depredations.***—Thread Blight has been one of the most common and perhaps one of the most destructive blights of the tea plant. Until recently it was usually neglected and laughed at as doing little or no harm. The result of this is seen in the fact that twenty to fifty per cent. of the bushes in a block were not unfrequently affected, thus reducing yield and ruining bushes. Now, we are glad to say, a change has come in the general attitude to this blight, and every effort is made to eradicate it.

Method of transmission.

796. The withered leaves, adhering to the bush, are the chief agents in the dispersion of the disease. We have repeatedly found tea leaves or jungle leaves, as, for instance, the *utengah*, adhering to bushes near a point where a new start had been given to the blight. It would thus seem that the disease is readily transmissible and may be diffused all over the garden if a few bushes are allowed to furnish withered and fungus-bearing leaves to be carried by the wind. These leaves, on coming in contact with a fresh plant, at once put out a small filament that unites the diseased structure to its new host.

Burn prunings.

797. ***Remedy.***—As a precautionary measure it should be insisted on that all prunings bearing even the smallest particle of thread blight should at once be burned. It is fatal to leave them lying about the garden, as the blight will inevitably then get spread to other bushes, and, beyond this, the conditions are produced in which the spores of the fungus are formed. Burying the prunings is little better. Cases are on record in which the roots of a plant have been attacked by blight spreading from buried prunings. We do not believe that underground infection is usual, and experiments have been instituted by Dr. Butler and one of the authors (H. H. M.) to test this point; but the fact that instances of such infection are on record is quite sufficient to make the burning of all thread-blighted prunings the bounden duty of every planter.

The Thread Blight.

THE THREAD BLIGHT.

798. The method of treatment generally adopted up to the present time is to cut out the parts affected, at the pruning season. If the blight occurs in the upper part of the bush only, it still remains the best system, but if the attack involves the lower part of the bush, and this method would mean very heavy pruning, we think better means of dealing with the blight have now been devised. It is well known that the smallest piece of thread left in a bush is quite sufficient to cause a new attack, and so if this method be carried out it needs the most careful and thorough work, for the internal thread which is not easily seen may go far in the bush below that which is visible on the outside, and so the whole pruning and mutilation of the bush be futile.

Cutting out.

Firing bushes.

799. An improvement on this method—because it was more certain—was the burning of the blighted bushes introduced into the Jorhat district, we believe, by Mr. F. H. Edwardo, of Heelcaka. It consisted in leaving the blighted bushes unpruned at the ordinary time of pruning, and then, immediately afterwards, putting straw under them, setting fire to this, and so killing the fungus. It involved, however, fairly heavy pruning afterwards. While excellent as to results it meant the cutting back of individual bushes in a plot—a proceeding which is always objectionable.

Lime and sulphur.

800. If this cutting back can be avoided and yet the blight killed, a distinct step in advance will have been taken, and hence another system was introduced by Mr. Anderson, who was at that time manager of Hukanpukri. This consists in the application of a liquid obtained by boiling together quicklime and sulphur with much water to the bushes at the pruning season. The mode of working was the following :—At the pruning of a plot all the bushes were left unpruned which showed any trace of the blight. Then a special gang of men went round, pruned the bushes as far as was feasible, removed the leaves, and then the mixture was painted on by brushes made of any material to be had. It was essential that this should be done thoroughly, the mixture being rubbed into the thread, but done properly the treatment was effective in about 90 per cent. of the cases. The results were so good that a circular was issued by one of the authors in December 1900, and the method is now in general use with successful results in nearly every case. Even when the cutting out method is still practised it would be well if the stumps were treated with this

Vegetable Parasites of the Tea Plant.

THE THREAD BLIGHT.

Preparation of lime and sulphur mixture.

mixture as a safeguard. The mixture is prepared as follows:— $7\frac{1}{2}$ lbs. of lime (quick and unslaked) are slaked with water, and then mixed with $2\frac{1}{2}$ lbs. of sulphur—water being then added to make the volume of the liquid up to ten gallons. The mixture is boiled in an iron vessel till the liquid becomes orange in colour and takes on an abominable smell (somewhat similar to that of rotten eggs), allowed to cool, and applied carefully and thoroughly with a brush or piece of jute tow to all the stems of the tea bush which show any sign of thread blight.

Chiswick compound.

Instead of this, it appears from recent information, that Chiswick Compound may be used with equally successful results. We have, however, no personal experience of its employment.

Kerosene and oil.

A third mixture has been used for painting stems affected with thread blight, *viz.*, a mixture of equal parts of kerosene and oil (say mustard oil). It certainly kills the thread, but beyond ascertaining this fact we have likewise no experience of the method.

Summary.

801. In summary therefore it may be said that when thread blight is only in the upper part of the bush it may be sufficient to cut out the parts affected. In any case it is wise to prune as low as possible without disturbing too much the symmetry of the bushes on the plot, and paint every part of the bush left with one of the mixtures above mentioned, though that made from lime and sulphur is the only one of which we have personal experience.

CEPHALEUROS MYCOIDEA. THE RED RUST.

142. Cephaleuros mycoidea, *Karsten.*

RED RUST; WHITE BLIGHT; "LEPROSY."

(SEE PLATES XXI AND XXII.)

References.—*Cunningham, Mycoidea parasitica, in Trans. Linn. Soc., 2nd series, Vol. I., 301-316, tabs. 42, 43; also An Entophytic Alga occurring on the leaves of Limnanthemum indicum, with notes on a Peculiarly Parasitic Variety of Mycoidea, in the Scientific Memoirs by Medical Officers of the Army of India, Part III., pp. 35, 40, pl. I; and Bark-blight caused by Cephaleuros virescens, Kunze, in Scientific Mems., etc., Part X., pp. 17-20, pl. III.; H. Marshall Ward, Trans. Linn. Soc. (1884), Vol. II., 2nd Series, Botany, pp. 87-115, Plates 18-20; Karsten, Ann. Jard. Bot. Burtenzorg, 1891; Diseases of Plants by Dr. Karl Freiherr von Tubeuf, transl. by W. G. Smith, 552; Tea Planter's Vade Mecum, 105-106; Massee, Diseases of Plants, 1899, p. 342; O. Collett, Planting Opinion, Aug. 21, 1900; H. H. Mann, Red Rust; A Serious Blight of the Tea Plant, Report to Ind. Tea Association, 1901.*

The Red Rust.

THE RED RUST.

Found in all districts in the plains in India.

Discovery.

802. ***History.***—So far as we can discover, this blight began to attract attention about 1880. It was then known as "White Blight," because of the peculiarity that the leaves of the twigs invaded by it were observed to become variegated and ultimately pure white, or as one writer remarked the bushes resemble "White Leprosy." It has since received the name of Red Rust, because of the red coloured diseased patches seen on the bark. We owe to Dr. D. D. Cunningham nearly all we know of the organism which causes the disease—at any rate in the form in which it is dangerous.

Has been getting worse.

803. The disease is one which has constantly been getting worse for many years and is now one of the most alarming the industry has to face. In the former edition it was stated that, at any rate as a serious blight of tea, that under consideration had a limited range in the tea districts of India. Now the state of affairs is certainly very different. We have ourselves found the dangerous form of the blight in practically every district in Assam. In Cachar it is at least as bad as in Assam. We have noticed it in Sylhet, in the Duars, and in the Terai. In fact, so far as all the districts in India are concerned except those in the hills, and here there is considerable doubt, there are none, probably, unaffected with the blight. One can go, according to recent observations made in conjunction with Dr. E. J. Butler, further and say that there are probably few gardens quite free from the dangerous form of the blight,—but it only becomes prominent when weakness of the bushes gives the chance for it to do serious damage.

Few gardens now free

Description

804. ***Description.***—On walking through tea gardens in almost all tea districts of India, especially such as have not very vigorous bushes, in the months of May and June and to a certain extent also in July and August, the eye is attracted by some of the bushes possessing a certain number of variegated leaves, partly yellow and partly green, more especially round the edges of the bush. The stems below these variegated leaves will, in ninety per cent. of the cases at least, be found to bear livid red or orange red spots in greater or less quantity. This is Red Rust. These red spots, on closer observation by holding the edge of the twig between the eye and the light, are seen to consist of a mass of filaments, enlarged at the tips, standing

Vegetable Parasites of the Tea Plant.

THE RED RUST.

up from the bark like a tiny forest. If the circumference of such a bush as we have described be further examined, it is most probable that more or less of the twigs will be found to be dead, until at last in bad cases the bushes have the appearance in June shown in Plate XXI, Nos. 1 and 2, and the dead twigs carry either red patches as described above or purple blotches from which most or all of the filaments have disappeared. These filaments form the fruiting organs of the blight which is the cause of the disease from which the bushes are suffering.

An alga and not a fungus.

805. But unlike the majority of the vegetable parasites indicated in the foregoing pages, this blight is not a fungus but an alga. That is to say, it belongs to the natural order of plants best known by the seaweeds and the fresh water algæ. In general terms, these may be said to differ from the fungi, by their more or less aquatic habit, by their being often highly coloured (frequently green), and by their being only very exceptionally parasitic. The blight with which we are concerned is one of those remarkable exceptions, for it is distinctly parasitic, and to the ordinary observer could hardly help being viewed as a fungus. But it is unfortunate that it has come to bear the name "Red Rust" since the term rust is usually restricted to one group of fungi with which this blight hardly bears even a superficial resemblance.

Leaf form.

806. ***Two phases in its life.***—There is another point that had better be here mentioned,—there are two widely different phases in the life of this alga; in one it is found on the leaves of the tea plant and is comparatively harmless; in the other it infests the bark and superficial structures of the young shoots, and is in that case a dangerous parasite. In its harmless condition it exists throughout Assam, in the Duars, Darjeeling and Ceylon. Indeed it exists throughout the tropical regions of India on an extensive series of widely different plants. In Assam it might almost be said to occur on any tree or bush the leaves of which have, like the tea plant, a fairly hard and polished epidermis on the upper surface. Thus,

On hard-leafed trees.

for example, it is common on the mango, the letchi, the *Nahor* (*Nagassa*), the *Satian*, the *Sum*, the *Adakuri*, the cinnamon and many others. We have never seen this leaf form of the blight on the *Sau*, the *Bukhain*, the *Sam* or other soft-leaved trees common in and around tea gardens.

The Red Rust.

807. Even in this harmless leaf form it may appear in two guises. The first of these consists in a number of orange red spots on the upper surface of the leaf, generally bearing a number of the same filaments as occur when the rust is seen on the stem. These will appear to be growing by a constantly widening rim and dying in the centre of the patch. **THE RED RUST. Orange Spots.**

The second form results from a combination of the alga with a fungus, when its appearance totally changes. Every planter is familiar with the hoary colour of the older leaves of tea or mango trees growing under shade. The irregular grey patches there found are composed of a lichen formed by the union of the alga we are considering with a black fungus with radiating cobweb-like arms which can often be seen on the leaves in addition. **Lichenous form.** *Conf. with para. 789.*

808. In both these leaf forms it seems, however, to be of little practical importance. The leaves ultimately die, but the tree is not appreciably injured, and for practical purposes the direct harm it does might almost be neglected, were it not for the fact that it is at any moment liable to change into the dangerous stem form, when the damage is serious in the extreme. **Leaf form not itself important.**

809. This form on the stem is, in fact, a much more deep-seated form of the blight, and as it continues to grow, the disc or main growing part of the alga that supports the external filaments is carried deeper and deeper into the tissue of the plant as each superficial layer becomes destroyed. The bark of the shoots is thus cracked (*see Plate XXII, No. 1*) and removed by the growth of the alga, and the ascending sap being intercepted, the leaves gradually give indications of decreasing vigour until ultimately the shoot is killed. **Bark form.** *Conf. with para. 824.*

810. ***Depredations.***—In short, when the red patches appear on young tea shoots, the following results occur:—

(1) The green stem becomes woody almost to the tip immediately, and the green succulent part disappears all but entirely. In one such young shoot examined, the woody part was $7\frac{1}{4}$ inches long, the green only $\frac{1}{8}$ inch; in an adjoining shoot not attacked, and apparently of about similar age, the woody part was 3 inches, the green 8 inches long. When the young stems in a bush become "wooded" up in this manner, Red Rust may be suspected. **Causes wooding-up of stem.**

Vegetable Parasites of the Tea Plant.

THE RED RUST.

(2) The leaves in all cases become yellowish and unhealthy, and in many instances, but not in all, take on the variegated "leprous" appearance previously described.

Leprous leaves.

(3) The stem or shoot where the patches occur becomes split in minute cracks (*Plate XXII, No. 1*), and the bark is destroyed as described above. Often the red patch is slightly raised and split at the edges or in the middle. The cause of this is following:—Although the fruiting organs of the alga causing the disease are above the bark and visible, yet the main part or "disc" of the alga is underneath the bark, and as it grows forces this up, the dislocation causing the minute cracks which appear in every direction.

Cracks in stem.

Shoot dies.

(4) The shoot becomes drier, ceases to grow, and finally dies.

811. After this has happened, or while it is in progress, the bush throws out another shoot from below the affected part. If this occurs early in the season, the new shoot will also probably be attacked, and the same cycle of changes take place. If, on the other hand, the new shoot is produced after the commencement of the rains, although it *may* be attacked in the same way, yet the chances are that it will not be so, and that it will be one of the flushing shoots of the bush for the remainder of the year. This apparent immunity is probably far more the result of the increased vigour of the shoots giving them the capacity of resisting the attack than of any inactivity of the disease during the rains. The smaller 'twiggy' shoots can be seen so attacked at almost any time till the end of the season.

After history of bush.

Appearance in autumn.

As the end of the rains approaches the striking livid red blotches of Red Rust disappear, only leaving, as a rule, a very few filaments (*see Plate XXII, No. 2*). At this time (October, November and December) the blight is much less easy to be seen than earlier, and would be overlooked in many cases if special search were not made for it. New shoots are occasionally attacked, even then, in the ordinary way, with the usual result.

Appearance of bush long affected.

812. The general result on a bush where the blight has been several years in operation without check, and which has not been heavy pruned, is to form, in the best part of the season, a narrow hard stemmed plant with a crown of green leaves. The bushes in fact get narrower and narrower, and the small size of the plants on a garden which has long been attacked by the blight is remarkable. Many a bush described as 'hidebound' has come into this condition through the

PLATE XXI. (*To face Page 400.*)

1. Bush badly attacked with Red Rust, June 1901.
(From Photograph by H. H. Mann.)

2. Bush badly attacked with Red Rust, June 1901.
(From Photograph by H. H. Mann.)

attacks of Red Rust, and we believe that a comparatively large amount of cutting down necessarily done in recent years in comparatively young tea has been caused by the unsuspected prevalence of this blight.

Blight on stem is not confined to tea.

813. It was formerly supposed that the stem form was almost, if not entirely, confined to tea. This supposition has now been entirely disproved, and it is probable that it occurs on almost as many trees as the leaf form. It is often seen on the *Sau* tree **(Albizzia stipulata)**, it occurs on the *Bogga medeloa* **(Tephrosia candida)** and on dozens of other plants all round and in the tea gardens. So universal is it that any attempt at dealing with the blight by isolation, by burning or cutting down round the plots may be dismissed at once as unlikely to produce any good results.

Predisposing causes to red rust.

814. Red Rust will probably be found in every tea garden in Assam. Why then does it not occur in dangerous amount and do serious damage in all estates? The fact that the distribution varies with garden, with climate, with attention, with manuring, renders it at first sight most probable that there are some conditions present in one case and not in another which lead to the excessive development of the blight. If these conditions can be determined, it is evident that we shall be on the track of a far more certain method of preventing or even dealing with the blight than any system of direct attack would be.

Weakness of bushes.

815. A close examination of the question from the point of view leads one to the strong opinion that the most important exciting cause of a bad attack is in weakness of the bushes, and in India at any rate the most common cause of weakness of the bush is in defective soil conditions. As occurring on the worst gardens, the soil may be described as a rather heavy loam, dark brown when wet, greyish when dry, containing much more clay than is usually found in the best tea soil. The surface is fairly friable down to a depth of 10 inches to one foot,—just so far, in fact, as the cultivation extends. Immediately below this is a hard impermeable clay subsoil forming what is usually known in agriculture as a 'pan.' Below this again is a slightly softer clay interspersed with the fragments of the dark red laterite rock usual in the locality. The gardens have none but surface drains. The results of these conditions are—

Subsoil pan.

(1) Owing to the 'pan' immediately below the cultivated depth and to the absence of drains, the top layer is nearly always (except

THE RED RUST.

in the rains) too dry and the lower layer too wet. As an example of this condition of things, I may say that a determination of moisture made in this subsoil at 3 feet deep in December 1900, when the surface was dry and powdery, gave 20lbs. water to the cubic foot, the total amount which it could contain when saturated being 27lbs.* This water was unavailable because of the more or less impermeable 'pan,' and even were it available, roots could not penetrate a soil so near saturation as the above figures show.

Lack of Drainage.

(2) Plants growing on such a soil are almost entirely dependent on the surface layer for moisture and for food—and their root development is almost entirely a surface one. This was found strikingly to be the case when bushes were dug up for this purpose. Plate I (*see page 37*), Nos. 1 and 2, from actual photographs, show what really was the case. The root system in fact consists in a spreading shallow mass of roots such as would be quite admissible, if sufficiently manured, in the English climate where the soil is always moist, but which is entirely out of place in a situation experiencing long droughts such as prevail in Nowgong or in Cachar. That the failure of the roots to descend was caused by the impervious nature of the ground was rendered certain by an examination of the roots themselves. In one case a root was observed proceeding directly downward, but on reaching the layer of soil in question, it suddenly was bent back on itself and came up again. Another root penetrated the layer for a few inches, becoming very rapidly thinner in the process, and then split into two, both of which went no further down but only horizontally. The extreme depth to which the roots penetrated was 18 inches to 2 feet into the soil.

Exhausted soil owing to shallow root.

816. These conditions are of course most unhealthy, but it remained to compare the amount of Red Rust here with that in gardens similarly situated, except that descending roots were produced. The surface soil appeared to be similar but the subsoil was lighter in texture and the land was drained. The bushes were about the same age, but the section had been recently topdressed with bheel soil. Here Red Rust was certainly found on a good number of bushes, but in no case did it amount to such an actually serious blight as on the gardens previously mentioned. Wider experience confirms this view. We have seen Red Rust bad on a light well-drained soil suit-

Comparison with other soil conditions.

* I am indebted to a report by Mr. Ede, of Silchar, for these figures.

PLATE XXII. *(To face Page 402.)*

1. Wood attacked by Red Rust showing cracks.
(From Photograph by H. H. Mann.)

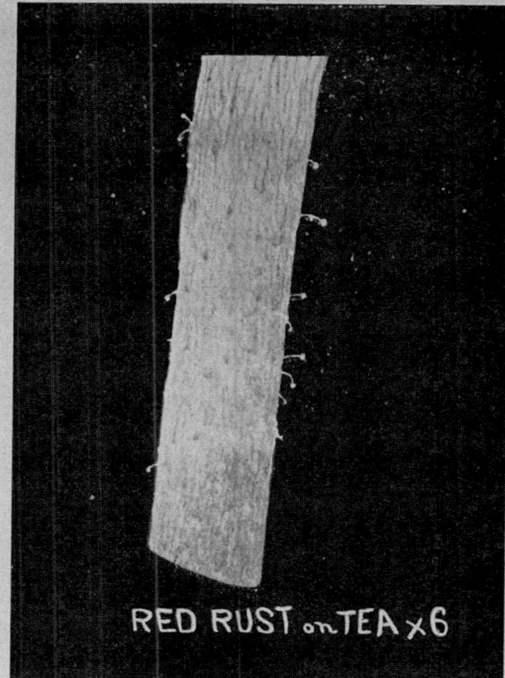

2. Red Rust on Twig (enlarged six diameters).
(From Photograph by T. H. Hall.)

The Red Rust.

THE RED RUST.

able for tea, but never to such an extent as to threaten the existence of a garden—as it has done in cases with soil such as I have described.

Heavy pruning.

817. Another striking example of the effect of soil conditions is furnished by the results of heavy pruning in different places. On the garden referred to above, some tea collar pruned one year had the new shoots covered with rust the following season : on another where the soil conditions were good, only heavy pruning had been done, and yet the plot practically free the year following. The treatment, if cutting hard is a cure, was nothing like so radical as in the former case, but the Red Rust was practically eradicated nevertheless.

There are undoubtedly other predisposing causes to attack by the disease, which we do not recognise, as well as those (like too long continued high pruning) which we know. But the state of the soil is the most important, and in dealing with the blight it is not likely that success will be achieved until this is put as nearly right as possible.

Methods of preventing attack.

818. ***Remedy—Methods of Preventing Attack.***—The conclusion is obvious. While the blight is of almost universal distribution, it will only enter as a serious disease where favourable conditions arise causing lack of vigour in the tea, the most notable being the lack of extended and deep root development in the soil, which results in rapid exhaustion of the shallow layer from which the food-supply is drawn, and in great susceptibility to drought. Is this a defect, however, which can be removed ? In many cases we think it is, and that the removal of this defect is the proper first step to the eradication of the blight.

Drainage needed.

819. The primary means of increasing deep root development is by deep draining. The worst gardens for Red Rust that we have seen have been undrained, badly drained, or drained only recently. The only garden we know where the blight have been regularly fought, and is in a fair way to be conquered, is one where drainage has formed one of the main lines of attack. The effect of a correct system of drainage is to remove excess of standing soil water, and in many cases it may be said that the depth of possible root development is determined by the depth of the drains. It has been argued that owing to the short rainfall in Nowgong or similar districts, drainage can hardly be needed there. As a matter of

Conf. with paras. 94-121.

Vegetable Parasites of the Tea Plant.

THE RED RUST.

Effect of drainage on roots.

fact, there is no district in the Indian tea area where it is more needed, for there the soil is stiffer and less permeable than is usual in the Assam valley, and consequently a hard pan is apt to form at the depth of the annual deep hoeing, below which is water which only very gradually gets away. Part of the land on a badly rusted garden was drained to 3′ 6″ in December one year, and the effect on the roots six months later, was already visible. On exposing the roots of several bushes, they already were found to penetrate to two feet six inches or three feet deep, as against an extreme of two feet on the undrained portion of the same plot of tea. It is then evident that the drained plot would in the future be much more independent of drought than the undrained, inasmuch as it had a larger extent of soil to tap for water and for food—an extent however which never contains enough water to prevent its root growth. Probably one bush would be able to utilise 60 to 70 cubic feet of soil, where its previous range only extended to 25 cubic feet.

Cultivation.

820. But drainage having been carried out, the greatest effort should be made to force the plant to utilise the new soil put at its disposal by very deep cultivation. or (what is probably in many cases as useful) ordinary deep cultivation and trenching 2 feet deep between alternate rows each year; by breaking up the 'pan' by growing trees among the tea; by green manuring with a deep rooted leguminous crop. *Sau* trees would naturally be recommended for growing in the tea area, and they to a certain extent fulfil the object in view, but on such soil as we have in mind they hardly seem to be deeply enough rooted to be an ideal for the purpose. Though the **Grevillea** has no manurial action like the *Sau*, yet it might be better for this purpose owing to its deep tap root. This is however distinctly a matter for experiment. For green manuring *Mati kalai* (**Phaseolus sp.**) is naturally the first plant thought of, but there seems some doubt on such land as we are discussing whether it is really very deep rooted. It needs experiment to decide the best leguminous crop for the purpose, but in the meantime *Mati kalai* should be used.

Growing trees.

Mati kalai.

Manures.

821. There are cases where drainage will not, however, suffice. The upper layers have become so exhausted and the lower layers are so poor that the bush has not the food necessary to give it vigour

THE RED RUST.

even if its root range is extended. In such cases manure in some form is essential. Manure alone, even, is of great value. On one plot, as poor, weak, and rusty as any, in one of the gardens visited, a new set of coolie lines were placed recently. Now, the part round these lines, though it contained a great deal of rust, seemed to be resisting it with much greater vigour than elsewhere, and it was here a rarity to see a bush of which half the foliage is killed—a common sight in the remainder of the section. Further, those gardens in Nowgong, with soil such as we have described as favourable to Red Rust, which have suffered least are those on which top-dressing and manuring has been most systematically carried out. Such manures should be used as will give vigour to the bushes, as, for example, top-dressing bheel soil material if good; cattle manure if available; oil cake if cattle manure cannot be obtained; or green manuring with '*Mati kalai*;'—all these being manures which increase the vigour of the tea bush and do not merely increase the yield.

Manures.

822. ***Methods of removing the blight.***—While we believe that the methods above indicated will suffice to prevent an attack of Red Rust or to prevent it, at any rate, from assuming serious proportions, yet, alone, they will not be sufficient to eradicate the blight. In such a case it will be equally necessary to remove the blight itself, and the most drastic methods have often been recommended for this purpose, such as collar-pruning and burning all the prunings, or even burning the bushes *in situ* on the plots. The great question in a case like this is whether, if these drastic measures are adopted, we have any guarantee that the disease is really eradicated, and whether milder methods will not bring about the same result. After a very careful study of the subject, we have come to the conclusion that, provided the conditions are otherwise favourable to the blight, cutting out the rust in any way, alone, without further treatment, is of little or no use,—indeed, that it is often worse than useless, and that the new shoots are often worse attacked than the old ones. We have already quoted one case, but they could be found over the whole of the badly blighted districts. To collar prune a seriously rusted plot without seeing that the soil conditions are good or attempting to prevent a new attack by spraying, or both, is a suicidal policy, and may result in a block of tea worse rusted and worse in every way than before.

Methods of direct attack.

Uselessness of cutting out the blight.

Vegetable Parasites of the Tea Plant.

THE RED RUST.

Bordeaux mixture sprayed.

823. In July 1901 we recommended that in rusty blocks the tea should be sprayed after pruning with Bordeaux Mixture or Sulphide of Potassium solution, the quantity required amounting to about 100 gallons per acre. This has been carried out on several gardens with very promising results. It cannot be expected that the Red Rust can be eradicated in a single season, but the amount can be very much reduced, and by continuing the treatment, the cost of which amounts to about 6 rupees an acre, the disease can be kept under control.

Principle of application.

824. The principle on which this method of application depends is as follows. If rust attacks a first year shoot, that shoot inevitably dies. A second year's shoot in our experience likewise always succumbs. But on older wood, this is not universally the case, though very often the attack is fatal even on these stems. The reason why this older wood is not always killed is shown by careful microscopic examination. If first or second year's affected shoots be examined, the alga is found to have perforated right into the interior of the shoot through the protective layer of corky tissue. In older wood this is, however, not always the case, and if the stem is vigorous, it may be able to throw off the disease before such penetration does take place. Hence the amount of pruning absolutely necessary in such cases seems to be indicated. On a plot of land badly affected with the blight, it would appear therefore sufficient to prune out the last two years' wood, removing all the small twiggy shoots which invariably contain Rust, and spray the remainder of the bush with Bordeaux Mixture or Sulphide of Potassium, taking care that every part is reached by the spray.

Safeguards.

825. ***Safeguards against fresh attacks.***—But though apparently satisfactory so far, this is not enough. Inasmuch as the whole jungle is crammed full of the blight, in the leaf form above described, and that hence the tea is always in danger of a fresh attack, it becomes necessary to watch the new shoots on the bushes treated as above. It would seem possible to have a few boys trained to recognise the red patches on the stems, and to have these boys going round and round the plots treated as above, from April to June, and putting a patch of Bordeaux Mixture on the spot attacked by the alga.

Spraying of stumps.

826. Whenever heavy pruning is carried out on a garden where Red Rust is found, we should make spraying of the stumps a *sine*

qua non. We have ourselves seen the benefit accruing from this treatment. In addition to this, all seedlings should be dipped in Bordeaux Mixture before being planted out either in new clearances or in filling vacancies, but especially in the latter case. Indeed it would be more than advisable to spray all vacancy in-fillings with Bordeaux Mixture two or three times every year for the first three years, as this is the *one* blight which nearly always ruins such plants. THE RED RUST.

Spraying of Sau trees.

827. As a further precaution it would be wise to spray the '*Sau*' trees in the gardens. The stems are so commonly covered with the blight under discussion, that if this is not done it becomes a question whether their danger is not greater than their value. But we see no great difficulty in checkmating the disease in the way we have indicated, especially as they are not usually planted less than 40 feet apart, and hence could not amount to more than 25 to 30 per acre. Previous to spraying it would do no harm if they were pruned considerably, only remembering that the '*Sau*' tree always dies back to a joint, and cutting accordingly.

Summary.

828. The results we have obtained, therefore, lead to the following conclusions so far as the practical treatment of the blight is concerned.

1. Red Rust is now one of the most widely extended of tea blights and though doing most damage in the Nowgong and Cachar districts, it can be seen almost everywhere on tea in India. Even when not noticed elsewhere, it can almost always be seen on the stems of plants used for filling up vacancies in old tea. A form, not itself of serious consequence, occurs almost everywhere on the leaves of the tea in the gardens.

2. The blight abounds in the jungle on the leaves of many trees, and on the stems of many more, but its entry into the tea garden as a serious blight is caused largely by weakness in the bushes. This is caused by too long continued high pruning, or more often by defective soil conditions leading to the formation of roots near the surface only, resulting in susceptibility to drought; and to exhaustion of the limited soil available for feeding purposes. These conditions of soil can largely be counteracted by—

(*a*) drainage,—deep drains not less than 3 feet deep are necessary;

Vegetable Parasites of the Tea Plant.

THE RED RUST.

(*b*) deep cultivation leading to the forcing of the roots into a lower layer; or trenching between the rows still deeper which has the same effect;

(*c*) growing deep-rooted trees among the tea;

(*d*) manuring by top dressing with bheel soil, by cattle manure, by oil cake, or by green crops.

(3) The blight itself can be dealt with by cutting out the last two years' wood at least, at pruning time, taking special pains to remove the small twiggy shoots in the bush, and spraying the bush thus pruned with Bordeaux Mixture, or Sulphide of Potassium solution, the former for preference. In fact it would probably be advisable to thus spray all cut-back tea in affected districts.

(4) The future should be safeguarded—

(*a*) by dipping all seedlings intended for transplanting into old tea in Bordeaux Mixture before planting out;

(*b*) by spraying or painting the '*Sau*' trees in the garden at pruning time with the same mixture if possible.

829. Treated by these methods it appears that the blight may be kept in hand. There will always be, inevitably, a trace of it in many gardens, but by the application of the means indicated, there seems a probability that the blight will not remain a serious one, while otherwise it will gradually, though with exceeding slowness, but yet inevitably, ruin many fine properties in all the tea districts of India.

NECTRIA DITISSIMA. THE TEA CANKER.

143. Nectria [ditissima (?)]

THE TEA CANKER.

(SEE PLATE XXIII, NOS. 1 AND 2.)

References.—*von Tubeuf, Diseases of Plants caused by Cryptogamic Parasites, Massee, Diseases of Plants, Indian Gardening and Planting, June 14, 1900.*

Found in Cachar, Assam, the Duars, and the Wynaad.

First found in Wynaad.

830. ***History.***—During the course of a tour in the Wynaad in 1899, one of the authors (G. W.) noticed swellings on and crackings of certain stems of tea. The disease proved to be a canker

PLATE XXIII. (*To face Page 409.*)

1. The Tea Canker on Young Twigs.
(From Photograph by H. H. Mann.)

2. The Tea Canker on Old Stems.
(From Photograph by H. H. Mann.)

The Tea Canker.

similar to those doing so much damage to Apple trees in England, to Cocoa in Ceylon, to Cinchona in India and to many other economic trees. The blight has since been reported as doing serious damage in Assam (North Lakhimpur and Jorhat), and in Cachar, and it has been found in the Duars. THE TEA CANKER.

831. ***Description.***—The disease is caused by a fungus which gains access to the living and growing layer of the stems just underneath the bark, but in every case there must have been previous injury by insects, by pruning, by lightning, or by other agents. It appears not to be capable of attacking a healthy uncut tea stem. Once it has found admission it travels up and down the stem in the living layer underneath the bark, and every now and then causes swellings that rupture the bark and come to the surface in order to fruit and produce the spores (seeds) by which it is spread. These spores ripen in abundance and blow about in the atmosphere all over the estate until they fall on another injured or cut surface when the story is repeated. Caused by fungus.

832. The appearance of such attacked stems is shown in Plate XXIII, both on the young and the old wood. In the former case the stem cracks and splits in every direction, and the young shoot has been described as appearing to have had a bad attack of hail,—which indeed often causes the injury which admits the canker. In the latter case it gives an open growing sore which spreads until it often rings the tree rendering collar-pruning necessary. Appearance of stems.

833. ***Depredations.***—The blight is already sufficiently serious and shows signs of spreading. Hitherto it is principally, though not entirely, found in low-lying gardens either of the bheel type, or consisting of heavy flats difficult to drain, or else where water was liable to back up. When it attacks the young stems it means the loss of all the new wood made in the year: when it is found on the old wood it means the loss of the bush, temporarily at any rate. On Low lands principally.

834. ***Remedy.***—There is one only cure, namely, to cut off and destroy when and where such stems are found as carry the fungus. But the prunings with canker on them must not be left on the ground as they will pour out their countless spores, and more actually continue to spread the disease than if left on the bush. All such prunings must be carried off and burned at once. It is, of course, impossible to avoid injuries to the bush. White ants are a Cure

Vegetable Parasites of the Tea Plant.

THE TEA CANKER.

fruitful source of such, and the simple act of pruning, however carefully performed, will leave openings for the introduction of the germs of canker. In gardens at all liable to it, it would well repay the cost to spray with Bordeaux Mixture (as for Red Rust) after pruning. This with careful pruning, and avoidance of snags, ought to keep (if the cankered stems are removed) the bushes free from this dangerous and spreading disease.

MARASMIUS SARMENTOSUS.

144. Marasmius sarmentosus, *Berk.*

THE HORSE HAIR BLIGHT.

Found in the Duars, Assam, and Cachar.

THE HORSE-HAIR BLIGHT.

835. During a tour in the Duars in 1900 one of the authors was shown a considerable number of bushes covered with festoons of what just resembled horse hair hanging round and sticking to the tea stems, —some of it just resembling a black thread on the branches. By some of the planters there it was said to be worse than thread-blight. Since that time we have received samples from Assam and also from Cachar— and in each case the effect was said to be similar to thread blight in that the stems and the leaves died.

Common in jungle.

So far the blight does not seem to have spread very much on the tea bushes. It is common in the jungle, being noticed more especially on **Terminalia tomentosa** trees. In any case the blight should be dealt with in a manner precisely similar to the method of treating thread blight with Lime and Sulphur.

145. THE DARJEELING STEM BLIGHT.

THE DARJEELING STEM BLIGHT.

836. In the higher parts of the Darjeeling district there will be noticed on almost every garden, a number of bushes dying from the centre, apparently without reason. It was never noticed below 4,000 feet, and appears often on isolated bushes all over the property. In some gardens it is one of the most serious blights on the place. On cutting one of the stems which is dying the centre of the wood appears to be turning black,—and this appearance, we are informed by Dr. Butler, is due to a fungus attacking the stem. It demands much more investigation, however, before it can be named, or a remedy recommended with any certainty. In the meantime, all that can be done is to cut out the stems affected below the part discoloured, and paint the stump with Stockholm tar. This is one of the blights which most urgently demand further investigation.

Only at high elevations.

PLATE XXIV. (*To face Page 411.*)

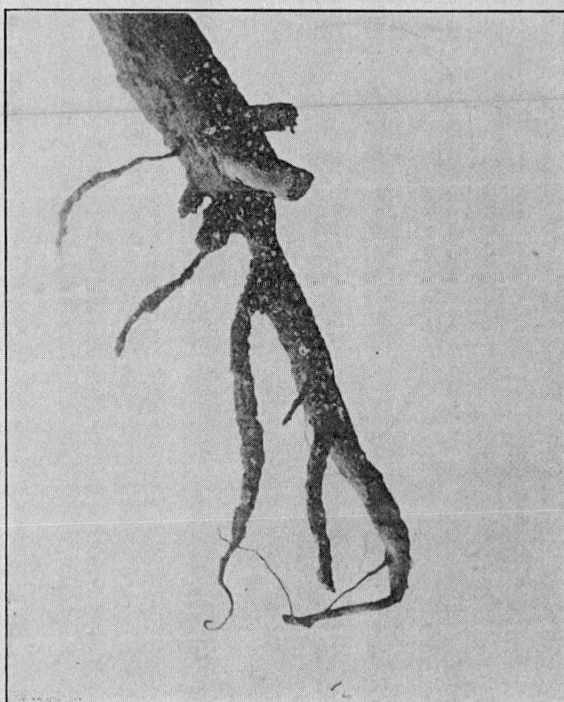

Stump Rot on Tea Root showing Incrustation.
(From Photograph by H. H. Mann.)

THE STUMP ROT.

CHAPTER XXI.

VEGETABLE PARASITES OF THE TEA PLANT—continued.

LXX.—Fungi on the Root.

146. Rosellinia sp.

ROSELLINIA SP.

THE ROOT FUNGUS: THE STUMP ROT.

THE STUMP ROT.

(SEE PLATE XXIV.)

References.—*Bamber, Chem. Agri. Tea, p. 256; Indian Forester, XIII. (1887), p. 290, 388; Massee. Kew Bull, 1896, p. 1; Cunningham, Sci. Mem. of Med. Off. of the Army in India, III., (1887), p. 8; X. p. 22; von Tubeuf, Diseases of Plants, 200; Hartig, Diseases of Trees, p. 78; Massee, Diseases of Plants, p. 45.*

Found in all districts.

837. ***History.***—Almost from the beginning of the tea industry in India the sudden dying of bushes after planting has been noted, but until Dr. Cunningham investigated the matter was little known as to its cause. Even he, however, owing to his being only able to use dried material, was unable to make out the life history of the blight. The fungus was further examined in 1897 by Mr. Massee, of Kew, and more information was obtained. In the former edition of this work, the opinion was expressed that there was evidence that the tea plant was attacked by three root fungi. One of these has been definitely isolated now and will be dealt with under a different heading; all the others seem to belong to the present species.

History.

Cunningham's investigations.

838. ***Description.***—It is a well known fact that certain shade trees within a garden, if killed or felled, cause the death of a number of tea bushes around their stumps. The trees with this evil reputation most frequently mentioned are the *Sum* (Machilus), *Bukhain* (Melia), *Madar* (Erythrina), *Simul* (Bombax), *Bela*, and to a certain extent *Nahor* or *Nagassa* (Mesua),—all of these except the *Nahor* being soft-wooded trees. The Grevillea must now be added to this list. If the tea bushes killed in this manner be dug up and examined, it will be seen that the roots are covered with a brown incrustation, under which is a fine white fungus mycelial thread, which has been sent to us, at least on one occasion, in mistake for thread blight on the roots. The appearance

Effect of dead tree stumps.

Brown incrustation on roots.

Vegetable Parasites of the Tea Plant.

THE STUMP ROT.

of the roots may vary considerably, and it is possible that even yet there may be more than one root fungus of this class.

Description.

839. In what is, at any rate, the most common form, the stump just underneath the ground is the principal point attacked, hence the name "stump rot." The effects "presented themselves externally in the form of numerous, conspicuous, irregularly-undulated swellings, which occur so closely over the base of the stem and origins of the larger roots as to be more or less completely confluent, whilst further out along the course of the roots they occurred in isolated patches. Where they were present, the bark no longer retained its normal smooth texture and grey colour, but was roughened, friable, and deep brown, owing to the mixture of earth derived from the surrounding soil with the disintegrated tissues. In certain sites masses of material of rusty-brown colour and spongy texture were visible in fissures of the surface, and, on removing portions of the disintegrating bark, these were seen to form portions of sheets and strands of similarly coloured material traversing the tissues in every direction. Such material was present throughout the entire thickness of the cortical tissues, and specially abundant at the level of the bast, where it was in many places spread out so as to form a continuous stratum over large areas. The wood appeared to be comparatively little affected, but was here and there interrupted by distinct wedge-shaped portions of a greyish tissue, with narrow, sinuous, blackish margins." (*Cunningham.*) These appearances are most prominent, usually, near the surface of the soil, as has been said, but they may penetrate much further down the smaller roots (as in the photograph shown.—*Plate XXIV*). The fungus is not sufficiently well known even yet for its history to be described in detail.

History of an attack.

840. The history of an attack seems to be somewhat as follows :—Nearly all Assam soil, especially forest soil, contains the spores of this fungus, but they are incapable of germinating on and growing in living root tissue. No sooner, however, does the root of a tree decay (after it has been cut down) than the fungus germinates on the remains, which produces a mycelium which then obtains the power of passing on to and growing on living root tissue. It creeps through the ground, therefore, from the tree root to the tea, and then on till a large number of tea bushes are destroyed in a constantly enlarging circle.

The Stump Rot.

THE STUMP ROT.

841. ***Depredations.***—The injury produced by this fungus is all but universal on forest land, and on grass land also round the few trees which have existed there. It has been found in every district, and is the most usual cause of the circles of vacancies so common on many gardens. A bush will one day appear to be unhealthy, then the leaves are seen to gradually wither to turn brown, and to fall off without showing any fungal disease on their surface. The vitality of the shoots may last a day or two longer, but then they die, and the whole operation of dying may only take a fortnight, though it may be prolonged considerably.

Remedies.

842. ***Remedy.***—There can be little doubt as to the best methods of dealing with this class of blight.

"Owing to the habit of the fungus in penetrating and spreading in the living tissues of the root of its victim, cure is practically outside the question when a plant is once permeated with mycelium; and keeping in view the varied modes of reproduction for facilitating the rapid spread of the disease, no efforts should be spared in the way of preventing such spreading, when the presence of the fungus is once detected."

Trench round plot attacked.

"Undoubtedly the most frequent and rapid mode of spreading is by means of the mycelium travelling in the soil, and a good method of isolating diseased patches is to cut a narrow trench, from nine inches to a foot deep round such, care being taken to throw the excavated soil into the diseased portion and not outside it. This method, which was first suggested by Hartig for the purpose of preventing the spread of subterranean fungi in the German forests, cannot be too strongly commended especially where the diseased patches are small in area. The amount of success depends entirely on the thoroughness, combined with an intelligent method of carrying out the work. Half attempts invariably result in a loss of capital without benefit. It may be enough to suggest that the disease may be spread by the spores of the fungus, or infected soil being carried by the shoes of labourers, by dirty tools, wheels of carts, animals, etc., from diseased centres. Diseased and fallen trees, and especially stumps and roots, should be at once destroyed by burning. The soil surrounding diseased stumps should be burned after the stumps have been removed, so as to destroy the smaller diseased portions of the root that remained behind.

Sulphur.

"A second preventive method, which has proved of service in France, is to lay bare the trunk as far below the surface of the soil as can be done without injury to the tree, and to densely coat the exposed trunk and adjoining soil with powdered sulphur. This should be repeated when the channel round the trunk becomes filled up with earth.

Stagnant water to be avoided.

"Stagnant water should not be allowed to remain in the soil, as this favours the spread of the fungus." (*Massee.*)

Antiseptics.

843. As the fungus generally attacks the tree roots which are the cause of the mischief just below the surface of the ground, it has been suggested by Dr. Butler that there may be great advantage in treating such roots with antiseptics when just cut down wherever it is imprac-

Vegetable Parasites of the Tea Plant.

THE STUMP ROT.

ticable to remove the whole of the roots down to the smaller parts. This might be done by cutting a hole in the top of the stump and putting in a solution of corrosive sublimate. This, in addition to its antiseptic properties, is one of the most penetrating liquids known, and would render quite impossible the growth of these root fungi over a considerable area of root. This is a matter for experiment, and we intend to try it in the near future. But, nevertheless, whenever possible we are confident that it would pay on cutting down a dangerous tree, to remove the whole of the roots, as it is the most radical and certain method of preventing the blight.

Not wise to plant again for a year.

844. After the death of a bush it is not wise to plant another immediately at the same spot for, if this is done, the chances are that this new plant will go out in a similar fashion to the first. The safest way is to burn the soil, as recommended by Mr. Massee, and being new soil for the new plant. An alternative is to mix the soil thoroughly with *quick* lime, and allow the hole where the plant has been as well as the soil to stand exposed to the atmosphere for a year, before putting in a new plant. When the new plant is introduced, it should be treated with Bordeaux Mixture for, say, 6 inches beneath the surface of the soil. In cases where it has been tried this method seems to have been usually successful, but too much lime must not be added or it will be probably found that the tea-bush planted on the spot will never be vigorous.

DIPLODIA VASINFECTA.

147. Diplodia sp. (*n. sp.*)

THE INTERNAL ROOT ROT.

THE INTERNAL ROOT ROT.

Found in Assam.

Bishnath District, Assam.

845. ***History.***—About a year ago a message was received from the Bishnath district, Assam, that bushes were dying out almost by wholesale in young tea on grass land, and no reason could be assigned for it. It further transpired that the whole of the bushes which were dying were planted with Dibrugarh village seed about three or four years previously. There was little to show on the surface of the roots to indicate why their death had occurred, and the material was made over to Dr. Butler. He shortly after reported that he had found a fungus inside the roots which penetrated the vessels of the root and which was the cause of the damage.

846. ***Description.***—As has been said, there is little to show on

The Internal Root Rot.

the surface of the root as to what is the cause of the death of the plants. The leaves of the plant take on a yellow appearance, in which the network of veins is very prominently seen (an appearance easily recognised after a little practice), and then they begin gradually to fall off and branch by branch the bush dies. THE INTERNAL ROOT ROT.

The fungus is wholly internal in the roots, and except for the very small fruiting organ, which rarely forms, it never comes to the surface of the root. Appearance of bushes.

847. ***Depredations.***—Its depredations have been very serious on the gardens which have been attacked. In one case it was calculated that thirty acres of plants in a four year old garden had died. In another, even more than this had been destroyed. In fact, without reference to position, wherever the Dibrugarh village seed had been used there the plant had died, though not usually until after the first pruning, say at three years old from seed. A similar case has been recently reported from Jorhat—the same class of seed was used four years ago, now the plants are dying out, and it may be, and is probably the case, that this blight is more widespread than has hitherto been known. Depredations.

848. ***Remedy.***—The most important preventive measure is to be particular as to the source of the seed used on a garden. None should on any account be employed whose source is not guaranteed. And by this we do not mean that it should bear a certain name, but that it should actually be the produce of the seed garden bearing that name. The matter is too serious to allow of any doubt in the matter, and an absolute guarantee should be insisted on. Remedy. Care in seed selection.

849. We think from experiments made in 1902 that it may be possible to cure this blight. Mr. C. T. Dunlop very kindly recently carried out, at Dr. Butler's suggestion, an experiment in which the roots of the affected bushes were opened in February, and the soil and roots were watered with a two per cent. solution of Sulphate of Iron (Ferrous Sulphate). Though bushes were dying all round and the bushes treated were already affected, none have died since which were then treated. The experiment was on too small a scale to be very certain of the result, but a further test on a larger area is to be carried out in the next year. Sulphate of iron.

850. Seeing that the fungus is almost entirely, if not entirely *inside* the root, that there is considerable evidence that it is carried

Vegetable Parasites of the Tea Plant.

THE INTERNAL ROOT ROT.

by seed, and that no bushes planted (of Manipuri jat) on the affected spots have since died, there seems little of any danger of putting in fresh plants where the old ones have gone out through the present fungus,—and this should be done, and we think can be done without danger, in all cases.

APPENDIX I.

The Insecticide and Fungicide materials mentioned in the text are prepared according to the following formulæ :—

Kerosene Emulsion.—Dissolve 1-1½ lbs. of soap in one gallon of water, and while the mixture is boiling (or nearly so), add two gallons of kerosene to the liquid obtained, and thoroughly mix with a syringe, or by passing through the spraying pump, until the whole forms a white creamy or buttery mixture. This mixture should keep for several days. When wanted for use, dilute the above quantity to thirty gallons.

This is suggested for use against the following insects :—

The Tea Aphis. (In this case make up to 80 gallons instead of 30 as above.)

The Tea Mosquito.

The Scale Insects.

Paris Green.—Make into a thin paint in a small quantity of water, adding powdered or quicklime equal to the amount of poison used. Strain the mixture into the spraying tank. Use at the rate of one pound to form 100 to 200 gallons of water.

This has been suggested by Mr. Green for use against the Tea Tortrix (Capua Coffearia), and may be also used in preparing a poisonous bait for crickets.

Chiswick Compound.—1. Twenty-five pounds to 200 gallons of water.

For use against Mosquito Blight.

2. Twelve and a half pounds to 200 gallons.

For use against Red Spider.

Fish Oil Soap.—One pound to one gallon of water.

For use against Scale Insects.

Gondal Fluid.—

1 part *dekamali* gum (the resin of Gardenia gummifera or Gardenia ludica).

2 parts asafœtida or *hingra.*

2 parts bazar aloes or *musubar.*

2 parts castor oil cake.

These are well compounded, mixed and kept in water for about a fortnight. When thoroughly united, and what may be called decomposed into a thickened compound, water is added in order to bring to the consistency of paint, and red ochre or some other similar red colour added.

It is not wise for a planter to make this mixture himself, as it can be bought ready made in Calcutta.

For use against White Ants.

Bordeaux Mixture.—Dissolve 3 pounds of "Agricultural Sulphate of Copper" in 23 gallons of water in a wooden tub (not in a metal vessel). In another vessel slake 3 pounds of quicklime, if possible freshly burnt, adding two gallons of water gradually This lime should form a turbid smooth liquid without any lumps. Finally add, gradu ally, the lime liquid to the sulphate of copper solution, stirring meanwhile. When thoroughly mixed, the liquid is ready for use, but must be kept stirred up.

For use against Red Rust, Brown Blight, and nearly all fungus diseases.

Sulphide of Potassium.—Dissolve 1 pound of "Liver of Sulphur" in 25 gallons of water in a wooden tub, and apply as with the Bordeaux Mixture. "Liver of Sulphur" must be kept in a closed bottle or tin.

For use against Red Rust.

APPENDIX II.

Glossary of Vernacular Terms.

"**Adakuri**"—Litsœa citrata.

"**Al**" dye—the dye obtained from Morinda citrifolia.

"**Banjhi**"—Barren.

"**Barota**"—Amatissa consorta.

"**Batea-banda-puk**"—Amatissa consorta.

"**Bhela**"—Semicarpus anacardium.

"**Bich-kalam**"—Middle-prune, that is to say, moderately heavy prune, cutting across the centre of the bush.

"**Bilauni**"—Mæsa indica.

"**Bogga medeloa**"—Tephrosia candida.

"**Bukhain**"—Melia azedarach.

"**Bunsu**"—Paspalum sanguinale.

"**Chibaung**"—Loranthus, occurring on tea.

"**Chilauni**"—Schima wallichii.

"**Ciru**"—Imperata arundinacea.

"**Dekamali**" gum—The resin of Gardenia gummifera or Gardenia ludica.

"**Doob**" grass—Cynodon dactylon.

"**Gold-mohur**" tree—Poinciana regia.

"**Hingra**"—Asafœtida.

"**Hullahs**"—Depressions or low-lying tracts in a tea garden, often partly under water, and through which streams usually run in the rainy season.

"**Ilami**"—Ageratum sp.

"**Kadam**"—Anthocephalus cadamba.

"**Kalai**"—Phaseolus mungo or aconitifolius.

"**Kodalli**"—A form of spade in which the digging part is at right angles to the handle.

"**Korkani**" Jungle—Land in which, owing to water, to white ants, and to various insects, the trees and plants are on mounds like ant hills and lower land is between.

"**Koroi**"—Albizzia odoratissima.

"**Kumla**"—Lachnosterna impressa.

"**Kur**"—Imperata arundinacea.

"**Loquat**"—Eriobotrya japonica.

"**Madar**"—Calatropis procera.

"**Mahua**" cake.—Oil Cake from Bassia latifolia.

"**Maj-kalam**"—Middle prune, that is to say, moderately heavy prune, cutting across the centre of the bush.

"**Mal-muriya**"—Mæsa indica.

"**Mati-kalai**"—Phaseolus mungo or aconitifolius.

"**Medeloa**"—Dalbergia assamica.

"**Musnbar**"—Bazaar aloes.
"**Nagassa**"—Mesua ferrea.
"**Nahor**"—Mesua ferrea.
"**Nullahs**"—Stream in a tea garden, generally running in a nullah, but often also merely meaning a drain.
"**Pan**"—Piper betle.
"**Peepul**"—Ficus religiosa.
"**Phaki**" leaf—Useless leaf, being the stipule of the new shoot.
"**Rogamulla**"—Loranthus,—a mistletoe-like plant found on tea bushes, especially in tea kept for seed.
"**Roghu-kadam**" Tree—Anthocephalus Cadamba.
"**Sal**" Tree—Shorea robusta.
"**Sam**" Tree—Artocarpus chaplasha.
"**Sapodilla**" Plum.—Achras sapota.
"**Satian**" Tree—Alstonia scholaris.
"**Shisham**" Tree—Dalbergia sissoo.
"**Sida**"—Sida rhombifolia.
"**Simul**" Tree—Bombax malabaricum.
"**Siris**" Trees—Various species of Albizzia trees.
"**Sum**" Tree—Machilus odoratissima.
"**Titaphul**"—Phlogocanthus thyrsiflorus.
"**Titiapat**"—Artemisia sp.
"**Tun**"—Cedrela toona.
"**Tur**"—Cajanus indicus.
"**Ulu**" Grass—Imperata arundinacea.
"**Utengah**"—Dillenia indica.

INDEX.

A

B

C

D

E

I

J

K

L

M

N

Q

R

S

T

U

V

W

X

Y

Z